Renoir.

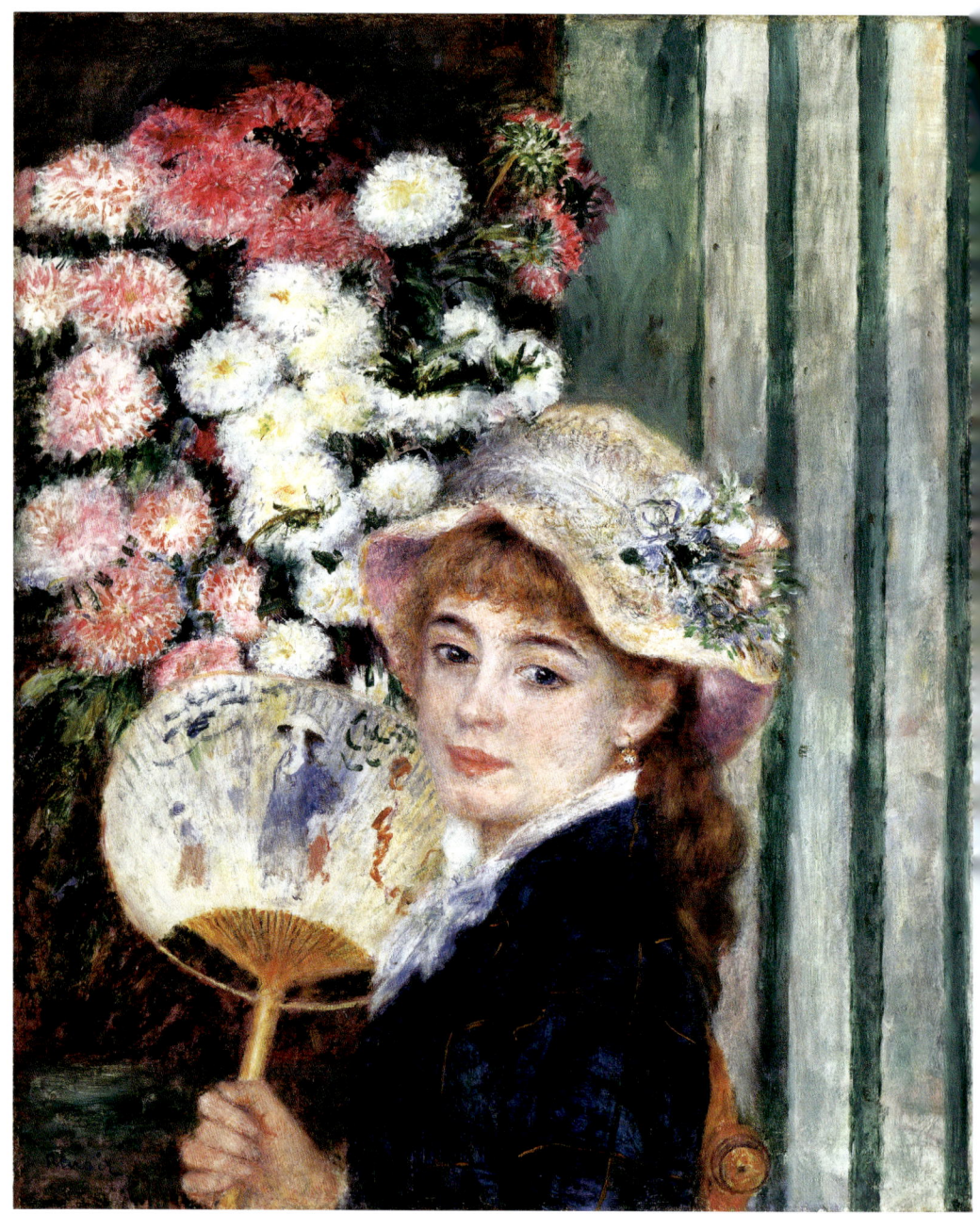

Gilles Néret

Renoir

Painter of Happiness

TASCHEN

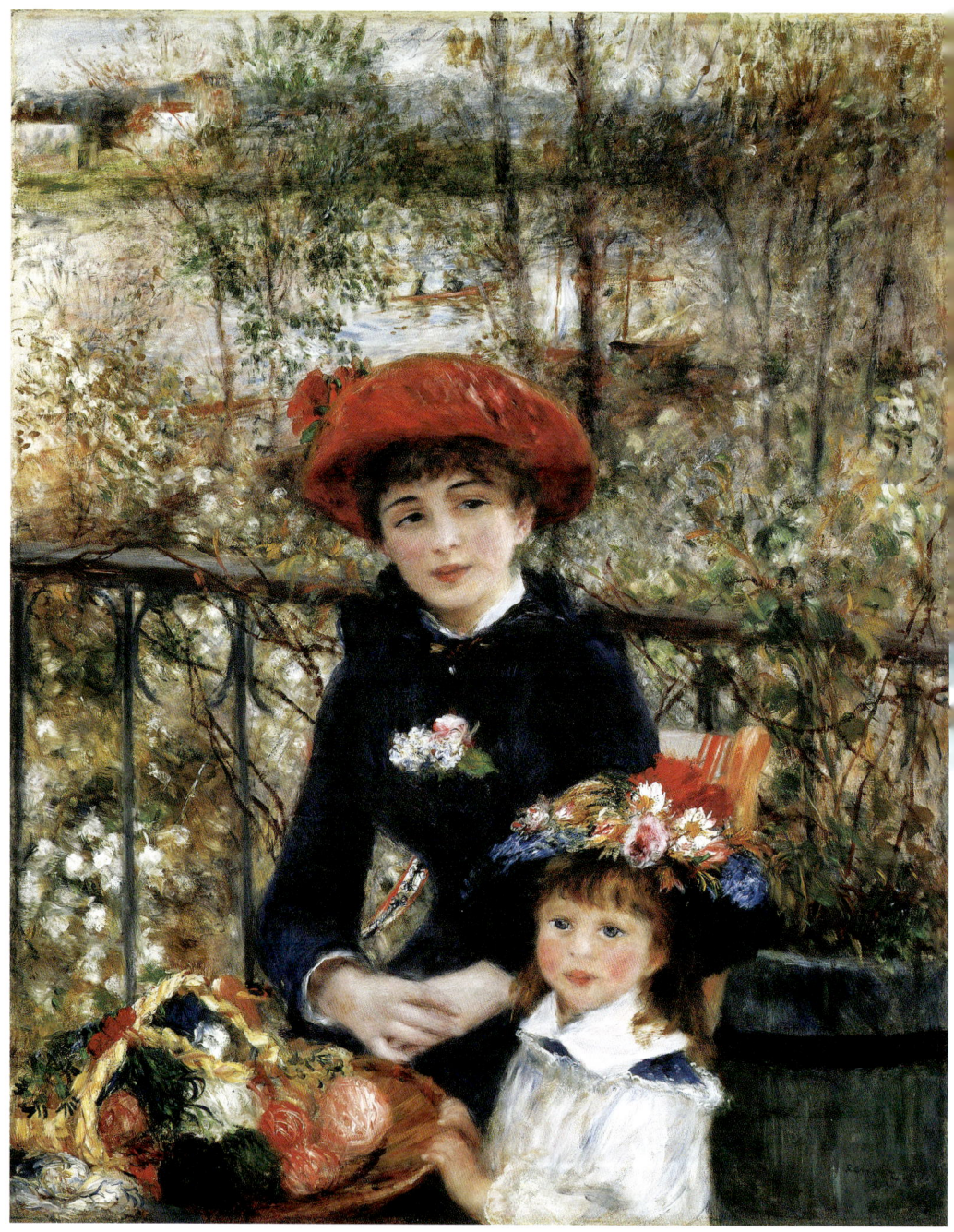

Contents

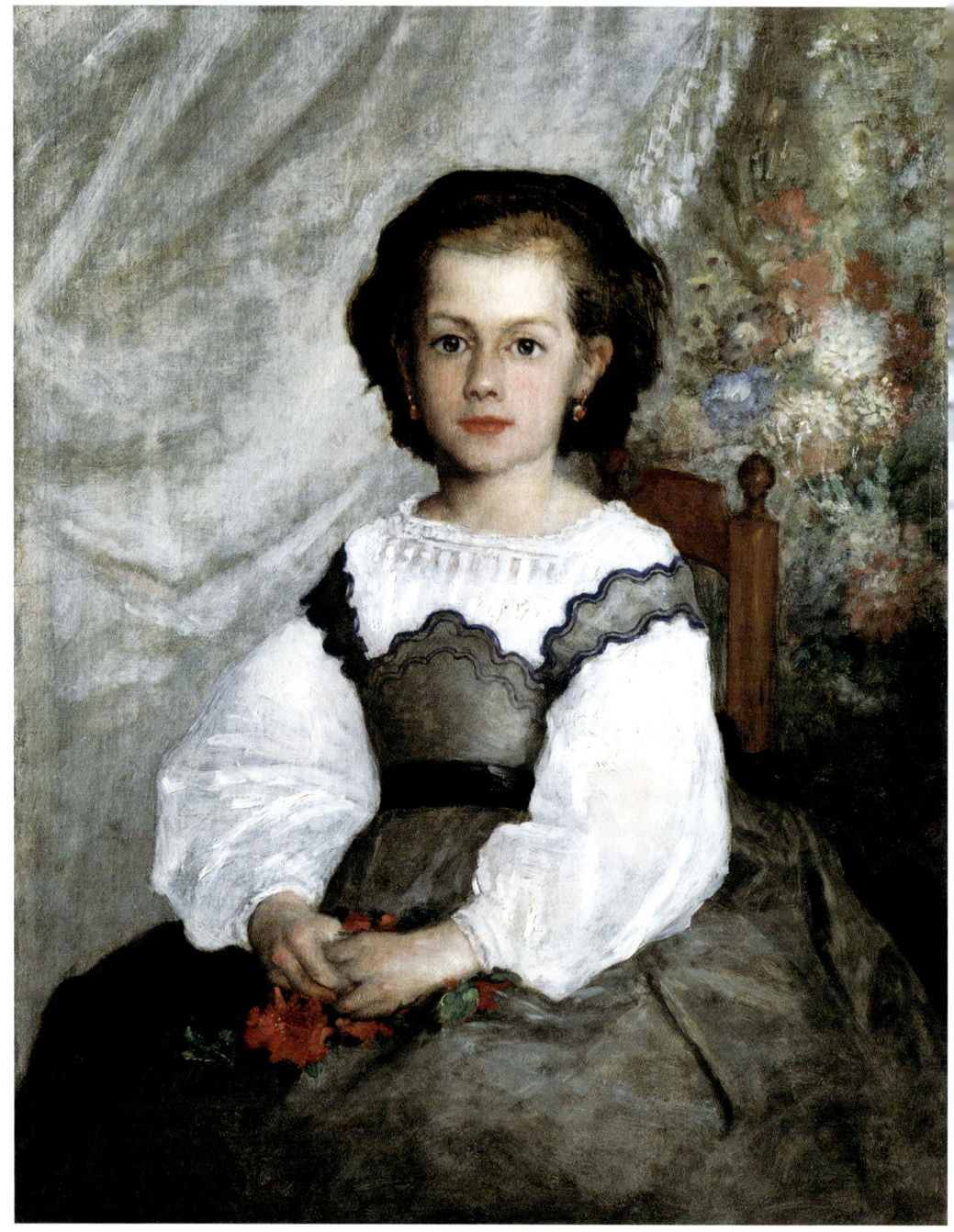

Mademoiselle Romaine Lacaux, 1864
Oil on canvas, 81.3 x 65 cm (32 x 25⅝ in.)
The Cleveland Museum of Art,
Gift of the Hanna Fund 1942

Of all the Impressionist painters, Renoir and
perhaps his friend, Berthe Morisot (1841–1895),
were the only ones who were capable of
representing the ingenuity, grace and freshness
of little girls whose natural mischievousness,
combined with shyness, he found so attractive.

A Decorator of China
1854–1870

If Renoir has now attained universal glory, if museums throughout the world are proud
to possess his works, if the public is willing to stand in line for hours to view each of his
many retrospectives, it is because this artist occupies a special place in the history of art and
epitomizes one of its key trends. In Renoir's work, art appears in its most delightful, luminous aspects, bursting with health and vitality. At a time when smiles were hard to come by,
this painter of happiness stood out like a beacon. "I am well aware," he would say, "that it is
difficult to accept that a painter can produce truly great works and remain happy. Simply
because Fragonard enjoyed a laugh, he came to be considered as a minor painter. People
given to laughter are never taken seriously. Art in a frock-coat, whether in painting, music,
or literature, will always carry the day".

Nowadays, the public is less easily led and agrees with Renoir. What Renoir's work offers
is a complete and self-contained world that is his alone, in the centre of which he has raised
an altar to womanhood. By indicating through his paintings what appears to be a predilection for "those she-fauns with bee-stung lips," as the French poet Stéphane Mallarmé
(1842–1898) described them, created more for kissing than for talking, Renoir invented a
new type of femininity. He allowed his women bathers and laundresses to step down from
Olympus and transformed his parlour maid, Gabrielle, into a pagan goddess, since this was
how he saw her in his imagination. Our vision of the world could never be the same again.
This was not lost on Marcel Proust, who observed: "Women pass in the street, different
from those that we formerly saw, because they are Renoirs, those Renoirs we persistently
refused to see as women". Picasso made a similar remark when describing the roosters

Frédéric Bazille (1841–1870)
**The Artist's Studio,
Rue de la Condamine,** 1870
Oil on canvas, 98 x 128 cm (38⅝ x 50½ in.)
Paris, Musée d'Orsay

Bazille, who was mown down by Prussian bullets at the
age of only twenty-nine but left a moving legacy in the
shape of his own version of *The Artist's Studio*, amused
himself by including all of his own paintings in it. The
female nude over the divan, is *The Toilette*; *Fisherman
Casting His Net* can be seen on the left. Manet, wearing
a hat, is the central figure. He is studying a painting on
the easel while a group of his friends – it is hard to say
which of them are, Renoir, Zola, Monet or Sisley –
surround him as their leader. A comparison between
these two renditions of the subject, both designed to
enhance Manet's prestige, illustrate Bazille's modernity
and the inspiration that Fantin-Latour drew from the
Dutch masters.

Henri Fantin-Latour (1836–1904)
A Studio at Batignolles, 1870
Oil on canvas,
204 x 273.5 cm (80⅜ x 107¾ in.)
Paris, Musée d'Orsay

Manet, shown here at his easel,
is the central figure in *A Studio at
Batignolles.* He is surrounded by the
younger generation of admirers who
have elected him their standard-bearer.
Behind the creator of *Olympia* (p. 166)
stand Otto Scholderer, Renoir, Zola,
Edmond Maître, Bazille and Monet.
Zacharie Astruc is seated. Fantin-
Latour owed his reputation to flower
paintings rather than portraits.
He was famous for painting roses
"like a woman's bosom" (Jacques-
Émile Blanche).

that he painted. "We must discover them", he said, "just as Corot discovered morning and
Renoir discovered young girls".

Throughout his long career, from the French defeat in the Franco-Prussian War to
the Treaty of Versailles, Renoir drew from the real world only what he enjoyed, and only
depicted the subjects that make people happy, such as children, fruit, shapely women, and
pleasant landscapes suffused with light. The historic events taking place in France, from the
Commune to World War I, seem to have left no trace on his work that has the timeless air of
a sensual, pagan celebration. It is surprising to note that, unlike the public, a section of the
intelligentsia and certain art critics have never ceased to condemn Renoir, not just during
his lifetime, but even subsequently. This reluctance to acknowledge his genius persists even
today. Some critics claim that Renoir is, at best, a worthy successor to the frivolous, eighteenth-century French tradition of Watteau, Boucher, Fragonard and others. As Salvador Dalí
said, "by dint of acting the genius … you become one". By dint of hearing and reading that he
was the spiritual heir to the masters he admired, Renoir accentuated the likenesses, though
in his case, he went beyond the bounds of Impressionism, and attained the eternal greatness
of classicism, adding to this mastery a *joie de vivre* that is lacking in Rubens, Titian, Ingres,
Delacroix, and Corot, his favourite exemplars whom he came eventually to equal.

When Renoir died in 1919, at the height of his fame, there were still some ready to belittle
a painter who, having renewed the link with Renaissance art, had succeeded in discovering
the nobility and simplicity of the art of antiquity. By the time he died, Renoir was, nevertheless, the most admired of the Impressionist painters. Michel Hoog, curator of the Musée de

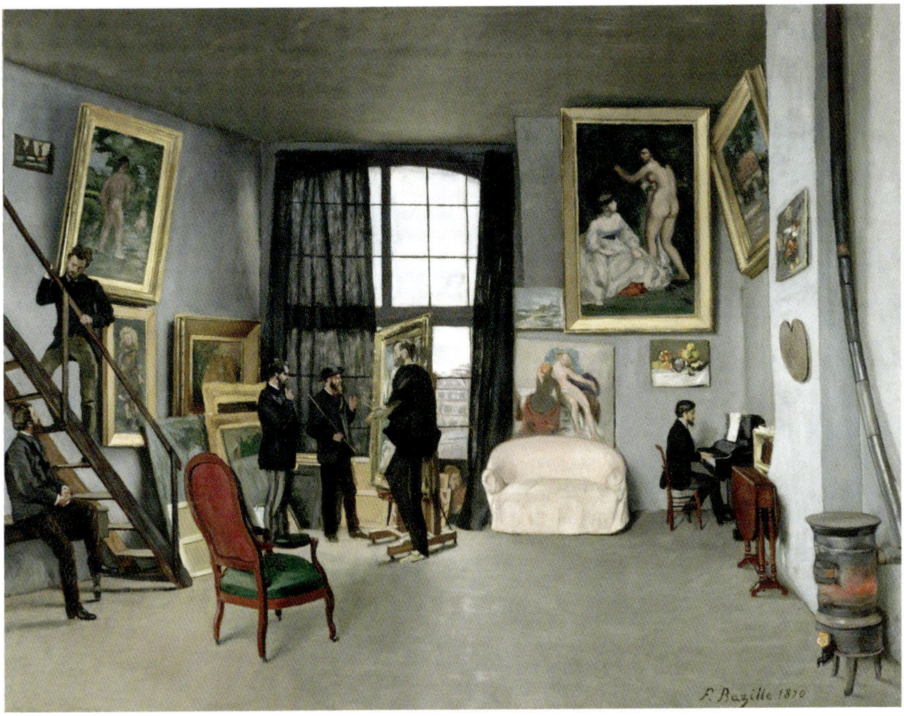
F. Bazille 1870

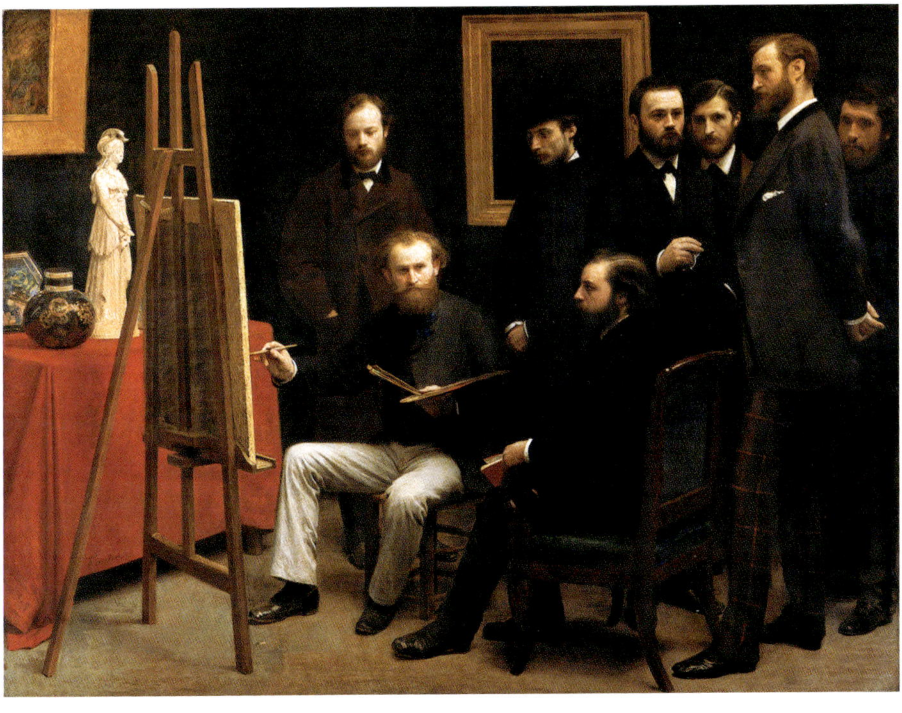

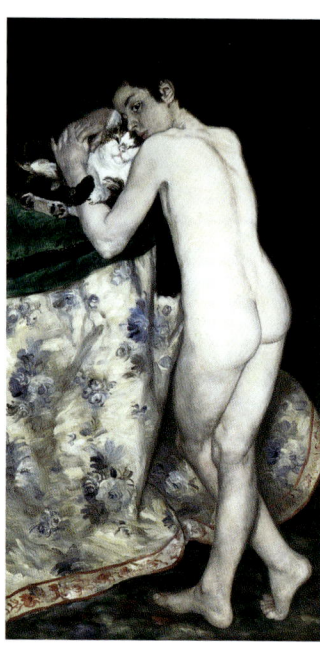

The Boy with the Cat, 1868
Oil on canvas, 123.5 x 66 cm (48⅝ x 26 in.)
Paris, Musée d'Orsay

This is the only male nude that Renoir ever
painted, and it is of a very young boy. The
painter was passionately interested in women
and recognised the fact by joking: "Even before
I could walk, I started to love women!"

French School
**Forty-three Portraits in
Gleyre's Studio**, c. 1856–1868
Oil on canvas,
114 x 146 cm (45 x 57½ in.)
Musée des Beaux-Arts de la Ville
de Paris, Petit Palais

l'Orangerie and lecturer at the École du Louvre, says that Renoir "is one of the few modern painters whom the 'non-specialist' (in the current jargon) knows, recognises, and *enjoys*". Renoir is himself responsible for this divorce between the advocates of what is "artistically correct," who are springing up everywhere, and popular taste. It is difficult to know what to make of an artist considered by himself and others to be the creator of art that is, in his own words, simple and uncomplicated. Cézanne is an artist whose work has produced many theses about its influence and role in art history. Gauguin and Van Gogh have frequently been the subjects of scholarly research, yet Renoir has been consigned forever to the rank of a "very popular artist".

"Renoir paints the way he breathes!" There is nothing to be added to this dictum of Octave Mirbeau. As the German art historian, Meier-Graefe, wrote in 1911, in the first monograph about Renoir: "He paints like the bird sings, like the sun shines, like the buds that burst into blossom. Never has anything been created with less artifice. It is the movement of the babe-in-arms toward its mother's breast". Michel Hoog, a more contemporary critic confirms: "The work of Auguste Renoir is decked out with every seductive charm; the skill is amazing and the technique is one of pure delight. The figures are graceful, the portrait sitters smile, the nudes are luminous and healthy and the children at play, there are flowers, fruits, and people strolling in the garden in spring … perhaps only the art of Matisse reflects an equally happy world". What so many people have failed to recognise is that this radiant exterior was created by means of intense, incessant toil, a permanent effort to progress and improve. It was through arduous daily exertion alone that an artist could successfully create

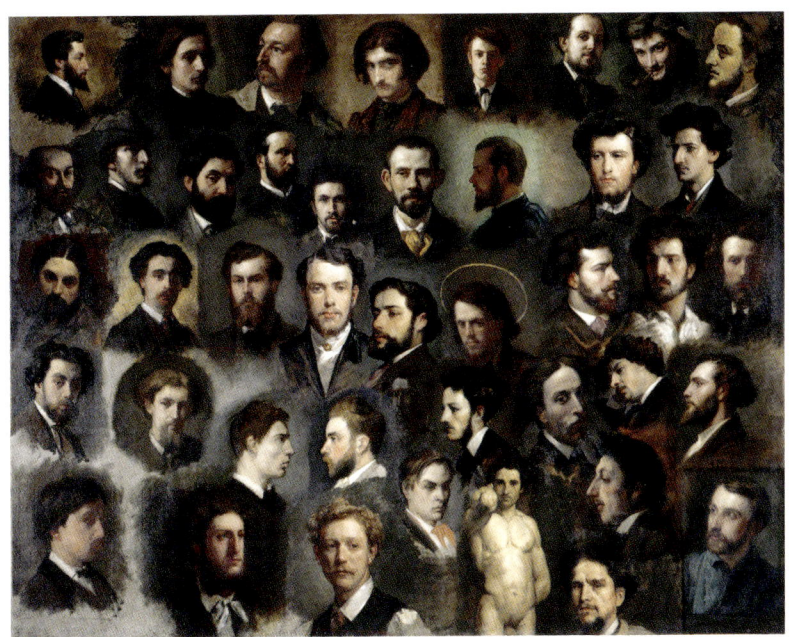

paintings that are so varied and numerous. Renoir himself admitted in around 1910 that "except in cases of force majeure, I don't think I have gone a single day without painting".

Renoir's genius also lies in the fact that he was able to retain a simple attitude towards his subjects, while trying constantly to perfect the basic gifts with which he had been born. He opted for the world of sense-perceptions, taking in with a keen but naïve eye the sights that the world offered him at every turn: "How difficult it is in a painting to find the exact moment at which to stop. A painting should not reek of its model and yet one ought to be able to smell the fragrance of nature. A painting should not be an official report. Personally, I like paintings that make me want to take a stroll through them if they are landscapes or run my hand over a nipple or a back if they are female figures." These statements were aimed more at winning over the public than at retaining the attention of the critics.

Renoir's work did not emerge from the void, spontaneously and instinctively, any more than the Impressionist revolution came about purely from observing the sun playing on the leaves of the trees or splattering human flesh with patches of light. Renoir and his successor Matisse, both masters of colour, constantly sought the optimum way of mastering the language of plastic art by creating perfect combinations of shape and colour, volume and contour. When Renoir was 72 years old he transformed a watercolour – with help of the sculptor Maillol's young pupil, Richard Guino – into a monumental sculpture, the *Venus Victrix* (p. 475), just as Matisse, at 80, produced his series of *Jazz* decoupages that finally enabled him "to cut out blocks of colour" in the same way as "sculptors carve directly into stone".

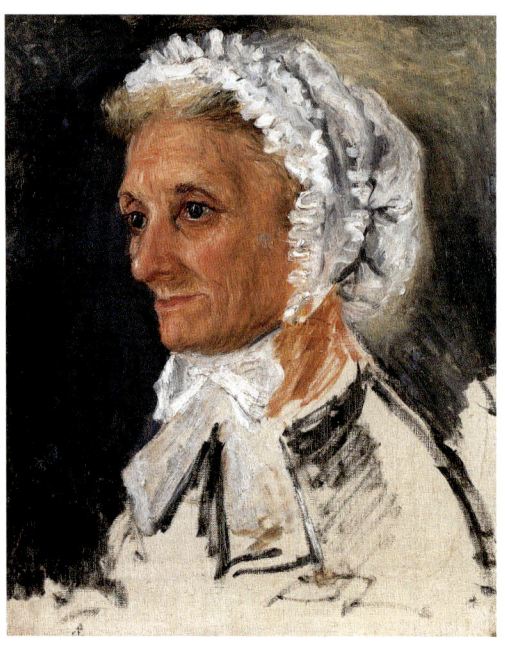

Portrait of the Artist's Mother, 1860
Oil on canvas, 45 x 38 cm (17¾ x 15 in.)
Private collection

The portraits of his parents are evidence of the progress that Renoir made in just a few years. Only nine years separate them. The portrait of his mother Marguerite (1807–1896) is executed sketchily with heavy use of the palette knife, under the influence of Courbet, from whom he seems to have learned much of what Van Gogh did. The portrait of his father Léonard (1799–1874), on the other hand, is very much in the Manet style. Renoir was still trying to find himself, but this time he was able to use a much more fluid style of painting and his touch was less restrained and more lively.

Portrait of the Artist's Father, 1869
Oil on canvas,
62.2 x 47 cm (24½ x 18⅝ in.)
Saint Louis Art Museum

Pissarro described Renoir as being "the most changeable of men". That is not the kind of thing guaranteed to make one popular either. We all like to pigeonhole people. It is useful and reassuring. The "Impressionist" label, for example, is ideal. It is conveniently vague, allowing artists as different as Cézanne and Gauguin to be lumped together. It also ignores the fact that for all the members of the movement, with the exception of Monet, impressionism only represented a very short period in their artistic lives. Renoir's Impressionist period only lasted a dozen years (1870–1882). It was at the very moment when this revolution in art, initially so scandalous and the object of such abuse, began to be accepted; when people were finally getting used to the movement and were beginning to appreciate the radiant beauty of Renoir's early style; when he had been distinguished from the other Impressionists by being called a "Romantic", in Baudelaire's sense of the term, and was coming to be considered as the true heir of eighteenth-century French painting, that Renoir chose to distance himself from the movement and explore other directions. What made his move so courageous was that his paintings were just beginning to sell. Pissarro despaired: "I had a long conversation with Renoir. He admitted to me that everyone, Durand and even former admirers, were berating him, deploring his attempts to emerge from his Romantic period and leave it behind."

Renoir ceaselessly questioned his past achievements, ignoring pleas to continue to work in the style of a previous period. Picasso also experienced this mania of the art world, which preferred his Blue and Pink periods to the Cubist one that succeeded them. Matisse was criticised for having turned into a bourgeois in Nice and for ceasing to be a Fauvist,

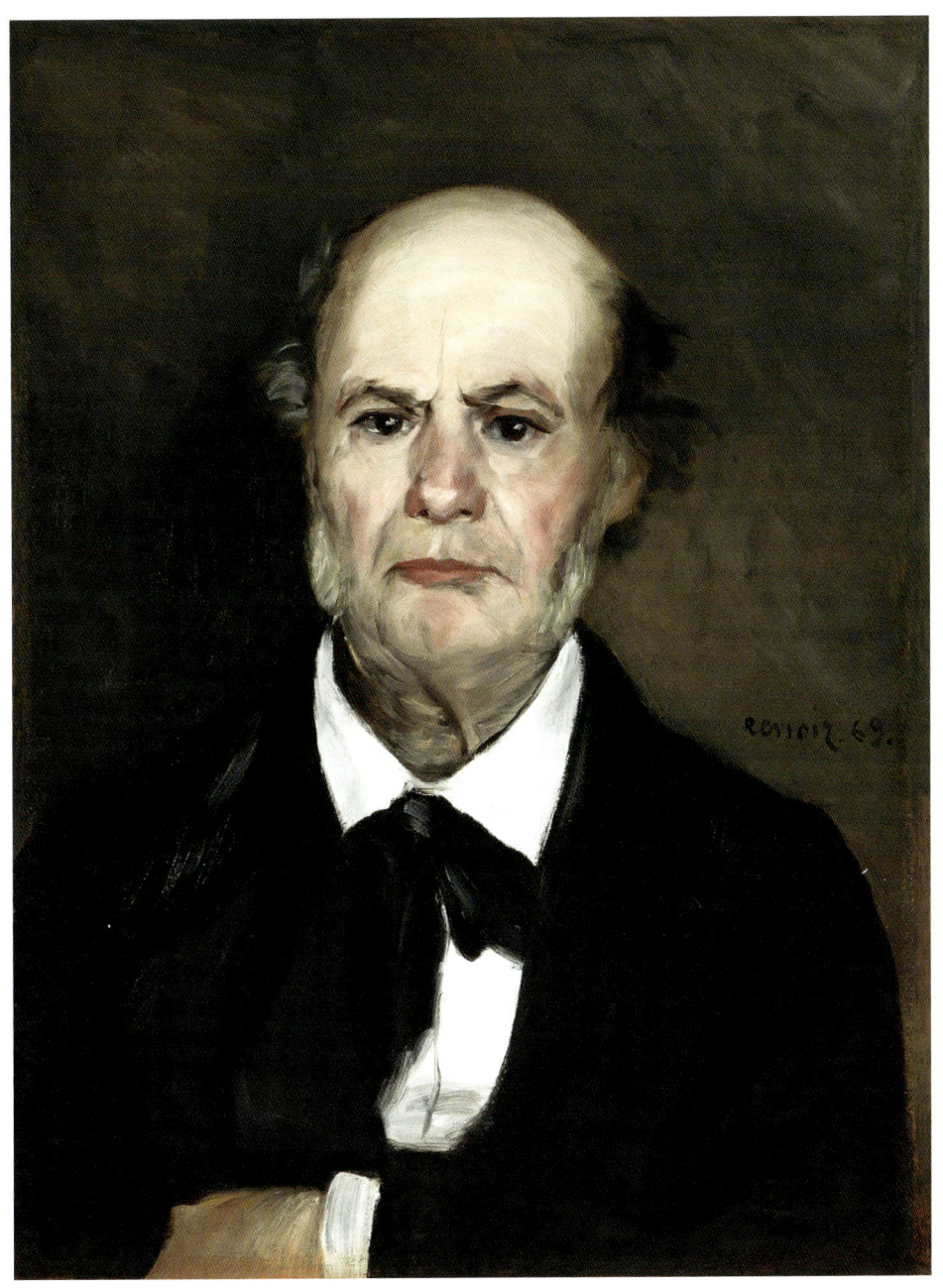

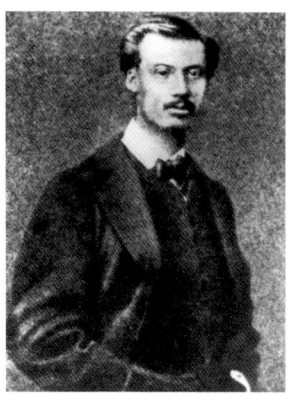

Pierre-Auguste Renoir, c. 1861

At the Inn of Mother Anthony, 1866
Oil on canvas, 194 x 131 cm (76½ x 51⅝ in.)
Stockholm, Nationalmuseum

"that dangerous troublemaker who previously maintained the supremacy of the French School throughout the world". These are only three painters among the many who have followed their own desires and scorned the idea of lingering in the past or of being revived by a conservative art world that is quick to congratulate them on their newly-acquired graces at one moment and equally prepared at another to blame them for having abandoned their former graces. The apparent ease with which Renoir created his paintings often leads to a misunderstanding of his work. When he left Impressionism behind, although he had already produced such masterpieces as *Le Moulin de la Galette* (pp. 114/115), *Madame Charpentier and Her Children* (pp. 388/389) and *The Luncheon of the Boating Party* (pp. 156/157), he considered that he could "neither paint nor draw" and, moving against the general trend, did not hesitate to abandon the style in which he had begun to enjoy success and make his name, modelling himself on more demanding old masters, whose style was as far removed as possible from his own temperament, such as Raphael in Rome and Ingres in the Louvre.

Renoir was "the most changeable of men", according to Pissarro, and this was reflected in his attitude toward his models. As the actress Jeanne Samary (1857–1890) observed, "Renoir is not the marrying type. He marries all the women he paints … with his paintbrush". This is another trait that Picasso was to echo. Picasso's work is no longer compartmentalised into analytical, hermetically-sealed slices or collages; the periods are now described as the Fernande, Olga, Marie-Thérèse, Dora, Françoise, or Jacqueline years. For Renoir too, painting and sexuality were one and the same thing. "The two words are synonymous", Picasso

14

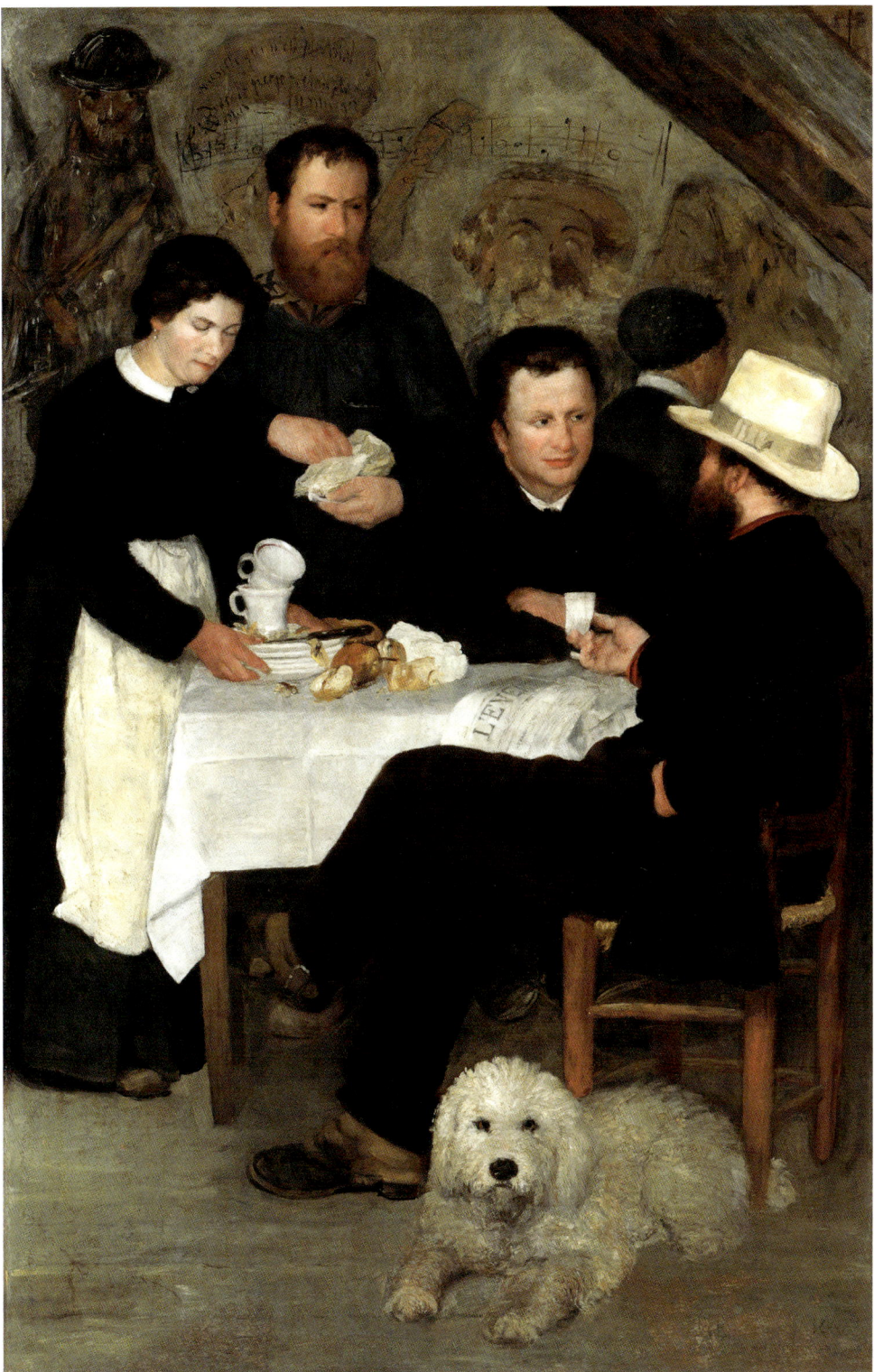

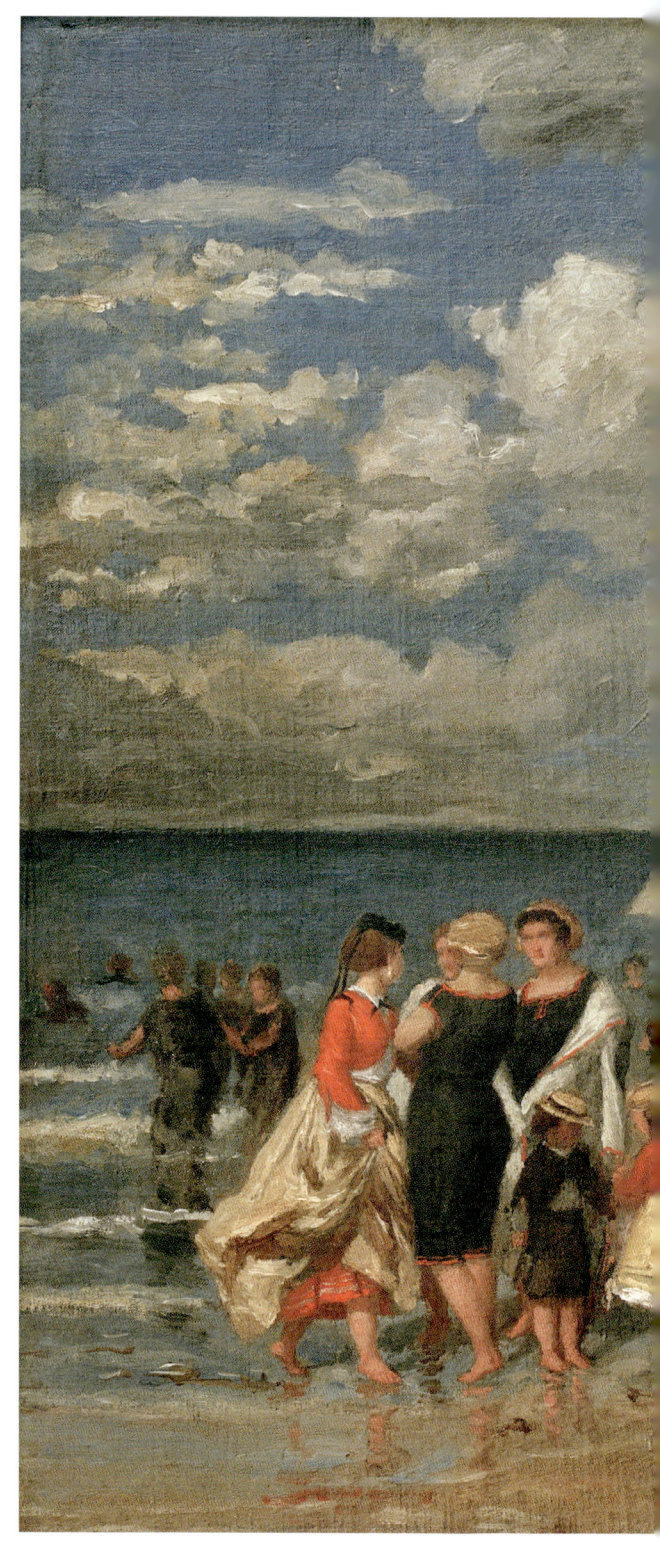

Return of a Boating Party, 1862
Oil on canvas,
50.8 x 61 cm (20 x 24 in.)
Private collection

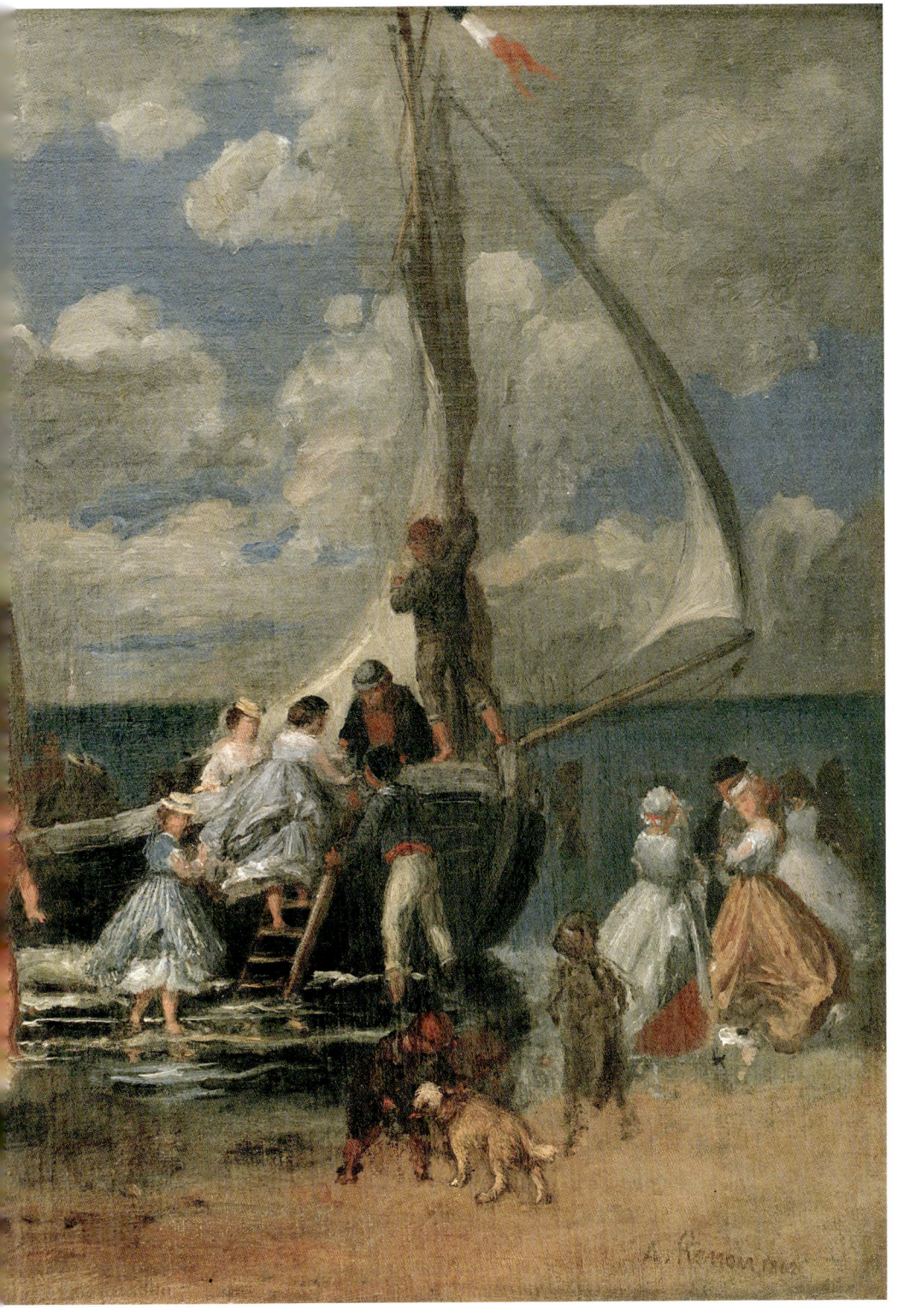

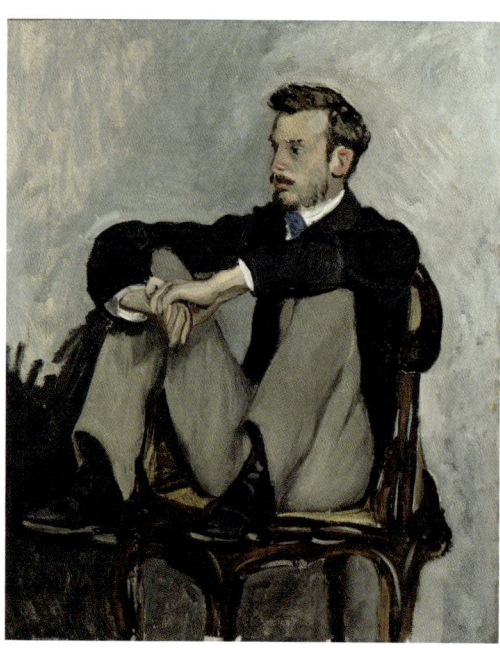

Frédéric Bazille
Portrait of Pierre-Auguste Renoir, 1867
Oil on canvas, 61.2 x 50 cm (24 x 19¾ in.)
Paris, Musée d'Orsay

Frédéric Bazille, 1867
Oil on canvas, 105 x 73.5 cm (41¼ x 29 in.)
Paris, Musée d'Orsay

once said to Jean Leymarie. Julius Meier-Graefe considers that Renoir shows us "a divine
feast of the flesh, still free of desire, not yet distorted by passion, idyllic, yet exuding a powerful sensuality". Jean Renoir, his son, reported his father's fears that "succeeding generations
would make love very badly. That would be a serious matter, for those who do not have
painting …!" In a letter to Albert André, his painter-friend in later life, Renoir stated: "Thanks
be for painting that, late in life, it still gives you illusions and sometimes even joy," a remark
that Picasso, who was something of a *voyeur* in later life, might just as well have made. To a
journalist who persisted in asking how he was still able to paint with hands that were so badly
deformed from rheumatism, he replied cheekily, "I actually paint with my dick …!"

   In the course of his long life, Renoir produced more than 5,000 paintings, a large
number of which are sketches and roughs whose commercial success has done his reputation the greatest disservice. When Japan was at the height of its economic boom, the
Renoir-loving Japanese bought his paintings by calculating the prices according to
whether the subject-matter was *portraiture* or *landscape*, regardless of the artistic quality
of the work. Renoir painted several hundred masterpieces – the most important of which
are reproduced in this book – and these are more than adequate testimony to his glory.
None of his work should be thrown away, but not all of it deserves to be on permanent display in the great museums of the world. If critics sometimes turned up their noses at him,
his fellow-artists, whose opinion surely counts for something, have all been admirers of
Renoir. Any of them would have awarded him the same accolade as Degas did Toulouse-
Lautrec: "You are clearly one of us!" Cézanne copied the *portrait* that Renoir painted of

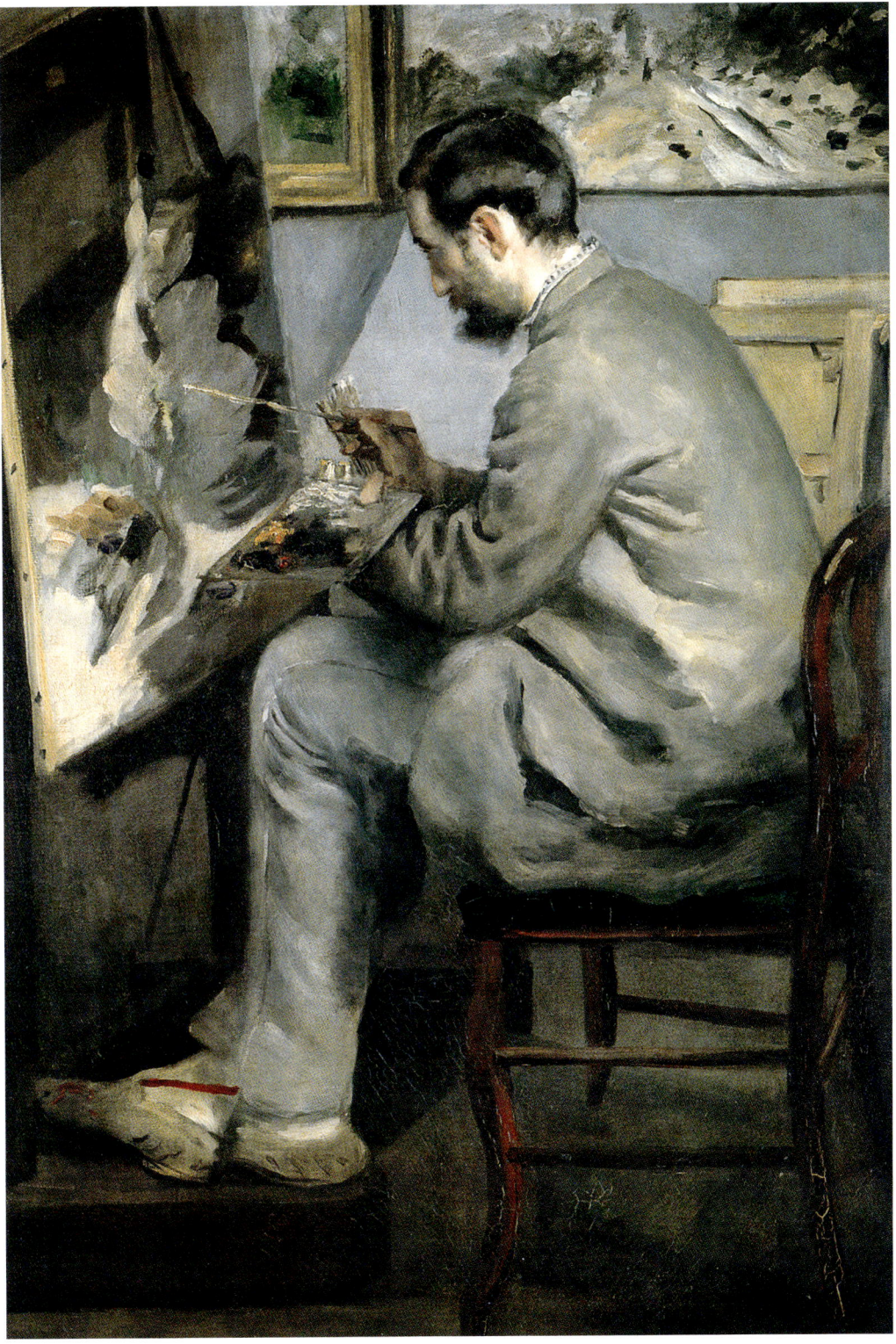

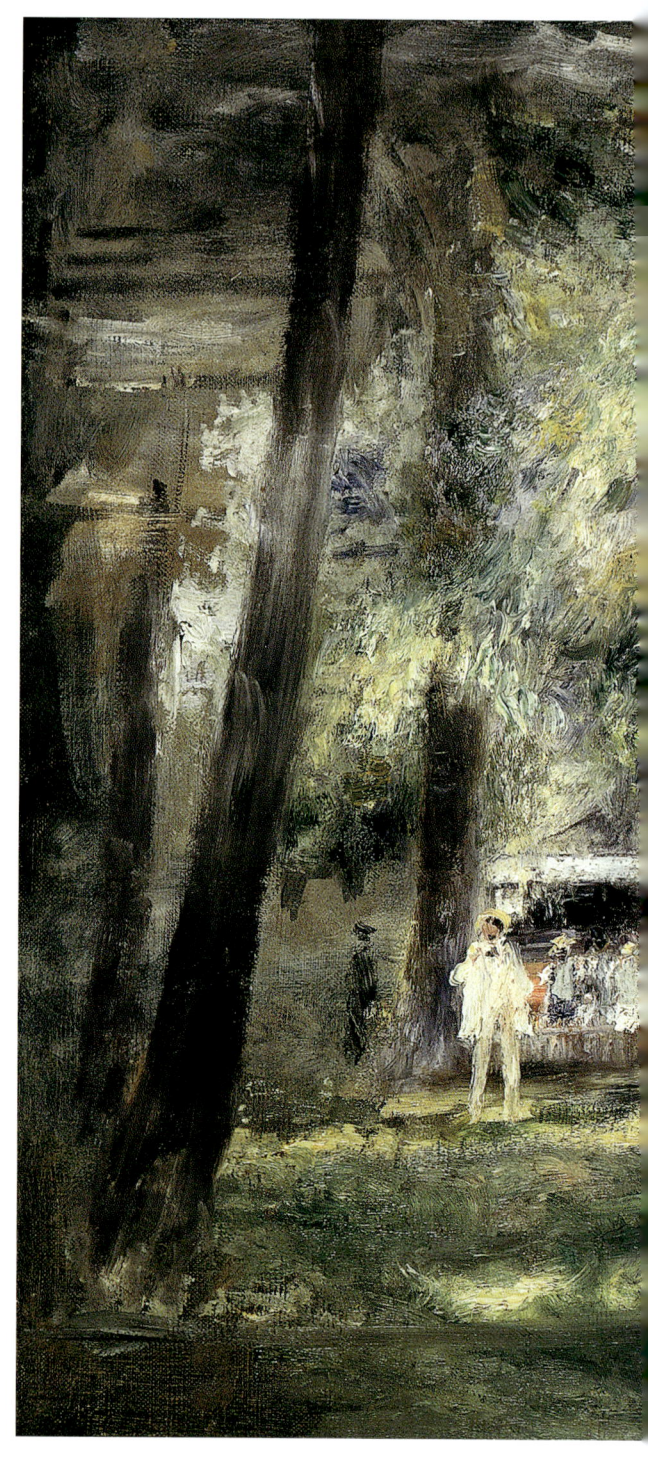

In the Saint-Cloud Park, 1866
Oil on canvas,
50 x 61 cm (19¾ x 24 in.)
Private collection

This meeting in a park at Saint-
Cloud, near Paris, preceded the
discovery of the delights of painting
in the open air, which would become
so important to the Impressionists.

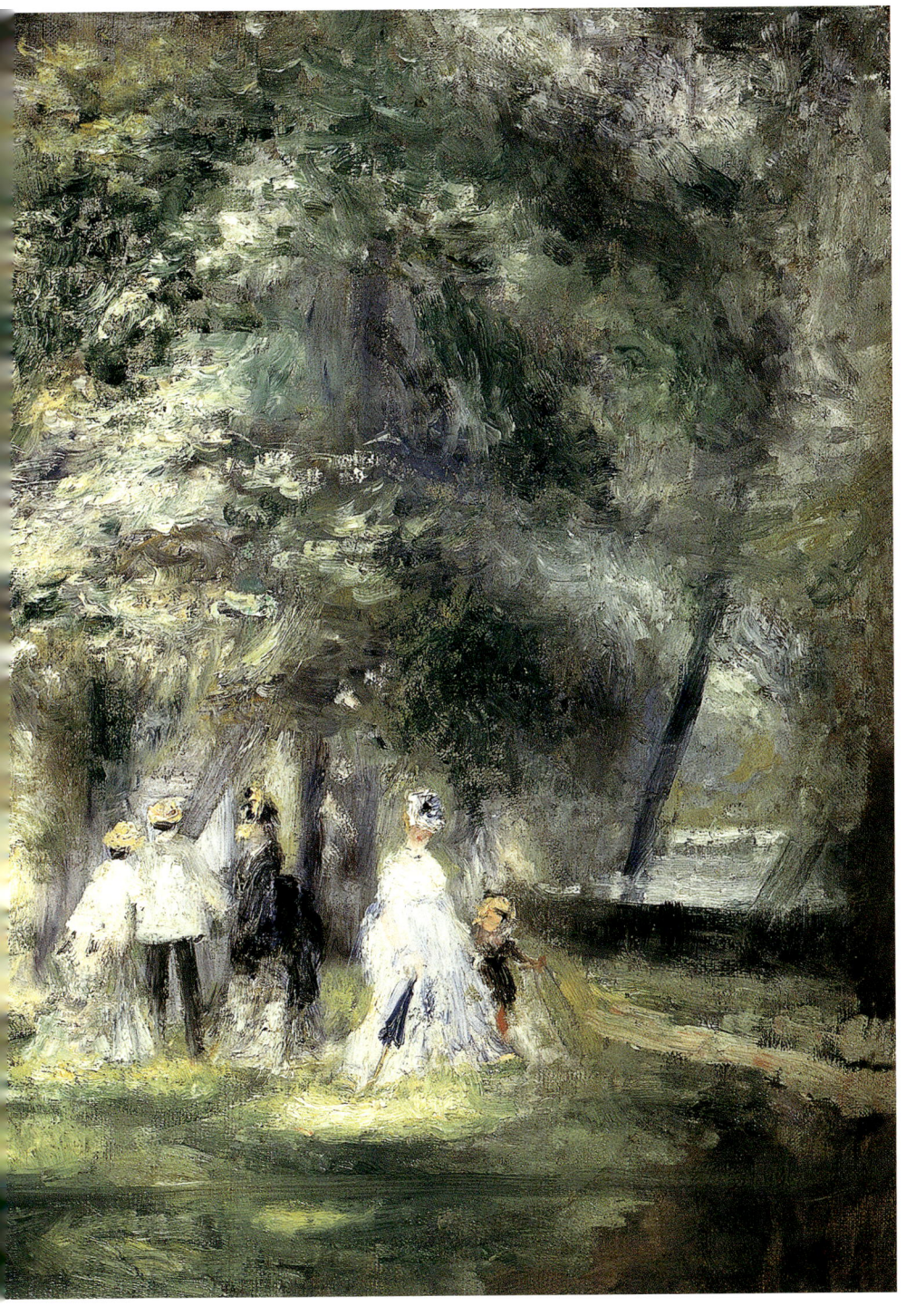

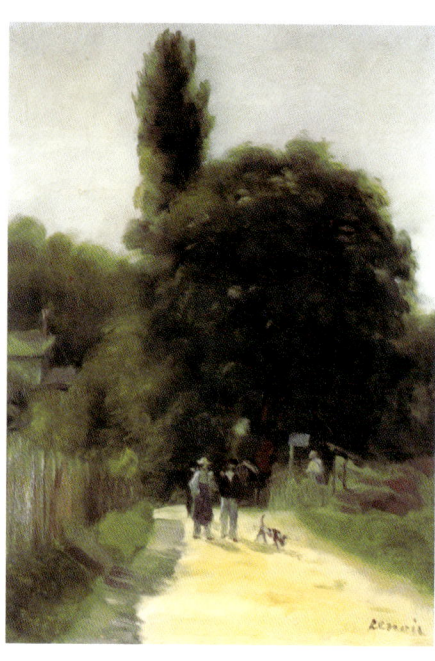

Landscape with Two Figures, 1865/66
Oil on canvas, 33 x 24.1 cm (13 x 9½ in.)
Private collection

**The Painter Jules Le Cœur Walking His Dogs
in the Forest of Fontainebleau**, 1866
Oil on canvas, 112 x 90 cm (44 x 35½ in.)
Museu de Arte de São Paulo,
Assis Chateaubriand

him (p. 224). Van Gogh frequently praised the "clean, pure" line of *The Great Bathers* (pp. 348/349). Bonnard admired Renoir's nudes and Matisse considered Renoir to be a "master of glaze and a portraitist with a gift of giving life to a subject every bit as great as Goya's". Picasso always had a Renoir in his possession and amused himself by improvising "something else" on Renoir's paintings, just as composers improvise on a theme in music. In 1926, Rouault wrote in his *Souvenirs intimes*: "glory to thee, Renoir, for so frequently being drunk on colour, when so many others were merely content with being moderately successful and dried up".

The French writer, André Lhote, suggests that Renoir himself was responsible for the "nightingale-painter" legend so as to disconcert journalists and critics who pestered him. In truth, Renoir was, above all, a great professional who considered himself to be "first and foremost a good craftsman". In his view, "painting is a craft, like cabinet-making," but "even the most cunning hand is only a servant to the thought". This was something he proved from the outset, by painting blinds for a patron who considered that his "skill was unnatural" but who wanted to go into partnership with him. He demonstrated it again when he decided to abandon poverty and become a fashionable portraitist accepted by the Salon, a position which he coveted since it would increase the value of the works exhibited. However, what critics overlook is the fact that this was merely one aspect of his constant professionalism which existed to serve his boundless *joie de vivre*. In Charles Gleyre's studio, where he first began to study fine art and where he met his future colleagues, Monet, Sisley, and Bazille, he "staggered" the studio owner and teacher, "a very respectable Swiss painter". Gleyre, on

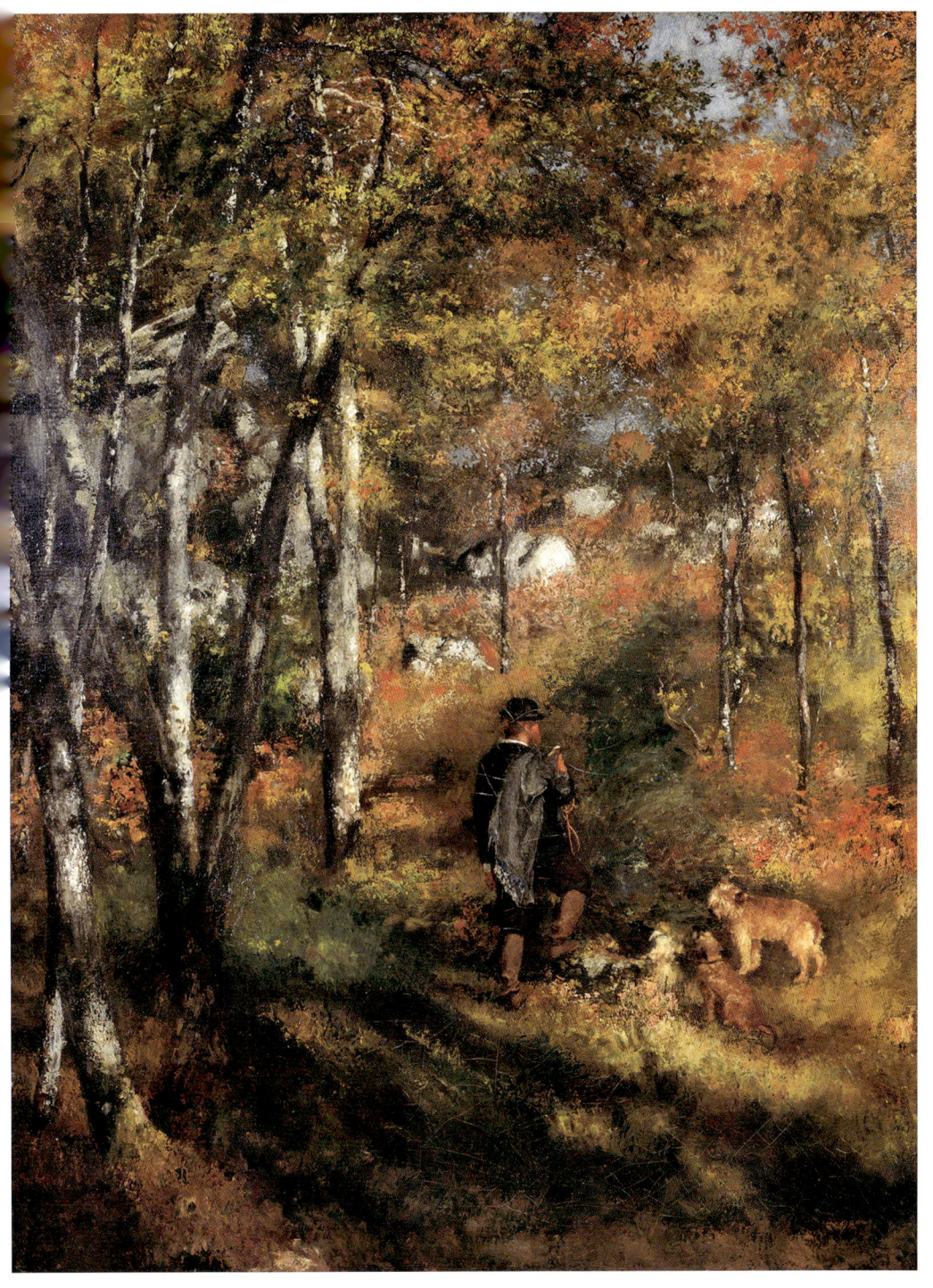

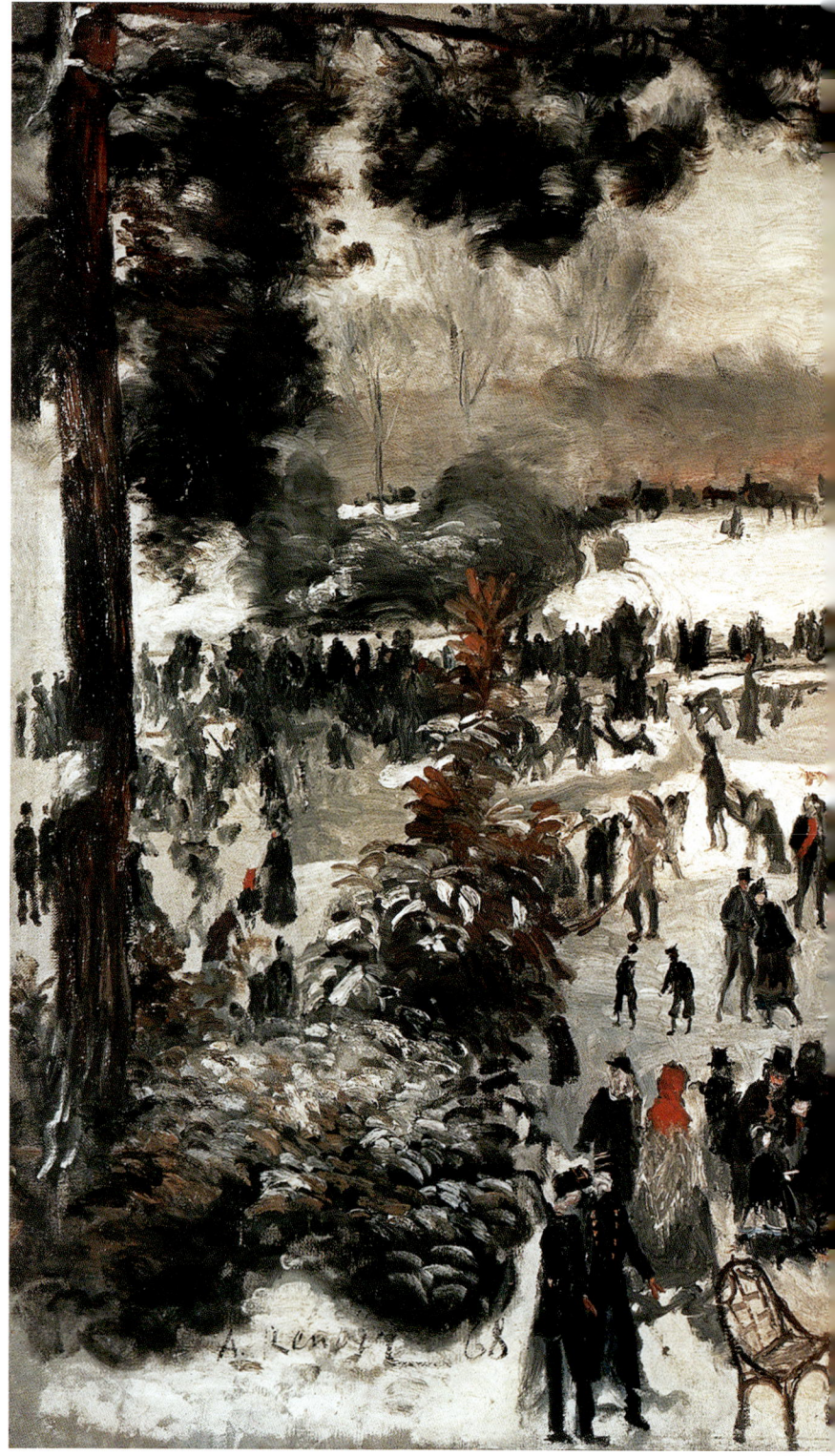

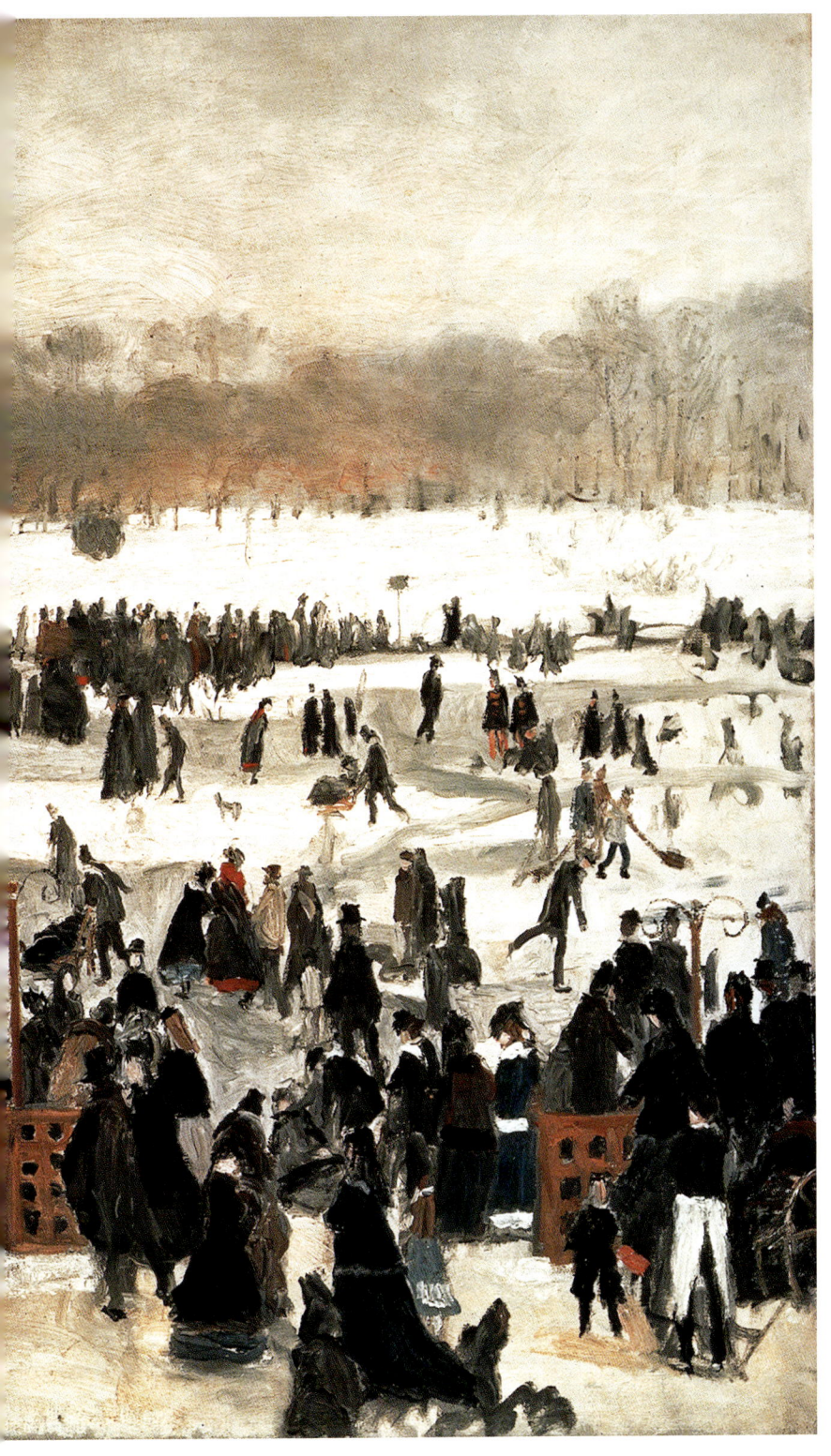

Skaters in the Bois de Boulogne, 1868
Oil on canvas, 72 x 90 cm (28⅜ x 35½ in.)
Private collection

Renoir did not like the snow, which he referred
to as "the leprosy of nature". Nevertheless, he
painted two or three winter landscapes, though
he dotted them with tiny figures designed to serve
as landmarks and introduce the warmth of life
into this frigid aspect of nature. Figures in a
landscape was to be one of his recurring themes.

**The Champs-Elysées during the 1867
Universal Exposition**, 1867
Oil on canvas, 76.5 x 130.2 cm (30⅛ x 51⅜ in.)
Private collection

his weekly visit, stopped by Renoir's easel. "Gleyre looked at my canvas, and coldly remarked, 'No doubt you are just having fun?' 'Of course I am!' I replied, 'And if I weren't having fun, I can assure you that I would stop doing it!' I don't think he quite understood". What he told his teacher he confirmed to his son, Jean, at the end of his life. "I can only paint if I enjoy it, and how can you possibly do so when you are always asking yourself whether what you are going to paint will make people grind their teeth?" Hence his much-quoted aphorism, "when Pissarro paints his views of Paris, he always puts in a funeral. Personally, I would have added a wedding". Taking the easy way out, critics have taken literally Renoir's boast that "whatever happens in my head is of no interest to me. I want to touch or at least see."

Pierre-Auguste Renoir was born in Limoges, France on 25 February 1841, the fourth of five children. His father, a bespoke tailor, had great difficulty making ends meet for his family. Despite this, Renoir had a happy childhood. In such an impoverished household, everyone had to become a breadwinner at an early age, but this need not mean going down the mine! In Pierre-Auguste's case, it was a toss-up between drawing, his talent for which was evident from the way he doodled all over his exercise books at school, and music, in which he was encouraged by Charles Gounod, the choirmaster at the church of Saint-Roch. This was after the family had left Limoges and settled in Paris where they hoped, if not to make their fortune, at least to be able to earn a better living. To make the most of his gifts, Pierre-Auguste was to become a china-painter, a good trade at the time. So at the age of thirteen, he was apprenticed to a studio of porcelain-painters. He hoped one day to find employment at the Sèvres porcelain factory. The eldest son, who was ten years older

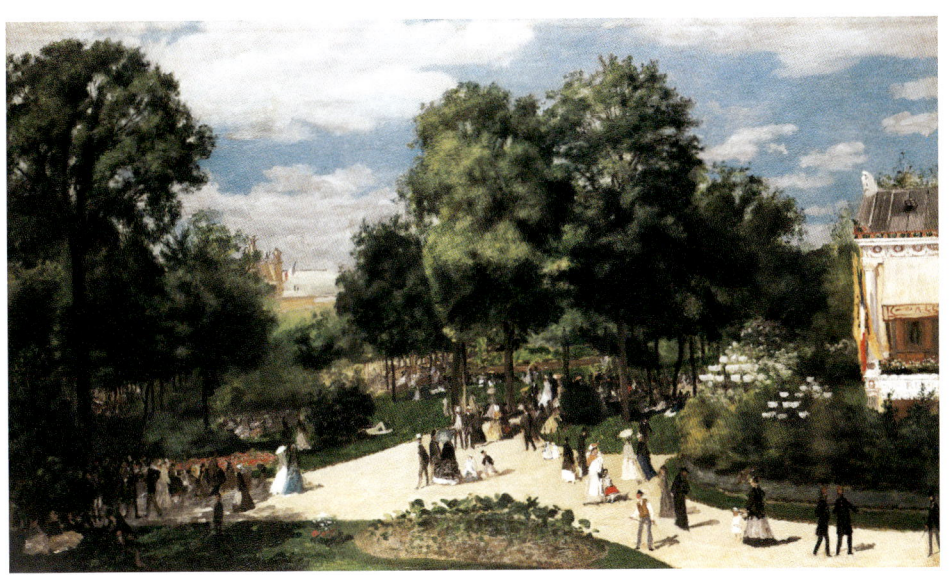

than the future painter, had chosen the occupation of heraldic engraver and was doing extremely well. The atmosphere in the family was artistic.

Using soft, rounded or pointed brushes and smooth colours, the young Renoir would sprinkle the white expanse of plates with little bouquets of flowers for which he was paid five sous per dozen. He once told the art dealer, Ambroise Vollard, that "when it was a matter of decorating large pieces, the bouquets of flowers were bigger. This meant a higher price could be charged, although it was still the very minimum, because the boss considered that it was in the interest of his 'artists' not to be overpaid. All of this china was destined for the East. When I felt surer of myself, I gave up the little bouquets and launched into figure work, still at the same miserable rate of pay. I remember that a profile of Marie-Antoinette brought me in eight sous". At lunchtime the young Renoir would go to the market at Les Halles where, standing next to the wine stalls selling beef and French fries, he would eat his homemade sandwich and marvel at the Fountain of the Innocents. He fell in love with the nudes sculpted by Jean Goujon, and retained a special affection for the sculptor that never deserted him. As early as his apprenticeship, the young Renoir was already influenced by the two major passions that dominated his work, the plasticity of the sculptor's art and the limpid colours that are the result of the play of light and that reached their zenith in the so-called "nacreous period".

Renoir worked so fast that the tiny coins accumulated in his pocket. Since his boss had no intention of paying a mere child the same wage as a grown man, he suggested hiring him as an employee at the exorbitant salary of a hundred and twenty francs a month. "A child, earning so much money! It's just not right!"

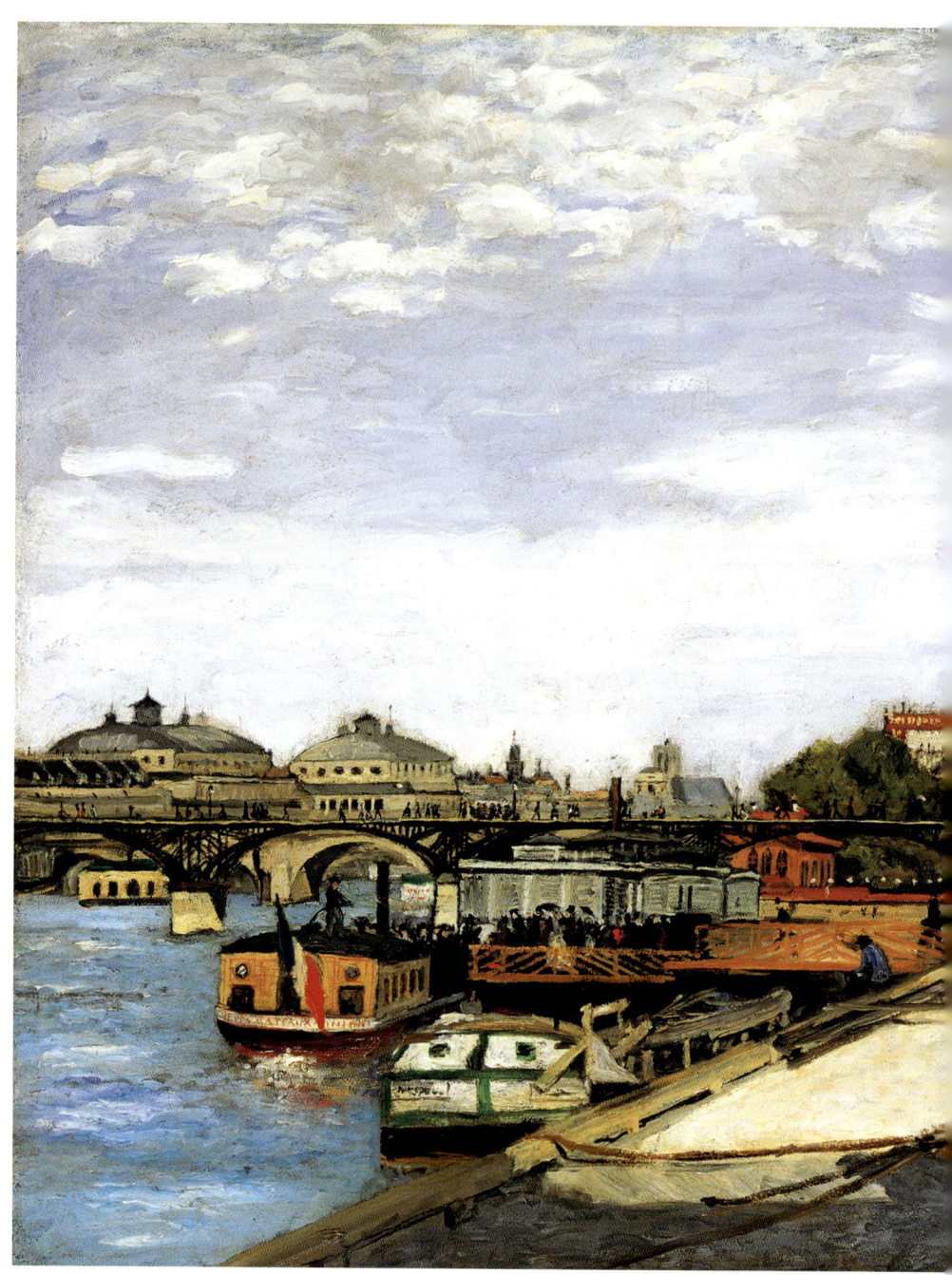

The Pont des Arts, Paris, 1867/68
Oil on canvas, 60.9 x 100.3 cm (24 x 39½ in.)
Pasadena, The Norton Simon Foundation

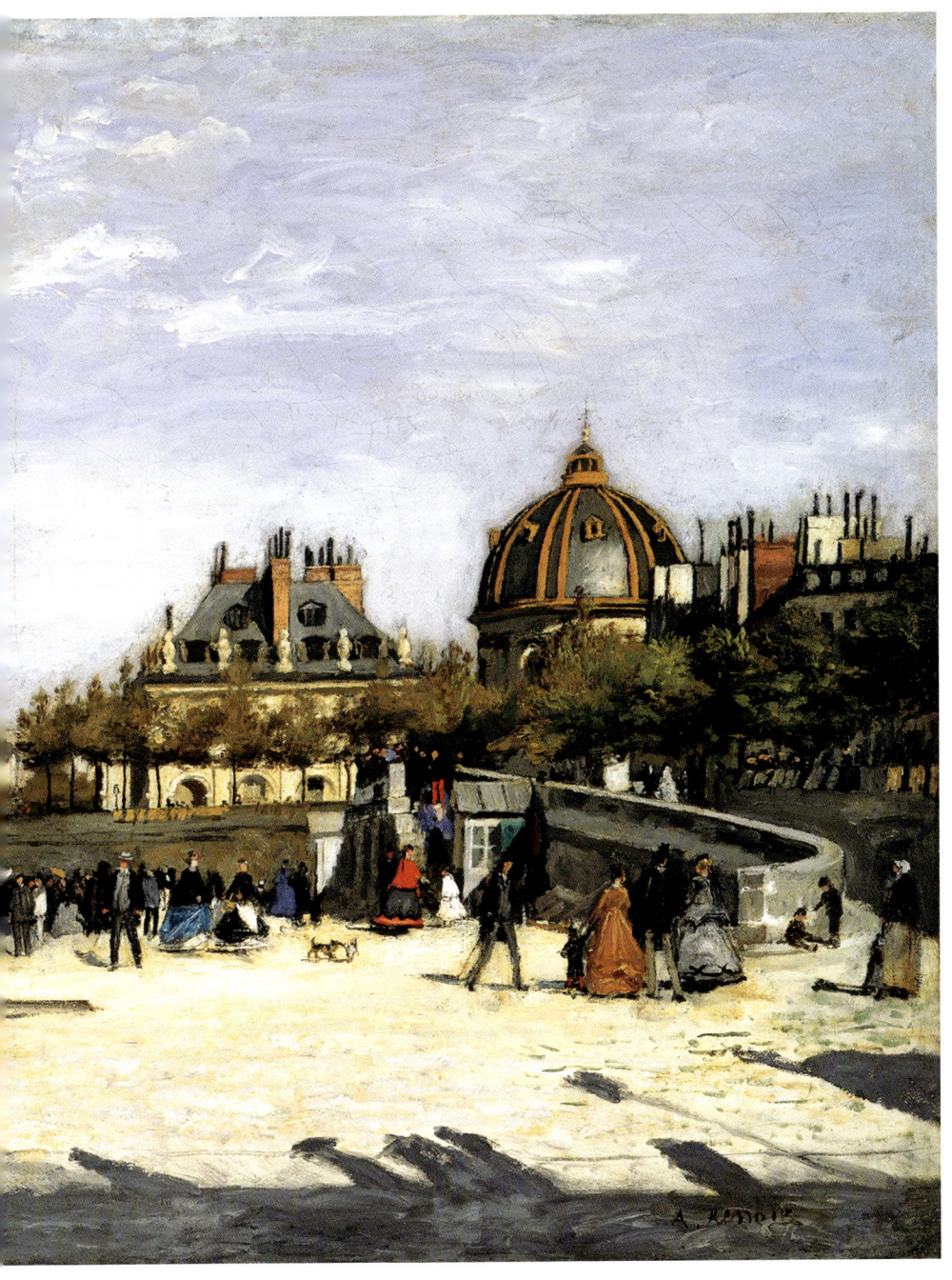

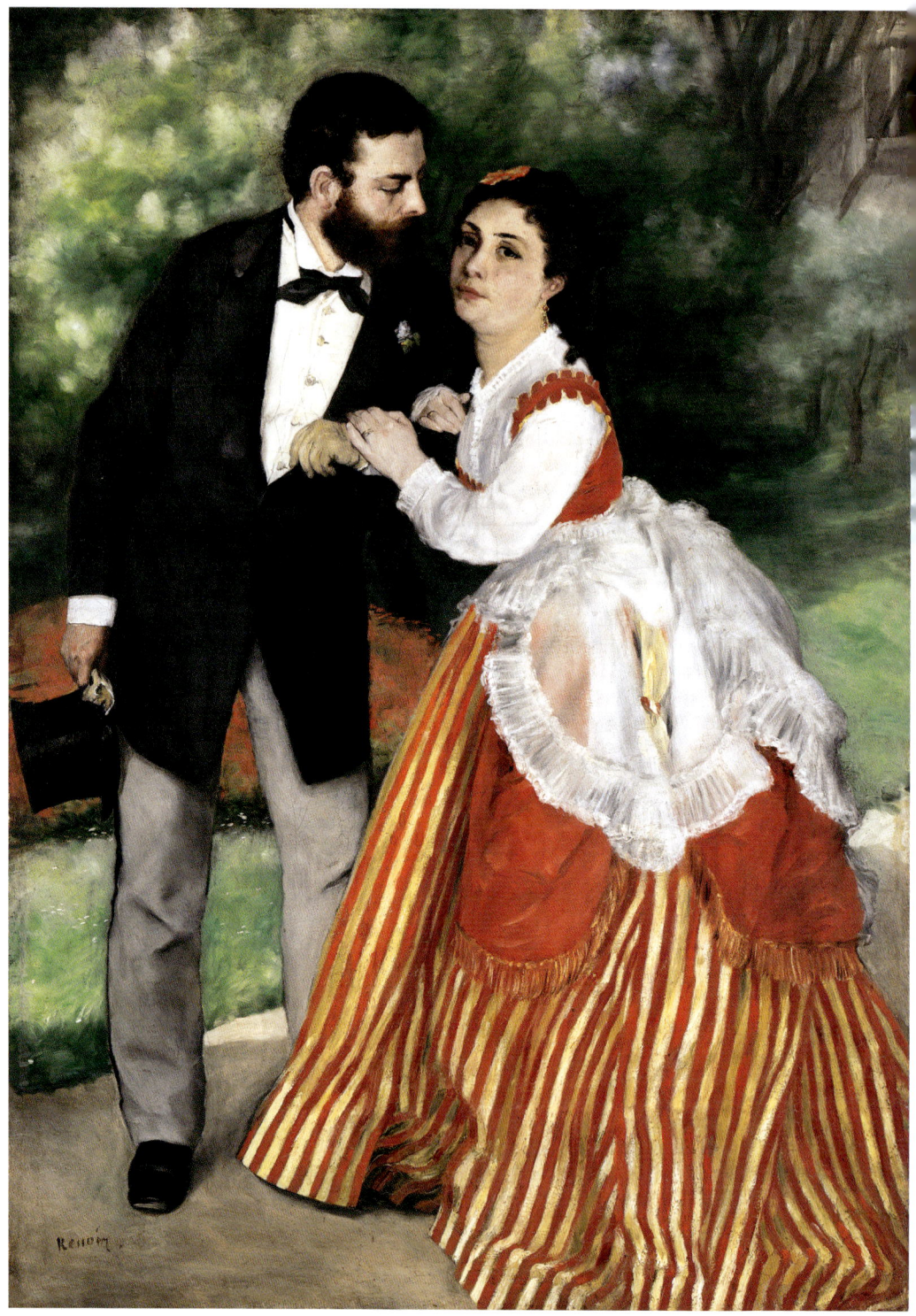

William Sisley, 1864
Oil on canvas,
81.5 x 65.5 cm (32 x 25⅞ in.)
Paris, Musée d'Orsay

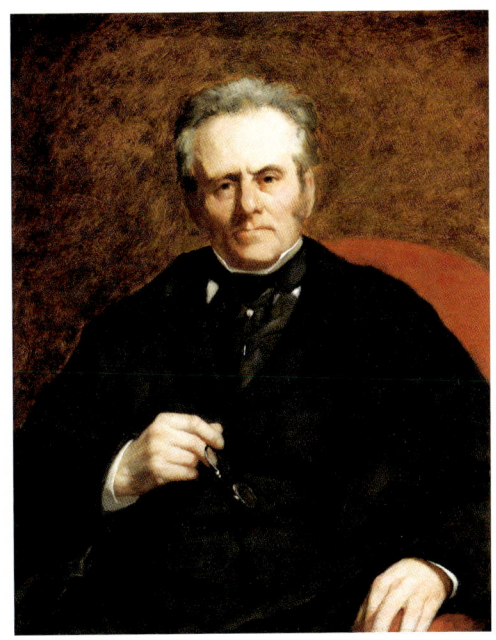

A Couple (Lise and Sisley), c. 1868
Oil on canvas,
105 x 75 cm (41¼ x 29½ in.)
Cologne, Wallraf-Richartz-Museum
& Fondation Corboud

Renoir and Alfred Sisley (1839–1899)
appear to have shared a mistress at
a certain period. Her name was Lise
Tréhot (1848–1922) and she is pictured
here. Renoir called this painting *Lise
et Sisley*.

On the advice of his older sister, Lisa, Renoir insisted on continuing to be paid at piecemeal rates. Inspired by a book given to him by his mother and entitled *The Gods of Olympus as Seen by the Great Painters*, he launched into producing his largest pieces of work. There were vases, for example, that he learned how to pot and fire himself and that he decorated with such subjects as "Venus against a background of clouds," creating a lovely effect. Jean Renoir owned an example of this work that has since disappeared. For a long time afterwards Renoir would recall this wonderful book of paintings of the Greek gods. He used it to paint in the style of Charles Gleyre (who had produced *Hercules at the Feet of Omphalos*, p. 34), creating one of his earliest paintings, an allegory entitled *Venus and Amor* (p. 35). At the end of his life he still remembered how, when living in a house called Les Collettes at Cagnes-sur-Mer, he transformed the laundresses and women bathers into earthly goddesses.

Unfortunately, mechanisation soon superseded craftsmanship, bringing in its wake the new public enthusiasm for the more methodical work of machines. The studio closed down. At the age of seventeen, Renoir had to look for other employment. He became a painter of fans. It was excellent training: "How many times have I copied *The Embarkation for Cythera*!" Renoir exclaimed to Vollard. "That is why the first painters with whose work I became familiar were Watteau, Lancret, and Boucher. More specifically I would say that Boucher's *Diana at the Bath* was the first painting to seize my imagination, and I have continued to love it throughout my life, as one does with first loves, even after one has been told that one ought not to love it because Boucher is 'nothing but a scene-painter'.

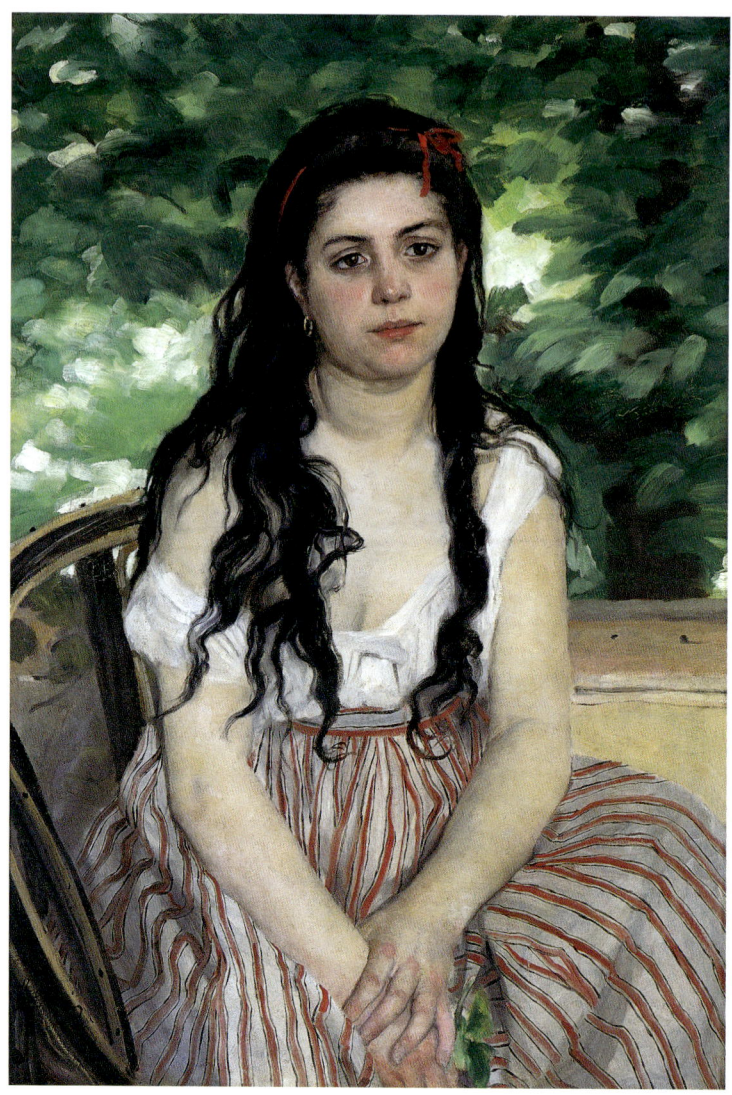

Summer, 1868
Oil on canvas, 85 x 59 cm (33½ x 23¼ in.)
Staatliche Museen zu Berlin, Nationalgalerie

The delightful young Lise Tréhot shared her life
with Renoir between 1866 and 1871. Renoir met
her through his friend, Jules Le Cœur, whose
young stepsister she was. He painted more than
twenty portraits of Lise, including *Diana* (p. 44),

Lise (p. 33), and *Odalisque* (pp. 50/51). Her
beautiful face, with its grave expression,
is seen for the last time in *Interior of a
Harem in Montmartre* (p. 47).

Lise, 1867
Oil on canvas, 184 x 115.5 cm (72½ x 45½ in.)
Essen, Museum Folkwang

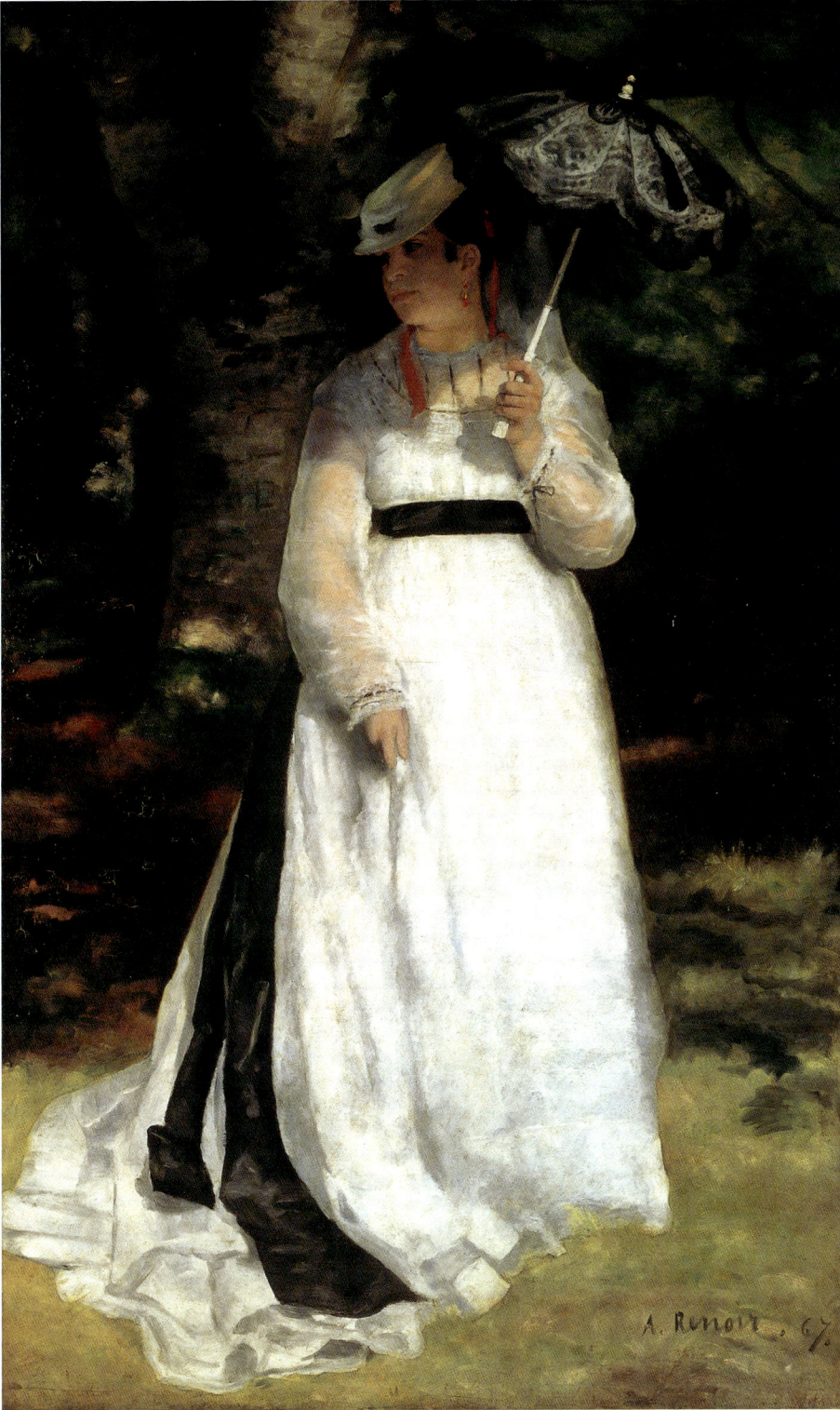

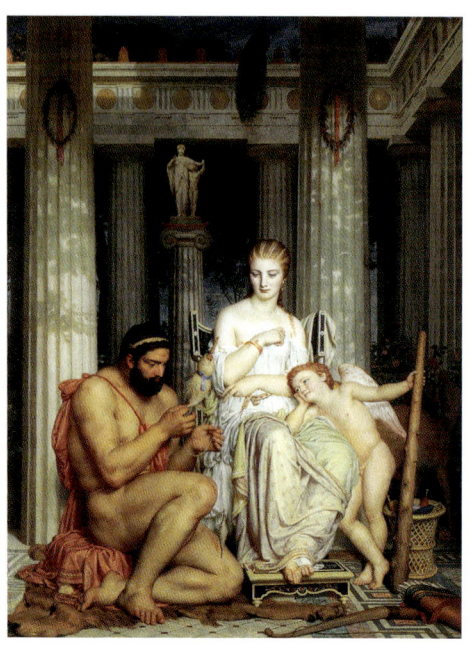

Charles Gleyre (1806–1874)
Hercules at the Feet of Omphalos, 1863
Oil on canvas, 145 x 111 cm (57 x 43¾ in.)
Neuchâtel, Musée d'Art et d'Histoire

Venus and Amor (Allegory), 1860
Oil on canvas, 46 x 38.1 cm (18⅛ x 15 in.)
Private collection

This first bather entering the water is still conventional in style and very much in the style of the period, but the subject is a foretaste of the personal vision of the future painter of *Bathers* and *Venus*.

A scene-painter, as if this were some kind of defect! Boucher is one of those painters who best understand the female form. He painted young buttocks and little dimples, which was just what was necessary. People will tell you, 'I prefer Titian to Boucher!' Well, so do I, of course! But, for all that, Boucher painted some very pretty women! A painter with a true appreciation of tits and bums is a saved man". This is where Renoir's third, and strongest, passion emerges, that which fills his whole work – love, which makes art joyful and loveable.

When the fan went out of fashion, Renoir began painting blinds designed to work as mobile stained glass windows, for Christian missionaries. "Once they reached their destination," explained Renoir, "these canvases, stretched over a frame, gave the Negroes the illusion that they were in a real church". Renoir mass-produced Virgins, magi, cherubs, and St Vincent de Paul, without first laying down a grid as other painters would, but instead drawing and painting the figures right on to the canvas with such dexterity and speed that the boss, frightened at having to pay him so much money, offered him a partnership. "Despite such tempting offers, I did not allow myself to be dazzled," concluded Renoir. By now, he had saved enough money to be able to live on it for a while (as long as he lived modestly), so "I went to learn 'great painting' from Gleyre, where live models could be studied". He enrolled simultaneously at the École Nationale Supérieure des Beaux-Arts, France's finest art school, where he made the acquaintance of the painter Fantin-Latour, who was destined to attract Renoir's attention because, in the words of Jacques-Émile Blanche, "he was unequalled in being able to paint roses like the breast of a woman". It was Fantin-Latour who brought Manet, Bazille, Monet, and Renoir together on the same canvas, in his famous painting of *A Studio at Batignolles* (p. 9 bottom).

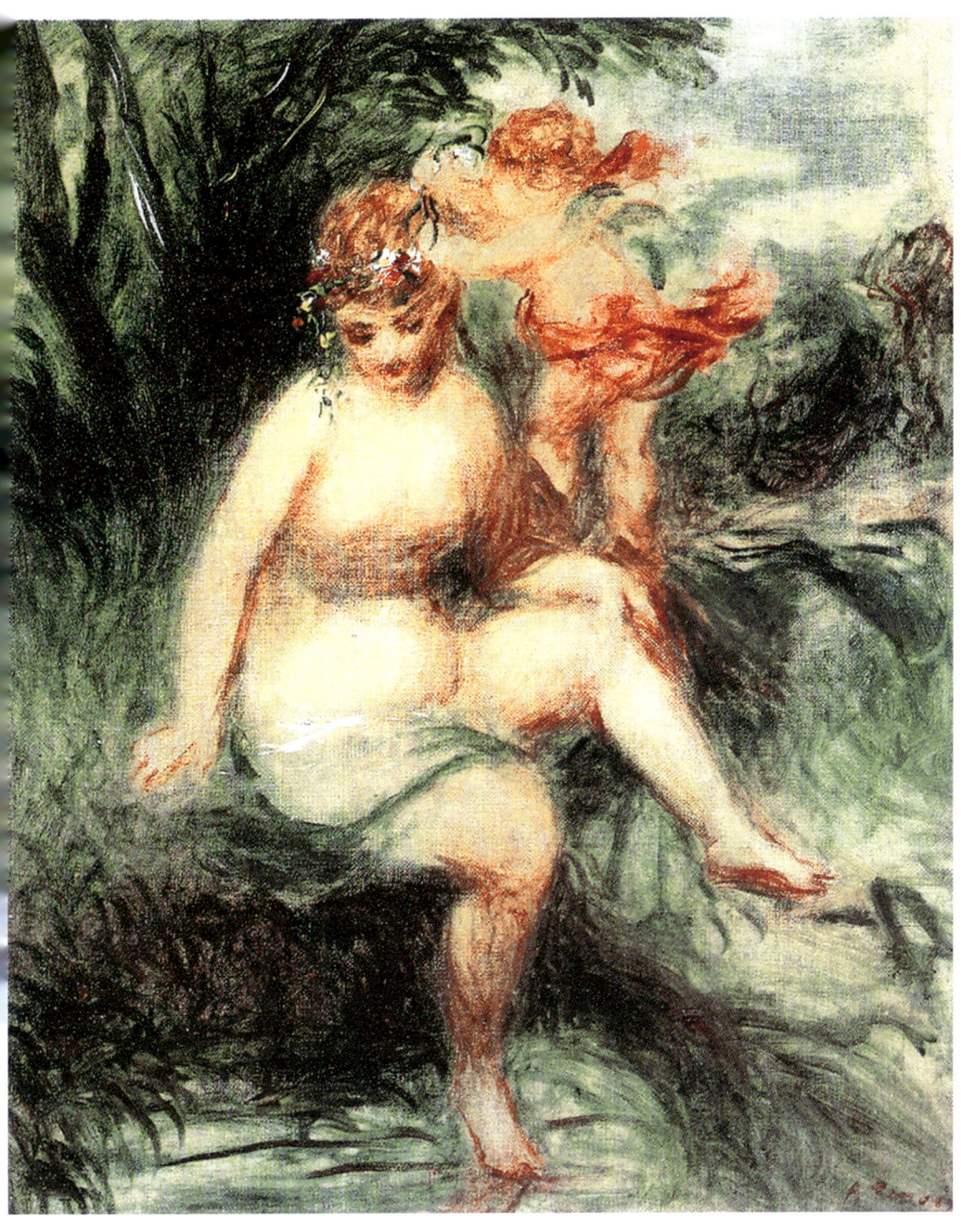

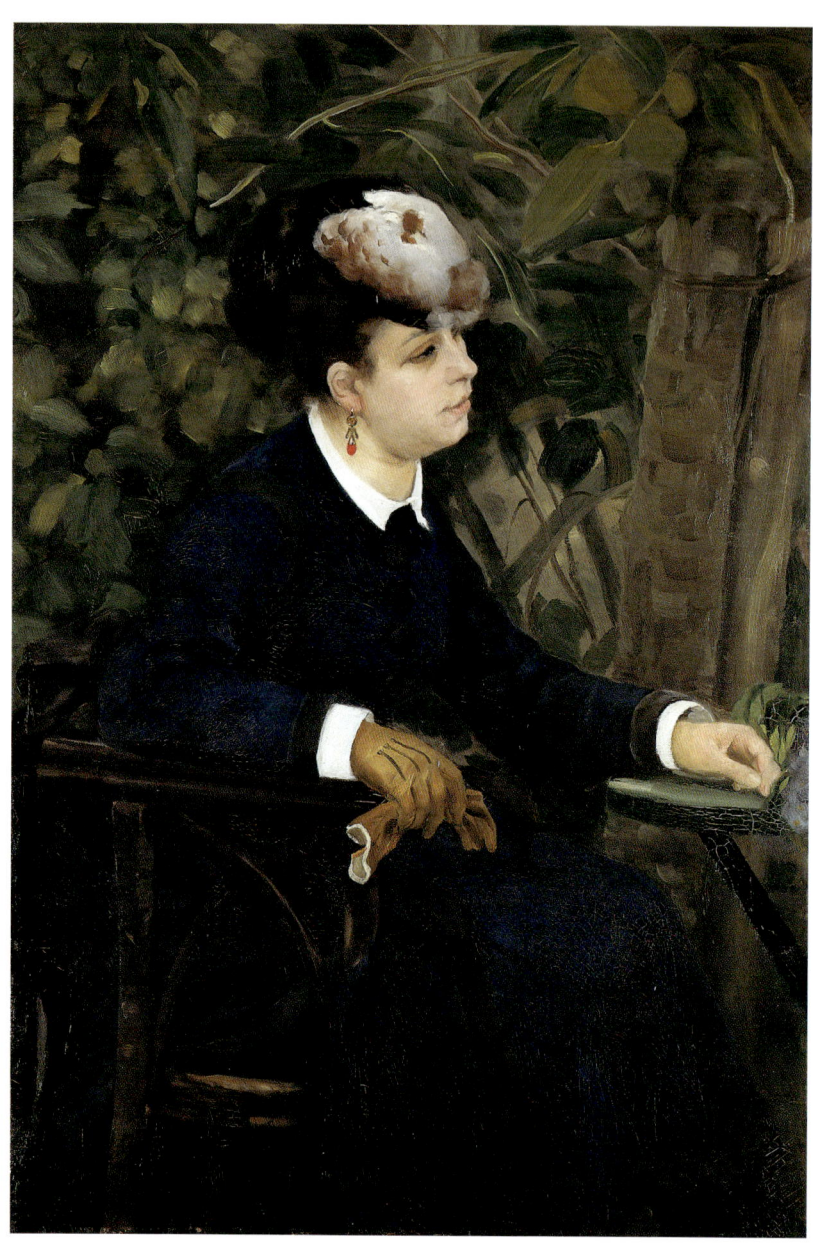

**Woman in a Garden
(Woman with a Seagull Feather)**, 1868
Oil on canvas, 105.5 x 73.4 cm (41⅝ x 29 in.)
Kunstmuseum Basel

Still Life, 1864
Oil on canvas,
130 x 98 cm (51¼ x 38⅝ in.)
Hamburger Kunsthalle

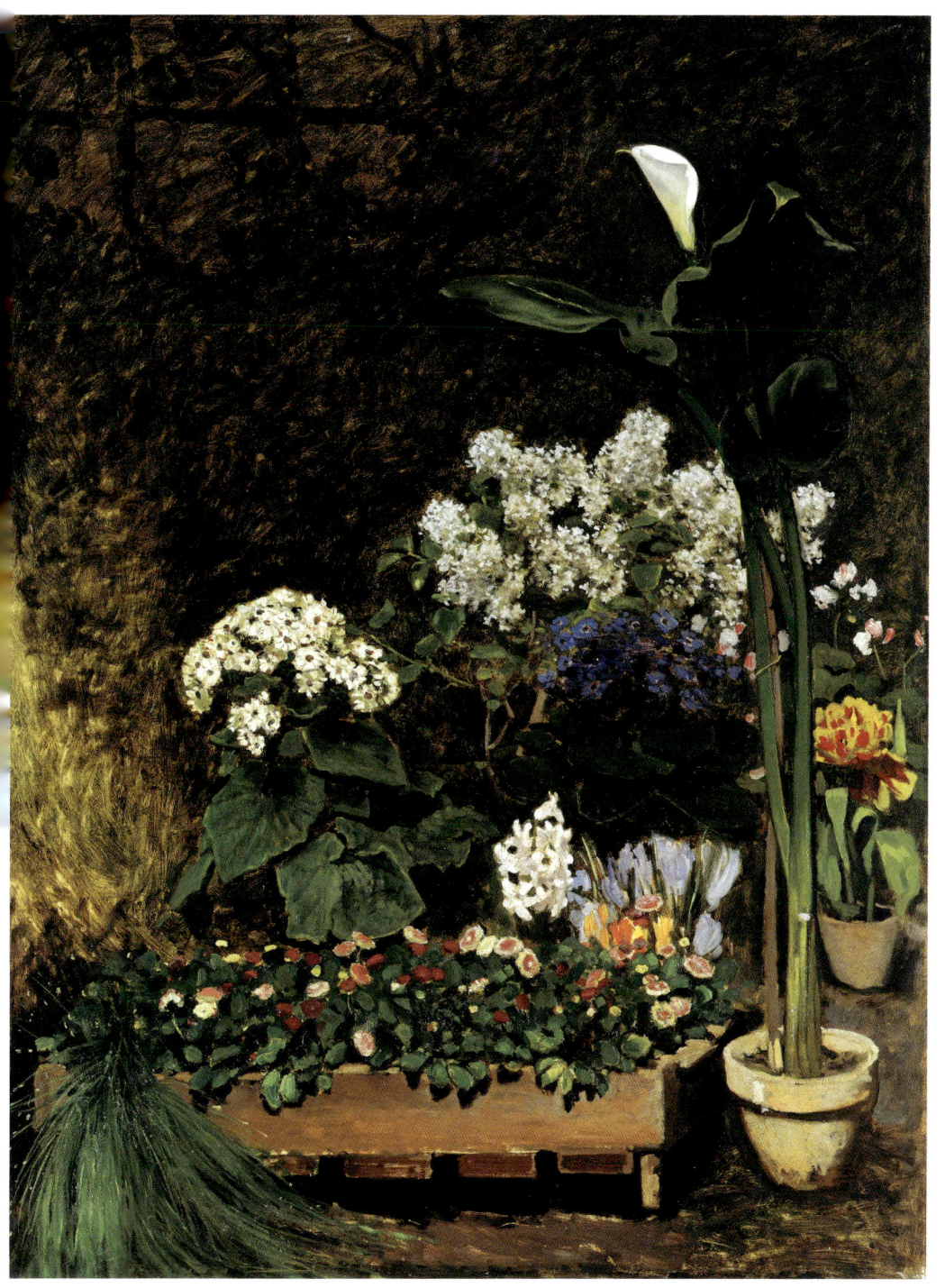

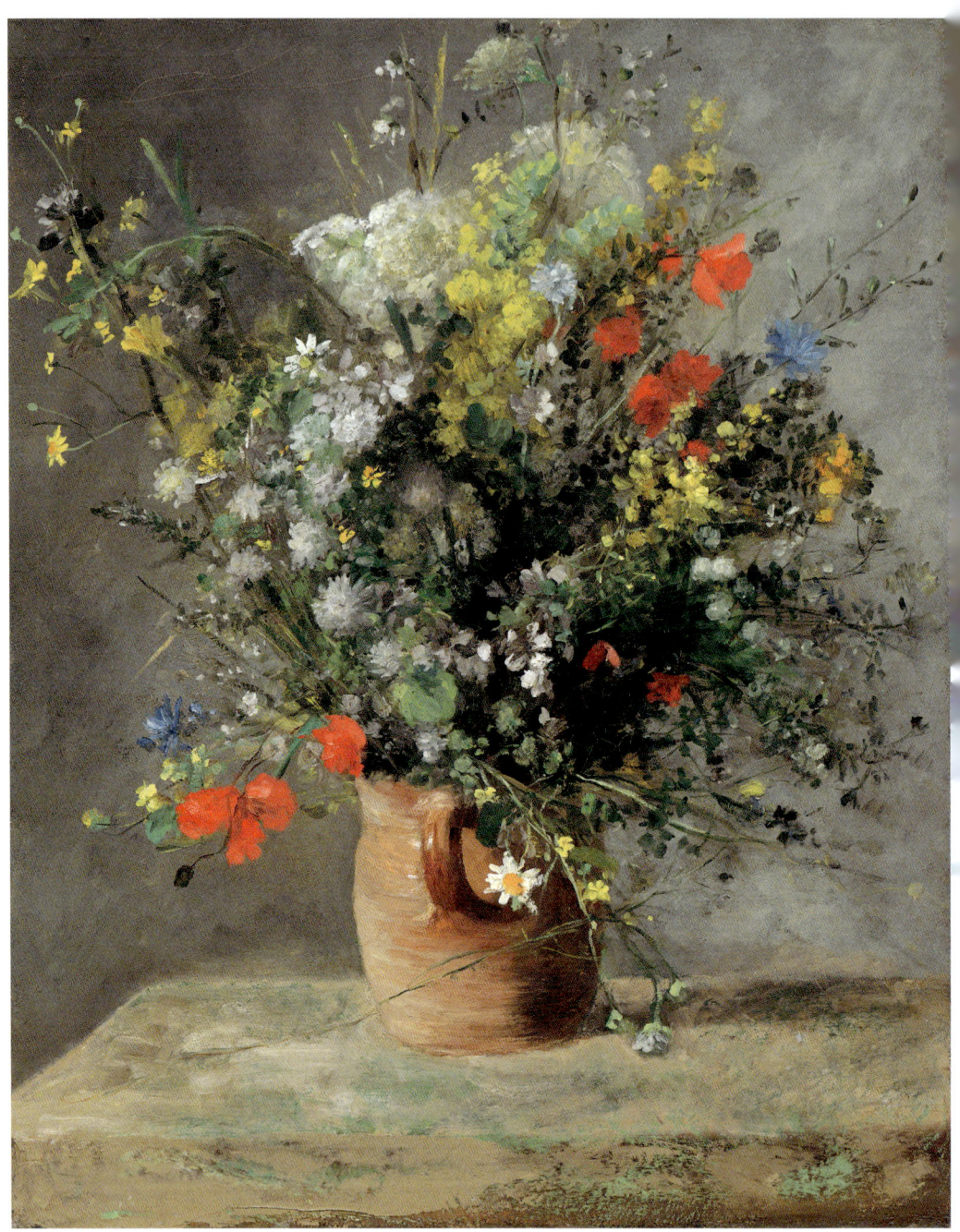

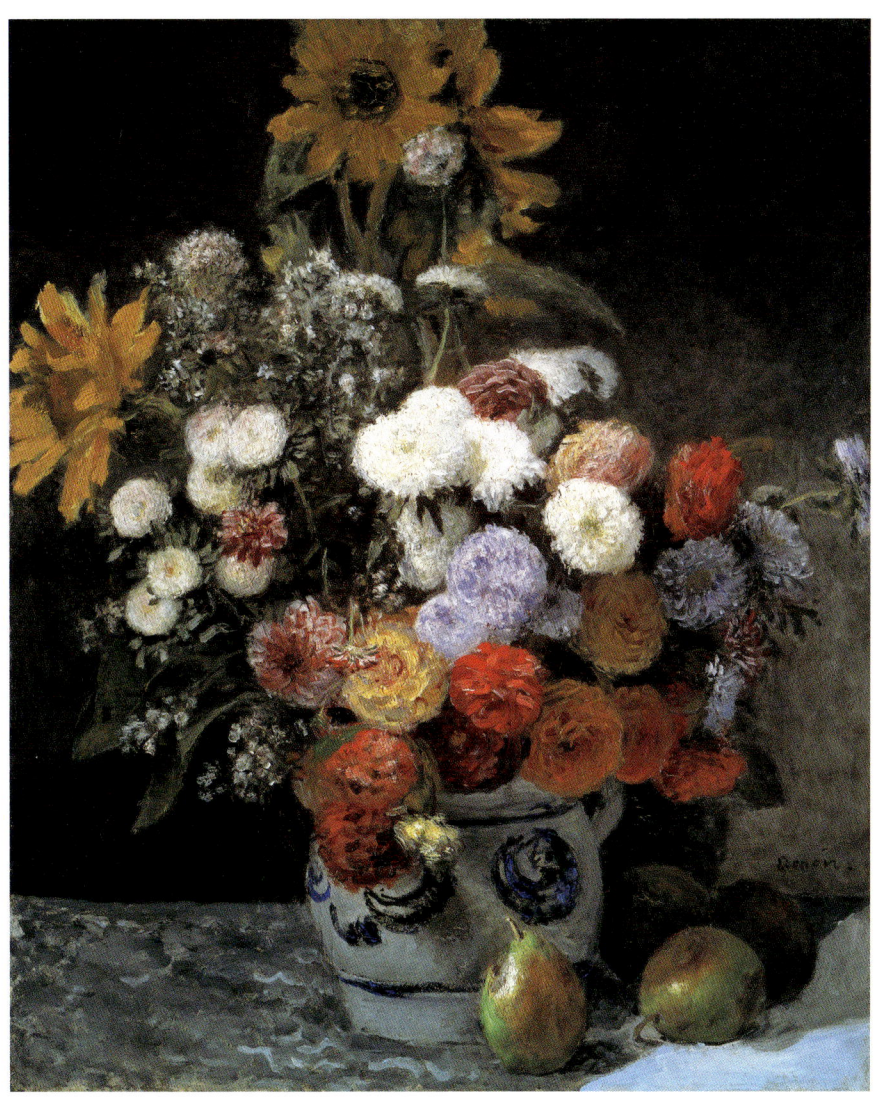

Flowers in a Vase, c. 1866
Oil on canvas,
81.3 x 65.1 cm (32 x 25¾ in.)
Washington D.C., National Gallery of Art,
Mr. and Mrs. Paul Mellon Collection

Mixed Flowers in an Earthenware Pot, c. 1869
Oil on paperboard mounted on canvas,
64.8 x 54.3 cm (25⅝ x 21½ in.)
Boston, Museum of Fine Arts,
Bequest of John T. Spaulding

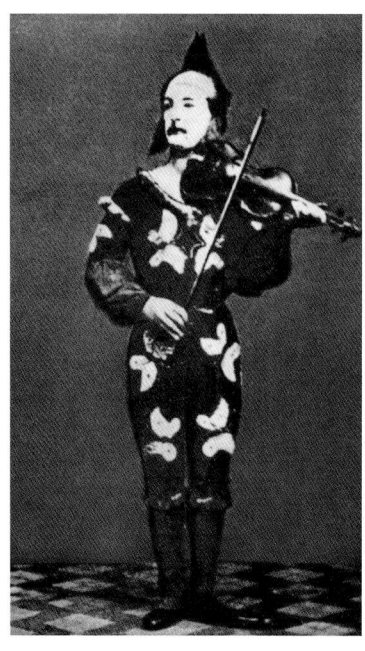

John Price, 1860

The Clown (John Price), 1868
Oil on canvas, 193.5 x 130 cm (76¼ x 51¼ in.)
Otterlo, Kröller-Müller Museum

"This man Gleyre was incapable of providing any assistance to his students!" Renoir once explained to Vollard, "but at least he had the decency to leave them alone to do exactly as they pleased". The four friends who had met at the studio took advantage of this freedom to go and paint in the open air, in the Forest of Fontainebleau, which at the time was the home of the Barbizon School. It was also where Millet, Rousseau, Daubigny, Dupré, Troyon, Díaz, and Corot came to seek inspiration. Monet originated from Le Havre where he had admired the work of the local painter Jongkind, by whom he swore; Sisley was under the influence of Corot, who would eventually become Renoir's idol and remain so for his entire life, though at the time, Renoir held Narcisso Virgilio Díaz de la Peña in greater admiration. "It should be said," he later explained as if to excuse himself, "that Díaz's painting, which later turned so dark, then shone as brightly as gemstones". One fateful day, in the forest, Renoir first met the great man. Riled by some ruffians who had made fun of the porcelain-painter's smock that he still wore when he worked, Renoir had hit out in a rage, but he was not tough enough to hold his own, and the brawl would have gone against him had a giant of a man not intervened on his side. Despite having a wooden leg, the man put Renoir's attackers to flight, threatening them by whirling his cane in the air menacingly. "I am a painter as well, my name is Díaz," he said, introducing himself, and studied Renoir's canvas. "That's not badly drawn, but for heaven's sake why do you paint with such dark colours?" From then on, Renoir painted in brighter colours, leaving dark ones out of his palette. Díaz's influence turned out to be transitory. The revelation of Courbet and Manet, as well as the power of Delacroix, monopolised Renoir's attention. Manet's paintings had scandalised the Salon des Refusés but had greatly impressed the group of artists at

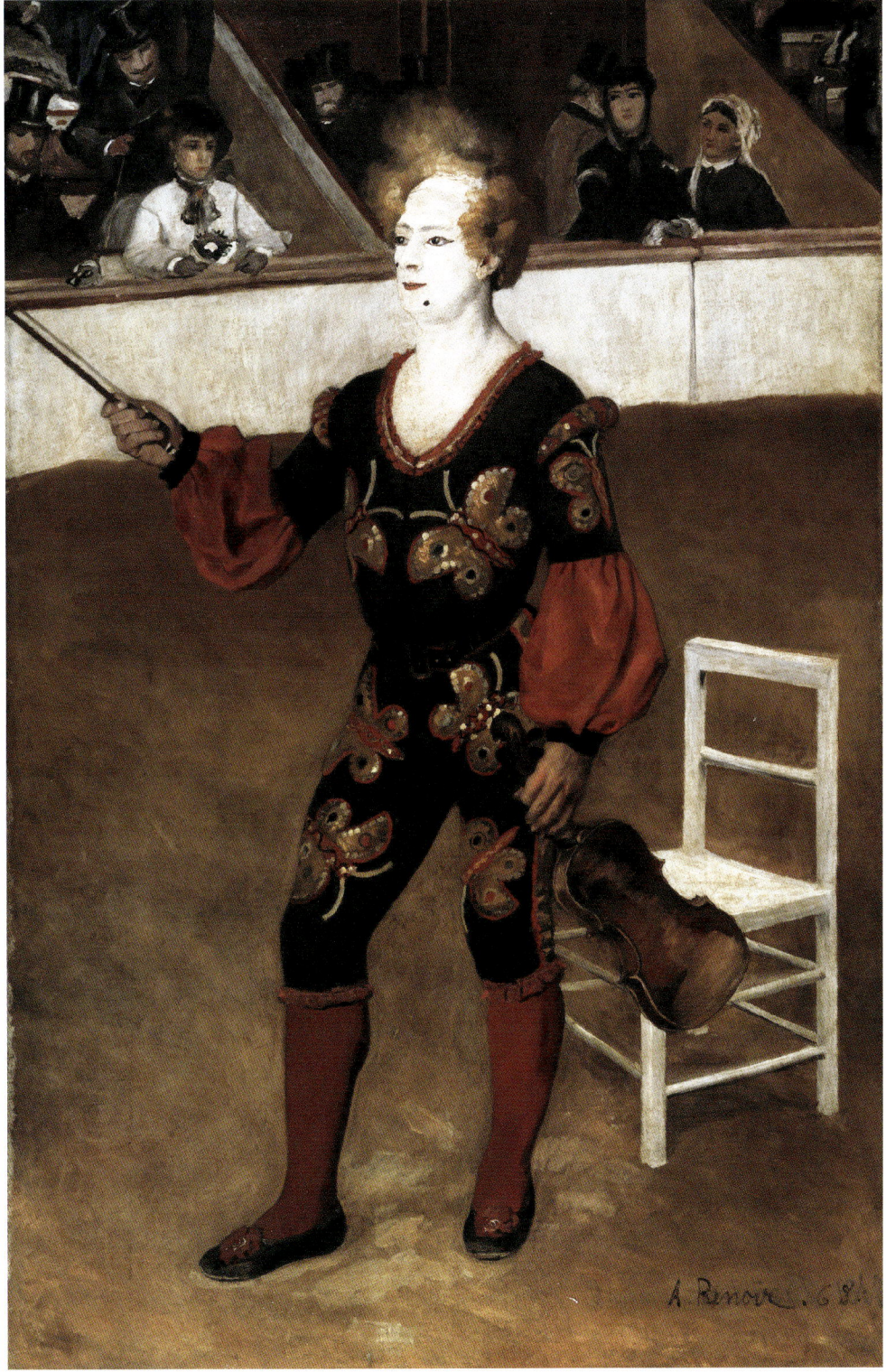

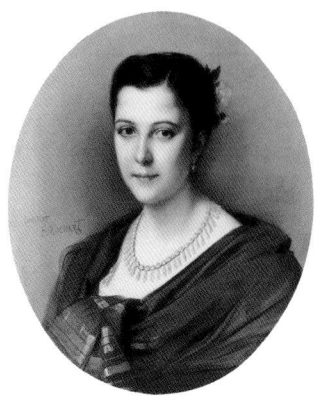

Constant-Joseph Brochart (1816–1899)
Clémentine Stora, c. 1880
Pastel, 68 x 57 cm (26⅞ x 22½ in.)
Private collection

PAGE 44
Diana, 1867
Oil on canvas, 199.5 x 129.5 cm (78½ x 51 in.)
Washington, D.C., National Gallery of Art,
Chester Dale Collection

PAGE 45
Bather with Griffon Terrier, 1870
Oil on canvas, 183.5 x 115 cm (72¼ x 45⅜ in.)
Museu de Arte de São Paulo,
Assis Chateaubriand

the Gleyre Studio, as well as their fellow-students at the Académie Suisse: Pissarro, Cézanne, and Guillaumin. It was then that the long-lasting friendship between Renoir and Cézanne was born. Renoir gained experience and learned lessons from the work of the masters whom he admired, but their influence was neither durable nor persistent. The personalities of Courbet and especially Manet were not compatible with his own. Manet was the standard-bearer of the emerging group, which was made up of those rebelling against the academic formula painting that then prevailed. It was Manet whose work was closest to the simplicity that each sought to acquire, but this was merely a stage beyond which they would all soon move, each according to his own temperament. Renoir's deep admiration for Rubens did not wane, and he copied the latter's *Portrait of Helena Fourment and Her Children* in the Louvre (1635/36).

Renoir's elder sister was married by now but she continued to look after her little brother and urged him to become a portrait painter, so that he would be able to live from his work. This excellent advice gradually enabled him to live comfortably. "That is exactly what I did," explained the painter. "The only problem was that my models were friends and so the portraits earned me nothing". Renoir was a dab hand at portraits. He had had plenty of practice at Gleyre's studio (cf. *Forty-three Portraits in Gleyre's Studio,* p. 11). He had already exhibited his *Esmeralda* at the salon, but later destroyed it in disgust at its dark palette. He graduated from a student to a promising young painter and finally received his first commissions to paint portraits. That of *Mademoiselle Romaine Lacaux* (p. 6) is probably the loveliest. This nine-year-old infanta in the Velázquez style was the daughter of an earthenware manufacturer whom Renoir had probably met when he was a porcelain-plate painter. Despite a

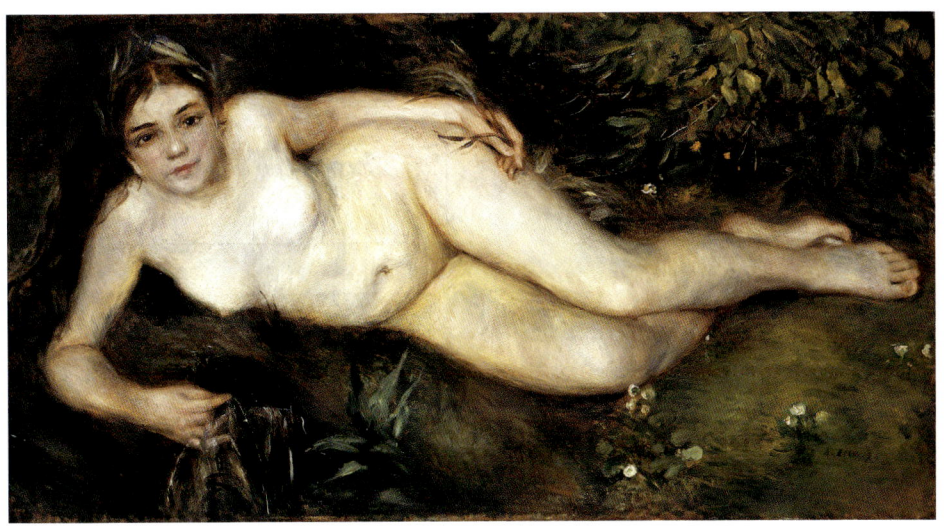

A Nymph by a Stream, 1869/70
Oil on canvas, 66.7 x 122.9 cm (26⅜ x 48½ in.)
London, The National Gallery

certain clumsiness, the twenty-three-year-old Renoir succeeded in creating a painting that already showed the features that would make him such a great portraitist. His apprenticeship in china painting can be seen in the satiny hues and shades of pink – which have an almost Chinese delicacy – of the face and hands. He daringly sought to reveal the flesh of the arms through the transparent silk sleeves. The solidity of the model and the extraordinary luminosity are already present. But it is Romaine Lacaux's (1855–1918) gaze that holds the viewer with a rare intensity and frankness that exude the very spirit of childhood. This was something to which Renoir would later devote himself with enthusiasm. Palpable here is the irrepressible love for human beings that always emanates from Renoir, his remarkable ability to capture the personality of the sitter. It is the same gift that enabled the former porcelain-painter to dash off magnificent well-structured bouquets in luscious profusion, radiating light and colour. Courbet's influence is ever-present beneath the surface of Renoir's work.

During the 1860s, Renoir produced a wealth of portraits, commissioned or otherwise. Firstly, there were those of his friends and colleagues, such as Bazille (p. 19), *A Couple* (p. 30), and William Sisley, Alfred's father (1799–1879; p. 31), all of which he intended to display at the 1865 Salon. The portrait of Sisley's father clearly shows the character of this shrewd and strict sixty-five-year-old Protestant businessman who had left London to settle in Paris, where his son was born. William Sisley was one of the first wealthy notables to be courted by Renoir. The portrait is competently done, rich in the ivory black that Renoir always used and that he treated as a prime colour, but he still had a long way to go before he could paint like his predecessors, Manet and Fantin-Latour.

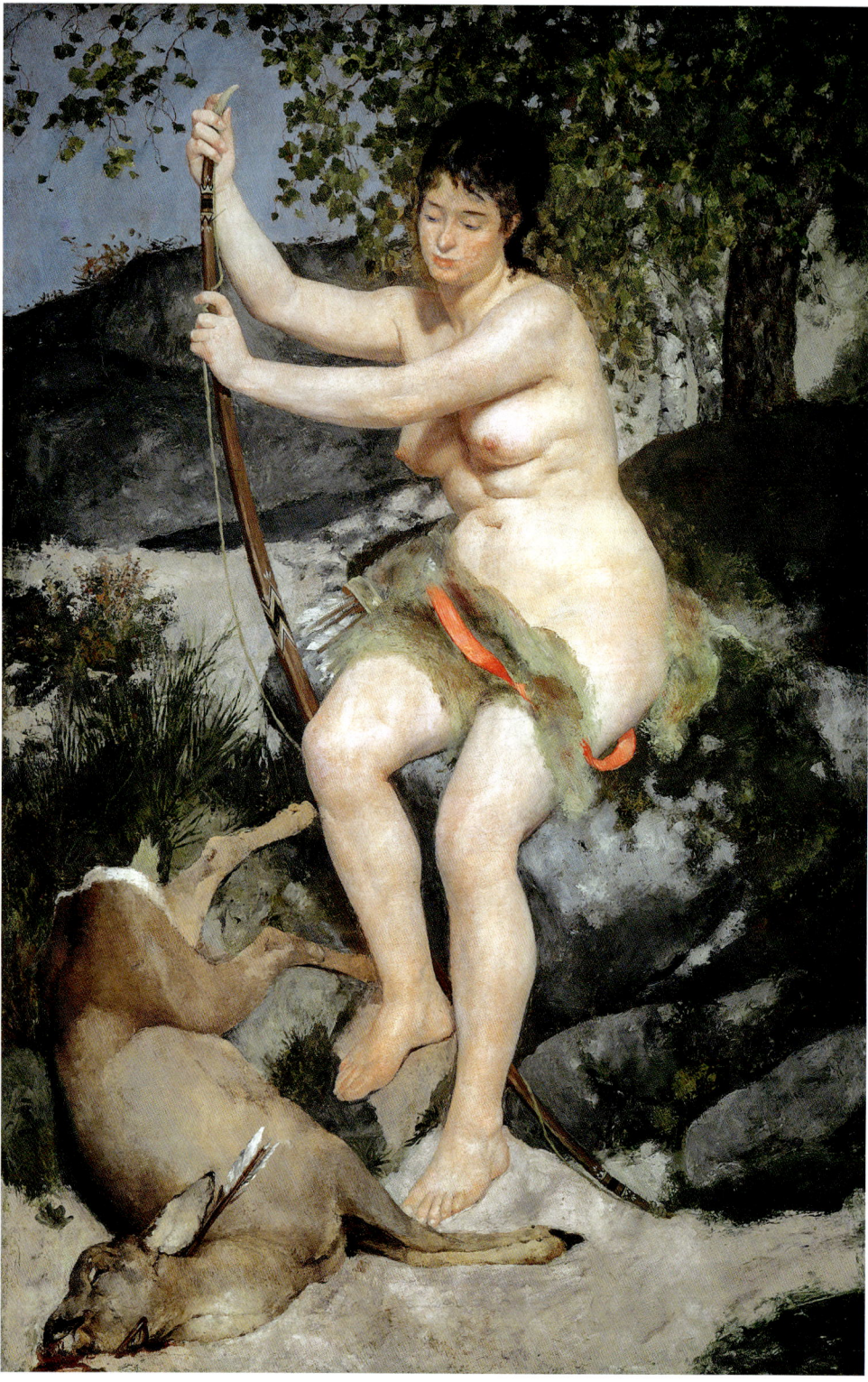

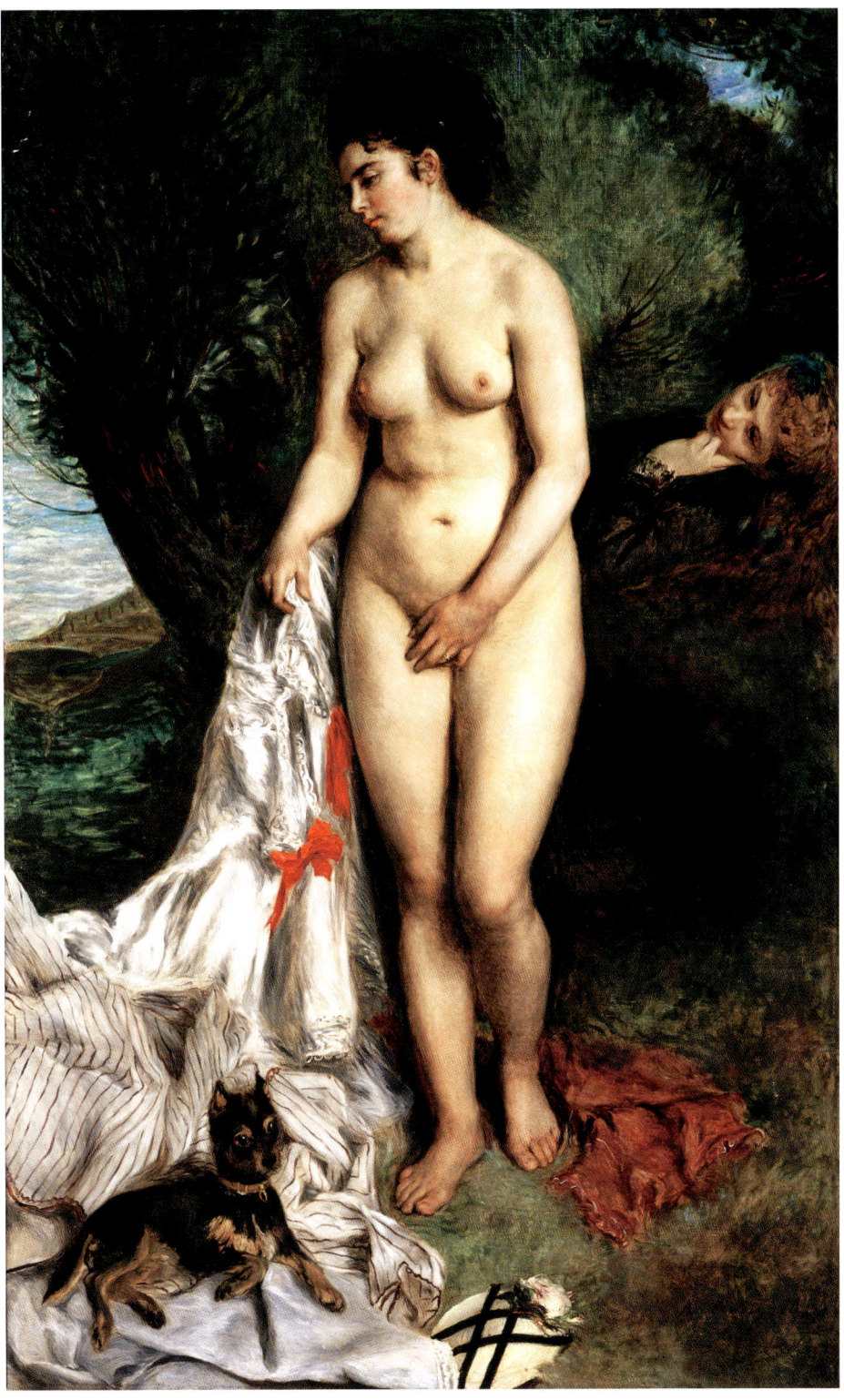

**Interior of a Harem in Montmartre
(Parisian Women Dressed as Algerians)**, 1872
Oil on canvas, 156 x 128.8 cm (61½ x 50¾ in.)
Tokyo, National Museum of Western Art,
Matsukata Collection

Renoir was still seeking his own style but had
moved on from the inspiration of Courbet to
Delacroix, whose palette he admired. The result
was this homage to the orientalism of Delacroix's
Women of Algiers (p. 48). Renoir would later
dismiss this type of genre painting, seeing it
merely as a youthful experiment and deploring
the fact that some of his admirers begged him
to continue to paint in this manner. On the advice
of Vollard, he "accidentally forgot" to take the
monumental *Harem* painting with him when he
moved house, but an honest concierge reminded
him that he had left it behind, forcing him to
spend 40 sous on sending a coach to have it
picked up!

Before the outbreak of the Franco-Prussian War in 1870, Renoir made several trips to
the Forest of Fontainebleau. He either stayed at the Auberge du Cheval Blanc, run by a man
called Paillard in Chailly-en-Brière, or at Mother Anthony's inn at Marlotte. He also benefited
on several occasions from the generous hospitality of his friend, Jules Le Cœur, who owned
a large property in Marlotte, where he lived with his mistress, Clémence Tréhot, daughter of
the postmaster of Ecquevilly, in the department of Seine-et-Oise. Jules Le Cœur's home not
only gave Renoir the opportunity of finding out what life was like in a wealthy household
that had a taste for art and literature, but it was here that he found his favourite model, who
was to be his companion for many years, Clémence's younger sister, the charming young
Lise Tréhot. The first time he met this young woman, whose rustic charm attracted him
immediately, Renoir begged her to come and pose for him. He painted more than twenty
portraits of Lise, standing in a park, sitting on the grass or seen sewing in an interior. She
appears as *Diana* (p. 44), in *Lise* (p. 33), in *Summer* she is standing against a background
of greenery (p. 32), with a seagull on her hat (*Woman in a Garden*, p. 36), and finally as an
Odalisque (pp. 50/51), a painting which could have borne Delacroix's signature.

There is a striking diversity in all these portraits of the same model. Renoir was after all
"the most changeable of men", as Pissarro described him. In several of the portraits of Lise,
Renoir remembers his aim to exhibit at the Salon and win fame. He resorts to a style still
traditional, with smooth brushstrokes and a rather dark palette, in order to win over the
jury. It is in the large expanses and the glazes that show the foundations of preparations
that he extends the colours with flat tints of warm brown, intense greens, and faded blues.

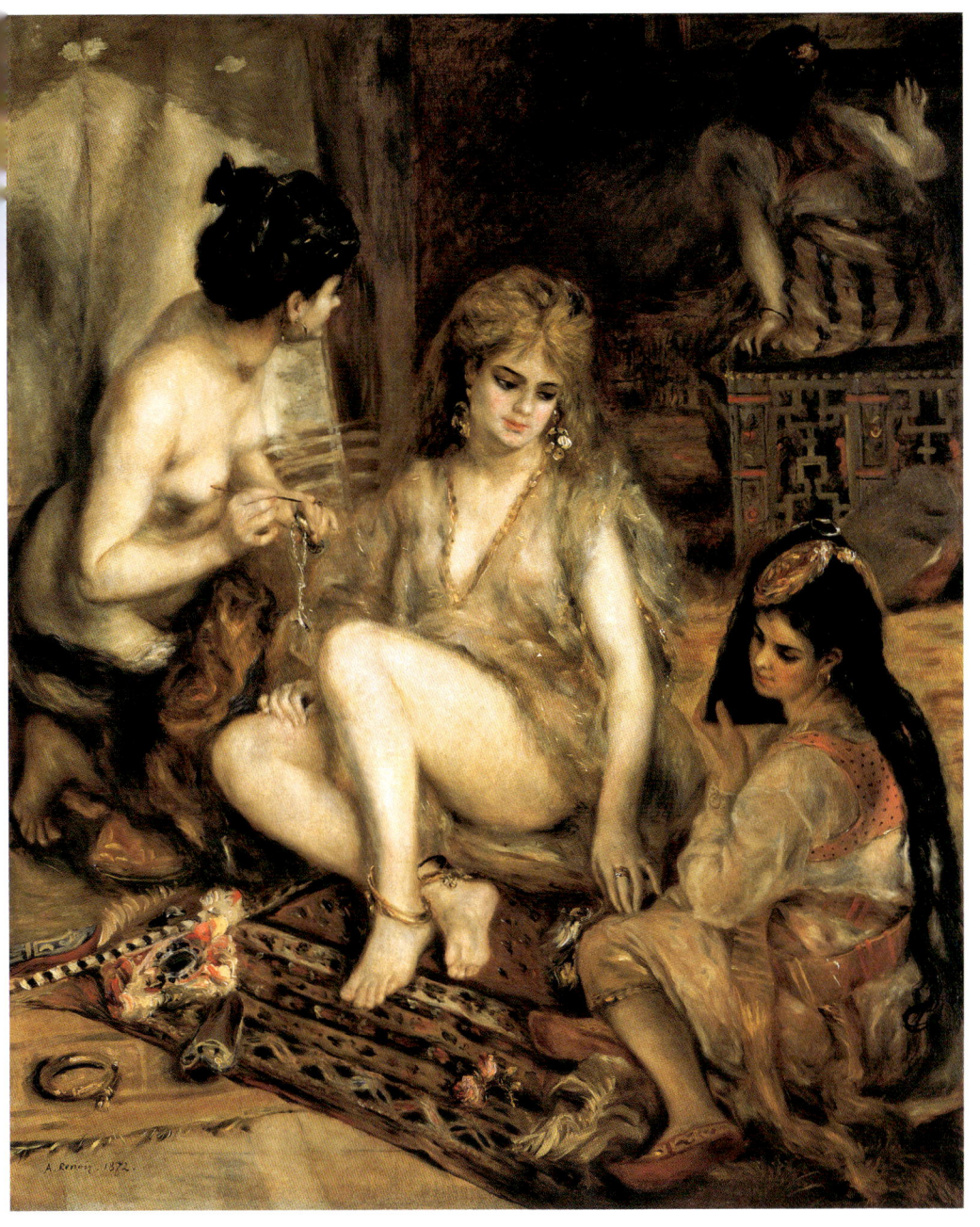

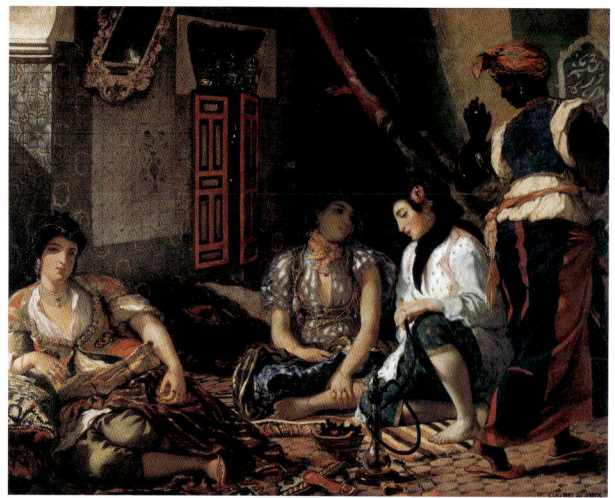

Eugène Delacroix (1798–1863)
Women of Algiers, 1834
Oil on canvas,
180 x 229 cm (70⅞ x 90¼ in.)
Paris, Musée du Louvre

**Algerian Woman
(Madame Clémentine Stora
in Algerian Dress)**, 1870
Oil on canvas,
84.5 x 59.7 cm (33⅜ x 23⅝ in.)
Fine Arts Museum of San
Francisco, Gift of Mr. and Mrs.
Prentis Cobb Hale in honor of
Thomas Carr Howe Jr.

In *Diana*, for example, he paints large areas of impasto, sometimes using a palette knife, and constructs a patchwork of colours that are reminiscent of the master of Ornans. Elsewhere, in *Lise*, *Summer*, *Woman in a Garden* or *The Walk* (p. 53), he uses more modern techniques, the precursors of those he employed in *Le Moulin de la Galette* (pp. 114/115). Having become a true believer in a bright palette, as Diaz had suggested, he rejected a bituminous preparatory background and placed his subject directly on the bare white canvas. He now used ochre and vermilion and replaced the earth colours of his early portraits with blues that combined poetry and light with the life of the shapes. In this way he attempts to combine what will later become Impressionism with his own classical temperament.

For the record, and for a better understanding of the conventions and tastes of the period, it is worth repeating Renoir's story of how he "had been about" to sell *Diana* to a visitor to his studio when they found themselves unable to come to an arrangement … because the would-be purchaser wanted to buy the deer alone! He was not interested in the rest of the picture. In fact, it was only for reasons of convention that the sensuous woman that Renoir wanted to paint had become a Diana. "All I wanted to do was produce a nude study, but such a painting would have been considered quite improper, so I placed an archery bow in the model's hand and a deer at her feet. I added an animal skin to make her nudity less shocking – and the painting became a Diana!" All of this he did just for a chance to exhibit at the 1867 Salon – which then, of course, rejected the painting out of hand.

It was while he was staying at Mother Anthony's that Renoir decided to throw in his lot with the "refusés", those other painters who had been rejected by the Salon. "*At the Inn of Mother*

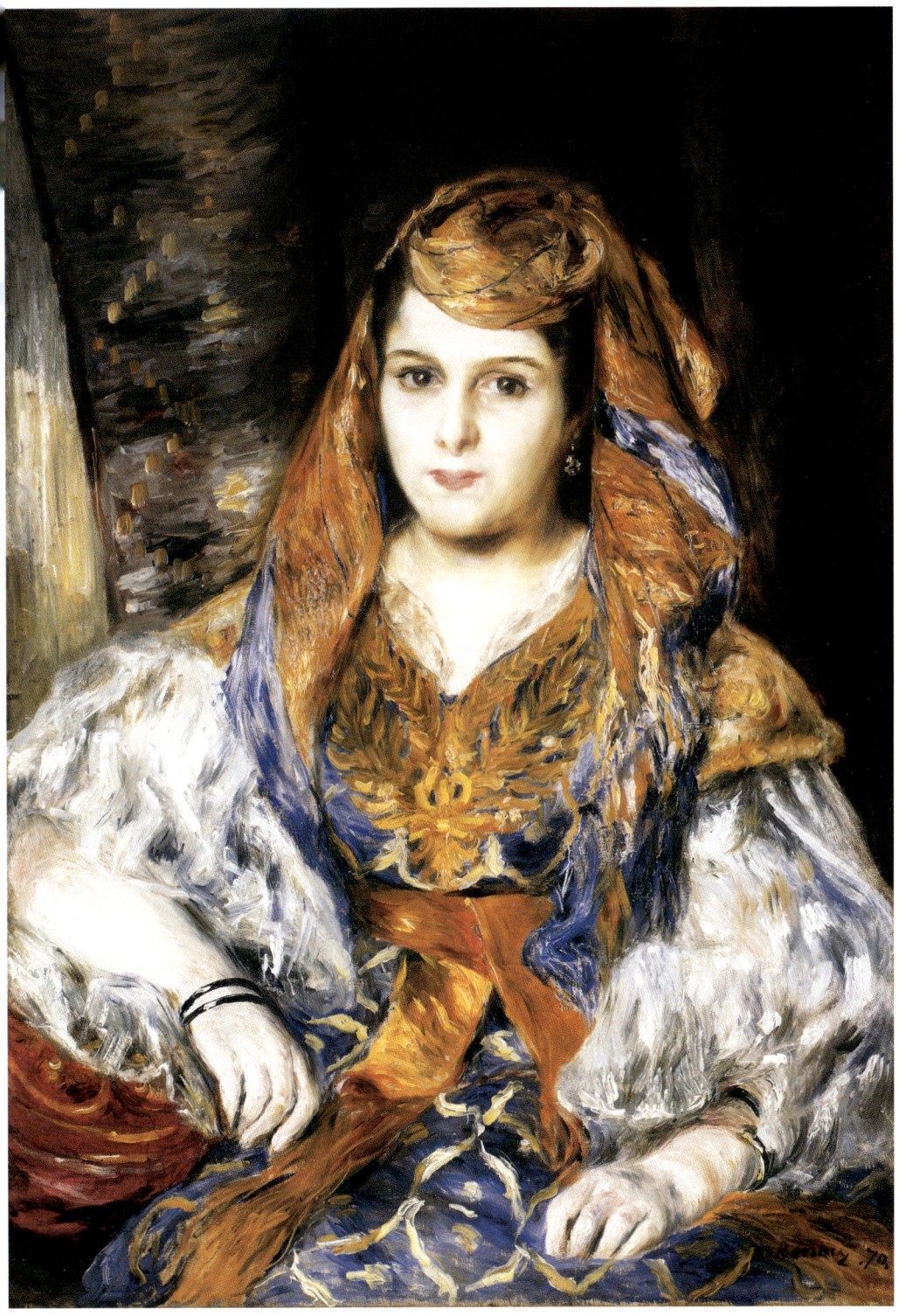

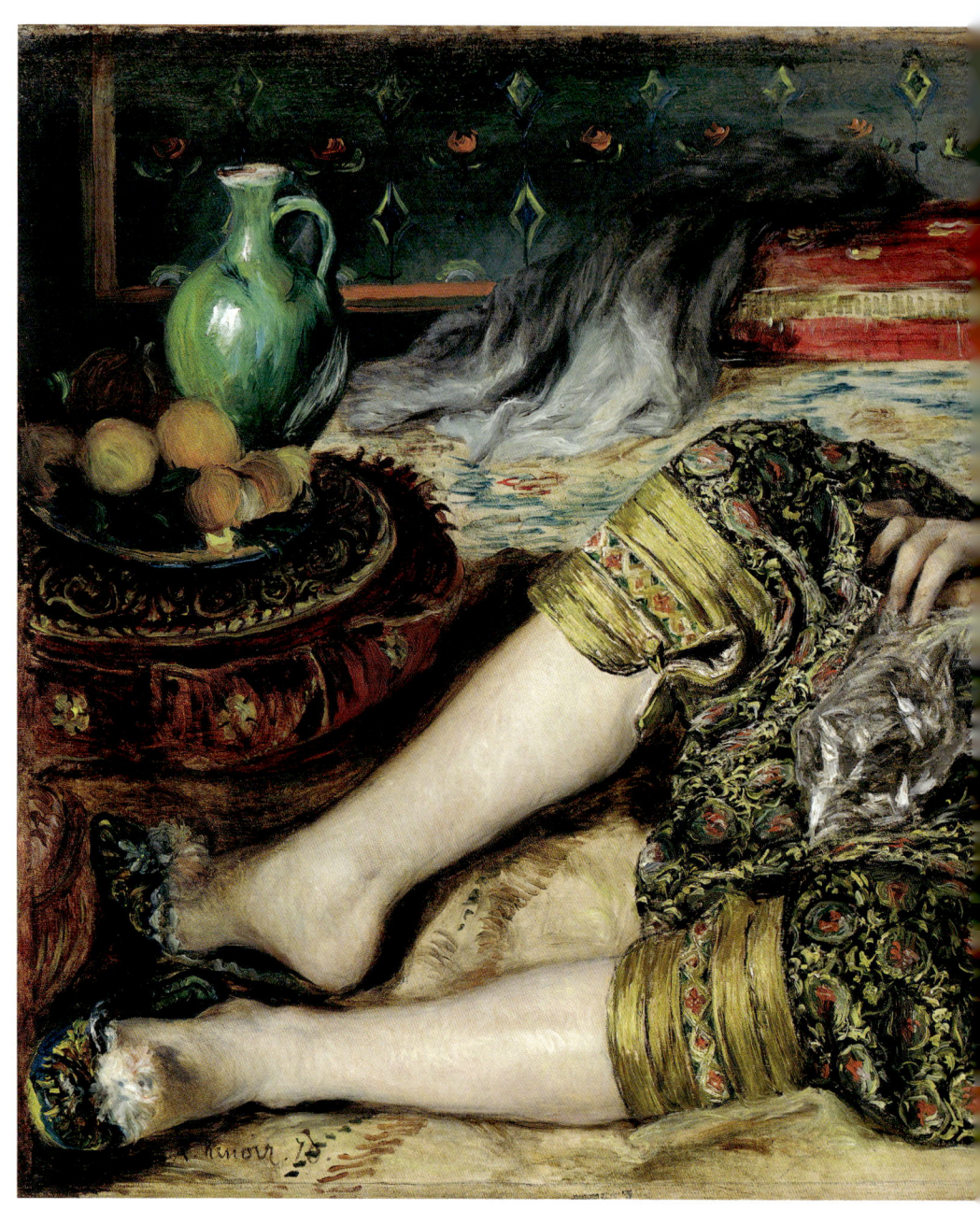

Odalisque, 1870
Oil on canvas, 69.2 x 122.6 cm (27¼ x 48¼ in.)
Washington, D.C., National Gallery of Art,
Chester Dale Collection

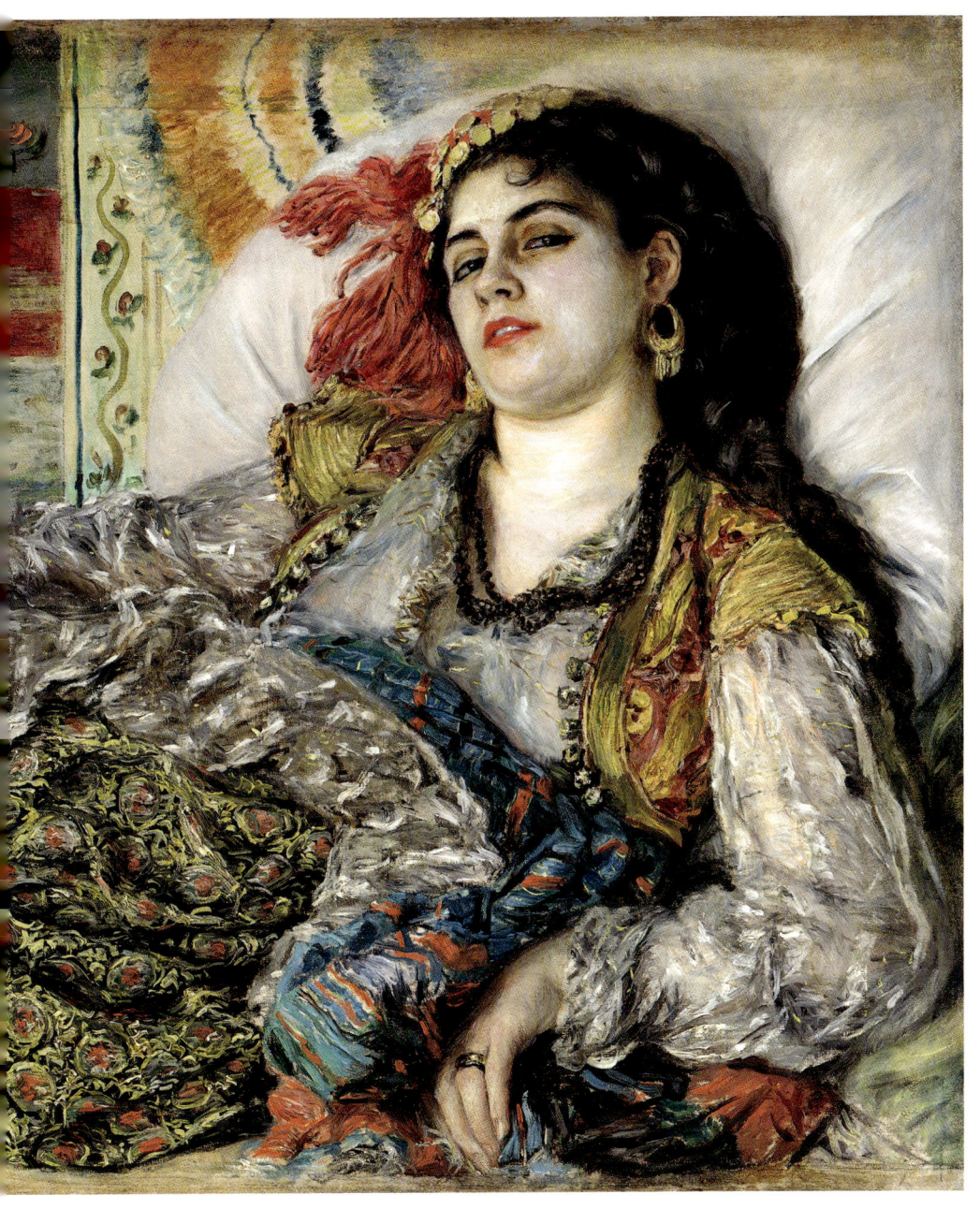

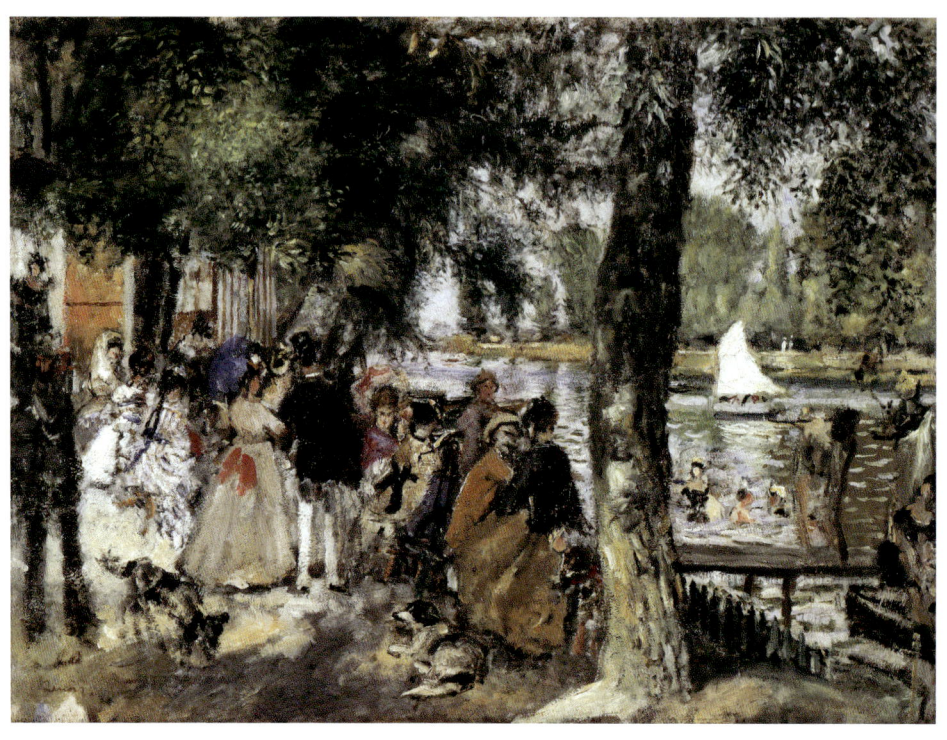

La Grenouillère, 1869
Oil on canvas, 59 x 80 cm (23¼ x 31½ in.)
Moscow, Pushkin Museum

La Grenouillère, painted by Renoir and Monet
standing side-by-side, marked the true beginnings
of Impressionism. The two friends could be said
to share not only their love for water and watery
landscapes but also the penury in which they
both lived at the time. "We don't eat every day,"
explained Renoir, but "Monet is good company".

Each of them was discovering his own temperament
and aspirations. In Monet's work, the figures are
of secondary importance to the water (p. 55).
Renoir, on the other hand, worked on the details.
The former was a more powerful painter, but the
latter showed more delicacy and subtlety.

The Walk, 1870
Oil on canvas,
81.3 x 64.8 cm (32 x 25⅝ in.)
Los Angeles, The J. Paul Getty Museum

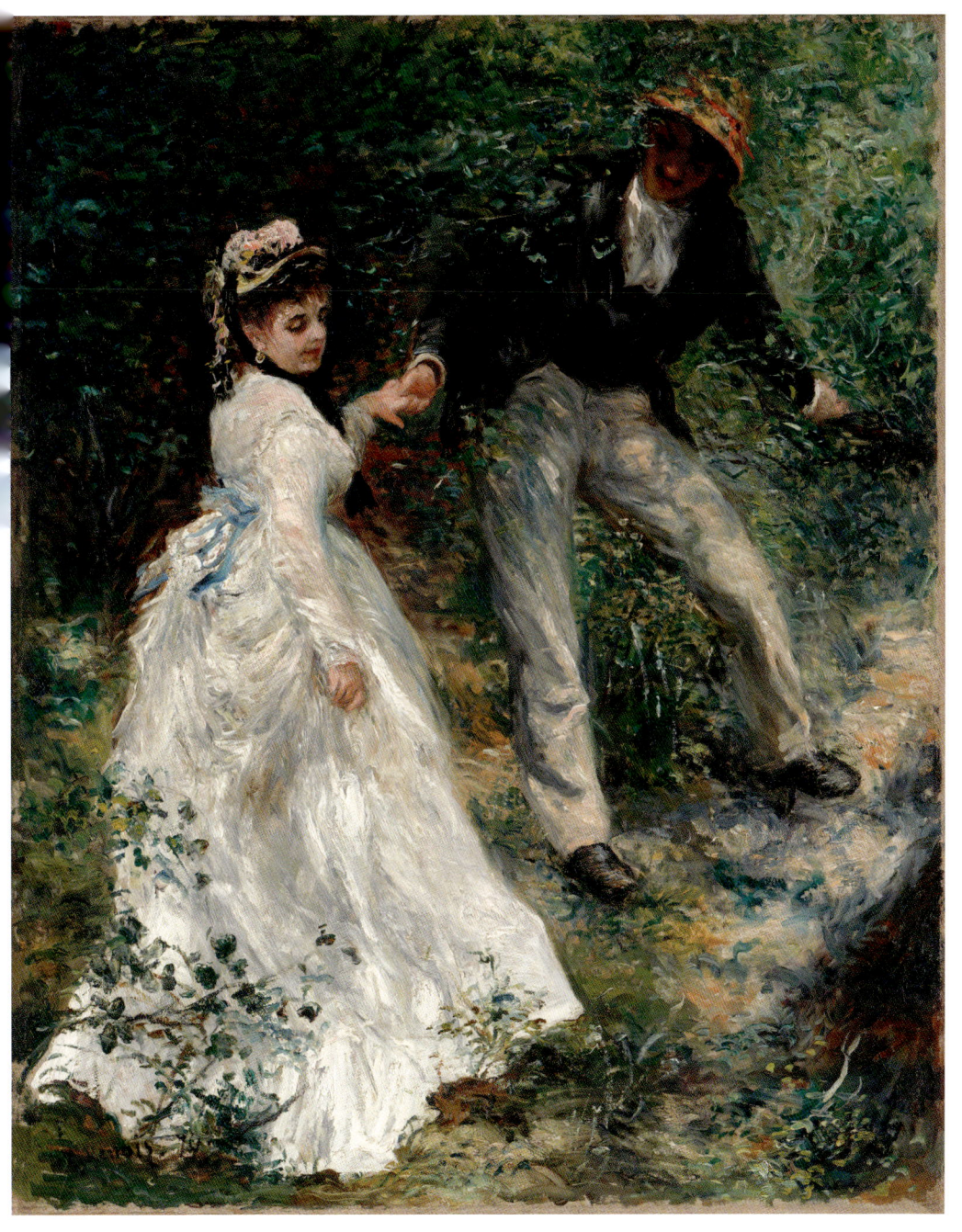

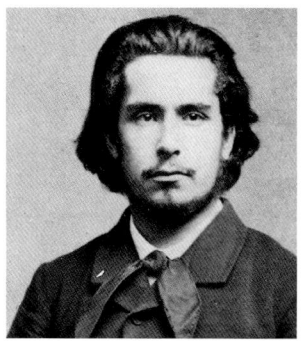

Claude Monet (1840–1926) in 1860

Claude Monet
La Grenouillère, 1869
Oil on canvas, 74.6 x 99.7 cm (29⅜ x 39⅜ in.)
New York, The Metropolitan Museum of Art,
H. O. Havemeyer Collection,
Bequest of Mrs. H. O. Havemeyer

Anthony (p. 15) is one of the paintings of which I have the most pleasant memories," Renoir
confided to Vollard in 1918. "It is not because I find this picture particularly exciting, but
because it reminds me so vividly of the excellent Mother Anthony and her inn at Marlotte,
a real village inn. I took as the subject of my painting the lounge that also served as a dining-
room. The old woman [with her back to the viewer, her hair tightly bound] in a kerchief is
Mother Anthony herself; the lovely girl … is the servant, Nana; the white poodle is Toto, who
had a wooden leg. I posed a few of my friends around the table including Sisley and Le Cœur.
The walls of the room, as I indicated in the picture, were covered in paintings that were stuck
directly on the wall. They were the unpretentious but often very excellent work of the local
regulars. Murger's silhouette, that I reproduced on the canvas in the top left, had been painted
by me". Colin B. Bailey, in his *Renoir's Portraits – Impressions of an Age* shows that Renoir's
painting is an overt political manifesto. He had started on this group portrait during the previous year, shortly after the jury of the 1866 Salon rejected his life-size painting entitled *Landscape
with Two Figures* (p. 22), and while he was finishing the painting entitled *The Painter Jules Le
Cœur Walking His Dogs in the Forest of Fontainebleau* (p. 23) for his friend Le Cœur. By placing
L'Evènement in a prominent position at the edge of the table of the Inn, Renoir was not only paying his respects to a young man of twenty-six called Zola, the only person to have defended the
"refusés" who did so in this newspaper as a result of which he was forced to resign, but he is also
expressing his solidarity with him, while tacitly acknowledging the power of the press.

Although Renoir spent most of his summers with his aged parents who had retired to
Ville-d'Avray or with Jules Le Cœur, in winter he often sought refuge at Marlotte, among

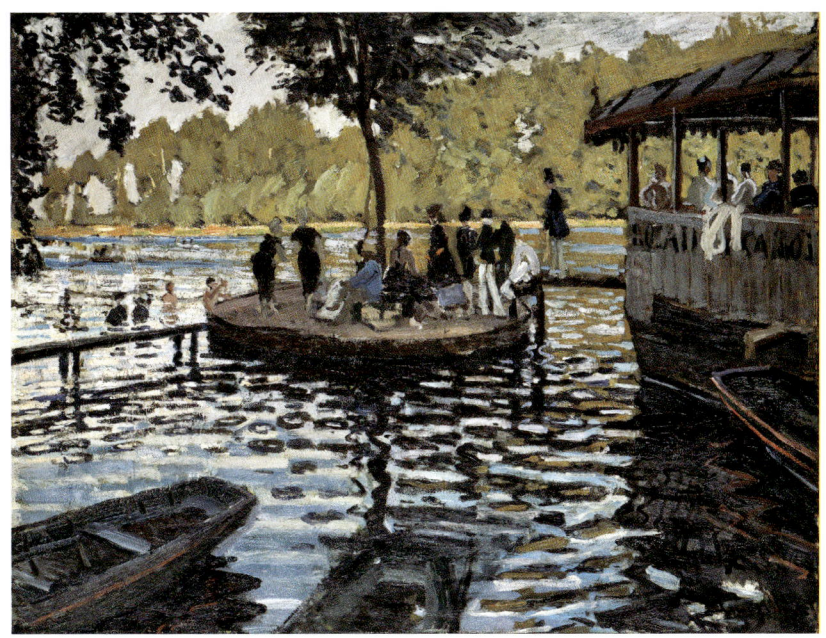

his wealthier friends. From 1867 through 1870, he shared a studio in Paris successively with Sisley, at the Porte Maillot, then with Frédéric Bazille, at first in the Rue Visconti, later at 9 Rue La Condamine in the Batignolles district. It was in Bazille's apartment that he painted the unusual and charming portrait of his friend, who was engaged in the painting *Frédéric Bazille* (p. 19). This was Renoir's way of thanking Bazille for having him as his roommate. Bazille had previously painted a portrait of his friend Renoir (p. 18), perched on a chair, looking dashing and relaxed. Renoir maliciously repaid the compliment by representing Bazille, who was a real dandy and always impeccably dressed, in a shabby, creased, paint-spattered suit. This was the only portrait by Renoir that Manet liked enough to hang on his wall. It was also featured in the second Impressionist exhibition as a symbol of group solidarity.

Monet claimed and kept for his whole life the most unusual, exuberant, "rainbow-like" and certainly the most pre-Impressionist portrait that Renoir painted in 1870, shortly before he enlisted to fight against the Prussians. This is the painting of *Madame Clémentine Stora in Algerian Dress* (p. 49). The sitter was a wealthy North African woman, the wife of a carpet-seller, who thought the portrait "horrible" and immediately resold it for 300 francs. This painting is the striking third contribution to the trilogy of homage to the orientalism of Delacroix and his *Women of Algiers* (p. 48). The first of these had Lise posing as an *Odalisque* (pp. 50/51) and the second is a monumental painting of Parisian women in Algerian costume, entitled *Interior of a Harem in Montmartre* (*Parisian Women Dressed as Algerians*; p. 47). In this painting, the grave and beautiful face of Lise Tréhot is seen for

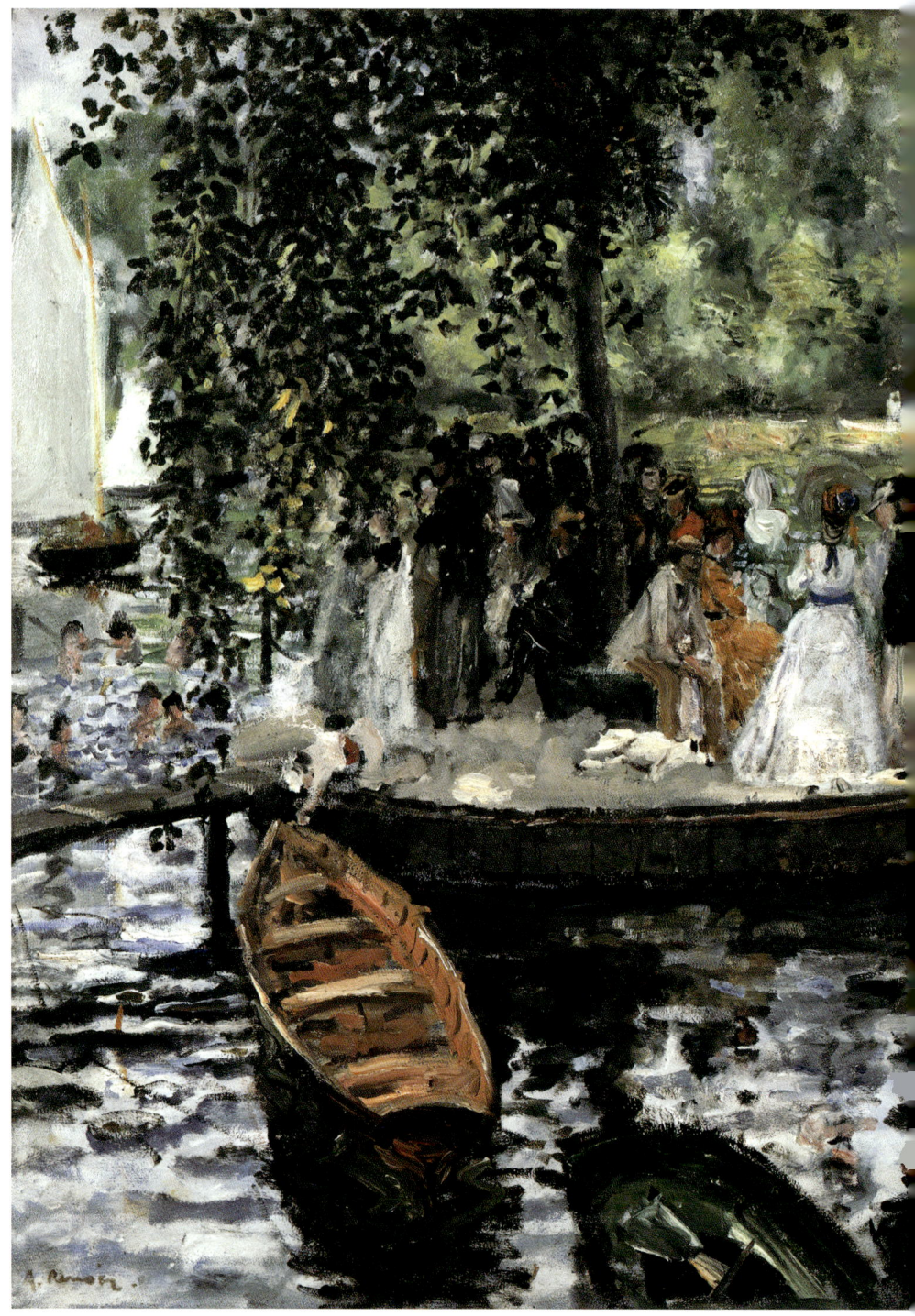

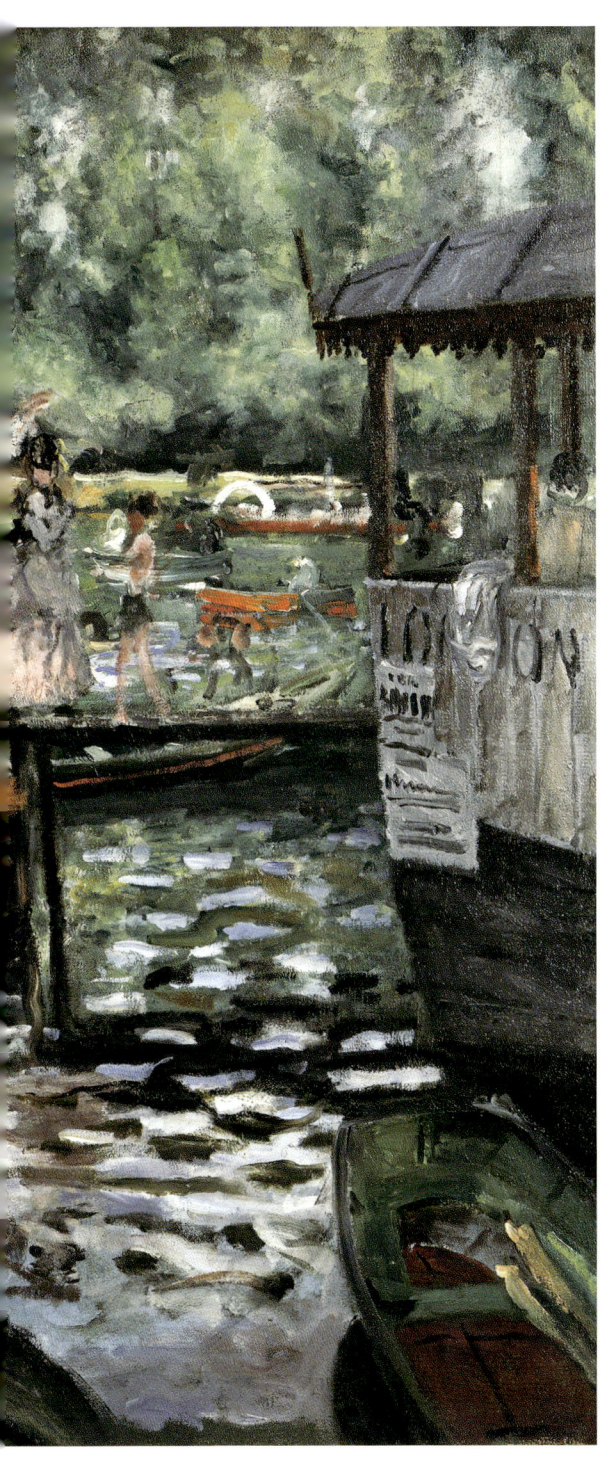

La Grenouillère, 1869
Oil on canvas, 66.5 x 81 cm (26¼ x 32 in.)
Stockholm, Nationalmuseum

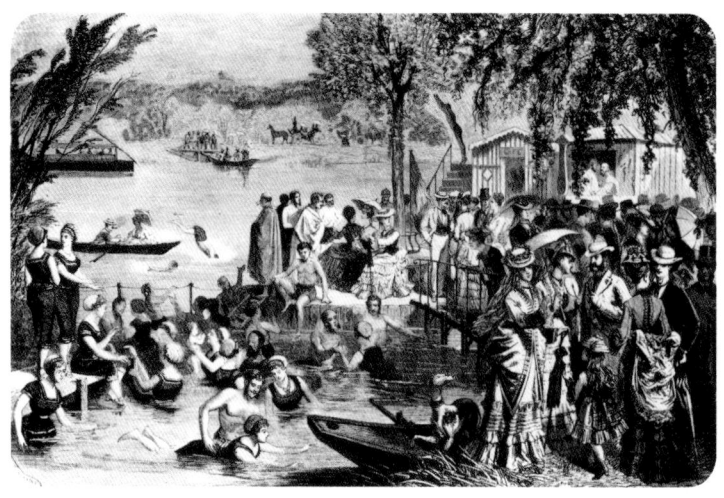

La Grenouillère, contemporary engraving

La Grenouillère, 1869
Oil on canvas, 65 x 92 cm (25⅝ x 36¼ in.)
Winterthur, Oskar Reinhart Collection
"Am Römerholz"

the last time; she was to leave him to marry a young architect, by whom she went on to have children. She never saw Renoir again. Renoir, true to himself, disavowed these paintings on which he had lavished such care, seeing them in later life as juvenilia that merely aimed to flatter "the perpetual demand of art-lovers for painting in an older style" – but what a style it was! He even did everything he could to "lose" the monumental *Harem*, deliberately leaving it behind when he moved house, until one day someone came running after him, shouting "your painting, I kept it, here, take it back …!" It was the faithful concierge of the building. Renoir bitterly resented paying 40 sous for a hansom-cab in which to deliver the painting to an auction house where it was sold in a lot for 500 francs.

Renoir's landscapes of the period more closely resemble those of Corot, whom he idolised in this field. There is also something of the influence of Jongkind, rather than Courbet or Manet. An example is his *The Champs-Elysées during the 1867 Universal Exposition* (p. 27) painted in 1867, though the subject-matter and ambitiousness of the painting recall *Music in the Tuileries* by Manet. Manet's painting is a manifesto of Baudelaire and modernity, concentrating mainly on the effect of the colours and shapes produced by the juxtaposition of the cylindrical top hats of the men and the corollas of the short capes and crinolines of the ladies. But Renoir was already creating one of his landscapes whose value resides in the silhouette figures passing through them. In this respect *The Pont des Arts, Paris* (pp. 28/29) and *Skaters in the Bois de Boulogne* (pp. 24/25), which Renoir proudly claimed to be his only winter landscape ("I have never been able to bear the cold … and even if the cold were bearable, why would one ever bother painting snow, that leprosy of nature?"), still hesitate

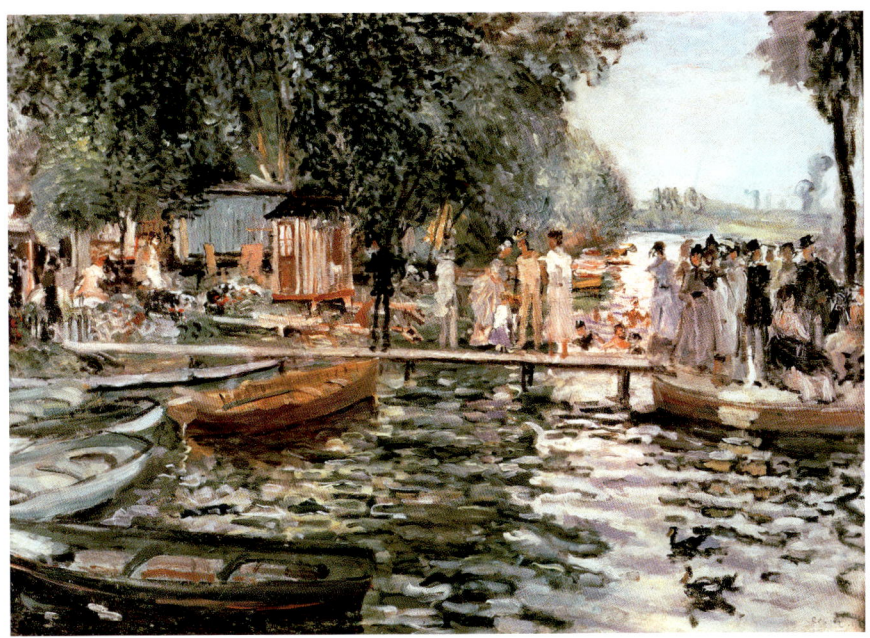

between a loosely structural composition in the style of Corot, and the very different tendencies and division of hues first perceptible in the views of *La Grenouillère* that were painted in the same years (pp. 52, 59, 56/57). The reflections of the landscape in water, with clearly distinct brushstrokes, used in *La Grenouillère* paintings, are no doubt the source of the separate brushstroke technique that was to become the hallmark of the Impressionist period.

Renoir and Monet painted *La Grenouillère* side by side, like brothers. It is the same watery landscape, seen from the same angle, on the same day and at the same time, yet each interprets it according to his temperament. In Monet's work (p. 50), the figures disappear and the water is the focal point. Throughout his life, Monet saw a reflection of life in the water, the image of an image, the mirroring and shimmering of a magic prism that would lead inexorably to the liquid and quasi-abstract mural-style *Waterlilies* of his final years. Ever since the myth of Orpheus, artists have always been tempted to try to pass through the looking glass. Renoir (pp. 56/57), on the other hand, emphasised the details, and especially the figures. For him, a landscape achieved its full significance only by being populated. It was the wondrous garden of humanity. Was it not the most handsome setting for a female nude? The water enticed the women to dive into it. Renoir's definition of La Grenouillère ["The Frog-Pond"] says it all: "It is so-called not because the place resembles a swamp but because, in the slang of the period, 'frog' was a term used to describe a young woman of the lower classes who was fairly free with her favours and would spend summer Sundays there with her athletic male companion".

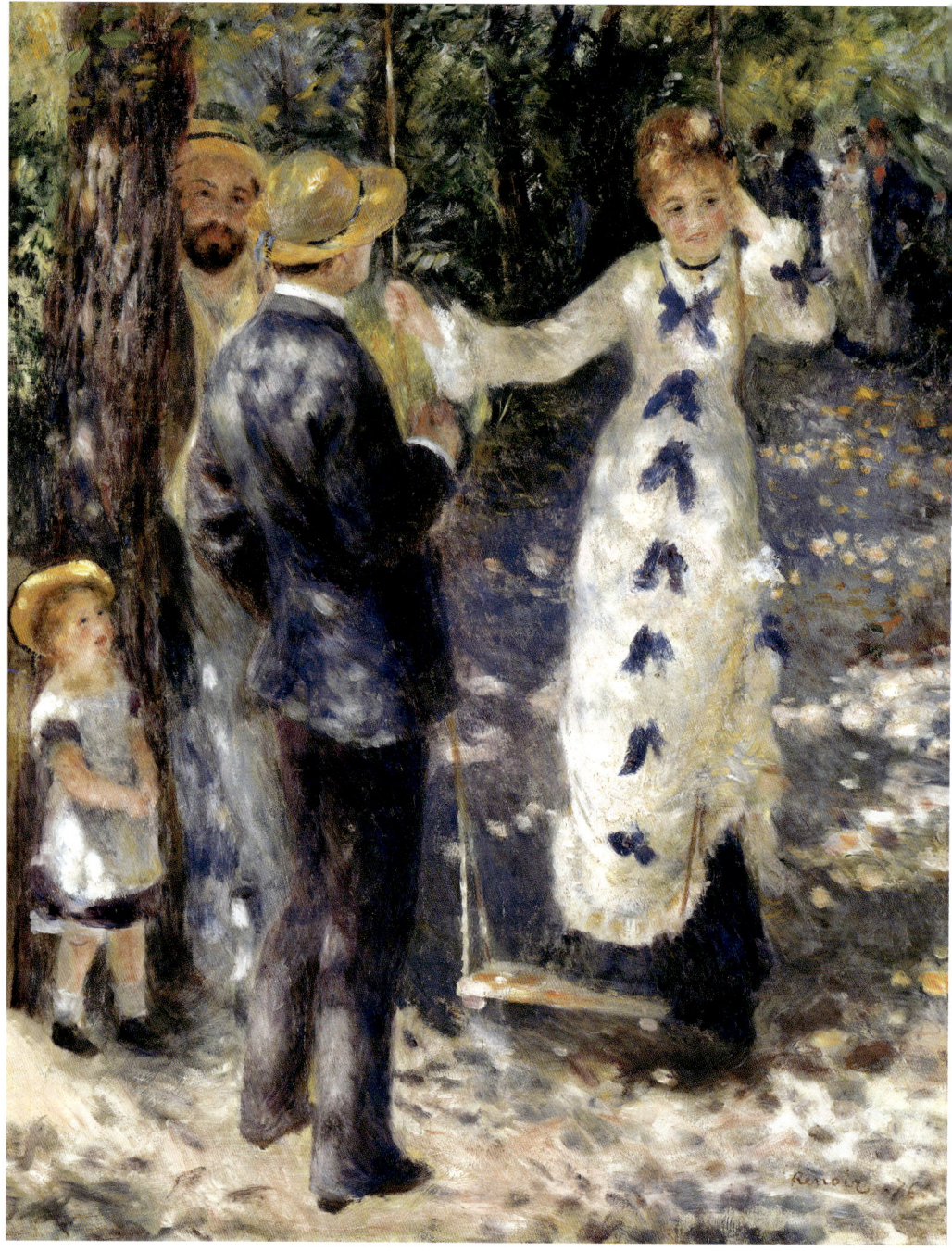

The Swing, 1876
Oil on canvas, 92 x 73 cm (36¼ x 28¾ in.)
Paris, Musée d'Orsay

Le Moulin de la Galette (pp. 114/115), *Nude
in the Sunlight* (p. 121) and *The Swing* constitute
the famous triptych of Renoir's works now
exhibited at the Musée d'Orsay in Paris. In fact,
the three paintings represent the Impressionists'
crowning achievement in their search for the light
and, at the same time, Renoir's road to discovery
that led, in his words, "to the end of the road
of Impressionism".

The Nightingale-painter
1870–1882

"Strive for intense light and shade, and the rest will come naturally". Édouard Manet's
advice was an accurate summary of his work at the time. It quickly became the rallying cry of a dozen or so young artists who, like him, were "wild about light" and who
managed to attract the opprobrium of the official art world during the twenty-year
Impressionist adventure. One can hardly expect to call into question the most firmly
established rules of Western art without causing a scandal. At a time when the canons
of artistic taste required polish and perfection, to exhibit paintings which looked like
collections of crude splashes or unfinished sketches at the Salon was simply out of the
question. The honourable members of the Institute and the distinguished professors
at the École des Beaux-Arts were in great earnest when they declared (as Gérôme,
to whom we owe such memorable works as *The Death of Caesar* and *Reception of the
Duke de Condé at Versailles*, did in 1894): "These people are trampling art underfoot.
People think it's a joke and tell me I am making a fuss about nothing. Well, I can tell
you, they're wrong. This is nothing less than the death of our country, France, as we
know it".

These "angry young men" were motivated by the best of intentions; worse still,
they were all of good family. Their story is reminiscent of those well-to-do children
who end up joining the Communist party. Bazille belonged to an old and wealthy
Protestant family and Degas to the financial aristocracy; Manet's father was a senior
civil servant and Cézanne's was a banker. The parents of both Monet and Pissarro
parents were affluent shopkeepers. Caillebotte, whose father was an industrialist, had

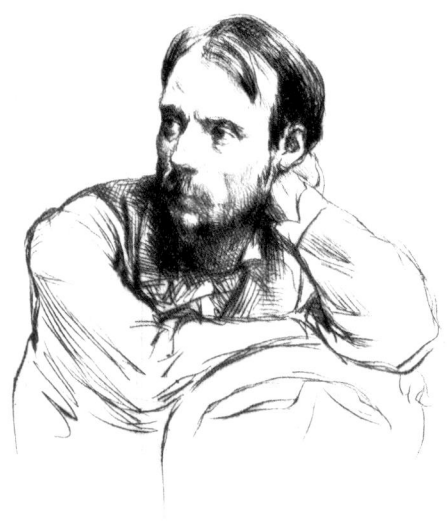

Marcellin Desboutins (1823–1902)
Pierre-Auguste Renoir, c. 1876/77
Etching, 15.9 x 11.1 cm (6⅜ x 4⅜ in.)
Paris, Bibliothèque nationale de France

money and Berthe Morisot was the daughter of a high court judge. The poor relation among them all was Renoir. The only thing that all of them really wanted, however, was to be loved by the general public and the critics alike. They sought official recognition from the Salons, proclaiming their "sincerity" while others condemned their "indecency".

These young people, who were soon to be dubbed "Impressionists", were no scientists. But they all knew the work of the French chemist Chevreul. He was in charge of the Gobelins tapestry factory and had studied the colours that could be produced by weaving different patterns into the same tapestry. Having observed that the juxtaposition of coloured objects changed their optical characteristics, he formulated the "law of simultaneous colour contrast". In his own way he too was an artist since he chose the range of coloured threads that was used to weave carpets and tapestries and sought to improve his results. His law can be summarised in two propositions: namely, that each colour tends to affect those adjacent to it with its complementary colour; and that, if two objects contain the same colour, placing them together has the effect of considerably attenuating the element they share. The fact that science had confirmed the empirical discoveries of these young painters encouraged them to break the sacrosanct rules of the past. Soon Seurat, with his Pointillism, would even attempt (in vain) to express the magic formula as an equation. But for now the future Impressionists were content merely to use the naked eye. "And what an eye they had!" exclaimed Cézanne. To a friend who quoted Amiel's aphorism, "a landscape is an emotional state", Degas retorted, "Oh no, a landscape is a *visual* state". Gone forever were the traditional

Édouard Manet (1832–1883)
Portrait of Émile Zola, 1868
Oil on canvas,
146 x 114 cm (57½ x 45 in.)
Paris, Musée d'Orsay

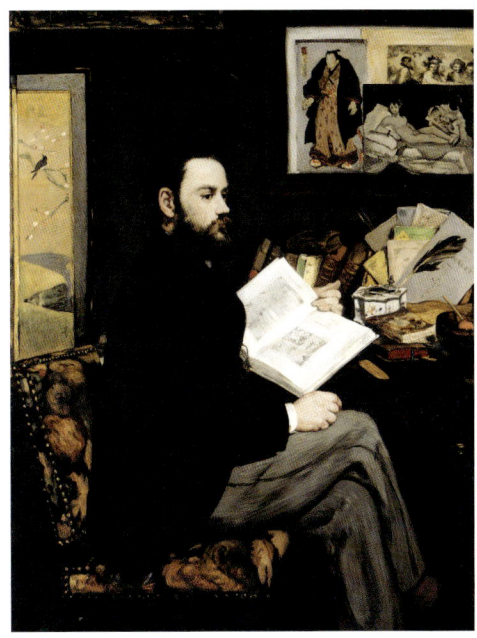

conventions of drawing, perspective, and studio lighting; shapes and distances could now be suggested solely through colour vibrations and contrasts. "I have spent my life 'weaving the rainbow'", explained Monet, the only member of the group to remain an Impressionist until his death, "treating light like a piece of embroidery".

When war broke out between France and Prussia on 18 July 1870, Renoir was hard at work. But when the threat of a Prussian invasion was imminent, he immediately enlisted in the Tenth Chasseurs regiment. Renoir was first sent to the garrison at Tarbes, and then to Libourne, where he fell victim to a serious illness. His uncle came and took him home to Bordeaux where he received life-saving treatment. During his time in the army he painted portraits of his captain, Édouard Bernier (p. 204), and his wife (p. 205). After the French defeat, Renoir spent two months at the château of family friends, teaching the daughter of the family to paint. He lived like a prince, spending days on end on horseback; his hosts were keen to have him to stay since they feared that he would be killed in the riots of the Paris Commune if he returned to the city. This was typical of the penniless young Renoir, who always seemed to find a well-lined nest in which to shelter. The whole group of young artists, who had been united by their shared views, had been temporarily dispersed. Manet, Degas and Bazille had joined the army like Renoir but Monet, Pissarro and Sisley, who was a British subject in any case, had left for England. There they discovered the paintings of Turner who taught them that the colour of snow is anything but white. They also met Paul Durand-Ruel, who was to become their dealer and saviour. Cézanne, meanwhile, was in hiding L'Estaque.

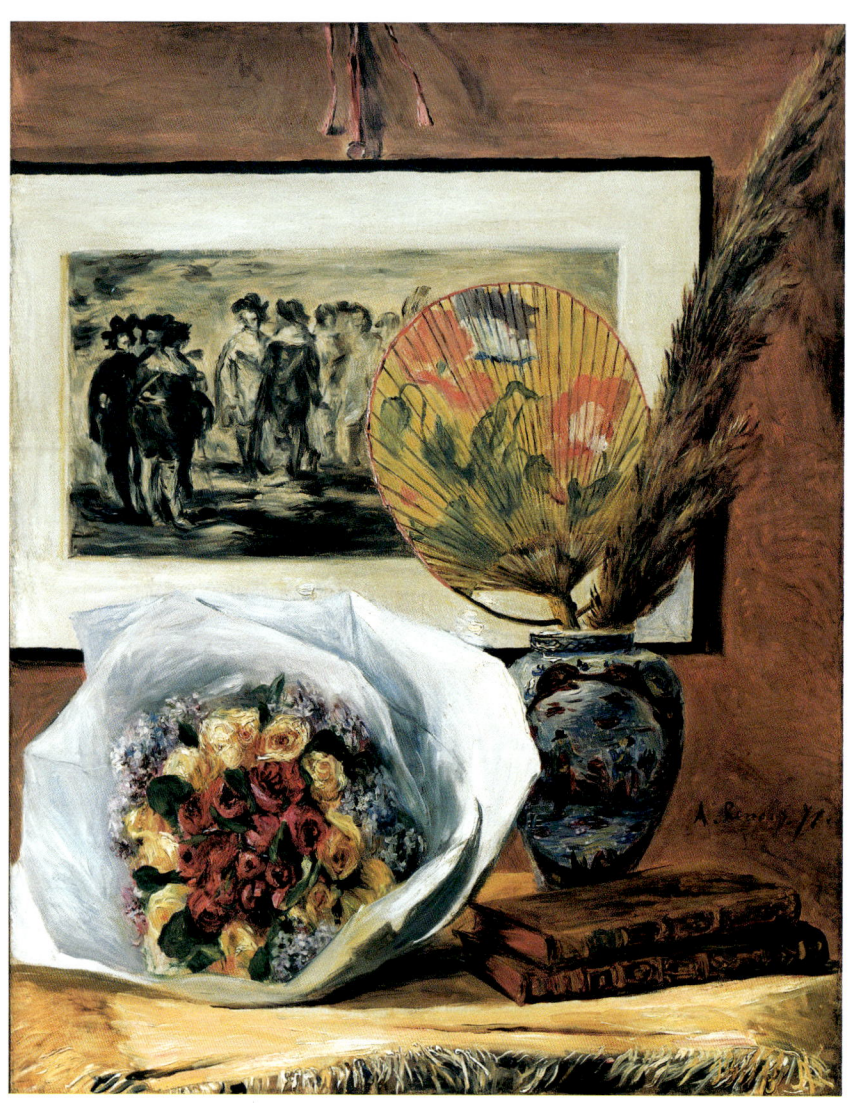

Still Life with Bouquet, 1871
Oil on canvas, 73.7 x 59.1 cm (29 x 23⅜ in.)
Houston, The Museum of Fine Arts,
Robert Lee Blaffer Memorial Collection,
Gift of Mrs. Sarah Campbell Blaffer

Rapha Maître, 1870/71
Oil on canvas, 130 x 83 cm (51¼ x 32¾ in.)
Private collection

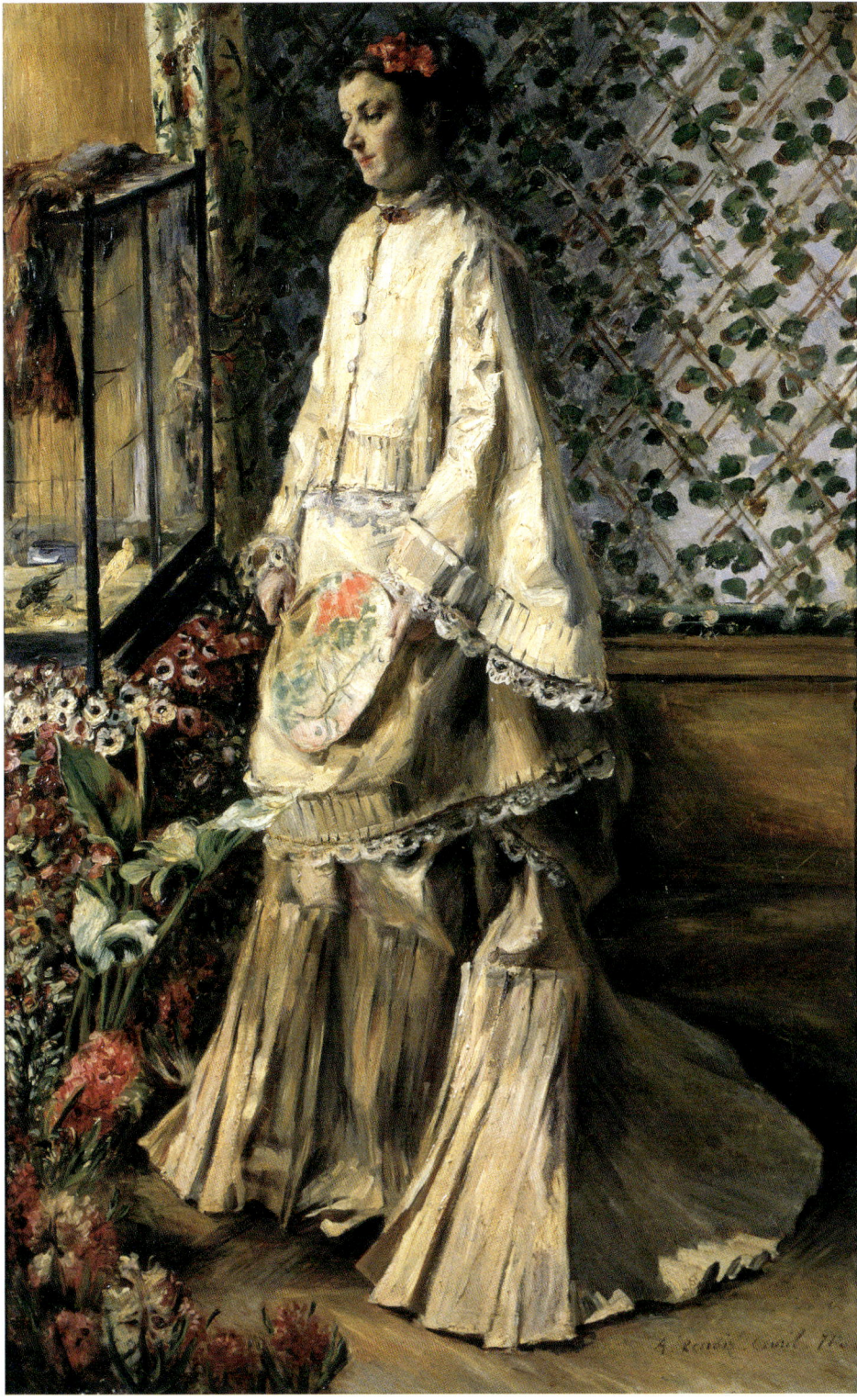

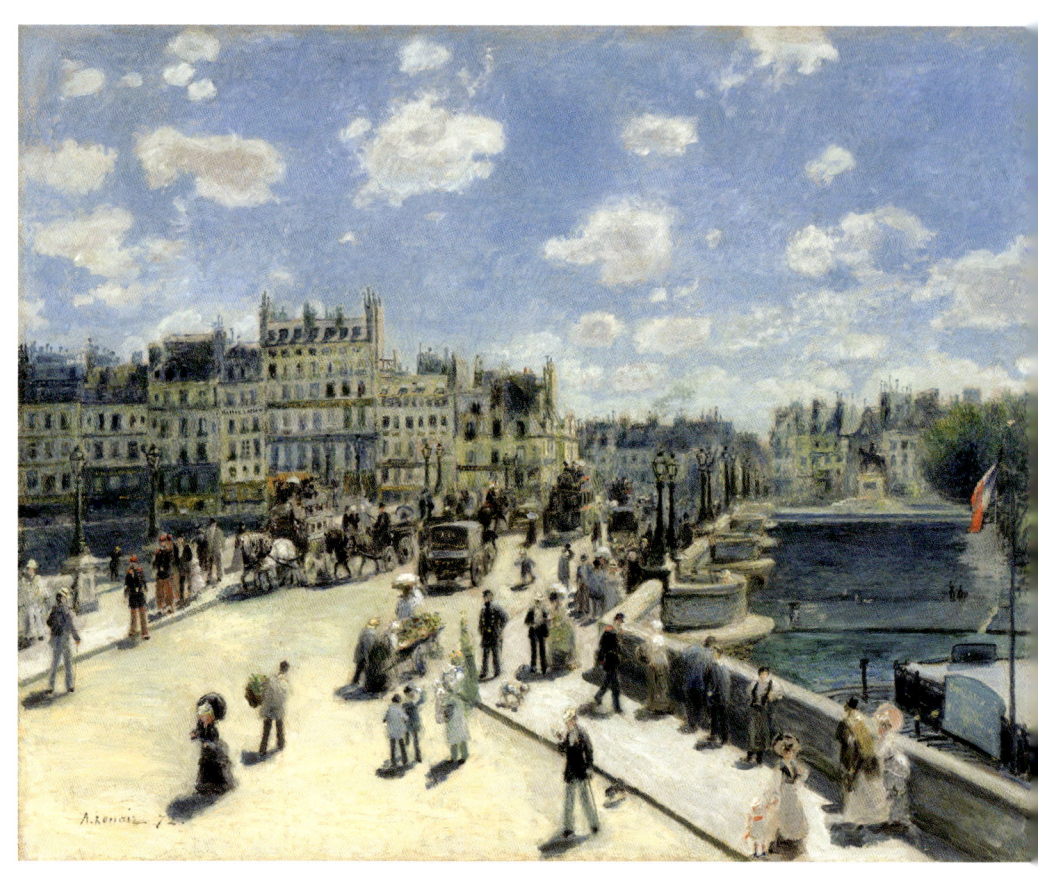

Pont-Neuf, **Paris**, 1872
Oil on canvas, 75.3 x 93.7 cm (29¾ x 37 in.)
Washington, D.C., National Gallery of Art,
Ailsa Mellon Bruce Collection

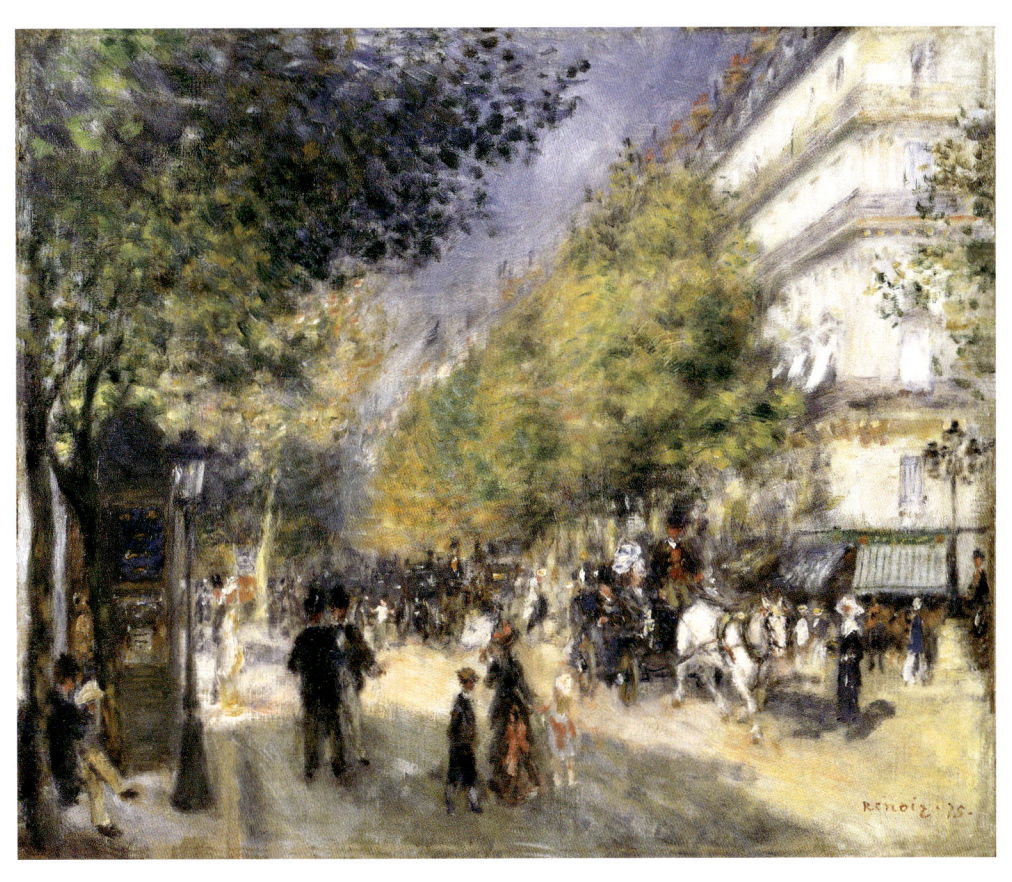

The Grands Boulevards, Paris, 1875
Oil on canvas, 52.1 x 63.5 cm (20⅝ x 25 in.)
Philadelphia Museum of Art,
The Henry P. McIlhenny Collection
in memory of Frances P. McIlhenny

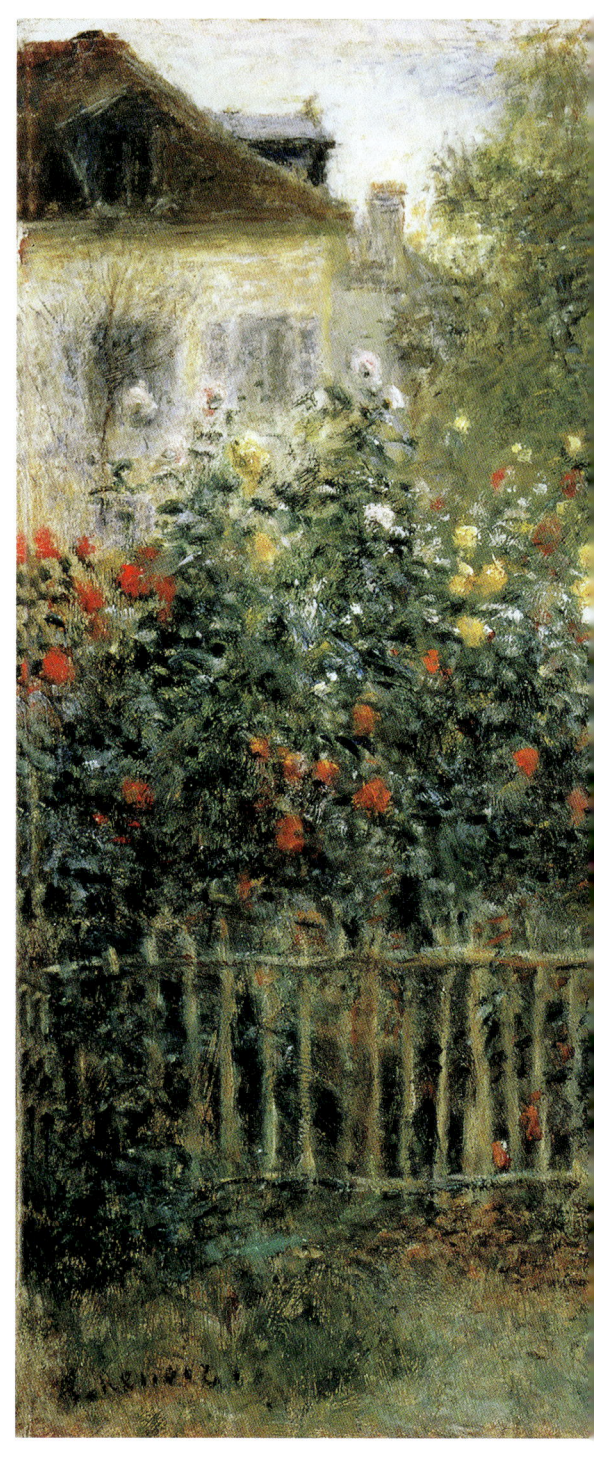

**Claude Monet Painting in
His Garden at Argenteuil**, 1873
Oil on canvas,
46.7 x 59.7 cm (18½ x 23⅝ in.)
Hartford, Connecticut, Wadsworth
Atheneum Museum of Art,
Bequest of Anne Parrish Titzell

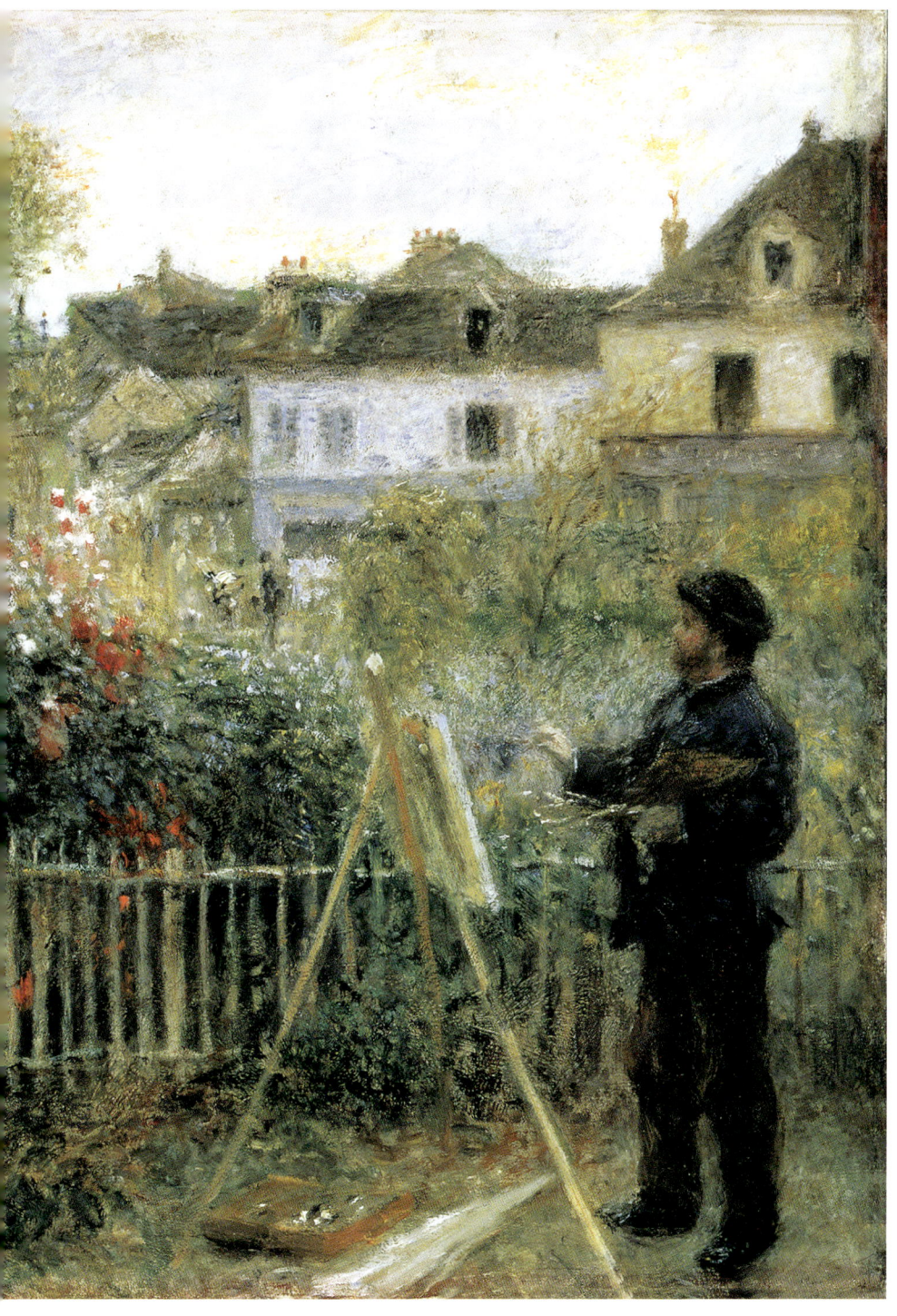

The Duck Pond, 1873
Oil on canvas,
50.8 x 62.2 cm (20 x 24½ in.)
Private collection

After the end of the Franco-Prussian War, life in Paris gradually returned to normal. Everyone came home and the group reformed. The only member missing was Bazille, who had been cut off in his prime at the battle of Beaune-la-Rolande. Realising that the next few years would be decisive, the group grew stronger. Manet had opened the way for them but it was Monet who now emerged as the leading member of the school. This was the Argenteuil period in which Impressionism assumed its true nature. As the Impressionists' friend Georges Rivière wrote: "Monet was really the life and soul of their little group at that time. It was he who revived their sometimes faltering spirits and who defended them from attack like a bull who may be annoyed by the banderillos but is never frightened. Renoir often declared that, at a time when everyone was heaping abuse upon the 'intransigents', Monet helped them most simply by retaining his composure and tenacity as well as his unshakeable belief that they would eventually triumph. In 1873, the attacks of the art critics had not yet attained the virulence that would soon be provoked by the small exhibition of the following year. But the indifference of art-lovers and the silence of the press were no less depressing for the young artists than the insults that greeted their first collective exhibition. In any case, the group formed by Claude Monet and his fellow-painters was, at that time, unbreakable."

Renoir was never attracted by theories, even new ones. He remained indifferent to the technique of colour modulation through the juxtaposition of splashes of colour and only adopted it gradually as his painting evolved. He was still strongly influenced by Manet and by the painting exhibited by Fantin-Latour at the 1870 salon, entitled

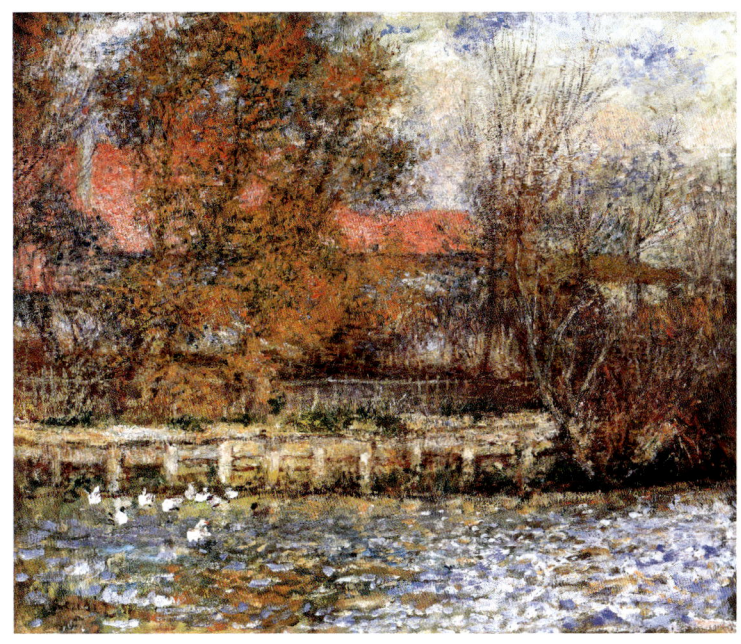

A Studio at Batignolles (p. 9 bottom). This homage to Manet was a painting in which Renoir himself was portrayed among Manet's friends. A year later, directly inspired by the *Portrait of Émile Zola* by Manet (p. 63), Renoir painted his own homage to the creator of *Olympia* in the form of a *Still Life with Bouquet* (p. 64). The bouquet was a direct reference to the one which the black maid presents to Olympia as a gift from an admirer – or rather a "client" (p. 166). This bouquet becomes a leitmotiv in several of Renoir's paintings such as *A Box at the Theater* (*At the Concert*; p. 171). The side-table is stacked with the same objects as in the portrait of Émile Zola: books, a Japanese fan, and a feather placed in a Chinese vase to echo the quill in the novelist's ink-well. The key to the painting is the engraving on the wall, a reference to the frame of the portrait of Zola in which Manet included a Japanese print and a reference to *Olympia*. Renoir has chosen his engraving carefully: it is a sketch entitled *The Little Knights*, and signed "pub. Manet after Velázquez", an etching by Manet of an oil painting in the Louvre then attributed to Velázquez. Manet seems to have attached great importance to this etching. In his own way then Renoir combines the work of two masters whom he greatly admired, Manet and Velázquez. He also alludes to Degas by cutting off the engraving frame at the left corner. Although Renoir seems to have been the least enthusiastic of the group about the prevailing fashion for all things Japanese, the Japanese fan reappears, on the wall this time, behind *Portrait of Madame Monet* (*Madame Claude Monet Reading*; p. 213). In *Girl with a Fan* (p. 2), however, it is merely an accessory and a pretext.

Young Girl on a Bench, 1875
Oil on canvas,
64 x 52 cm (25¼ x 20½ in.)
Private collection

The two portraits of *Rapha Maître* (pp. 65 and 79) attempt to create a sharp contrast between light and shade. They show that Renoir was still strongly under the influence of Manet as late as 1871, although he did not achieve the vigour and frankness of his older colleague. His model was Camille, nicknamed Rapha, the mistress of his friend Louis-Edmond Maître, "a dilettante who, had he possessed a large fortune, would have been the most intelligent of patrons". He was Bazille's travelling companion and a great friend of Fantin-Latour, and commissioned the first of these portraits from Renoir (p. 65). The portrait, he claimed, would "turn the heads of the art-collectors of the future". It is full-length and shows Rapha, dressed in the latest fashion, standing in an opulent apartment in front of a birdcage lit by a window. This picture was painted at the height of the Paris Commune disturbances, when there were barricades up in the Place de la Concorde, just around the corner. A civil war was in progress and Paris stank of gunpowder. Yet Renoir's painting typically does not contain so much as a hint of these social upheavals. We are simply offered the peaceful atmosphere of an elegant home. Meier-Graefe severely criticised the painting, describing it as "the form of a Renoir without its content". This is a fair assessment since Renoir had not yet found his true Impressionist style.

The second painting (p. 79) is simply a small study of a head produced by Renoir for his own pleasure. Its format and intimate nature suggest an intimate acquaintance with the model. Renoir would later severely criticise portraits of this kind as "daubs". But the critic Colin B. Bailey notes that "disdain was not shared by the following generation.

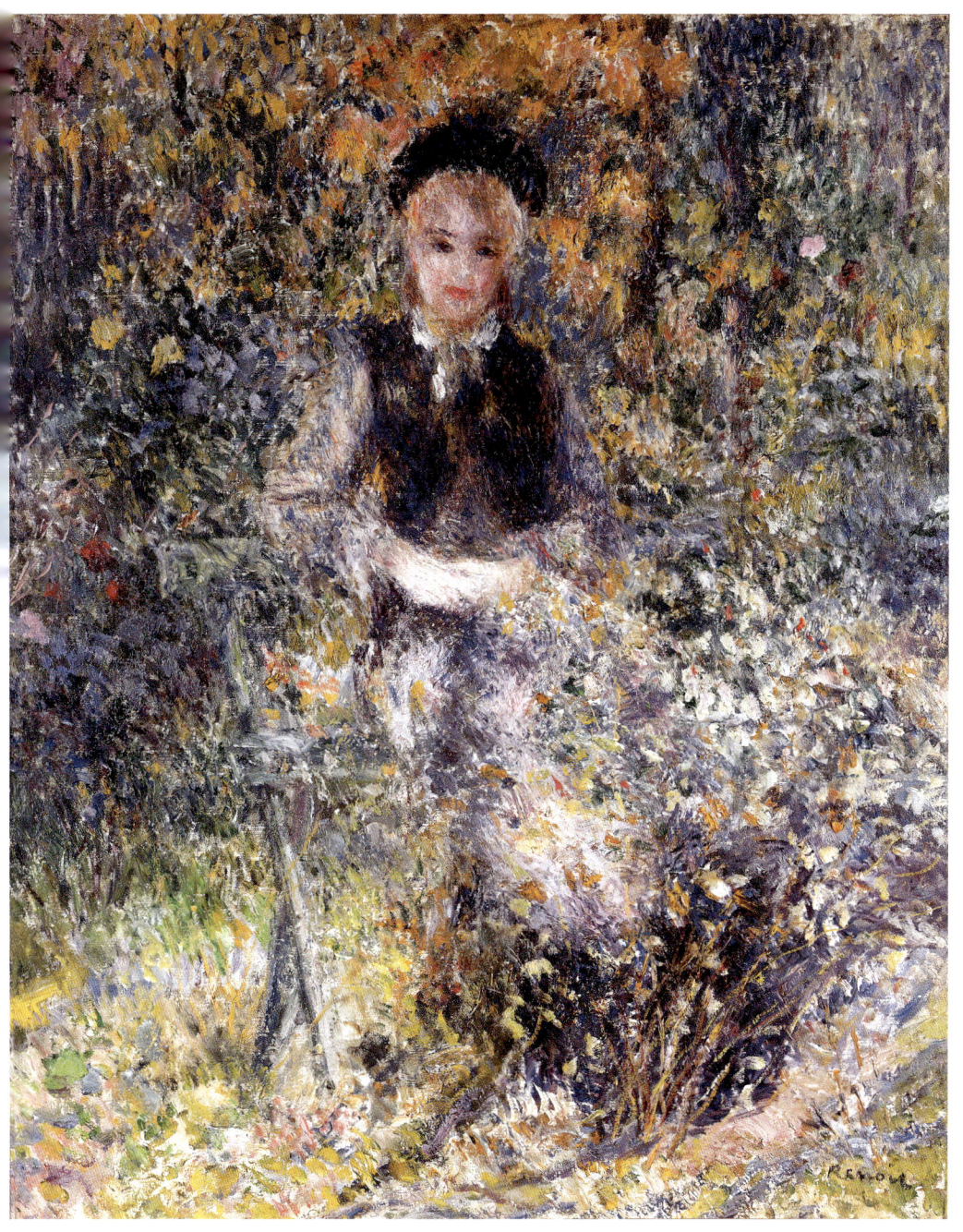

PAGES 76/77
**Madame Monet Reading
"Le Figaro"**, 1872–1874
Oil on canvas, 53 x 71.7 cm (20⅞ x 28¼ in.)
Lissabon, Fundação Calouste
Gulbenkian Museu

Woman with a Parasol in a Garden, 1875
Oil on canvas, 54.5 x 65 cm (21½ x 25⅝ in.)
Madrid, Museo Nacional
Thyssen-Bornemisza

When he painted in the open air, Renoir's
brushwork resembled that of Monet.
Thus, *Woman with a Parasol in a Garden*
could have been the work of either one
of them. When Renoir worked alone, he
painted most of his landscapes by spreading
the colour in a thin wash in which the
brushstrokes merged into each other.
But when he painted *The Duck Pond* (p. 71)
or *The Seine at Argenteuil* (pp. 84/85),
side-by-side with Monet, just as they had
worked on their versions of *La Grenouillère*
(pp. 56/57) in 1870, whether it was their
friendship, the effect of painting outdoors
or the fact that they saw the scene from the
same point of view, Renoir miraculously
began separating his brushstrokes in the
manner of Pissarro.

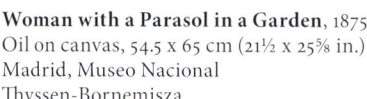

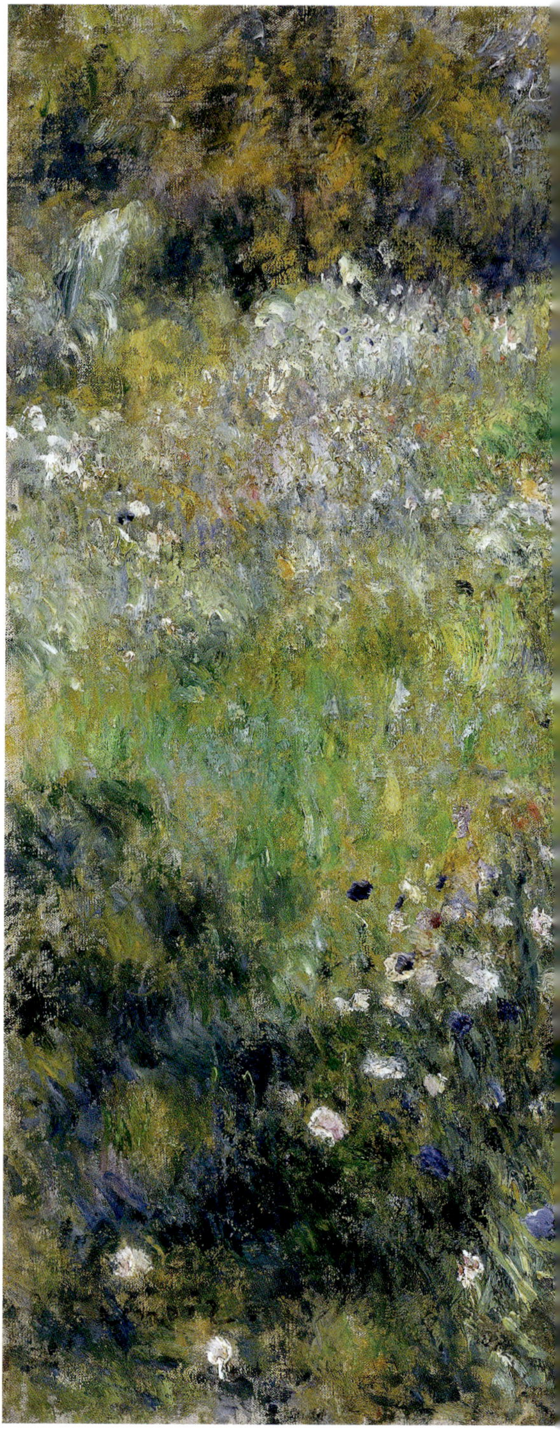

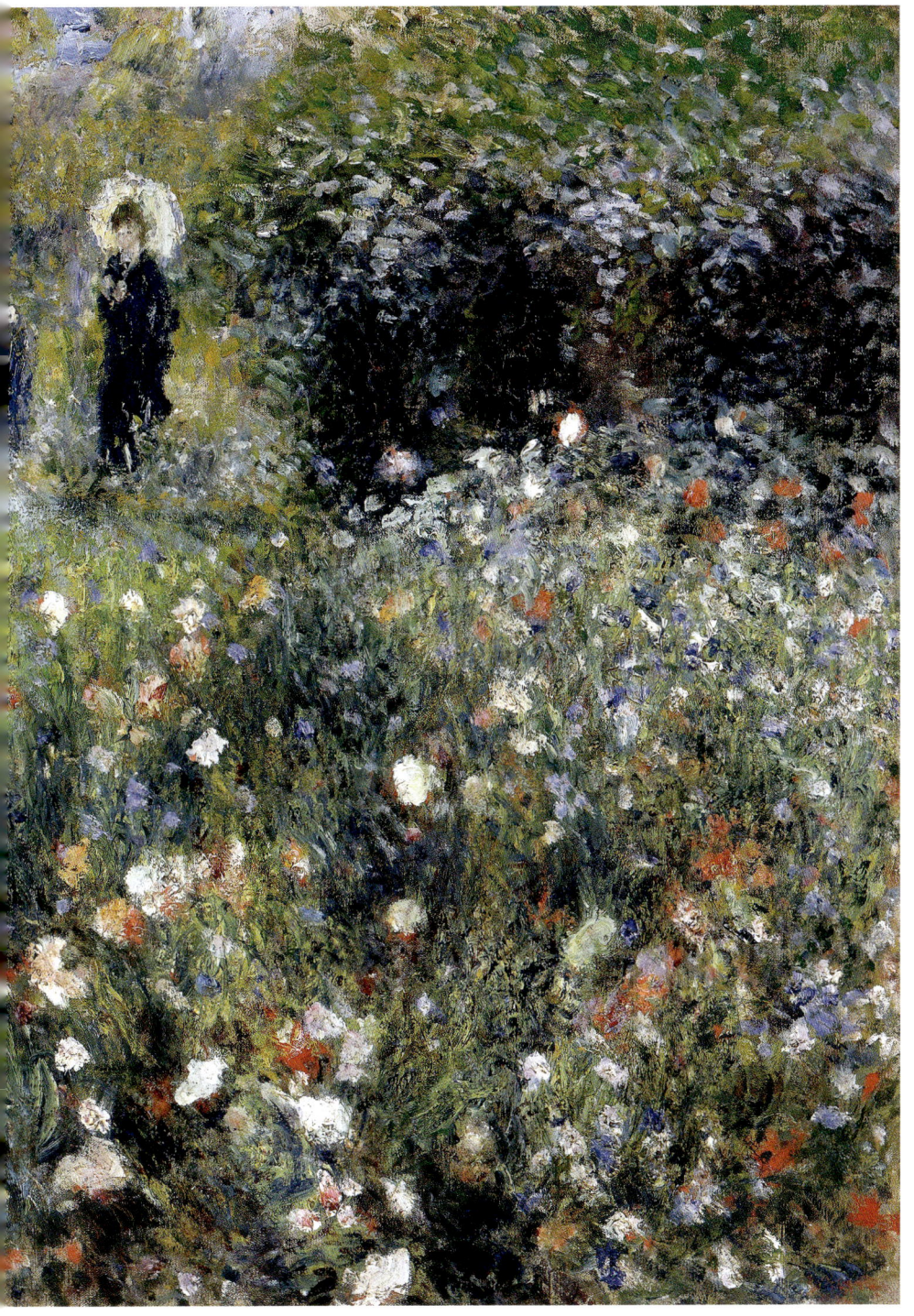

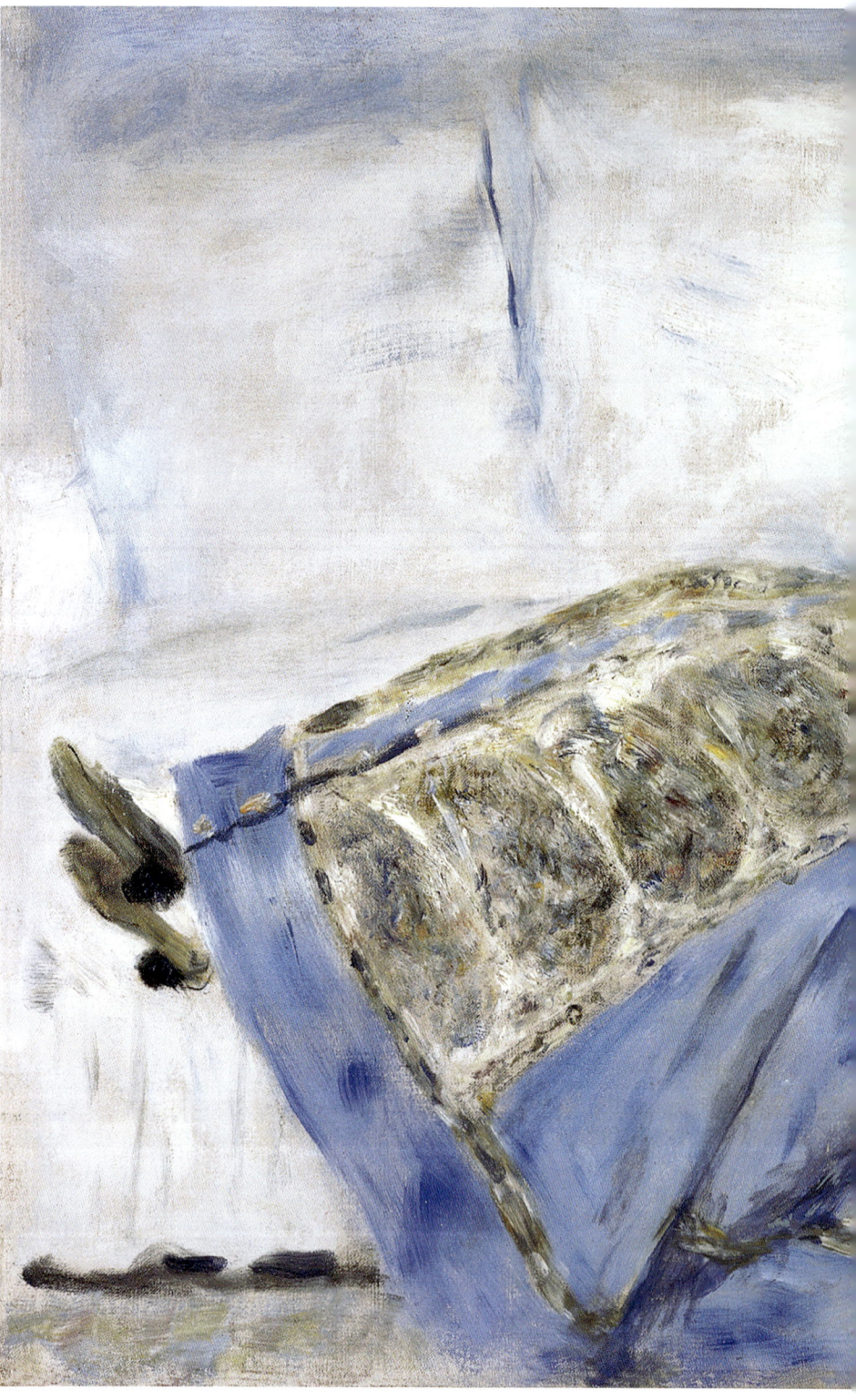

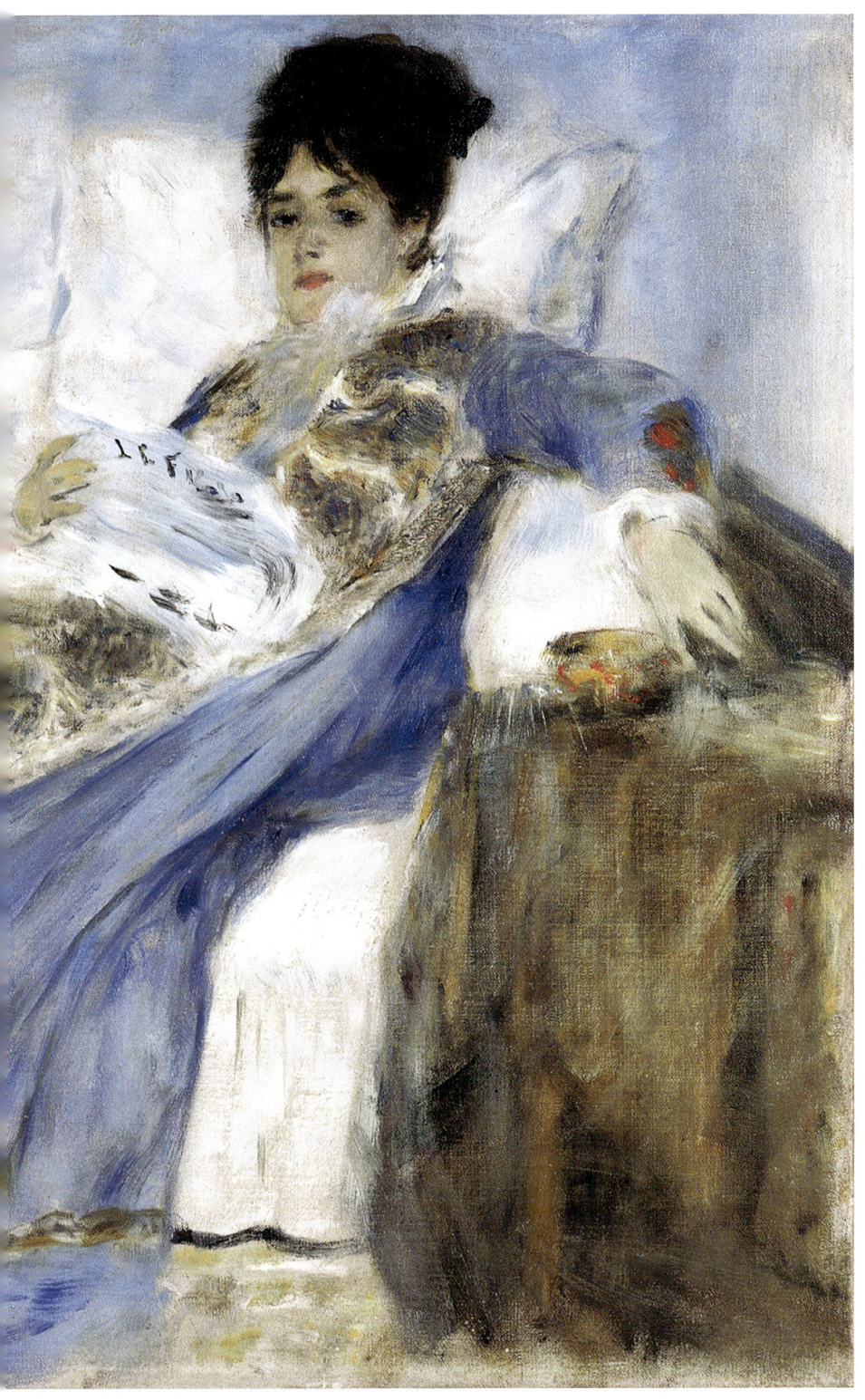

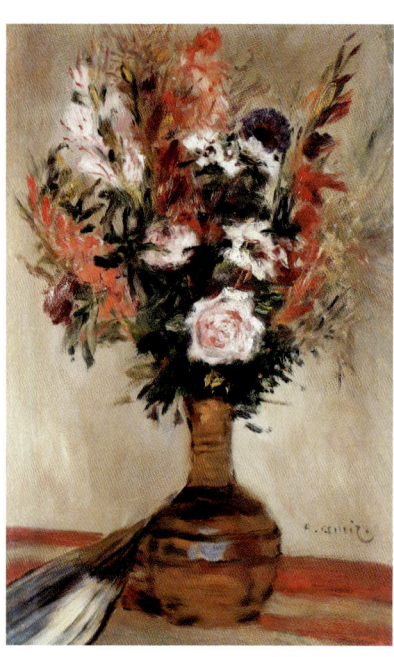

Roses in a Vase, 1872
Oil on canvas,
66 x 41 cm (26 x 16¼ in.)
Private collection

Rapha Maître, 1870/71
Oil on canvas,
37.5 x 32.4 cm (14⅞ x 12⅞ in.)
Northampton, Massachusetts,
Smith College Museum of Art

Proust may even have drawn inspiration from the large portrait of Rapha Maître for his description of the narrow hallway, in the home of Odette de Crécy, which 'was framed by a garden trellis […] edged along its length by a rectangular tub full of chrysanthemums'". Bailey claims that Matisse "paid a dual homage to Renoir by reproducing the lower part of this painting in his two portraits of Auguste Pellerin, the inventor of Tip margarine who, by the end of his life, possessed no fewer than 92 Cézannes and had just become at that time the proud owner of Renoir's *Rapha Maître*".

Manet's influence is evident in the *Ride in the Bois de Boulogne* (p. 209), an even larger canvas painted in 1873 and featuring the wife of Captain Darras, Henriette Darras (1837–1910). The painting shows certain weaknesses in the rendering of the horses, which are rather more Degas's forte. When Renoir went against his nature and undertook "large projects" designed to be exhibited at the Salon – with which he was obsessed –, the attempt was doomed to failure. He had great admiration for Delacroix's *Women of Algiers* (p. 48) which, he claimed "smelled of the very incense of the seraglio" and about which he said later in his life, to Berthe Morisot's daughter Julie Manet, after gazing long and hard at the painting: "After you have done something like that, you can sleep peacefully". But his own interpretation of the subject, *Interior of a Harem in Montmartre* (*Parisian Women Dressed as Algerians*; p. 47), was rejected for the 1872 Salon. The *Ride in the Bois de Boulogne*, which had also been conceived with the Salon specifically in mind, was in turn rejected in 1873. Paul Signac, a great admirer of Renoir, nevertheless criticised the painting, which was inspired by a work of Delacroix on the

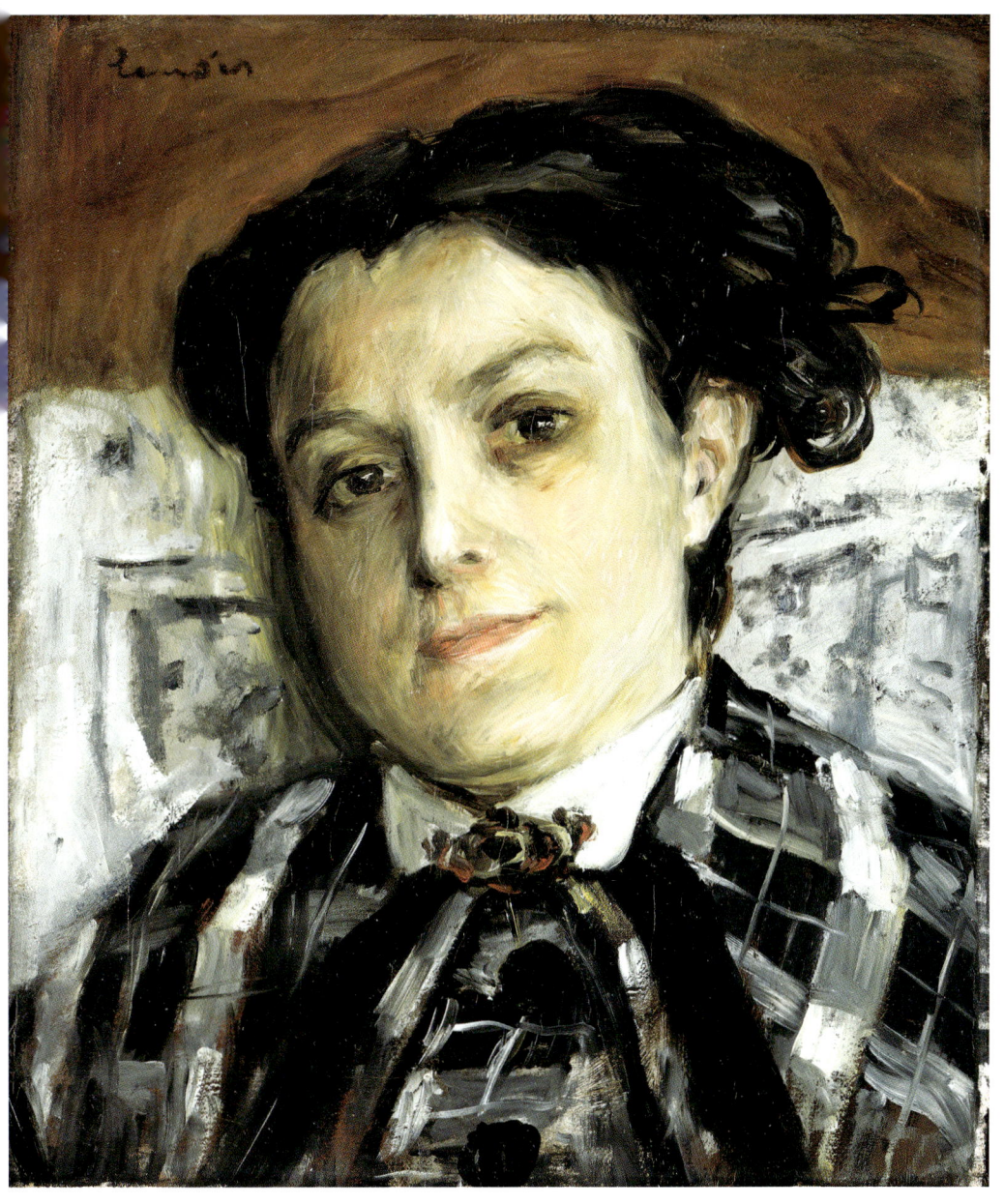

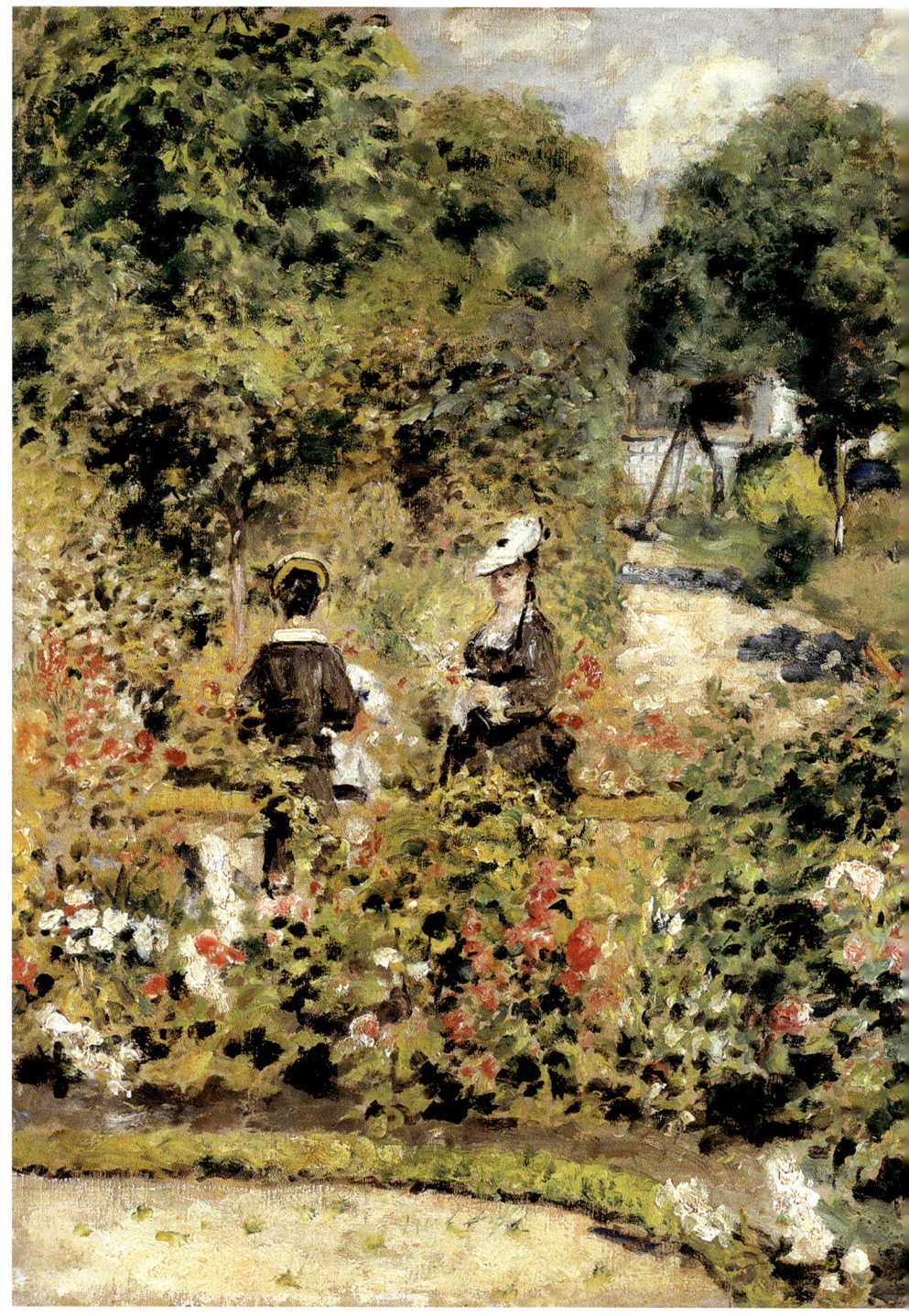

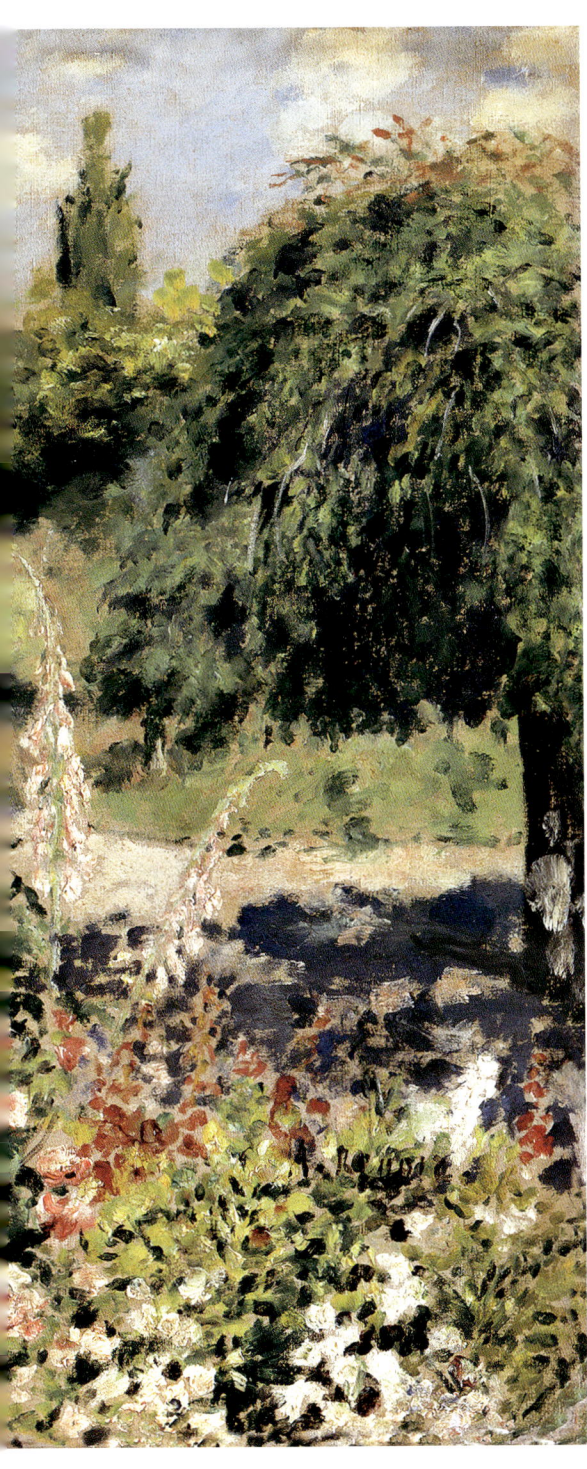

Garden at Fontenay, c. 1873/74
Oil on canvas, 51 x 62 cm (20 x 24½ in.)
Winterthur, Oskar Reinhart Collection
"Am Römerholz"

The Seine at Argenteuil, 1874
Oil on canvas, 50.2 x 65.4 cm (19⅞ x 25¾ in.)
Portland Art Museum,
Bequest of Winslow B. Ayer

As in the case of *The Duck Pond* (p. 71), Renoir
and Monet had both set up their easels on the
bank of the Seine at Petit-Gennevilliers, not far
from the bridge at Argenteuil. Both intended to
paint a view of a sailing-barge moored on the
Seine at Argenteuil. Here again, Monet's style
did not emulate Renoir's, rather the opposite, as
here Renoir fragments his brushstrokes much
more than usual in an attempt to reproduce the
coloured reflections on the water.

Boating at Argenteuil, 1873
Oil on canvas, 50 x 61 cm (19¾ x 24 in.)
Private collection

same subject: "It combines wholly unsuccessful parts with others that are quite pretty.
The sensuous charm of Renoir's women is already there. You can tell that he loves buttocks, nipples and flesh glimpsed through gauze. The scene is more reminiscent of a
brothel than a harem."

However, this pastiche is evidence of Renoir's attraction to the rich colour schemes
and enthralling subject-matter of Delacroix. Claude Roger-Marx rightly points out that
Renoir was using Delacroix to try and rediscover the lost technique of the Venetian
painters and Peter Paul Rubens, and that this presages his eventual abandonment of
Impressionism. Renoir had come to believe in shape, and the creation of shape, after
studying the *Fountain of the Innocents* and the nudes of Jean Goujon. He loved to fashion alluring and silky portraits. These and his interiors came only gradually to embrace
the Impressionist philosophy. The same cannot be said of his landscape paintings, in
which Renoir fell much more heavily under Monet's influence. The Impressionists
were inventing the first urban landscapes, panoramic and bird's eye views of the boulevards of Paris and the Pont-Neuf, which would continue to inspire them until the turn
of the century. Some even collaborated on paintings, as Pissarro and Cézanne did in
The Hermitage at Pontoise, in which Cézanne concentrated on the landscape, leaving
Pissarro to add the figures.

In 1854, the Emperor Napoleon III, in an attempt to fulfil an old ambition of the kings
of France to link the two palaces of the Louvre and the Tuileries, ordered the demolition
of the houses that stood in the Louvre and the Carousel courtyards. He was equally

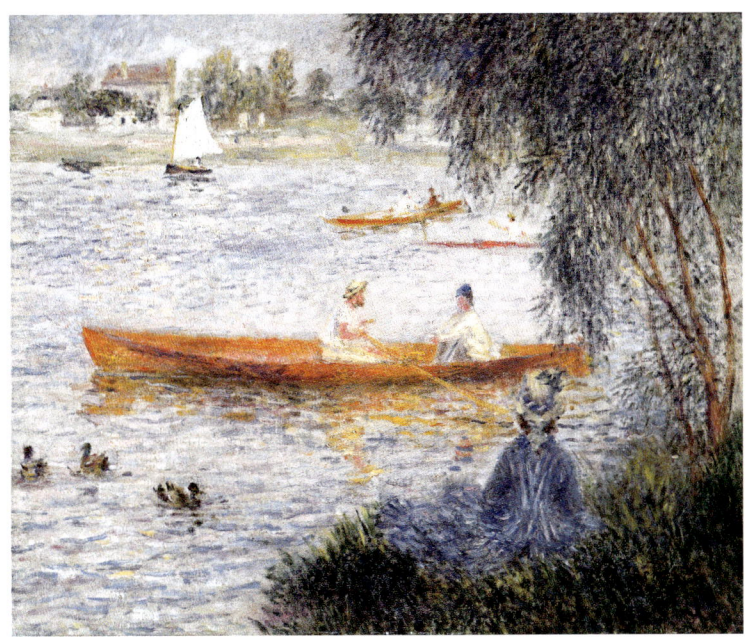

keen to do away with the invasive and volatile proletariat that industrialisation had produced. Napoleon had become emperor three years previously after a coup d'état which cost the lives of nearly two hundred workers at the barricades. There were riots in 1869 and the first Communist International was held in 1864. The year 1848 saw the publication of a pamphlet that began with the immortal line, "A spectre haunts Europe: the spectre of Communism", and ended with the call: "Workers of the world, unite!" This was the 'Communist Manifesto', published by Karl Marx and Friedrich Engels. Paris had a population of two million at the time, 500,000 of whom were workers by the end of the Empire; of these 112,000 were women. They were paid two francs for a full day's work at a time when an attic room cost 120 francs to rent. The renovations of Baron Haussmann, who created the *grands boulevards* and Les Halles – "the stomach of the city", as Zola described it – as well as Garnier's brand-new opera house, caused Paris to become known throughout the world as "the city of light". The most striking product of this urban facelift was a distinct separation between the working-class districts, on the outskirts of the city, and the wealthier inner-city districts. Haussmann's first objective as Prefect of the Seine département, in which Paris was situated, was to eradicate the teeming slums and open up the city by creating those wide, straight thoroughfares (or "grands boulevards") – one of which bears his name – which would also make it easier to quell any popular uprising.

The makeover of Paris by Napoleon III also included, finally, an attempt to revive his faltering popularity by staging the first Universal Exposition in 1867. The city had

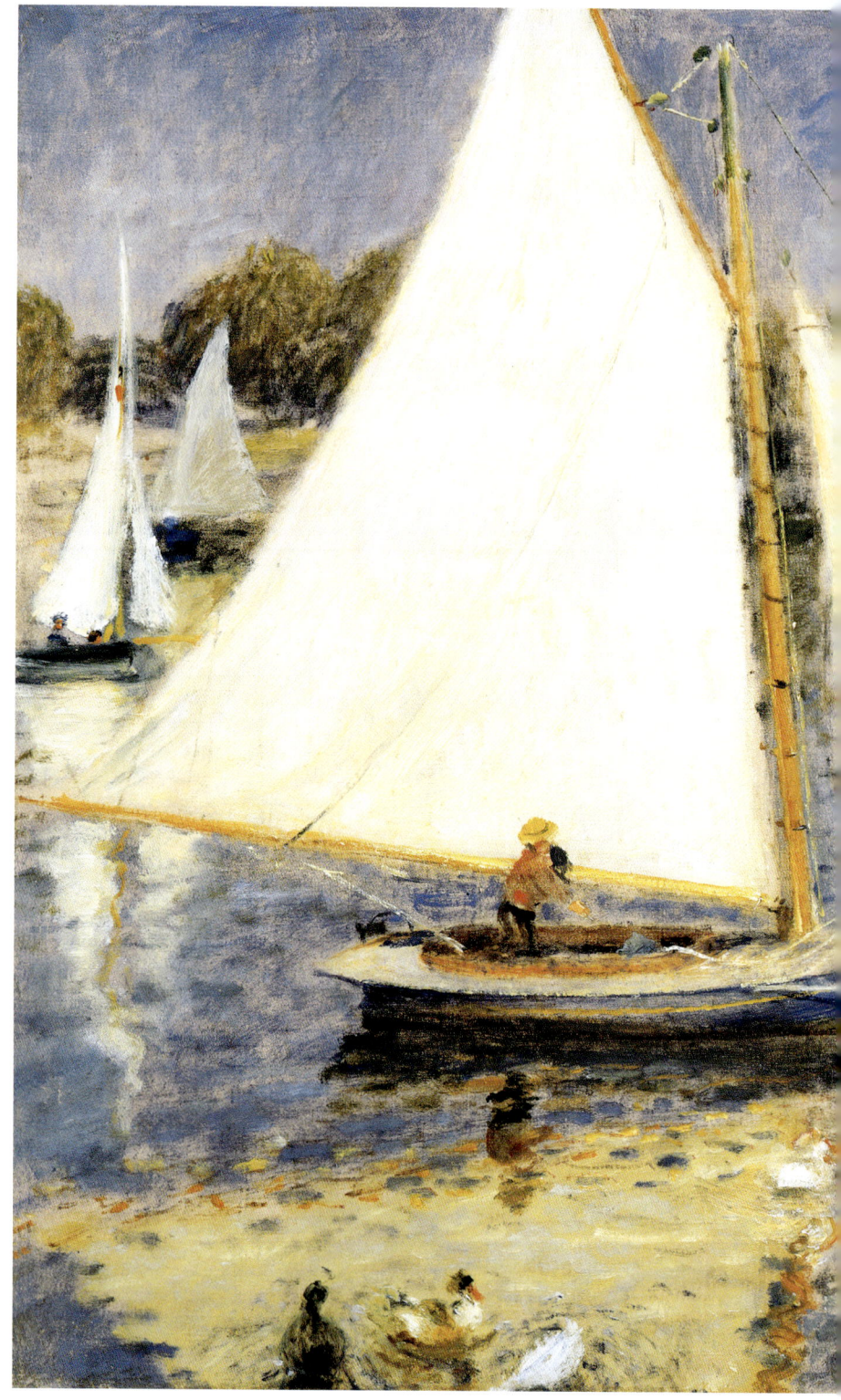

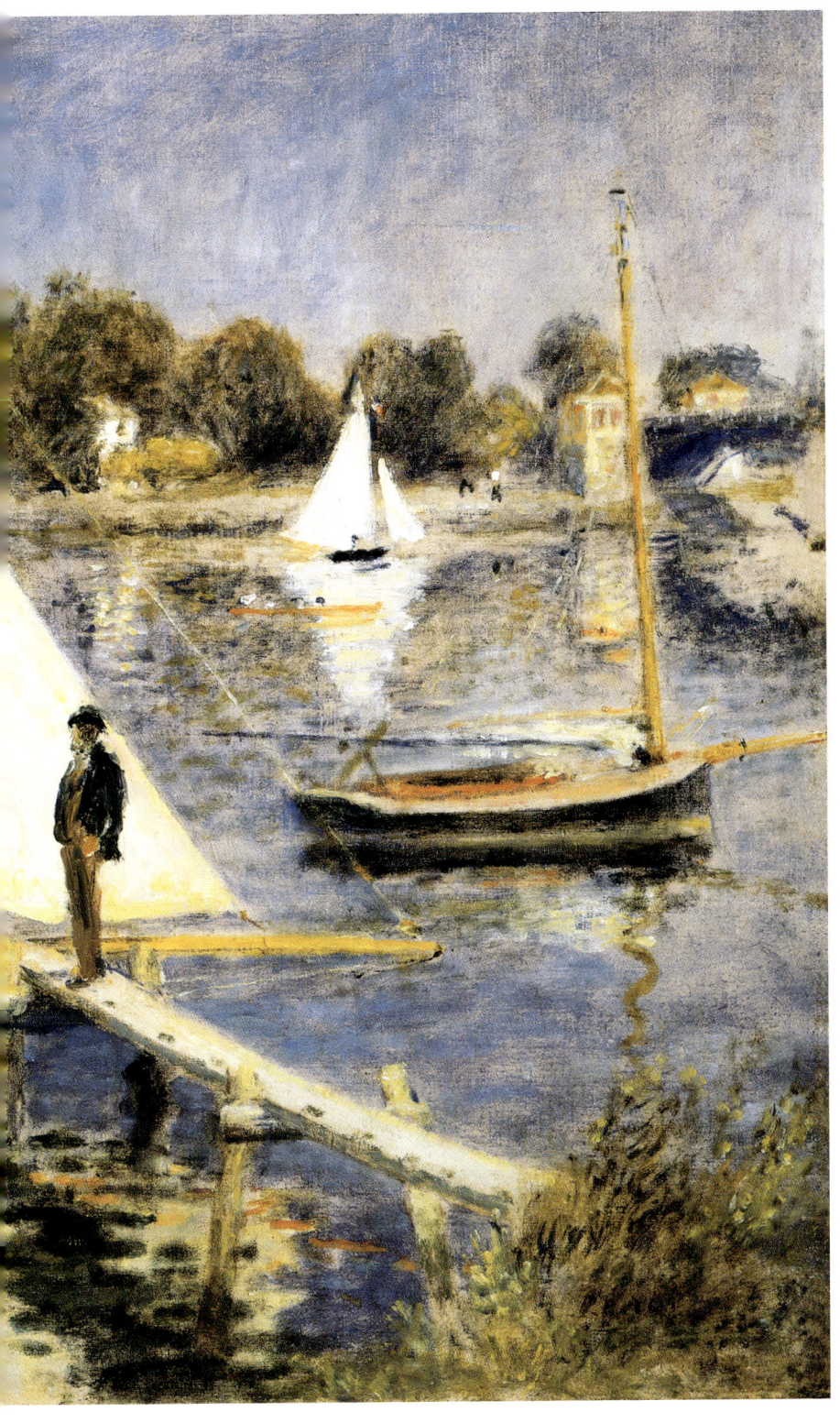

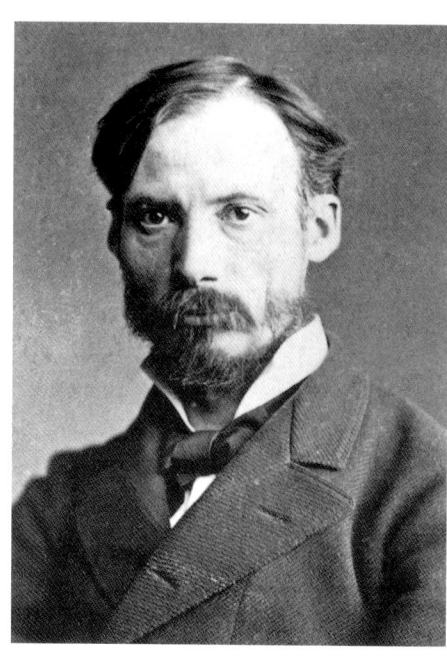

Renoir at the age of thirty-four, 1875

The Theatre Box, 1874
Oil on canvas, 80 x 63.5 cm (31½ x 25 in.)
London, The Courtauld Institute of Art

become "a huge harlot" in the words of Charles Baudelaire. Photographed by Félix Nadar from his hot-air balloon, it was now compact, orderly, huge and gleaming. At its heart were the dense crowds of people that covered the pavements and the terraces. The new painters considered it a "joy to choose one's residence among the multitude, in the rippling, fleeting movements of the infinite". This is how Baudelaire described Constantin Guys, whom he considered to be the embodiment of "modernity" with his desire to "marry the crowds". In his preface to *Le Spleen de Paris*, the poet noted that this passion for crowds ought to give rise to a new language, a poetic prose that would be "flexible and abrupt" enough to reflect "living in enormous cities". It ought also to produce a new type of painting. "In the minutiae of daily life, in the everyday metamorphoses of external things, there is a rapid movement which requires of the artist an equal velocity of execution".

Manet painted views of Paris, and especially the Rue Mosnier where he had his studio, using a technique so supple that it looked instantaneous. It consisted of rapid cross-hatchings and was probably his most direct contribution to Impressionism. The Impressionists, who owe him so much, learned direct observation from him. He learned from them in turn that "shadow is obtained not only by darkening the local colour, but also by breaking the light up in a particular area or on planes in which only cool colours can be perceived and fixed"(R. Rey). In 1866, Monet clambered over the rooftops of the Louvre facing Saint-Germain-l'Auxerrois to paint the first panoramic views of Paris. This was Haussmann's brand new Paris, with its new buildings, its people

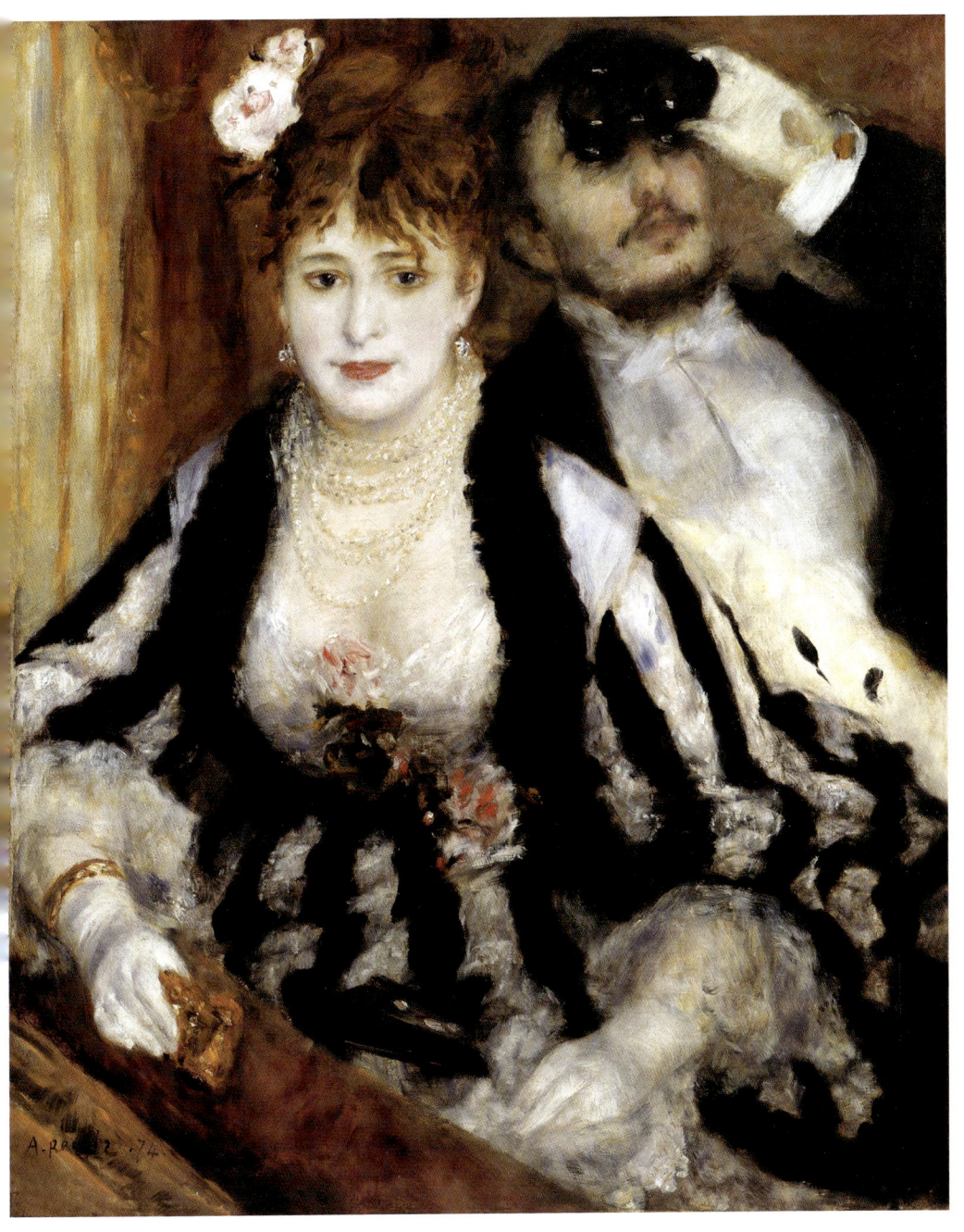

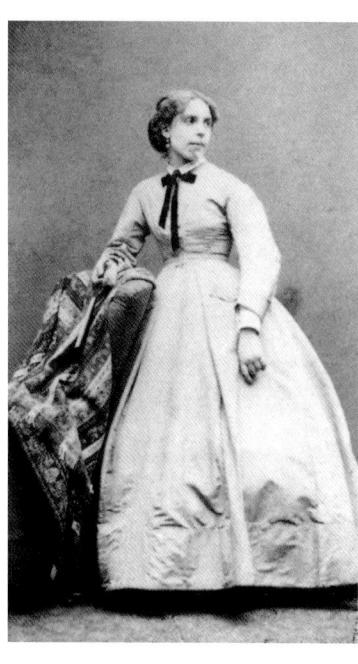

Henriette Henriot (1857–1944),
photographed by Étienne Carjat
Paris, Bibliothèque de l'Arsenal,
Collection Rondelet

The Parisian Woman (Henriette Henriot), 1874
Oil on canvas, 163.2 x 108.3 cm (64⅜ x 42¾ in.)
Cardiff, National Museum of Wales

The Parisian Woman belongs to what might be
called "the Henriette Henriot period". Henriette
Henriot was an actress at the Odéon theatre and
Renoir's favourite model who was also the object
of his affections in the 1870s. She features in at
least eleven of Renoir's paintings. Jean Prouvaire,
a critic writing in the magazine *Le Rappel*, who
liked Renoir's work and had a sense of humour,
saw in the three paintings Renoir submitted for the
first exhibition by the group, *The Dancer* (p. 93),
The Parisian Woman, and *The Theatre Box* (p. 87),
"the three stages through which the ladies of
Paris pass", from teenager to *cocotte*.

strolling through the streets, its coaches and numerous figures, all of them seen from
above. Renoir could only be enchanted. He had not anticipated this new fashion for
painting Parisian cityscapes. In 1867, he painted a view of the *The Pont des Arts, Paris*
(pp. 28/29) and *The Champs-Elysées during the 1867 Universal Exposition* (p. 27), and
then in 1868 he followed it up with *Skaters in the Bois de Boulogne* (pp. 24/25). In 1872
Renoir finally completed his *Pont-Neuf, Paris* (p. 66), which was influenced by the
paintings that Monet had done from a window in the Louvre Colonnade. Only then did
Corot's influence on Renoir come to be superseded by his Impressionist development
which can be glimpsed in the vibration of the elements bathed in sunlight as well as
the general blue-tinted harmony. The brushwork is still a long way from the individual
strokes that he would use a year later when he painted *The Duck Pond* (p. 71) side-by-side
with Claude Monet, just as they had already painted *La Grenouillère* together. However,
his style in this painting may for all that remain even closer to his nature.

Renoir's brother Edmond had started a career in journalism, only to see it interrupted by the Franco-Prussian War in which both brothers enlisted. He returned to
journalism after the French defeat and the Commune. Edmond found his brother's
work more and more to his liking. He posed for him (*The Theatre Box,* p. 87) and
helped him as he had done when his brother was executing the view of the *Pont-Neuf*.
In 1939–1940, he explained to John Rewald what his contribution had been. "We had
established our headquarters on the landing of a little café in the corner of the Quai du
Louvre which was much closer to the Seine than the buildings which have been erected

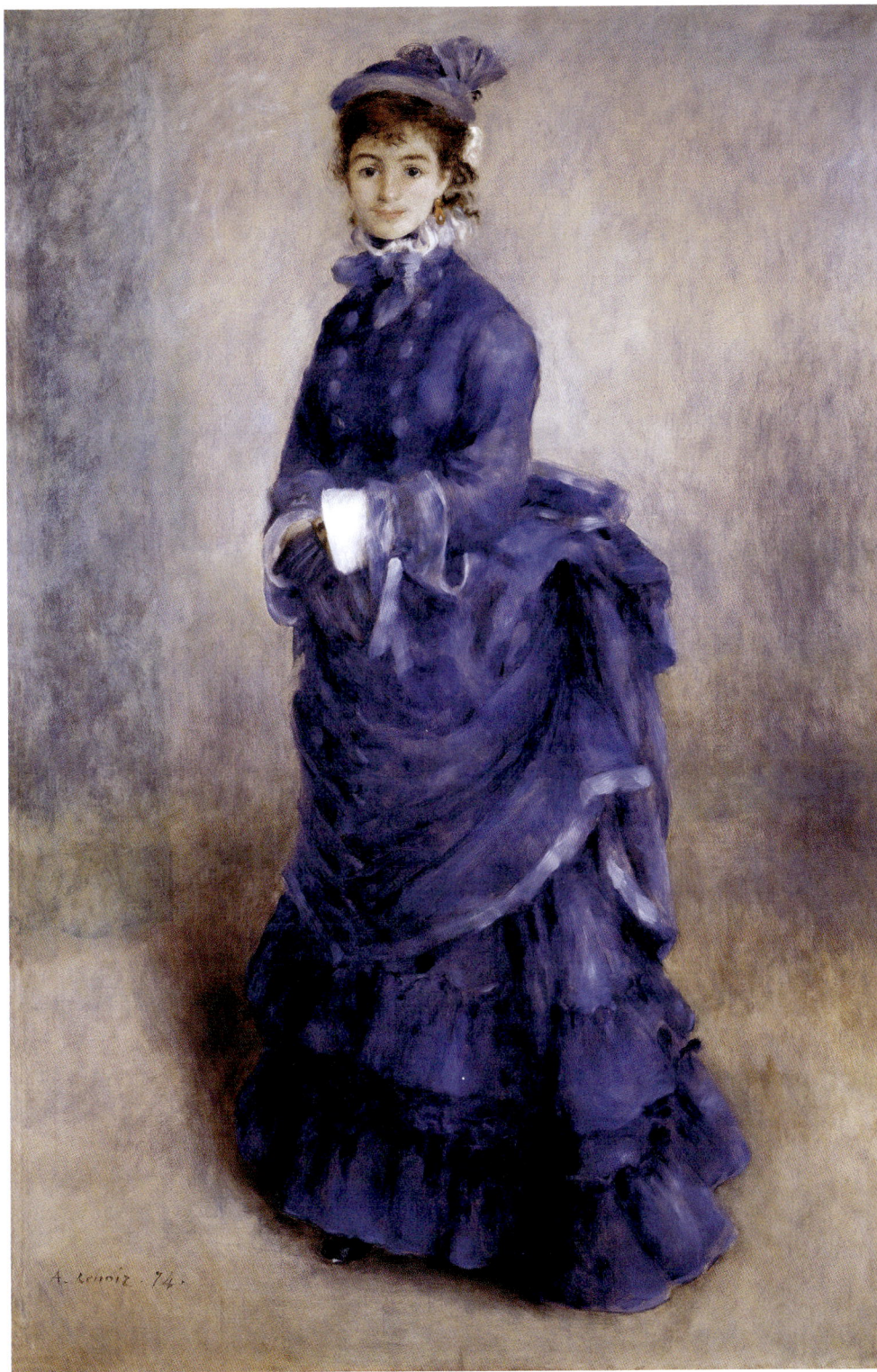

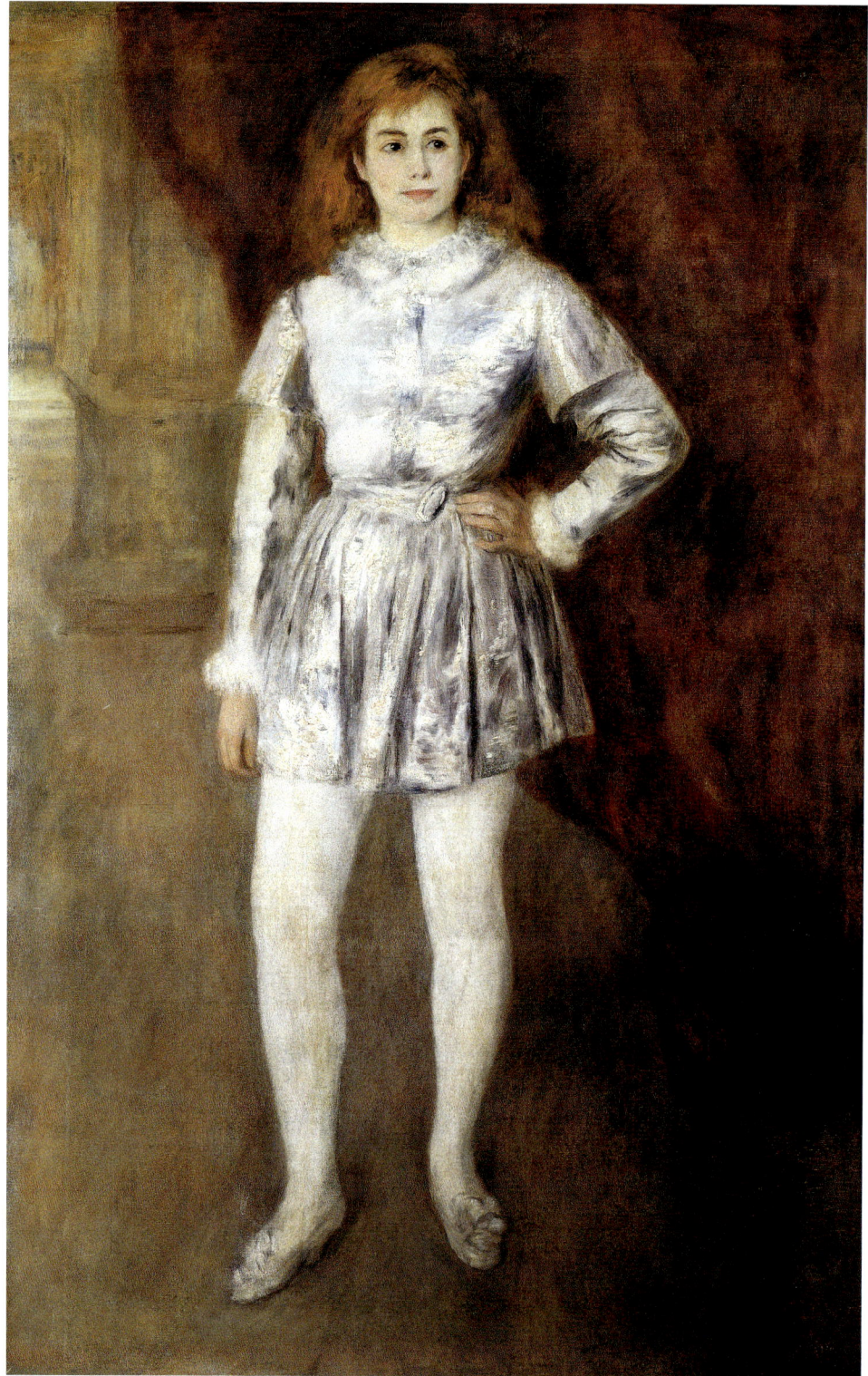

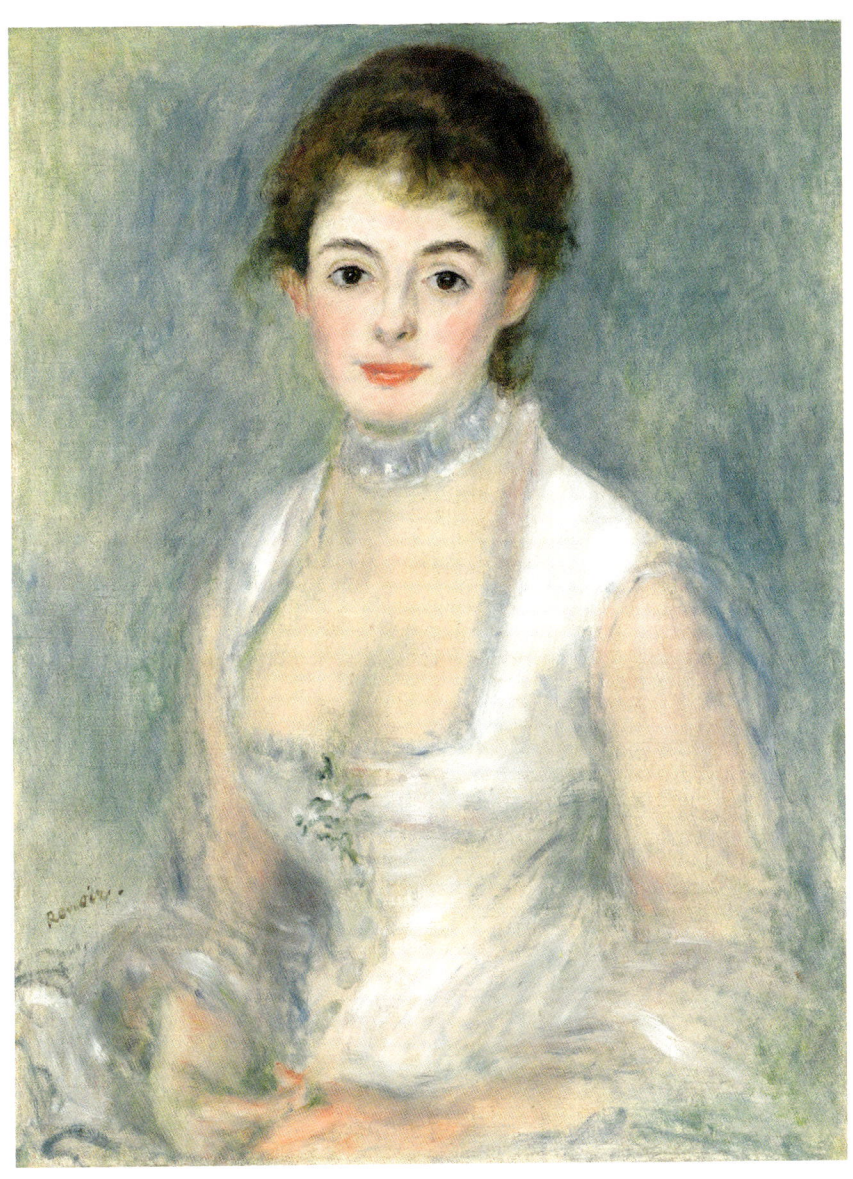

Madame Henriot in Costume,
c. 1875–1877
Oil on canvas, 161.3 x 104.8 cm (63⅝ x 41⅜ in.)
Columbus Museum of Art,
Museum Purchase, Howald Fund

Madame Henriot, c. 1876
Oil on canvas, 65.8 x 49.5 cm (26 x 19½ in.)
Washington, D.C., National Gallery of Art,
Gift of Adele R. Levy Fund, Inc.

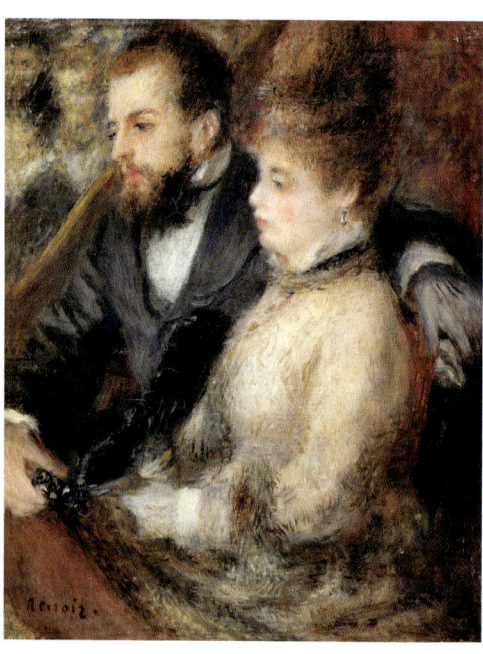

Box at the Theatre, c. 1873
Oil on canvas,
27 x 22 cm (10¾ x 8¾ in.)
Private collection

The Dancer, 1874
Oil on canvas,
142.5 x 94.5 cm (56⅛ x 37¼ in.)
Washington, D.C., National Gallery
of Art, Widener Collection

on the site since then. For the price of two coffees, at ten centimes each, we could sit in the café for hours. From there, Auguste had a commanding view of the bridge and, after noting the ground, the parapets, the houses in the distance, the Place Dauphine and the statue of Henri IV, he would enjoy sketching the passers-by, the traffic and the crowds. During this time, I would scribble away except when he told me to go to the bridge and get the passers-by to pause." "Edmond Renoir would ask a man the time", explained Rewald, "or a woman for directions to a particular street, requesting all kinds of useless information in order to give his brother sufficient time to complete his sketch."

Produced three years later, *The Grands Boulevards, Paris* (p. 67) is much more frankly Impressionist in the vaporous effect of the light. At the same period Renoir was adopting a more traditional attitude to his portrait-painting and his interiors. Yet he continued to change and evolve his own personal style, which disconcerted those purists who preferred short brushstrokes. He mixed his styles in his own way, sometimes using a spread-out, blended technique and at other times employing discrete brushstrokes. His subtle way of using brushstrokes by delicately blending them produced an effect of scintillating light through a kind of haziness that is Renoir's own. The extreme diversity of skills and techniques used by Renoir, depending on his mood, are exemplified in two views he painted of the *Place de la Trinité* (1875). One has stronger brushstrokes but in the other the brushwork is more delicate. By painting from a window, Renoir avoided having to plant his easel in the middle of the crowds. The result is a bird's eye view, which changes the framing of the scene and provides dynamic foreshortenings that

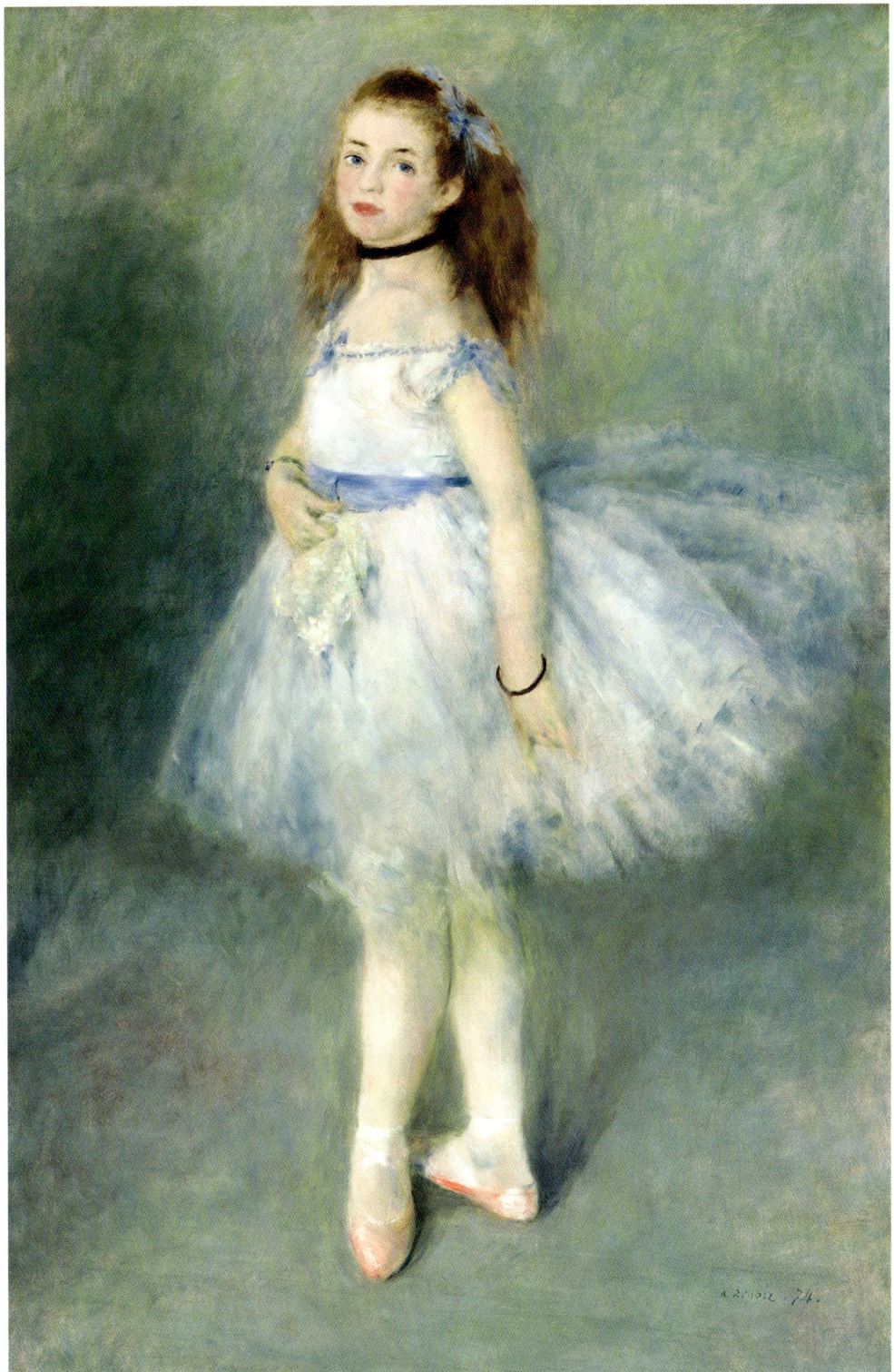

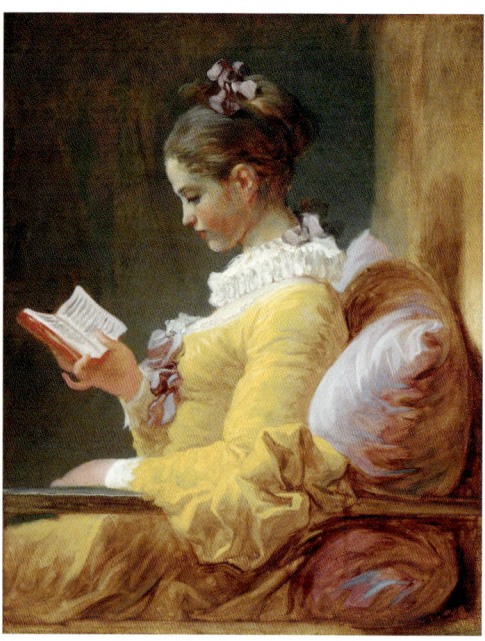

Jean-Honoré Fragonard (1732–1806)
Young Girl Reading, c. 1769
Oil on canvas, 81.1 x 64.8 cm (32 x 25⅝ in.)
Washington, D.C., National Gallery of Art,
Gift of Mrs. Mellon Bruce in memory of
her father, Andrew W. Mellon

look forward, before the creation of cinema and its use of tracking shots. The spectator no longer sees the subject from a distance but has the impression of mingling with the crowd and becoming a part of city life. The Impressionists behaved in just the same way in the city as they did in the country. They rejected contours as illusions and tried to do nothing in their paintings but capture vibrations. One critic talked of "a large number of dark blurs at the bottom of the painting", representing the passers-by, but another understood better what they were trying to achieve. "Never before has the extreme animation of the highway been captured in this way, the teeming crowd pouring over the asphalt and the cars in the road, the waving of the branches of the trees along the boulevard in the dust and light, the elusive, fleeting, instantaneous movement in all its prodigious fluidity."

Impressionism, nevertheless, worked better in the countryside. In 1873, Renoir and Monet shared the same subject-matter on several occasions, including *The Duck Pond* (p. 71), and the moored yacht in *The Seine at Argenteuil* (pp. 84/85), as they had done earlier when they painted *La Grenouillère*. The first of these is painted in small, thick brushstrokes, a technique invented by Pissarro, while the second uses wider, more dis-parate strokes. In both cases, Monet and Renoir use the same technique. Is it friendship, the open air, or identical study of the subject-matter that link Renoir and Monet at this moment? The fact is that when Renoir works alone, he paints most of his landscapes by spreading the colour in a thin wash in which the brushstrokes melt into each other, but when he works with Monet, the disjointed strokes miraculously reappear. The two

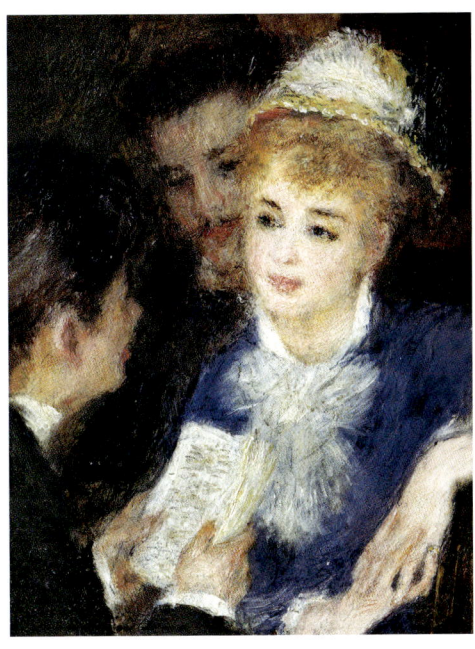

Reading the Part, c. 1876/77
Oil on wood, 9 x 7 cm (3⅝ x 2⅞ in.)
Reims, Musée des Beaux-Arts

depictions of *The Duck Pond* are almost twins, and when preparing to paint *The Seine at Argenteuil*, the two artists planted their easels on the bank at Petit-Gennevilliers, not far from the bridge at Argenteuil. In the latter case, Monet is not emulating Renoir. It is Renoir who, with his talent for flexibility and even mimicry, breaks up his brushstrokes more than usual in an attempt to render the multicoloured reflections on the water. His technique remains very slightly more fluid, making certain shady spots more alluring. Monet, as he is wont to do, plays with more marked contrasts.

Similarly, when Renoir painted *Claude Monet Painting in His Garden at Argenteuil* (pp. 68/69), he adopted his friend's vibrant and belligerent technique as if to please him. Monet is painting in front of a mass of multicoloured dahlias, which seem to be his subject. He did indeed treat this subject in *Monet's Garden in Argenteuil* (also known as *The Dahlias*). The two friends were therefore not standing or sitting together as they usually did, but working at different angles. Renoir paints the location faithfully and represents the narrowness of the garden hemmed in by houses, while in Monet's picture the dahlias are the central feature, designed to hide the surrounding dwellings. Monet transforms his garden into an earthly paradise while Renoir, with a hint of mockery, emphasises the lack of privacy in these suburban surroundings, the legacy of Baron Haussmann's building work.

Renoir's affection for Monet and his wife, and his admiration for the way in which Monet was now leading the fight, is translated into a series of portraits. Some of these are outdoor and others traditional, using the theme of reading. Borrowing this from Fragonard's *Young*

Woman Reading, 1874–1876
Oil on canvas, 46.5 x 38.5 cm (18¼ x 15¼ in.)
Paris, Musée d'Orsay

Renoir did not need to find excuses for
painting portraits. Even if the subject-matter
was hackneyed, his pictorial language and
expression were fresh and innovative.
He flagrantly borrowed the theme of
Young Girl Reading (p. 94). This was one of
a series of girls reading books or newspapers
or studying a part in a play. The readers
included Madame Monet (pp. 76/77, 213)
as well as Madame Chocquet (p. 119).

Girl Reading (p. 94), Renoir never paints the husband and wife together. He would use
the same classic pose to paint a succession of portraits of little girls or young women
reading – including Madame Choquet – or sewing, embroidering, and picking flowers.
A sunshade replaced the heavy paraphernalia of the bow, arrow and dead hind by which
a nude was transformed into a Diana. Renoir could be accused of being too conventional in his choice of poses for his models. After all, paintings of interiors in which
beautiful Parisian women recline on sofas, reading, were popularised by such second-
rate artists as Firmin-Girard, his fellow student at the Gleyre studio. But as Colin B.
Bailey remarks, "These comparisons, of which so many could be made, remind us that
if Renoir lacks originality in his choice of subjects, his pictorial language and means of
expression indicate a truly innovative spirit. His use of colour is exuberant and allusions
to Japanese influence are very discreet".

The ties of friendship between Renoir and Monet that had existed since both studied under Gleyre were strained by the enforced separation of the war as well perhaps
as by Renoir's obstinate attempts to have his work accepted by the Salon. In *Renoir's
Portraits*, Colin B. Bailey mentions another possible reason for the closeness of the two
painters and offers another context into which the portraits of Monet by Renoir should
be placed. "From April 1873, Monet had been campaigning for a new system of exhibiting and selling works of art. This was a sufficiently controversial subject of discussion
at Argenteuil for Zola to mention it to his colleague Paul Alexis. Alexis wrote about it
enthusiastically on 5 May 1873 in the radical *L'Avenir national* (The Future of the Nation),

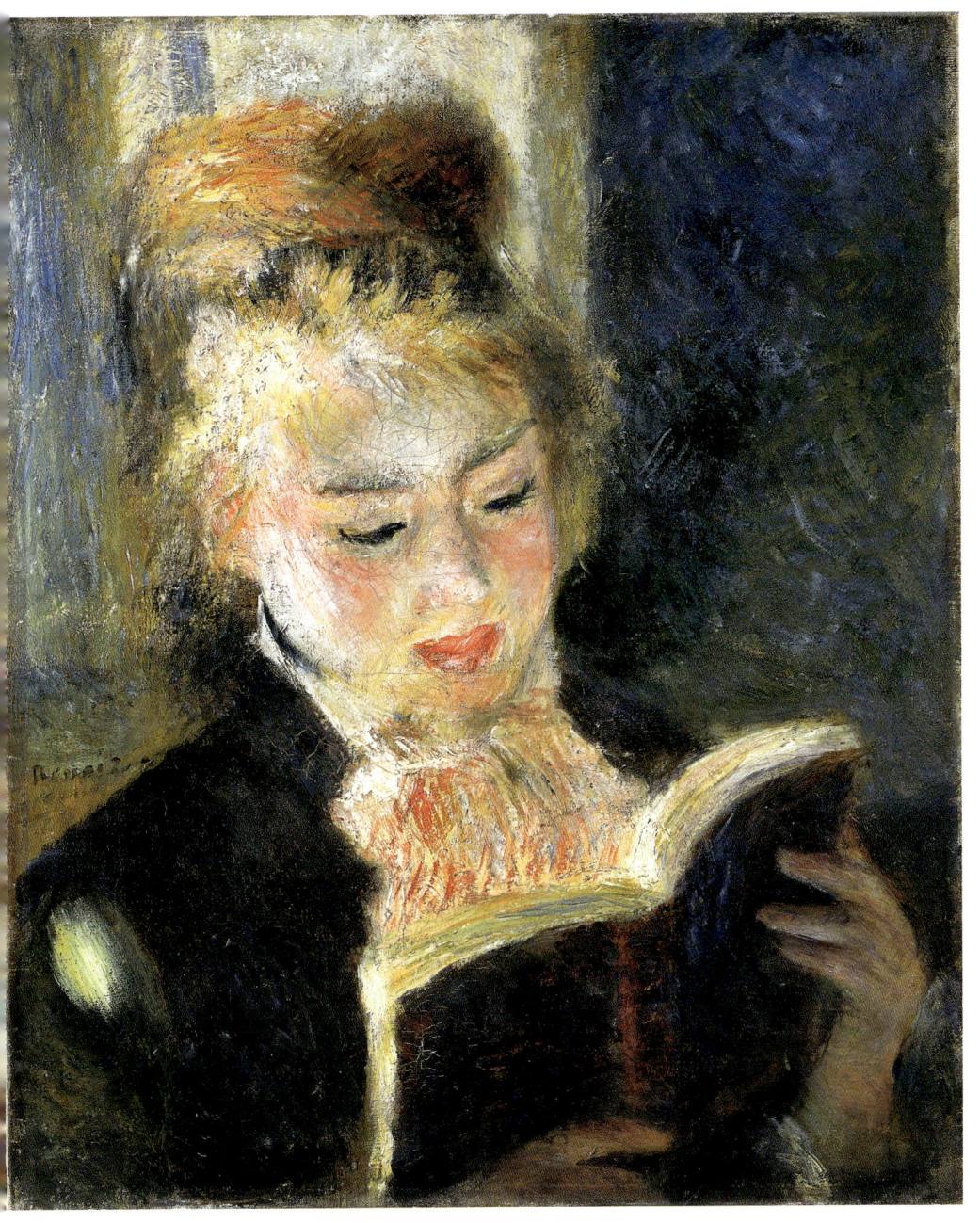

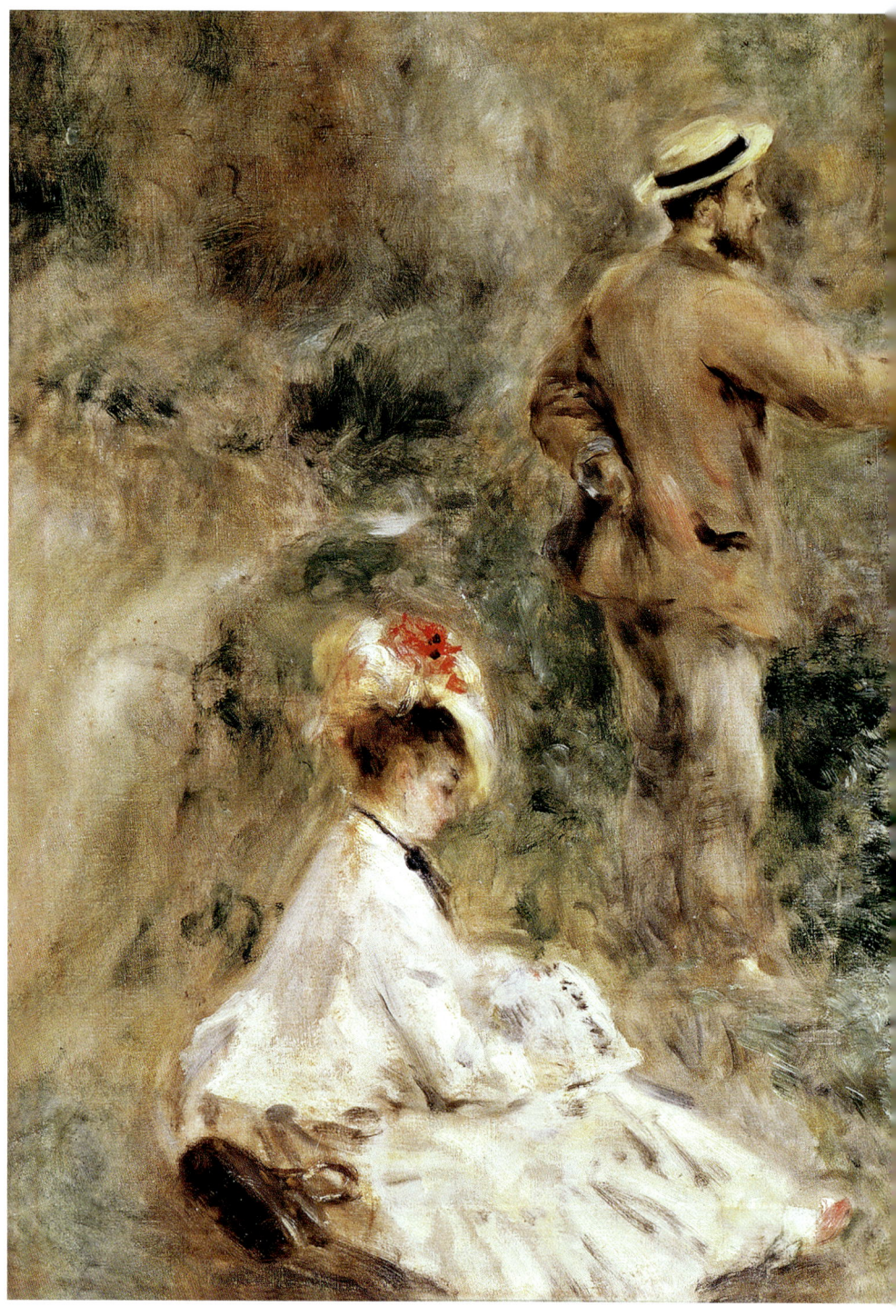

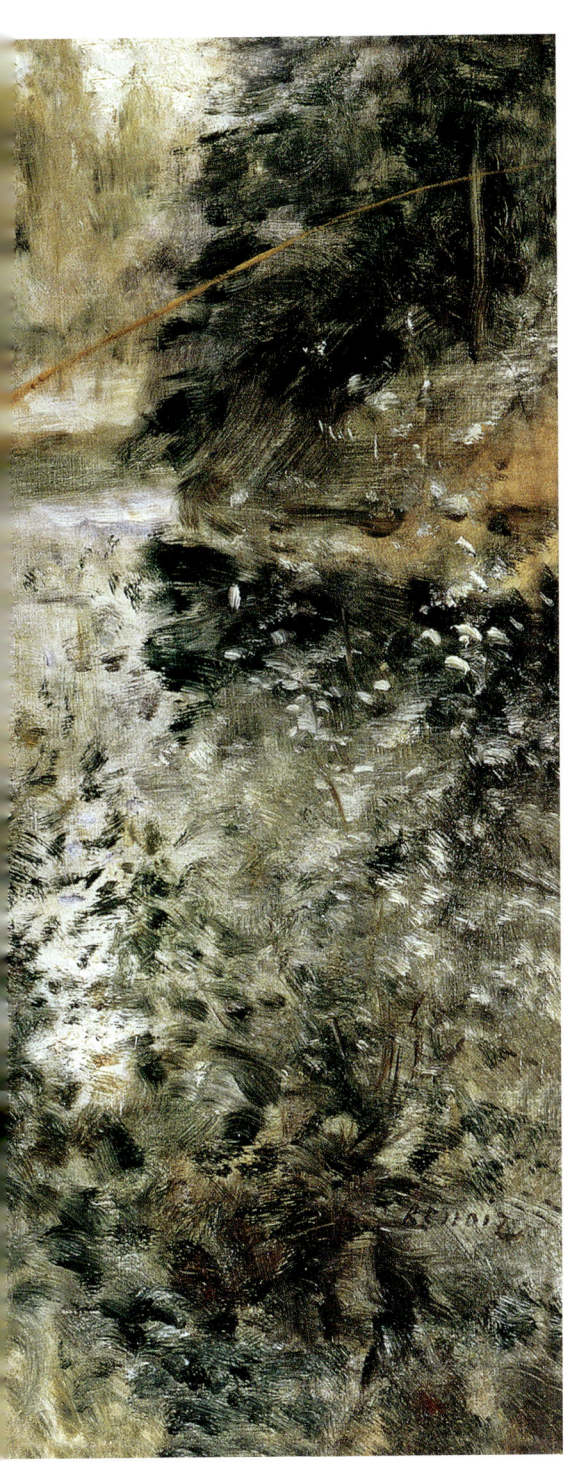

The Fisherman, 1874
Oil on canvas, 54 x 64 cm (21⅜ x 25¼ in.)
Private collection

The Fisherman was bought at auction by the
publisher Charpentier who then wanted to
meet the painter; the encounter led to a firm
friendship and Renoir's subsequent success.

By the Fireside, 1875
Oil on canvas,
61.5 x 50.6 cm (24¼ x 20 in.)
Staatsgalerie Stuttgart

claiming that 'this powerful idea, first entertained by an association of artists, is taking shape." Yet, although Pissarro, Jongkind and Sisley were among its founder members, Renoir did not attend the initial meetings. Since the Salon was stubbornly refusing to open its doors to him, he seems to have reflected, why not become involved in the project until something better comes along? In the absence of any enthusiasm or fellow-feeling, Renoir may have offered his portraits of Monet as his contribution to the project. They offered a "living symbol of the independent artist" to be used for publicity purposes.

Renoir turned all his attention to the project. The portraits reflect it with their allusions to a radical bohemianism which contrasts with the conservatism of the population at large. In *Claude Monet* (p. 212), and *Claude Monet Reading* (p. 214), Monet is in his working clothes. He is shown smoking a pipe, like Courbet, rather than the cigarette that any self-respecting urban fop would have sported at the time. When he is shown reading a newspaper, it is *L'Événement*, which had just published the articles of the association of the new joint stock company. According to Jean Renoir, his father "had at first regarded Monet as a dandy who would refuse to climb on his stool at the Gleyre studio and rejected the advances of the female students saying 'I'm sorry, but I only sleep with duchesses or maidservants ... the ideal would be a maidservant duchess', and wore impeccably ironed white shirts with lace-edged cuffs". Monet was indeed a fastidious dresser, as can be seen in all photographs of him. Renoir offered a different image of him, carefully choosing his props, in the form of a pipe, a little hat, a jacket with a velvet

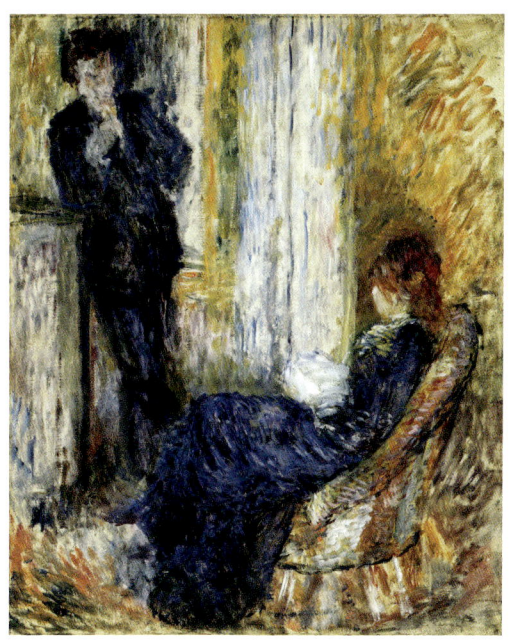

collar that did not reveal the white shirt underneath and a spartan décor, symbolising the artist's integrity. Renoir also shows him with his work tool, the palette, in his hand in *Claude Monet with Palette* (p. 216), a composition that makes a certain concession to tradition. He even sketched Monet in workman's clothes in a pastel, *Claude Monet Standing* (1873), which could have been used on a propaganda poster. In the first portrait, *Claude Monet*, the artist is reading a paperback just as, in *Madame Claude Monet Reading* (p. 213), Madame Monet is turning the pages of a popular novel. The second *Claude Monet Reading* advertises *L'Événement* and in *Madame Monet Reading "Le Figaro"* (pp. 76/77) the subject is holding the newspaper *Le Figaro* in her hand. Such details might always come in handy.

In all his outdoor scenes, Renoir adopts the short rapid brushstrokes of the Impressionists which favour colour and scatter shapes to make the figure blend into the décor. This is the case with many of his paintings of the period such as *Girl Gathering Flowers* (c. 1872) or *Young Girl on a Bench* (p. 73). As soon as the portrait is painted indoors, Renoir expresses himself far more characteristically. An exception is *Camille Monet* (p. 215), which is very conventionally painted and was quite clearly destined for the Salon. A much more original work is *Madame Monet Reading "Le Figaro"* (pp. 76/77), which reflects Manet's deep and lasting influence in its elegant clarity and vigorous attack. This is a successful attempt to reduce painting to that which can be grasped in a sideways glance, a study of an instantaneous glimpse. Camille Monet raises her eyes for a second from what she is reading and the artist notes, almost in shorthand, the

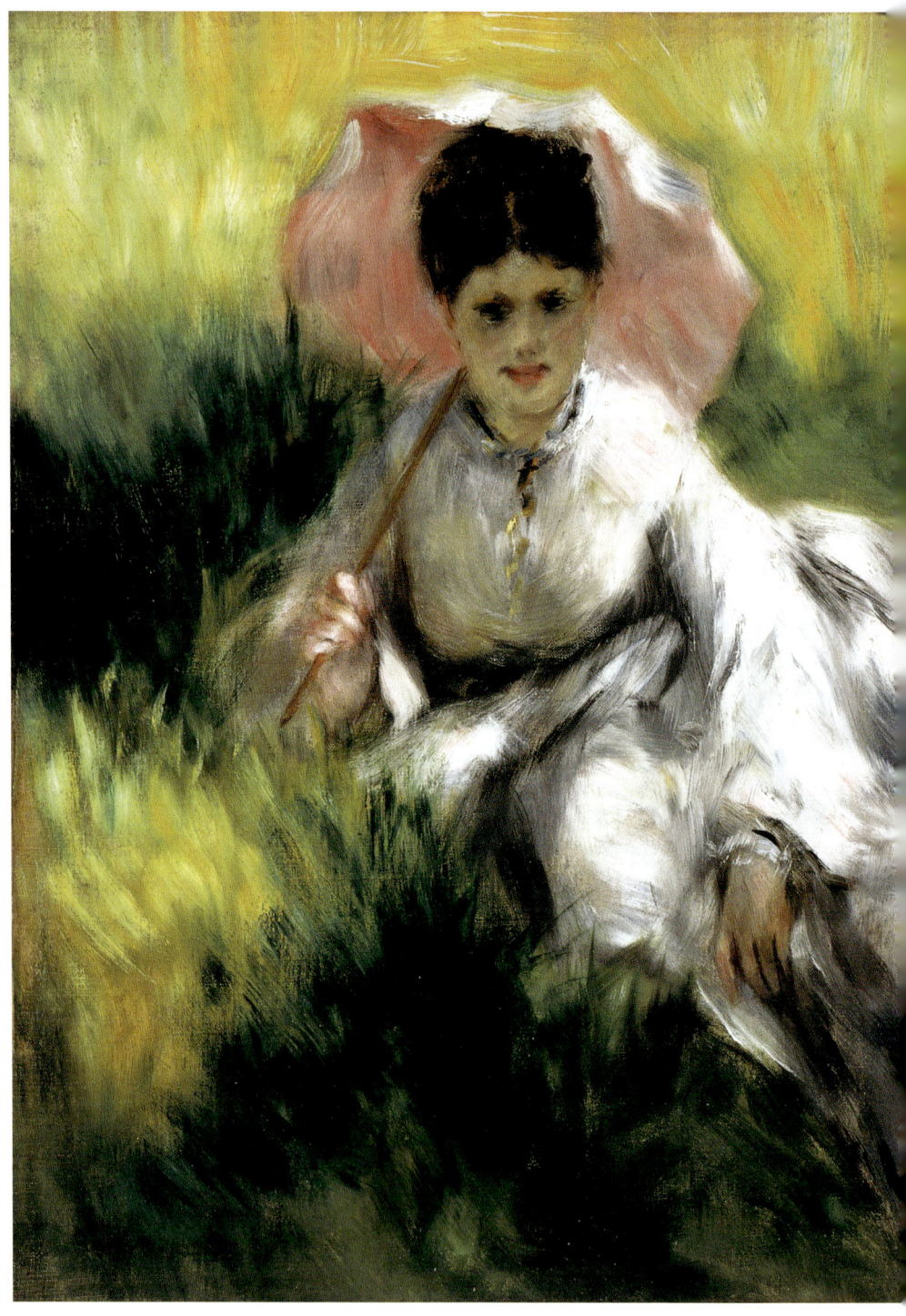

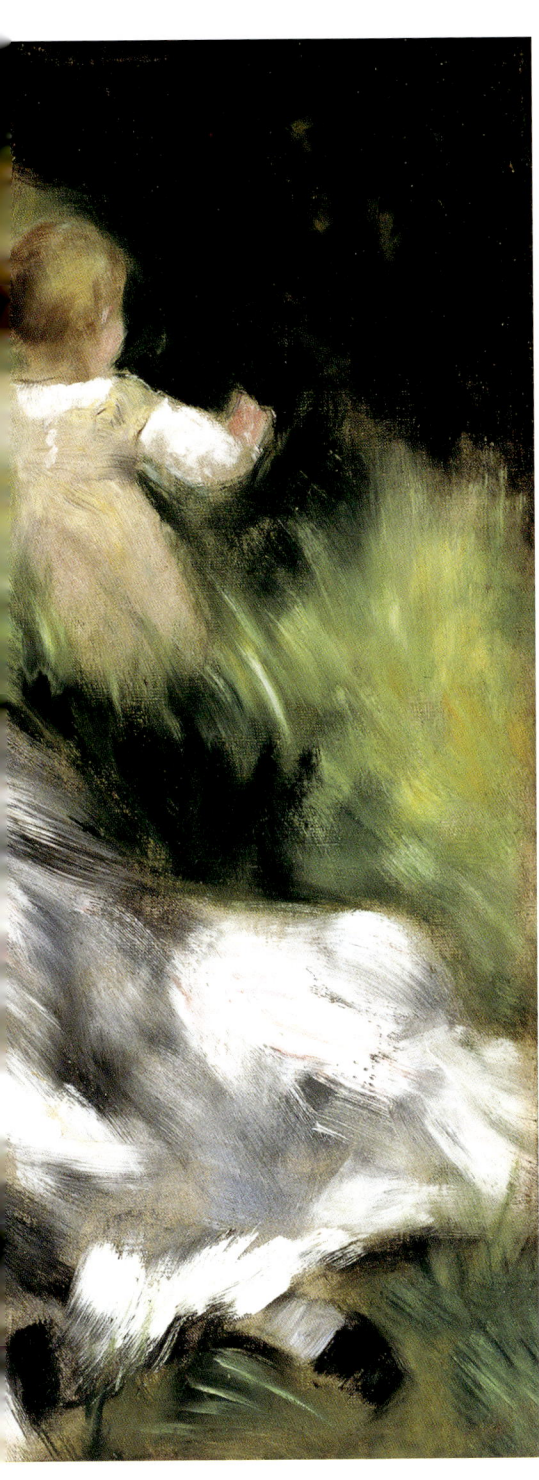

**Woman with a Parasol and Small Child
on a Sunlit Hillside**, c. 1874–1876
Oil on canvas, 47 x 56.2 cm (18⅝ x 22¼ in.)
Boston, Museum of Fine Arts,
Bequest of John T. Spaulding

Madame Monet and Her Son, 1874
Oil on canvas, 50.4 x 68 cm (19⅞ x 26⅞ in.)
Washington, D. C., National Gallery of Art,
Ailsa Mellon Bruce Collection

principal shapes and areas of colour. There is hardly any modelling: sharp colour contrasts and values determine the features, the hair and the details of her housecoat. The silhouette, which cuts diagonally across the composition, is carefully calculated. The upper half of the painting briefly sketches cushions and a wall so that the face can stand out against them; the lower half, consisting of sketched details, highlights the shape of the body. This tour de force clearly bears Renoir's hallmark. The student has become his master's equal, and may even have outdone him. This work is full of grace and vivacity and shows a total mastery of technique. Similarly, in *Claude Monet Reading* (p. 214) – a portrait which Monet possessed all his life – the brushstrokes become visible, the colours are intensified and highlighting is visible. The orange dotted in the model's beard and the blue smoke from his pipe were the very features of which the professional art critics so thoroughly disapproved.

Renoir's friendship with Monet and Manet, who he met in the garden at Argenteuil, also produced *Madame Monet and Her Son* (p. 105), which has become a legend in the annals of Impressionism. Monet took a wicked delight in telling the story of the painting: "This delightful painting by Renoir, which I am so happy to own today, is a portrait of my first wife. It was painted in our garden at Argenteuil on a day when Manet, attracted by the colour and light, had decided to produce an outdoor painting showing figures under the trees. Renoir arrived in the middle of the sitting. He too was captivated by the charm of the hour. He asked me for my palette, a brush and canvas, and there he was painting beside Manet, who watched him out of the corner of his eye,

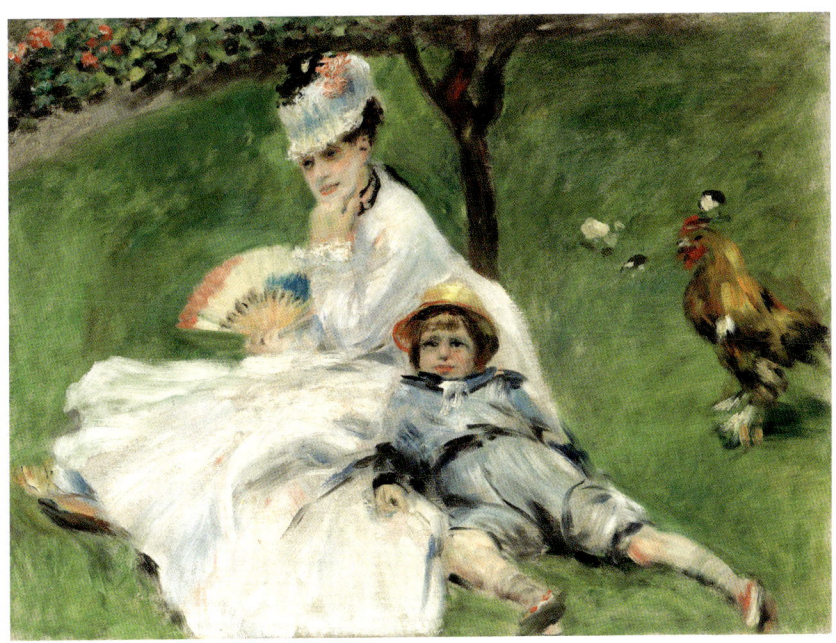

glancing at him from time to time and eventually walking over to the canvas. He grimaced, sidled up to me and, pointing at Renoir, whispered in my ear: 'that fellow has no talent whatsoever! If you really were a friend of his, you would tell him to give up painting!' Wasn't that amusing of Manet?"

We will never know whether or not Manet was joking. Rewald claims that Monet only told the story to annoy his friend. The ploy was unsuccessful because Renoir used to laugh at the story himself. He claimed that Manet, who owned his portrait of Bazille painting (p. 19), would say of his subsequent paintings, "Oh no! This is no longer Bazille's portrait at all!", to indicate his disapproval, which so many others shared, of Renoir's new style. Renoir constantly sought to perfect his technique by drawing inspiration from Manet whose emphasis on colour he greatly admired. He strove for improvement, and especially in the area in which he excelled, portraits of women. He teased Manet in turn, claiming that he had no idea about how to paint women, and wondering who could ever want to sleep with his Olympia.

The painting that Manet did that day is generally cited as the first in which he showed himself more open to the influence of his younger colleagues by working outdoors and opting for a freer and brighter palette. Renoir's painting is actually better than Manet's, it could be argued, since he had had more practice at the exercise. Its lively spontaneity is missing from Manet's painstaking *The Monet Family in the Garden* (1874). Renoir's version is daring and dynamic, more of a sketch than a carefully worked composition. He had rarely better captured an ephemeral scene in a few brushstrokes: Camille's face

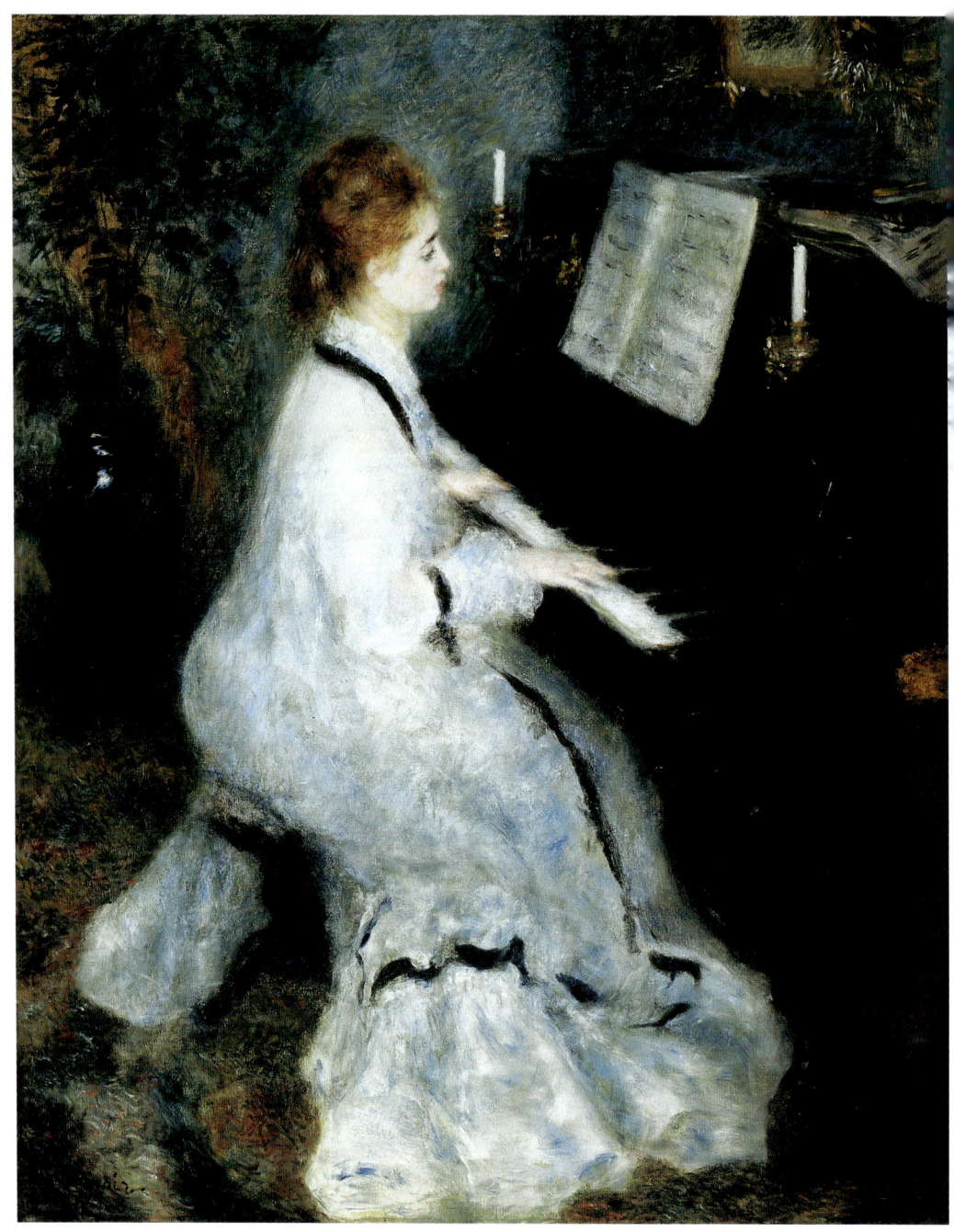

Woman with a Cat, c. 1875
Oil on canvas,
56 x 46.4 cm (22 x 18⅜ in.)
Washington, D.C., National
Gallery of Art, Gift of Mr. and
Mrs. Benjamin E. Levy

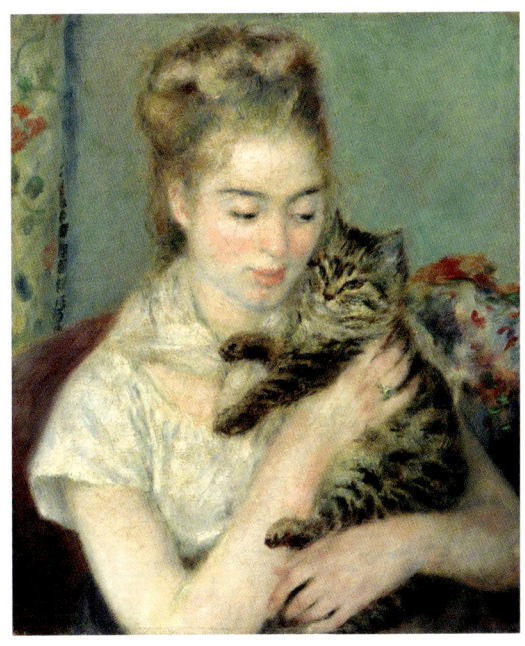

Woman at the Piano, 1875/76
Oil on canvas,
93 x 74 cm (36⅝ x 29¼ in.)
The Art Institute of Chicago,
Mr. and Mrs. Martin
A. Ryerson Collection

is rendered in no more than a few lines. Manet's composition looks stilted in comparison, despite its innovative technique and variety of tones. Renoir never missed an opportunity of making fun of Monet for putting on aristocratic airs and graces. He had emphasised the artificiality of the suburban garden of which his friend was so proud. In this painting he maliciously suggests the proximity of Monet's cramped garden to the neighbouring farmyard. With a few dashes of orange he adds a handsome cockerel, which struts around as if it were in its own backyard.

Renoir used the same virtuosity to sketch a small picture of a young woman, thought to be Camille Monet, half-lying in the grass; while a blond child runs away behind her. *Woman with a Parasol and Small Child on a Sunlit Hillside* (pp. 102/103) is painted in long, silky strokes of the kind that Renoir preferred to the crude little dabs he had used before. The painting is charming and illustrates the diversity of techniques that Renoir had now mastered and could use whenever the fancy took him. Traces of Manet remain but are attenuated by details typical of Renoir, such as the bluish shadows in the white dress or the way in which the face is isolated under the unfurled sunshade and framed by the light filtering through the grass. Pissarro called Renoir "the most changeable of men" and, from 1873 onwards, he was no longer a slave to his techniques. He could change and combine them with consummate skill in the service of his feelings. Examples are to be found in landscapes such as *Woman with a Parasol in a Garden* (pp. 74/75), *The Harvesters* (1874) or even *Garden at Fontenay* (pp. 80/81). Renoir uses flickering strokes or long, thick ones to emphasise either the landscape

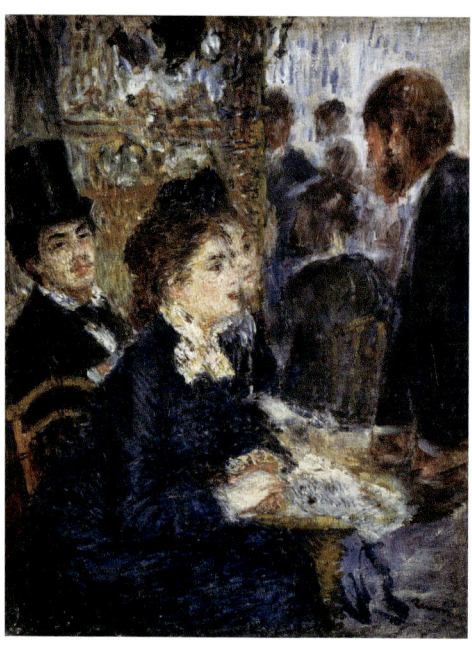

At the Café, c. 1877
Oil on canvas, 35.7 x 27.5 cm (14 x 10⅞ in.)
Otterlo, Kröller-Müller Museum

Young Woman with a Veil, c. 1875
Oil on canvas,
61.3 x 50.8 cm (24¼ x 20 in.)
Paris, Musée d'Orsay

or the figures. To produce a watery landscape with reflections in the water, such as in *Boating at Argenteuil* (p. 83), he spreads the colours in a thin wash and allows his brush-strokes to mingle.

Denis Rouart summarises Renoir's landscape work as follows: "Throughout his Impressionist period, Renoir had an astonishing range of techniques. He laid his colours on the canvas either in thick strokes, or a thin wash, or separate brushstrokes, or else in strokes that melt into one another". Renoir's outdoor painting shows definite signs of a move towards Impressionism. Other paintings however recall Manet of course as well as Titian, Rubens, and Watteau. Denis Rouart continues: "His paintings cannot be attached to a period. They are simply great, and Impressionist only in manner." Rouart is referring, of course, to such works as *The Theatre Box* (p. 87), *The Parisian Woman* (p. 89) and *The Dancer* (p. 93).

In September 1873, Renoir took up residence in Montmartre where he rented a garret at 35 Rue Saint-Georges. There the painter began two of his most famous canvases, *The Theatre Box* and *The Dancer*, which he completed in 1874. Six months later, from mid-April to mid-May 1874, he participated in the first Impressionist exhibition. The famous joint stock company, the Société Anonyme des Artistes Peintres, Sculpteurs, Graveurs, had finally been launched. The exhibition was held at the gallery of the photographer Nadar at 35 Boulevard des Capucines in Paris. Arranging the exhibition proved a mammoth task. Bazille came up with the idea first and after the Franco-Prussian War Monet took it up. The members of "Monet's gang" had agreed to form

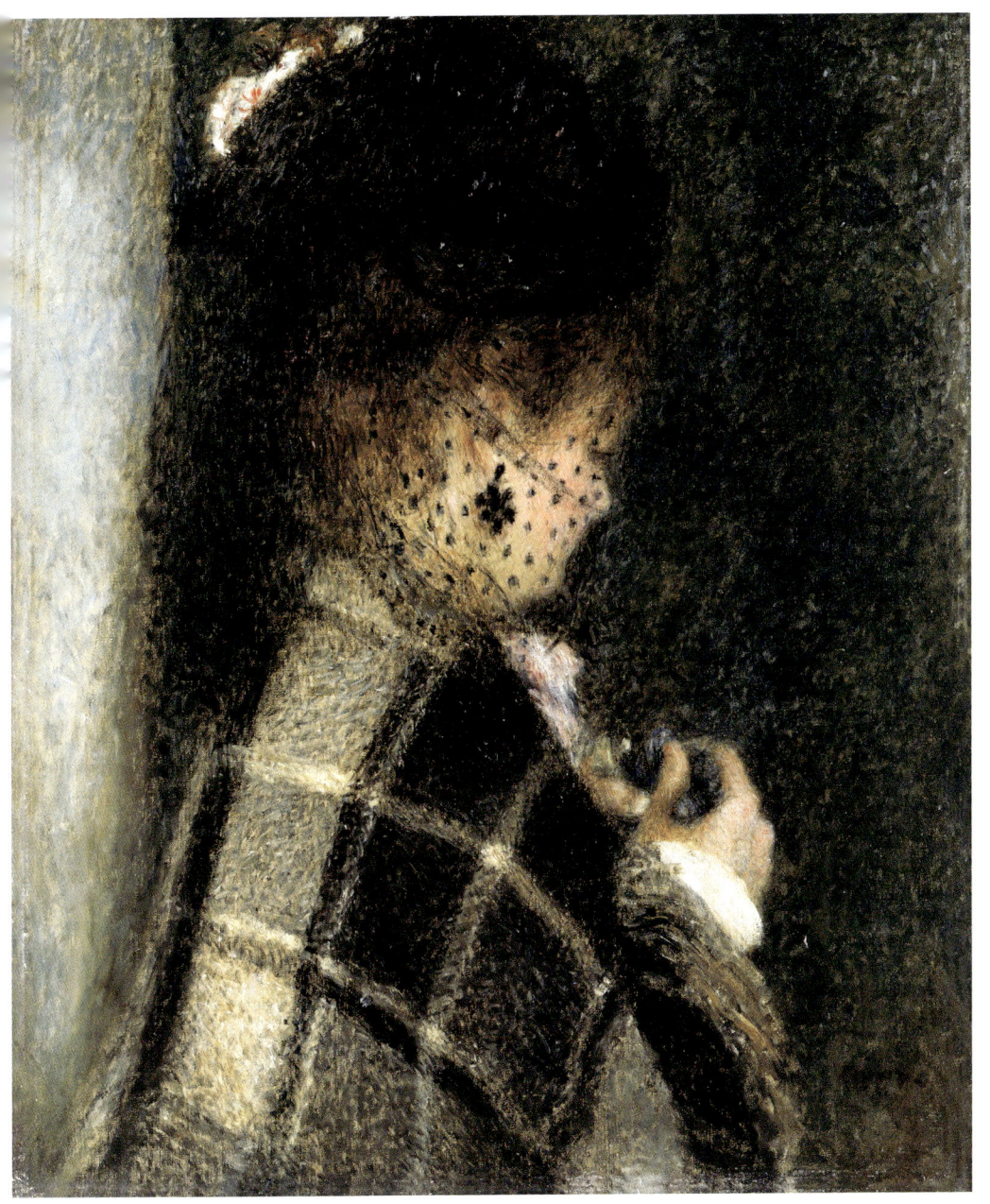

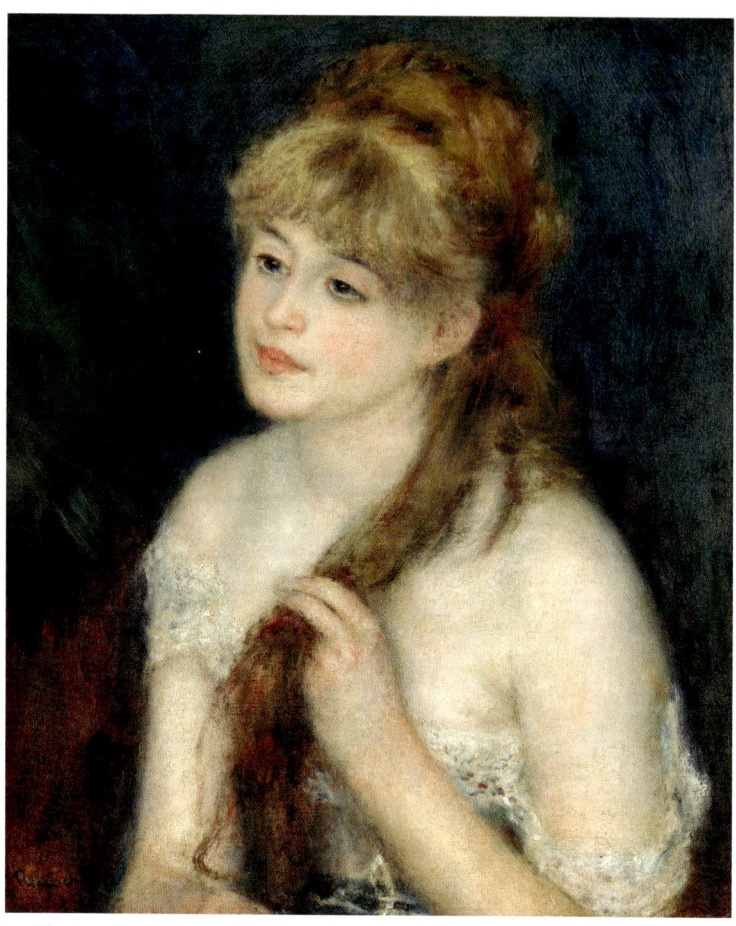

Young Woman Braiding Her Hair, 1876
Oil on canvas, 55.5 x 46 cm (21⅞ x 18⅛ in.)
Washington, D. C., National Gallery of Art,
Ailsa Mellon Bruce Collection

Renoir and Titian were both obsessed with
women's hair. The paintings by Titian that Renoir
most admired, including *Venus, The Virgin, Flora,
Bacchante, Ariadne* and *Madonna with a Rabbit*,
were those in which the model sported luxuriant
tresses. His *Penitent Magdalene* (p. 176) focuses
on the abundant hair that betrays the sensuality
and delicious sensation of the locks touching the
erogenous zones of her naked flesh, a delight that
can be detected from her ecstatic, heavenwards

gaze. Mary Magdalene is a female type that makes
her appearance in so many of Renoir's portraits,
clothed or unclothed, from *Young Woman Seated*
in which she has her fingers in her mouth to
Young Woman Braiding Her Hair in which she is
caressing her tresses. The numerous Bathers have
all loosened their hair and are often playing with
it, all of which are reminiscent of Titian's *Venus
Rising from the Sea* ("*Venus Anadyomene*"; p. 350).

Young Woman Seated, c. 1876/77
Oil on canvas, 66 x 55.5 cm (26 x 21⅞ in.)
The Barber Institute of Fine Arts,
University of Birmingham

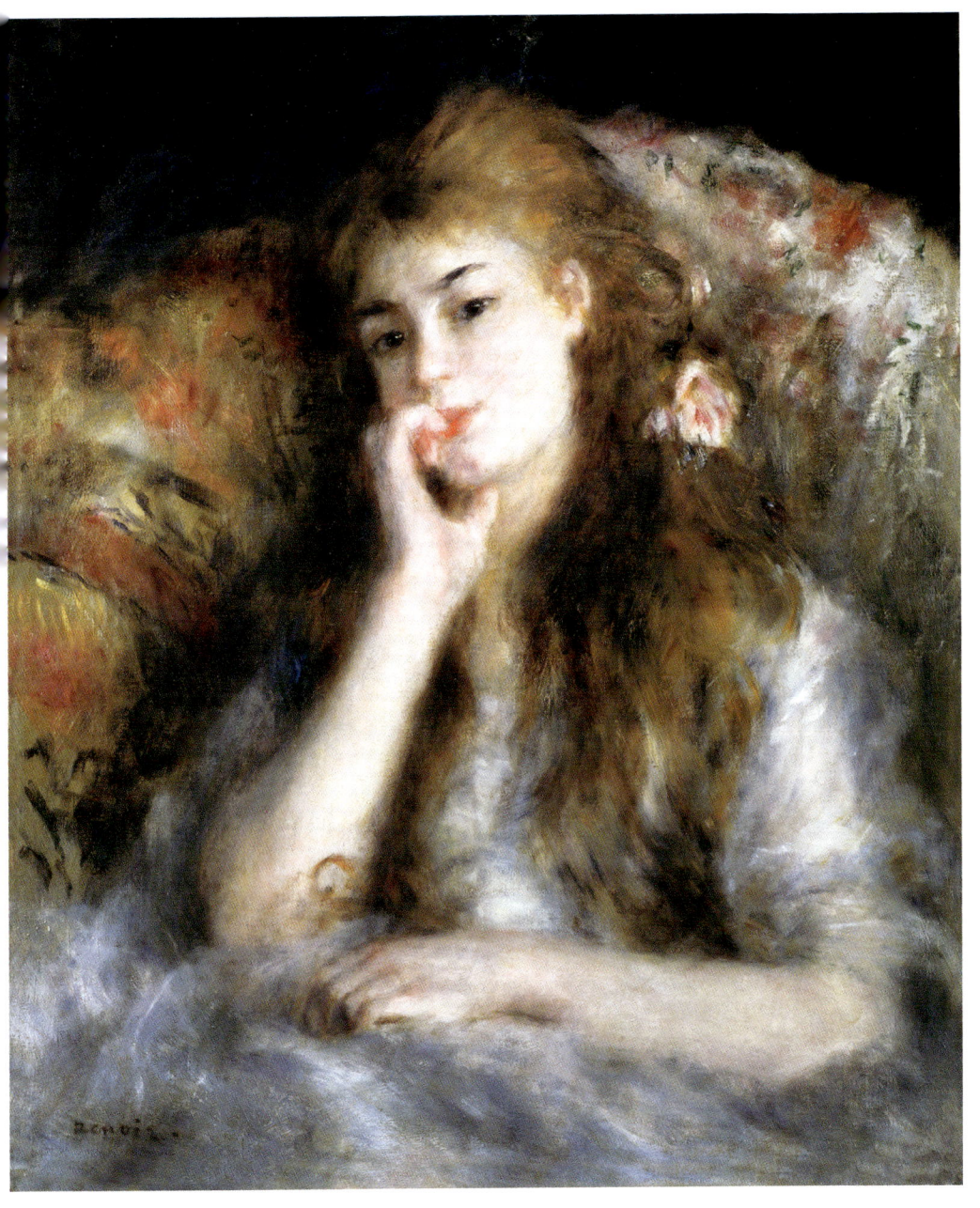

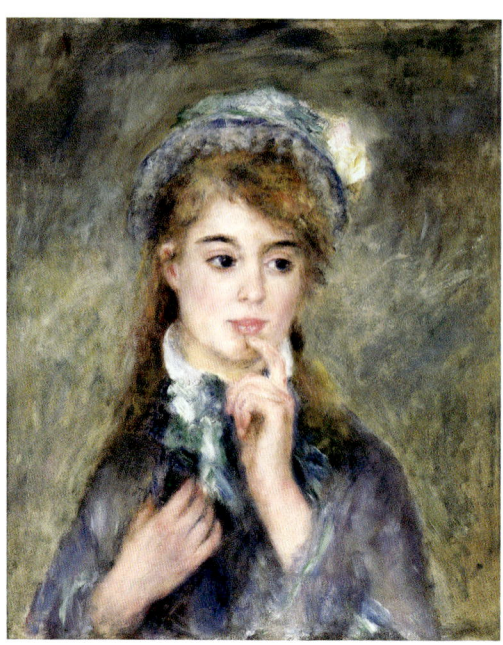

**Portrait of a Young Woman
(L'Ingenue)**, c. 1874
Oil on canvas, 55.7 x 46.4 cm (22 x 18⅜ in.)
Williamstown, Massachusetts, The Clark

The First Outing, 1876/77
Oil on canvas,
65 x 49.5 cm (25½ x 19½ in.)
London, The National Gallery

a group and exhibit together; but they shared no common aesthetic or conception of painting. Pierre Cabanne describes it succinctly: "Fauvism and Cubism were relatively long-lasting movements governed by a single mindset and vision. The same cannot be said of Impressionism. The more deeply the term 'Impressionist' became entrenched, then the greater the distance that the artists put between themselves and the 'Impression'. In this way they all sought – though each in his or her own way – to define a new set of resources with which to translate nature and modern life into art. Impressionism was never a coherent movement, since the term was used to embrace artists as diverse as Monet and Degas, Cézanne and Boudin, Alphonse Legros and Gauguin, Sisley and Caillebotte, Renoir and Seurat. It was not a doctrine and its protagonists never shared a common agenda. The only link between them was the contempt in which they were held, the hostility of the critics and the authorities towards them, and their lack of commercial success. When the principal Impressionists finally became well-known, the collective exhibitions ceased."

One might indeed wonder whether or not the Impressionists ever actually existed. Manet, their unwilling standard-bearer, actually remained distant from them. He sympathised with their efforts but refused to exhibit with any of them, Cézanne, famously, in particular. Degas took part in all the "Impressionist" exhibitions, except that of 1888, yet no painter is further from the "Impressionist" concept of painting outdoors and in bright light. He took offence at being labelled an Impressionist and had nothing but contempt for the expression of direct feeling that Monet, Renoir and Sisley sought to

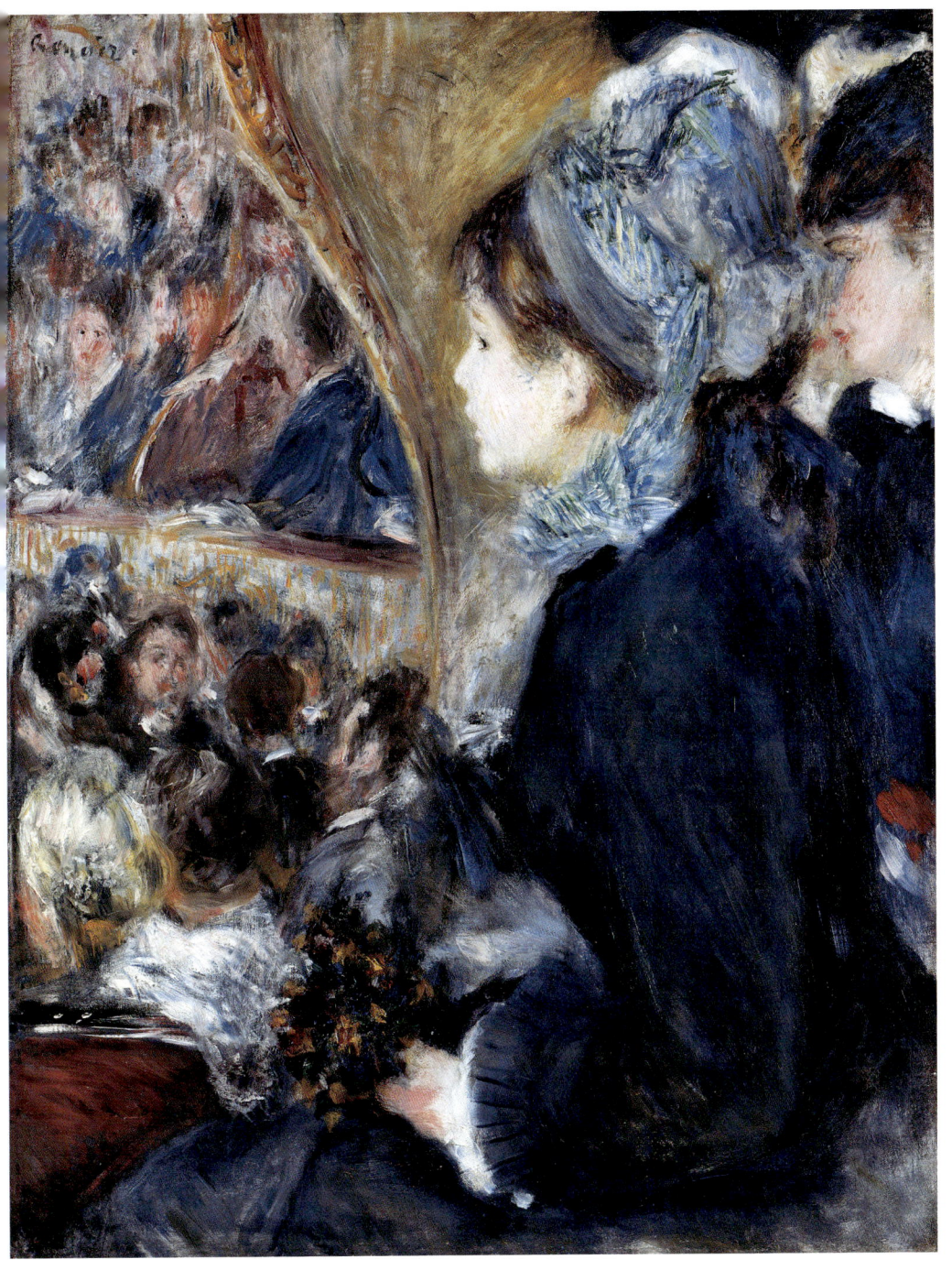

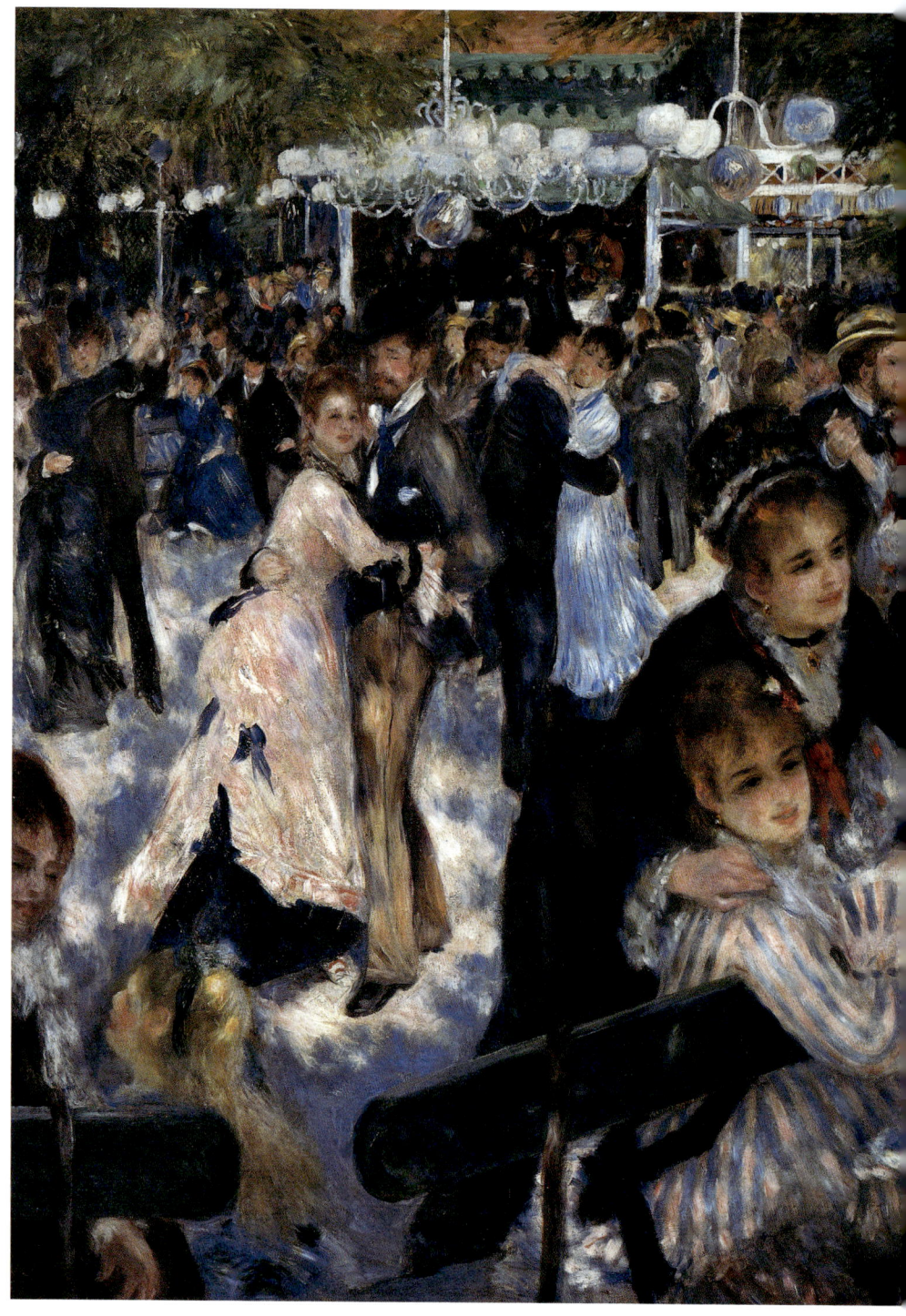

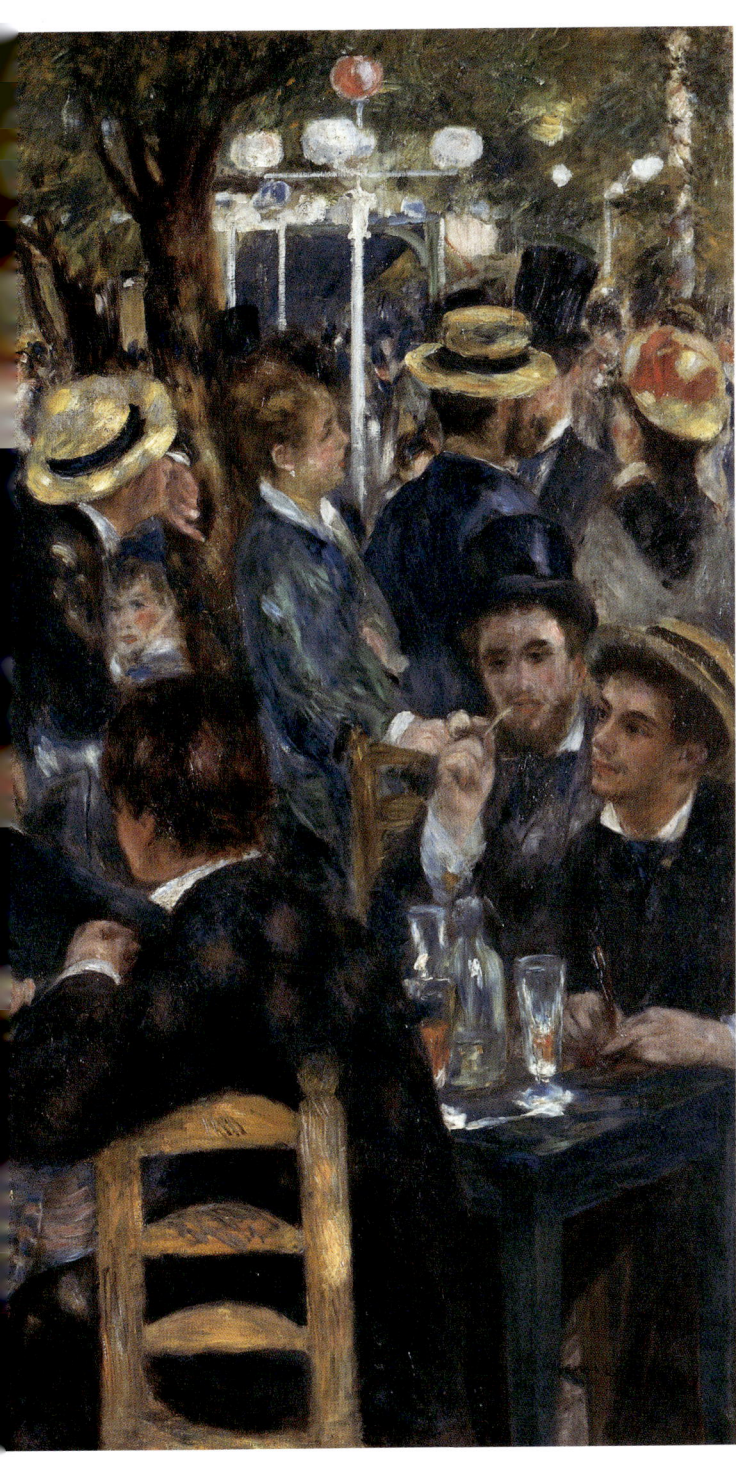

**Le Moulin de
la Galette**, 1876
Oil on canvas,
131.5 x 176.5 cm
(51⅞ x 69½ in.)
Paris, Musée d'Orsay

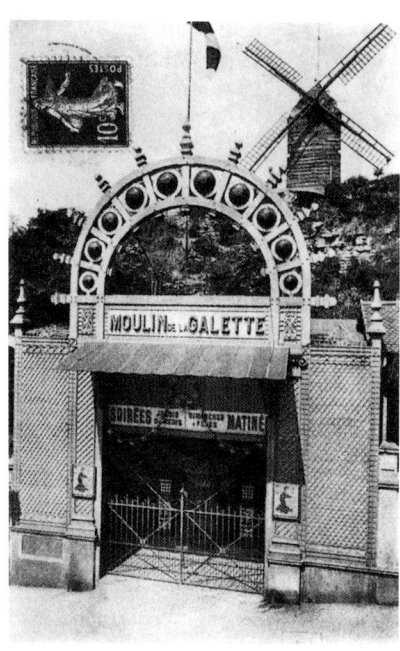

The Moulin de la Galette
Contemporary photograph

The Moulin de la Galette – unlike the Moulin Rouge, that temple of vice in which the French Cancan originated, immortalized by Toulouse-Lautrec – was simply a local dance-hall frequented by the young people of semi-rural Montmartre. The Sunday hop drew a large crowd. Renoir loved the gaiety and unpretentiousness of the atmosphere in this local tavern. He recruited his models from among his friends and their female companions who were milliners, dressmakers or flower-sellers. The atmosphere inspired Renoir to produce one of his greatest works in his quest for a luminous setting, his famous *Le Moulin de la Galette* (pp. 114/115).

The Bower – In the Garden (Under the Trees at the Moulin de la Galette), 1876
Oil on canvas,
81 x 65 cm (32 x 25⅝ in.)
Moscow, Pushkin Museum

convey. Degas always thought that painting needed to go beyond impressions, which could never be anything but rapid and misleading. No artist could ever become great 'by accident'. This view Renoir eventually came to share. With his customary acerbic wit Degas hoped for "the creation of a police force whose job it is to prosecute landscape artists". What he shared with the other exhibitors was contempt for the official institutions and the Salon and a taste for pale colour schemes and depictions of modern life. The greatest exponents of Impressionism, such as Cézanne and Gauguin, soon began producing the works for which they would become famous. Cézanne prepared the way for the Cubism of Pablo Picasso's *Demoiselles d'Avignon* (1907); Gauguin looked forward to Henri Matisse and the Fauves. Renoir, the ever-changing individualist, was only a committed Impressionist – if indeed he ever was – during the period 1870 to 1882. He had no particular method and swore no allegiance to any style or trend. His only credo was vitality and *joie de vivre*. Picasso's expression of impatience with 'styles' ("down with style! Does God have a style?") might have been Renoir's. Picasso confided to André Malraux that he had once smoked hashish, at Bateau-Lavoir. "It was disgusting! For hours on end, I felt sure that I would always paint in the same way!" Malraux concluded that, for the painter of *Guernica* (1937), "continuity of style was hell on earth." Renoir felt the same way.

"Monet's gang" had nothing in common, as has already been noted, other than the contempt in which the critics, the establishment, and the public all held them. The crushing defeat and huge scandal that resulted from the first Impressionist exhibition

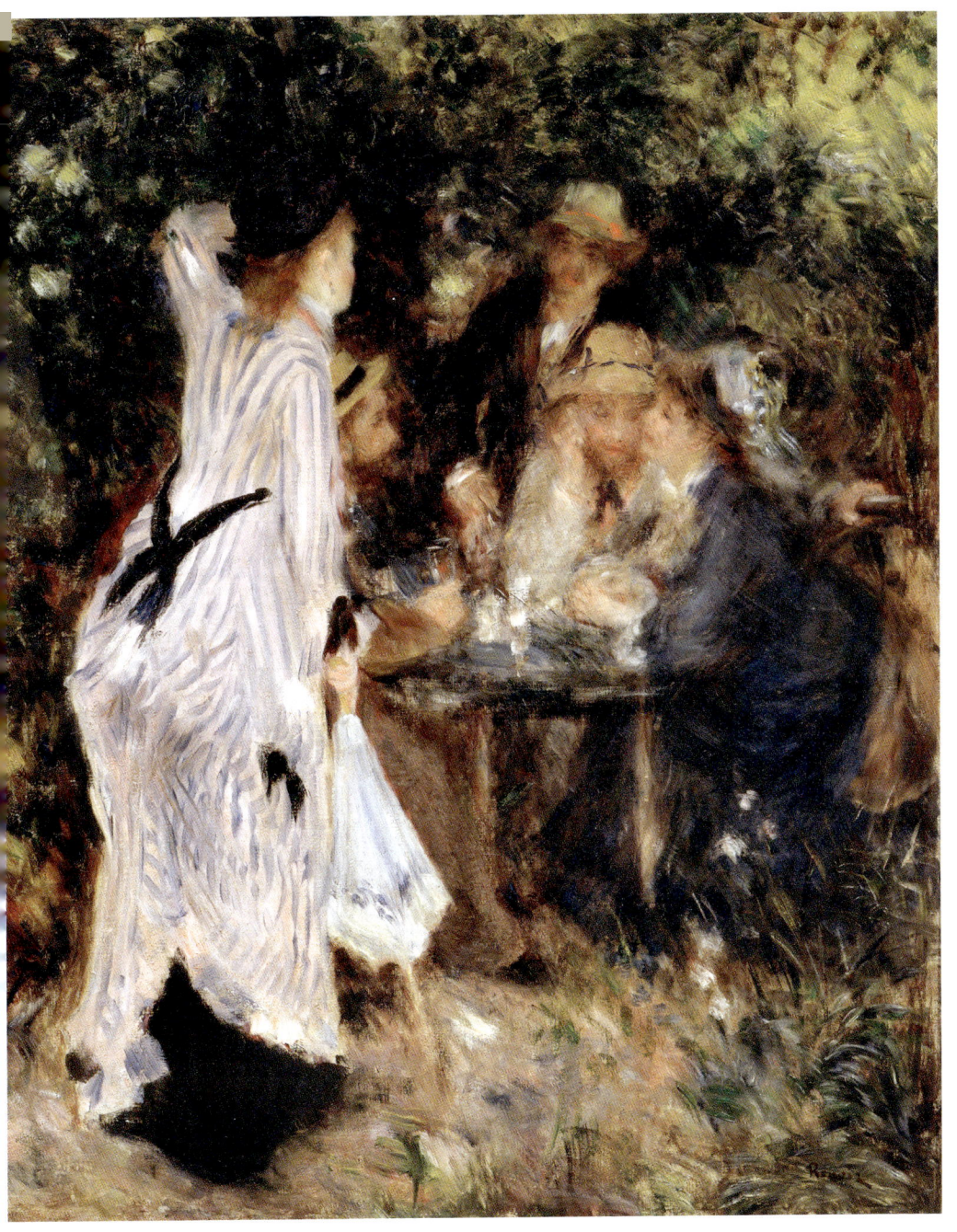

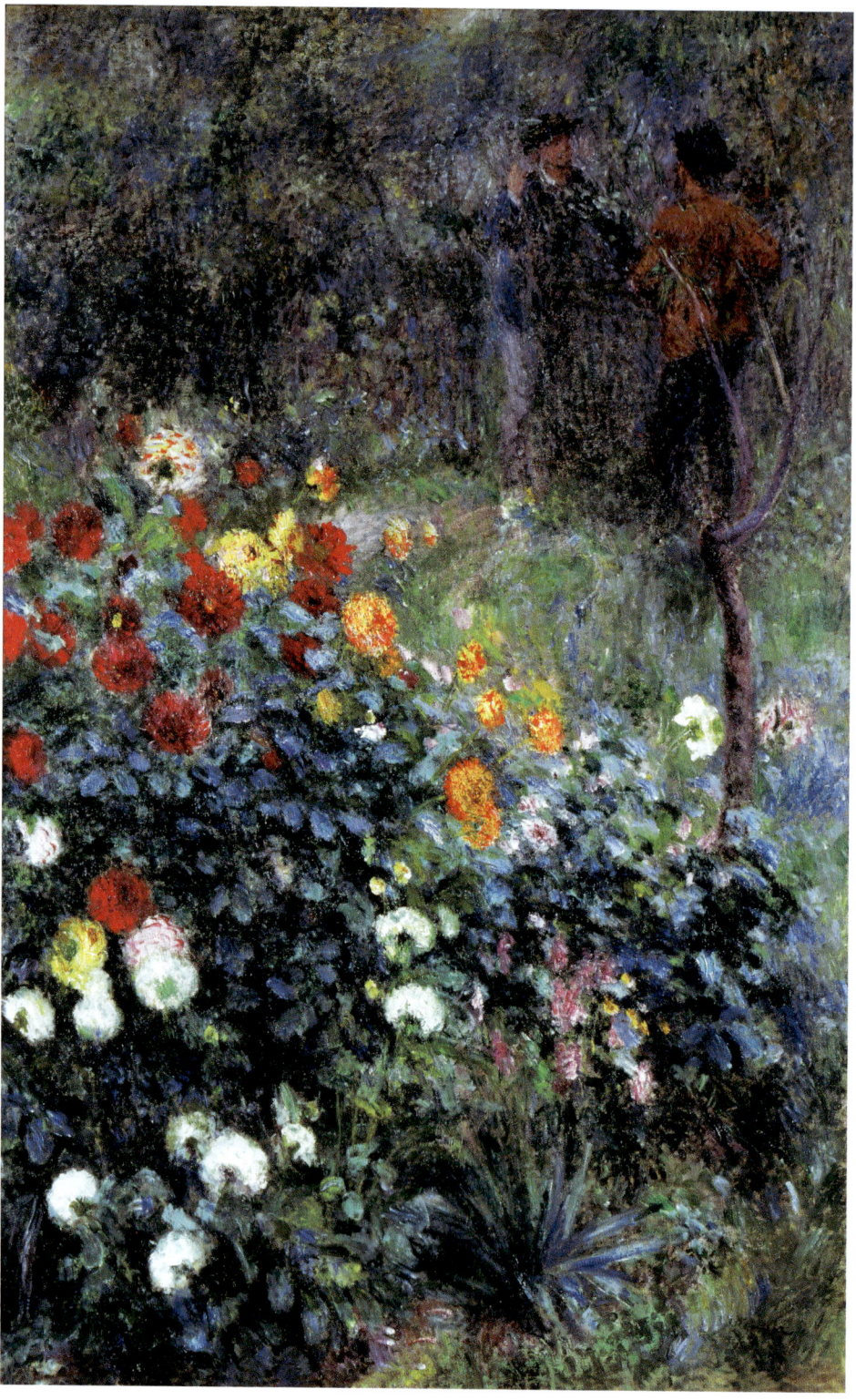

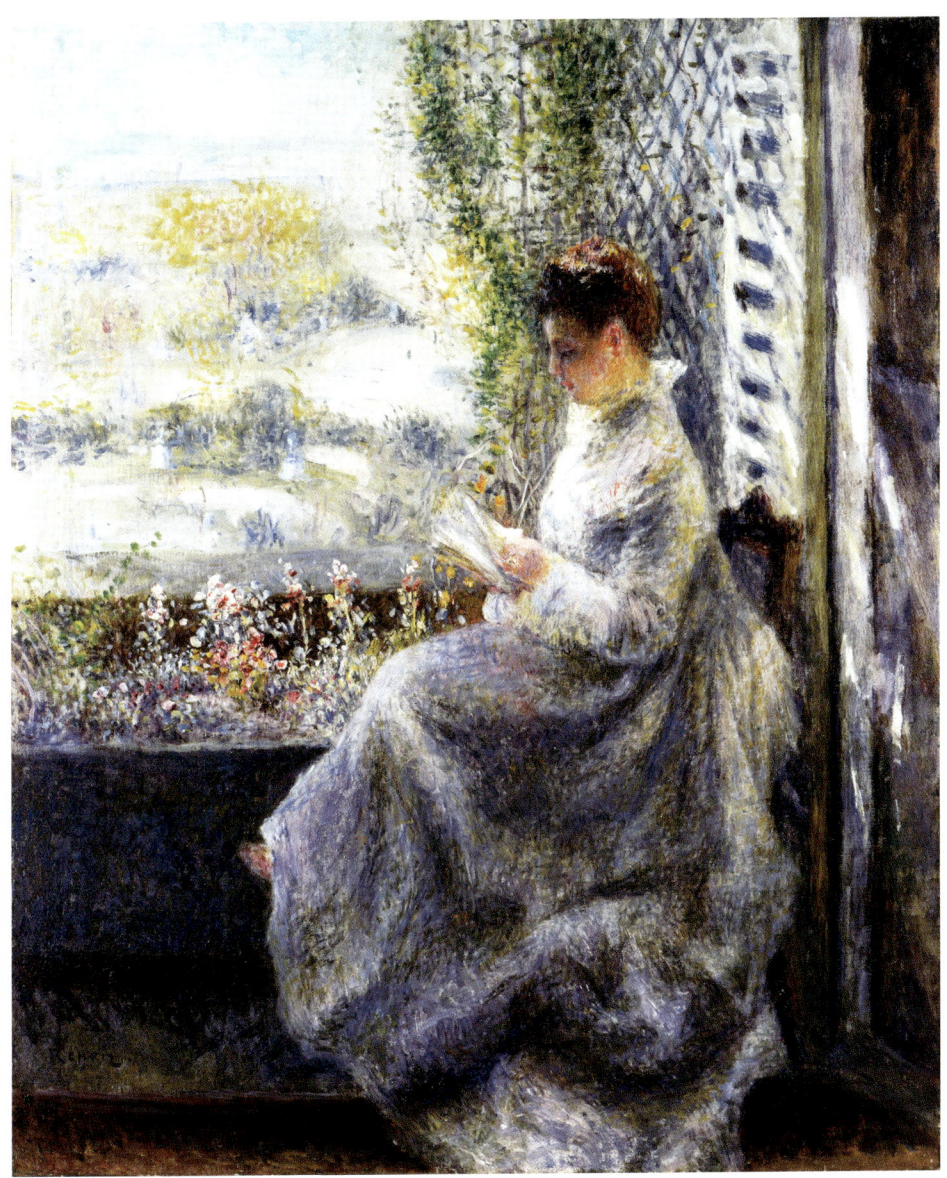

The Garden in the Rue Cortot, Montmartre, 1876
Oil on canvas, 154.3 x 88.9 cm (60¾ x 35 in.)
Pittsburgh, Carnegie Museum of Art, Acquired
through the generosity of Mrs. Alan M. Scaife

Madame Chocquet Reading, 1876
Oil on canvas, 65 x 54 cm (25⅝ x 21⅜ in.)
Private collection

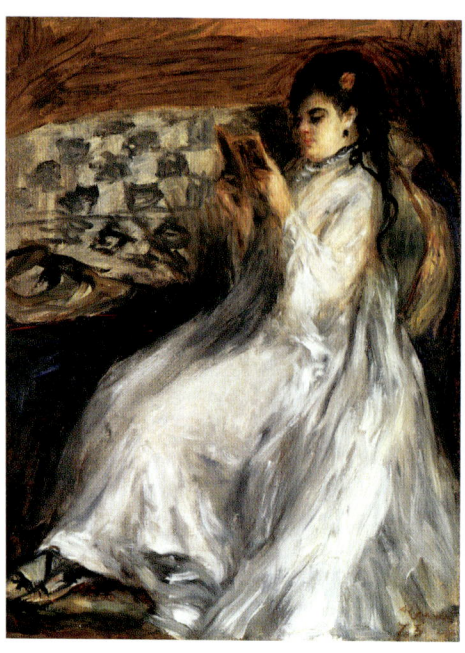

Young Woman Reading, c. 1873
Oil on canvas, 35.5 x 27.5 cm (14 x 10⅞ in.)
Private collection

Nude in the Sunlight, c. 1876
Oil on canvas,
81 x 65 cm (32 x 25⅝ in.)
Paris, Musée d'Orsay

left them more united than ever. The pejorative term "Impressionism", which they all disliked, stuck. Edmond Renoir, the painter's brother, once remarked to Monet, standing in front of one of his paintings, that their titles were rather dull. To humour him Monet suggested that he call this one "an Impression". Louis Leroy, the art critic of *Le Charivari*, who made up for his lack of taste with a good sense of humour, commented: "He called it an Impression? I thought as much. I said to myself that since I was impressed, there must have been some kind of impression in there". The killer sentence had been written. Later in the article he made his fictional interlocutor, a painter called Vincent, say: "I am an Impression on legs, the vengeful palette knife".

The article was designed to ridicule the exhibition and set the tone. A vicious press campaign was orchestrated against the "rebels" in the course of which the term "Impressionist", coined by Leroy, was adopted. The singularly blinkered Jules Clareti even applied it to Manet's painting *The Railway* exhibited in that same year at the Salon! Imagine the painter's fury when he read in *Le Bien Public* (The Commonwealth) on 25 June that he was the "master of the school of blotches"! Despite the hatred of those to whom the term was applied, "Impressionism" soon became a convenient label for them. Some decided to turn this pejorative term into a positive definition. So it was that Georges Rivière wrote in the publication entitled *Impressionism*, published on 6 April 1877: "Treating the tonality of a subject rather than the subject itself is what distinguishes the Impressionists from other painters". Renoir happened to be a friend of Rivière and is extensively cited in his article in support of its aesthetic position.

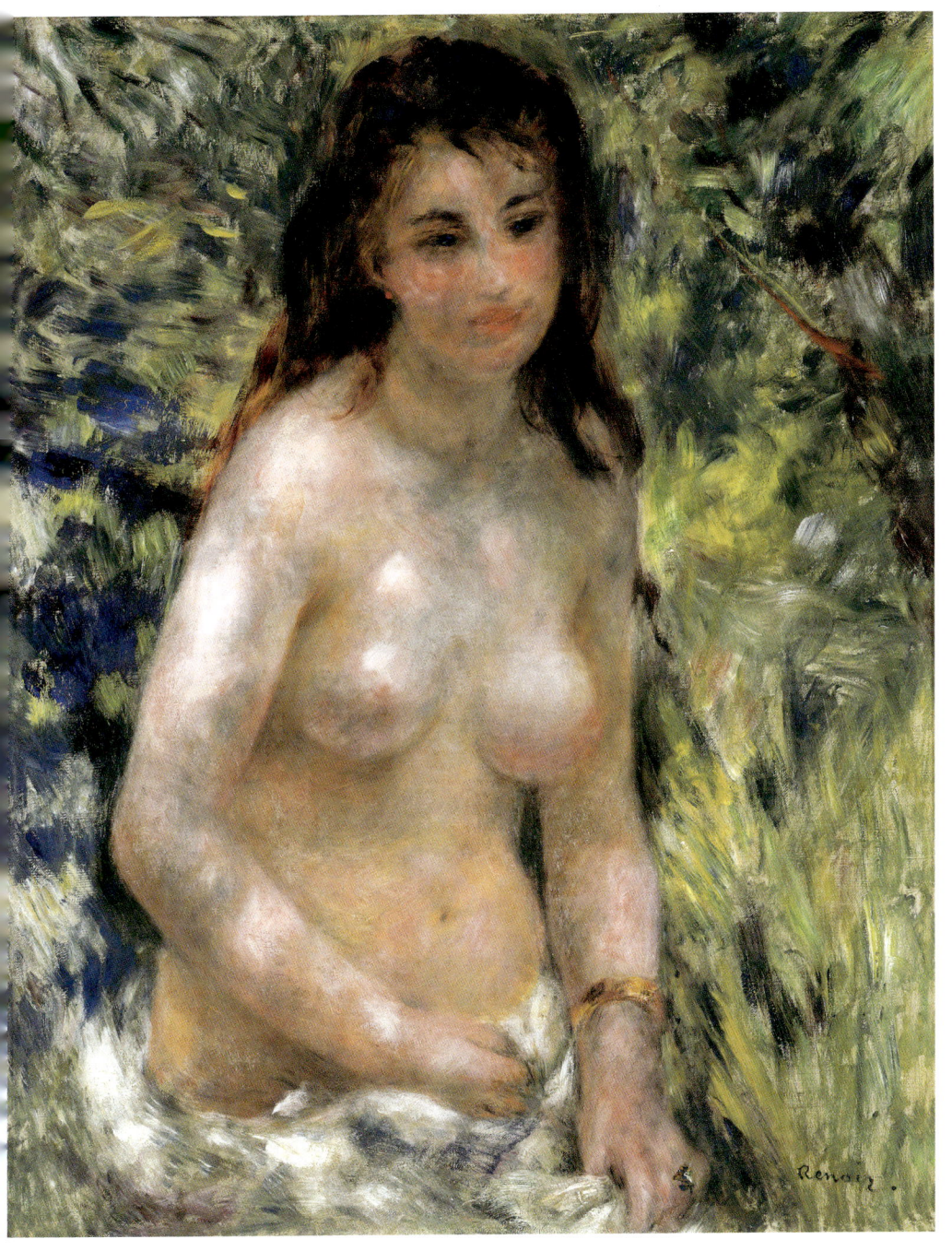

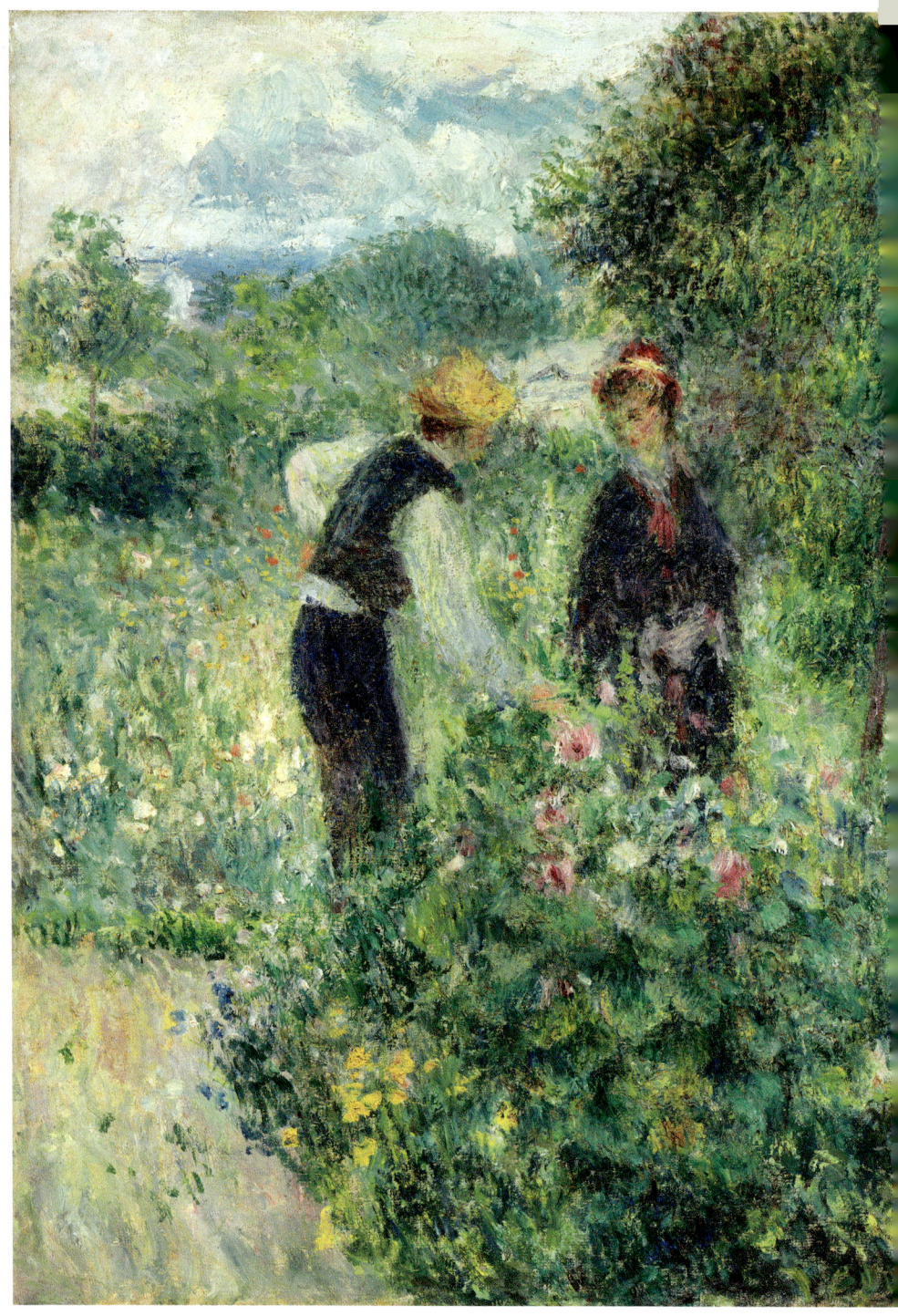

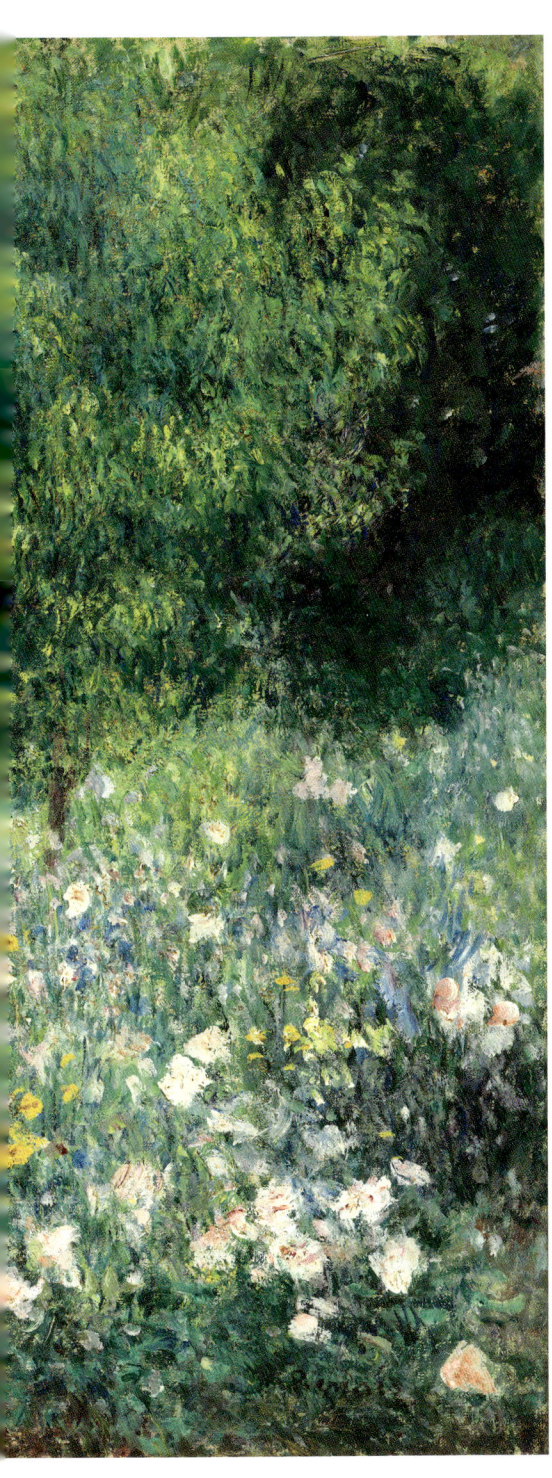

Picking Flowers, 1875
Oil on canvas, 54.3 x 65.2 cm (21½ x 25¾ in.)
Washington, D.C., National Gallery of Art,
Ailsa Mellon Bruce Collection

Banks of the Seine at Champrosay, 1876
Oil on canvas,
54.6 x 66 cm (21½ x 26 in.)
Paris, Musée d'Orsay

The 1877 exhibition was called "Impressionist" in spite of protest from Edgar Degas. Théodore Duret published the first seminal work about the group, entitled *The Impressionist Painters*, the following year. He stressed the influence of Courbet, Corot and Manet and demonstrated the similarity of their work to Japanese prints. Duret wrote monographs about those that he considered to be the true leaders of the movement – Monet, Sisley, Pissarro, Renoir and Berthe Morisot. The term "Impressionist" entered into common usage, though some continued to use it pejoratively. Meilhac and Halévy staged a musical in 1877 at the Variétés called *The Grasshopper* in which the main character was an Impressionist or "Intentionist" whose paintings could be viewed just as well upside down as the right way up. (It was not incidentally until Abstraction, and Kandinsky's famous watercolour of 1911, that this actually came to pass.) The Impressionists themselves explained reluctantly that what was "Impressionist" about their exhibitions was that they contained neither epic, allegorical, oriental, historical nor genre paintings. To Louis Leroy's delight they turned his ironic epithet into the banner under which they all rallied.

Renoir was represented in the infamous 1877 exhibition by *The Dancer* (p. 93), *The Theatre Box* (p. 87), *The Parisian Woman* (p. 89), *The Harvesters*, *Flowers* (a still life), *Head of a Woman* and an unidentified *Sketch*. Renoir did not receive a bad press and was spared Leroy's venom. He even received a few compliments, albeit backhanded ones. *The Dancer* attracted the most attention. Jean Prouvaire, for instance, wrote in *Le Rappel* (Recall): "Renoir's *Young Dancer* is a delightful portrait. With her dark red hair, her

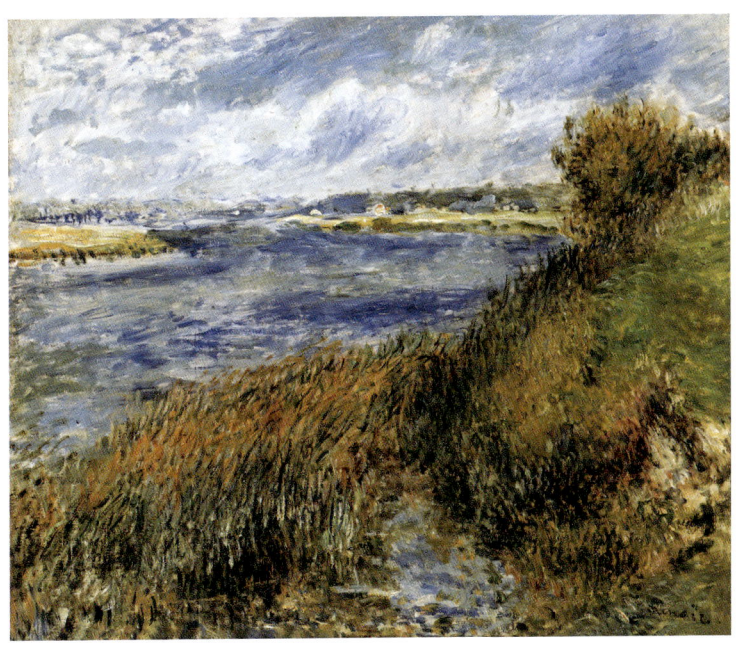

pallid complexion and bright red lips, she recalls the *Woman Aged Thirteen* so cruelly described by Théodore de Banville in his *Parisian Women from Paris (Les Parisiennes de Paris)*. Thanks to her precocious exertions, her legs have thickened already and her feet are not nearly pretty enough in her pink satin shoes. But her long, thin stockings are those of a child, and below her boyish chest she sports a blue first communion sash, which flutters down over her ballerina skirt. Is she still a little girl? Probably. Is she already a woman? Perhaps. But is she a girl? Never!". The dancer's legs clearly did not meet with approval. The wicked Louis Leroy lamented them in *Le Charivari*: "What a pity it is that the painter, who has some understanding of colour, cannot draw better! The legs of his dancer are as flaccid as the gauze of her petticoats."

Armand Sylvestre, writing in *L'Opinion nationale* (National Opinion), used both stick and carrot. "Renoir's *Dancer* and *Parisian Woman* are no more than two rough sketches. The face should never be treated in this cowardly way. Despite this reservation, the general tone is charming. The heads are reminiscent of English painting and Francisco de Goya, and the fabrics are merely washed in a diluted and undifferentiated impasto. The whole effect is more or less attractive but remains no more than promising. It takes more than these intangible features to do justice to the real world. There is only one thing worse than mistaking reality for a shadow, and that is mistaking a shadow for reality. Let these criticisms not obscure the fact that none of our established school of painters could produce a face equal in distinction, finesse, and accuracy, the face of the *Dancer*."

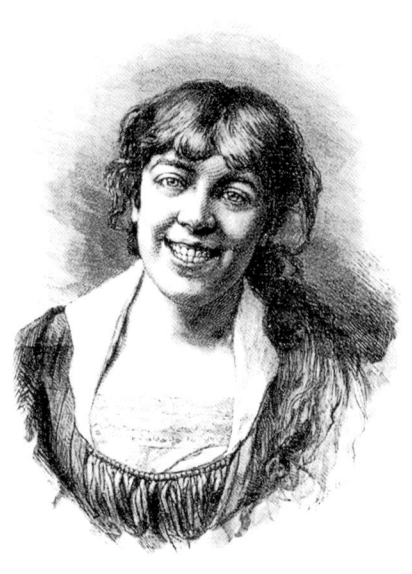

Jeanne Samary in the role of Antoinette in
L'Étincelle. Reproduced from *L'Illustration*,
13 December, 1879

Bust of Jeanne Samary (Day-dreaming), 1877
Oil on canvas, 56 x 47 cm (22 x 18⅝ in.)
Moscow, Pushkin Museum

At the time, Jeanne Samary was as famous an
actress as Sarah Bernhardt. For three years,
Renoir spoke of her as "little Samary... who is the
delight of women and especially men". The painter
enhanced her reputation and his association with
her enabled him to climb the rungs of the social
ladder. *Jeanne Samary* (p. 130) was exhibited
at the 1879 Salon, at the same time as *Madame
Charpentier and Her Children* (pp. 388/389).
But the picture was hung "too high-up and badly
placed" while the portrait of Madame Charpentier
was in the place of honour, thanks to the social
standing of the model. "She is very nice, but she
has terrible 'salt-cellars'", exclaimed Marguerite
Charpentier of Samary.

Marc de Mointifaud was unconditional in his praise in the review *L'Artiste* (The Artist):
"When viewed from a distance, from the back of the third room on the ground floor
(say), the *Dancer* is strikingly original, a sort of watery dilution moulded in terrestrial
forms. There is nothing more alive than the pink carnations, and the gauze dress blends
in wonderfully with their luminous tones. This is the realism of the great schools of
painting, which understand that there is no need to trivialise nature when trying to
interpret it".

The Theatre Box (p. 87) has become one of the symbols of Impressionism. Paul Jamot
calls it "the masterpiece of all Renoir's masterpieces because its novelty and unexpect-
edness surprise us while everything else demands comparison with the greatest of
the Old Masters". But it attracted little attention from the critics at the 1874 exhibition.
Prouvaire sees in it the image of the "tart", one of those women "whose cheeks are
whitened with pearly white, and whose eyes are lit up with banal excitement: a woman
as delicious as she is stupid". None of this would have shocked Renoir, who claimed
to be attracted to illiterate women. Montifaud talked of "a face borrowed from the
world of elegance", which is not necessarily a contradiction. The woman in the painting was Nini Lopez, nicknamed "Gueule-de-Raie" (Fish-face), one of the painter's
old friends, who had a delightful face despite her hideous nickname. She posed as the
young woman who everyone admires while her companion (Edmond Renoir) squints
through his opera glasses at the spectators in the neighbouring boxes. The storyline
is thin in comparison with the painting itself. Nini also posed for one of Renoir's most

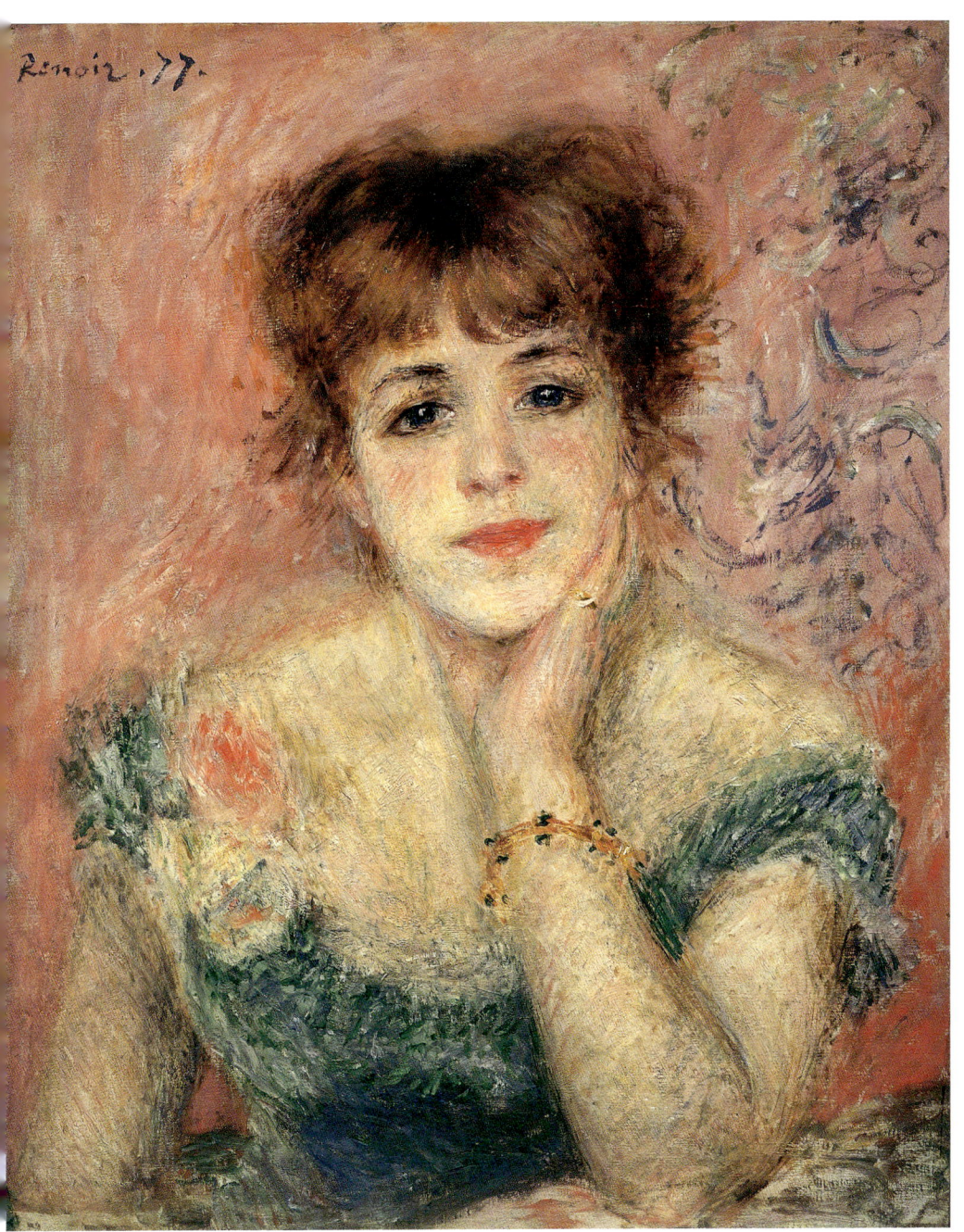

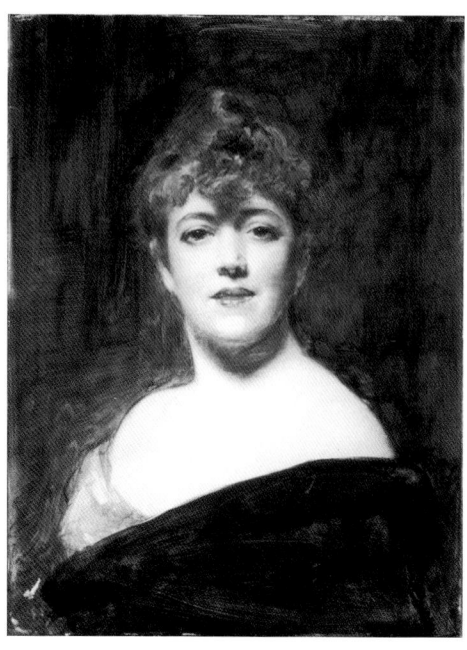

Émile Auguste Carolus-Duran
(1837–1917)
Jeanne Samary, c. 1885
Oil on canvas, 65 x 49 cm (25⅝ x 19⅜ in.)
Paris, Musée de la Comédie-Française

Jeanne Samary, 1877
Oil on canvas, 46 x 40 cm (18⅛ x 15¾ in.)
Paris, Musée de la Comédie-Française

moving female portraits, *Portrait of a Woman* (*Nini Fish-face*; p. 211). There is a smaller version of the same subject entitled *Box at the Theatre* (p. 92). It was a favourite trick of Renoir's to produce not a sketch but rather a repeat performance for an admirer of his work. It shows how Renoir could adapt his technique to the smaller format when necessary, substituting the long smooth strokes of the larger painting for the small, nervous dabs more suited to the small format.

The elegant *Parisian Woman* (p. 89) belongs to what could be called "the Henriette Henriot" period. The actress, whom Renoir held in great affection, was his favourite model in the 1870s. She features in at least 11 of his paintings between 1874 and 1876, as well as in three full-length formal portraits representing elegant bourgeois life. The first time that it was exhibited Jean Prouvaire, writing in *Le Rappel*, celebrated the portrait's wit. He claimed to have discovered in *The Dancer, The Parisian Woman* and *The Theatre Box* "the three stages through which the ladies of Paris pass, from teenager to tart". He realised that this had not been the artist's intention. But he could not resist concocting a storyline: "You can see the tip of her boot, peeping out like a little black mouse. Her hat is tipped over one ear in a coquettish manner and her dress is too tight. Nothing is more irritating than a closed door. Is the painting a portrait? I fear so. The face is both disconcertingly old and puerile, and the smile is false. Yet the impression conveyed has a certain naivety. The subject looks like she is doing all she can to remain chaste. The dress, which is very well painted, is of a celestial blue." On 16 February 1898, Paul Signac wrote in his diary: "Vuillard was kind enough to take me to visit the Rouart collection

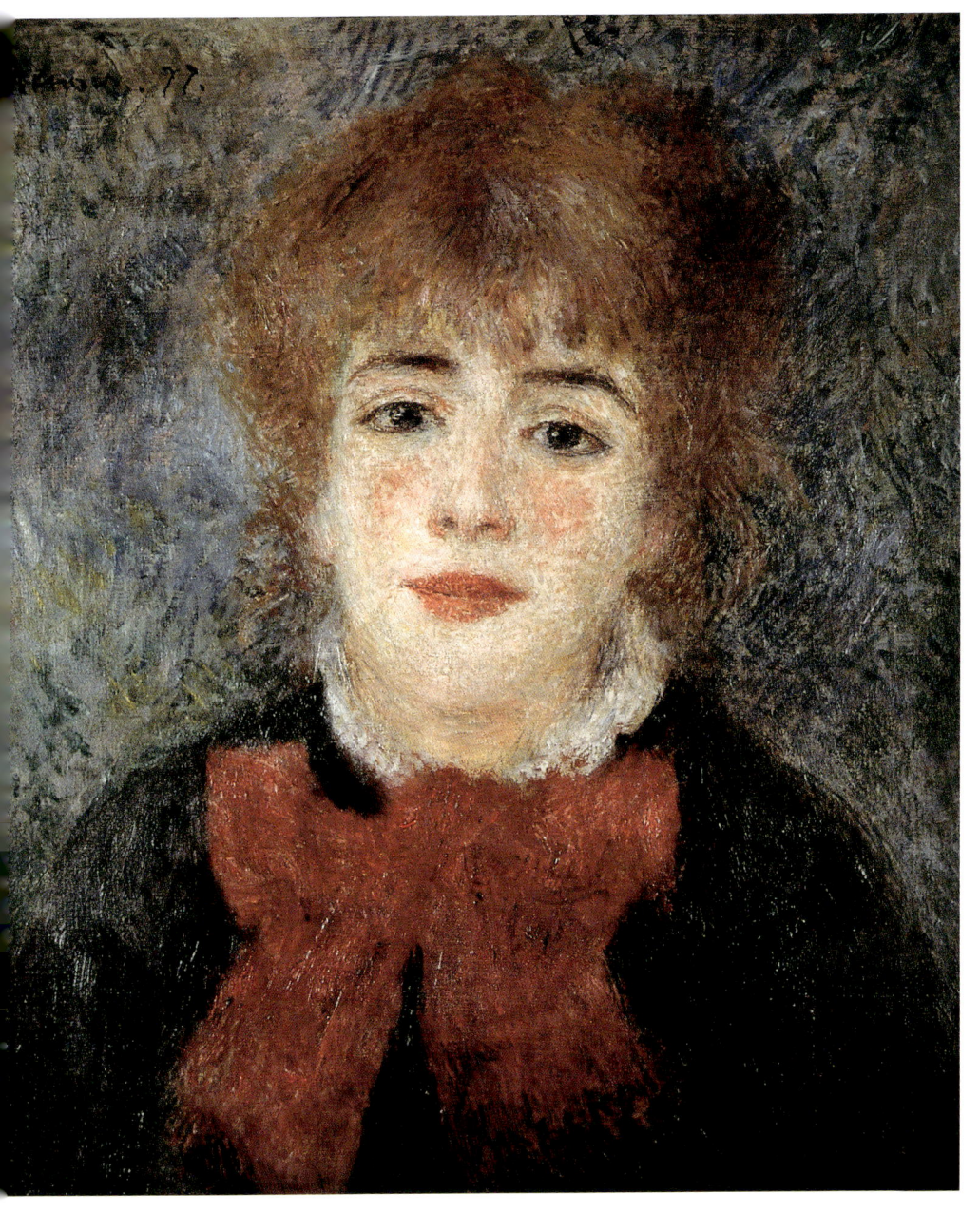

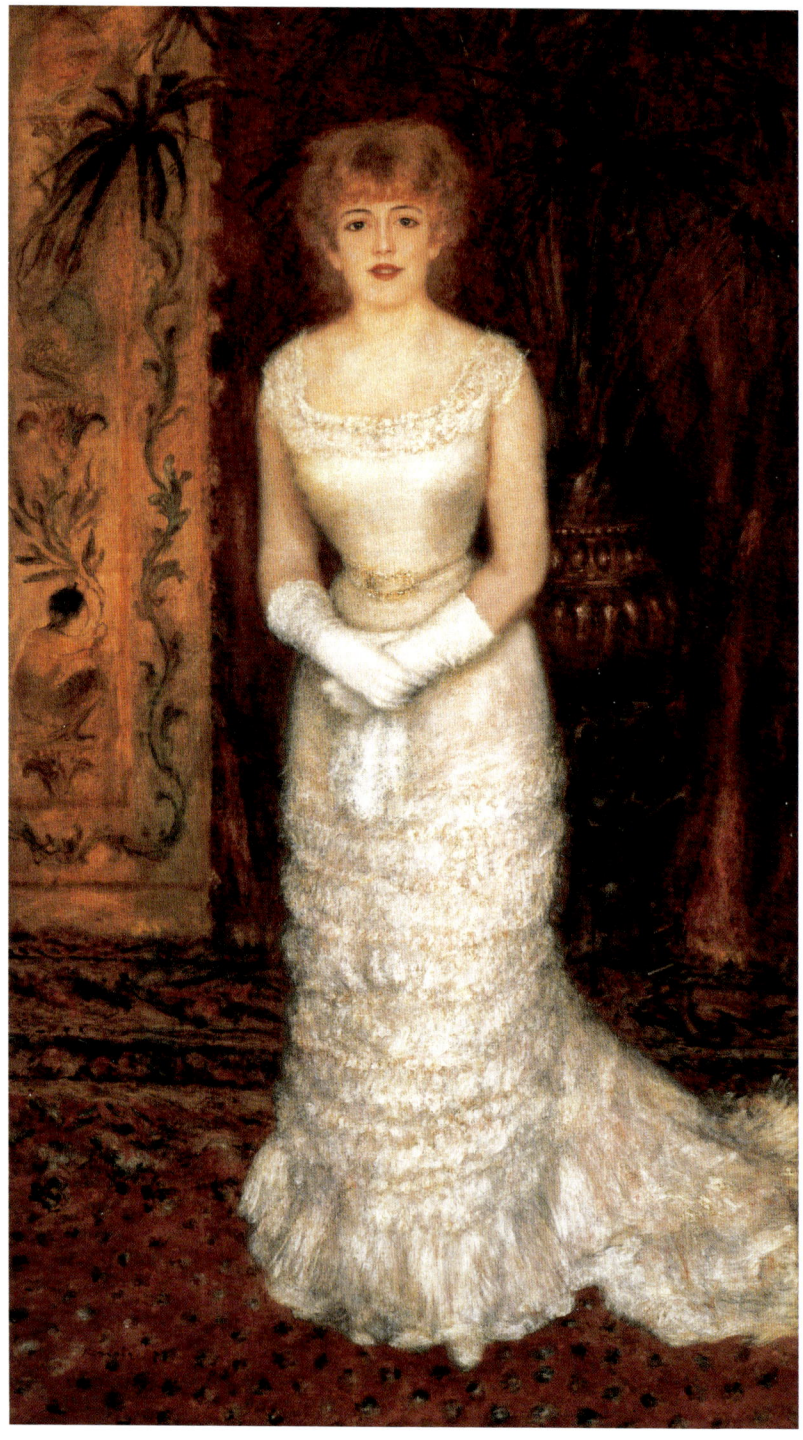

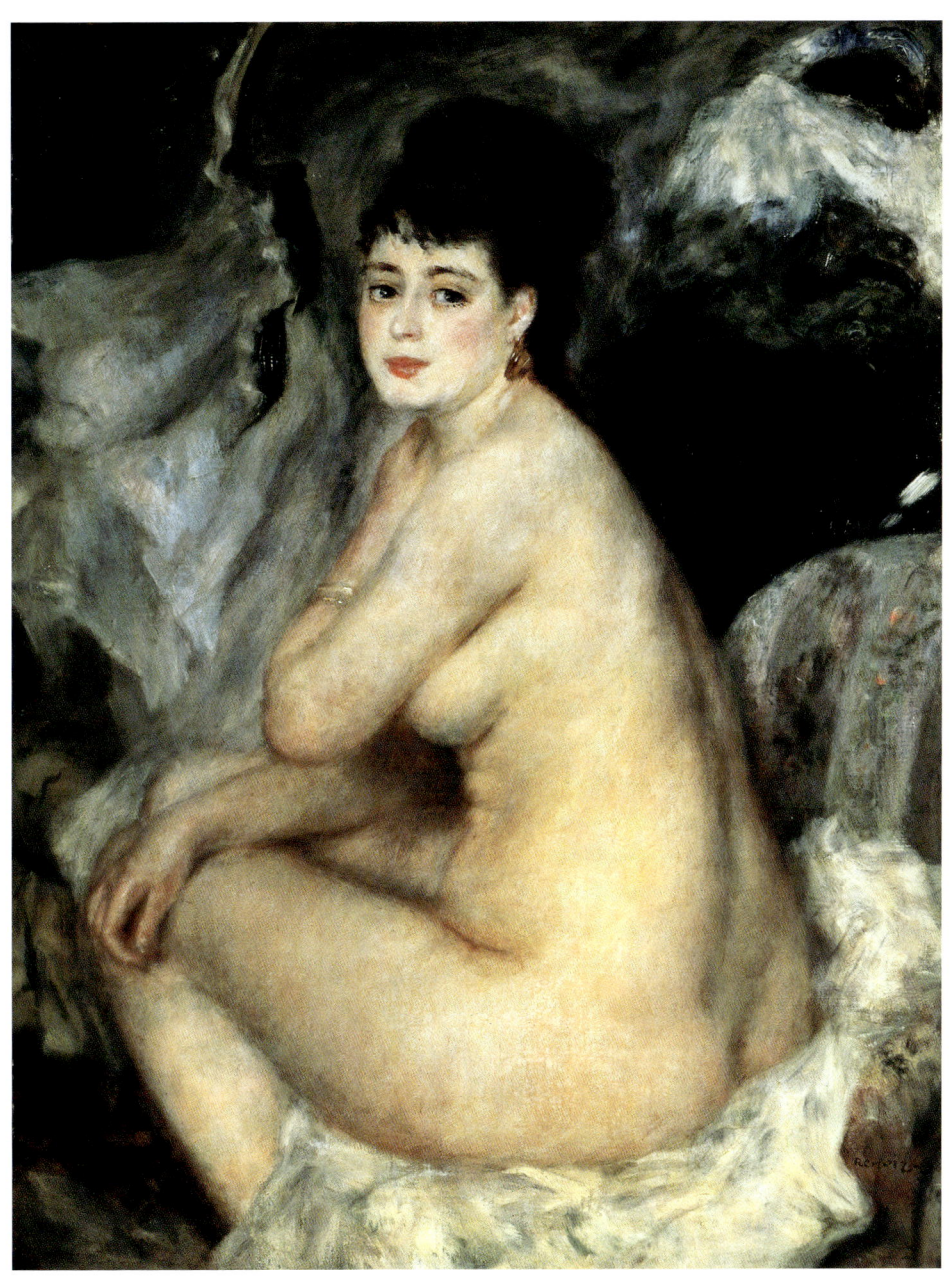

Jeanne Samary, 1878
Oil on canvas, 174 x 105 cm (68⅝ x 41⅜ in.)
Saint Petersburg, Hermitage Museum

Nude Seated on a Sofa, 1876
Oil on canvas, 92 x 73 cm (36¼ x 28¾ in.)
Moscow, Pushkin Museum

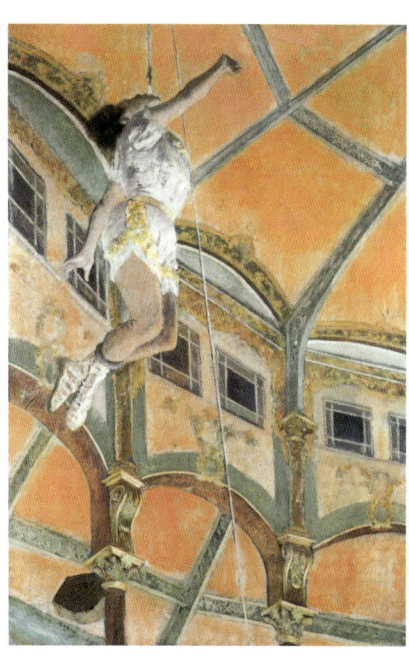

Edgar Degas (1834–1917)
Mlle La La at the Circus Fernando, 1879
Oil on canvas, 117 x 77 cm (46 x 30⅜ in.)
London, The National Gallery

**Acrobats at the Cirque Fernando
(Francisca and Angelina Wartenberg)**, 1879
Oil on canvas, 131.2 x 99.2 cm (51¾ x 39 in.)
The Art Institute of Chicago,
Potter Palmer Collection

… I saw so much that I came out in a daze. My clearest memories are those of a sketch by Delacroix… and a large portrait of a woman in blue by Renoir painted in 1874. The dress is an intense, pure blue, which brings out by contrast in the flesh tones a yellowish colour with a greenish reflection. The play of colour is admirably noted. It is simple, beautiful, and fresh. The painting was created twenty years ago. But it still looks as if it has just been painted …"

Henriette Henriot was a repertory actress with an undistinguished reputation. She had acted in *Macbeth* at the Odéon theatre and taken the part of Eva in Sardou's play *Dora* at the Gymnase theatre. But that all changed when she met the extraordinary actor and director, Antoine, who founded the avant-garde Théâtre-libre in the Rue Blanche in March 1887. The works of the Naturalists and the Parnassians were performed there. Henriette became one of it main stars and was always offered the role of the tart. Renoir represents her as an actress in his *Madame Henriot in Costume* (p. 90). She stands in front of a red curtain and receives applause, dressed in a page's costume. Renoir and Henriette both seem to have wanted to make their name in the theatre, she as an actress and he as a portraitist-chronicler. This would soon cause him to produce a masterpiece, the full-length portrait of *Jeanne Samary* (p. 130), who was the leading lady at the Comédie-Française. The painting was exhibited at the Salon in 1879. Renoir was in the habit of giving a goodbye portrait to his mistresses when they parted company. For Lise Tréhot he painted *Lise in a White Shawl* and, for Henriette, the Washington portrait (p. 91). It was the most handsome tribute that he could have paid her and she

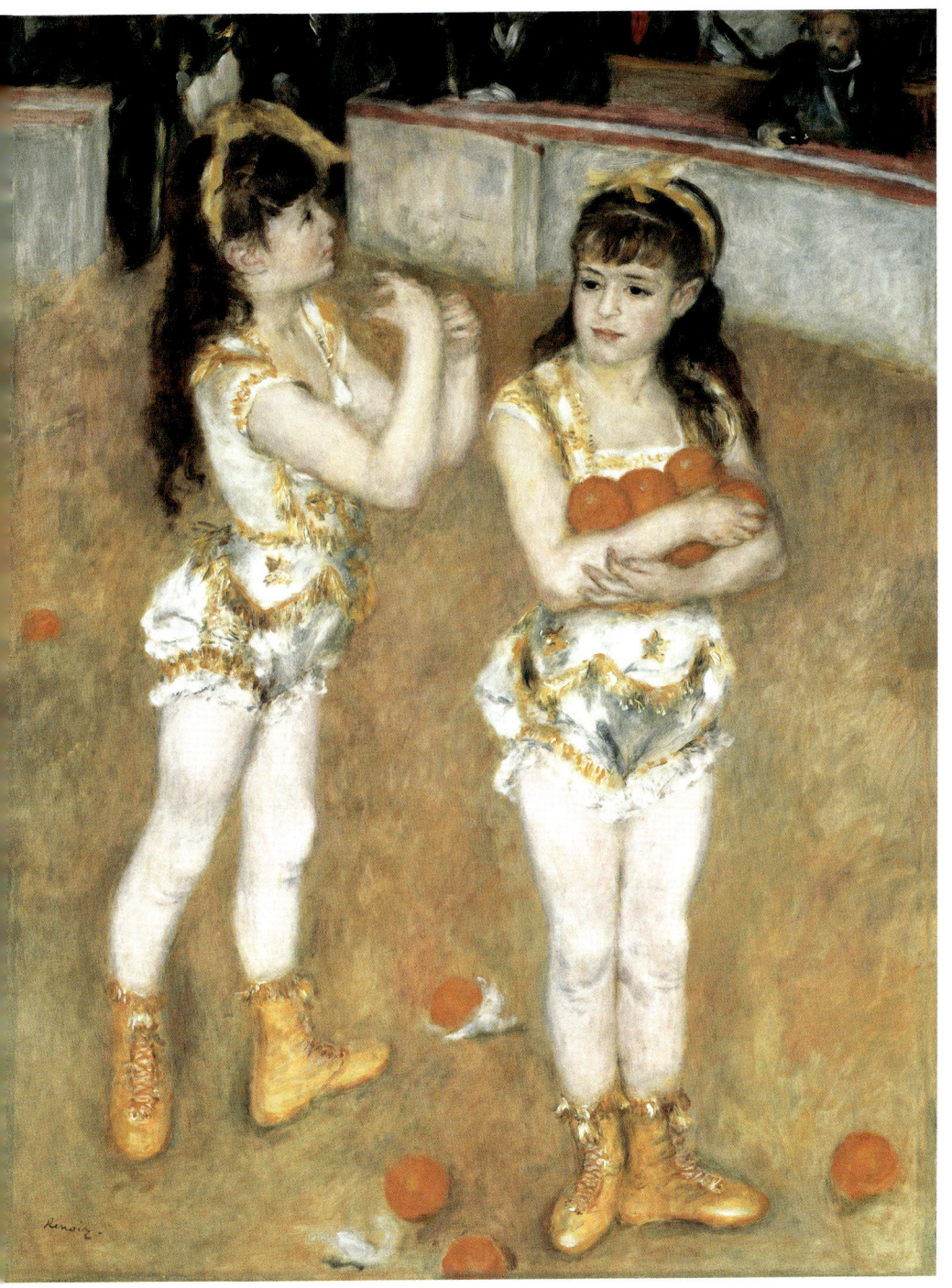

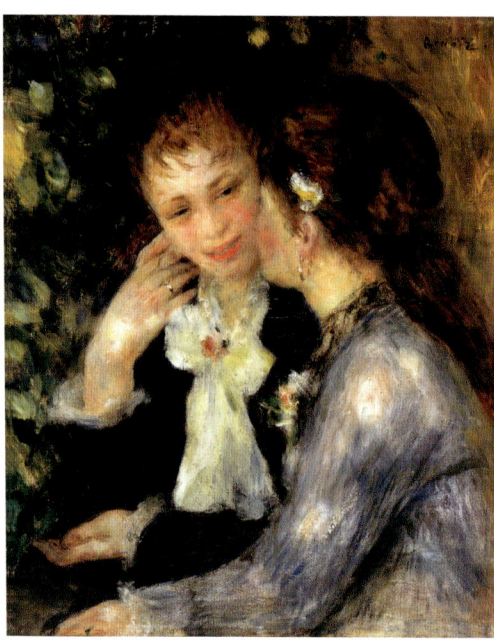

Confidences, c. 1876–1878
Oil on canvas, 61.5 x 50.5 cm (24¼ x 20 in.)
Winterthur, Oskar Reinhart Collection
"Am Römerholz"

Leaving the Conservatory, 1876/77
Oil on canvas,
187.5 x 117.5 cm (73⅞ x 46⅜ in.)
Philadelphia, The Barnes Foundation

kept it. The exceptionally fine treatment of the silk and gauze renders them diaphanous, and the portrait is one of the most striking that Renoir produced in the 1870s. The colour flows, and the eyes, lips, and intertwined fingers are voluptuously depicted. Painting white upon white, he explained to Vollard, "is exceedingly difficult. But nothing is more exciting to paint and produces a more lovely effect". Comparing a contemporary photograph of the model (p. 88) with the Renoir portrait shows, as always, that all physical defects have disappeared to leave an image that is all elegance and charm. The shapes are soft and supple, the bosom is fuller, and the transparent sleeves of the dress hint at bare arms. The spectator can only wonder at Renoir's good taste. Who else but he could have so miraculously captured the delicate and ineffable beauty – in fact the very essence – of womanhood? In such an ideal of happiness it is hard to see the portrait of a living and breathing human being. Other painters, and Renoir's favourite trio (Watteau, Boucher and Fragonard) in particular, were capable of rendering charm and delicacy on the canvas. Yet they rarely succeeded in conveying the abstract vision of a personality while preserving the physical presence of the sitter. Renoir's time as a porcelain-painter must have helped him to reproduce the sparkle of the eyes or the opalescence of the flesh. The result is a work of imagination that Renoir alone could have achieved.

Renoir loved Paris. In 1874, he abandoned the outer suburbs of Bougival and Argenteuil and moved into the centre of Paris. He needed to resolve his serious financial difficulties and hoped to meet collectors and obtain portrait commissions in Paris. He took up residence in Montmartre and would repair, at the end of a day's painting, to

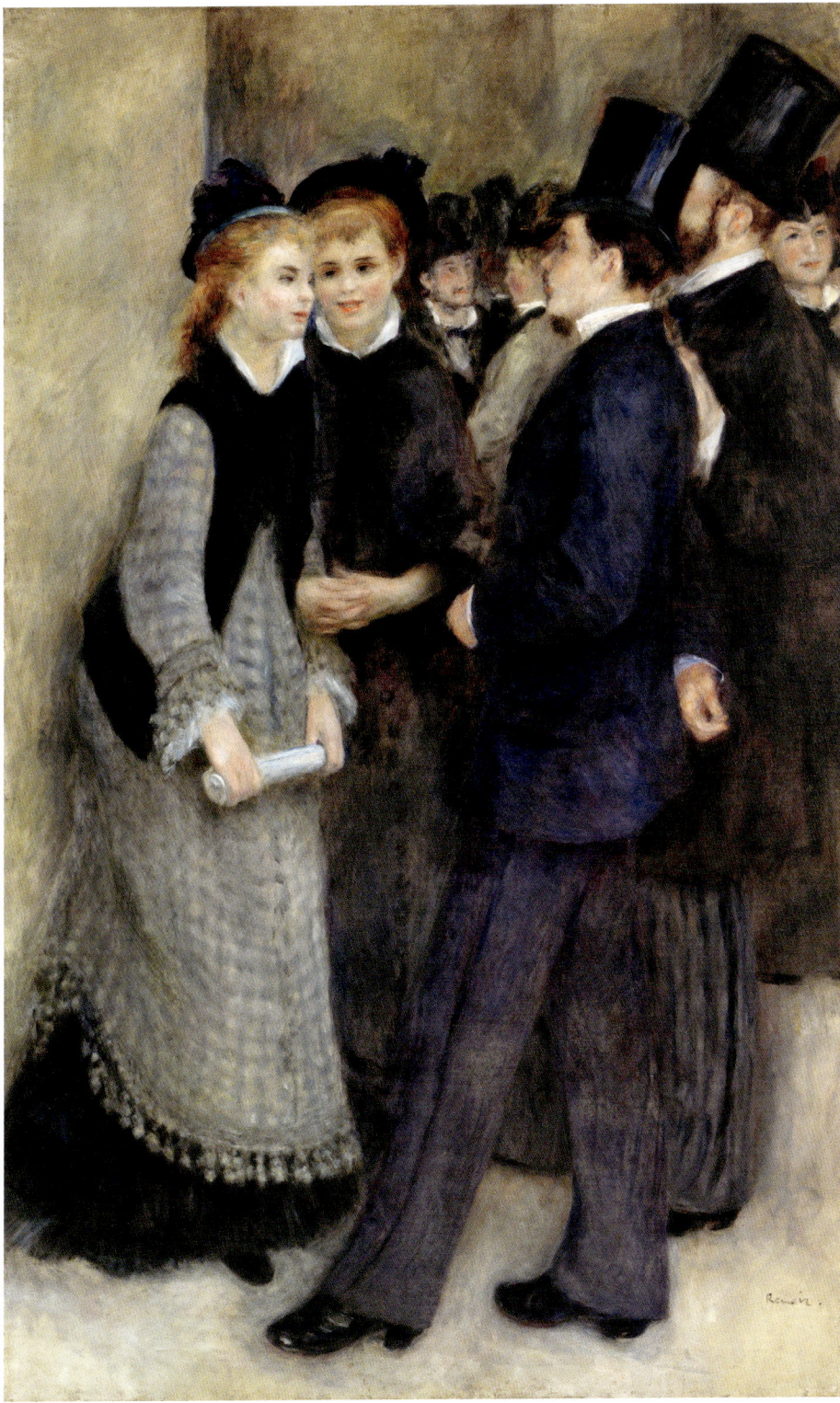

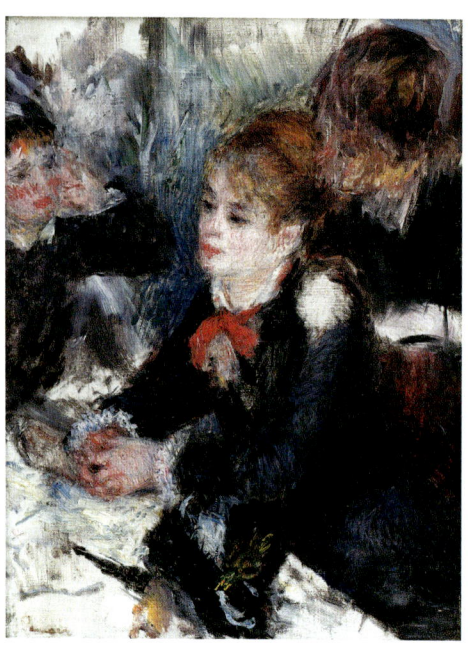

At the Milliner's, 1878
Oil on canvas, 32.9 x 24.8 cm (13 x 9⅞ in.)
Cambridge, Massachusetts,
Harvard Art Museums/Fogg Museum,
Bequest of Annie Swan Coburn

Young Girl Reading, 1880
Oil on canvas,
57 x 47.5 cm (22½ x 18¾ in.)
Frankfurt am Main, Städel Museum

a café in the Place Pigalle called La Nouvelle Athènes. It was a favourite meeting place for the independent painters and their friends. Here he met not only his seniors, Degas and Manet, but also up-and-coming painters such as Franc-Lamy, Norbert Goeneutte and Frédéric Cordey. Renoir also made friends there with the composer Emmanuel Chabrier, the musician Cabaner and a civil servant in the Ministry of Finance named Georges Rivière, who was to become his best biographer. In an attempt to resolve his money problems after the failure of the Nadar exhibition, Renoir persuaded his friends to organise a public auction of their paintings.

The first sale was held on 24 March 1875 at the famous Hôtel Drouot auction house. It provoked such a violent hostility from the public that the police had to be called. The sale itself was deeply disappointing. Renoir's twenty paintings fetched 2,251 francs, a mere 100 francs per painting. The sale at least attracted the interest of two collectors who would turn out to be his salvation. Victor Chocquet (1821–1891), a senior official in the Customs Office, was an enthusiast hitherto unknown to the group. "Monsieur Choquet", Renoir later told Ambroise Vollard, "happened to be at the Hôtel Drouot when our paintings were exhibited. He tried to find some likenesses in my paintings to those of Delacroix, whom he worshipped. On the evening of the sale he wrote to me, complimenting me on my painting, and asking me if I would agree to paint the portrait of Madame Chocquet (1837–1899). I accepted his offer with alacrity". Chocquet went on to commission several portraits of himself, his wife and his daughter, Marie-Sophie, who died while still a child. He became one of the painter's most vociferous defenders.

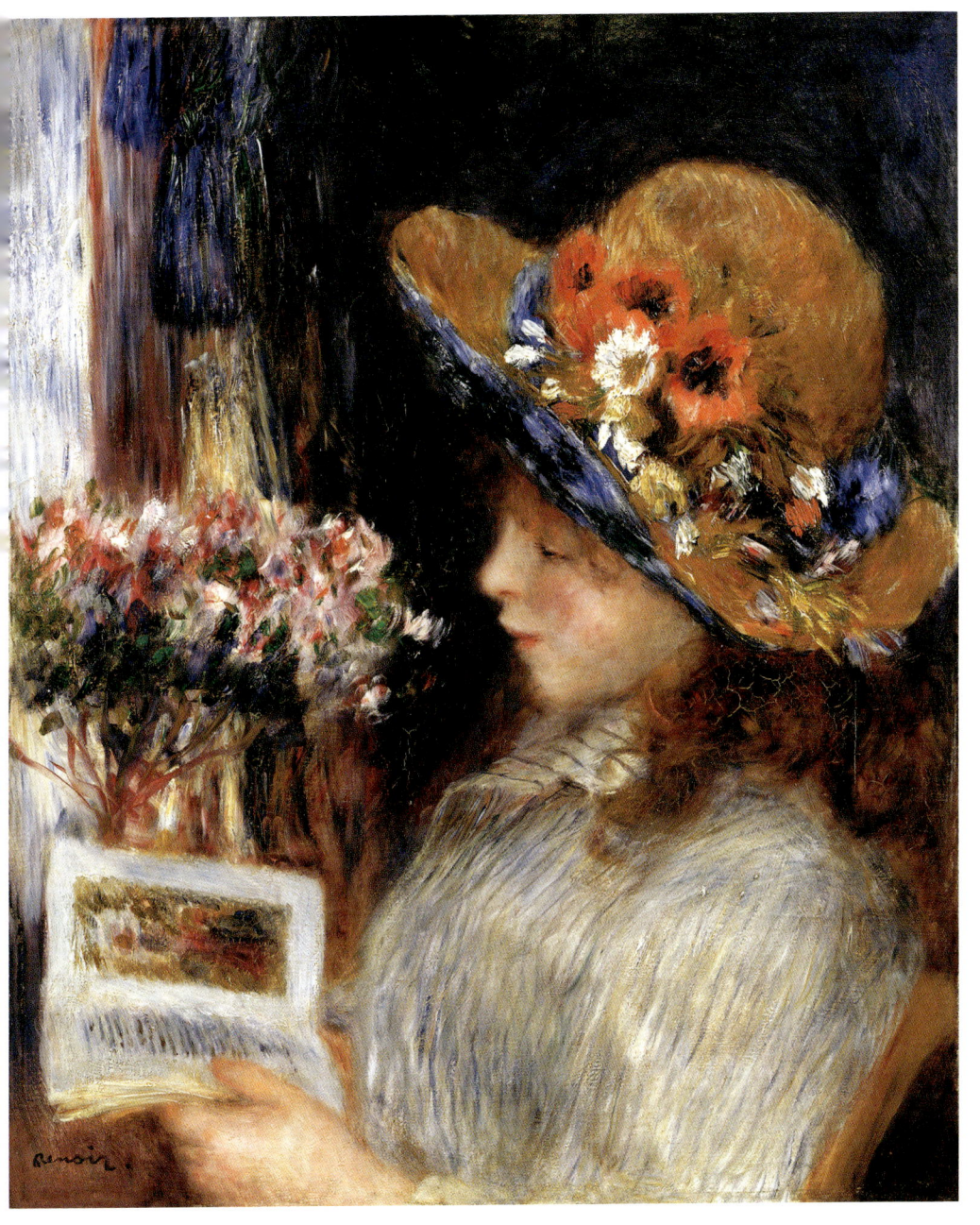

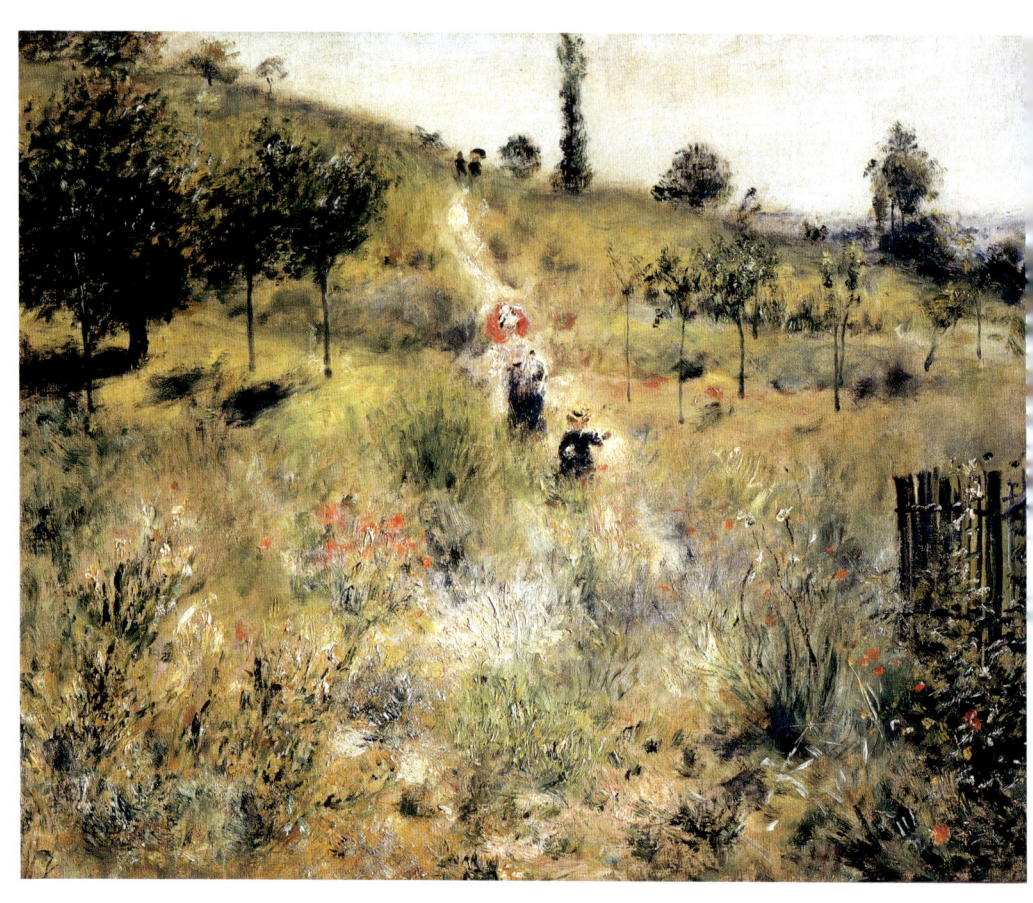

Country Footpath in the Summer, c. 1875
Oil on canvas, 60 x 74 cm (23½ x 29¼ in.)
Paris, Musée d'Orsay

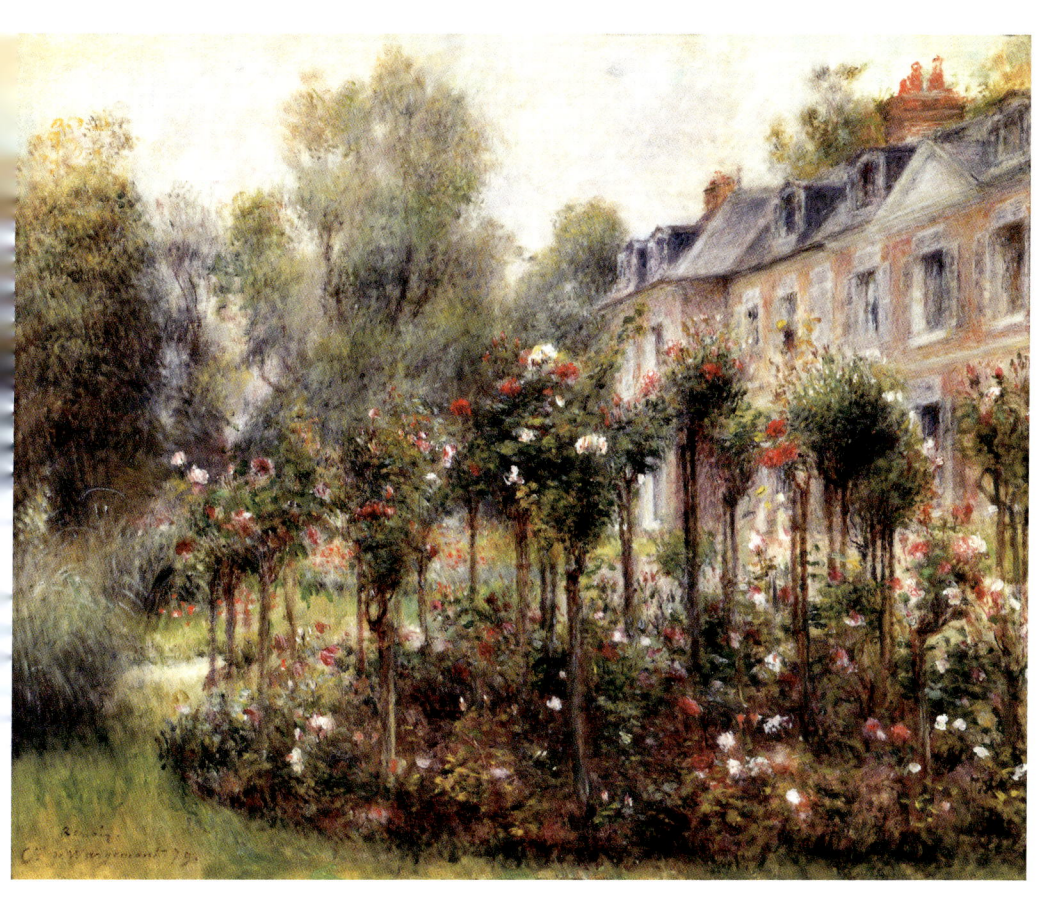

The Rose Garden at Wargemont, 1879
Oil on canvas, 63.5 x 80 cm (25 x 31½ in.)
Private collection

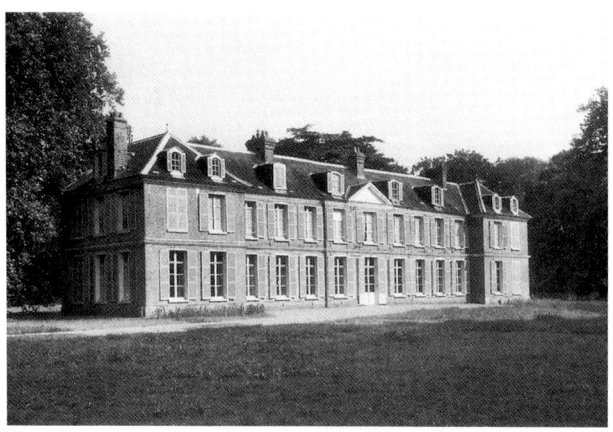

The Château de Wargemont, near Dieppe,
Normandy

Seascape, 1879
Oil on canvas, 72.6 x 91.6 cm (28⅝ x 36 in.)
The Art Institute of Chicago,
Potter Palmer Collection

With his meagre resources, Chocquet bought paintings from Renoir, Cézanne and
other Impressionists long before the general public came to appreciate them. He
amassed a magnificent collection, worthy of any museum, which was broken up after
his death.

Renoir produced two portraits of Choquet, one of which is now in the Fogg Museum
in Cambridge (p. 219). This is the type of affectionate portrait at which Renoir was so
good, and shows how touched the artist was by the enthusiasm, sensitivity and kindness
of the model. Its delicate tone and lightness of touch show the artist's authentic style
at this period, so different to the rigid style of his portraits commissioned by wealthy
clients. His affection for Choquet combines with his mastery of technique to produce
a friendly, relaxed portrait. Cézanne also painted a portrait of Victor Choquet (p. 218),
which enables us to compare what Renoir liked about Choquet with what Cézanne
saw in him. In Cézanne's version the pose is very similar but one is immediately struck
by the crude, almost brutal, style and his preoccupation with the presence of bones
beneath the flesh. Renoir seeks to capture the personality of the subject. Cézanne sees
Choquet as an object to be painted, no different to a pitcher or an apple. Perhaps what
all inspired portraitists do is paint themselves as much as their models. Flaubert after
all claimed that the character of Madame Bovary was based upon himself. *Madame
Chocquet Reading* (p. 119), painted in 1876, and *Young Woman Reading* (p. 120), painted
around 1873, show how far Renoir had come in his attempt to free himself from Manet's
pervasive influence and find a mode of self-expression. Manet's influence has been so

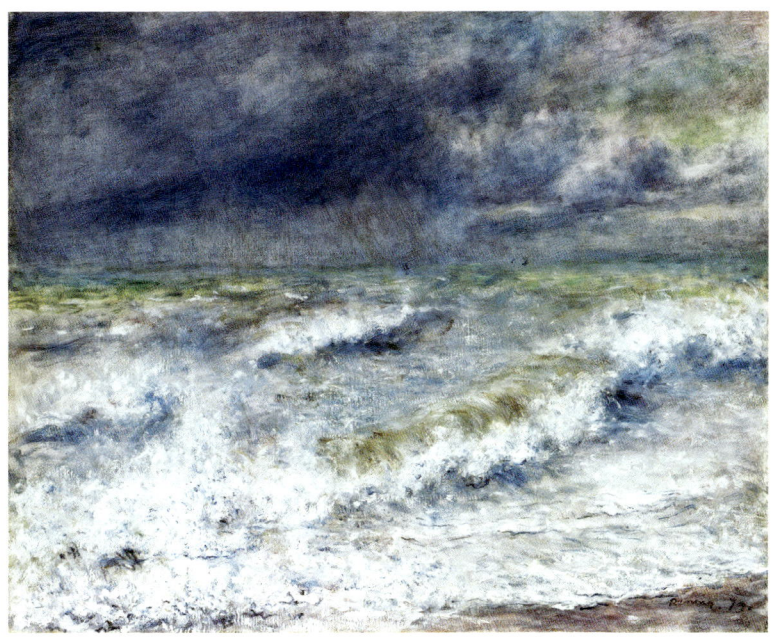

"atomised" that model and décor are one. This is Renoir at his most Impressionist – with all the weaknesses which he would subsequently correct – but no doubt what Chocquet expected of him at the time. At this time Renoir often yielded to the temptation of 'atomising' female forms along with the décor. Only by using black as a colour – which he did throughout – could he show, through the broken shapes, the model's almond-shaped eyes. These he painted as if they were the reflection of life itself. The period of "atomised" portraits includes *Woman at the Piano* (p. 106), painted in 1875/76 whose subject matter is as traditional as the theme of reading. The composition however is original and contains a veiled allusion to Degas: the painter dominates his model, an effect emphasised by the vase on the ground in the upper left corner. The sitter for this typical scene from contemporary middle-class life is unknown, as ought to be the case for an Impressionist work, in that it should contain no anecdotal subject-matter or storyline. The woman is, however, typical of the kind that Renoir admired. This is no doubt the painting that was shown at the second Impressionist group exhibition in 1876.

Money problems were not the only reason which kept Renoir in Paris during this period. Renoir is arguably more of a painter of Paris than any of the other Impressionists. This is the case not because of his panoramas since all of his friends, from Monet and Pissarro to Sisley, tackled these. He differed from them in his love of street scenes, which united Parisian life, both working- and middle-class, in all its facets. Renoir himself straddled both classes. As a young apprentice porcelain-painter he used to linger on the Boulevard du Temple, known as the "Crime Boulevard". Whether his subject

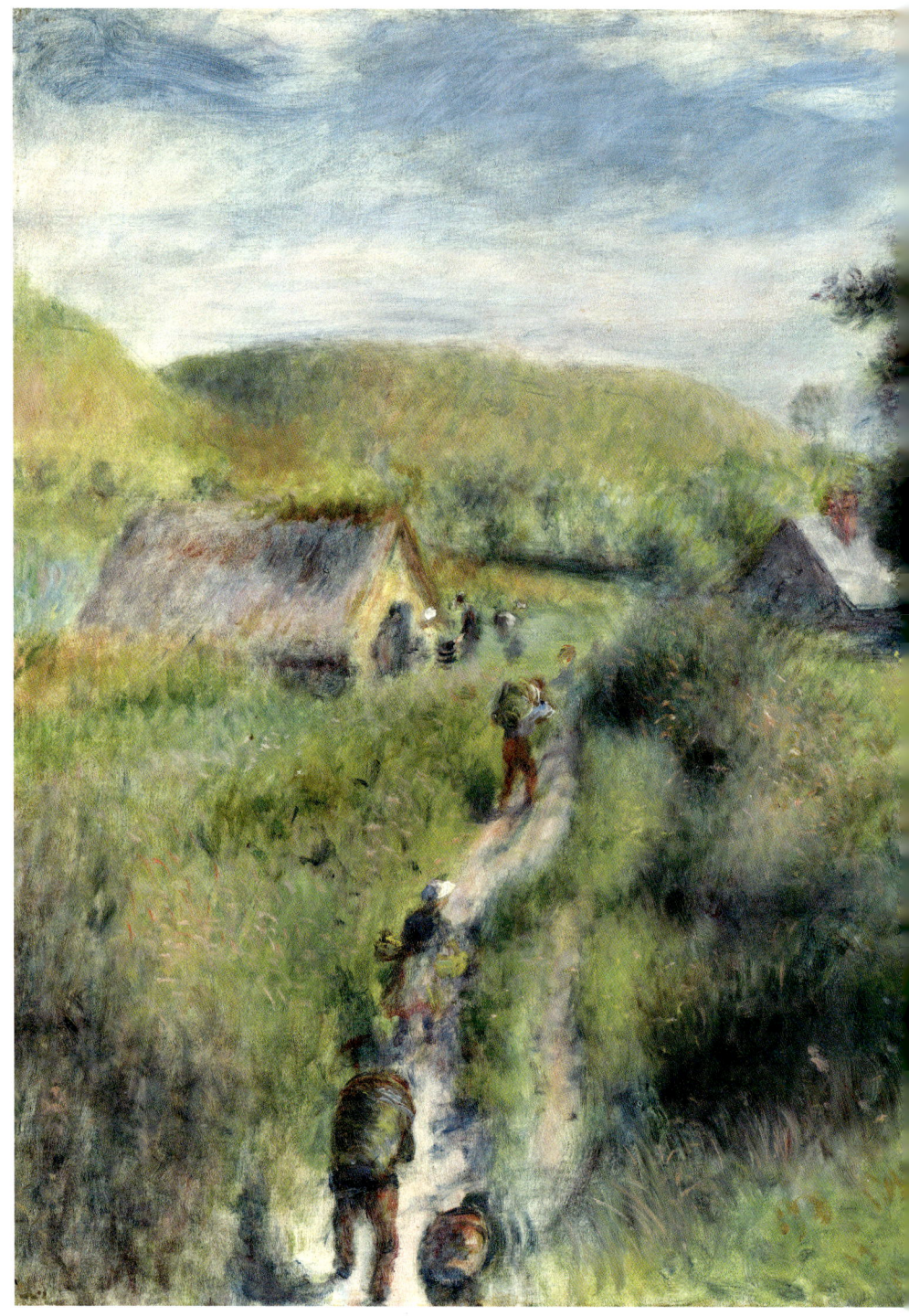

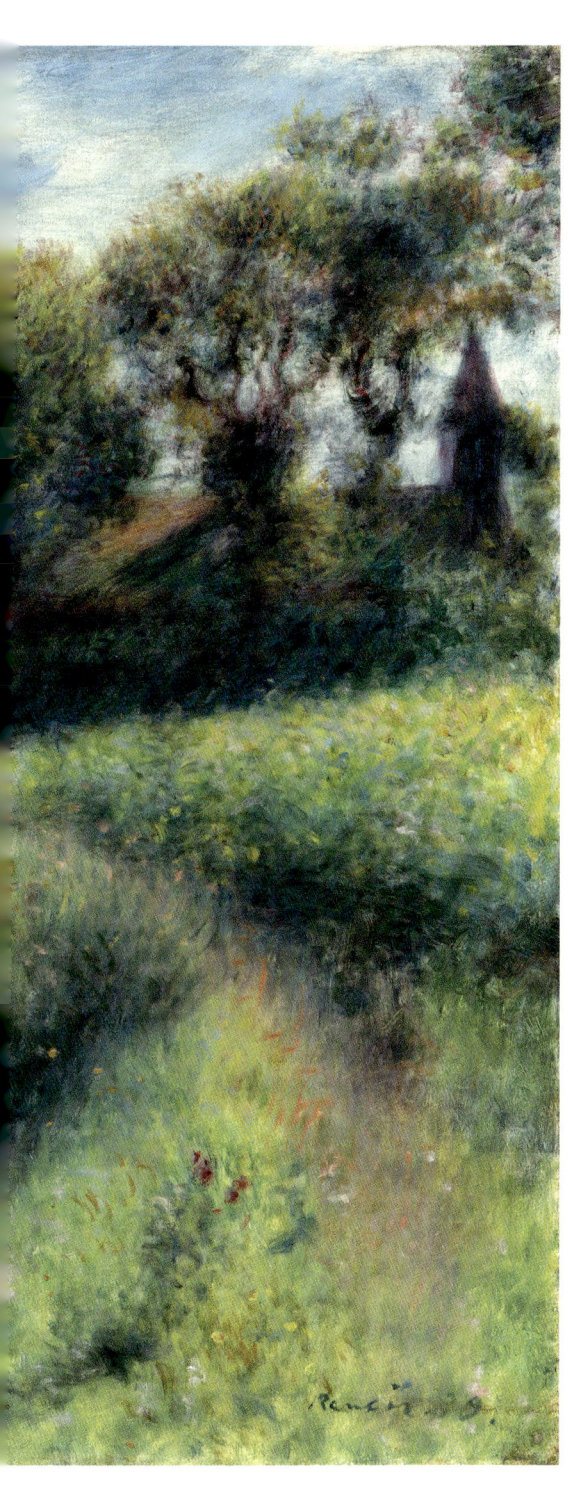

The Mussel Harvest, 1879
Oil on canvas, 54.2 x 65.4 cm (21⅜ x 25¾ in.)
Washington, D.C., National Gallery of Art,
Gift of Margaret Seligman Lewisohn in
memory of her husband, Sam A. Lewisohn

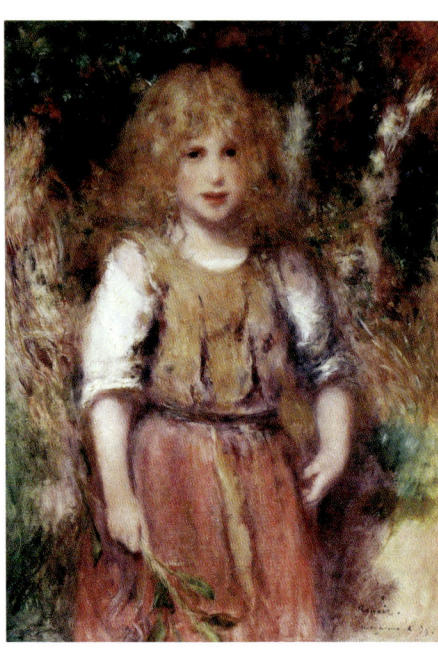

Gypsy Girl, 1879
Oil on canvas, 73 x 54 cm (28¾ x 21⅜ in.)
Private collection

The fisherman's granddaughter was painted at
Wargemont. Renoir loved her red hair and
included her in the painting of *Mussel-Fishers
at Berneval* (p. 397).

Place Clichy, c. 1880
Oil on canvas, 65 x 54 cm (25⅝ x 21⅜ in.)
Cambridge, The Fitzwilliam Museum

was the shop-girls of Montmartre or the elegant ladies riding in the Bois de Boulogne,
the Moulin de la Galette or the receptions held by his publisher Georges Charpentier,
Renoir always depicted the scene in the same way. He focused on the human figures and
their world. He once calmly told Gleyre, who took the remark as a joke, that he painted
purely for pleasure and that he painted only that which gave him pleasure. For Renoir,
Paris was the greatest of pleasures.

Renoir differs from the other Impressionists in the importance he attributes to the
human individual and the pre-eminence of portraiture in all his work. The Impressionists, with the exception of Degas and Cézanne, painted almost nothing but landscapes.
Human beings appear in the landscape as if by chance and are more often than not
reduced to a silhouette, a splash of colour in space of no more importance than any other
object. They simply allow a dab of contrasting colour to be added in a certain place.
Renoir, more even than Cézanne or Degas, most frequently chooses the human being
as his subject. For Cézanne, as Marcel Brion puts it, "any portrait, even a self-portrait, is
no more than an arrangement of lines, volumes and colours, the opportunity to create
a particular organic architecture in which life is gradually frozen and turned to stone".
Cézanne saw no difference between the *Bathers* and the view of the rocky crags that
he painted at L'Estaque. His landscapes are portraits, and his portraits, landscapes. It
was his declared ambition to penetrate the very geological foundations of the landscape
and "marry the shoulders of the hills to the curves of women". As for Degas, human
beings were a subject of profound indifference, if not contempt, to him. They provided

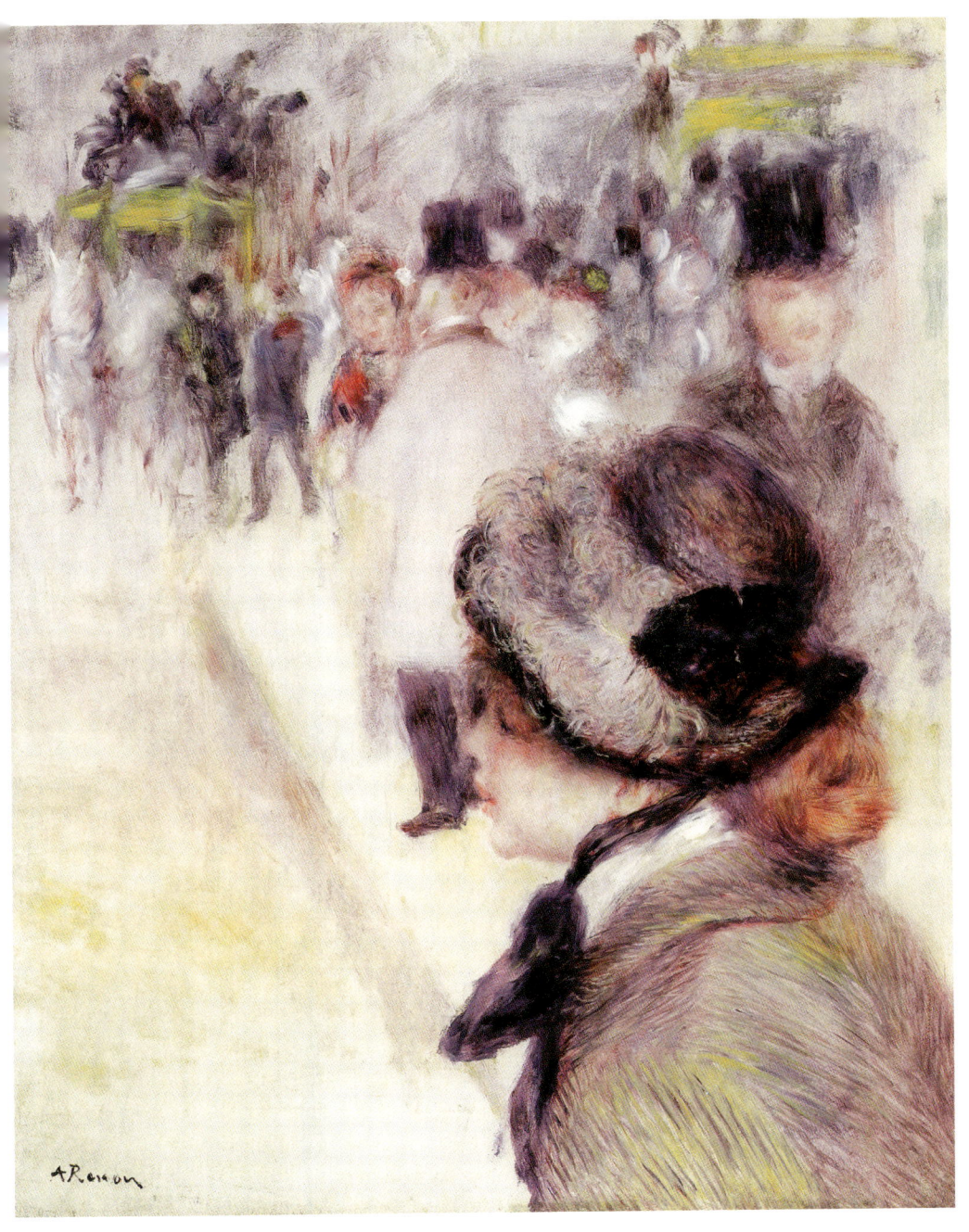

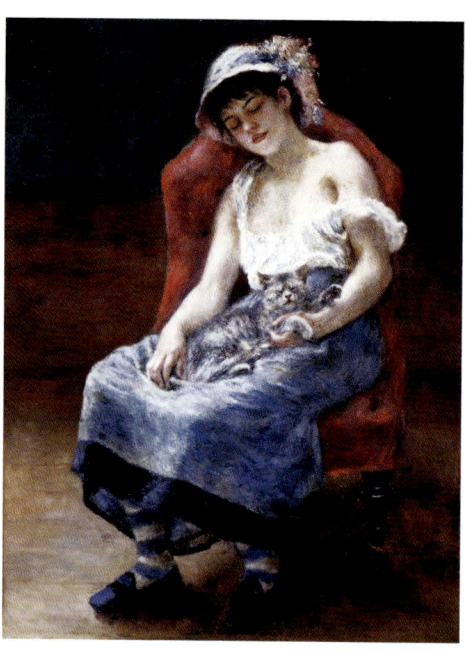

Sleeping Girl, 1880
Oil on canvas, 120.3 x 92 cm (47⅜ x 36¼ in.)
Williamstown, Massachusetts, The Clark

Young Woman Sewing, 1879
Oil on canvas, 61.4 x 50.5 cm (24¼ x 20 in.)
The Art Institute of Chicago, Mr. and Mrs.
Lewis Larned Coburn Memorial Collection

no more than a useful pretext for painting. Degas had mapped out an ambitious plan for himself. This plan, which he hoped would enable him to exploit a certain number of themes, resembled a spare parts catalogue more than a social studies textbook. It included musicians and their instruments; bakers' wives surrounded by variously shaped loaves and cakes; the gestures involved in manual labour; hairdresser's hands in action; the leg movements of dancers, which he often painted in isolation from the rest of the body, and the symptoms of physical exhaustion in laundresses. Degas excused for this aesthetic research by claiming: "People call me the painter of ballet dancers, but no one understands that for me the dancer is merely a pretext for painting pretty fabrics and conveying movement". He once greeted a wealthy patron of the opera for carrying off a dancer with the cynical reproach: "Sir, you have no right to take away our tools!" He once told the mother of the composer Ludovic Halévy: "Louise, I should like to paint your portrait. You have been *drawn* so often". Renoir was altogether less blasé. For him, a female breast was neither a hill nor a spare part. "A breast", he once said, "is round and warm". "If God had not created breasts, I don't think that I would ever have become a painter!"

Renoir found in the streets of Paris an inexhaustible supply of extraordinarily diverse female models. In painting the Parisian women as he saw them and as he got to know them, often intimately, he created – as Marcel Proust remarked – a new type of ideal femininity. The same can be said of very few other painters. After Sandro Botticelli and Piero della Francesca, a new type of feminine beauty did not emerge

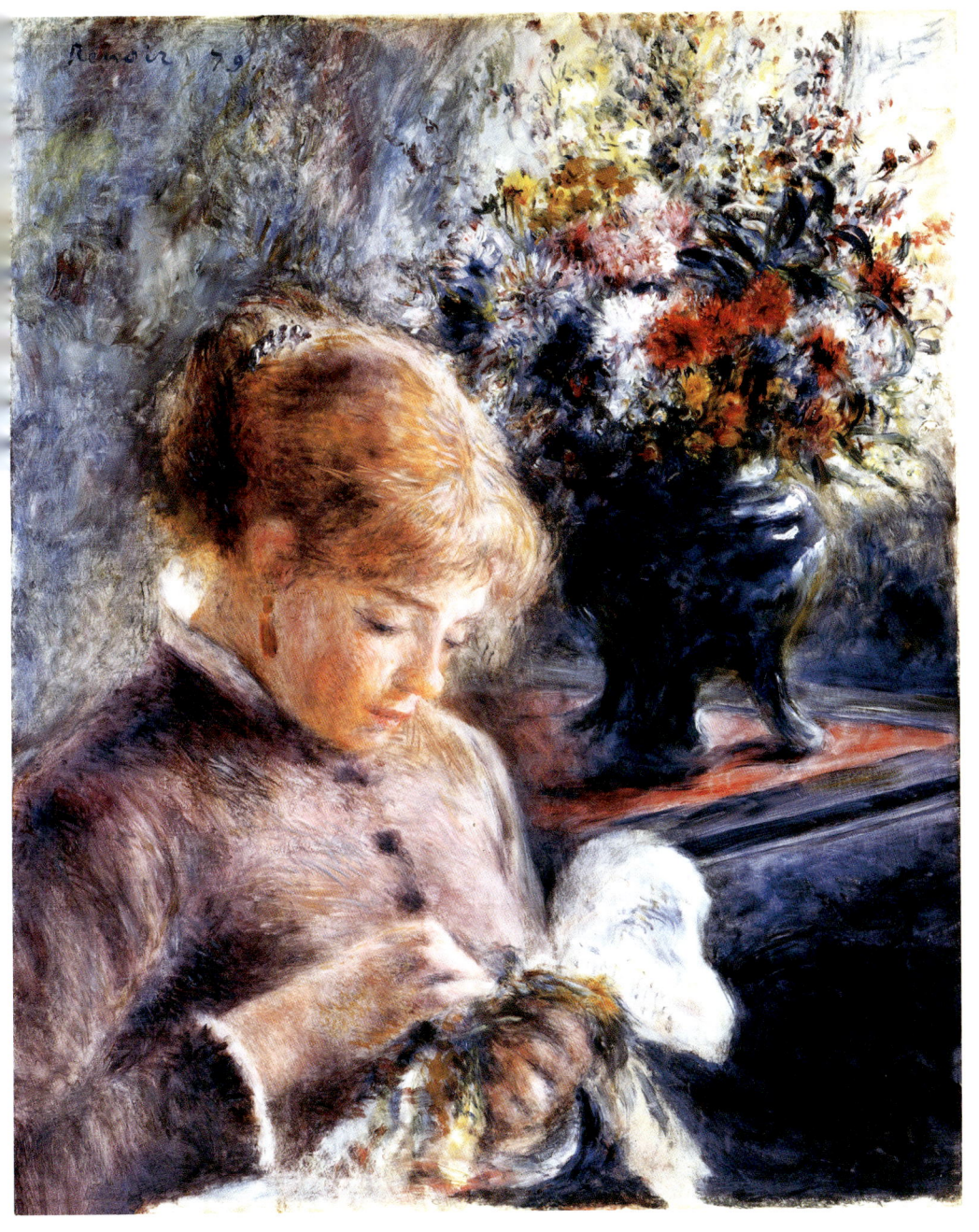

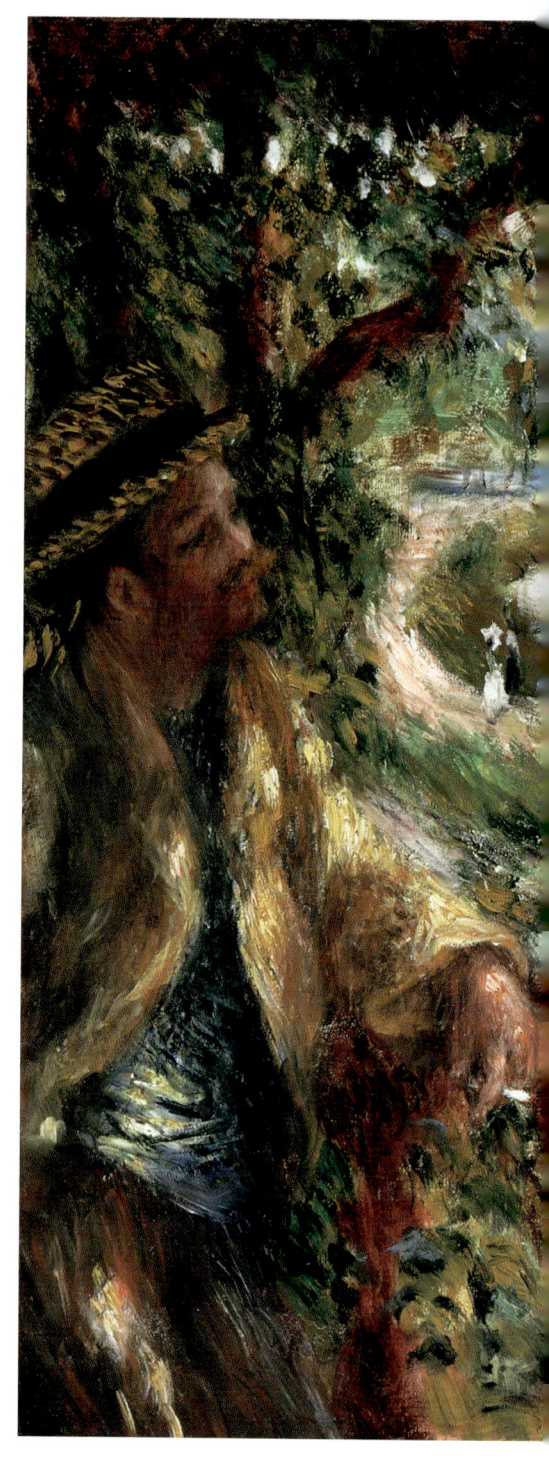

Near the Lake, 1879/80
Oil on canvas,
47.5 x 56.4 cm (18¾ x 22¼ in.)
The Art Institute of Chicago,
Potter Palmer Collection

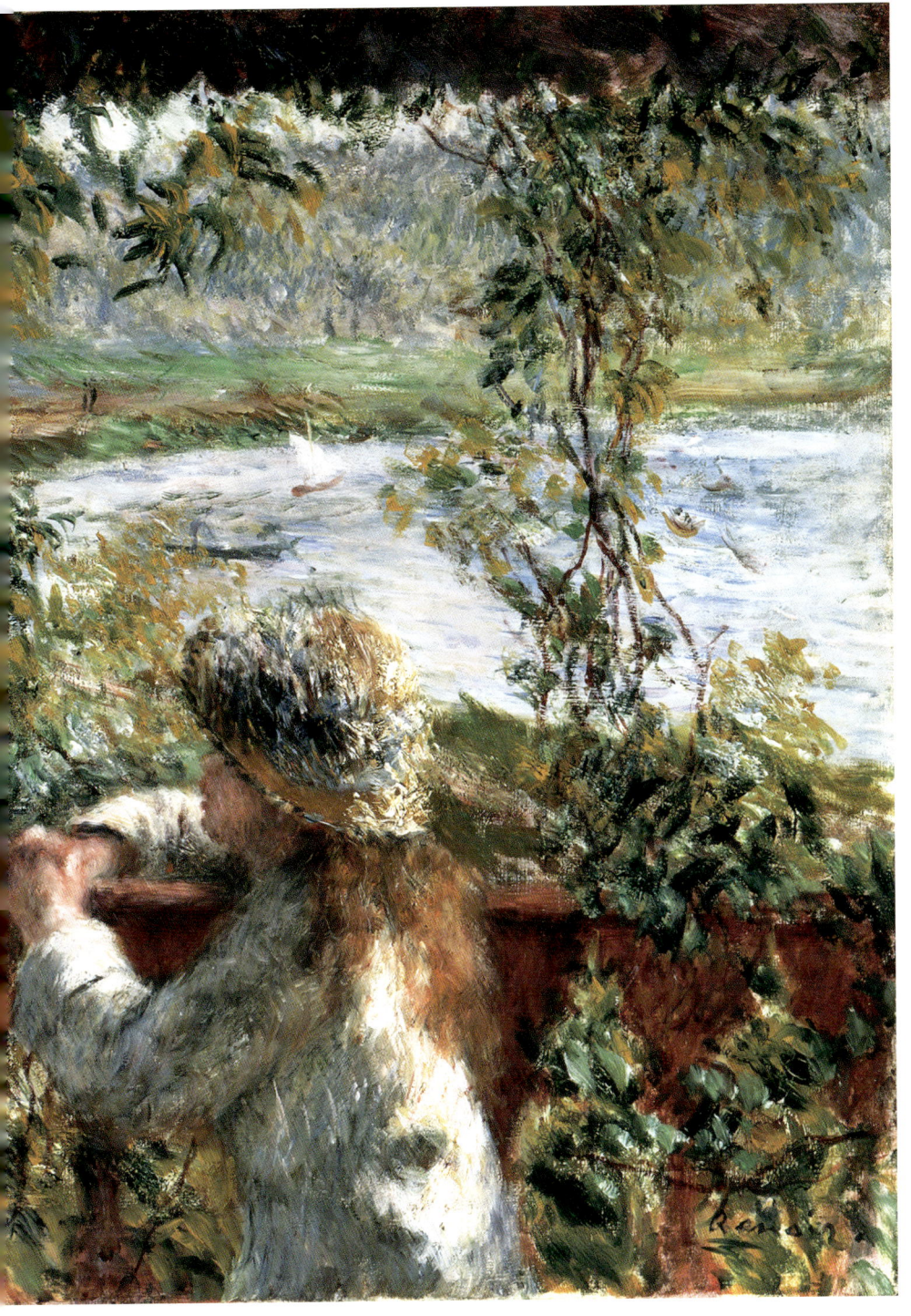

After the Luncheon, 1879
Oil on canvas, 100.5 x 81.3 cm (39⅝ x 32 in.)
Frankfurt am Main, Städel Museum

This is the scene in the garden of Olivier's tavern
in Montmartre. The woman holding a glass is the
actress, Ellen Andrée (1857–1925); one of Renoir's
favourite models is seen standing. The man
lighting a cigarette is Edmond, the painter's
younger brother.

until the advent of Veronese and Tintoretto. Renoir was preceded by Ingres and succeeded by Henri Matisse. It can be said, without excessive patriotism, that the qualities (and defects) that Ingres, Renoir and Matisse recorded have a common ancestry in a long French tradition. Ingres is commonly though to be the leading exponent of Classicism. When he painted a woman's portrait, such as that of *Madame Moitessier* (p. 266), the Classical Ingres suddenly becomes a Romantic painter. A painting such as *The Turkish Bath* (1863) has a new erotic force which breaks Ingres's classical mould apart. Flesh and fabric intermingle; the clothes and body become one. The shoulders and arms have the texture of silk and velvet; the pleats of the skirt are like folds in the skin. Some of Ingres's women look like they are about to step out of their dresses. These portraits, like those of Renoir and Matisse, proclaim the nude as the highest form of artistic expression.

The art critic Gaëtan Picon makes the same observation: "Nothing is sharper or more subtle, more 'Ingresque' in fact, than the point at which neck meets necklace or velvet meets flesh, the contact between a shawl and a lock of hair or between a breast and the top of the corsage, the sight of an arm emerging from a long glove. These portraits of women have a particular radiance because they are painted, as nudes more openly are, in the full light of desire." Picon might equally have been referring to Ingres, Renoir or Matisse.

The numerous apple-cheeked women that Renoir created, with their childish round features, avoid looking monotonous or banal because the painter gives them

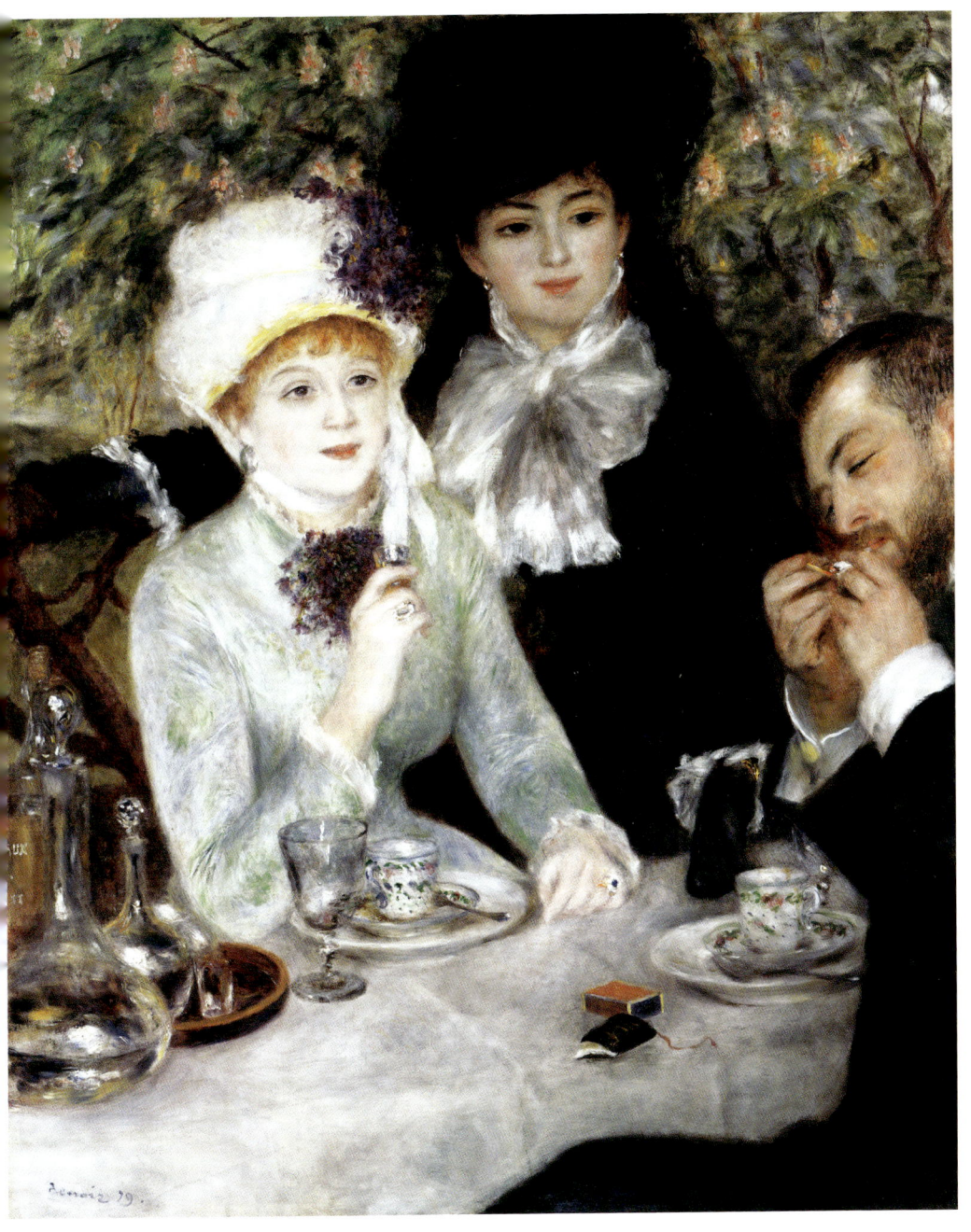

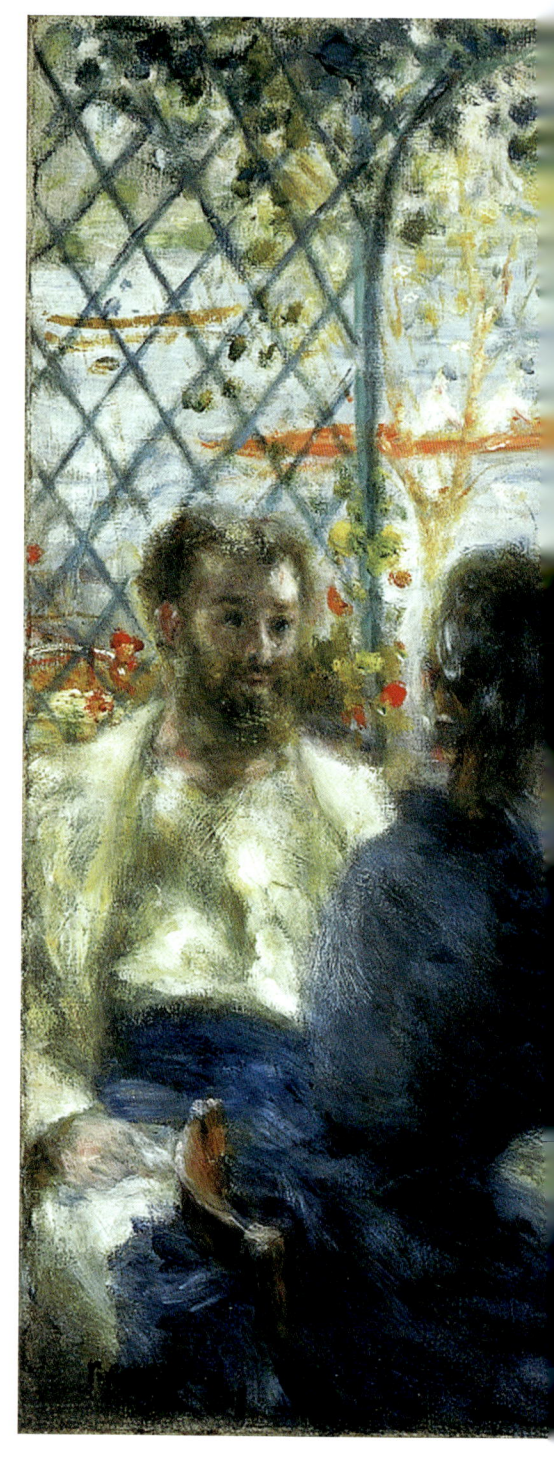

Lunch at the Restaurant Fournaise
(The Rowers' Lunch), 1875
Oil on canvas,
55 x 65.9 cm (21¾ x 26 in.)
The Art Institute of Chicago,
Potter Palmer Collection

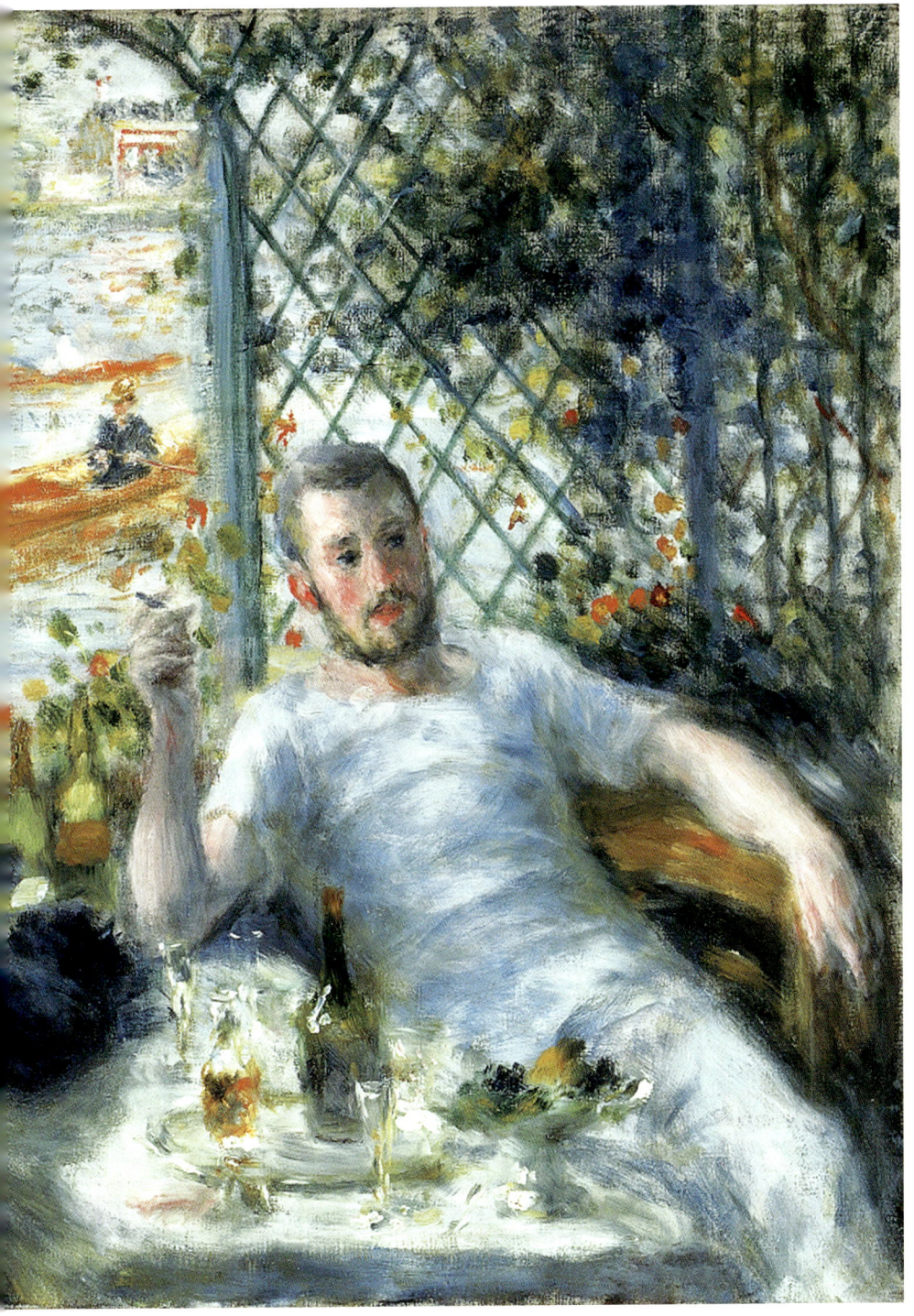

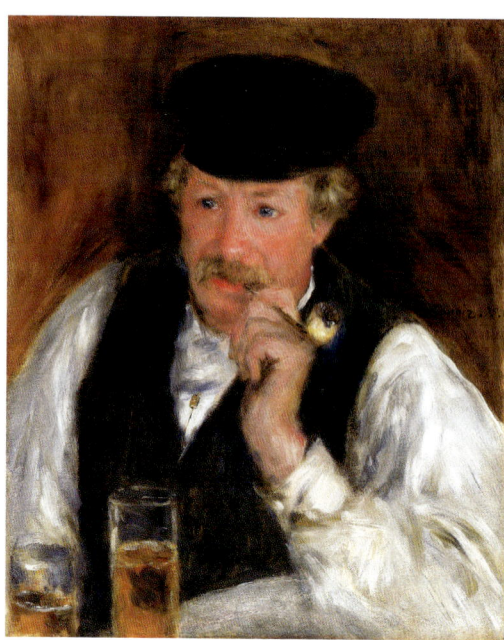

Père Fournaise, 1875
Oil on canvas,
56.2 x 47 cm (22¼ x 18⅝ in.)
Williamstown, Massachusetts,
The Clark

such warmth and vitality. His favourite models were working-class girls, the seamstresses and milliners who were always to be found in the cafés of Montmartre. Where a
naturalistic painter would find misery and exhaustion, Renoir perceives their unspoilt
beauty, innocent sensuality and sheer *joie de vivre*. *Place Clichy* (p. 145) and the *Two
Girls* (p. 169), sitting on a café terrace, are glimpses of Renoir's Paris. In painting after
painting incarnations of the same feminine grace look out at us and – at his behest –
beckon us in. They remain apparently unconscious of the desire that they arouse in
us. *Place Clichy* (c. 1880) has two unusual features. First of all, as Jamot has correctly
observed, a new type of model appears in this painting. She has a doll-like face, which
is one of the features which Picasso claims to have been "discovered" by Renoir in girls.
These faces appear on all sorts of models, and are to be found in abundance in *The
Luncheon of the Boating Party* (pp. 156/157), which is the crowning glory of Renoir's
Impressionist legacy. They reappear in *Dance in the City, Dance in the Country* and
Dance at Bougival (pp. 285 to 287), painted just before the Ingres-influenced period
when Renoir began to have doubts about this style.

The second particularity is the composition of the painting: the figure of the young
woman stands out strikingly in the foreground, detailed with a precision that under-
lines the empty space on the left and the colourful blur of the crowds in the middle
ground. Here Degas shows the influence of Japanese prints and photographic techniques that one also finds in early cinema. Note that this work, which looks like one
of pure spontaneity, was in fact produced after a series of preparatory studies. The

sketch *At the Café* (p. 108) was produced with considerable brio and impasto; it is an example of Renoir's liking for the small format. The man in the top hat is usually identified as Georges Rivière, while the two young women are the painter's usual models. This evocation of café life, so much a part of artistic circles from the Café Guerbois to the Nouvelle-Athènes, reflects his Impressionist desire spontaneously to "record", as his brother Edmond wrote in an article published in 1879, "a faithful picture of modern life".

Works of this period often look like snapshots of an image that Renoir found striking. This is Renoir in action, suddenly glimpsing a model at rest in a sunny corner of the studio and, struck by the light playing on her face, grabbing a canvas in order to seize the moment before the young girl is even aware what is happening. The result is *Woman Reading* (p. 97). She had "skin that absorbed light", Renoir remembered. He painted the scene before it could escape him, transforming it into a stunning work of art. This *Woman Reading* is obviously very similar to *Young Girl Reading* by Fragonard (p. 94). The same light, reflected by their books, lights up the foreheads of both readers, rendering the shadows on the face transparent. Renoir's Impressionist side reveals a wonderful variety of fresh and subtle tints. Renoir's work is never livelier nor happier than when he combines the best of Fragonard and Impressionism. *Reading the Part* (p. 95) or *Young Girl Reading* (p. 137) are in the same vein. The themes are also a pretext and there is the same rapid, raised brushwork in the eyes, the eyebrows and the lips, which draws us into a magical kingdom of colour and delivers instances of pure happiness.

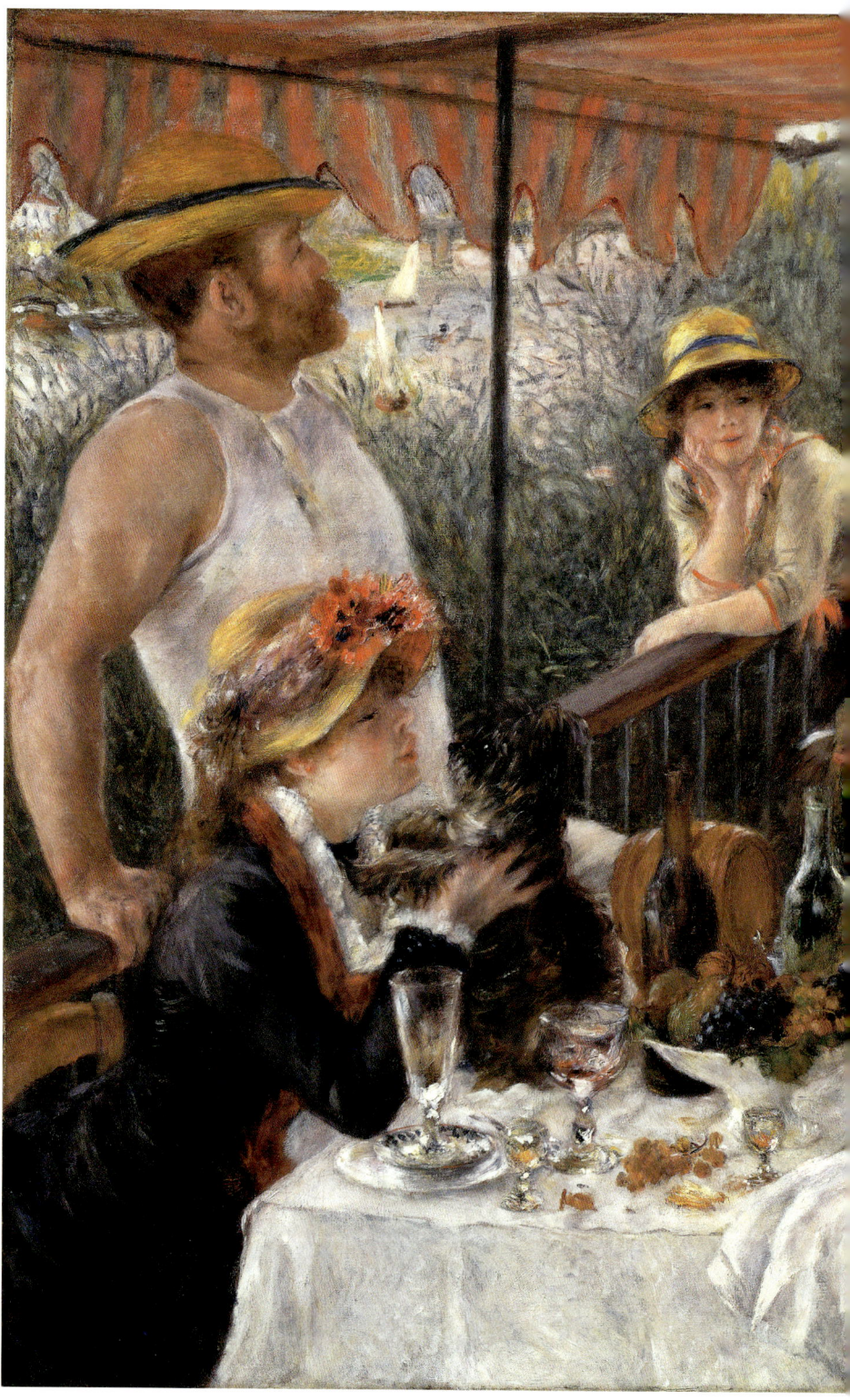

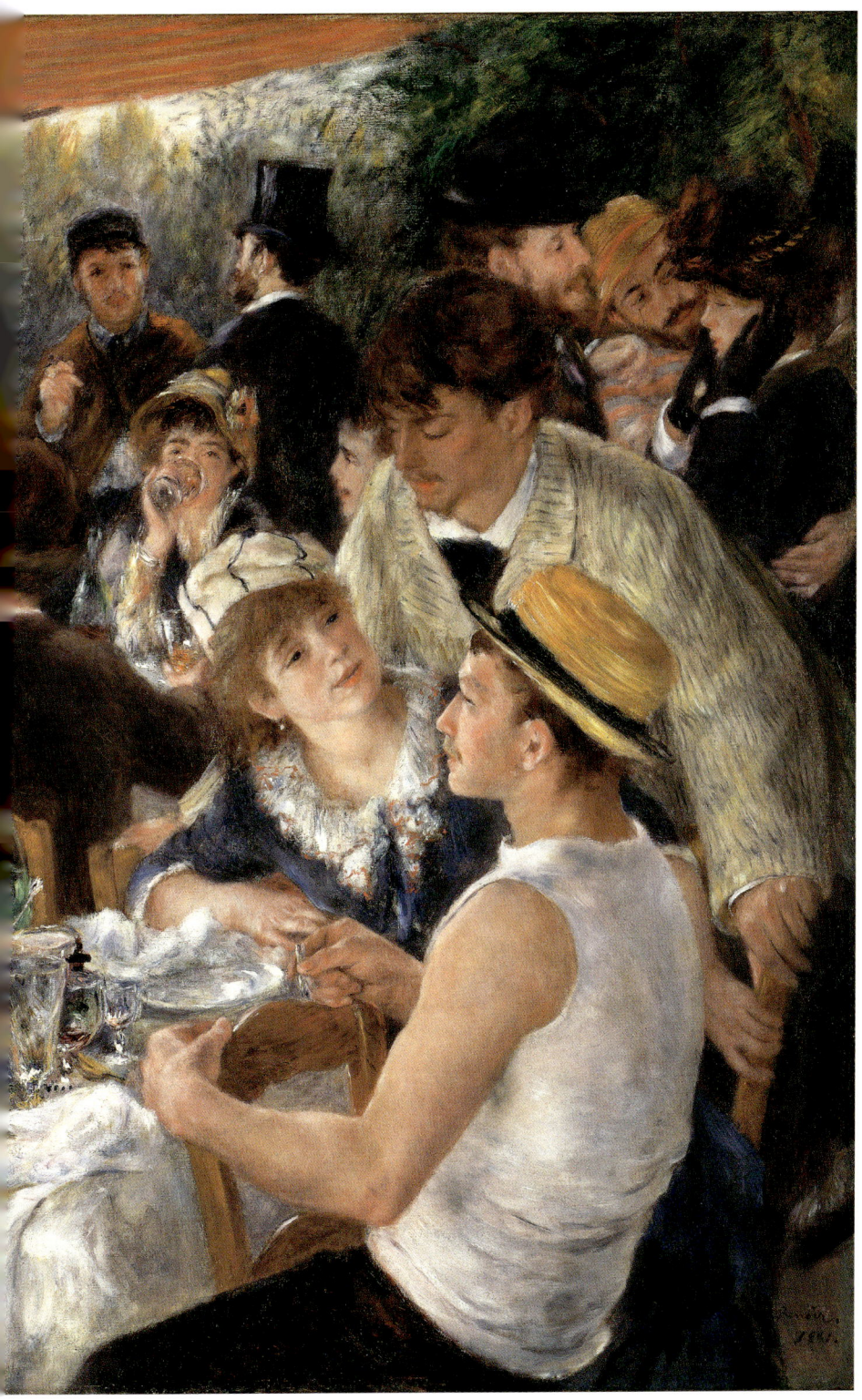

The Luncheon of the Boating Party, 1880/81
Oil on canvas, 130.2 x 175.6 cm (51⅜ x 69¼ in.)
Washington, D. C., The Phillips Collection

Alphonsine Fournaise, 1879
Oil on canvas,
73 x 93 cm (28¾ x 36⅝ in.)
Paris, Musée d'Orsay

Renoir was less interested in events on stage in the theatre than in the audience, dressed in opera gowns and bathed in the artificial light. The star of the show in *The Theatre Box* (p. 87) is the woman in the audience in all her splendour, rouged and powdered, dressed in silk, lace and jewellery. She herself is "exhibited" like a jewel in this sumptuous setting. Here again, the theme is a mere pretext and one used frequently by Renoir. A slightly different version of it is found in *At the Concert*, also called *A Box at the Theater* (p. 171). A mere corner of the stage curtain on the left justifies the title; the arrangement of the drapery is what matters. The bouquet borrowed from *Olympia* (p. 166) is included in recognition of Manet. It completes the trio of bouquets in the painting which include the faces of the young woman and the girl. The eye is drawn to their mouths, hair, eyes, and the pearly glow of their skin. The rest simply enhance these features. According to tradition, the models are the wife and daughter of Turquet, the Undersecretary of State for Fine Arts and a man who does not appear to have looked with much favour on the "independents". Renoir would have reflected on the need to put himself in the good books of such a man. The subject, style and social standing of the models of the painting are that required of submissions to the official jury of the Salon. The same pretext as in theatre box also served for *The First Outing* (p. 113). Two years had passed since the first *Box at the Opera* and the scene in the middle ground has become bucolic, with new emphasis lent to the *Olympia* bouquet, which is held by a charming girl in the foreground dressed in her Sunday best. She is the focus of attention, with her doll-like profile, the freshness of her complexion and the wide-eyed look

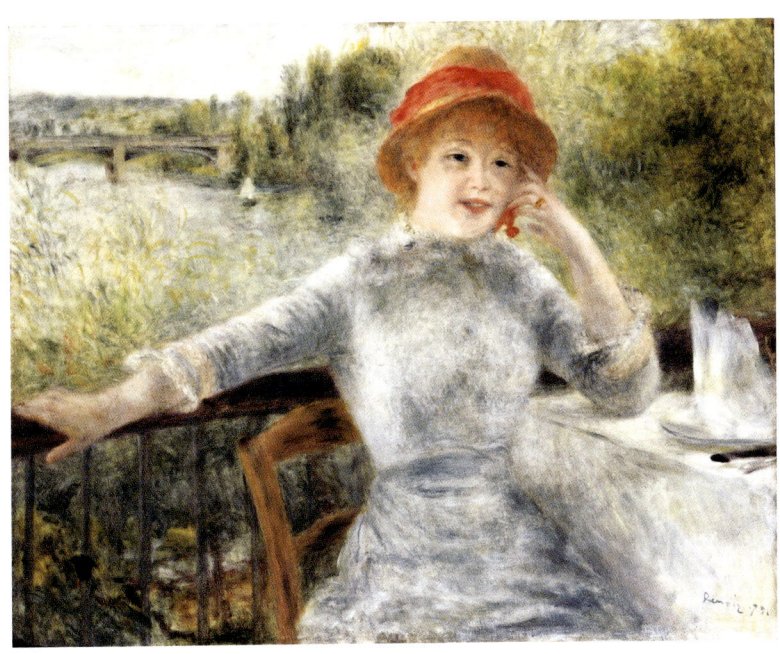

of a young girl astonished by her first trip to the theatre. The curved line of the box is repeated in the front of her jacket, adding solidity to a painting full of implied movement and sound. Matisse would often use curves in the same way. It is amusing to compare *The First Outing* with *Young Woman with a Veil* (p. 109). The reversed silhouette is the same, but this is no young girl with the right to hold Manet's bouquet so the pretext of the theatre box has been omitted. Instead she is given a veil, allowing the painter to play with effects of transparency.

What do young girls dream about? This is the question raised by the girl in *Young Woman Seated* (p. 111). She looks like she is day-dreaming as she sucks a finger while the other hand rests on a barely visible knee. Renoir tried to defend himself in vain when he told Albert André: "It horrified me to learn that one of my canvases had come to be called *The Thought*. That girl never had a thought in her life. She lived like a bird." This is hard to take at face value coming from Renoir, the "nightingale-painter" who wanted everyone to believe that he didn't have a single idea in his mind and that all he wanted was "to touch, or at least, see." One thing, indeed, is certain: he was a true sensualist with a passion for women. *Young Woman Braiding Her Hair* (p. 110), which belongs to the same series of profiles as *Young Woman Seated* and *Portrait of a Young Woman* (p. 112) – who also has her fingers at her mouth and holds her breast in the other hand – are not as innocent as they look. One's own temperament is the worst form of betrayal. Michelangelo long rejected the Pope's request for him to paint the ceiling of the Sistine Chapel on the grounds that he was merely a sculptor. But in fact he was afraid of being

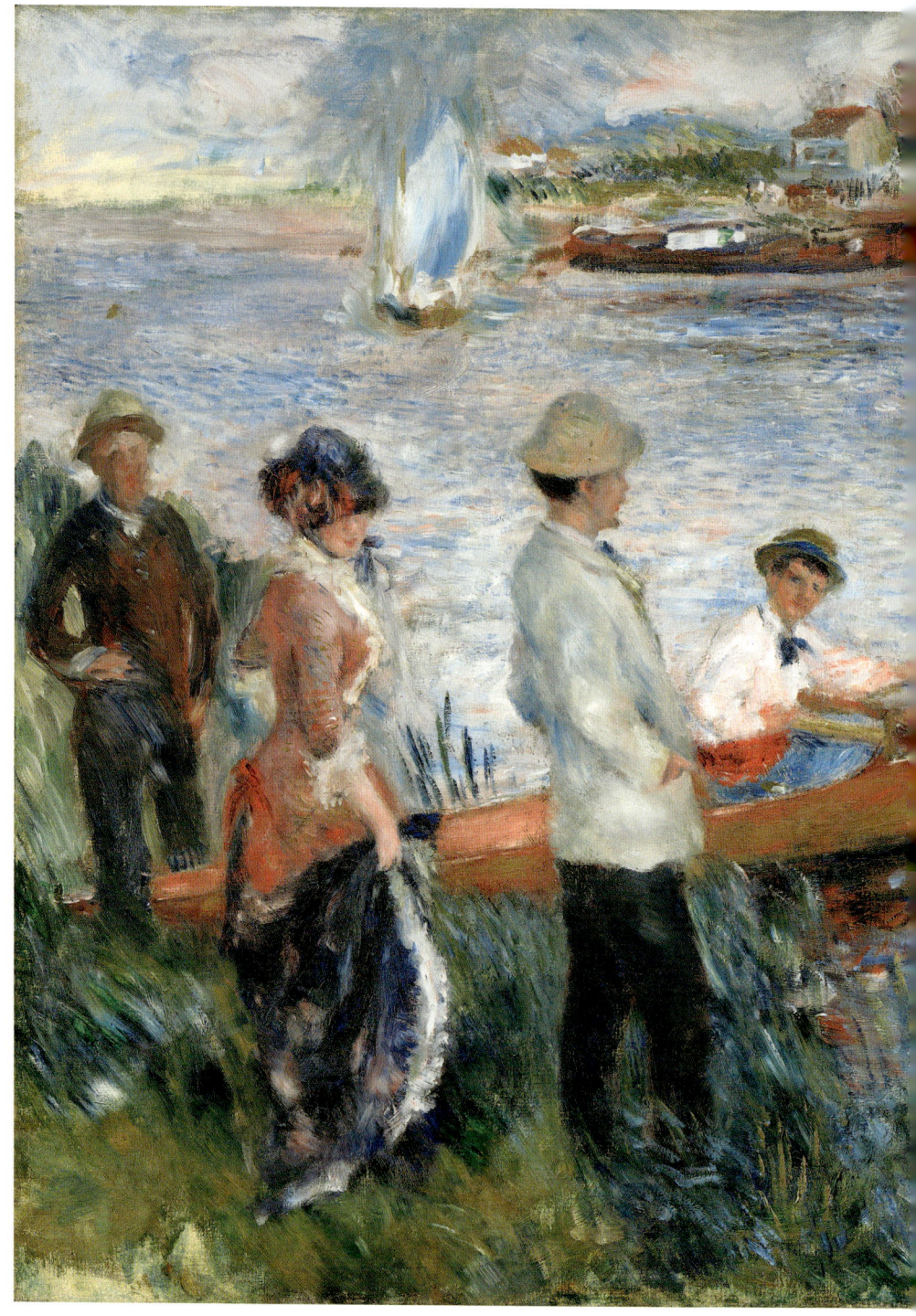

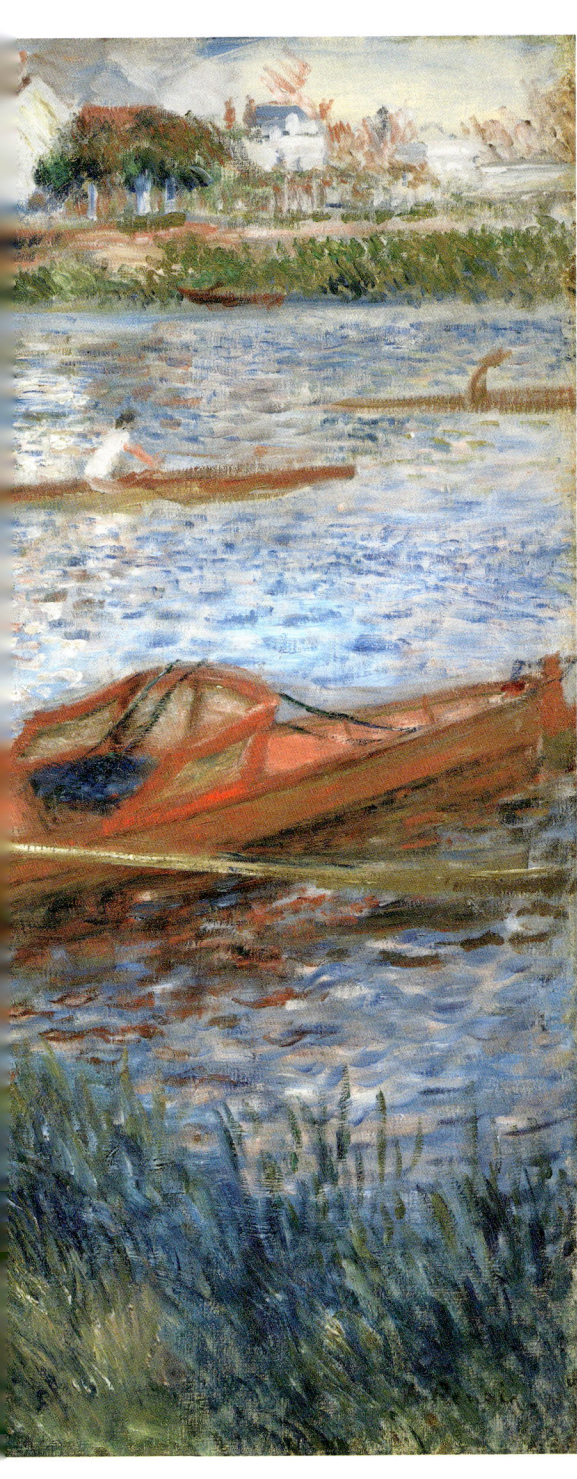

Oarsmen at Chatou, 1879
Oil on canvas,
81.2 x 100.2 cm (32 x 39½ in.)
Washington, D.C.,
National Gallery of Art

betrayed by his paintings; and one has only to look at the *Ignudi*, the handsome naked youths with which he sprinkled the vault of the church, to see his fears realised. The long feminine manes that Renoir loved to paint – and that are found in abundance in his paintings of nudes and bathers – were mentioned by Baudelaire, who knew all about fetishes, in his poem 'The Mane' in *Les Fleurs du mal*: "A whole world, distant, absent, almost deceased, / Lives in the depths of this fragrant forest! / As other spirits sail upon waves of music / Mine, oh my love, Swims in your perfume." Anyone who is attracted to one particular part of the body – the lips, the hair, the face or the legs – is a fetishist. Museums and galleries are full of fetishes. Renoir had them all: for legs and thighs, like Boucher and Fragonard, and for breasts like Rubens. He was one in the long line of those who admire the female backside from Albrecht Dürer, Raphael, Velázquez and Rubens through Boucher and Courbet to Picasso, Dalí and Andy Warhol. In his love of long, silky hair he also found himself in good company, with Botticelli, Dürer, Titian, Chassériau, Puvis de Chavanne, Toulouse-Lautrec (redheads only), Degas and Balthus. The same names crop up again and again. Rubens had several such fetishes, including one for fur, and his *Venus with a Fur* would inspire Sacher-Masoch.

But Titian – whom Renoir admired unconditionally – had the greatest fetish for female hair. Renoir pays him constant homage. His *Blonde Bather* (p. 338), *Bather Arranging Her Hair* (p. 345), and his greatest masterpiece, *The Great Bathers* (pp. 348/349) all pay tribute to Titian's *Venus Rising from the Sea* ("*Venus Anadyomene*"; p. 350). Many of Renoir's female portraits, whether clothed or naked, are inspired by *The Penitent Magdalene* by

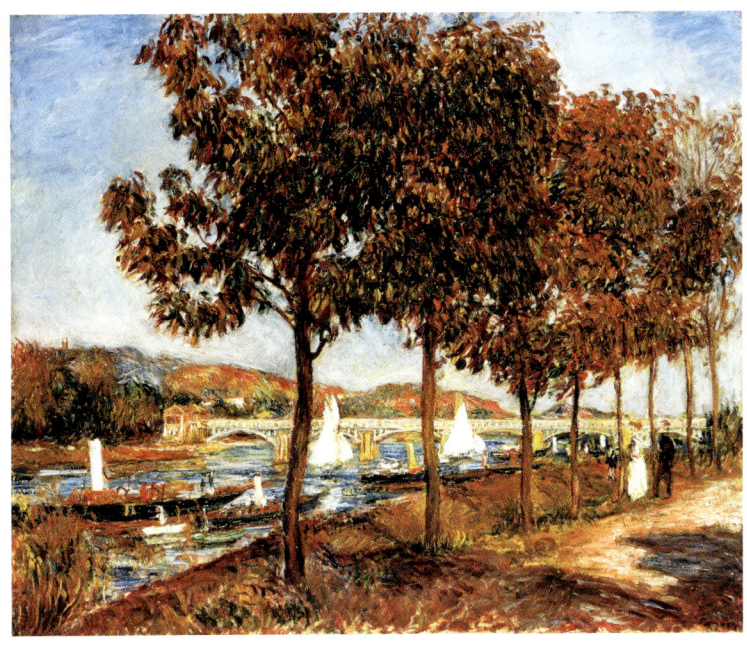

Titian (p. 176). Renoir's Magdalene is merely a pretext for showing her abundant tresses whose purpose is ostensibly to clothe her modesty. In reality, the painting not only emphasises her exposed charms but betrays the pleasure that her magnificent mane of hair causes her where it touches her naked body. Her delight is evident in her ecstatic gaze heavenwards. Note in passing that it was Titian's *Venus of Urbino* that Manet used as a model for his famous *Olympia.* But Manet replaced the dog, placed by Titian at the feet of his Venus, with a black cat standing in the same spot with its tail in the air! What the critics made of this should come as no surprise. No detail added by such a meticulous painter could be innocent. Renoir introduced cats into his paintings on occasion and they too were the cause of mirth. A cat is hugged lovingly in the arms of the *Woman with a Cat* (p. 107), who gazes into space. Another lies on the warm lap of *Sleeping Girl* (p. 146). One is left to wonder what they too are dreaming about.

Renoir used the opulent surroundings of a theatre auditorium as a backdrop for the "star" of his paintings, the spectator. But he loved the world of the stage itself, the actors, actresses, ballerinas and even the less polished circus performers. Lautrec or Degas often show the chaos behind the scenes, the difficulties of the profession, the exhausting exercises which were the price to be paid for a brief instant of glory. Just as Renoir conceals the toil and anguish which his more ambitious paintings cost him, so he ignores the off-stage exertions of the ballerinas or jugglers and concentrates on capturing their ingenuity and grace. This is the case with the young acrobats and jugglers of the *Acrobats at the Cirque Fernando* (p. 133), whom he chose as the subject

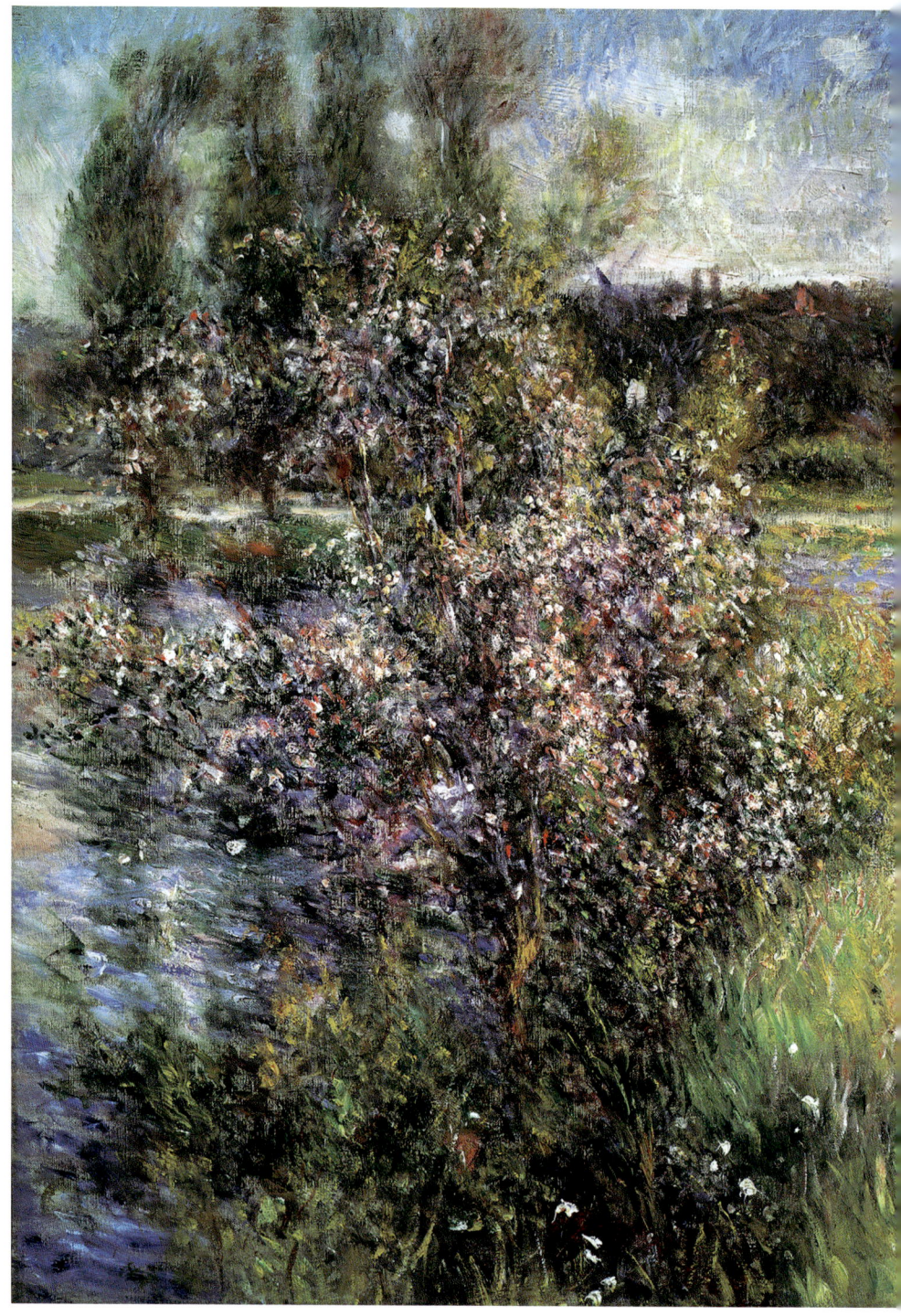

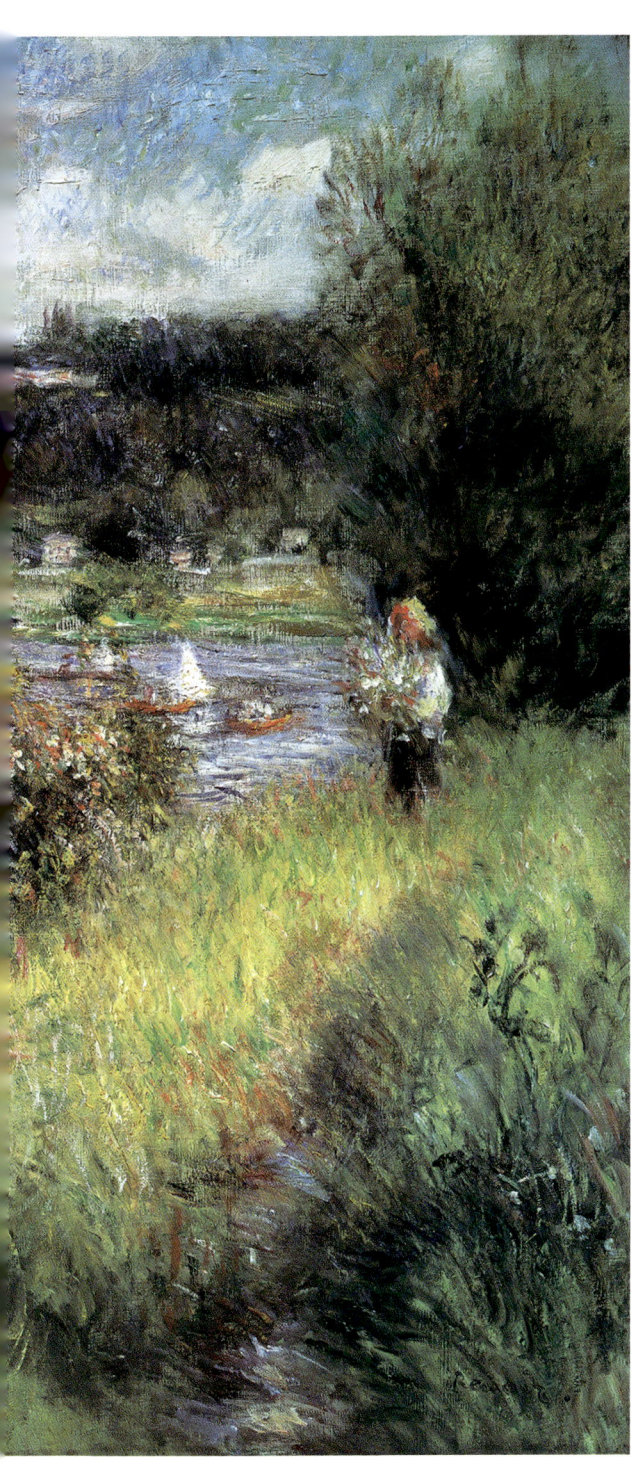

The Seine at Chatou, 1881
Oil on canvas,
73.3 x 92.4 cm (28⅞ x 36½ in.)
Boston, Museum of Fine Arts,
Gift of Arthur Brewster Emmons

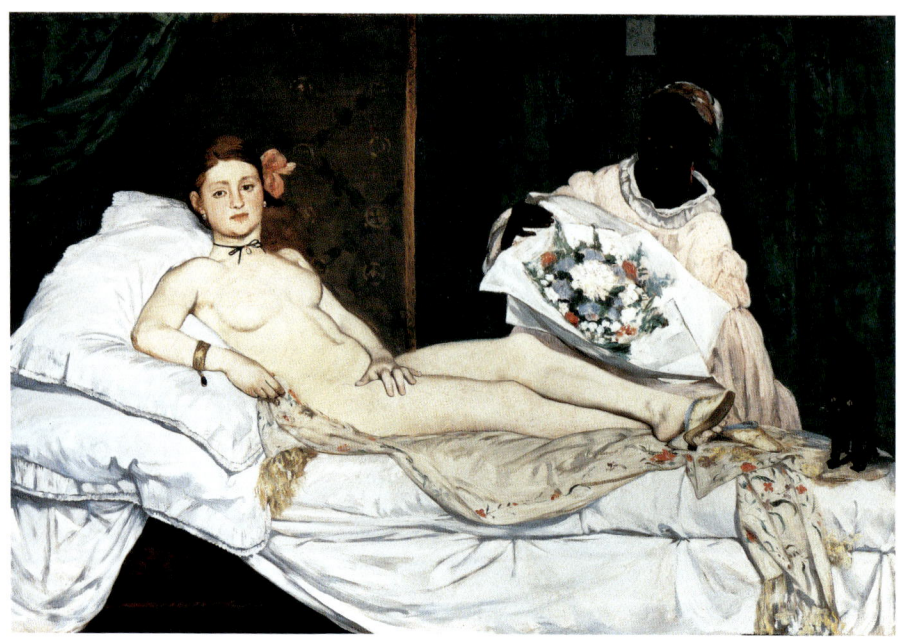

of this delightful portrait. They are shown close-up and in bird's eye view at the moment when, happy and relaxed, they receive their deserved applause from the audience. Degas who preferred to show an acrobat deep in his exertions (*Mlle La La at the Circus Fernando,* p. 132) and his dancers are "little monkey girls", in the words of Edmond de Goncourt, "pursuing their graceful contortions". Not a trace of sadness or worry is to be seen on the faces of the young girls in *Leaving the Conservatory* (p. 135), but merely the confidence that one day they will become great actresses like Jeanne Samary, of whom Renoir left three main portraits (pp. 127, 129 and 130). She was a talented actress whom he admired, of course, but he was even more sensitive to her charm as a woman, her gaiety and spontaneity. These qualities were very similar to his own. But to them she added another, and one that was irresistible to him: a magnificent head of golden hair and a radiant complexion which, as he used to say, "lit up everything around her".

In her day, Jeanne Samary was as famous as Sarah Bernhardt, and painting her after the adorable but unknown Henriette Henriot was a real step up the social ladder for Renoir. For three years she was his "little Samary, a joy to women and, above all, to men". She inspired no fewer than twelve oil portraits. Their association ended in 1880, when the actress began to prefer the more worldly realists who specialised in painting her in the great female roles of the Comédie-Française, and would enhance her reputation. Jules Bastien-Lepage, Carolus-Duran and Louise Abbéma each painted her portrait (Carolus-Duran's version is reproduced on p. 128). No doubt it was for love

Édouard Manet
Olympia, 1863
Oil on canvas, 130.5 x 191 cm (51½ x 75¼ in.)
Paris, Musée d'Orsay

of Renoir that made the famous actress "hold on" for three years because, unlike the academic painters who followed him, Renoir did not enjoy the performances of the Théâtre-Français. He rarely went and deliberately omitted anything from his paintings that might make them look like scenes from a play. Jeanne Samary had been a precocious child. She entered the Conservatory at the age of fourteen, and four years later won the first prize for acting at the Théâtre-Français. She was the pet of all the journalists one of whom wrote in 1877: "Mademoiselle Samary is gradually taking over all the soubrette parts in the repertoire". She received the award known as the Sociétariat de la Comédie-Française in 1879, two months before her thirty-second birthday. *Bust of Jeanne Samary,* also called *Day-dreaming* (p. 127), was exhibited at the third Impressionist exhibition in 1879.

This portrait, like *Jeanne Samary* (p. 129), is "Impressionist" in character. Samary disapproved, believing that it would do nothing for her reputation. But it is a delightful portrait, an array of sparkling colours. It was thought to be a good likeness of the subject but also rather "strange". Émile Zola claimed that "the success of the exhibition was the head of Mademoiselle Samary, all blonde and full of laughter". Flor O'Squarr was enraptured by the rendering which he found "as pink, fresh, spruce, clear, graceful and as sweet as the model." But it was considered to be no more than a study. The critic Véron demanded to know where Renoir had ever seen arms as rough as if they were covered in scales. The next time he painted her, Renoir tried to please his mistress and appease the critics. He submitted a more ambitious painting of Jeanne to the 1879 Salon. *Jeanne*

Two Girls, 1881/82
Oil on canvas, 81.3 x 65.2 cm (32 x 25¾ in.)
Moscow, Pushkin Museum

Samary (p. 130) is a full-length portrait of the actress in a ballgown. Unfortunately, the painting was "too high up and badly hung", so that it almost escaped the notice of the critics, while Louise Abbéma's *Samary* was hung in the best spot, in the same room as Bastien-Lepage's *Sarah Bernhardt*, and attracted all the attention. The actress wanted nothing to do with the painting, and it remained in Renoir's studio until it was bought by Durand-Ruel eight years after it had been painted. "She is very nice but look at her 'salt-cellars!'" Marguerite Charpentier is said to have exclaimed in jealousy when she saw the painting.

Renoir had taken the young actress, who was "short, plump, pink and round-faced" and whom people liked to compare to "a plump little quail", and transformed her into an elegant young woman, svelte and sensual though with a reserved exterior. It was, in fact, the crude, infectious laugh with which she used to show off her perfect teeth that most pleased the critics. Although Joris-Karl Huysmans did not appreciate her "constant, unbearable laugh", the delighted critics claimed that it was "Molière's laugh, the spark of contemporary dramatic art" and that she had an "impish mouth with the prettiest teeth in the world". Judging by photos, engravings and even the portrait by Carolus-Duran, it is obvious that Renoir, as usual, prettified the model considerably. He refined her chin, which was as "strong as a page-boy's", softened her wide-eyed, short-sighted stare, and masked her vulgarity. He made her heavy, untidy mass of hair look "as if it had arrived on a breath of spring air". One might well ask why Samary, who was as famous and talented as Sarah Bernhardt in her day, has not remained as famous

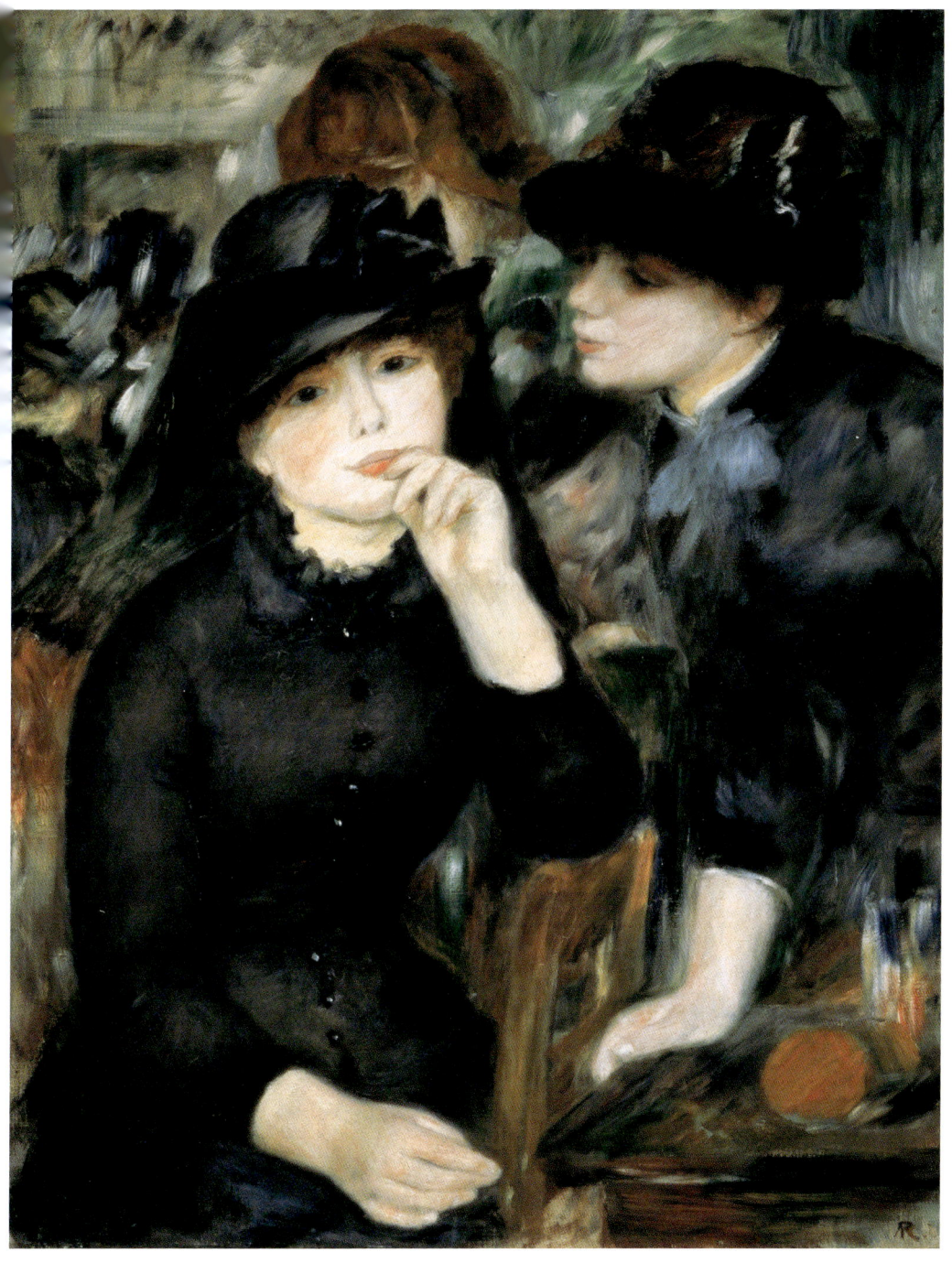

169

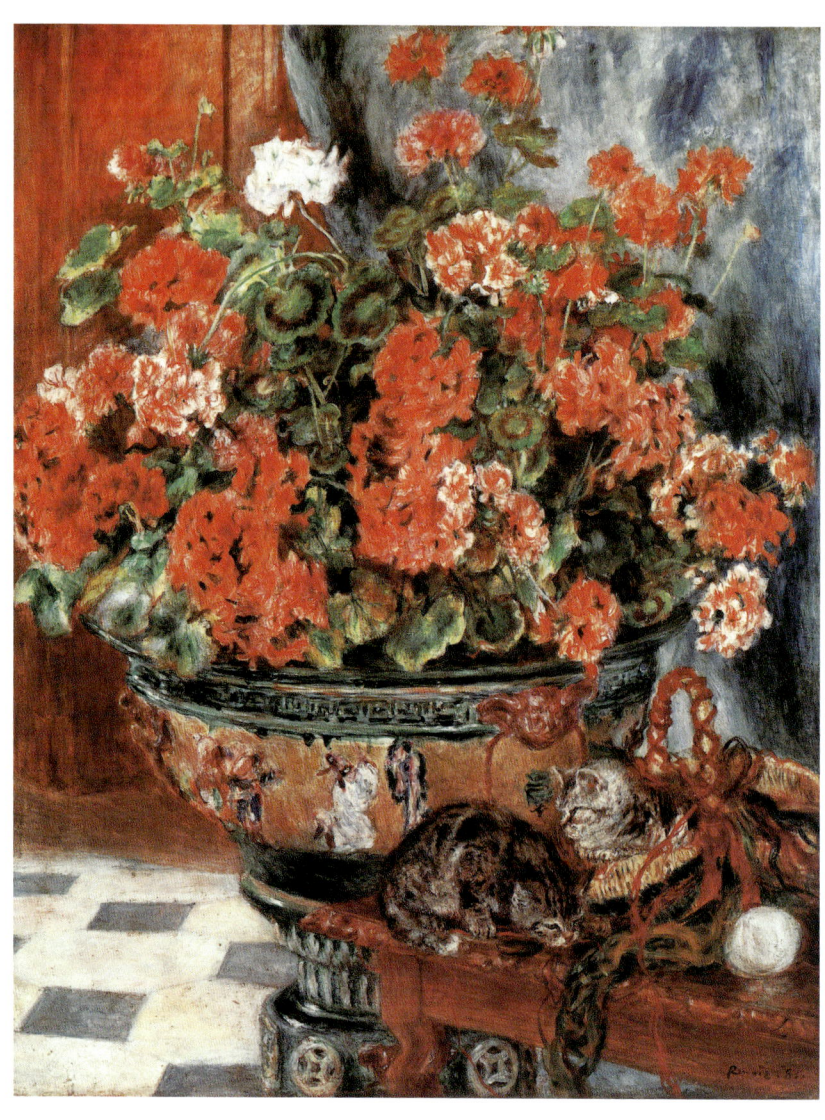

Flowers and Cats, 1880
Oil on canvas,
92.7 x 73.7 cm (36½ x 29 in.)
Private collection

A Box at the Theater (At the Concert), 1880
Oil on canvas, 99.4 x 80.7 cm (39¼ x 31⅞ in.)
Williamstown, Massachusetts, The Clark

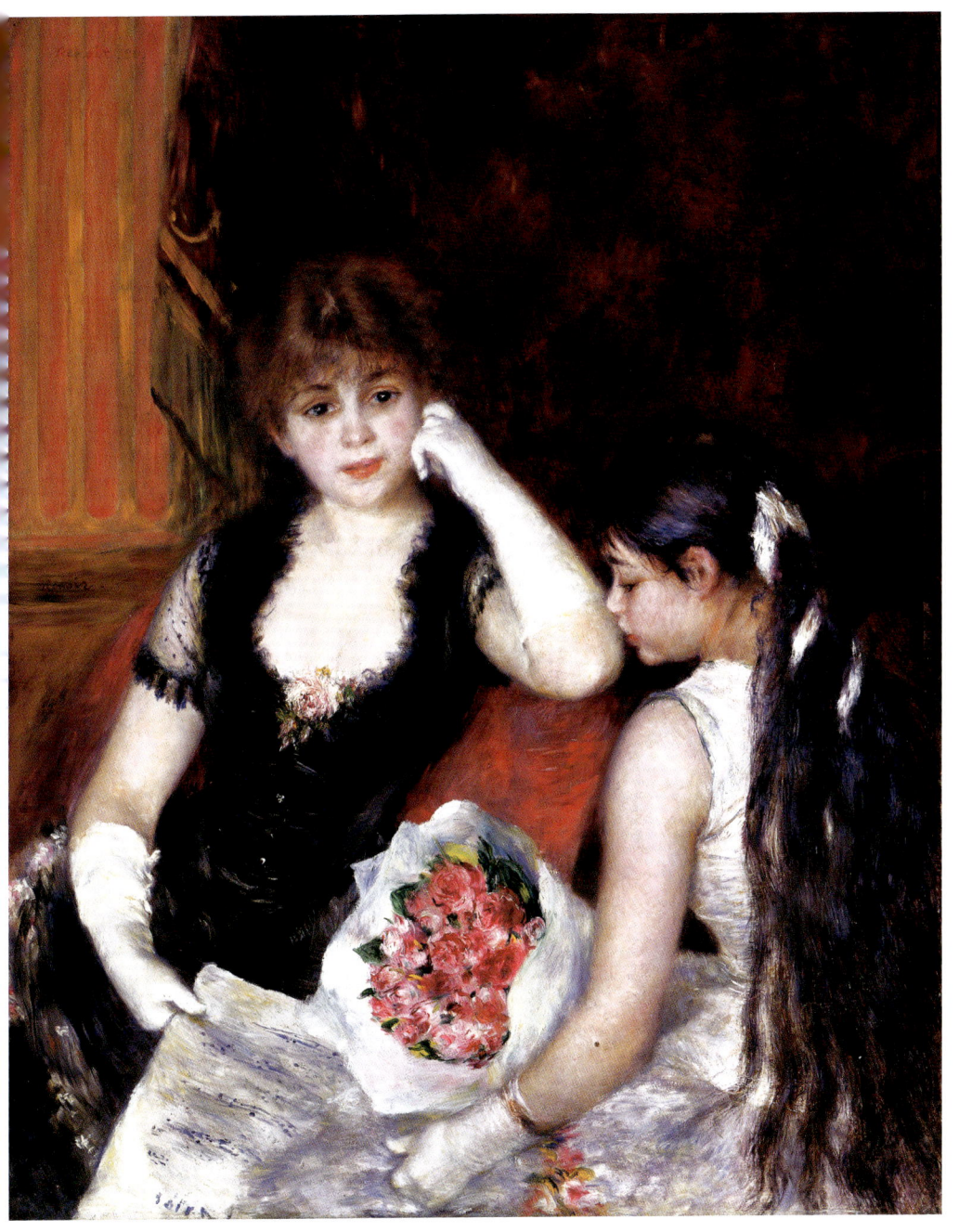

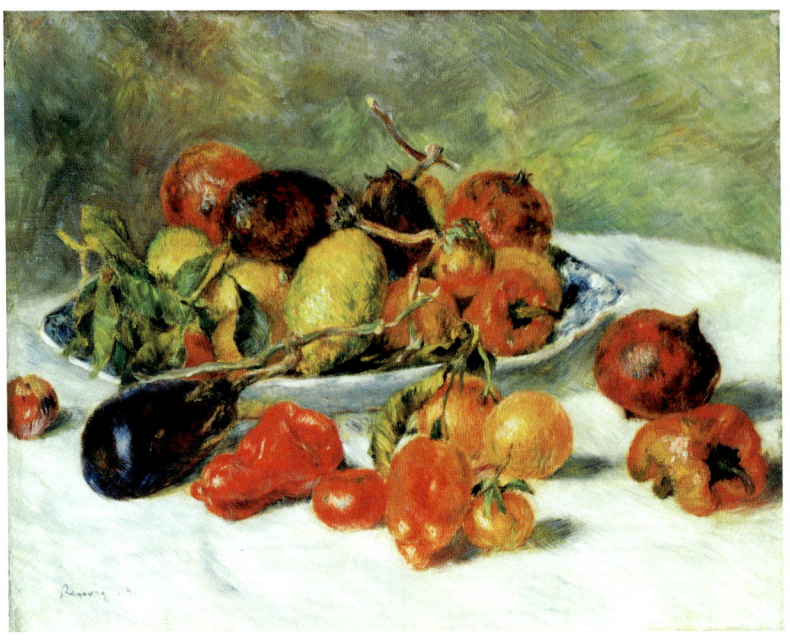

as "the Divine Sarah". The reason is simple: the precocious Samary even died precociously, at the age of thirty-three, from typhoid fever. Renoir has at least left us an image, of the laughing soubrette metamorphosed into a classy actress, which is endowed with "all the grace and application that eighteenth-century artists put into their portraits of their favourite stars".

Renoir's efforts were now beginning to be rewarded. His disastrous financial situation gradually improved, thanks mainly to his friends who were at the same time enthusiasts of his work and dealers in his paintings. There was Chocquet, Gustave Caillebotte who painted alongside the Impressionists and their favourite dealer, Durand-Ruel, who had hitherto sold paintings of the Barbizon School. During the Franco-Prussian War, he had met Pissarro, Sisley and Monet in London and fell in love with their work. He bought their paintings and exhibited them in Paris, but finding that they were not appreciated by the French, he sent them to London where they met with greater success. It was not until 1873 that he first met Renoir who was to remember the event with gratitude. "In 1873 a momentous event occurred in my life when I made the acquaintance of Durand-Ruel, the greatest dealer in paintings I have known, and the only one who believed in me." Unfortunately, Durand-Ruel faced ruin after taking on his new recruits and, for the moment at least, abandoned them to their fate. In April 1875 Renoir received what was for him the huge sum of 1,200 francs, the most he had ever been paid for a painting, for a large composition entitled *The Walk* (p. 53). Thanks to this unexpected windfall, he was able to rent two rooms in the garret, and

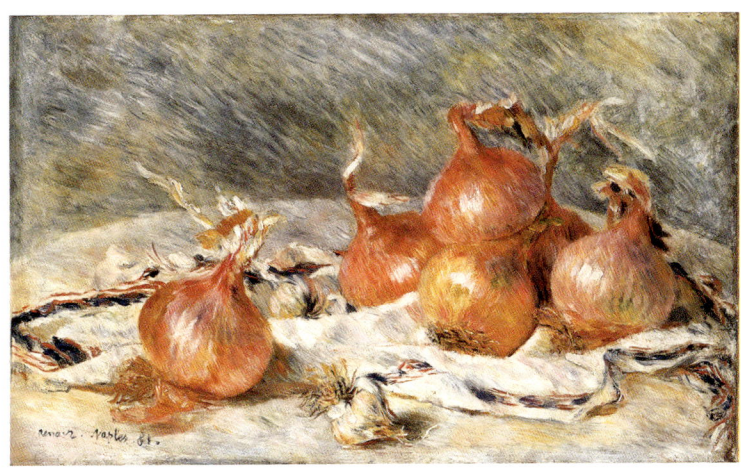

Fruits of the Midi, 1881
Oil on canvas, 51 x 65 cm (20 x 25⅝ in.)
The Art Institute of Chicago,
Mr. and Mrs. Martin A. Ryerson Collection

Onions, 1881
Oil on canvas, 39.1 x 60.6 cm (15½ x 23⅞ in.)
Williamstown, Massachusetts, The Clark

an old stable on the ground floor, of an eighteenth-century building at 12 Rue Cortot in Montmartre. In the charming but neglected garden behind the house, Renoir painted the portraits of Henriette Henriot, Nini Lopez (known as "Fish-face") and Claude Monet working in the open air. The money also enabled him to work on projects dear to his heart, some of which were to be very important, such as *The Swing* (p. 60), *Nude in the Sunlight* (p. 121) and the famous *Moulin de la Galette* (pp. 114/115) which he later claimed had taken him to the "very limits of Impressionism". These three paintings, which are closely related to each other in terms of the alternate lighting of areas of shade and patches of sunlight formed by light filtering through the trees, form a sort of triptych in the Musée d'Orsay in Paris. They are the crowning glory of the Impressionists' research into the effects of light.

The Moulin de la Galette (p. 116) was the local dance-hall at which the young people of Montmartre gathered on Sunday evenings. Renoir loved the lively, unpretentious atmosphere here as he had done at La Grenouillère. He recorded this local dive for posterity and so made it the symbol of the happy-go-lucky life of the period. He recruited his models among his male friends and their female companions who were milliners, dressmakers or florists. He would often take the canvas from his garden to the Moulin in order to work on the spot. But *The Garden in the Rue Cortot, Montmartre* (p. 118), which he also put on canvas, remained his favourite spot for painting and it is here that he devised and executed *The Swing* as well as *Nude in the Sunlight*. The effects of sunlight and shade are a great Impressionist theme and Renoir's triptych is a major

Portrait of Alfred Bérard with His Dog, 1881
Oil on canvas, 65.2 x 51.1 cm (25¾ x 20⅛ in.)
Philadelphia Museum of Art,
The Mr. and Mrs. Carroll S. Tyson, Jr., Collection

achievement in this area. A confirmed individualist, he does not approach the theme in the same way as his friends but with his own skills and techniques: rather than using the detached brushstrokes so dear to his friend Monet, he makes the strokes melt into each other, a technique which improved from painting to painting. In order to obtain the shimmering effect that links the figures to each other in a halo of pale or dark splashes of colour, he would use a criss-cross strike, in which successive layers of paint were superimposed, which was faithful to the blocks of colour and expressed the luminous atmosphere in which the figures were bathed. The overall harmony of *Le Moulin de la Galette* is bluish, as is that of *The Swing*, which looks like an enlarged detail from the *Moulin*. The *Nude in the Sunlight*, however, looks more like a bather who is sheltering from the sun, and the colour scheme and the texture of this nude alike suggest the delicate shades of shells. The pearly glow and lustrous shapes are a major feature of the painting in which the rounded forms echo one another. This painting is another example of Renoir breaking the Impressionists' first rule of painting outdoors, since *Nude in the Sunlight* was painted entirely in studio lighting. Renoir used traditional techniques but with a masterful freedom that makes this nude comparable to those he would paint twenty years later. Only an unpleasant fool such as Albert Wolff, the critic of *Le Figaro*, could possibly see in this painting "a pile of flesh in the process of decomposition".

The whole of Renoir's efforts in the last years of his Impressionist phase were dedicated to light. *The Bower*, also called *In the Garden* (*Under the Trees at the Moulin de la*

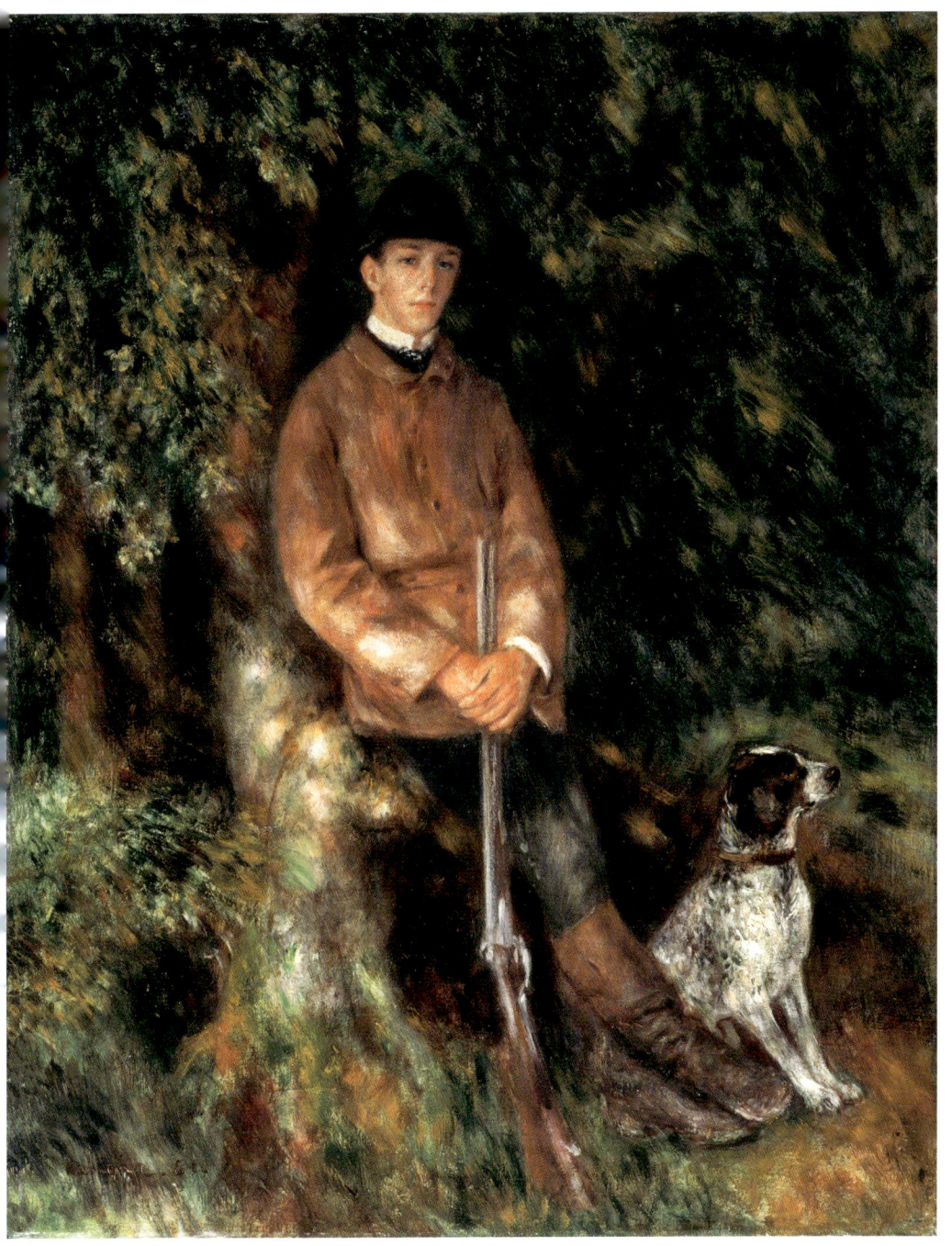

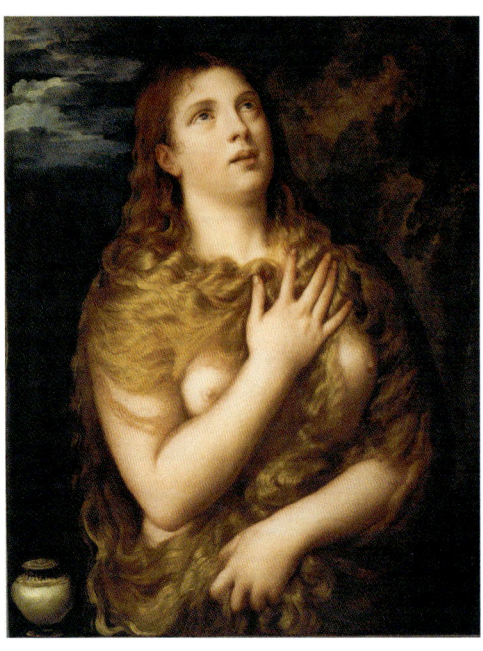

Titian (c. 1488–1576)
The Penitent Magdalene, c. 1530–1535
Oil on canvas, 85.8 x 69.5 cm (33⅞ x 27⅜ in.)
Florenz, Palazzo Pitti, Galleria Palatina

Nude, c. 1880
Oil on canvas,
81.4 x 64.9 cm (32 x 25⅝ in.)
Paris, Musée Rodin

Galette; (p. 117), *The Lovers* (c. 1875), *Young Man and Young Woman* (c. 1876), *Gypsy Girl* (p. 144) and *Madame Renoir with a Dog* (1880) are all treated in the same way as the triptych. Renoir confers homogeneity on the faces in the half-indistinct background in which he envelops them, but his manner is more fluid than that of the Impressionists who, with their dabs of colour, would have dissolved them completely in light. He too almost does so, however, and this posed a problem that had been worrying him for a long time. He did not mind using this effect in landscapes, which he did not consider to be true subjects. He took sheer pleasure in melting the brilliant light of a beautiful day into a huge bouquet of undergrowth sprinkled with a few umbelliferous plants, adding a few poppies for their splashes of red, as in *Country Footpath in the Summer* (p. 138), which could equally have been done by Monet, or in *Picking Flowers* (pp. 122/123). He gave free rein to Impressionism *à la* Monet in these landscapes where there were no houses, no trees, hardly any sky and the figures were barely visible. But he was dissatisfied by the illusionist effects of colours that come to seem unreal in the play of luminous vibration. He was sorry to have lost the magnificent Anna, his model for *Nude in the Sunlight*, who had also posed for *The Garden in the Rue Cortot, Montmartre* (p. 118), in which she is devoured by anthropophagous foliage. He began to see that the Impressionists were playing a dangerous game, and that light, by dissolving shape and tone, ends by draining things of their substance. It leads painting down a blind alley. Landscapes did not interest Renoir as much as interiors. The human form, which was most important to him, needed to be saved.

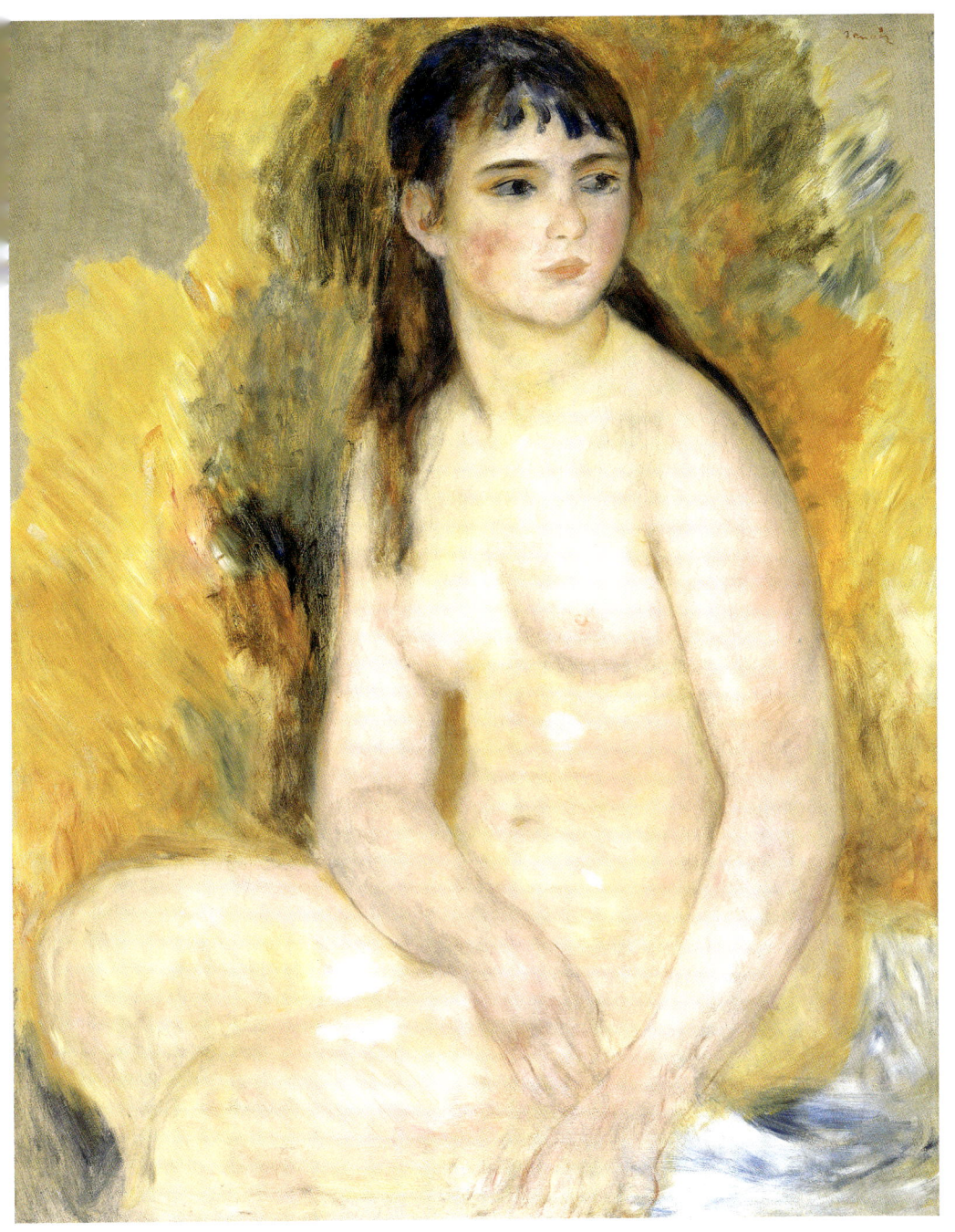

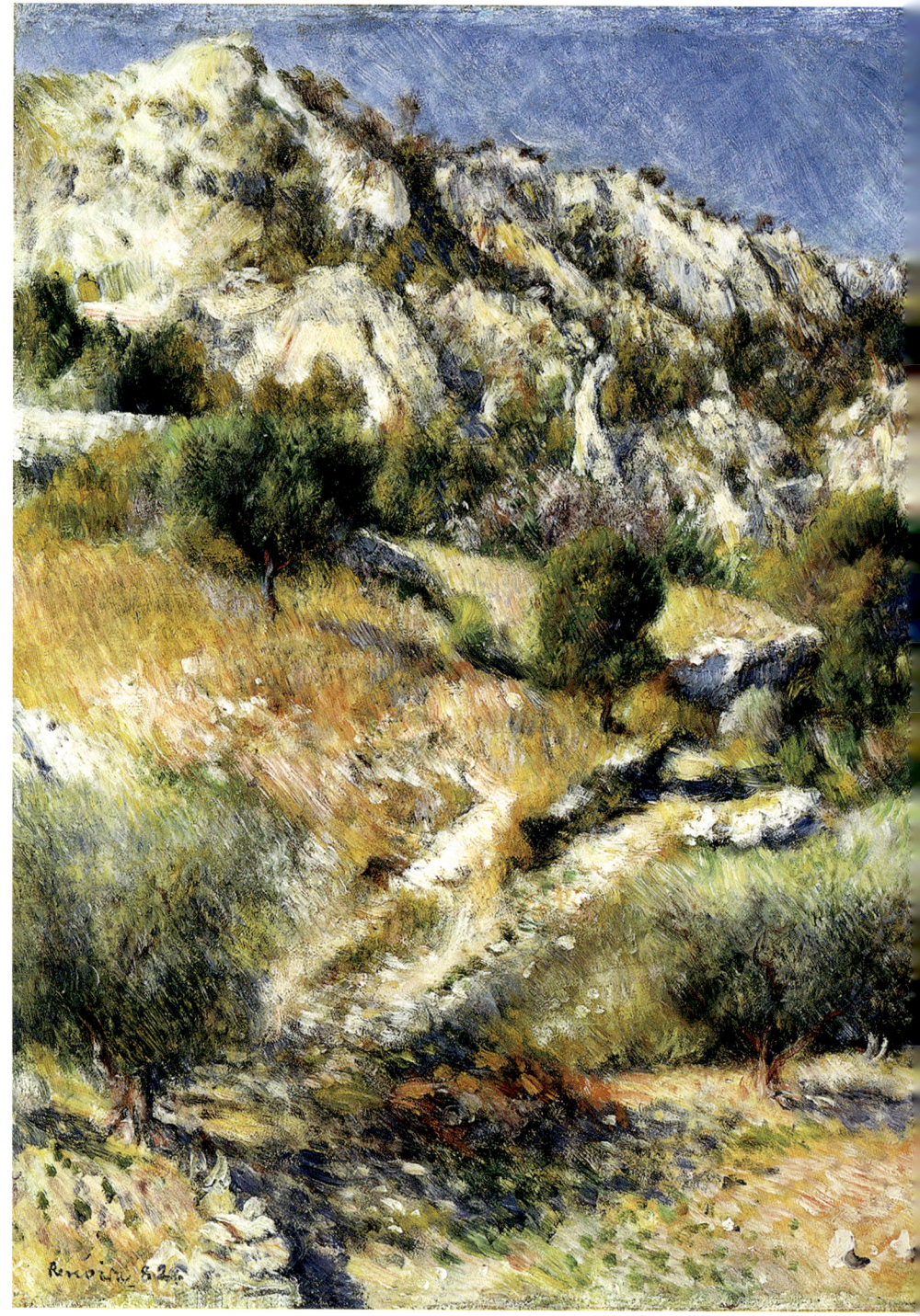

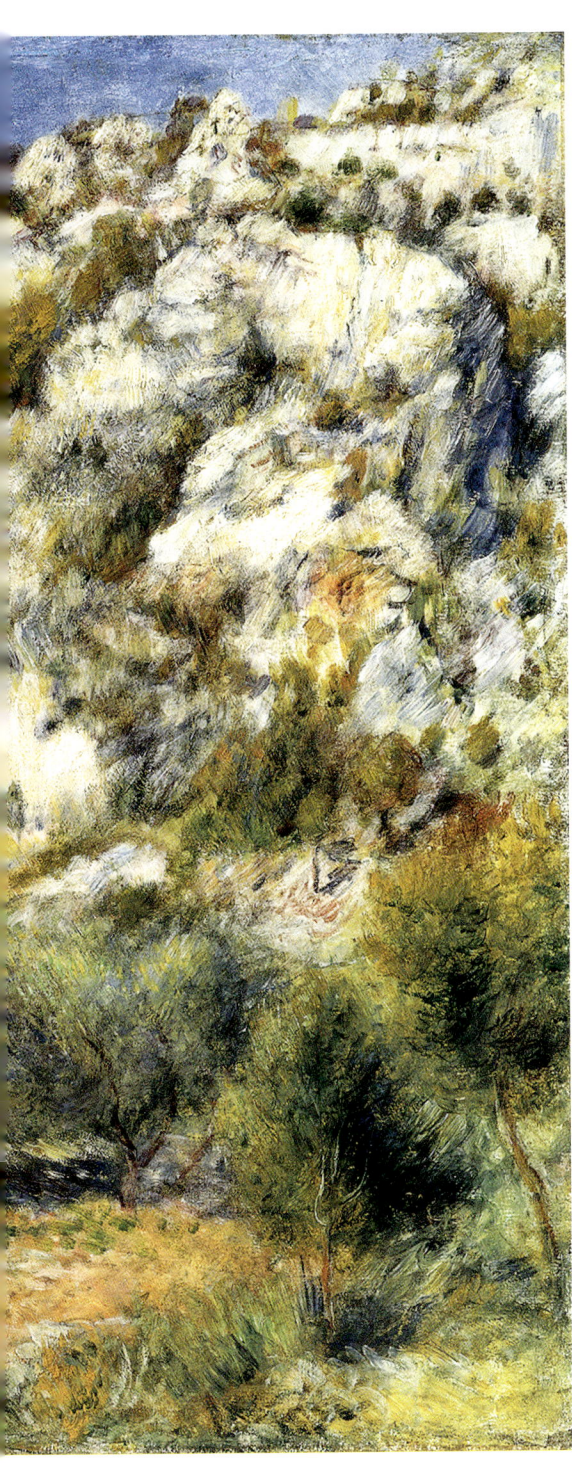

Rocky Crags at L'Estaque, 1882
Oil on canvas, 66.4 x 81 cm (26¼ x 32 in.)
Boston, Museum of Fine Arts,
Juliana Cheney Edwards Collection

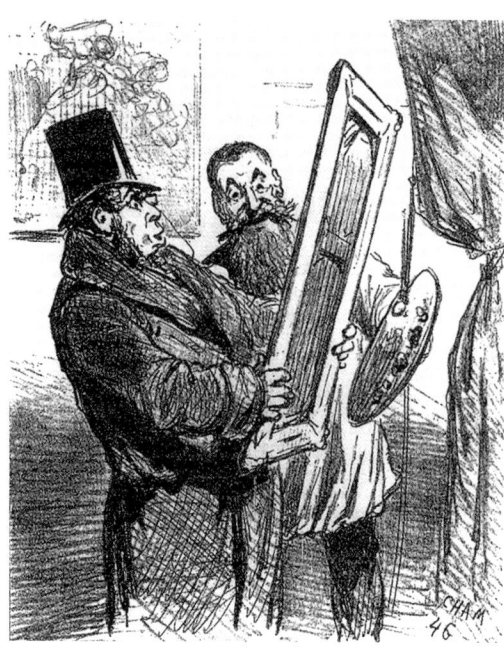

Caricature by Cham in the magazine
Le Charivari, Third Impressionist exhibition
in 1877: "But are all of these corpses? Yes,
unfortunately I can't manage to convey
the smell."

Bay of Naples, Evening, 1881
Oil on canvas,
57.9 x 80.8 cm (22⅞ x 31⅞ in.)
Williamstown, Massachusetts,
The Clark

For Pierre Cabanne, "Renoir above all expressed the idea that painting needed to be less subject to the variations of the moment and less aggressive towards the taste of the public." He was worried about the future and asked the statesman Gambetta for a post as curator of a provincial museum. Yet 1875 was to prove his *annus mirabilis*. Charged with dissolving the Impressionists' joint stock company, which had liabilities of 3,713 francs but only 277 francs in the bank, he organised another sale on 24 March at the Hôtel Drouot. The collection included twenty Monets, twenty-one Sisleys, twelve Berthe Morisots and twenty Renoirs. The sale was a disaster, bringing in only 1,1491 francs, an average of 160 francs per painting. But at the sale he met Chocquet, which was a start, and Charpentier, which was even better. The great-nephew of Charpentier, Michel Robida, tells how his great-uncle happened to be at the auction house and bought a Renoir painting, *The Fisherman* (pp. 98/99), for 180 francs. He wanted to meet the painter and invited him to visit him to his house. The Charpentiers had one of the most brilliant salons in Paris at their home in the Rue de Grenelle. Gambetta and Clémenceau were favoured political visitors, Zola, Flaubert, Goncourt, Daudet, Barbey d'Aurevilly and Marcel Proust were literary guests, the Duchesse de Rohan, the Duchesse d'Uzès, Countess Potocka, Robert de Montesquiou were high-society friends and Sarah Bernhardt, Jeanne Samary and Yvette Guilbert were actresses and frequent guests. Among the painters, there were the academics such as Henner, Bonnat and Carolus-Duran, who now mingled with the Charpentiers' new friends, the Impressionists, Manet, Monet, Sisley, Pissarro and Cézanne.

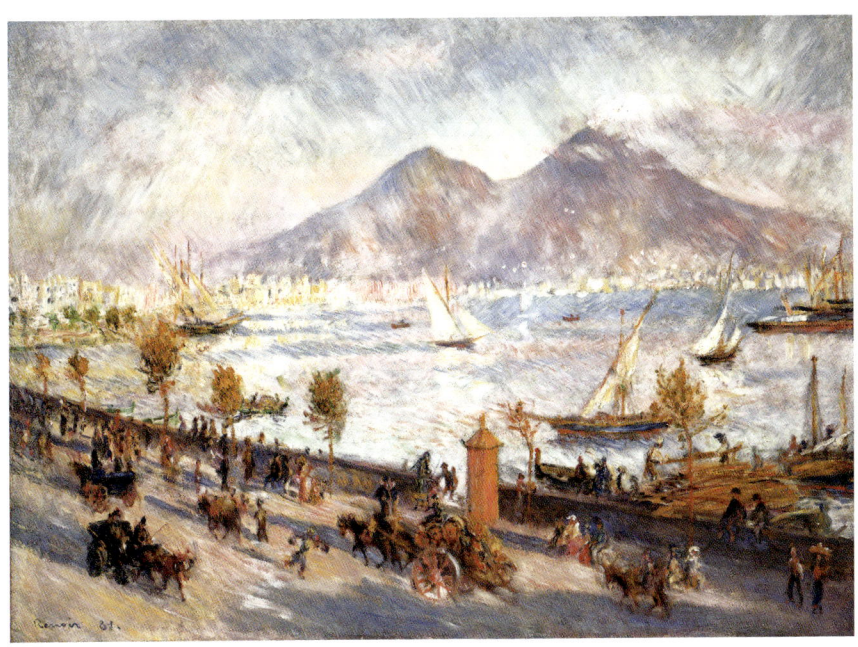

Renoir had found his hunting ground. The wealthy Charpentiers immediately commissioned him to paint portraits of their children, Paul and Georgette (pp. 390, 391). Madame Charpentier, who was keen to help, sometimes asked him to design their menus, decorate a frame, or produce a pastel portrait of her daughter Jane. Then one day she commissioned a large painting entitled *Madame Charpentier and Her Children* (pp. 388/389). The painting was hung at the 1879 Salon; it was Renoir's first great success. In this the Charpentiers, who had lots of useful contacts, no doubt played a large part. The wonderful portrait of *Jeanne Samary* (p. 130), whom Renoir had met at the Charpentiers, was poorly hung, high up on the dado rail, in a corner. Madame Charpentier's portrait was hung in the place of honour. In view of the social standing of his models, success was certain. The jury at last came out in favour of Renoir. After all his efforts, he thoroughly deserved it.

This stroke of good fortune led to many more. A whole series of commissions followed to paint the portraits of friends of the Charpentiers, beginning with that of *Madame Alphonse Daudet* (p. 200), whom Renoir painted at Champrosay during a three-week stay at the home of the famous author of *Letters from My Windmill*. He was also invited to Wargemont, near Dieppe, where he stayed in a small château belonging to a diplomat by the name of Bérard, who commissioned murals, a landscape featuring *The Rose Garden at Wargemont* (p. 139), numerous portraits of his children (pp. 396, 399, 400/401, 403, 404), and even a painting of his cats playing beside a planter containing flowers in the corridor of his château entitled *Flowers and Cats* (p. 170). Ridiculed

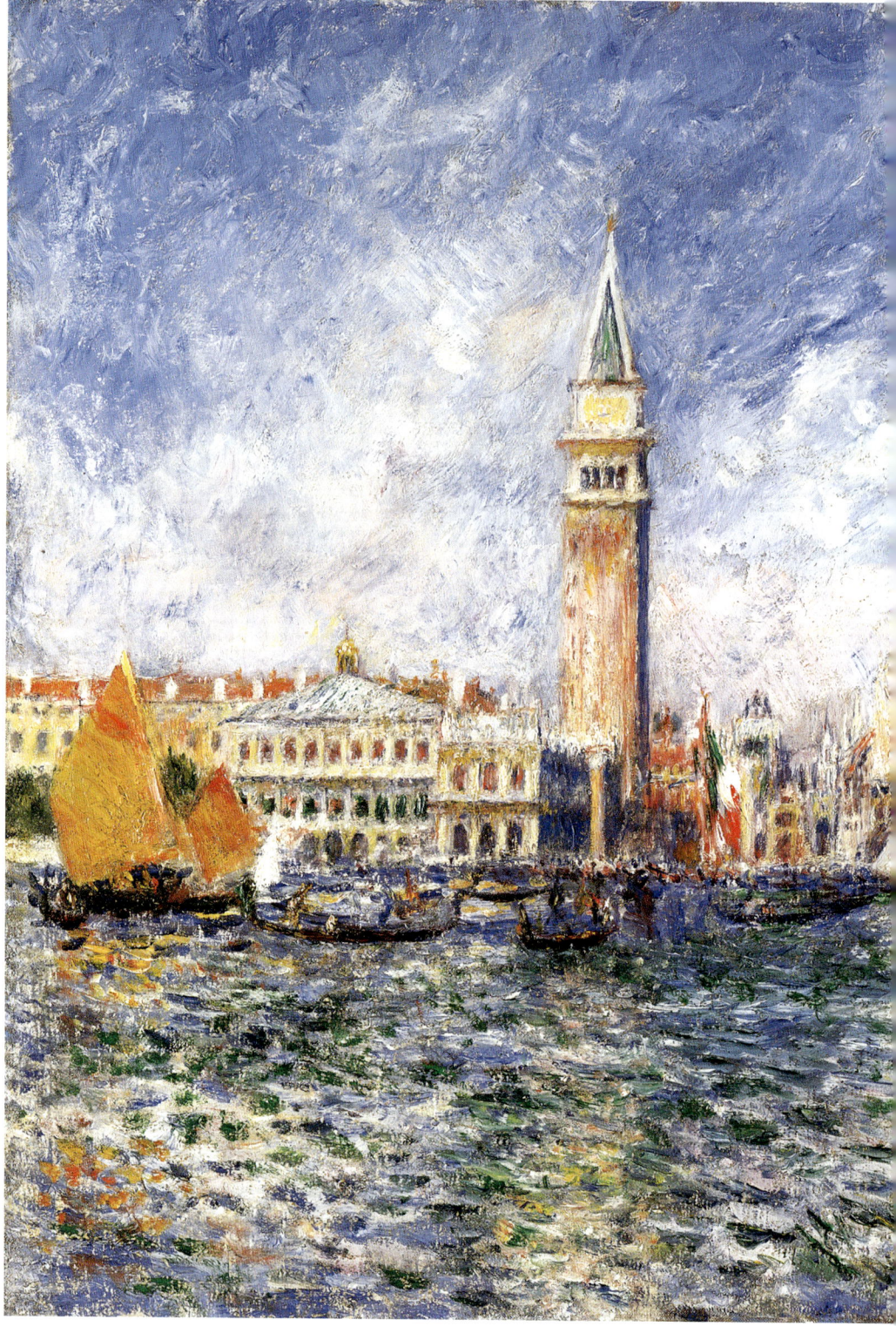

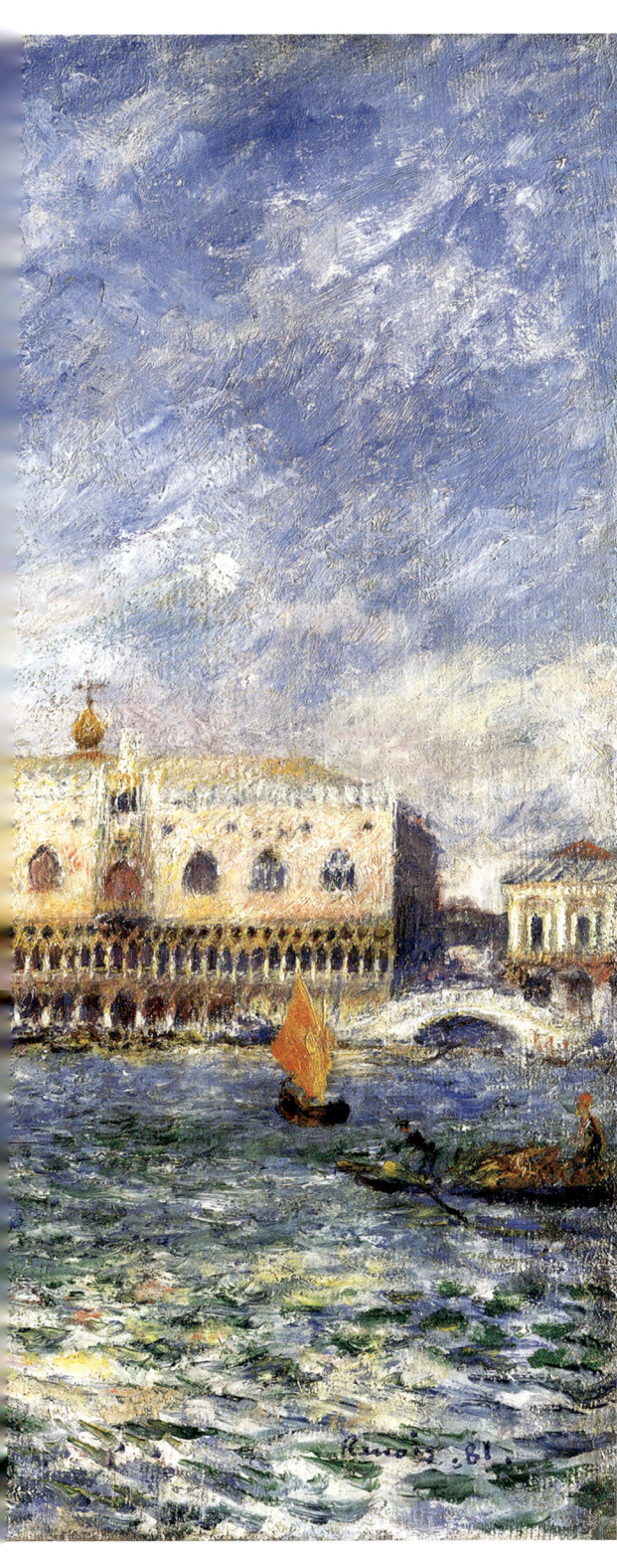

Venice, The Doge's Palace, 1881
Oil on canvas,
54.5 x 65.7 cm (21½ x 26 in.)
Williamstown, Massachusetts,
The Clark

**The Piazza San Marco,
Venice**, 1881
Oil on canvas,
65.4 x 81.3 cm (25¾ x 32 in.)
The Minneapolis
Institute of Arts,
The John R. Van Derlip Fund

PAGE 186
Claude Monet
Grand Canal, Venice, 1908
Oil on canvas,
73.7 x 92.4 cm (29 x 36½ in.)
Boston, Museum of
Fine Arts

PAGE 187
Claude Monet
Impression, Sunrise, 1872
Oil on canvas,
48 x 63 cm (19 x 24⅞ in.)
Paris, Musée
Marmottan Monet

PAGES 188/189
Venice – Fog, 1881
Oil on canvas,
45.5 x 60.5 cm (18 x 23⅞ in.)
Washington, D.C.,
The Kreeger Museum

184

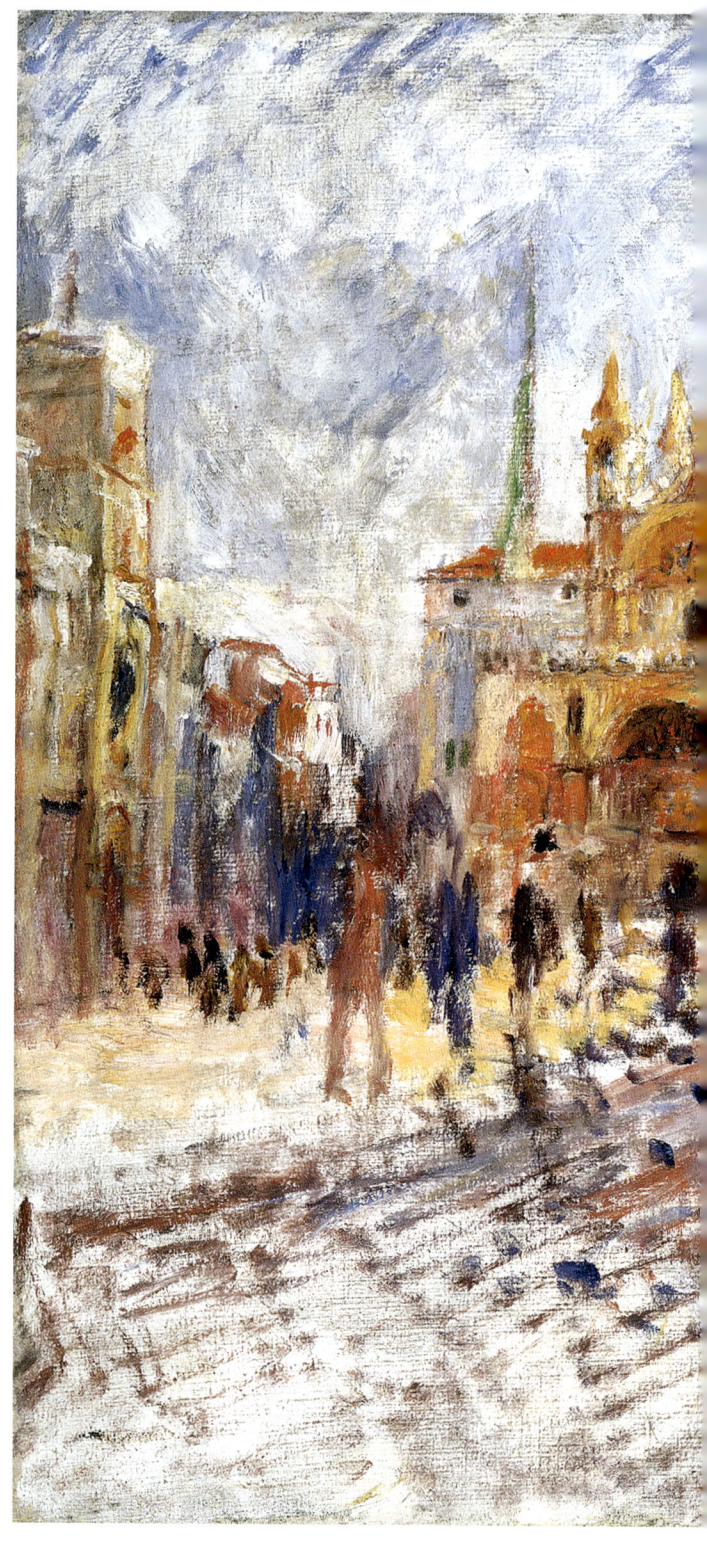

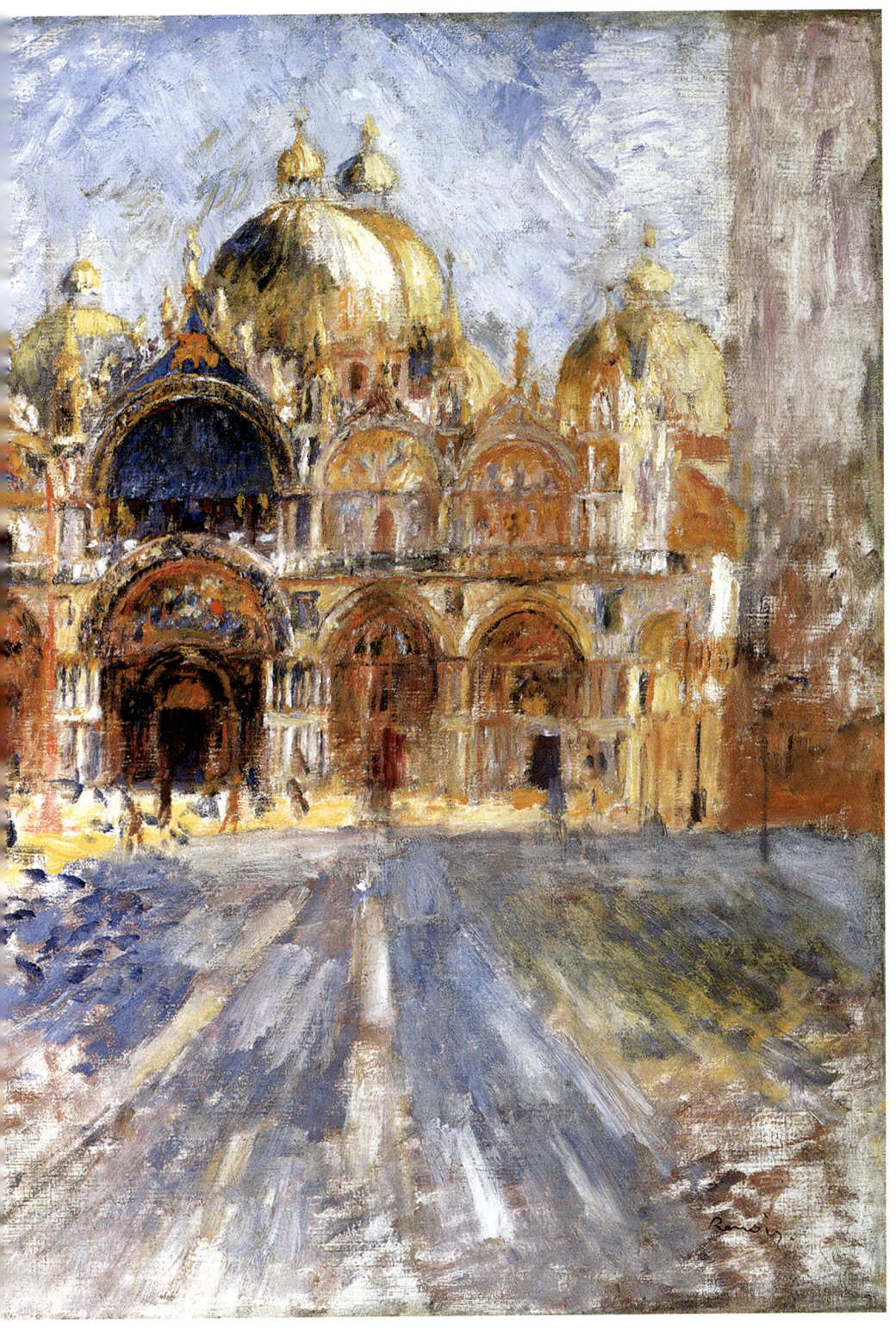

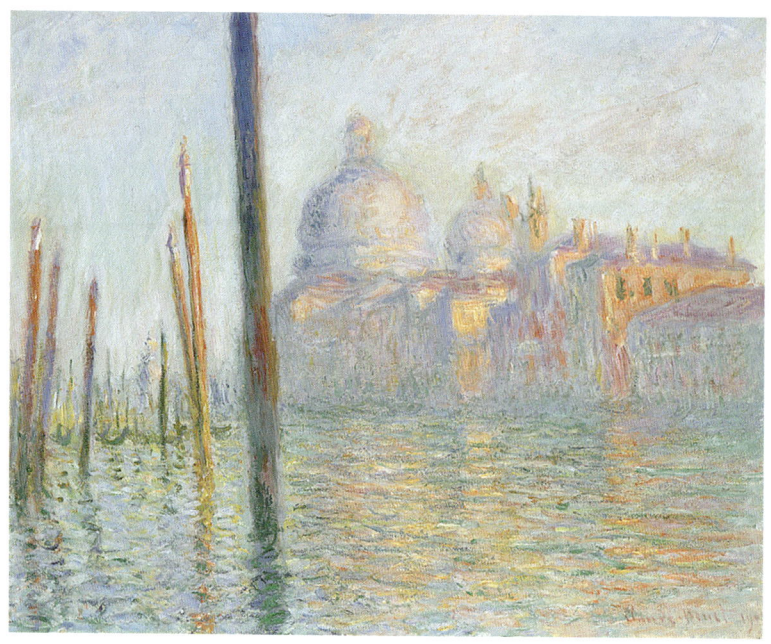

and insulted when he had participated in the Impressionist exhibitions, Renoir was now praised to the skies at the Salon for paintings that would have had scorn poured on them elsewhere. The art-critic Bertall congratulated him in *L'Artist* "for having broken with the nihilists of the Avenue de l'Opéra". Another journalist, Burty, remarked with relief in *La République Française*: "In my opinion he took too long to make the necessary concessions to firmness of rendering". Renoir's friends knew too well how hard their fight was to hold him guilty for his so-called repudiation. "Renoir is having great success at the Salon", Pissarro wrote to another friend of the group, the pastry chef Eugène Murer. I think that he is making a name for himself. Thank goodness for that! Poverty is very, very hard." Charles Bigot wrote ironically in *La Revue bleue* (The Blue Review): "Renoir did not need to be asked twice before he converted."

When he was not invited to dine by Murer or Charpentier, Renoir took his meals at "Camille's place", a dairy in the Rue Saint-Georges. Here in February 1880 he met a young milliner from Essoyes, in the Aube district. Her name was Aline Charigot, and she was twenty years old. He was getting on for forty. She lived with her mother who had worked as a dressmaker since her husband had left her and gone to the United States. Renoir's studio was close by, and the young Aline often came to pose for him. She knew nothing about painting but was fascinated by Renoir. He would only say of her "she makes you want to scratch her nape". On Sundays, the couple would visit Chatou or La Grenouillère. "She would tread on the grass without even damaging it", he remembered. It was during such an outing that he painted her sitting in the middle

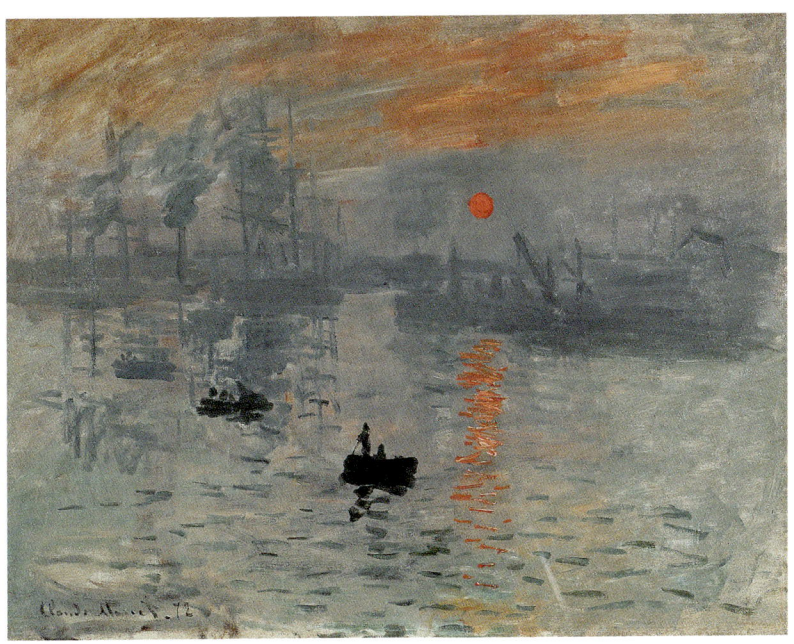

of a field with her dog (*Madame Renoir with a Dog*). In the summer of 1880, Renoir stayed at the inn of Père Fournaise at Chatou several times. It was a popular rendezvous with boating-parties and their friends. A year previously he had painted a delightful portrait of the daughter of the lemonade-seller, *Alphonsine Fournaise* (p. 159), sitting on the terrace of the family restaurant. This time he wanted to produce in the same context a large-scale work, which would equal and even surpass *Le Moulin de la Galette* (pp. 114/115). "I could not resist getting rid of any ornamental backdrops and concentrate instead on producing the painting of rowers that I had long wanted to do", wrote the painter to his friend Paul Bérard. "I am getting on now and do not want to put off this little celebration which I might not be able to manage later on. From time to time, one must attempt things that are beyond one's capacities".

According to Jean Renoir, *The Luncheon of the Boating Party* (pp. 156/157) "is the crowning glory of a long series of paintings, studies and drawings executed at La Grenouillère. The Fournaise family had become his friends. Madame and Mademoiselle Fournaise feature in several of the paintings. He also painted *Père Fournaise* (p. 154). They rarely presented Renoir with the bill. 'You have left us this landscape instead', they would say. My father insisted that his paintings were worthless. 'What does that matter. They are beautiful. And anyway, we need to put something on the wall to hide the damp patches'. My father would smile whenever he thought of those delightful innkeepers, and say to me, 'if only all art-lovers were like that!' He left them several paintings that later became valuable. The Fournaise family were not the only ones in the same situation. I could

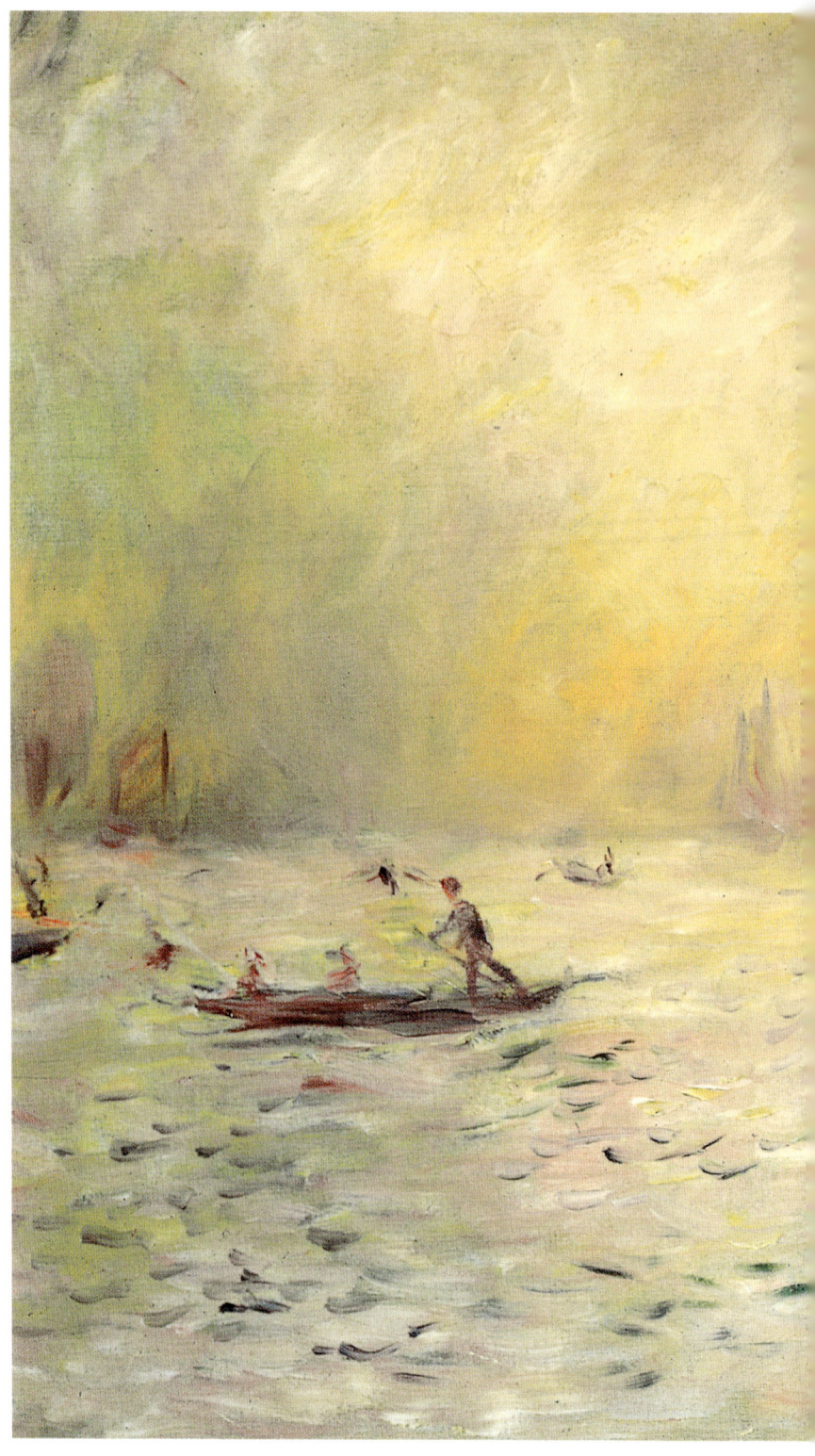

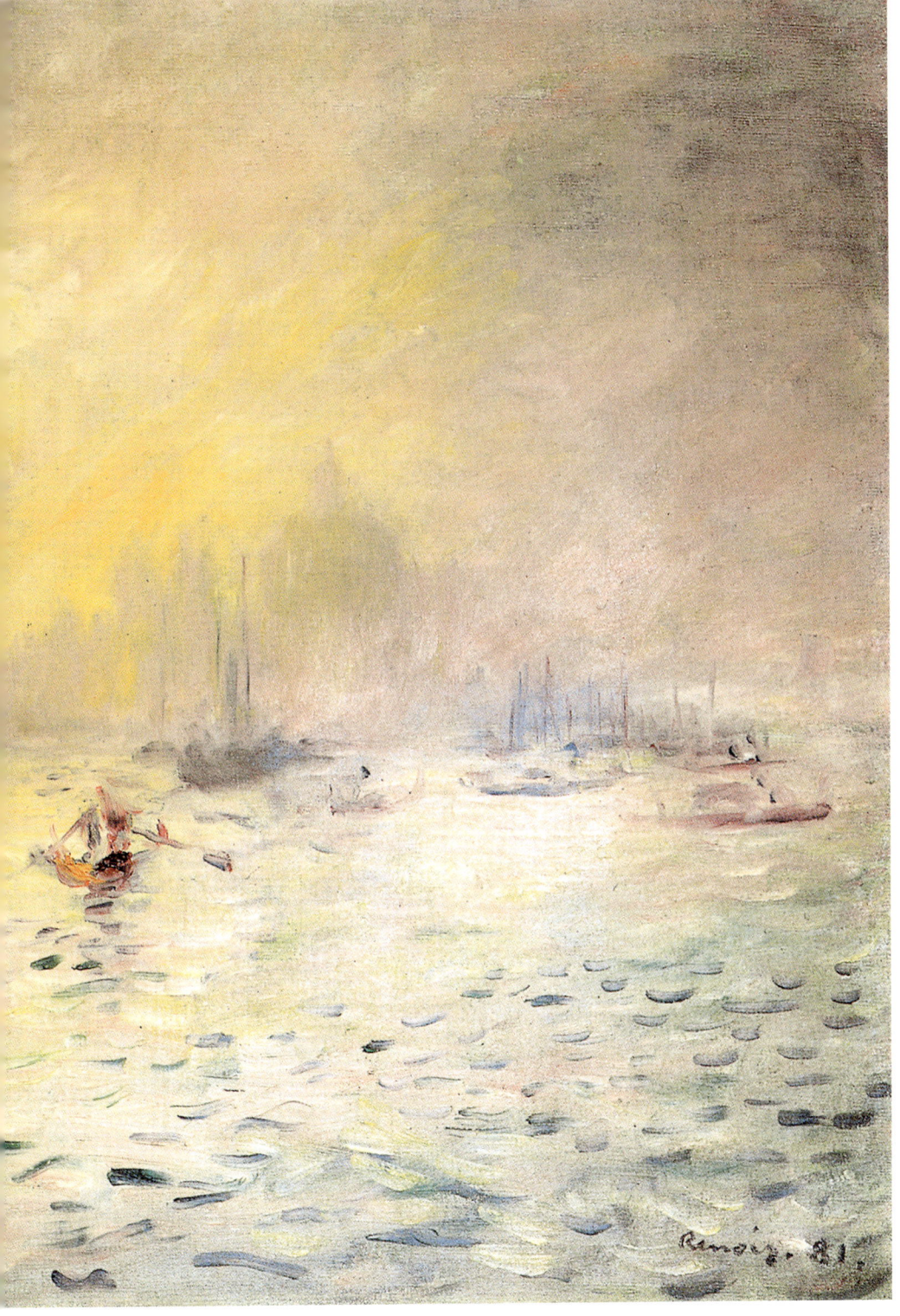

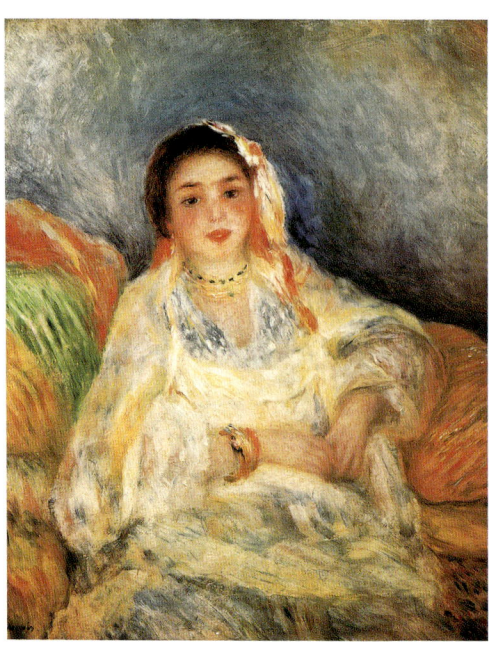

Algerian Woman Seated, 1881
Oil on canvas, 55 x 46 cm (21¾ x 18⅛ in.)
Private collection

Girl with a Fan, 1881
Oil on canvas,
65 x 50 cm (25⅝ x 19¾ in.)
Saint Petersburg,
Hermitage Museum

mention other large families who owned paintings that Renoir had left behind with them and which later got them out of a difficult financial situation, even ruin. 'I'm lucky', he used to say, 'I can do favours for friends and it costs me nothing!' When he stayed at the Fournaise inn my father sometimes used to meet Maupassant. The two men liked each other but admitted they had nothing in common. Renoir would say of the writer, 'he sees everything in black!' And Guy de Maupassant would say of the painter, 'he sees everything through rose-tinted spectacles!' They did agreed about one thing though. 'Maupassant is quite mad!' Renoir would say; 'Renoir is mad!' was Maupassant's conclusion. It took Renoir several years to bring the project to fruition. He was working on several paintings at a time, and was making sketches of the subject which he found unsatisfactory. In the summer of 1881, he made up his mind. 'I'm off for lunch', he said. I am not sure who all the models were. Lhote is definitely there at the back, wearing a top hat. Lestringuez is leaning over a friend who may be Rivière. The young women leaning her elbows on the balustrade is Alphonsine Fournaise, 'la belle Alphonsine', as the customers at her parents' restaurant used to call her. She died in 1935 at the age of ninety-two, completely ruined because she had invested all her money in Russian bonds. The woman drinking is little Henriot, the woman looking at Lestringuez must be Ellen André. The woman in the foreground stroking a little dog is my mother."

The atmosphere of a restaurant on the banks of the Seine replaces that of a dance-hall in Montmartre. Renoir concentrated here on a particular effect of the light filtered by the canvas of the awning and produced a rich evocation of a sunny summer's day on

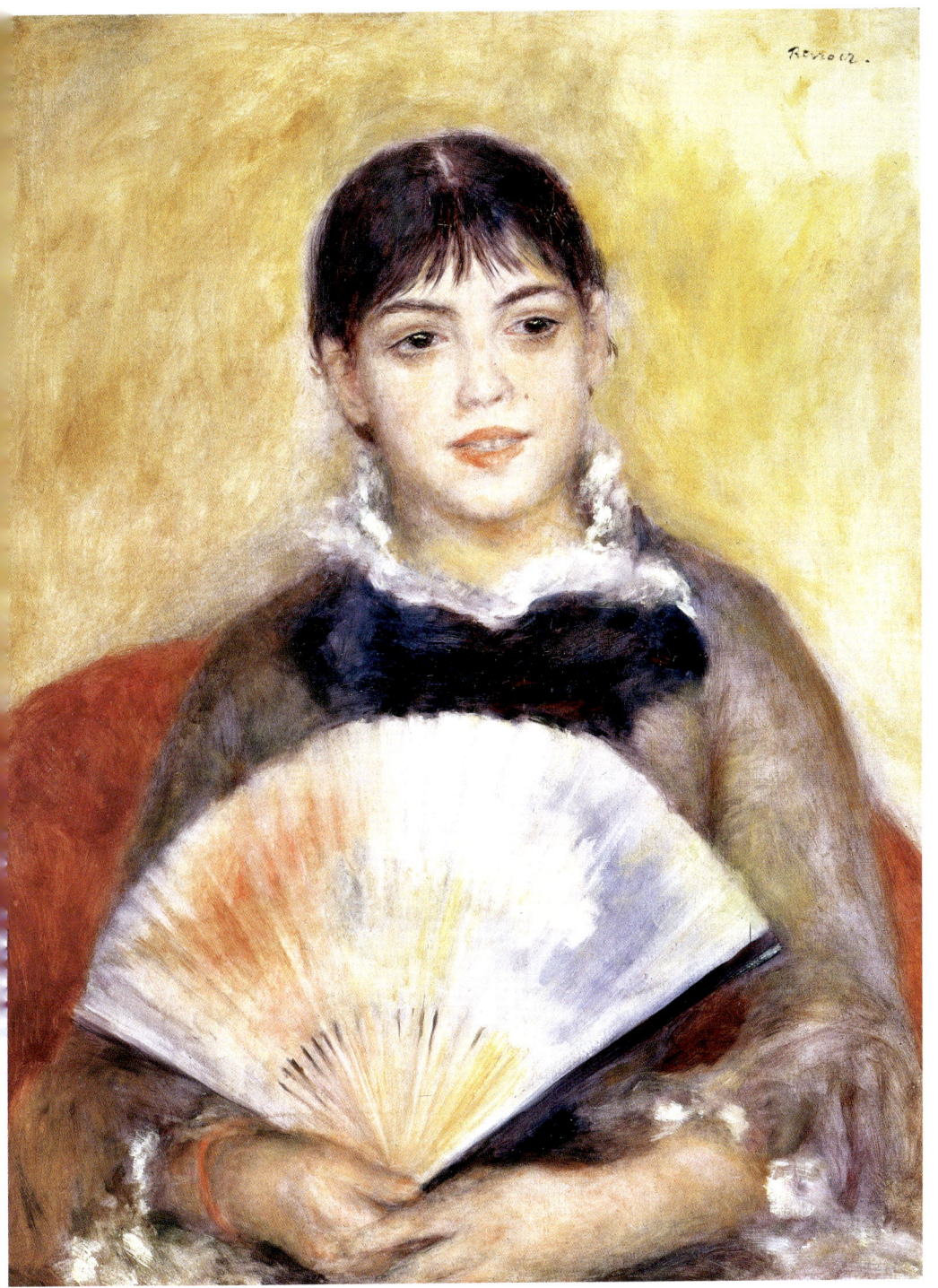

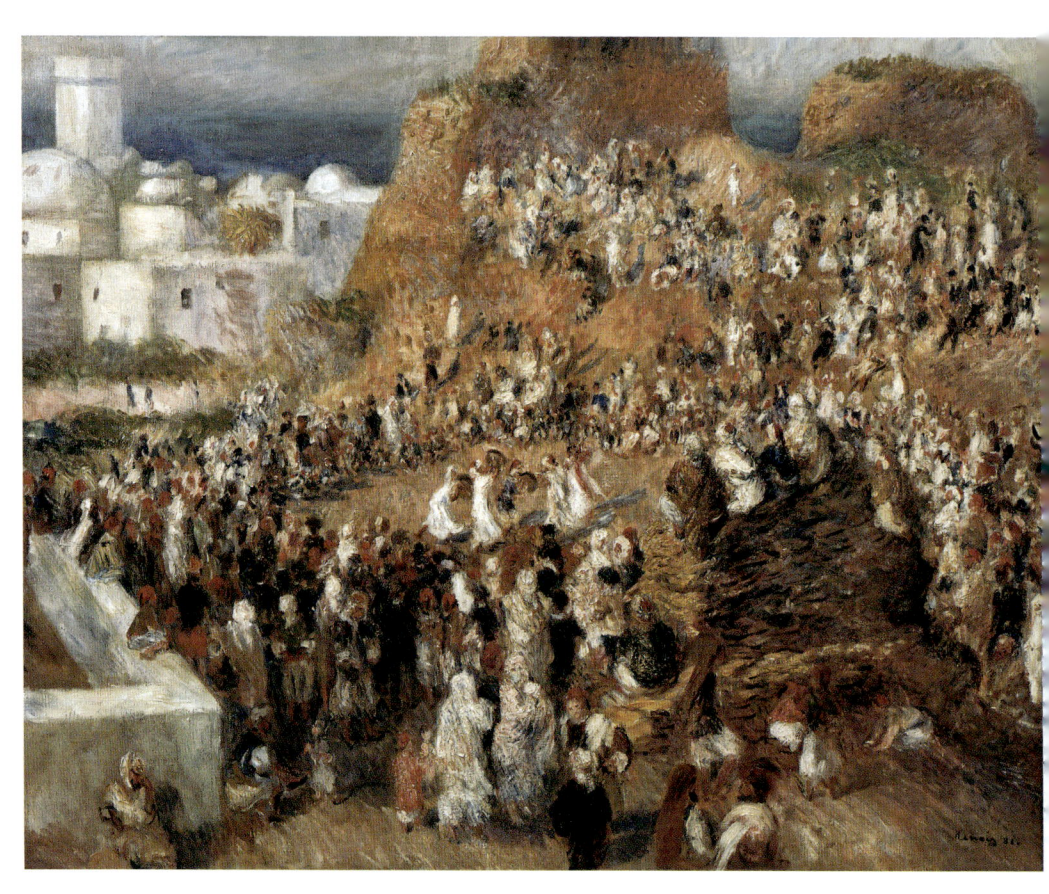

The Mosque (Arab Festival), 1881
Oil on canvas,
73.5 x 92.5 cm (29 x 36½ in.)
Paris, Musée d'Orsay

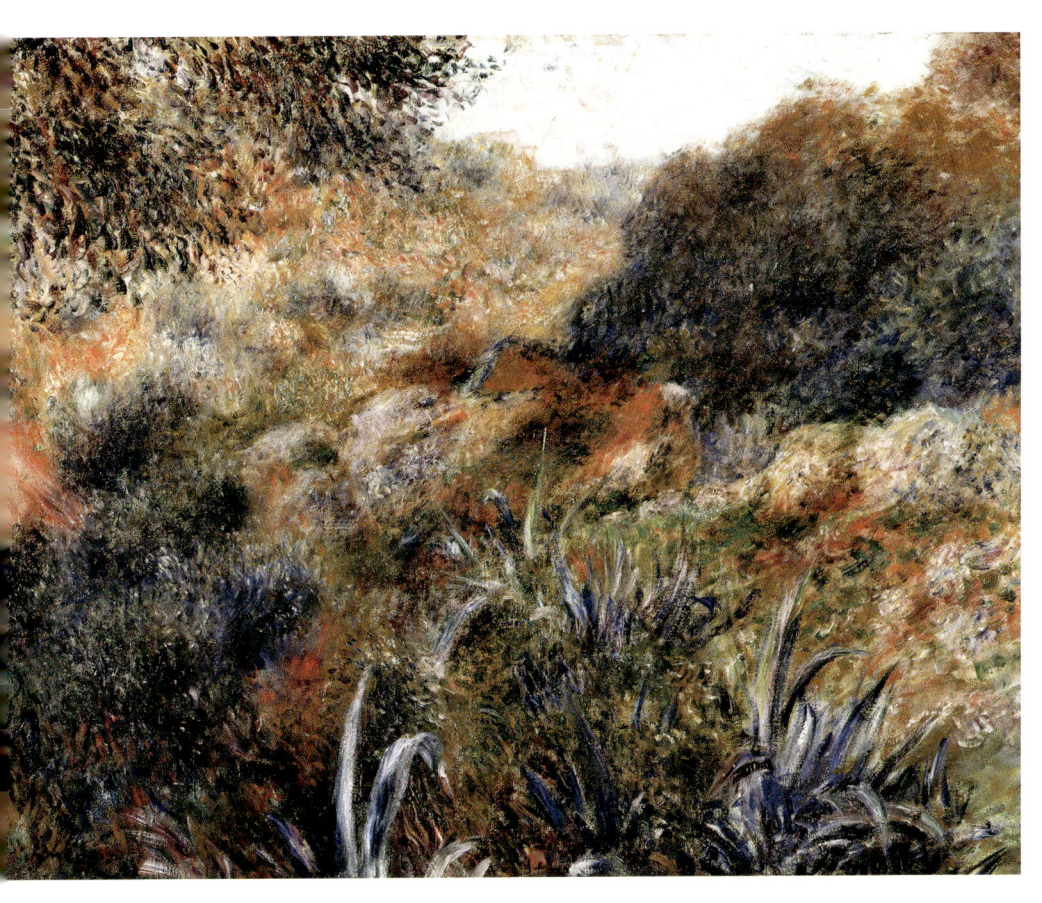

Algerian Landscape:
Wild Woman Ravine, 1881
Oil on canvas, 65 x 81.5 cm (25⅝ x 32 in.)
Paris, Musée d'Orsay

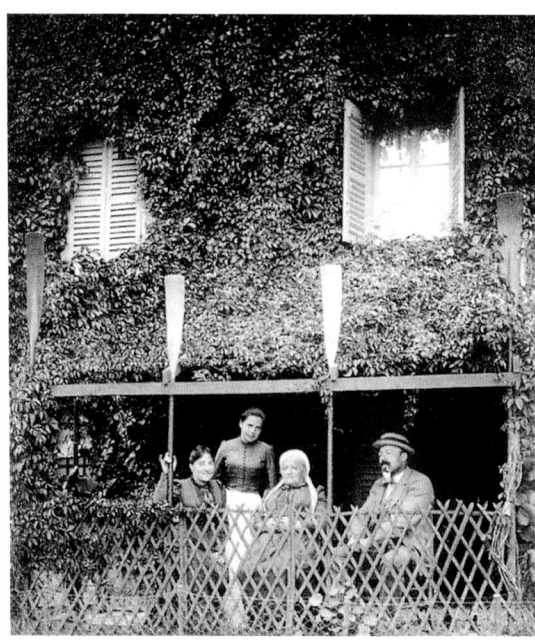

the banks of the Seine. He had never before succeeded so perfectly in painting human figures that are clearly individuals with their particular gestures and poses. The picture is a veritable portrait gallery. It contains certain moments of bravura such as the still life of the meal, Aline Charigot's (1859–1915) face and her dog, and the movement of the woman raising a glass to her lips while the other, on the right, is gazing lovingly at her companion, the rower. Denis Rouart says of this painting that "the fruit and wine bottles on the white tablecloth have a richness and brilliance worthy of the best Flemish painters. But for all that they contribute to the airy shimmering effect, which is achieved by the play of light on the objects and the slightly blurred outlines, and which is typical of Renoir at his most subtle." This was Renoir's last and most brilliant image of all the things that he was shortly simultaneously to give up: bohemian living, his youth and, above all, Impressionism.

By the autumn of 1880, Renoir's financial worries had disappeared as if by magic. The artist's fame as a portraitist had spread far and wide. "I began a portrait this morning, I will begin another one this evening and then I will probably go on to a third one", he wrote to his patron, Madame Charpentier. Thanks to Paul Bérard, the diplomat, he had met a banker, Georges Grimpel, who immediately commissioned paintings of his son and two daughters. He also met a man called Cahen d'Anvers (1846–1903) who wanted him to paint his eldest daughter, Irène, with her fiery tresses (p. 407), as well as her two younger sisters, Aline and Elizabeth (p. 406). This drew criticism from Degas: "You have no character at all, Renoir! I simply cannot accept painting on commission.

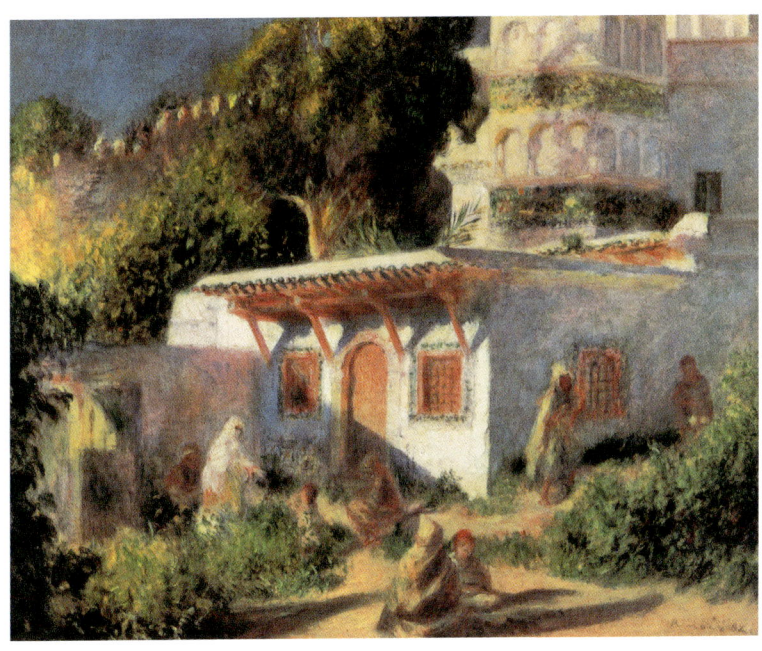

You're working for the money, aren't you?", he said. Michel Robida wanted to know if Renoir was going to marry Aline. Aline had invited Renoir to stay with her family in Essoyes, where he could work in peace. The thought of making a commitment of this sort made Renoir panic, and he went off to Algeria for six weeks in the spring of 1881 with his friend Cordey. He was tired of Paris and all his portrait commissions. He needed to "renew the way he saw things". Following in the footsteps of Delacroix, he discovered in North Africa, despite the lack of sunshine, "an extraordinary richness of nature". He painted several figures of native women (pp. 190, 196) and landscapes such as *Algerian Landscape: Wild Woman Ravine* (p. 193) and *The Mosque,* also called *Arab Festival* (p. 192). He went back to Algiers again in 1882, to recover from a bad attack of influenza that he had caught while painting out of doors with Cézanne. He painted young Arab women such as *Algerian Woman* as well as landscapes, *Mosque at Algiers* (p. 195) and *The Test Garden in Algiers.*

Between these two trips, he decided to go and seek inspiration in Italy. He was still suffering from an artistic and moral crisis of confidence. He visited Milan and Venice where he painted *Venice, The Doge's Palace* (pp. 182/183), *The Piazza San Marco, Venice* (pp. 184/185), and *Gondola in Venice* (1881) on the Grand Canal. Curiously he also painted a seascape *Venice – Fog* (pp. 188/189) in a sort of nostalgic homage to Monet's *Impression, Sunrise* (p. 216). From Venice he moved to Florence where he was amazed by *Virgin with a Chair* by Raphael in the Pitti Palace. In Rome he studied the frescoes of the Farnese and the treasures of the Vatican.

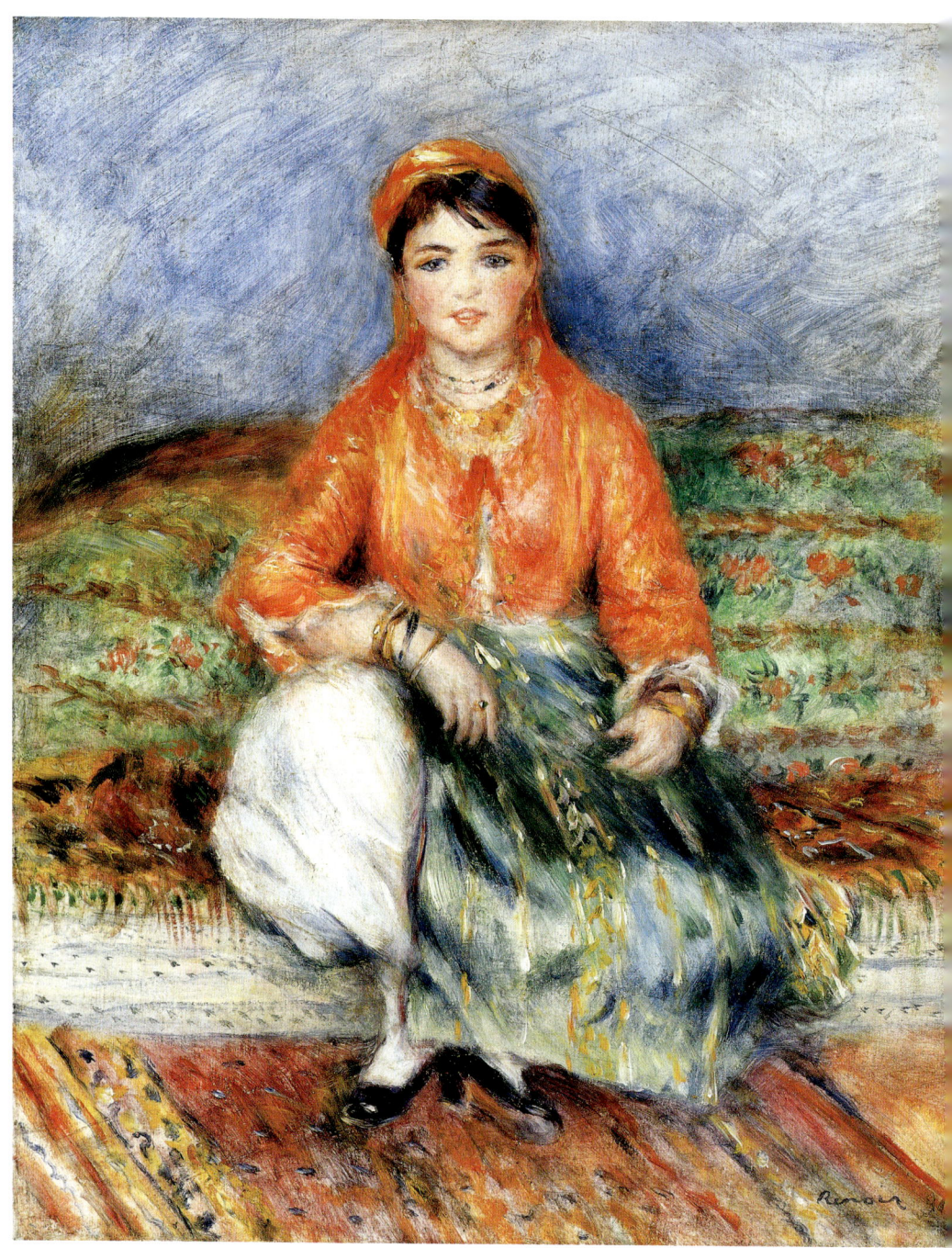

From the Trinacria inn in Naples, where he painted *Bay of Naples, Evening* (p. 181), which bears a strange resemblance to a Hiroshige print, he wrote a long letter on 21 November 1881 to Paul Durand-Ruel which clearly demonstrates his anxiety: "I am like a child at school faced with a blank page on which I am preparing to write when wham! It's got an ink-blot on it. At the age of forty I am still producing ink-blots. I went to see the Raphaels in Rome. They are very beautiful and I ought to have seen them earlier. Raphael is full of knowledge and wisdom: he was not trying to do impossible things as I am. But it is truly beautiful".

In December, Renoir visited Calabria, Pompei and Sorrento. His stay in Capri produced some nudes including a masterpiece, *Blonde Bather* (p. 338), which he painted from a fishing-boat in the bay in brilliant sunshine. On 12 January 1882 Renoir left Naples for Sicily to paint a portrait of Richard Wagner (1813–1883; p. 252), which a lawyer-friend and music-lover, Lascoux, had commissioned. After a rough crossing, he reached Palermo. Wagner, who lived in the Hôtel des Palmes, was in the process of putting the finishing touches to the score of *Parsifal* and thought that he could get rid of him by only according him a thirty-five minute interview. Renoir sketched a very striking portrait of the composer in the time allowed. "Ah!", cried Wagner, "I look like a Protestant priest".

On his return from Italy Renoir stopped near Marseilles to spend a few days at the Hôtel des Bains in L'Estaque. From there, he wrote to Durand-Ruel: "I am staying in L'Estaque, a little place like Asnières, but at the seaside. It is very beautiful and I am

Child with a Bird (Mademoiselle Fleury in Algerian Costume), 1882
Oil on canvas, 126.4 x 78.1 cm (49⅞ x 30¾ in.)
Williamstown, Massachusetts, The Clark

going to stay here for another fortnight. It would be a real pity to leave this lovely place without bringing back something and the weather is wonderful. It is spring but with gentle sunshine and no wind, which is rare in Marseilles. I met Cézanne here and we are going to work together." The two old friends painted two views of *Rocky Crags at L'Estaque* (pp. 178/179), which are of course very different from each other. Painting in the open air left Renoir suffering from a bad attack of influenza which soon degenerated into pneumonia. The mild Mediterranean climate helped him to recover quickly and soon he was back in Paris.

Aline, he learnt with delight, had been waiting for him patiently while he was away on his travels. The painter and the young woman decided to set up home together in about May 1882. With Aline deciding to spend it with him, life would never be the same again for Renoir. Nor would his painting.

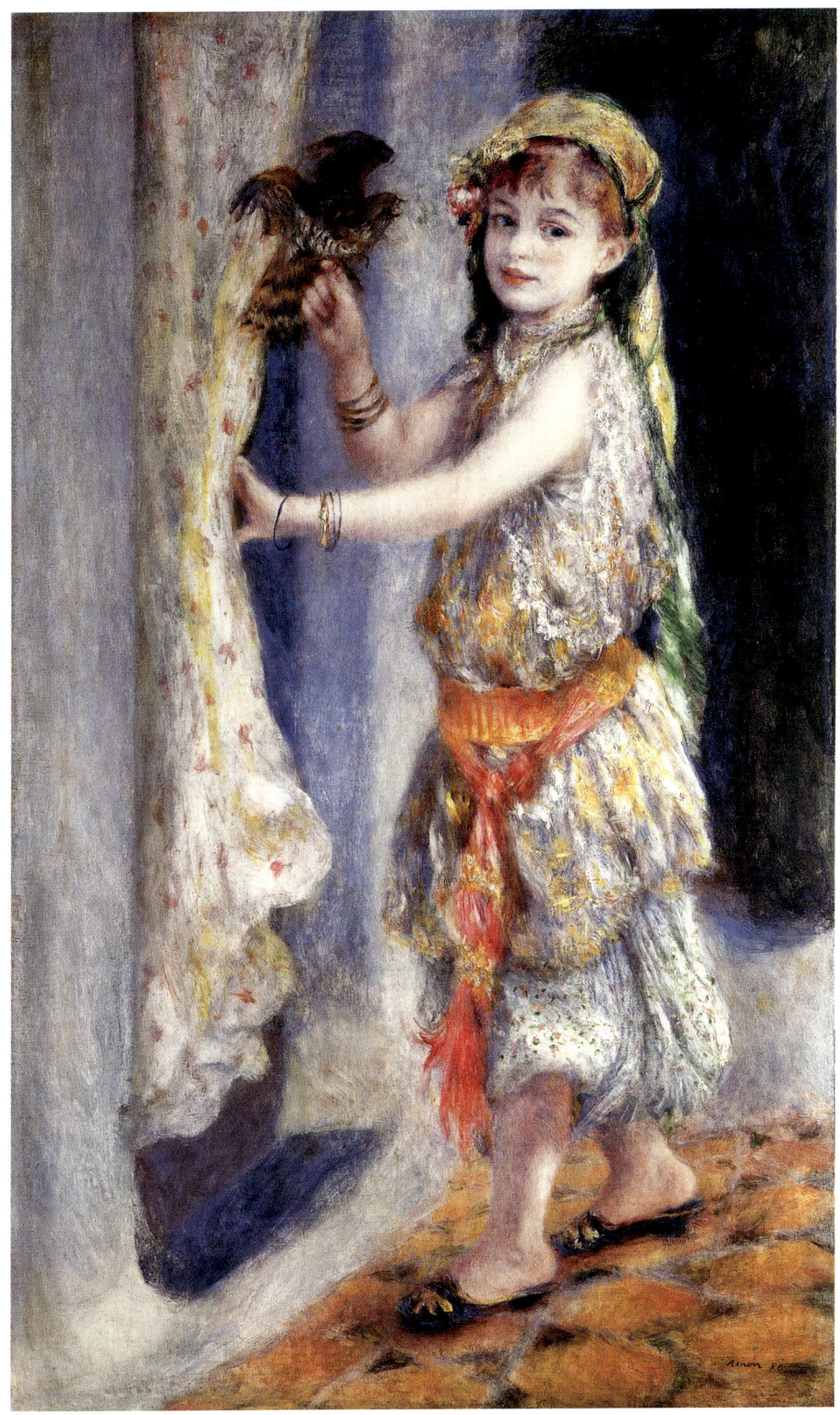

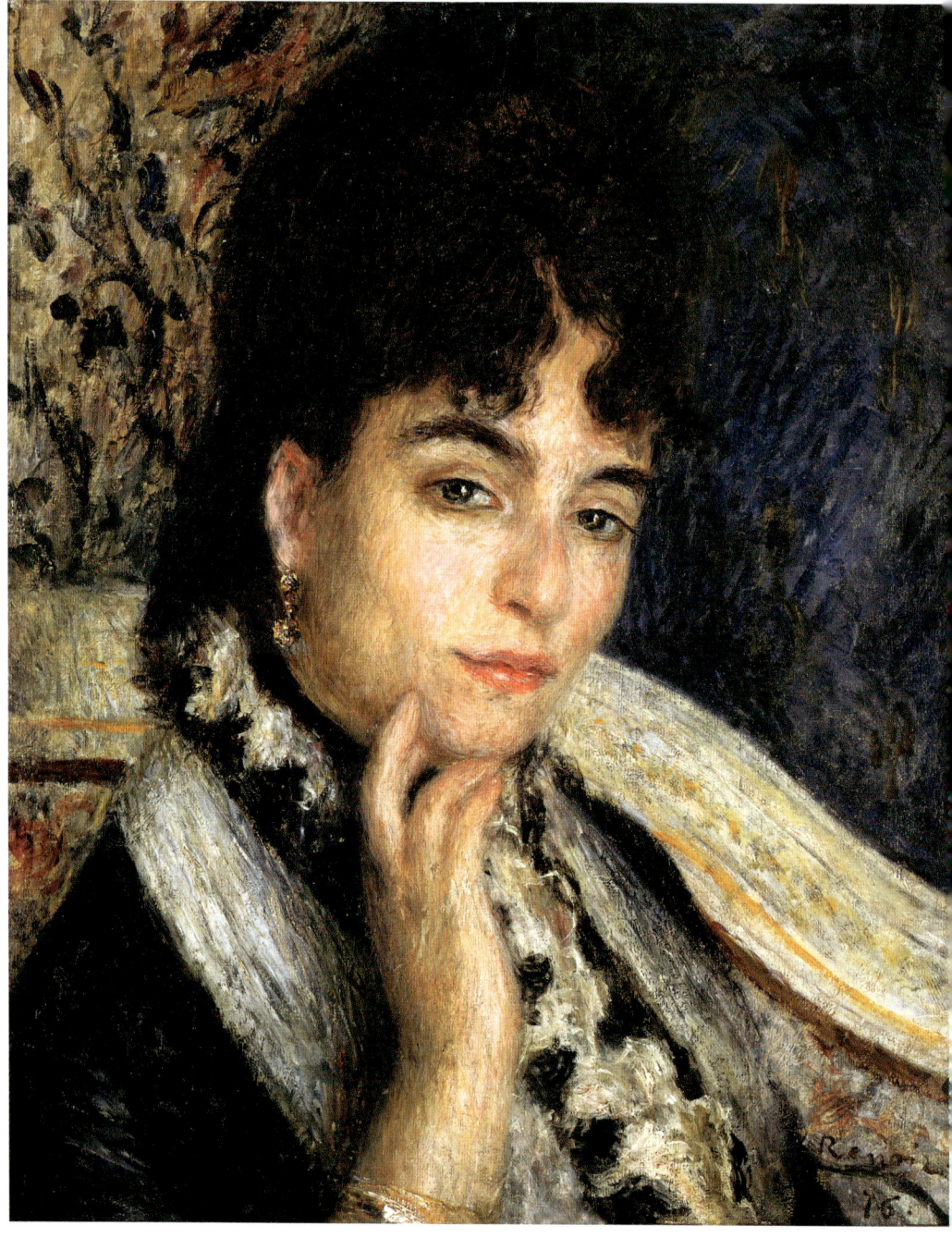

Madame Alphonse Daudet, 1876
Oil on canvas, 46.2 x 38 cm (18¼ x 15 in.)
Paris, Musée d'Orsay

The Portrait King
1864 –1885

Baudelaire hailed Renoir as the painter who would draw out the epic quality of modern life and understand the grandeur and poetry of neckties and patent leather boots. The Impressionists, who were "wild about light" and about painting, shared his view. But their "modernity" did not become the fashion as they had hoped; instead it caused a scandal. They based their work on the Old Masters, as Manet had done; they drew deeply on works by Rubens and Carrache for inspiration in their landscape paintings; they even set their sights on moving up to "higher" genres and exhibiting their work at the Salon. But all to no avail. As soon as they tried to execute their good intentions, these vanished into thin air, and something quite different emerged. Unconsciously, they refused to conform to official taste and chose freedom.

   The Impressionists' all-powerful enemy was the petit bourgeois, as personified by the eponymous hero of Alfred Jarry's groundbreaking parody *Ubu-Roi*. Ubu sums up his materialistic outlook when he describes his ideal way of life as "eating tripe all the time and riding around in a coach". In *À rebours* (Against Nature), Joris-Karl Huysmans described the French bourgeois as "self-assured and jovially in control, thanks to the power of his money and the contagion of his stupidity". "His rise", Huysmans concluded, "has caused the crushing of intelligence, the annihilation of probity, and the death of art." When the Impressionists first entered the fray it was the middle-class philistine who ruled the roost. Zola claimed that "the contemporary philanthropist" was just such a person and the life and soul of every panel of judges. "Your wife is the vigilant and affectionate guardian of your safe, O middle-class man", Baudelaire said mockingly

Mademoiselle Sicot, 1865
Oil on canvas, 116 x 89.5 cm (45¾ x 35¼ in.)
Washington, D.C., National Gallery of Art,
Chester Dale Collection

Under the influence of Gleyre and his fellow
mediocre painters who were members of the
Academy, Renoir was still painting portraits
against a very dark background. Yet he
demonstrated that he was already a brilliant
painter of the human face, who might even
become fashionable – unless he fell into the
Impressionist trap, of course – with this
elegant portrait of Mademoiselle Sicot,
a young Parisian actress.

in 'Rockets'. "She shall never be anything more than the ideal of the kept woman. Your
precociously nubile daughter shall dream in her cradle of being sold for a million".
Gauguin complained that everything in France was rotten, people and art alike, and
left for Tahiti. The cultural symbols of the Louis XV period were eagerly snapped up by
the *nouveaux riches*, bourgeois, fake aristocrats and captains of industry. They wanted
a cultural context that expressed continuity and timelessness. The present needed to be
ennobled and the past made bourgeois. Baudelaire again expressed it ironically: "It is
not merely a matter of transposing the banality of life into a Greek setting". This pasteboard nobility is the *Zeitgeist*. Napoleon III was recorded for all posterity in a photograph in which he pretended to be on horseback by sitting on a plush-covered stool.
His beautiful wife, the Empress Eugénie de Montijo de Guzman, and her ladies-in-
waiting sail along in their crinolines, which are overloaded with flounces and artificial
flowers, in the painting by the German Franz Xaver Winterhalter. They look as if they
were about to drop anchor in front of his easel.

The Russian Tsar, the King of Prussia – against whom the French would soon go to
war – and Queen Victoria all visited Paris, where they danced to the melodies of Offenbach,
rode on horseback, skated on the frozen lake in the Bois de Boulogne, and went to the
Théâtre-Français to see Sarah Bernhardt in *The Lady with Camellias* or Hortense Schneider
in *The Beautiful Helen*. Ingres was by now a senator, President of the École des Beaux-
Arts, and an artistic dictator who ordered that nature be copied scrupulously in the manner of the Old Masters. His permanent reference to the past reassured the ruling classes.

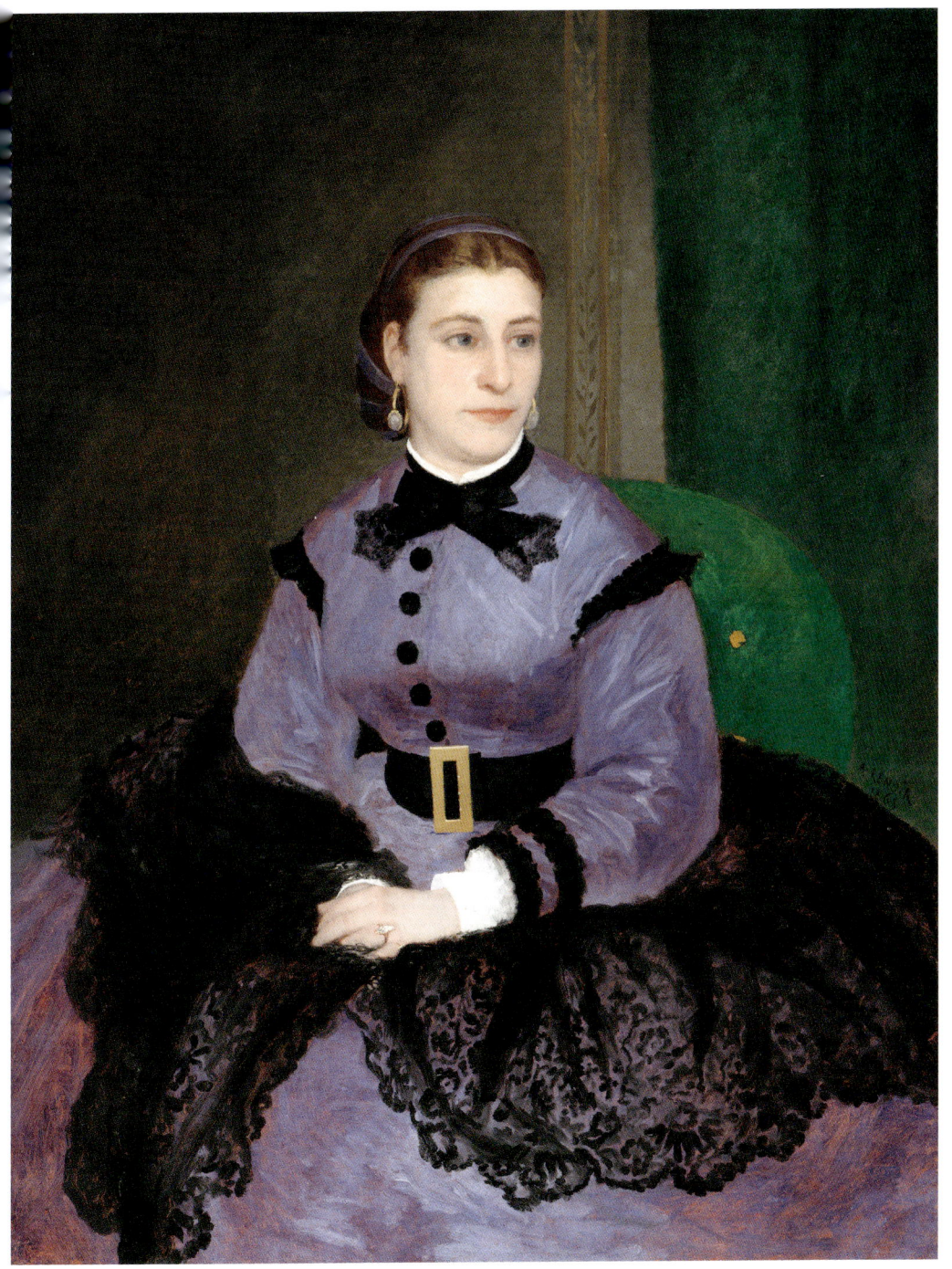

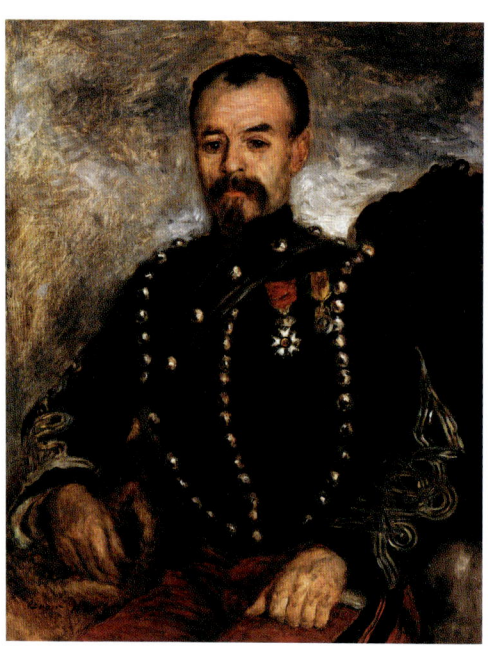

Captain Édouard Bernier
(formerly entitled **Captain Paul Darras**), 1871
Oil on canvas, 81 x 65 cm (32 x 25⅝ in.)
Staatliche Kunstsammlungen Dresden,
Gemäldegalerie Neue Meister

Madame Édouard Bernier
(**Marie-Octavie-Stéphanie Laurens**), 1871
Oil on canvas, 78.1 x 62.2 cm (30¾ x 24½ in.)
New York, The Metropolitan Museum of Art

The Universal Exposition of 1867 marked the apogee of France's Second Empire and confirmed Paris as the world capital of luxury and fashion. The 1889 exhibition, which was dominated by the brand-new Eiffel Tower, was a grandiose celebration of the marriage between art and industry. The colonial conquests promised ample raw materials and new markets for finished goods. In this period, elegant beauties of the type painted by Carolus-Duran (p. 210) were confronted with the first horseless carriages, railway trains, and photography.

"A helmet is a hat, / And they look good in that; / The fireman's own headgear / Looks just like soldier wear". This was the piece of doggerel with which art school students mocked the warriors who, wearing nothing but shiny classical helmets, figured in the epic paintings of David and the academicians who emulated him. These were the painters known as the "Pompiers" (firemen) because of their bombastic style. The chief culprits were Meissonier (whom Degas dubbed "a giant among dwarves") and Delaroche. Rodin's verdict was final: "Ugliness in art is everything which is false, artificial, and tries to be pretty instead of expressive; which is cloying and full of vapid airs and graces, which bends and arches for no apparent reason; everything which has no soul and no truth but merely parades a mendacious beauty." William Randolph Hearst, the American press baron whom Orson Welles incarnated in *Citizen Kane*, and the department store magnate A. T. Stewart were the kind of vulgarians who admired this style of art. They frequently purchased paintings worth tens of thousands of dollars by telegram, without ever having seen them. This, incidentally, should be food for thought for those contemporary artists whose work is currently fetching ridiculous prices across the Atlantic.

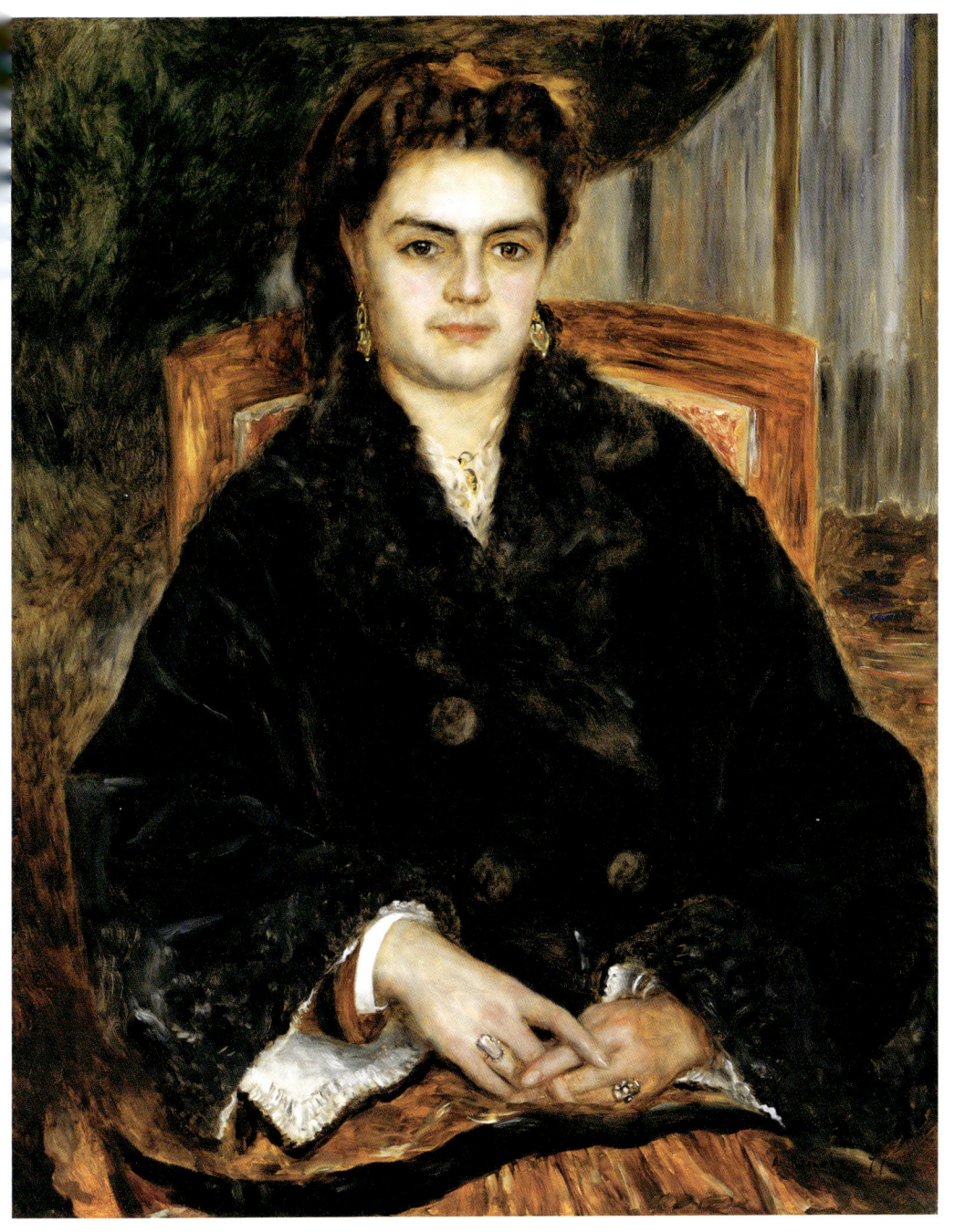

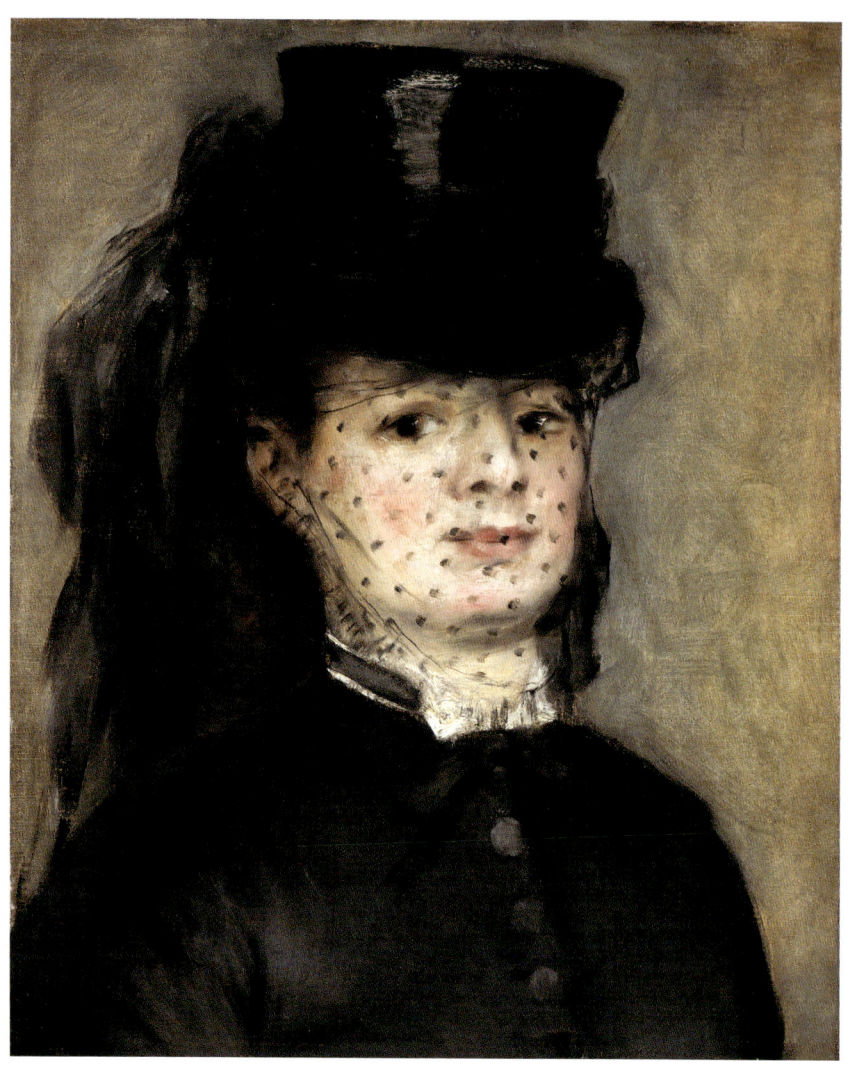

Madame Darras, c. 1868
Oil on canvas, 48 x 40 cm (19 x 15¾ in.)
Paris, Musée d'Orsay

Through Le Cœur, Renoir made the acquaintance
of Captain Paul Darras and his young wife
Henriette, who commissioned him to paint their
portraits. Renoir was delighted to accept the job
of painting this delightful couple and painted

Madame Darras which had the magnetism
and power of a portrait by Manet.

Woman with Parakeet, 1871
Oil on canvas,
92.1 x 65.1 cm (36⅜ x 25¾ in.)
New York, Solomon R. Guggenheim Museum,
Thannhauser Collection,
Gift of Justin K. Thannhauser

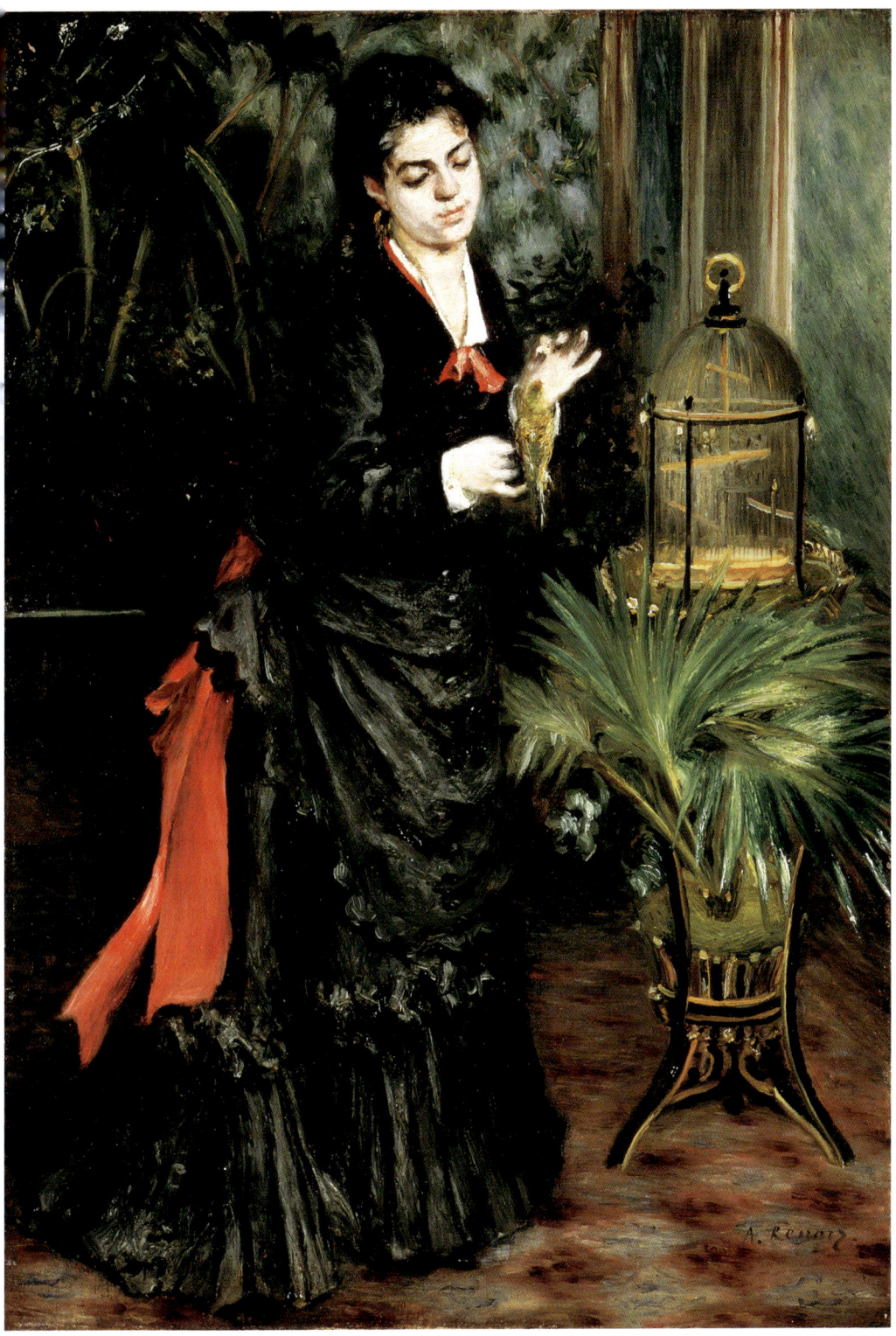

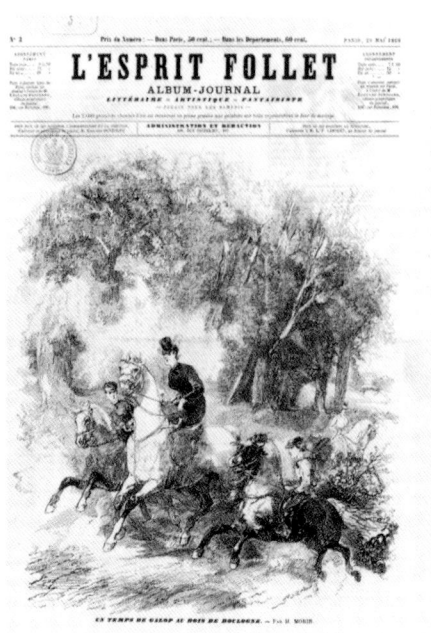

EN TEMPS DE GALOP AU BOIS DE BOULOGNE. — Par H. MORIN.

Edmond Morin (1824–1882)
A Gallop in the Bois de Boulogne,
cover of *L'Esprit Follet*, May 1869

Renoir was never successful in his depictions
of high society. The Bois de Boulogne was not
Montmartre, and this haunt of the smart set
where subtle games of seduction were played by
the upper class (as shown in the cover and title
of *L'Esprit Follet*) was quite foreign to him. The
elegant equestrian portrait of Sophie Croizette,
Sarah Bernhardt's rival at the Comédie-Française,
painted by his brother-in-law Carolus-Duran
(exclusively a society painter) won all the accolades
at the 1873 Salon. Fortunately, *Ride in the Bois
de Boulogne (Madame Henriette Darras)* was
Renoir's last attempt at academic painting.

**Ride in the Bois de Boulogne
(Madame Henriette Darras)**, 1873
Oil on canvas, 261.5 x 226 cm (102⅞ x 89 in.)
Hamburger Kunsthalle

"Every minute is worth a hundred francs", Bouguereau remarked when at the
height of his fame to the young Othon Friesz. Meissonier built himself an opulent
neo-Renaissance palace in the Place Malesherbes thanks to the astronomical sums that
his immaculately turned-out historical paintings fetched. The nouveaux riches wasted
absurd sums on the productions of this pasteboard Hollywood; ownership of one of
them considerably enhanced one's prestige. It took months of arduous toil to finish one
of these "enormous slices of bread-and-butter", to use Boudin's expression: every detail –
down to the soldiers' uniforms – needed to be correct. A painter who had been accepted
by the Salon knew that his career was safe. A gold medal was worth 4,000 francs and a
silver medal 1,500 francs. The awards made by the jury set the going rate for painters. A
painting rejected by the Salon was impossible to sell but one that had been accepted saw
its value increase threefold. "The Salon is the real battleground, the place where you face
the enemy", proclaimed Manet himself. When rejected by it in 1869, he wrote to a friend:
"This fatal rejection has taken the bread out of my mouth. Despite my reasonable prices,
dealers and collectors have turned their backs on me. It is sad to see how little interest
there is in a piece of art of no commercial value".

Edith Wharton and the architect Ogden Codman argued in *The Decoration of Houses*,
published in 1897, that if only the taste of the wealthy could be improved, then the general
level of taste would follow suit. This presupposes, as James Harding points out, "both that
the taste of the wealthy is some sort of yardstick and that it was in a poor state at the time".
Any artist who wanted to win the Rome Prize had no option but to use a theme drawn

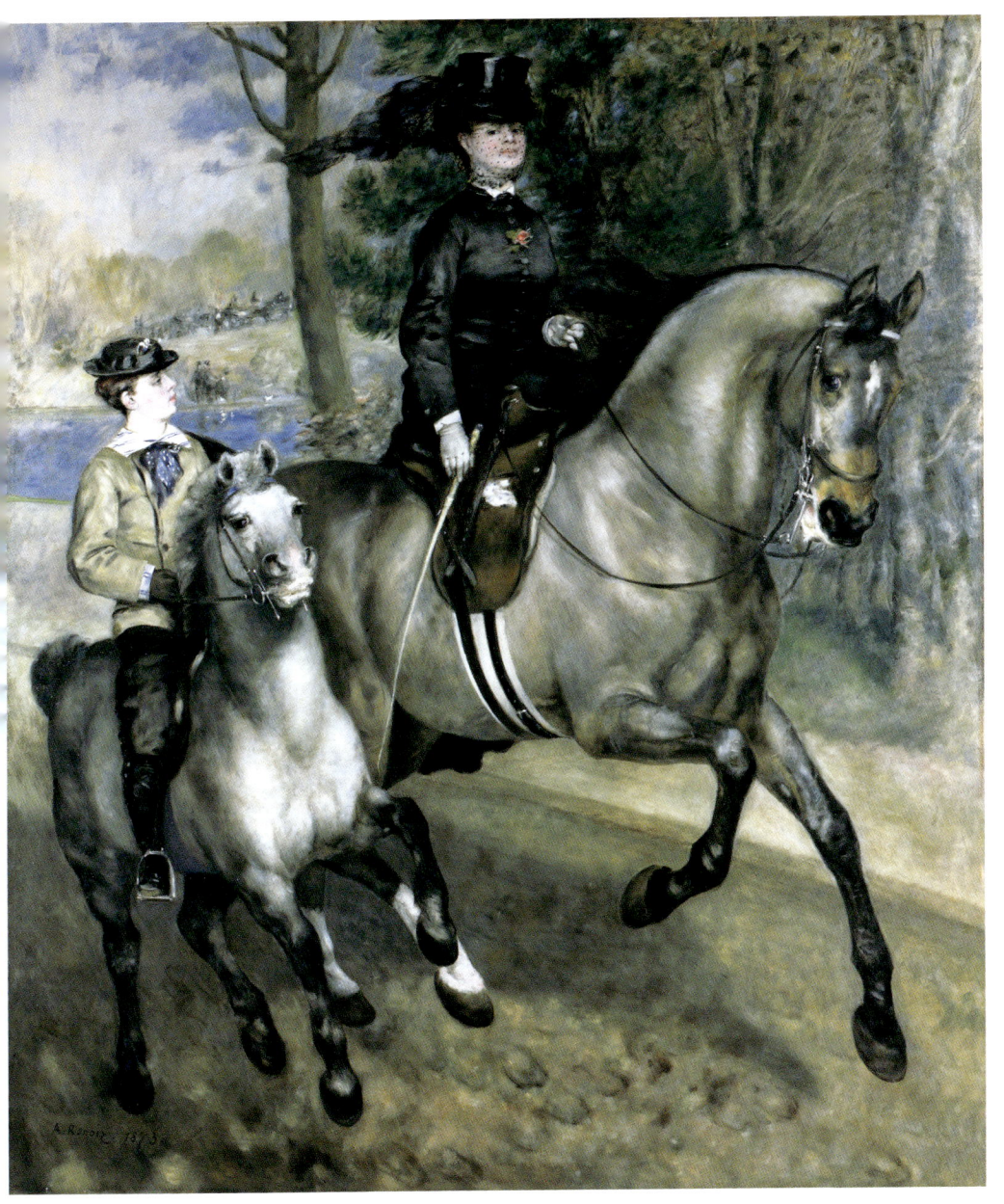

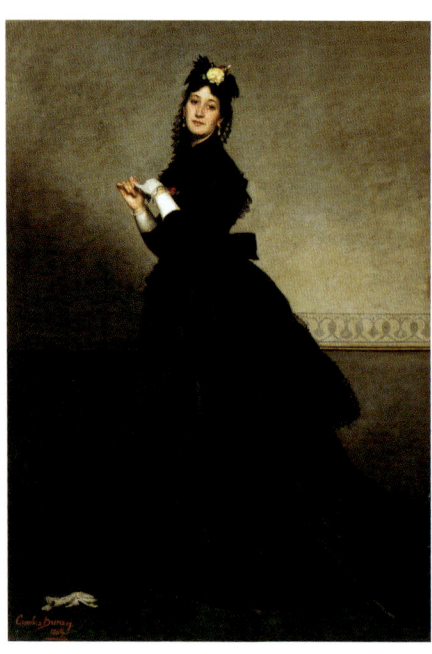

Émile Auguste Carolus-Duran
Woman with a Glove (The Artist's Wife), 1869
Oil on canvas, 228 x 164 cm (89⅞ x 64⅝ in.)
Paris, Musée d'Orsay

**Portrait of a Woman
(Nini Fish-face)**, c. 1874
Oil on canvas,
32 x 24 cm (12⅝ x 9½ in.)
Private collection

from classical antiquity, mythology, or the Bible. Commissions from the French state were only awarded for classical subjects with a high moral value, such as appropriately glorious episodes from French history. These epic works are housed in their own museum, which was founded by King Louis-Philippe at Versailles. A brief visit to this dinosaurs' graveyard today reveals works by Gros, Delacroix and David. Landscapes were then considered a minor genre. Gleyre, who was a neoclassical painter although a tolerant one, reminded his students Bazille, Monet, Renoir and Sisley that "when executing a figure, one should always think of antiquity. Nature is a perfectly fine object of study, but it is of no real interest. Style, you see, is all that counts." Leon Gambetta, a Republican and Speaker of the French parliament, was invited by Charpentier to one of his dinners. Charpentier tried to get Gambetta to commission from Renoir decorations of public buildings by arguing that he would revive the art of frescoes to the glory of the French Republic. Jean Renoir recalled the incident. "The famous orator took Renoir to one side. 'We cannot give you commissions', he told him. 'We cannot give any to you or your friends. The government would be in danger of falling'. 'Don't you like our paintings?', Renoir replied. 'Certainly I do. I consider it to be the only form of painting that counts and that the commissions we give are worthless. But that's the way it is.' My father pursued the point. 'What do you mean by that?' 'You are revolutionaries!', Gambetta replied. 'And what about you?', Renoir retorted. 'That's just it', replied Gambetta. 'We will only be forgiven for our origins, the opinions we hold, and for having succeeded in passing democratic laws, if we jettison everything that is trivial. It is better to keep the Republic alive with bad painting than to see it die with great art.'"

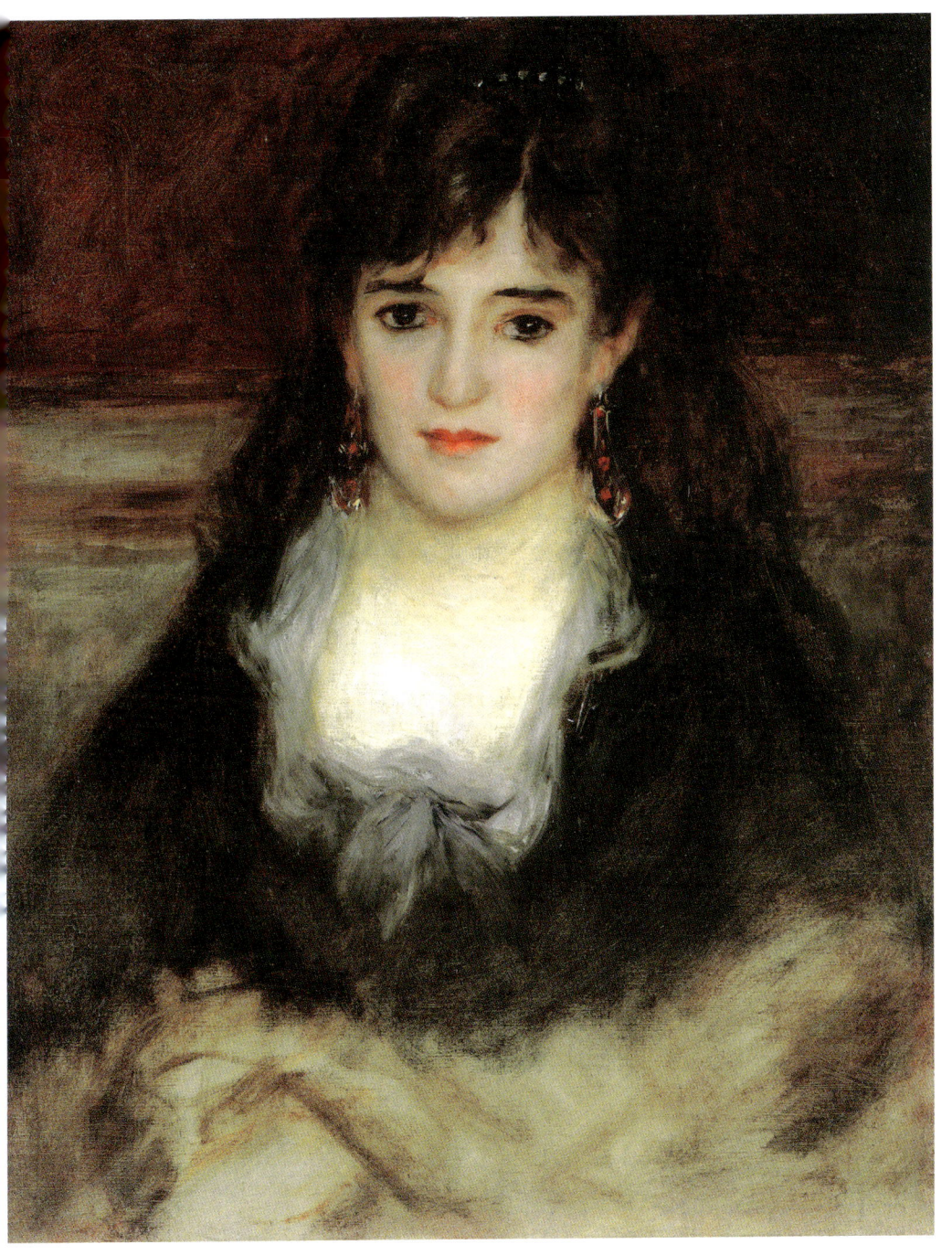

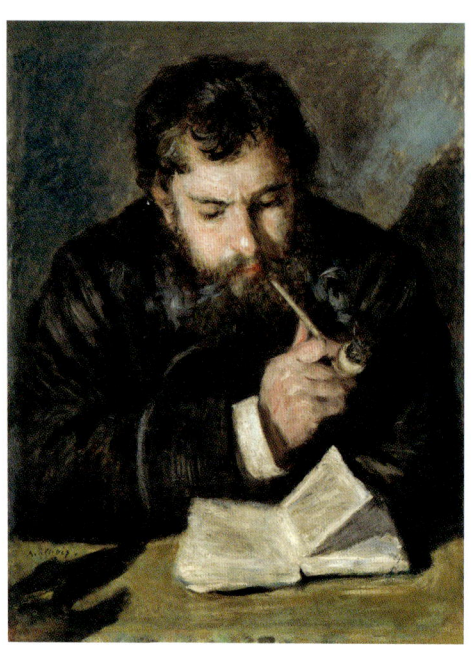

Claude Monet, 1872
Oil on canvas, 65 x 50 cm (25⅝ x 19¾ in.)
Washington, D.C., National Gallery of Art,
Mr. and Mrs. Paul Mellon Collection

**Portrait of Madame Monet
(Madame Claude Monet Reading)**, c. 1874
Oil on canvas, 61.7 x 50.3 cm (24⅜ x 19⅞ in.)
Williamstown, Massachusetts, The Clark

Renoir understood the rules of the game. He remembered the advice given to him by his older sister, that he should paint portraits if he wanted to make a decent living. He decided to exhibit at the Salon of 1881 despite knowing that his fellow-painters would consider him a traitor to their cause. "There are hardly fifteen art-lovers in the whole of Paris who are capable of liking a painter without the Salon's seal of approval", he explained to Durand-Ruel. "There are 80,000 who will not buy so much as a nose from a painter without it. That is why I submit two portraits every year, few as that may be. I don't want to fall into the trap of believing that something is bad just because it is in the wrong place or to waste my time berating the Salon. I don't even want to appear to be doing so. I believe that one must try to paint as well as possible. That's all there is to it. Had I been accused of neglecting my art or sacrificing my ideas to ambition, then I would be able to understand my critics. But since this is not the case, no one can accuse me of anything. I am currently busy doing good things as usual. I want to produce wonderful paintings for you that you will be able to sell for a very high price. I hope and think that it won't take me long to achieve. I have kept my distance from successful painters to find my true position. I think that I have now found what I was looking for. I may be mistaken but I would be very surprised if I were. Be patient and I will soon prove to you, I hope, that it is possible to send works to the Salon and still paint well. I beg you to plead my cause with my friends. The paintings I send to the Salon are purely commercial. Think of them as those kinds of medicine which may do no good but certainly do no harm".

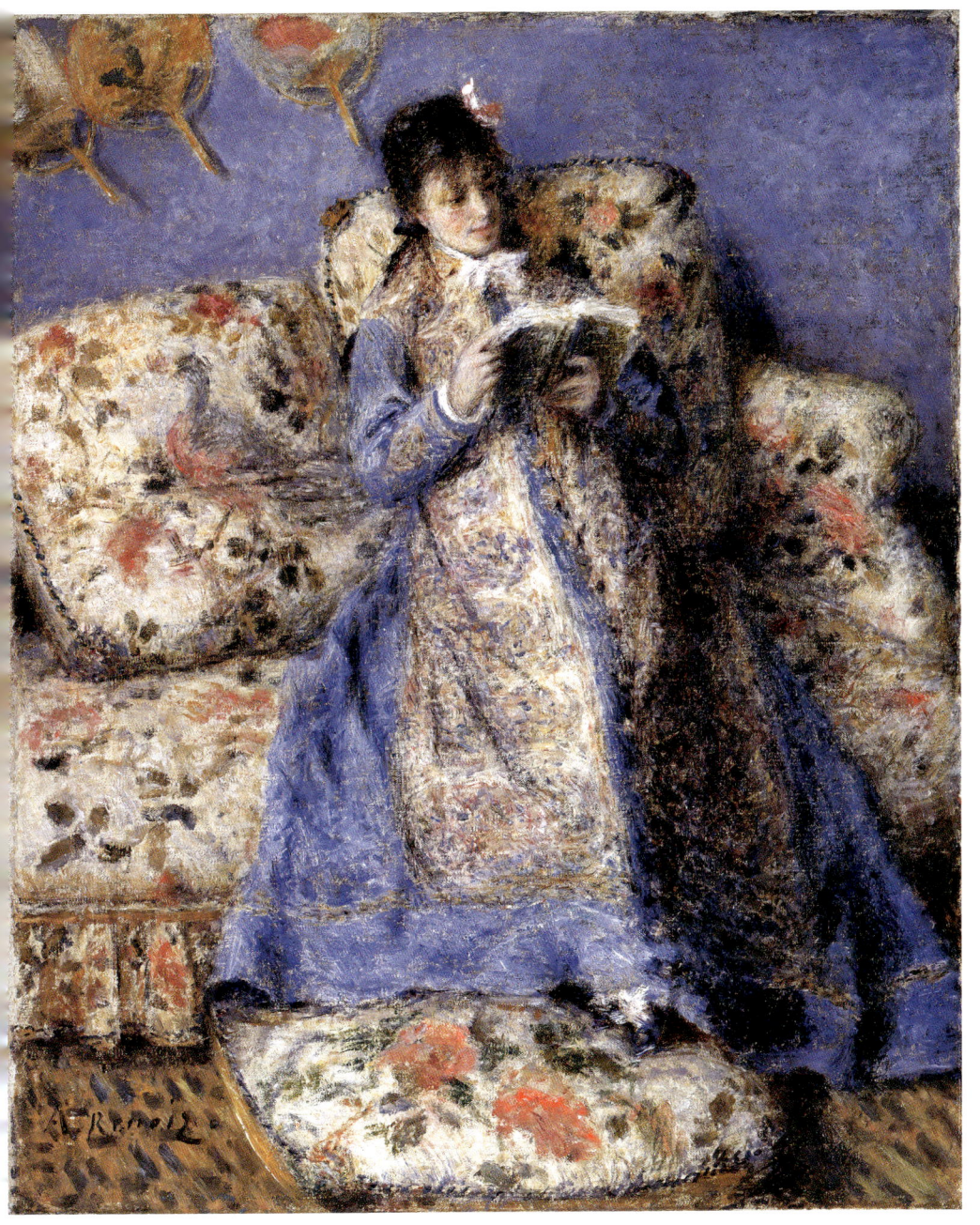

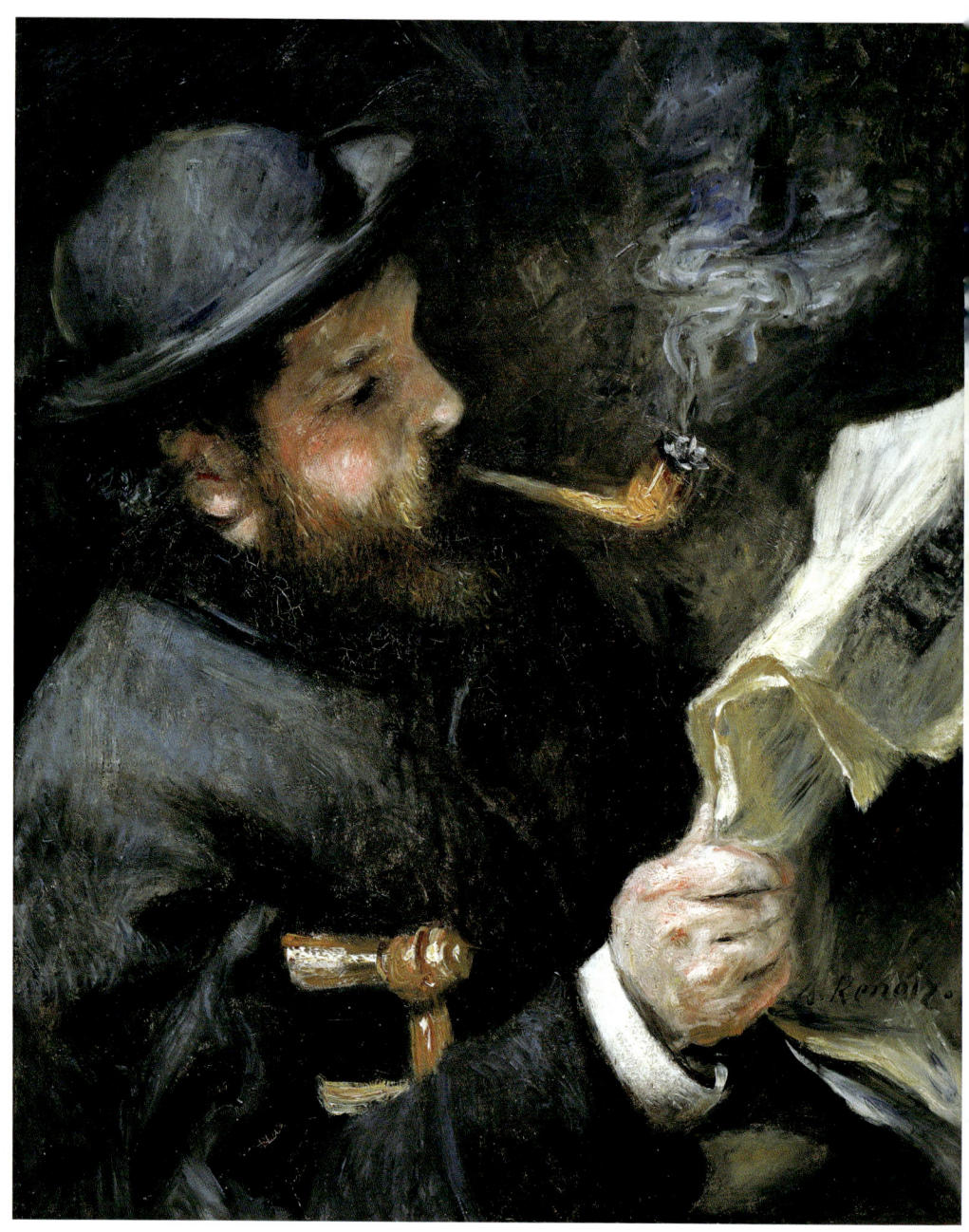

Claude Monet Reading, c. 1873
Oil on canvas, 61 x 50 cm (24 x 19¾ in.)
Paris, Musée Marmottan Monet

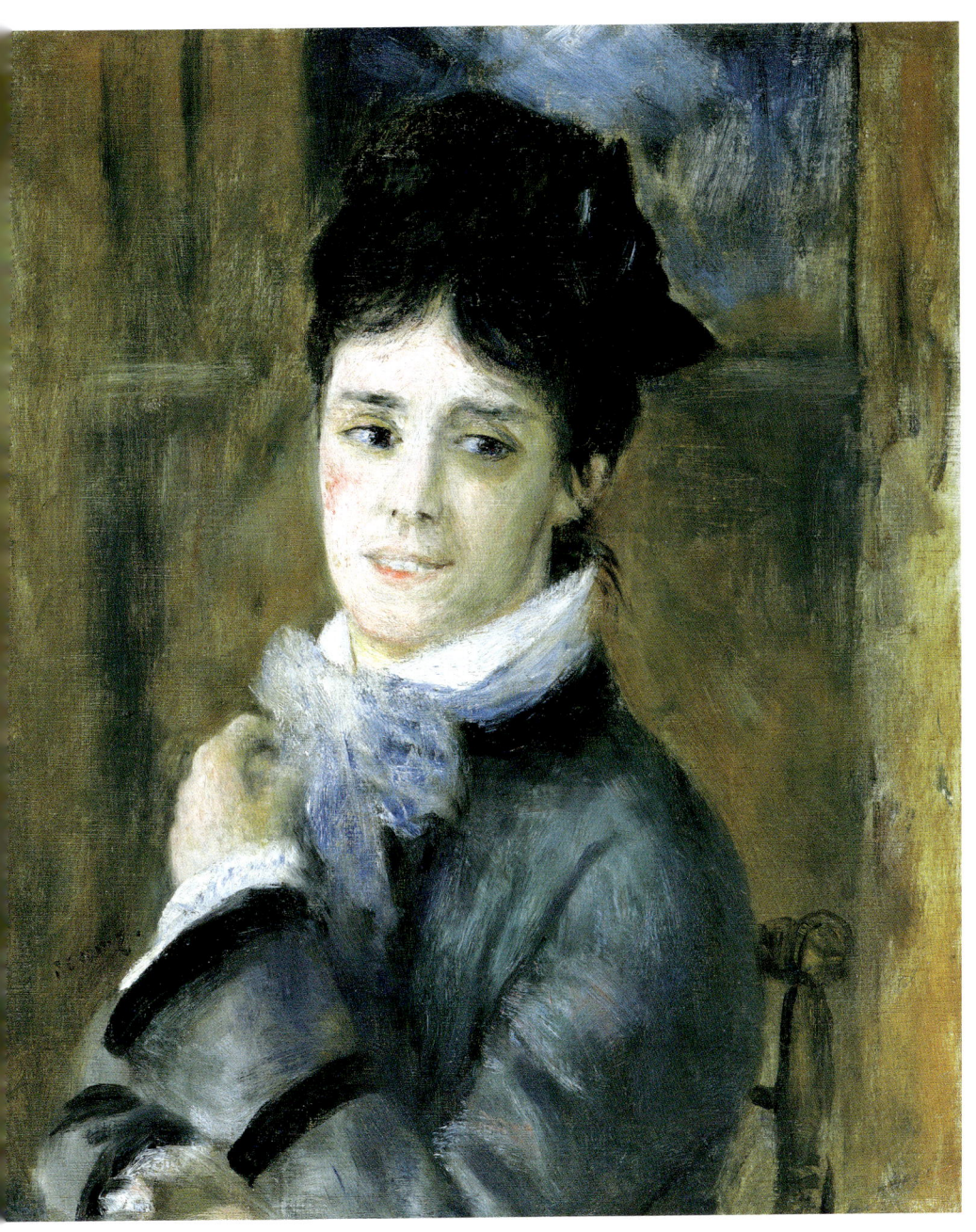

Camille Monet, c. 1873
Oil on canvas, 61 x 50 cm (24 x 19¾ in.)
Paris, Musée Marmottan Monet

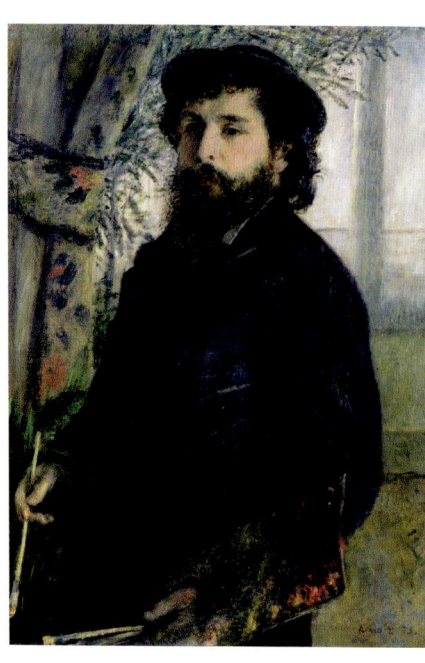

Claude Monet with Palette, 1875
Oil on canvas, 84 x 60.5 cm (33 x 23⅞ in.)
Paris, Musée d'Orsay

Charles Le Cœur, c. 1872
Oil on canvas,
42.8 x 29.2 cm (16⅞ x 11½ in.)
Paris, Musée d'Orsay

Degas told Renoir that he had no moral fibre. "You are just working for the money, aren't you? You tour the châteaux with Charles Ephrussi and in no time you will be exhibiting at the Mirlitons like Bouguereau!" Renoir took a different view: "Art-collectors make painting what it is. French painting is the work of Chocquet, and we owe the achievements of Italian painting to a few Borgias, Medicis, and other tyrants whom God gave a taste for colour". "The summit of bourgeois art is the portrait", Théodore Duret stated in 1867. The caricaturists had a field day. In depicting his pot-bellied plutocrat – the type dubbed by Baudelaire "the eternal bespectacled Eskimo" – Honoré Daumier has him exclaim: "It's flattering to have one's portrait on show at an exhibition". Or: "There is no question, that is my shape all right … but I shall always regret the fact that the artist was obstinate enough not to reproduce my glasses and my detachable collar!" Zola saw that the portrait would contribute to the renewal of contemporary art and that the mediocrity of contemporary portraitists alone prevented this from happening. When Renoir decided, in mid-career, to try his hand at fashionable Parisian portraiture, he revolutionised the form by treating it with the same freedom that his friends were bringing to landscape painting. His personal preferences even coincided with the conventions governing portraiture. The issue of how much the portrait should actually look like the sitter was a case in point. In his commissioned portraits Renoir transformed the personality of the sitter, especially if she were a woman, into one of the quintessential Renoir types. He did this without distorting her and whether she was a *grisette*, a member of the bourgeoisie, or a high society lady. He did complain, however,

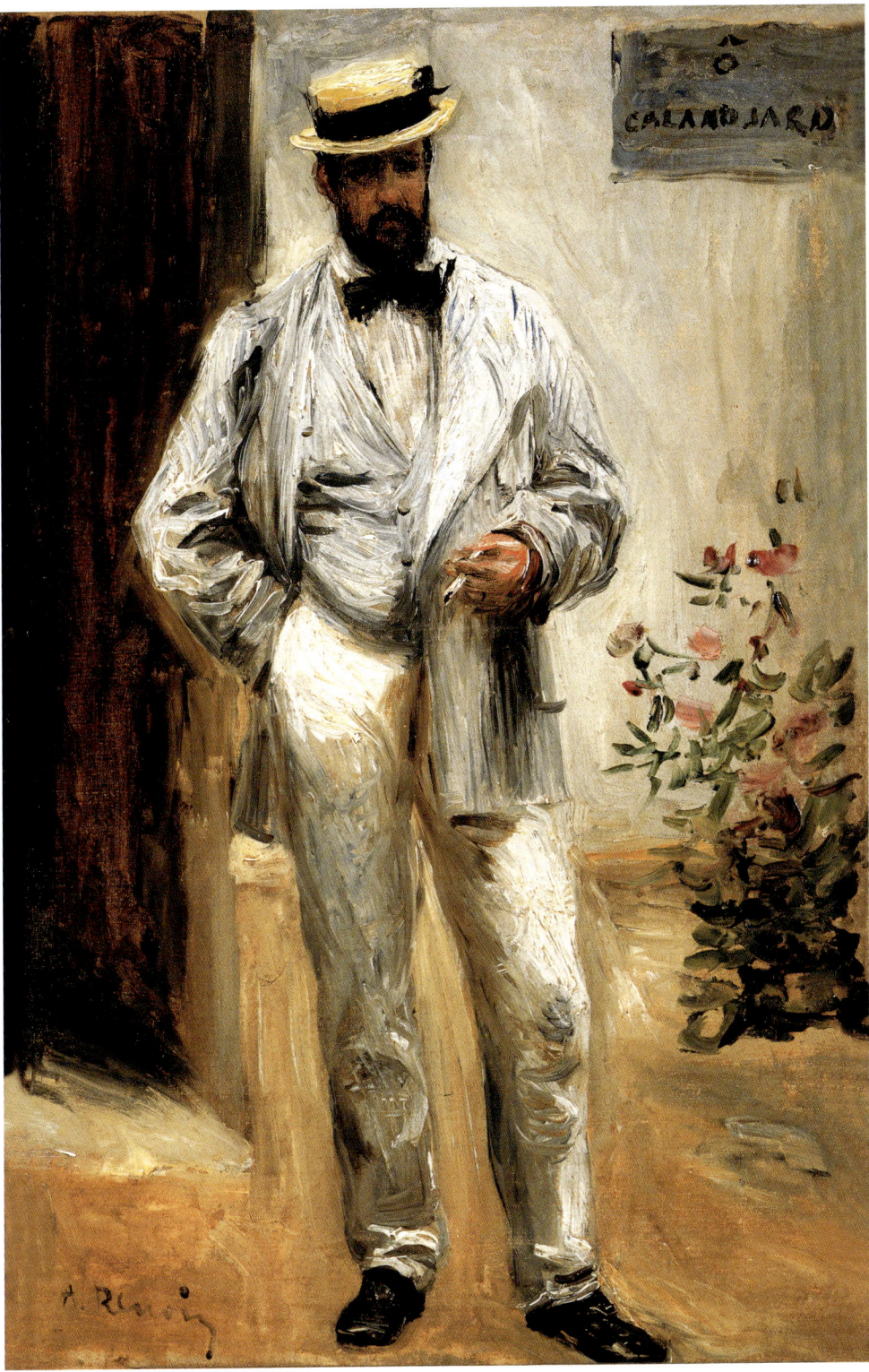

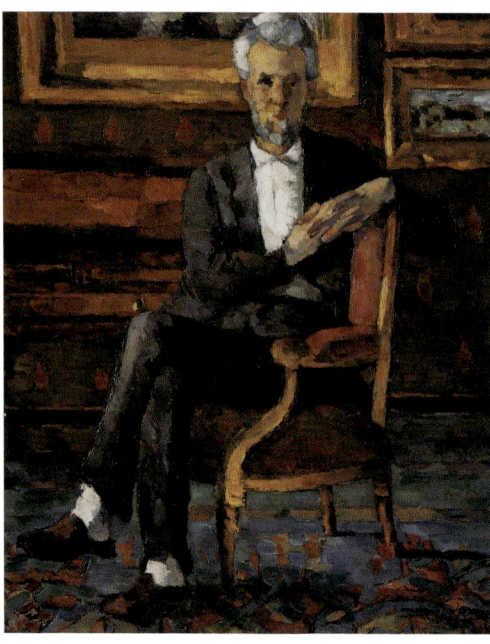

Paul Cézanne (1839–1906)
Victor Chocquet Seated, c. 1877
Oil on canvas, 45.7 x 38.1 cm (18 x 15 in.)
Columbus Museum of Art

Victor Chocquet, c. 1875
Oil on canvas, 53 x 43.5 cm (20⅞ x 17¼ in.)
Cambridge, Massachusetts,
Harvard Art Museums/Fogg Museum,
Bequest of Grenville L. Winthrop

of having to paint "the decadent flesh of society women" rather than humble work-ing-class girls. In this, he differed from his friend Zola, the chief advocate of naturalism and author of the novel *The Grog Shop*, which Renoir illustrated in 1878. "Zola imagines that he is depicting the common people when he says that they are smelly", he told Vollard. Renoir lived in a working-class neighbourhood, Montmartre, and was a regular at the local Moulin de la Galette. Hearing working people described as "atrocious beings" filled him with indignation. He offered a utopian vision of a society striving for equality and social harmony. He endows actresses and circus artistes with the same charm as *chatelaines* and society belles. The offspring of small traders are treated with the same tenderness as the spoiled children of bankers, doctors, and provincial senators.

Portraiture was no easy task for Renoir. He tried not only to reproduce the features, volumes and colours of the face as accurately as he could, but also to express the model's inner personality. Renoir once explained to the artist Paule Gobillard all of the difficulties encountered by the portraitist. "Portraits are impossible", he said. "The first portraitist who comes along will take twenty-five sous from you to do your nose, eyes, and mouth. Then a painter interferes, and the likeness disappears. The family is never satisfied and does not see the true colour of the hair or eyes, nor the tone produced by the reflections, the setting, and the light at various times of day". Despite these difficul-ties Renoir succeeded in pleasing his patrons. This was largely due to the fact that the painter happened to like his models personally. The paintings of *Madame Charpentier and Her Children* (pp. 388/389) or *Victor Chocquet* (p. 219) are successful for precisely

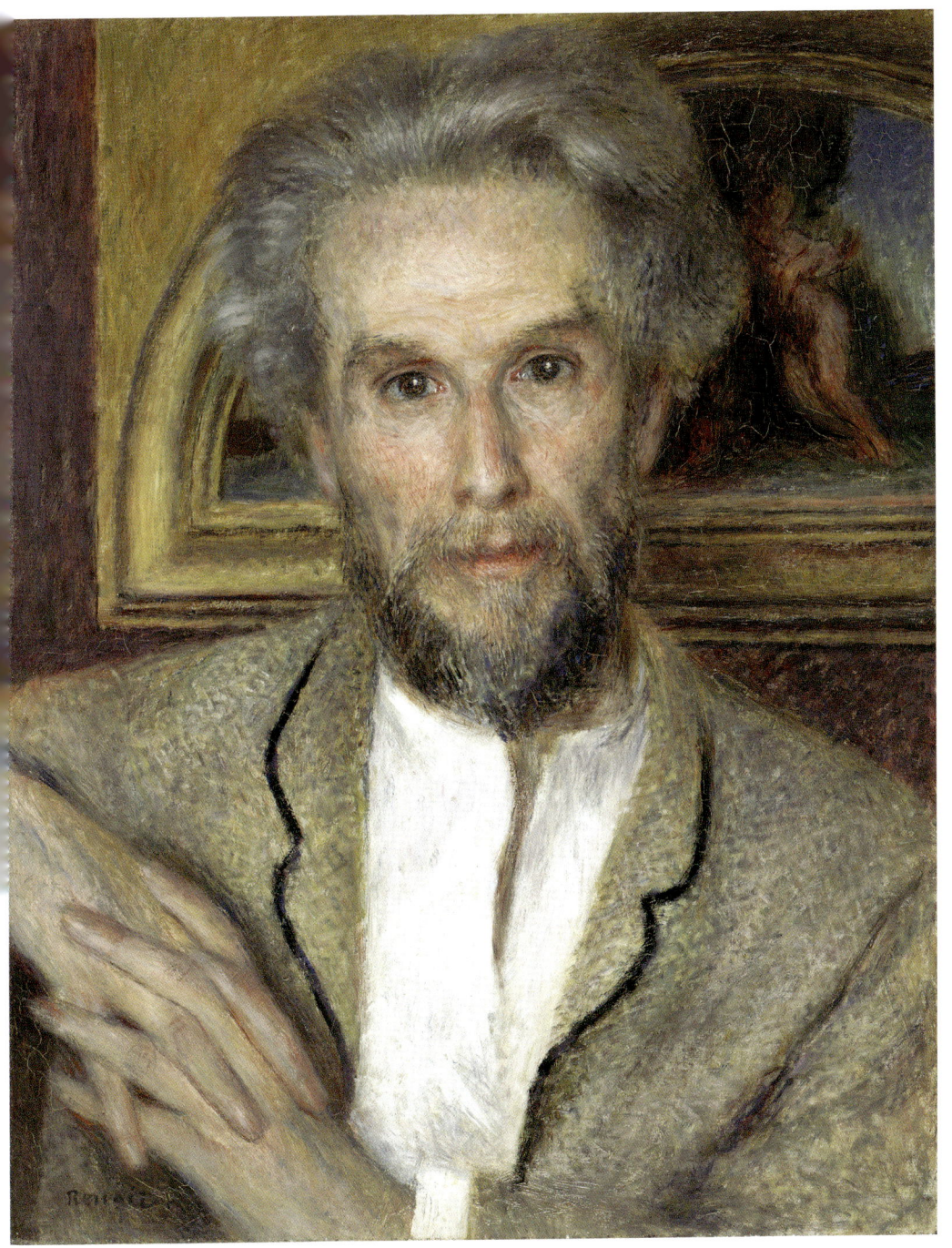

that reason. His portraits of children are among the best ever produced and make those of the greatest Old Masters look stilted and frigid. The explanation is simple. Renoir was under the spell of youth: he adored its freshness, its ingenuous beauty, and the feelings of indescribable tenderness that children, especially little girls, inspire. "Stop him from painting any more portraits and keep him on landscapes!" was Degas's spiteful comment. He did not share Renoir's conception of portraiture and took delight in condemning the painter's newfound success after *Madame Charpentier and Her Children* had been accorded the place of honour at the Salon. His friend's acid remarks did not prevent Renoir from working extensively on portraits between 1864 and 1885. François Daulte has catalogued no fewer than 397 compositions during this period, of which 164 were portraits and 161 genre paintings. Renoir decided to send his portraits to the Salon each year. *The Daughters of Catulle Mendès* (p. 321) was the last portrait that he exhibited, in 1890. If he painted so many portraits during this period it was because he hoped to earn a steadier income from them than he could have expected from landscapes. He hoped also to win recognition and fame. That he did so is best explained by his desire to portray humans as individuals. Portraits, much more so than landscapes, made this possible.

"I have always tried", he explained, "to paint human beings in the same way as beautiful pieces of fruit". His favourite models were the women he loved and his best clients soon became his friends. Even his nude studies are almost always of people who were part of his life. The ties of affection woven between the painter and his subjects were

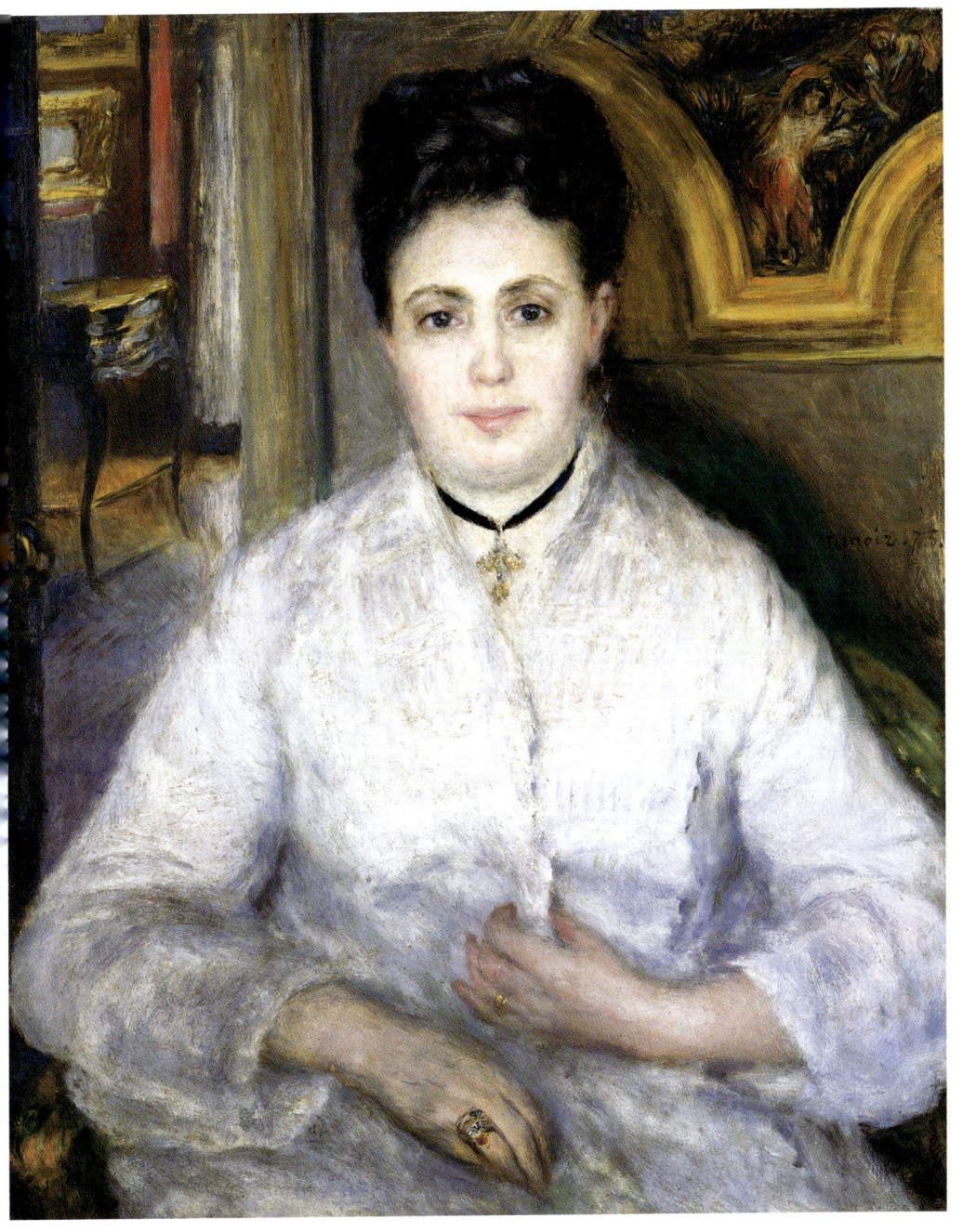

221

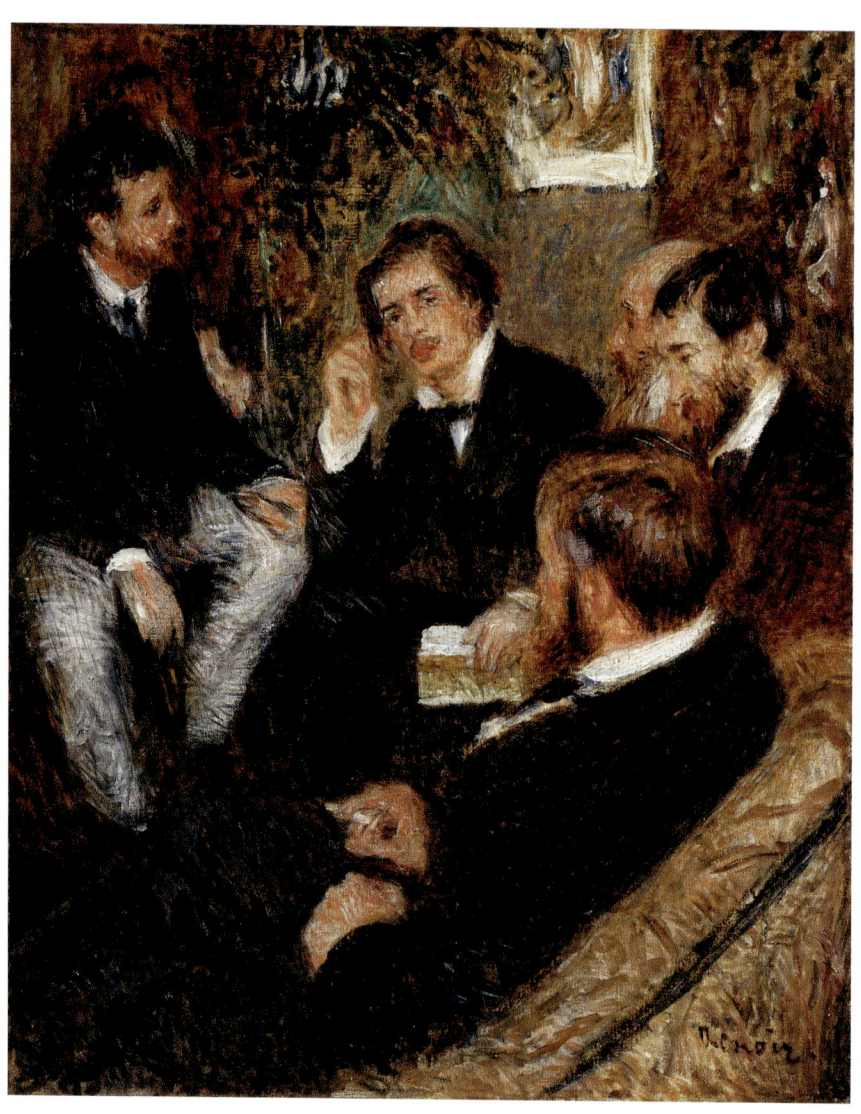

At Renoir's Home, rue St-Georges (formerly
The Artist's Studio, rue St-Georges), 1876
Oil on canvas, 46 x 38.1 cm (18⅛ x 15 in.)
Pasadena, Norton Simon Art Foundation

Alfred Sisley, 1876
Oil on canvas, 66.2 x 54.8 cm (26 x 21⅝ in.)
The Art Institute of Chicago, Mr. and Mrs.
Lewis Larned Coburn Memorial Collection

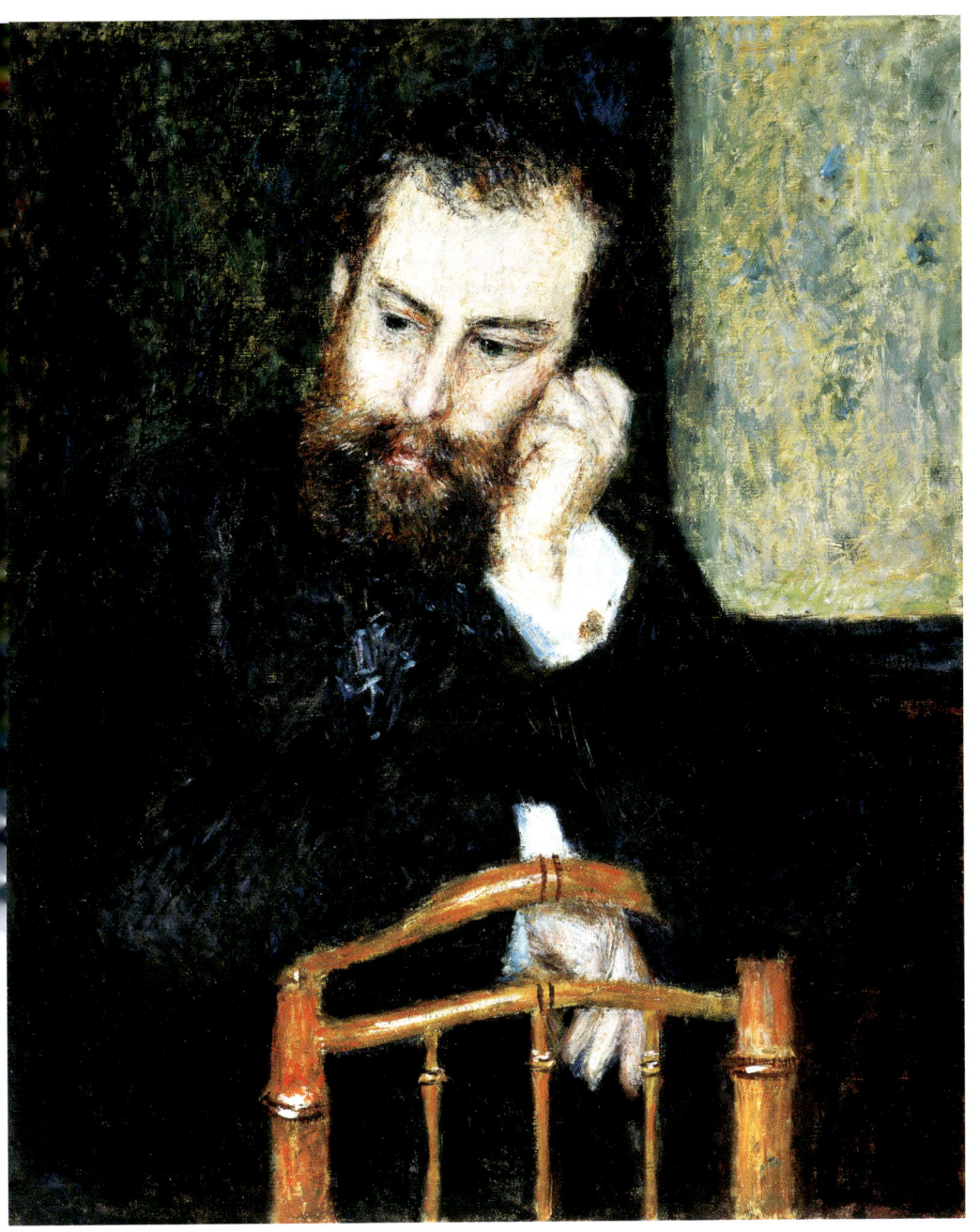

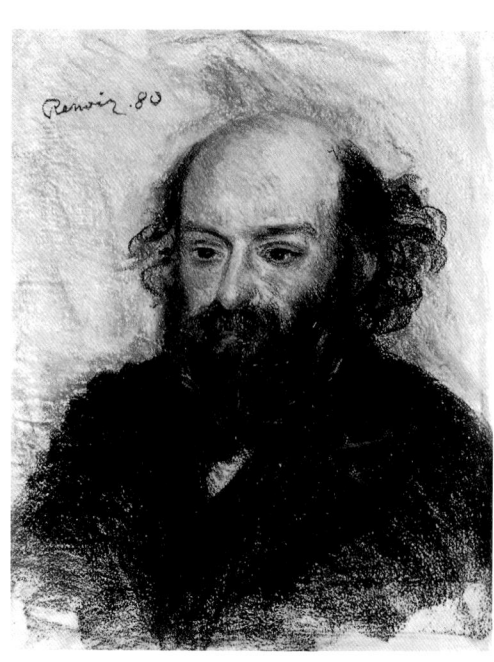

Paul Cézanne, 1880
Pastel, 55.5 x 43.5 cm (21⅞ x 17¼ in.)
Private collection

Self-Portrait, 1876
Oil on canvas, 73.3 x 57.3 cm (28⅞ x 22⅝ in.)
Cambridge, Massachusetts, Harvard Art
Museums/Fogg Museum, Bequest from the
Collection of Maurice Wertheim

born of his need to choose sitters whom he liked. The result is a special charm that
radiates from the finished painting. His male portraits are less likeable than those
he did of women. Renoir was permanently in love with women and transferred the
luminous radiance he found in them onto the canvas. One could imagine a life of
Renoir which analysed the stages of his development purely in terms of the human
faces he portrayed. It would need to include not only the women he encountered
during his lifetime – as one can study Picasso – but also the friends who enabled him
to flourish. According to Raymond Cogniat, this approach would produce a division
into four major periods. "The first would stretch from his beginnings as a painter to
the early years of Impressionism, including the family scenes and portraits of relatives
and friends. The first commissioned portraits would mark the second period. This is
the moment when Renoir entered the new social milieu of his patrons – publishers,
art dealers, and others – who belonged to the enlightened middle-classes. He offered
them a pictorial confirmation of the pleasant life they led. Then comes the period of
the more strictly organised paintings. These are created in a more restrained style in
which, without loss of spontaneous feeling, the portrait is defined more severely – as
much by the more definite style of drawing as by the clarity of the modelling. The
fourth period starts at the moment when Renoir decided to release himself from this
deliberate constraint. This was the time of total independence when he recruited his
entire entourage – his children, his wife and the maid, Gabrielle – to express the serenity and joy of painting."

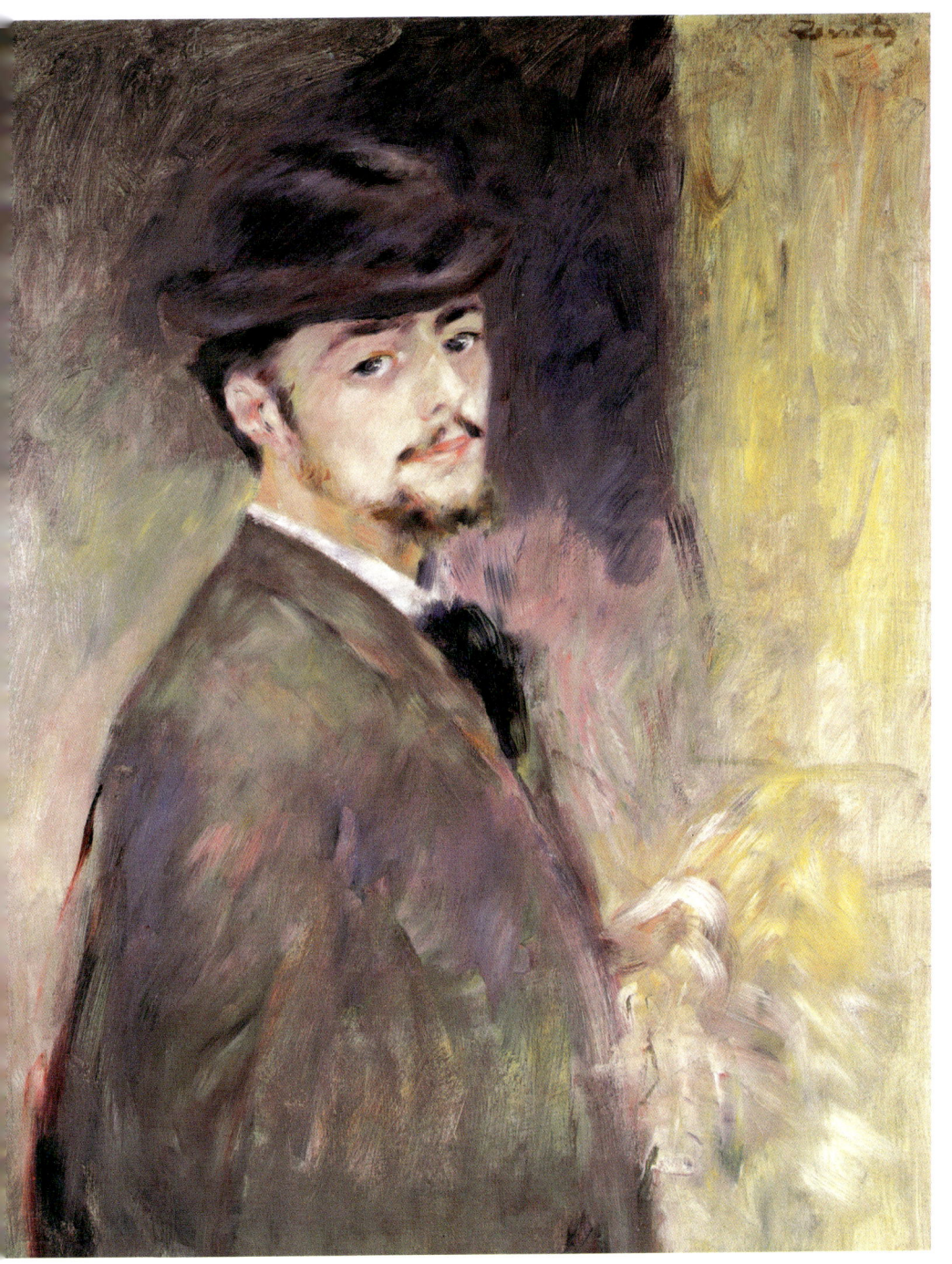

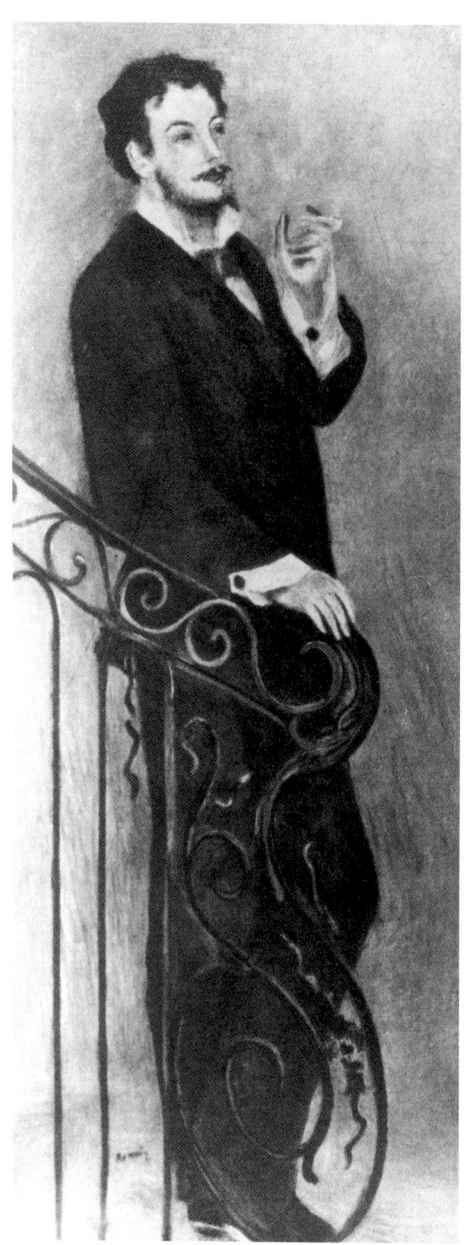

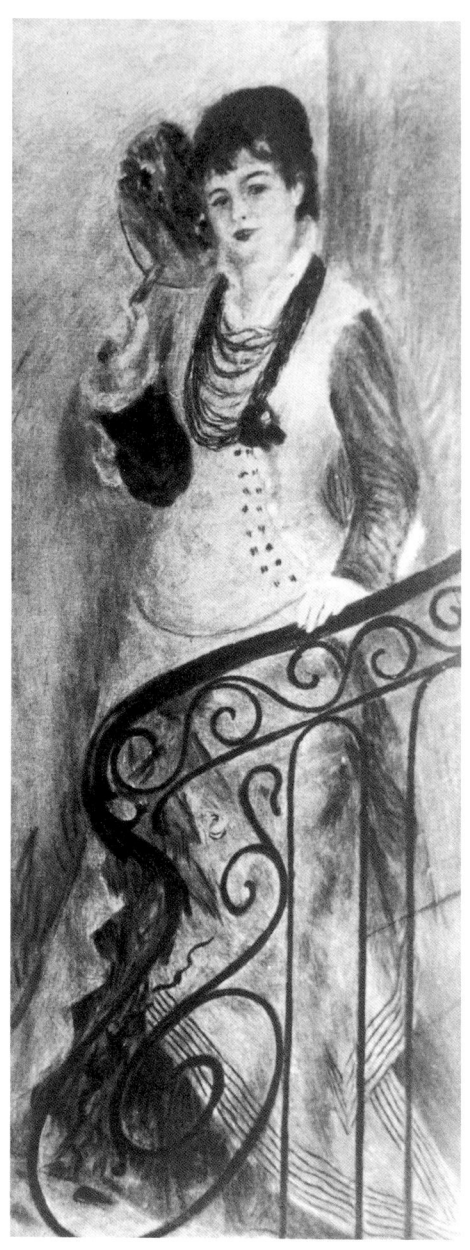

Man on the Staircase, c. 1876
Oil on canvas,
167.5 x 65.3 cm (66 x 25¾ in.)
Saint Petersburg, Hermitage Museum

Woman on the Staircase, c. 1876
Oil on canvas,
167.5 x 65.3 cm (66 x 25¾ in.)
Saint Petersburg, Hermitage Museum

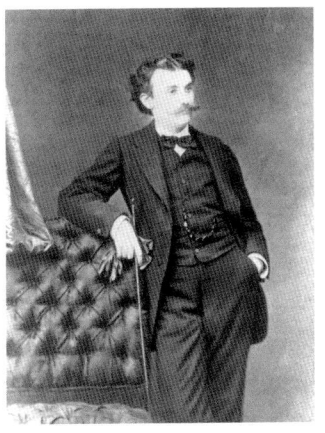

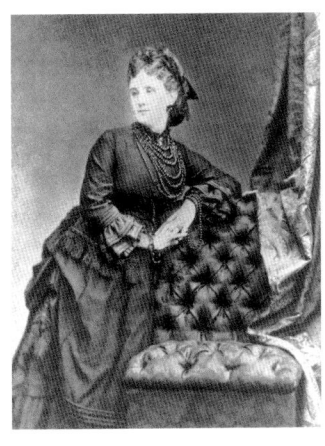

Georges Charpentier
(1846–1905), c. 1876

Marguerite Charpentier
(1848–1904), c. 1876

Much of Renoir's best early work already indicates his preference for portraiture over landscapes. These are the portraits produced from 1863 onwards, during his stay near Fontainebleau with Monet, Bazille and Sisley. His first painting of a child, *Mademoiselle Romaine Lacaux* (p. 6), dates from this period. So too does the large composition in which Renoir brought his friends Sisley and Jules Le Cœur around the same table, *At the Inn of Mother Anthony* (p. 15). The Franco-Prussian War of 1870 left Renoir no time to develop further his technique and style as a portraitist. Renoir at this time shows a warlike predilection in his choice of models and 'Pompier'-style attention to detail in rendering the jewels and fur coat of *Madame Édouard Bernier* (*Marie-Octavie-Stéphanie Laurens*; p. 205). The same can be said of the medals, brass buttons and gleaming 'frogs' worn by her husband, *Captain Édouard Bernier* – formerly entitled *Captain Paul Darras* (p. 204).

Renoir's technique is uncertain, though Manet's influence is present in his use of black and choice of palette. Renoir's excuse was that he had fallen seriously ill during his time in the Tenth Mounted Chasseurs and was still in convalescence. His brief experience of military life may account for his migration towards the "higher genre" indicated by Manet's *The Fife Player*. This painting, which Courbet described as a "play-ing-card", was rejected for the 1866 Salon but was recalled in 1882 by *The Bugler*. Manet placed himself in the vanguard by deliberately distancing himself from academic con-vention. He made the figure stand out against the background with surprising clarity and a minimum of resources. Renoir seems to have forgotten his pre-war attempts to

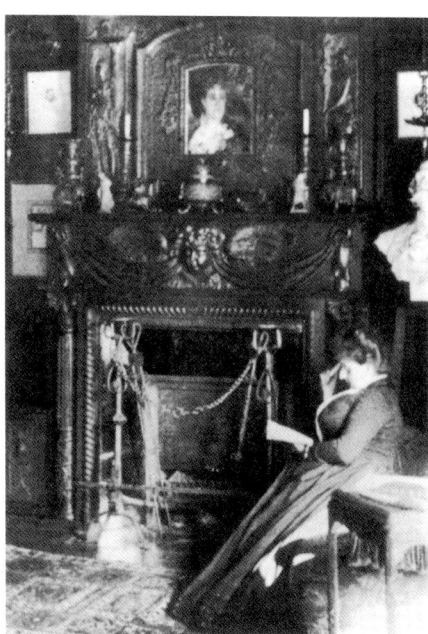

Madame Georges Charpentier, c. 1890,
photographed in her drawing room

Madame Georges Charpentier, 1876/77
Oil on canvas, 46 x 38 cm (18⅛ x 15 in.)
Paris, Musée d'Orsay

lighten his palette, as he had done so successfully in the charming portrait of *Madame Clémentine Stora in Algerian Dress* painted in 1870 (p. 49), and to have returned to old-fashioned composition. Note that there is a change of attribution in the title. The models for these two portraits were long thought to be Captain Darras and his wife Henriette because the captain posed several times for Renoir, especially for his portrait on horseback. Colin B. Bailey, in his *Renoir's Portraits – Impressions of an Age*, has corrected this mistake. The real sitters are another officer whom Renoir met during the war and his wife. Captain and Madame Bernier (1838–1920) were of humbler origin. These portraits barely reflect the character of the sitters but are stylised in the manner of the Salon painters. But one could in no way mistake the face of Madame Bernier (1838–1920; p. 205) for that of Henriette Darras in the portrait *Madame Darras* (p. 206) painted in 1873, which has the allure and strength of a true Manet.

Renoir appears to have returned to good health and so do his portraits. Impressionism reappears in the colour and small brushstrokes of *Woman with a Parrot* even if these are, as usual, less intense than in the landscapes. The year 1873 was fruitful. It marks the painting of Renoir's best Impressionist portraits, such as *Claude Monet Painting in His Garden at Argenteuil* (pp. 68/69), *Madame Claude Monet Reading* (p. 213), *Claude Monet* (p. 212), *Claude Monet Reading* (p. 214), and another portrait of *Camille Monet* (p. 215). These individual portraits all show his affection for the Monets. At the same time they are a kind of group manifesto in anticipation of the first Impressionist exhibition, which took place in 1874.

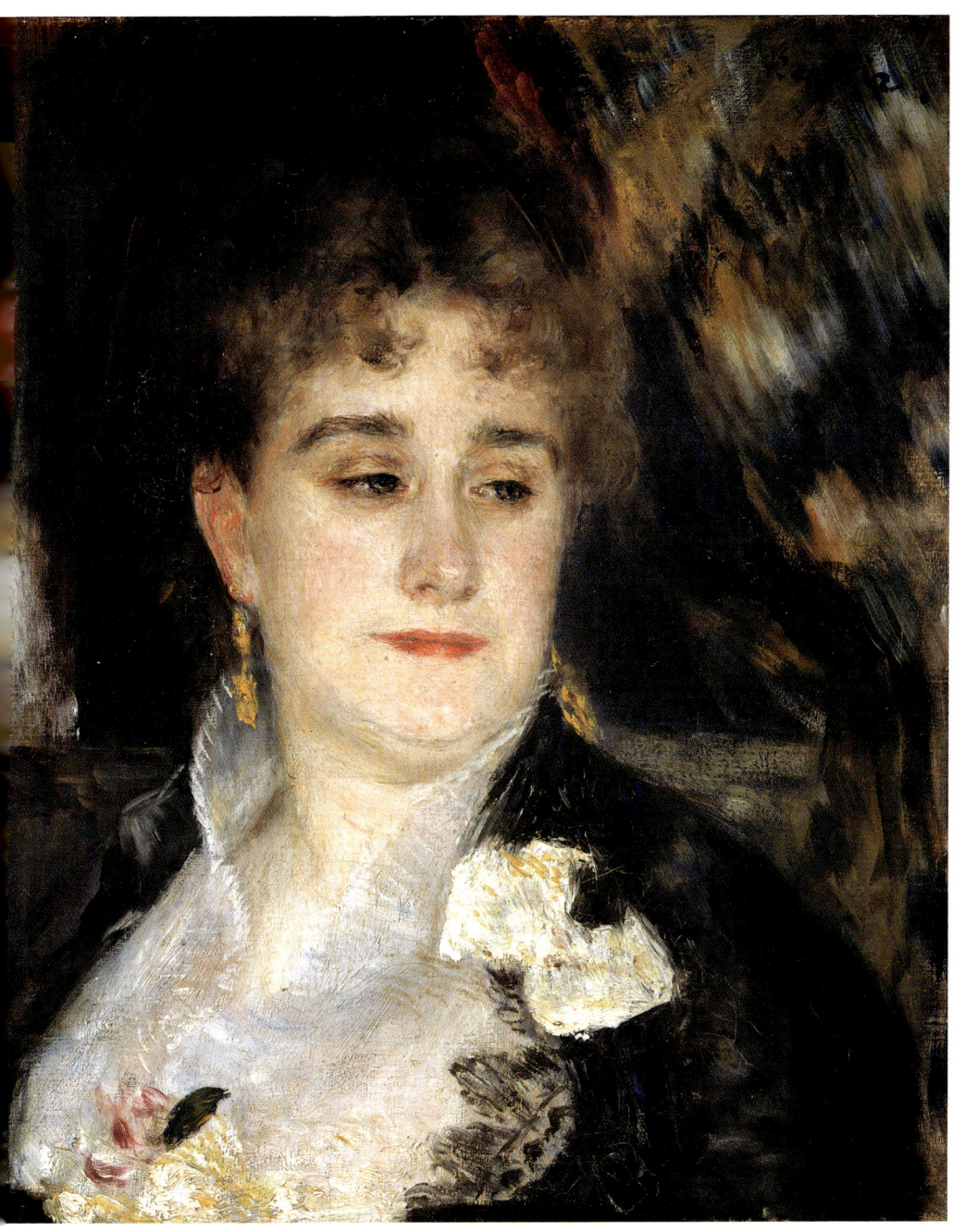

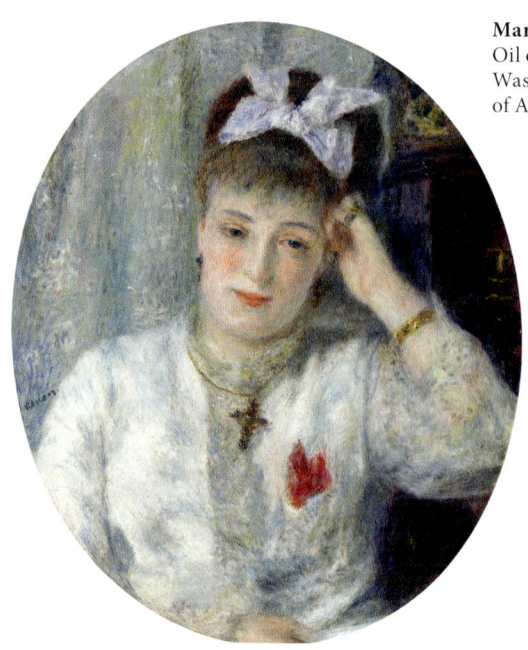

Marie Murer, 1877
Oil on canvas, 67.6 x 57.1 cm (26⅝ x 22½ in.)
Washington, D.C., National Gallery
of Art, Chester Dale Collection

Eugène Murer, 1877
Oil on canvas, 47 x 39.4 cm (18⅝ x 15⅝ in.)
New York, The Metropolitan Museum
of Art, The Walter H. and Leonore
Annenberg Collection, Bequest of
Walter H. Annenberg

Ride in the Bois de Boulogne (p. 209), for which the real Henriette Darras posed, looks today like a monumental farewell to the fumblings of youth. It is a huge contraption of almost three metres in width. It attempts to rival Degas in the depiction of the horses but is above all redolent of the academician Carolus-Duran, an old friend of the Charpentiers and the darling of the Salons. Renoir attempts here the style of the fashionable painters of high society. The ambitious Manet also tried his hand at it when he depicted *Marie Lefébure as an Amazon.* Yet the static elegance of Carolus-Duran's equestrian portrait, *At the Seaside, Sophie Croizette on Horseback*, makes it by far the most successful and reflects a certain Parisian chic that still eluded Renoir. Sophie Croizette, Carolus-Duran's sister-in-law, also happened to be Sarah Bernhardt's main rival at the Comédie-Française. This was yet another society painting to be acclaimed at the 1873 Salon. The Bois de Boulogne, meanwhile, was becoming synonymous with acts of seduction.

Edmond Morin's engraving *A Gallop in the Bois de Boulogne* (p. 208), which adorned the cover of the aptly-named publication *L'Esprit Follet,* alludes to the fact openly. Yet Renoir's "bread-and-butter" painting contains not the faintest hint of these games of seduction. This is a serious omission; Renoir has not yet "caught on". The elegant Bois de Boulogne was not Montmartre: it was still a foreign country to him. Renoir admitted to Berthe Morisot that, as he was not used to painting horses, he had copied from those who knew better. He may have had Velázquez in mind, or the steeds depicted by Rubens, or Delacroix's horses which chase Heliodorus out of the Temple in the church

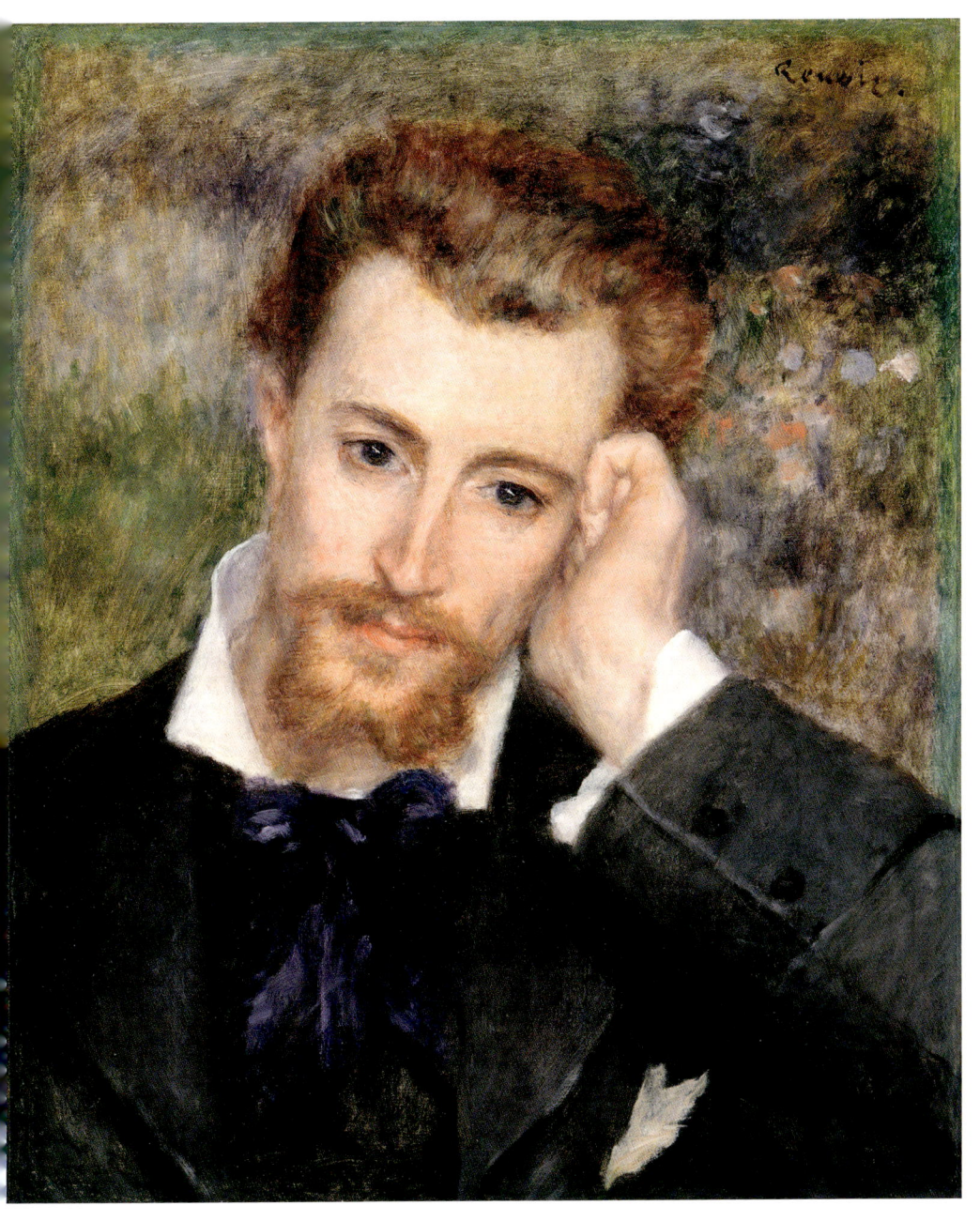

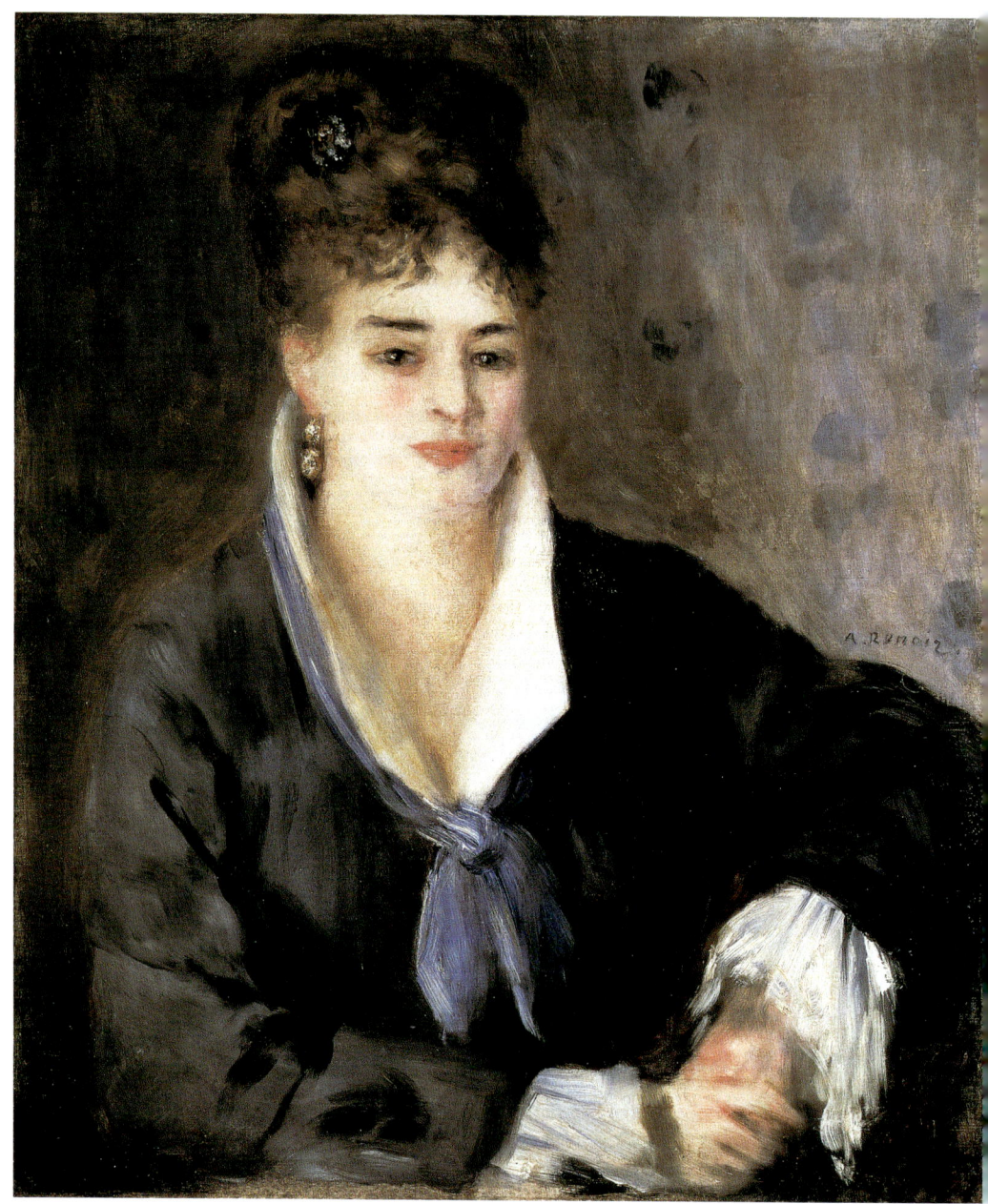

Lady in a Black Dress, c. 1876
Oil on canvas,
65.5 x 55.5 cm (25⅞ x 21⅞ in.)
Saint Petersburg, Hermitage Museum

of Saint-Sulpice. Perhaps he also copied the illustrations, in *L'Esprit Follet*, of women riding side-saddle, accompanied by their mounted cavaliers. What Degas would have had to say about the horses' hooves does not bear thinking about. The art critics of the day, who never missed an opportunity for getting it wrong, praised the work and Stanislas-Henri Rouart, an industrialist and discerning collector, acquired the painting in 1874 for the sum of 2,000 francs. The painting has enjoyed less success since then. Meier-Graefe considered that Renoir had moved away from Impressionism and taken "a backwards step in the direction of *Diana*" (p. 44). Rewald described it as a "gigantic but rather conventional painting". White summed it up when he called it Renoir's "last academic, realist work".

Carolus-Duran was far from being the clumsiest of the academicians. They sought inspiration from Velázquez, Van Dyck and Courbet. But Degas's judgement, "they shoot away at us while rifling through our pockets", is telling. Their historical paintings were too meticulous, their orientalism too gaudy, their Spanish works too fake, and their realism too saccharine. On the other hand, they included virtuoso portraitists among their number. Carolus-Duran's *Woman with a Glove* (*The Artist's Wife*; p. 210), famous for its technique and colour scheme, was so successful that he became over-whelmed with commissions. Despite his preference for ancient models, he became the most admired portrait-painter of his time. Clairin, a mediocre historical painter, was also a virtuoso portraitist. His friend Sarah Bernhardt insisted on being immor-talised by him, and he did so with talent, putting her in a daring pose. Charles Garnier

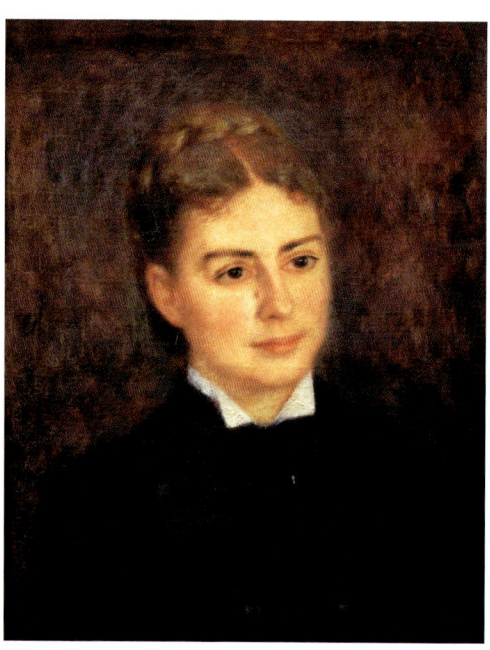

Madame Paul Bérard, 1879
Oil on canvas, 49.5 x 40 cm (19½ x 15¾ in.)
Paris, Musée d'Orsay,
on loan to the Château-Musée de Dieppe

Paul Bérard, 1880
Oil on canvas,
50 x 40 cm (19¾ x 15¾ in.)
Private collection

commissioned him to paint three high ceilings for the Paris Opera house. These works are well-executed and could almost be called modern in style, if Baudelaire's definition of modernism is adopted, although they cannot be said to be great art in the Manet tradition. Baudelaire considered modernity to be an all-embracing concept. It covered "dress, hairstyles and even gestures, expressions and smiles (each era has its look, its expression and its smile). Is there a man alive who, whether in the street, at the theatre, or in the Bois [de Boulogne], has not taken a cool enjoyment from the fact that he is immaculately dressed and who has not been transported by the beauty of a woman in a dress, making the two into an indivisible whole?"

When he painted his *Portrait of a Woman* (*Nini Fish-face*; p. 211) in 1874, Renoir was still thinking (no doubt enviously) of his rival, the acclaimed academician with pots of money. He reverts here to a style that is still traditional in its smooth execution and somber colour scheme. The transparent glaze of the background shows off his talents as a porcelain-painter. Nini also posed for *The Theatre Box* (p. 87) in 1874, the year of the first Impressionist exhibition. On this occasion Renoir puts one over his high society rivals. He succeeds in bringing to a painting done in artificial light the palette and freer brushstrokes of his landscapes. He conveys with unique skill the magic of milky flesh. As soon as he used a close friend rather than a client as his model, Renoir was able to relax. He used every means at his disposal to capture her beauty. Fragonard and Manet had preceded him in this and he in turn would inspire Matisse and Picasso in their depictions of feminine beauty.

234

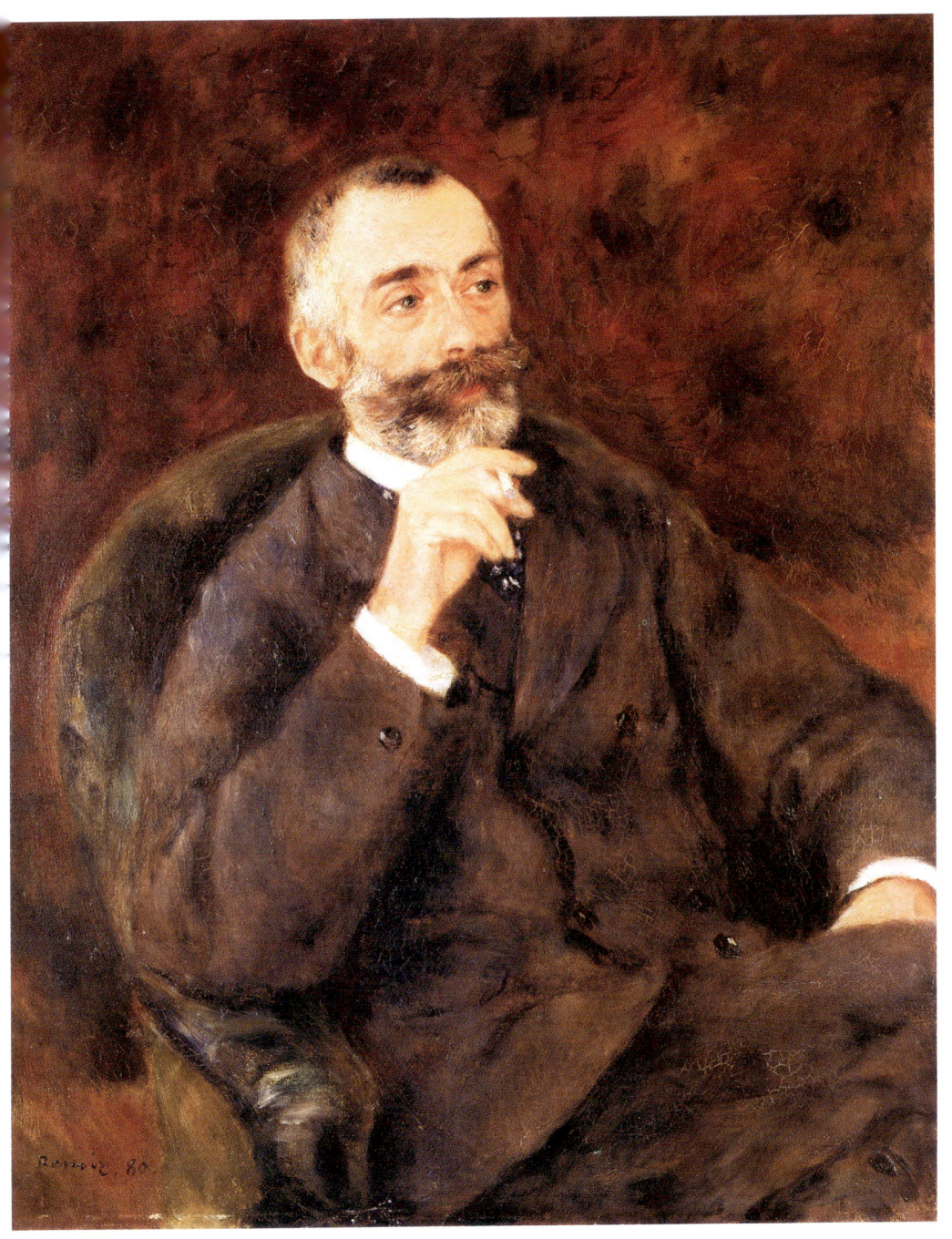

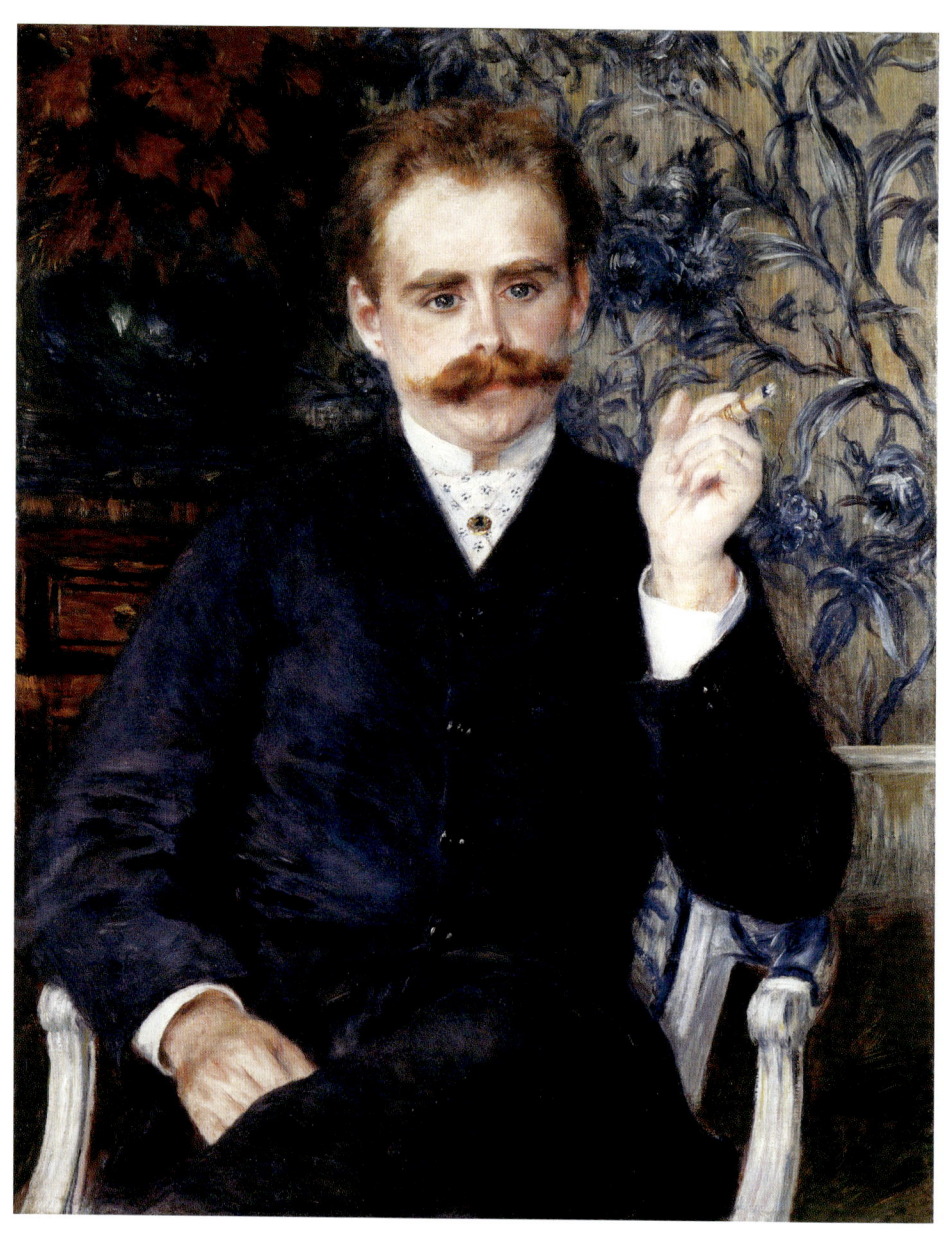

Albert Cahen d'Anvers, 1881
Oil on canvas, 80 x 63.8 cm (31½ x 25⅛ in.)
Los Angeles, The J. Paul Getty Museum

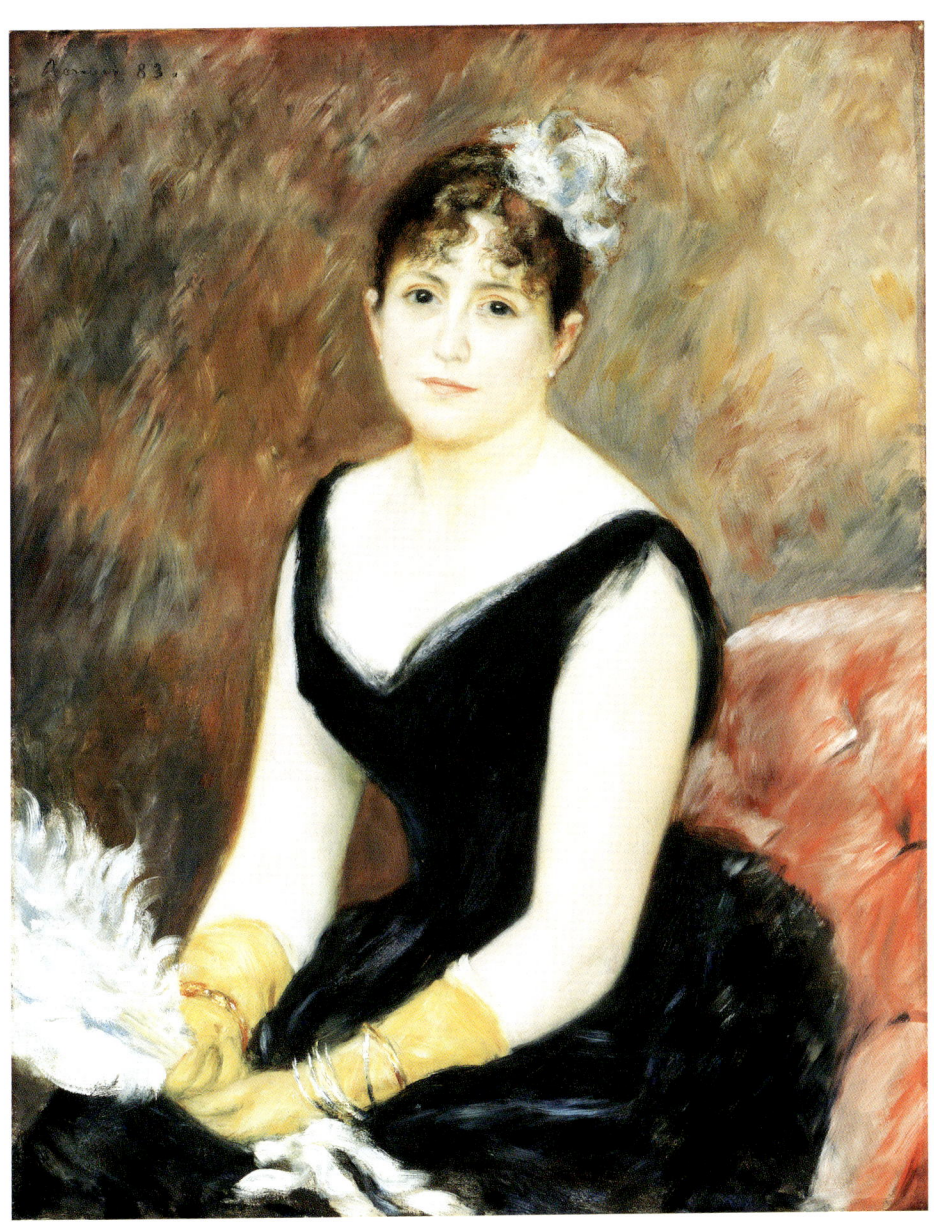

Madame Léon Clapisson, 1883
Oil on canvas, 81.2 x 65.3 cm (32 x 25¾ in.)
The Art Institute of Chicago,
Mr. and Mrs. Martin A. Ryerson Collection

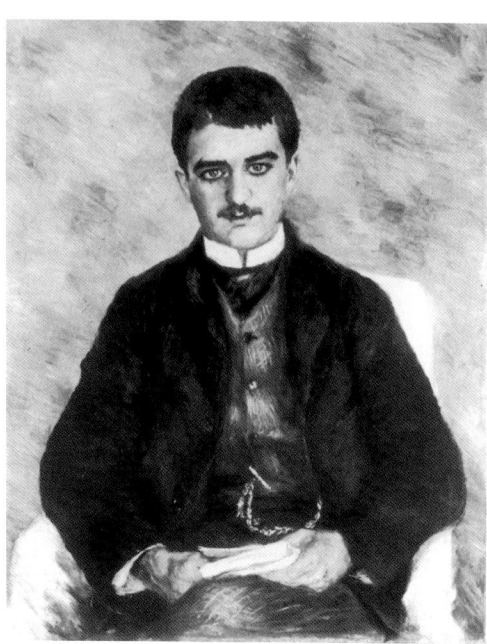

Joseph Durand-Ruel, 1882
Oil on canvas,
81 x 65 cm (32 x 25⅝ in.)
Private collection

In 1874, with the portrait of *Charles Le Cœur* (p. 217), Renoir resolutely entered the world of "new painting". Using small brushstrokes, hatching and cross-hatching, he creates a vivid portrait of his architect friend with whom he clearly had many good times and who helped him out at a time when collectors were hardly falling over themselves to buy his paintings. Le Cœur worked for the state but also built private homes for his wealthy friends, among them Prince Georges Bibesco. He commissioned Renoir to produce the interior decorations and in particular the ceilings for the Bibesco mansion. This improved the state of Renoir's finances to no end. This friendly and fruitful relationship, however, came to an abrupt but typical end when he was banned from the house for making advances to the Le Cœurs' eldest daughter.

The painter's rapid development in this period is particularly striking: in the course of a single year he changes from a style very reminiscent of Manet to one that would be dubbed "romantic Impressionism". *Claude Monet with Palette* (p. 216) and *Alfred Sisley* (p. 223) both show evidence of a transition from coarse brushstrokes to fine hatching that resembles the technique used in pastels. The strokes melt into one another, giving these portraits their vibrancy; the shapes and volumes obtained are the result of subtle gradations in a particularly daring palette. Renoir was always ready to change from one style to another or to combine them as he saw fit. Even the critics eventually succumbed to the charm of Renoir's portraits of women and children. They began praising his "lively art", his "agile and witty brush", and "that cheerful grace that makes colour so bewitching". Gradually his portraits revealed the inner man. This makes his portraits

Madame Joseph Durand-Ruel, 1911
Oil on canvas,
92 x 73 cm (36¼ x 28¾ in.)
Private collection

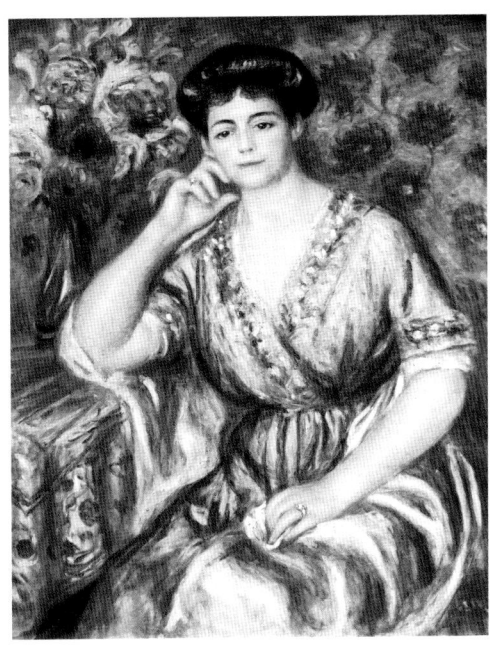

so different from Cézanne's organic architectures or Van Gogh's tormented lyricism. Renoir strove to marry the achievements of Impressionism with light classical painting. "There is nothing new in my paintings; they follow on from the eighteenth century", he explained. This situation lasted until the day when, as Jean Renoir writes in his memoirs, "the birth of his son sent all his theories flying. All of the ideas he had formulated in the Nouvelle Athènes café were suddenly undone by a fold in a baby's thigh".

For the moment, his two tendencies continued to alternate. One *Self-Portrait*, painted in the mid-1876s (p. 225), can be compared with a photograph taken of him at the same age (p. 86). They show a Renoir who looks much younger than his thirty-five years, contemplating the world with a sad and shy expression. In a few brushstrokes, the artist captures his own likeness and unease. "His self-portrait reminds me of the best Goyas, while being stamped with the same personality", Armand Sylvestre wrote, with the *Self-Portrait* on the frontispiece of the *Caprices* in mind. Lefort's remark about Goya could only have pleased Renoir and shown him that he was on the right track. "Goya's tendencies make him essentially a modern man", he wrote. "His style of portraiture, habits of composition, and the way in which he interprets the light are the techniques of the past – but equally of the future". Critics also talk of an "intensity of expression in Renoir which is reminiscent of Rembrandt". It is as if the two painters shared a desire to study themselves in front of a mirror at certain moments in their lives. Of course, Renoir did not produce anything like the ninety self-portraits through which Rembrandt chronicled his slow decline from the triumph of youth to the semi-senility of old age, through

The Daughters of Durand-Ruel, 1882
Oil on canvas, 81.3 x 65.4 cm (32 x 25¾ in.)
Norfolk, Virginia, Chrysler Museum of Art,
Gift of Walter P. Chrysler, Jr.
in memory of Thelma Chrysler Foy

periods of scepticism, defiance, sadness, vulnerability and courage, until the ravages of alcohol and madness finally caught up with him. Rembrandt's particular experience of self-portraiture cannot be generalised. What Rembrandt sees in himself makes him bitter, as it does those who look at his self-portraits. Renoir shares the same goal of self-exploration; but his conclusions are optimistic and even angelic. Each portrait of his maid, Gabrielle, is a hymn to blossoming femininity and his peasant girls have the features and allure of a *Venus Triumphant*. In the *Self-Portrait* (p. 225) that he painted at the age of thirty-five, the wrinkles revealed by the contemporary photograph (p. 86) have been brushed away. In the one that he painted eighteen years later (p. 253), the same care is taken to remove the stigmata of age and illness. Photographs, taken shortly afterwards, belie the image.

In a diary entry for 1899, Julie Manet reported that Renoir was finishing "a very handsome self-portrait. At first he made himself look a little too hard and wrinkled; we demanded that he remove a few wrinkles and now it is a better likeness. 'I think these look too much like calf's eyes', he told me." Renoir's self-portrait reveals, beneath the outward show of amiability, physical frailties and worries about old age and illness. He was fifty-eight years old by this time and his rheumatism was worsening in a prelude to the arthritis that would confine him to his wheelchair at the end of his life (p. 483). Even then, according to Thadée Nathanson's description, he remained constantly restless: "He comes back and goes away again, sits down and gets up, then when he is standing up, he sits down again, rises from his chair and searches for the cigarette that he

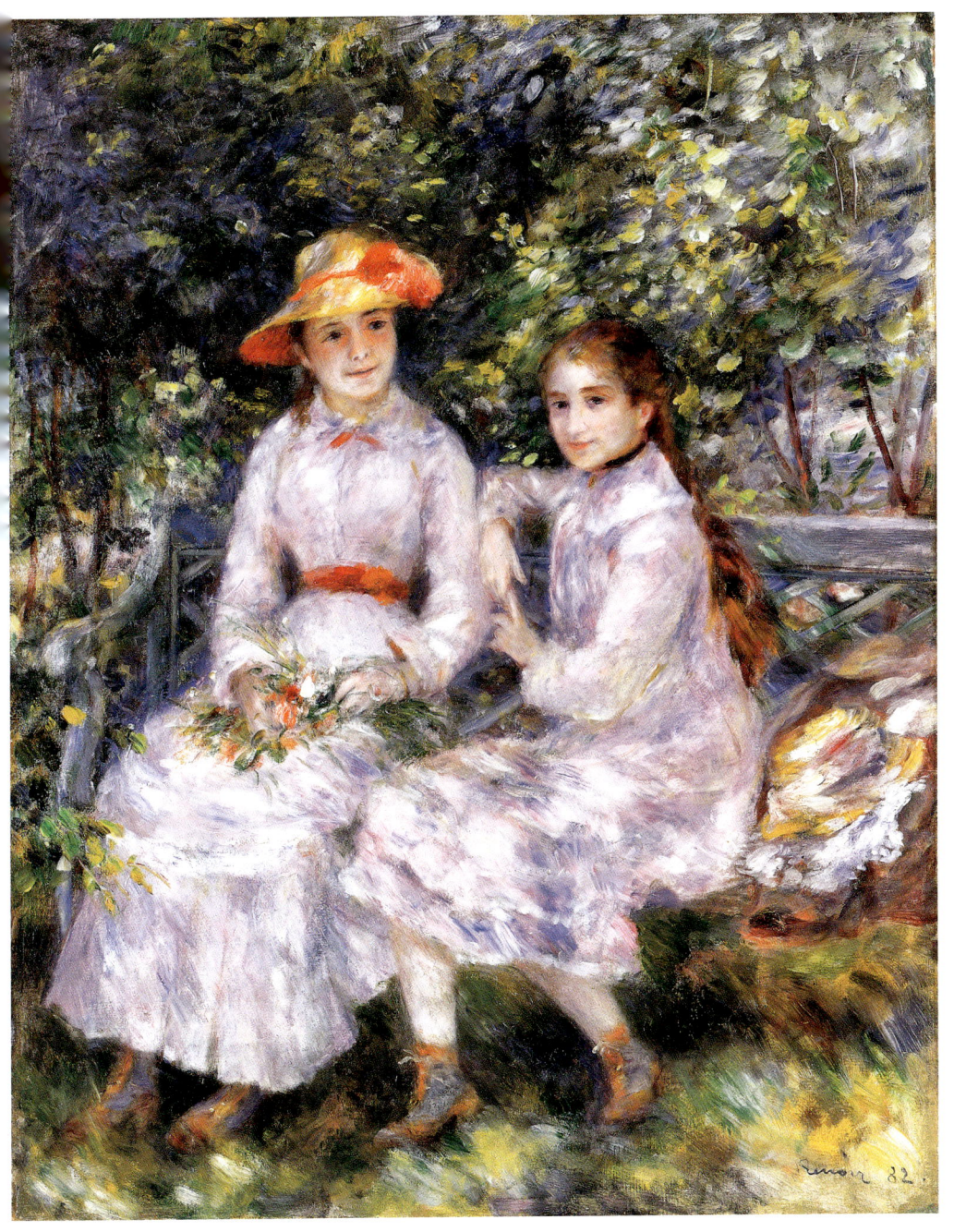

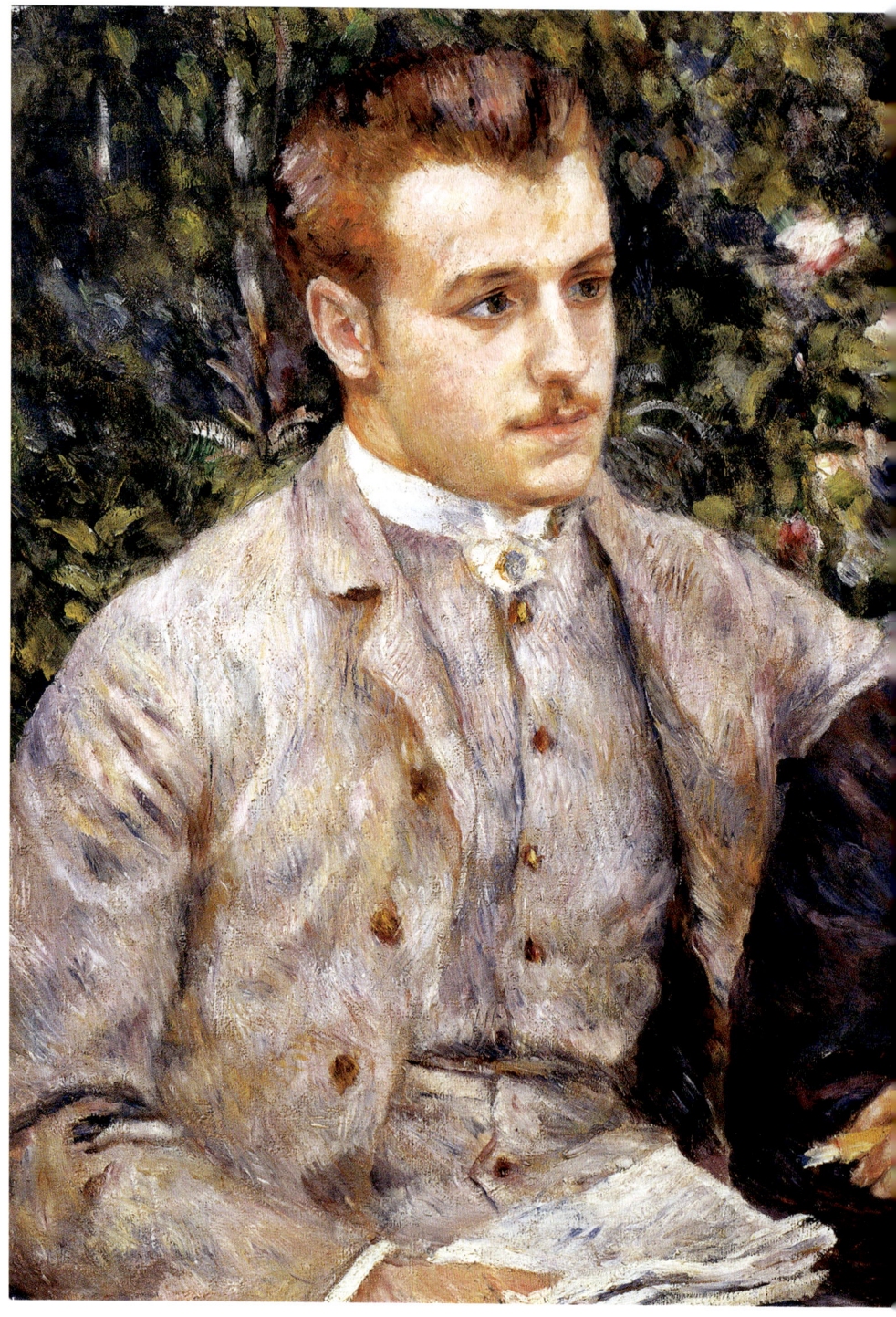

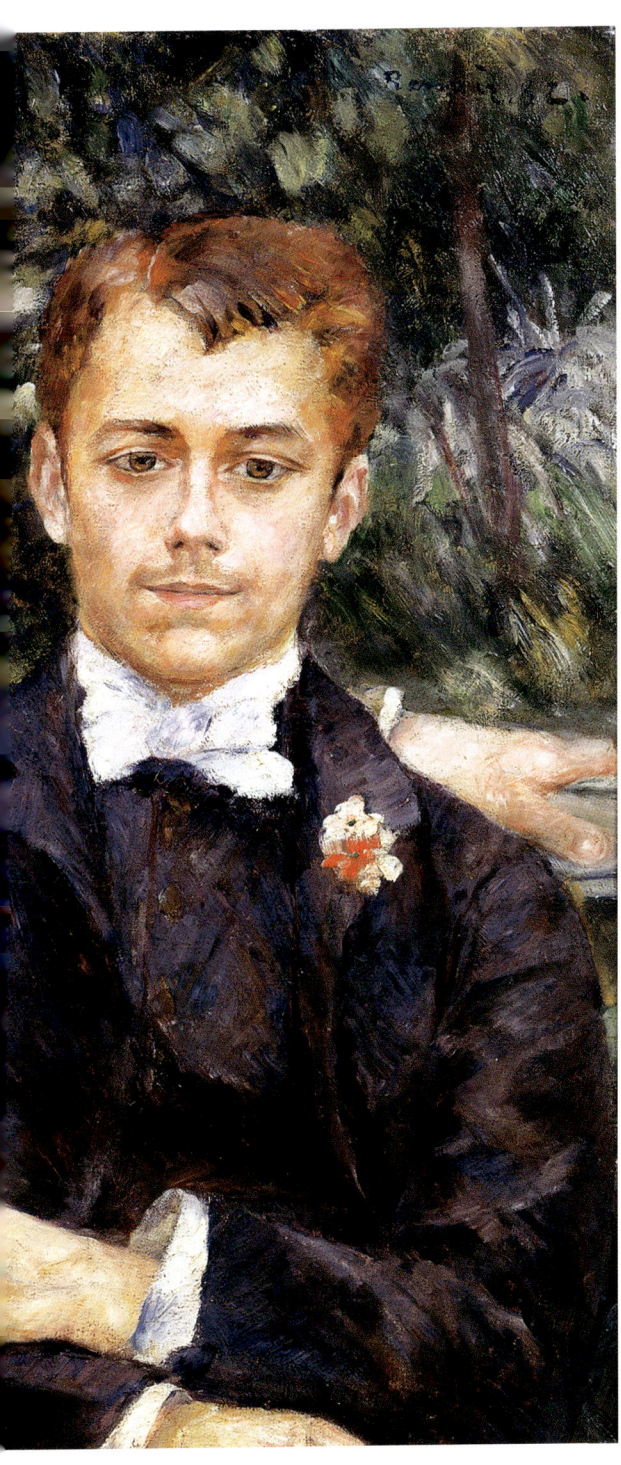

**Charles and Georges
Durand-Ruel**, 1882
Oil on canvas,
65 x 81 cm (25⅝ x 32 in.)
Private collection

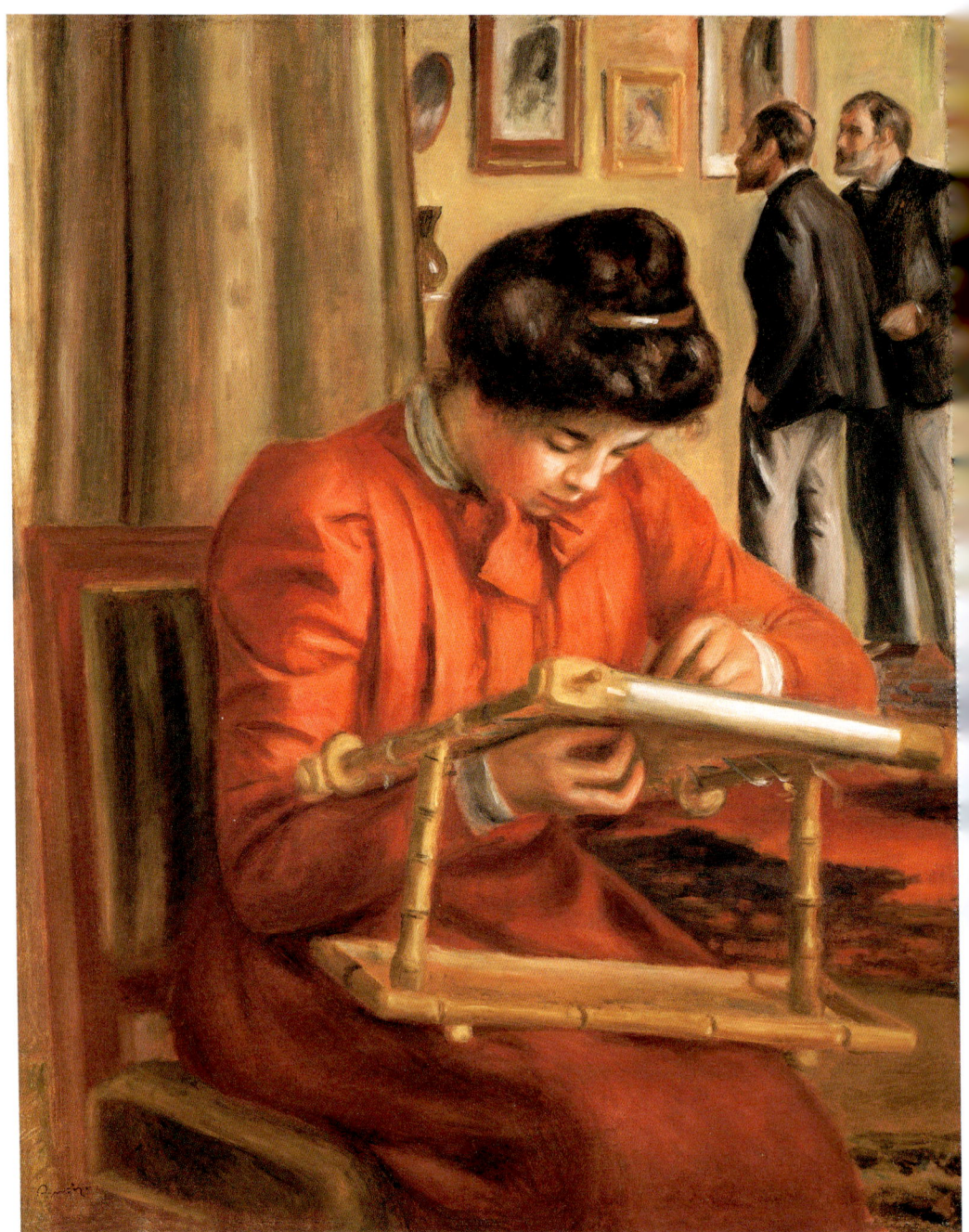

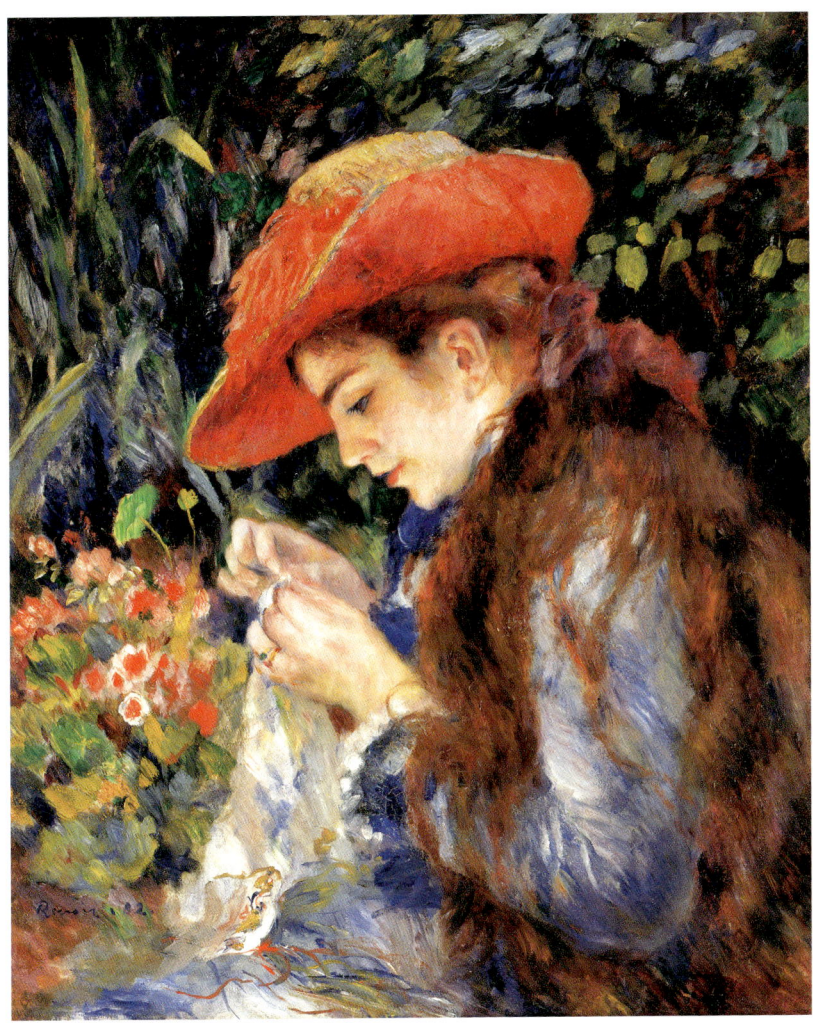

Christine Lerolle Embroidering, c. 1895–1898
Oil on canvas, 81.6 x 65.7 cm (32¼ x 25⅞ in.)
Columbus Museum of Art,
Gift of Howard D. and Babette L. Sirak,
the Donors to the Campaign for Enduring
Excellence, and the Derby Fund

Marie-Thérèse Durand-Ruel Sewing, 1882
Oil on canvas, 64.9 x 54 cm (25⅝ x 21⅜ in.)
Williamstown, Massachusetts, The Clark

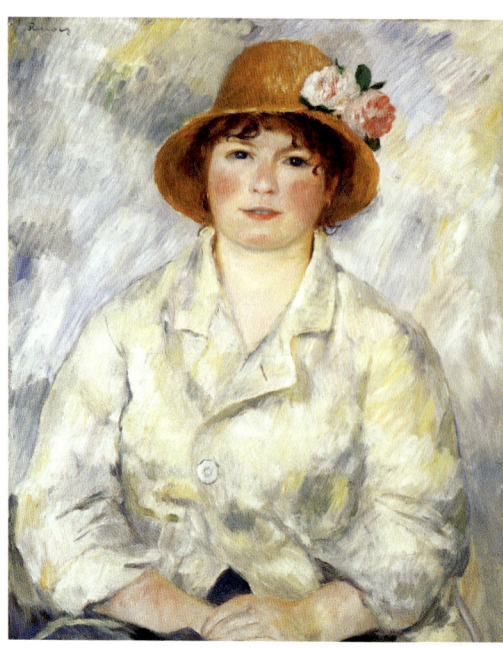

**Portrait of Aline Charigot
(later Madame Renoir)**, c. 1885
Oil on canvas, 65.4 x 54 cm (25¾ x 21⅜ in.)
Philadelphia Museum of Art,
The W. P. Wilstach Collection

Mlle Charlotte Berthier, 1883
Oil on canvas,
92.1 x 73 cm (36⅜ x 28¾ in.)
Washington, D.C.,
National Gallery of Art,
Gift of Angelika Wertheim Frink

must have left on a wooden stool, or maybe over there, or on the easel – no, it's there
on the table. Then he decides to roll another one anyway which he will probably lose
before he finds a way of lighting it anyway." "There was something of the old Arab
about my father", Jean Renoir recalled. The *Self-Portrait* that he painted at the age of
sixty-nine (p. 257) reveals an idealised vision. The deep lines that furrowed his face
around 1912 (see the photograph on p. 476) have been wiped away by his paintbrush.
Renoir's customary restlessness and worry are, however, clearly visible. Another *Self-
Portrait,* painted in the same year, is more honest. It shows a man who is gentle and calm
but very old. Even though he is condemned to a wheelchair, he maintains a luminous
serenity which belies the crippling physical pain he was suffering. His eyes continue
to look at life in its true brilliance, and his work continues to extract from the outside
world only what he enjoys.

Camille Pissarro described Renoir as "the most changeable of men". This description
fits the hesitation in his portraits between Impressionist brushstroke technique and
the more melting "romantic" look that he had perfected. This hesitation, according
to Théodore Duret, caused him to suffer a thought-provoking setback: "Renoir was
commissioned to paint the portrait of Madame Clapisson. The first portrait of her that
he produced (*Among the Roses,* 1882) was executed in very pale tones with brightly
coloured flowers surrounding the model. It was far too daring. He had to keep it
and paint a second one in darker tones (*Madame Léon Clapisson*, p. 237), which was
accepted. Since the model in the rejected portrait was altered beyond recognition, it

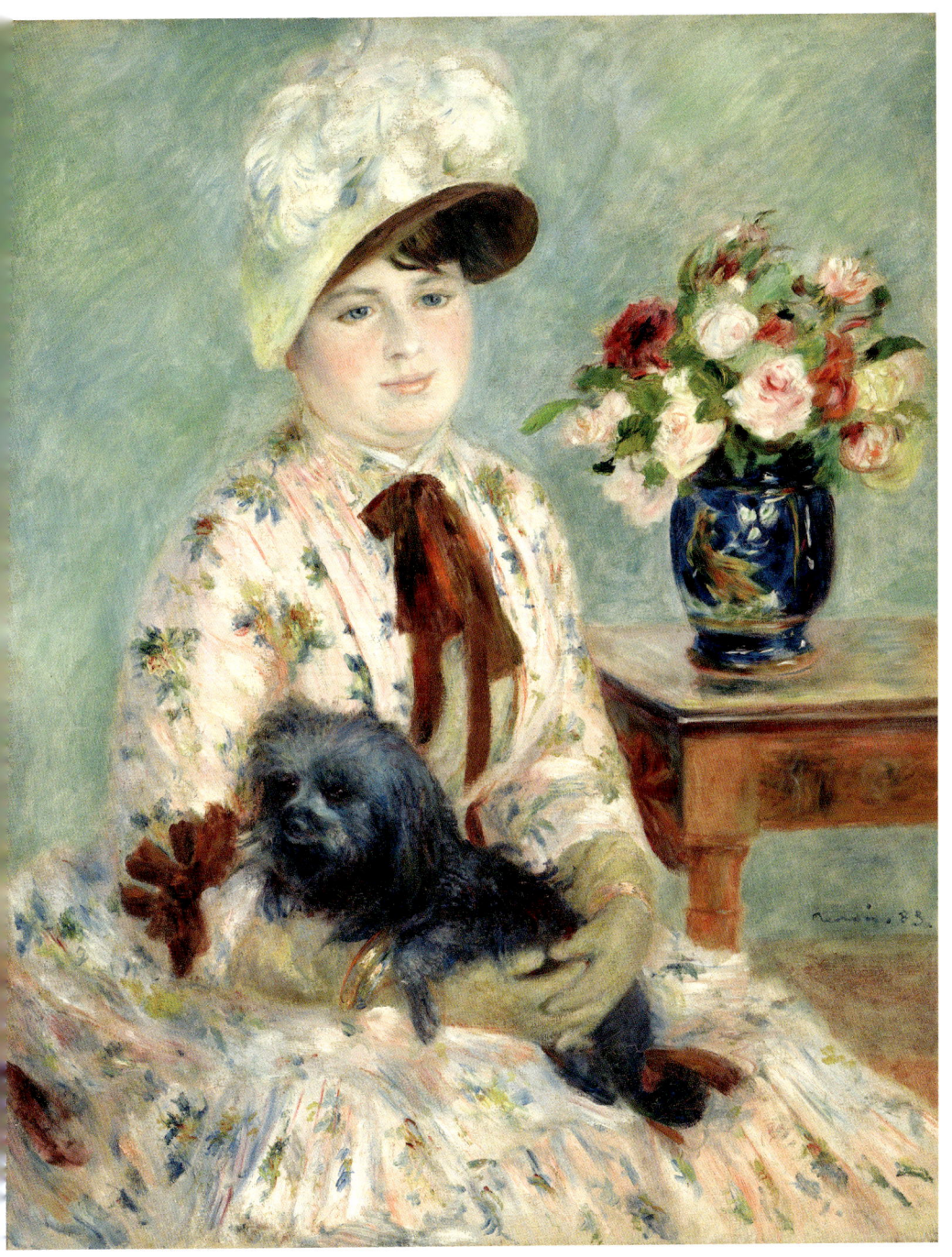

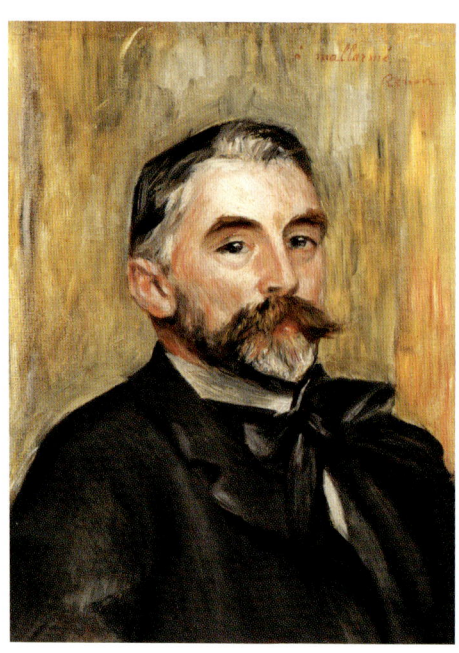

Stéphane Mallarmé, 1892
Oil on canvas,
50 x 40 cm (19¾ x 15¾ in.)
Paris, Musée d'Orsay

**Berthe Morisot and Her
Daughter Julie Manet**, 1894
Oil on canvas,
81 x 65 cm (32 x 25⅝ in.)
Private collection

was possible to sell it. It was one of Renoir's first works to end up in America." The twin portraits of Madame Clapisson clearly illustrate the way in which Renoir's portrait painting developed between his Impressionist and his Ingres period. The portrait of *Madame de Senonnes* (1814–1816), in purely classical style, became his source of inspiration. Raymond Cogniat notes that "Renoir began to understand the use of accepting, and even imposing on himself, certain constraints. Despite the fact that he had hitherto espoused theories that favoured the greatest measure of freedom, this gave him the means to paint much more rigorously". Renoir later said that Madame Charpentier was the person who had helped him to make the decisive step. Finding himself accused of having made too many U-turns, a certain politician once made an observation which is apposite here: "The weathervane never changes, only the wind", he said. Renoir himself never changed; he remained simple and affectionate. It was his technique, and the type of models that he painted, which gradually altered. Elegant children or society women now replaced his friends from his bohemian days and their partners. But the painter's vision remained as serene as ever. The fact that the work was commissioned had no effect on the vivacity of his palette. He had come of age both as a painter and as a man. Access to cultivated and liberal society was extremely important for him. Not only did it finally allow him to escape poverty – a significant development – but it also produced a harmony between the material conditions of his life and the moral character of his painting. This explains the impression of comfort and sincerity that Renoir's work exudes at every stage of his career.

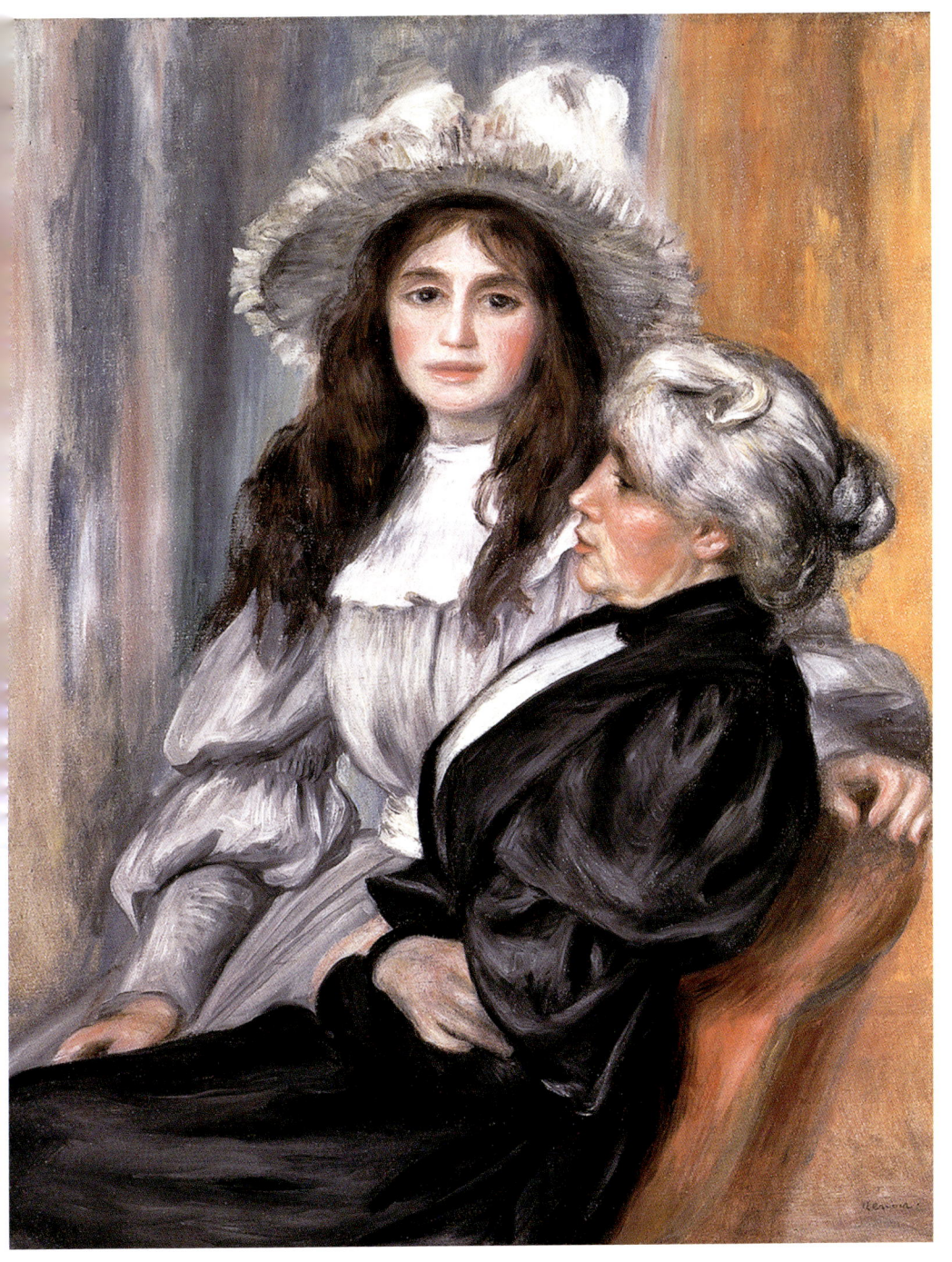

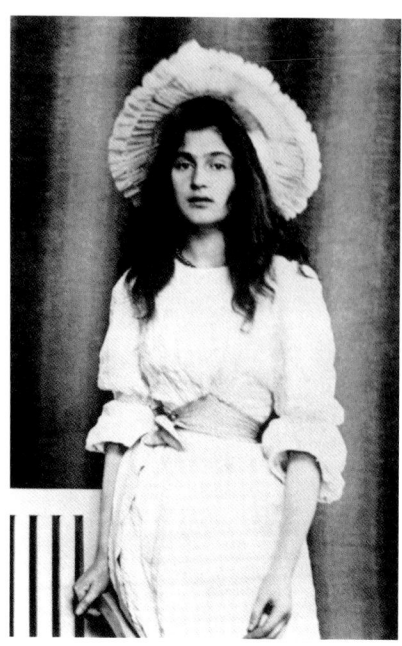

Julie Manet (1878–1966) in 1894

Julie Manet, 1894
Oil on canvas,
55 x 46 cm (21¾ x 18⅛ in.)
Paris, Musée Marmottan Monet

Renoir found it no surprise when he was accepted into the wealthy social circles from which he had hitherto been excluded. He felt perfectly at ease in them. Georges Rivière explains why: "Although Renoir did not enjoy society gatherings, he loved his visits to Madame Charpentier. At her house he found himself in an intelligent milieu from which she, with her customary tact and grace, banished everything which was depressing and boring." Renoir was something of a chameleon. Whether among old friends or at a society reception he could adapt to his environment. "Compare compositions such as *Moulin de la Galette* or *Rowers at Bougival* on the one hand", Raymond Cogniat observes, "with the portraits of the Charpentier or Bérard families, or even of Jeanne Samary, on the other. You will notice instantly that despite the huge social gap between these different people, they are all equals in the eyes of the painter. Renoir gives freshness and spontaneity to each figure, so the two series of paintings do not contradict each other in any way. They prove Renoir's ability to leave his mark on everything he tackled and to remove all vulgarity from working class pastimes and all formality from upper class ones. What makes Renoir an exceptional portraitist is that he succeeds in removing from all his models any artificiality resulting from their social status. He always succeeds in releasing his sitter from all sense of constraint. Those who have placed their memories on record invariably emphasise the patience and kindness he showed to gain their trust."

Renoir's greatest weakness was for women. Although he recognized no difference between the rich and poor, he certainly did between men and women. His portraits

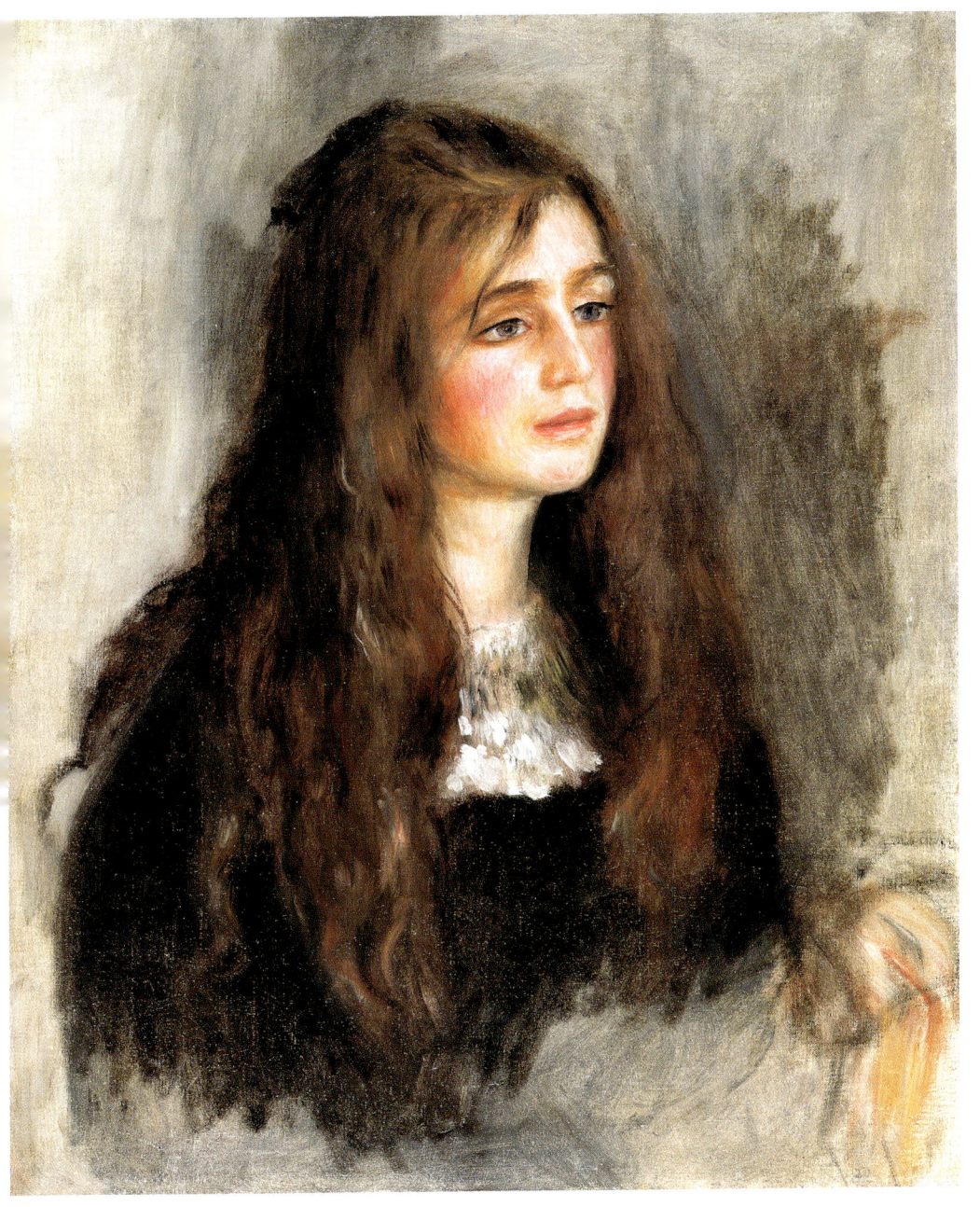

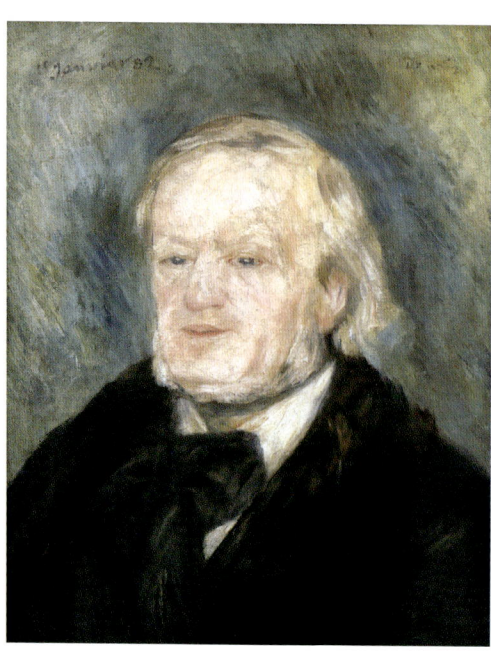

Richard Wagner, 1882
Oil on canvas,
51.3 x 44.7 cm (20¼ x 17⅝ in.)
Paris, Musée d'Orsay

Self-Portrait, 1899
Oil on canvas,
41.4 x 33.7 cm (16⅜ x 13⅜ in.)
Williamstown, Massachusetts,
The Clark

are proof of this. Human beings are not objects or tools for Renoir, as they were for Cézanne or Degas. But if Michelangelo had a taste for the handsome young men that he painted, Renoir's preference was for attractive women. This explains why his portraits of men are often judged to be of less interest than the ones he did of women. He never tries to probe beyond the appearance of his masculine models. None of them possess that luminous radiance that he found, and represented, in women. The sole exceptions to this rule are children. Renoir was clearly in love with womanhood in general; he liked and befriended men but never felt their charm. Jean Renoir noted that his father, giving free rein to his inclinations at the end of his life, told him: "'I can only bear women around me.' They certainly returned his affection. My father blossomed both physically and temperamentally in the company of women. The voices of men tired him; women's voices he found relaxing. He insisted that the maids should be allowed to sing, laugh, and make noises around him as he worked. The more childish their songs were, the more delighted he was by them."

The portrait of *Stéphane Mallarmé* (p. 248), a close friend who did much for him and the other Impressionists, is a beautiful mask, almost a sculpture in fact. But it says nothing about Mallarmé, the most important poet of the Symbolist movement in whose subtle language the music of the words is as important as their meaning. Renoir's preference for women sometimes led him to "feminise" his male models. He scrupulously respected both the physical features and the character of his subject, or at least his public face. But sympathy and affection were more important. The satiny texture of

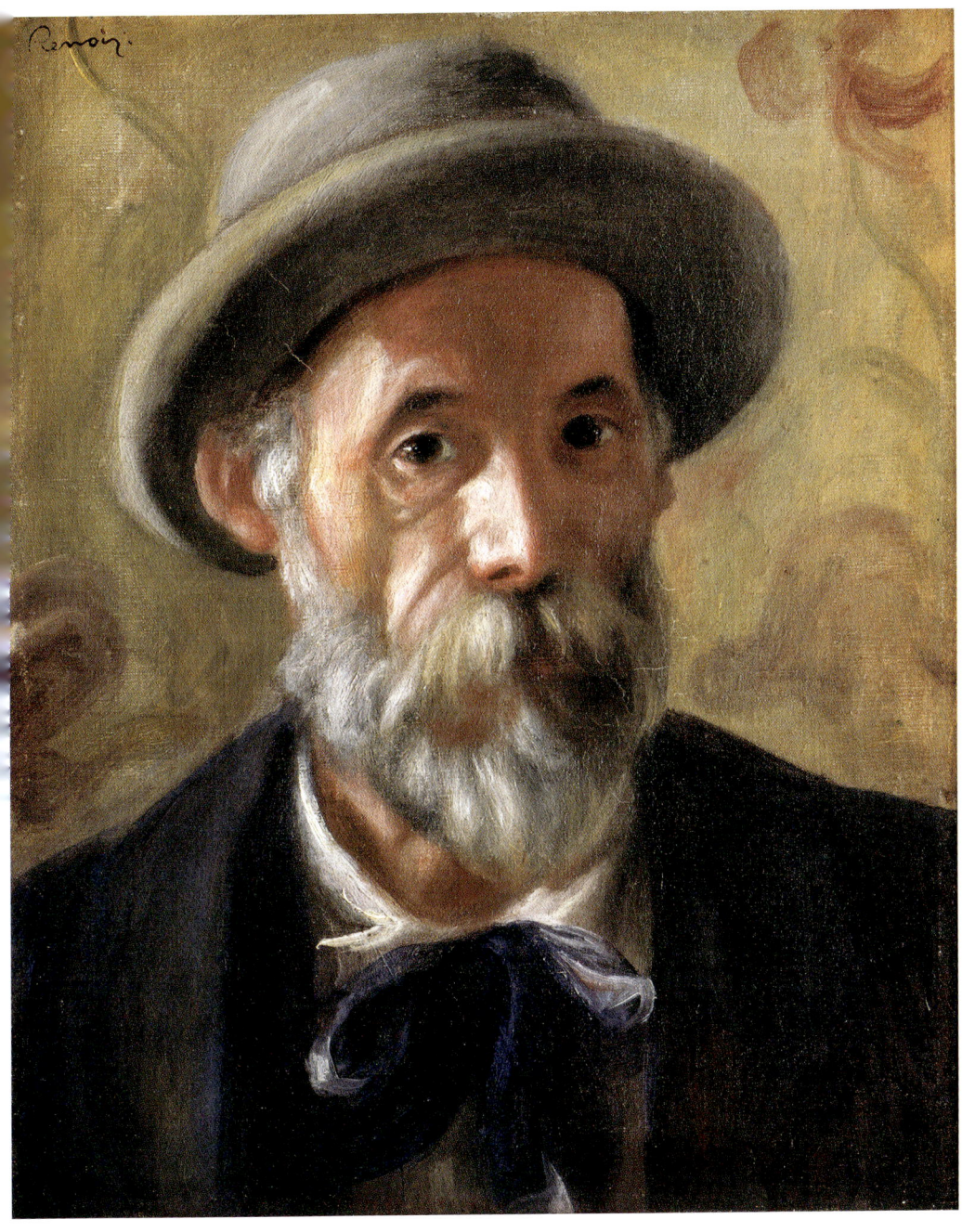

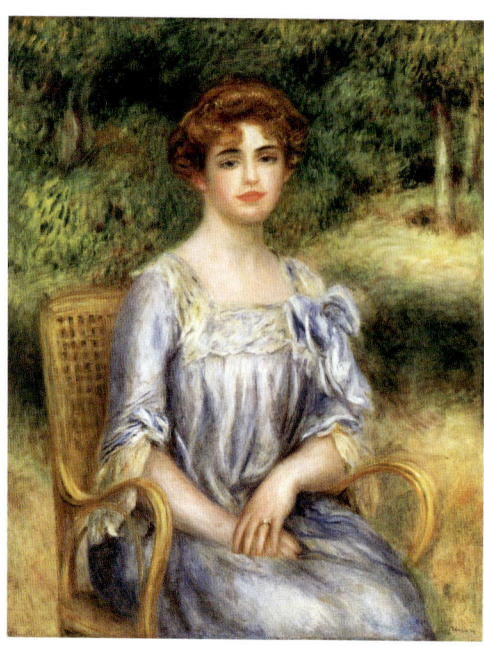

**Madame Gaston Bernheim de Villers,
née Suzanne Adler**, 1901
Oil on canvas, 92 x 73 cm (36¼ x 28¾ in.)
Paris, Musée d'Orsay

Misia Sert, 1904
Oil on canvas,
92.1 x 73 cm (36⅜ x 28¾ in.)
London, The National Gallery

the skin is rendered in tiny brushstrokes with extreme delicacy. He made all his models look younger and more attractive by erasing their wrinkles and softening any sign of surliness. This is even true of the portrait of *Richard Wagner* (1882, p. 252), which is known to have been painted in the thirty-five minutes that the musician granted him, and of the portrait of *Paul Cézanne* (1880, p. 224). The latter was so intriguingly different from the self-portraits that Cézanne had done that Cézanne copied it and kept it for the rest of his life. Where Renoir took no more than thirty-five minutes to paint a portrait, Cézanne is known to have needed forty sittings before he was satisfied with the merest shirt-front.

Renoir's brother Edmond recorded his virtuosity and speed in completing a portrait: "He worked with such prodigious virtuosity that he only needed a single sitting with the model. She would then leave her seat, come over and study the canvas, and say that she thought the image was a very good likeness. But he always expected to be asked to return. Auguste accepted this as a necessary evil, but in his second visit he would only ever retouch the painting, sometimes merely completing the background and certain details of the dress, without making any changes to the face. We talked about this. 'What you have to understand is that nothing is as mobile as a face', he confided to me. 'Even if the features remain constant, the physiognomy changes with every twist and turn of the face. The eyes may be more or less tired. The forehead may be wrinkled with care, the hair may not always be arranged in the same way, and the smile, which was so natural today, may look forced tomorrow. Should I reproduce these changes? No, I should not!'"

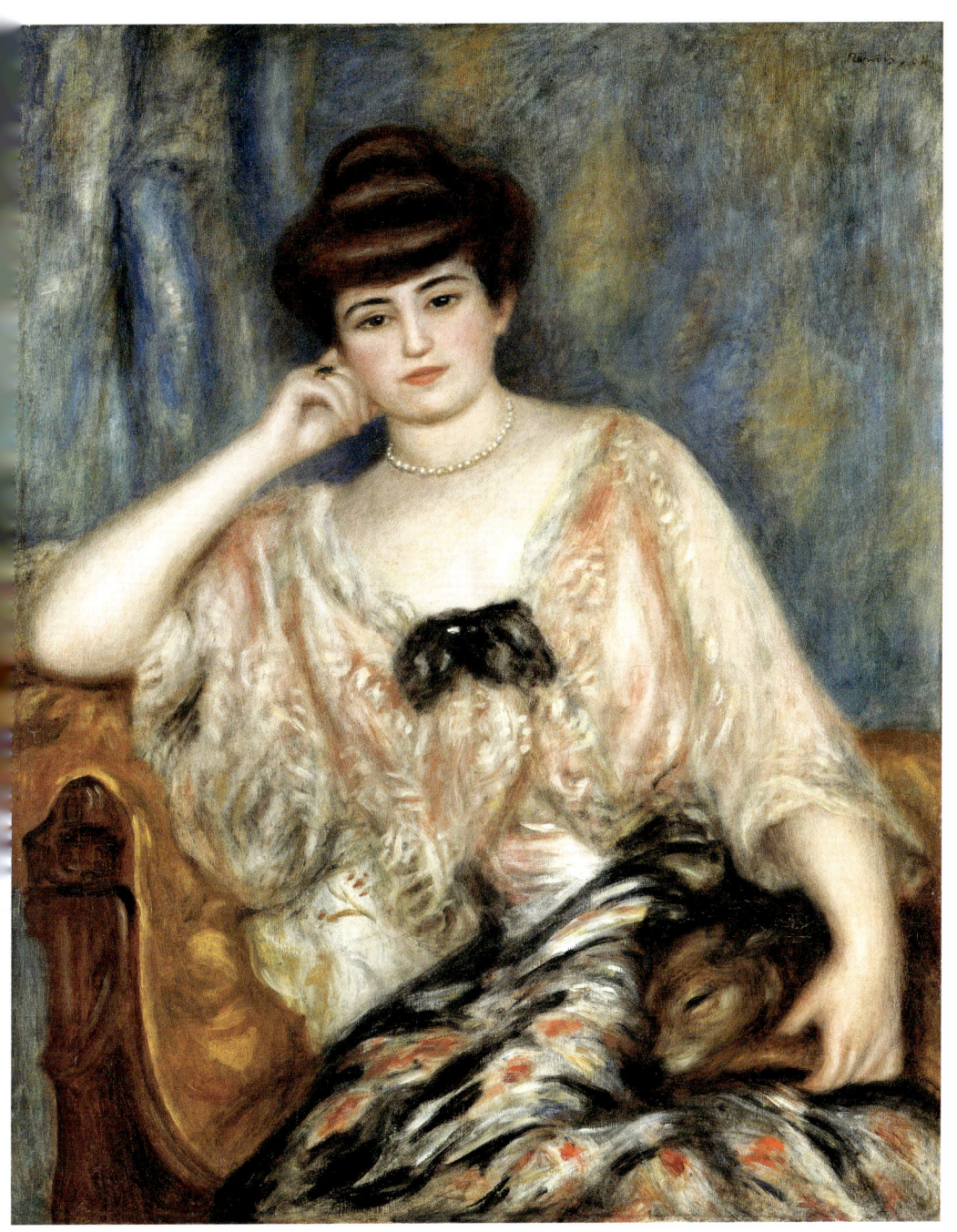

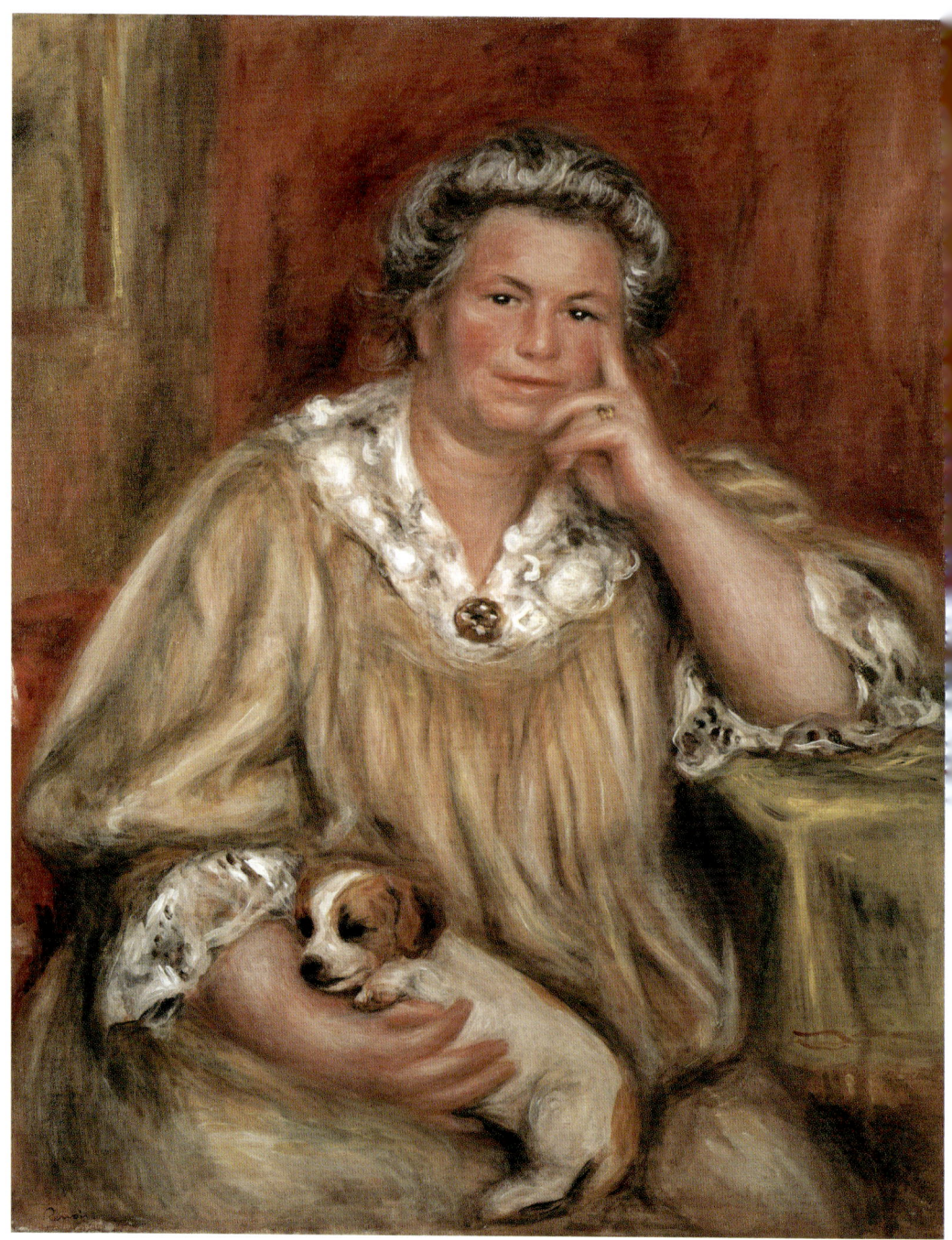

256

Self-Portrait, 1910
Oil on canvas,
45.7 x 38.1 cm (18 x 15 in.)
Private collection

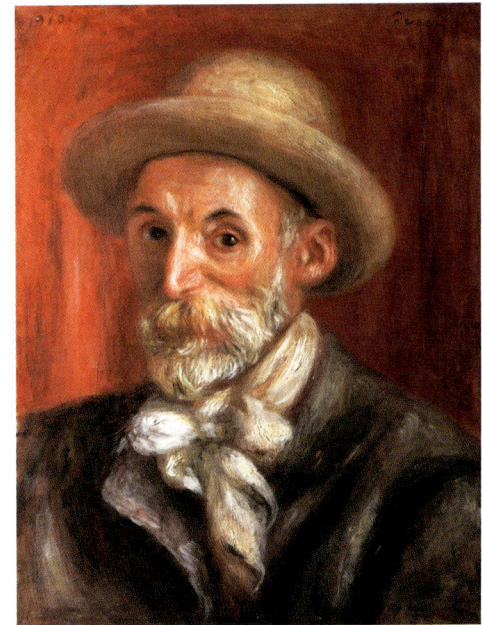

Madame Renoir, c. 1910
Oil on canvas, 81.2 x 65 cm (32 x 25½ in.)
Hartford, Wadsworth Atheneum Museum
of Art, The Ella Gallup Sumner and
Mary Catlin Sumner Collection Fund

With his typical brio, freshness and good humour, Renoir sketched in light washes of applied colour the face of *Wilhelm Mühlfeld* (p. 261), whom he barely knew and with whom he could not converse in his mother tongue. The photographs of Wilhelm Mühlfeld (p. 260) and Paul Durand-Ruel (p. 259) confirm that Renoir faithfully reproduced his models' features while making them younger, softer, and more expressive. There is fellow feeling in the German's expression. A deep affection emanates from his portrait of *Paul Durand-Ruel* (p. 258), the old man he loved so dearly and who, he wrote, "loved art and championed artists even before they died". The Impressionists, and Renoir in particular, owed so much to the man they affectionately called "Old Durand" or "the Saint Vincent de Paul of the Impressionists". One year before his death, Monet, who had become extremely wealthy by then, told René Gimpel that he had an outstanding debt of gratitude to Durand-Ruel. "He was the only person who fed me when I was hungry", Monet explained. The dealer and his sons went on performing services, especially financial ones, for the ageing artists, paying their rent, renewing their insurance policies, and taking care of charitable donations. Occasionally, Durand reprimanded Renoir (justifiably), as people still do today, for having signed sketches or incomplete works which might cause the value of his paintings to fall. Renoir was still worried about being "short" of money. "And how did you make your money, pray tell?" he retorted. "You have no other business operation than this, to the best of my knowledge!" The two men quarrelled on the occasion of the seventh Impressionist exhibition. Renoir wanted to stop exhibiting his works next to those of Pissarro and Gauguin,

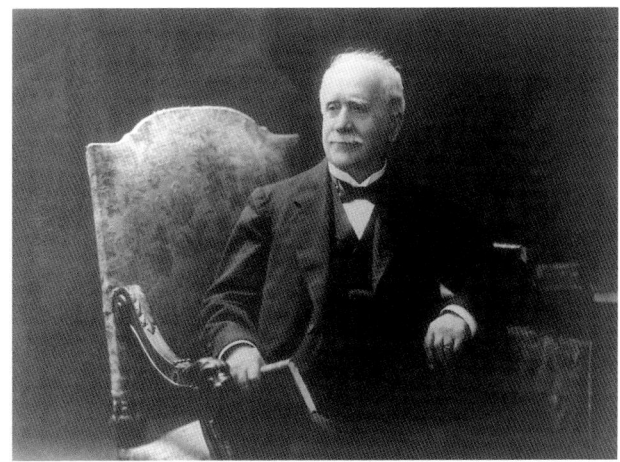

Paul Durand-Ruel (1831–1922),
c. 1910, photographed by
Eugène Pizon

Paul Durand-Ruel, 1910
Oil on canvas,
65 x 54 cm (25⅝ x 21⅜ in.)
Private collection

preferring the official Salon. "I only have one aim in life", he wrote to Durand-Ruel, "and that is to make the value of my paintings rise. Exhibiting with Pissarro, Gauguin and Guillaumin would be like exhibiting for charity. What is even worse is that Pissarro has invited the Russian Lavrof or some other revolutionary to take part. The public doesn't like the smell of politics and at my age I am not going to start becoming a revolutionary. Only a revolutionary would want to be in the company of an Israelite like Pissarro. They all know that I have made a great leap forward because of the Salon and are determined to make me lose everything I have gained […] If you get rid of these people and put me alongside artists such as Monet, Sisley, and Morisot, I'll be at your service. That would not be politics anymore but pure art." Renoir's conclusion was uncompromising: "The paintings of mine that you own are your property, so I cannot stop you from doing what you want with them. But I will not be the one exhibiting them".

Renoir feared that Durand-Ruel would be angry with him and refuse to handle his paintings, but his anxieties were dispelled when the dealer commissioned portraits of his five children. Renoir produced masterpieces for him. He took advantage of his situation to seek revenge for the affront he had received from the Salon when it rejected his first portrait of Madame Clapisson. He painted the portraits in full sunlight, using the multi-coloured palette that he was developing along with greater precision in his drawing. This marked the start of his Ingres period, which nostalgic admirers regretted, harking back to his earlier romanticism. Not even Durand-Ruel liked his new style. This came as no surprise to Renoir who realised that the style of his latest canvases

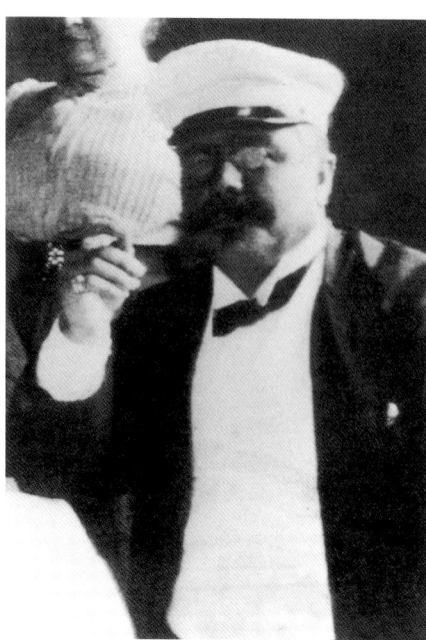

Wilhelm Mühlfeld
(1851–1912), c. 1901

Portrait of Wilhelm Mühlfeld, 1910
Oil on canvas,
55 x 45.8 cm (21¾ x 18 in.)
Southampton City Art Gallery

made them impossible to sell for the time being. They needed to be "bottled" for at least a year. He even jokingly promised to visit Bonnat's studio. Bonnat was the most famous of the fashionable portraitists of the period, whose students, led by Lautrec, defined his particular talent by singing: "Painting a frock-coat? / You know how to: / You give it the colour of boots / Against a background of pooh." "In a year or two", Renoir added, "I'll be raking in 30,000,000,000,000 a year. Don't talk to me about portraits in sunlight anymore. A nice black background is best!"

The setting for the portraits of Durand-Ruel's children is described by Jacques-Émile Blanche. "They posed for Renoir in a garden on the Rouen coast, beneath chestnut trees with fluttering leaves; the sunlight dappled their cheeks with reflections incompatible with the 'flat modelling' of studio light." Dappled natural light had been a specialty of Renoir's Impressionist period and reached its zenith in the "triptych" of *Le Moulin de la Galette* (pp. 114/115), *The Swing* (p. 60), and *Nude in the Sunlight* (p. 121). But on this occasion he takes care to prevent the light from dispersing the figures by defining their contours and their facial features clearly. Renoir seeks, here more than ever, to merge an Impressionist vision with the structure and solidity that he perceived in the art of the past. He had taken a long trip to Italy the previous year to replenish his artistic resources and extend his visual repertoire. Raphael's frescoes, which he found "admirable in their simplicity and grandeur", those in the Naples Museum, and the sculpted public monuments impressed him greatly. He wrote to his friend Bérard of his enthusiasm: "Sculptors have all the luck. Their statues stand in the sun and, when their shape is pure, they

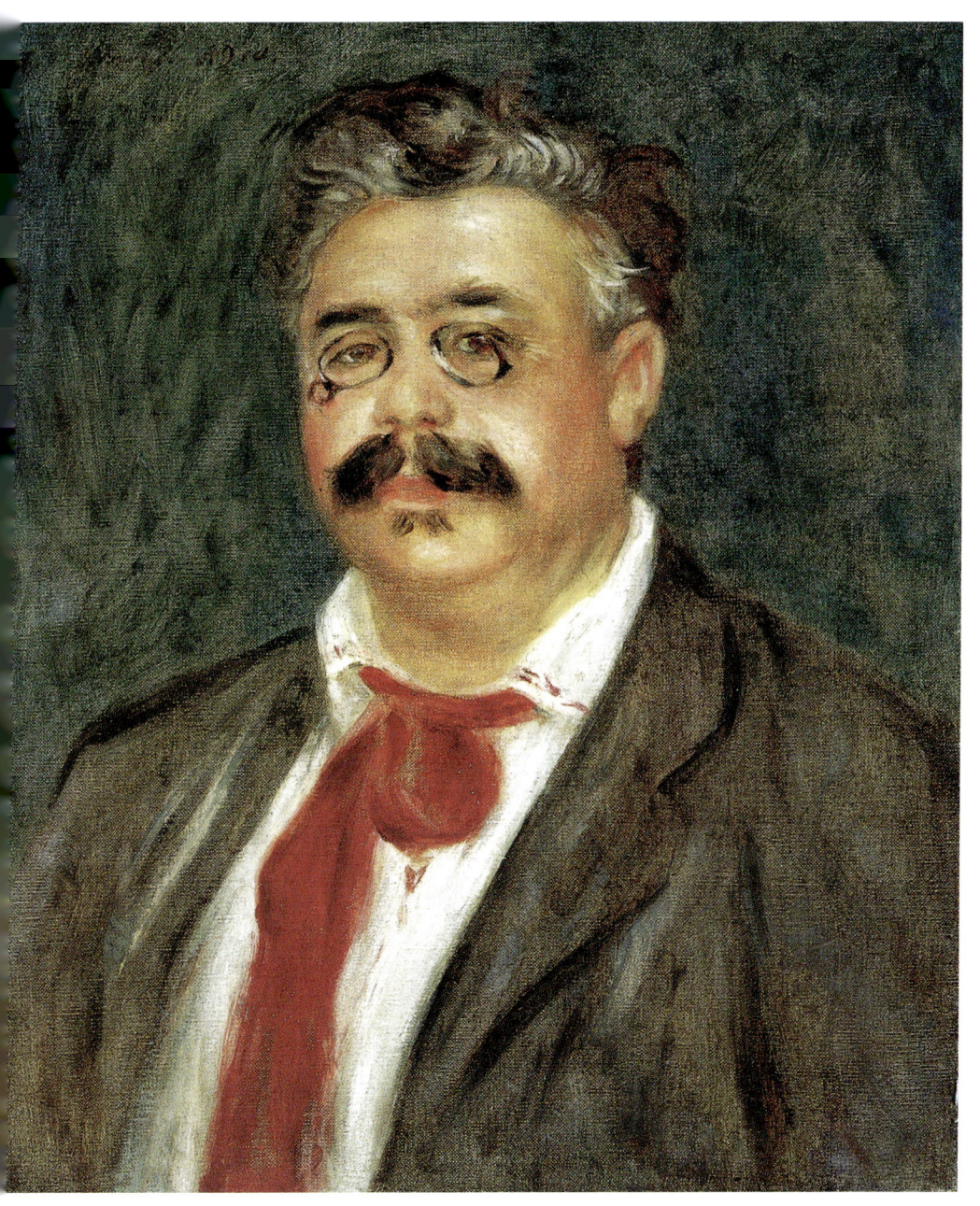

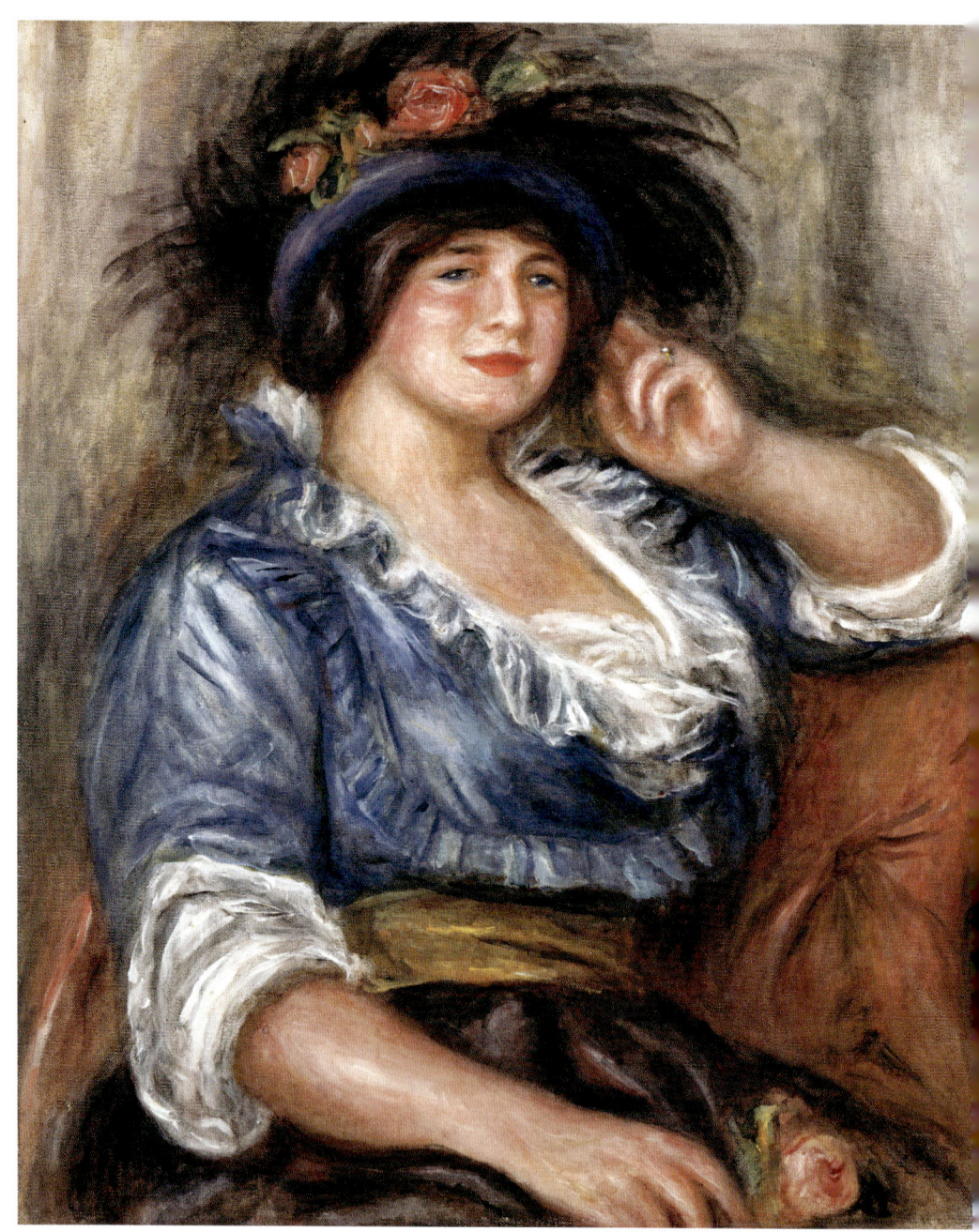

Henri Matisse (1869–1954)
Woman in Blue, 1937
Oil on canvas,
93 x 73.6 cm (36⅝ x 29 in.)
Private collection

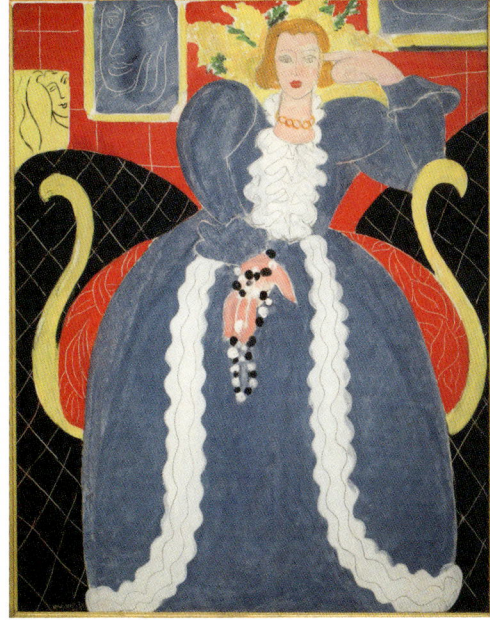

Madame Colonna Romano, c. 1913
Oil on canvas,
65.2 x 54.5 cm (25¾ x 21½ in.)
Paris, Musée d'Orsay

form part of the light itself. They exist in nature just like a tree does." The various portraits of the Durand-Ruel children (pp. 241, 242/243, 245) are Renoir's initial response to his desire to paint something resembling outdoor sculptures. He would one day create his own sculptures with the help of the sculptor Richard Guino, who translated his drawings into three dimensions (pp. 472 and 473). Matisse would in turn sculpt colour by making paper cutouts in works such as his *découpage* entitled *Jazz*. Renoir had not yet reached the stage of *Children in the Afternoon at Wargemont* (pp. 276/277), nor of *The Great Bathers* (pp. 348/349), manifesto paintings created under the influence of the painter of *The Source* or *The Large Odalisque*. He tended to tackle his portraits as bas-reliefs or frescoes. He did this in order to produce "great harmonies", as he wrote to his confidante Madame Charpentier, "without bothering with those minor details that extinguish the sun instead of setting it on fire".

It was Ambroise Vollard – portrayed by him caressing a small Maillol nude (p. 269) – who "found hands" for the aged, crippled Renoir. He procured the services of Maillol's best student, Guino, and encouraged Renoir to convert his dreams into monuments – as well as hard cash for Vollard himself. "That man never misses a trick!" René Gimpel noted in his diary, having seen Renoir with him at Les Collettes. "One day, he brought him a bundle of fish from the market, threw it down on the table, and said: 'paint that for me'. Renoir, amused, got down to work and when he had finished Vollard took the canvas. On another occasion, Vollard suddenly appeared before the painter dressed as a toreador and Renoir, excited by the colour, painted his portrait."

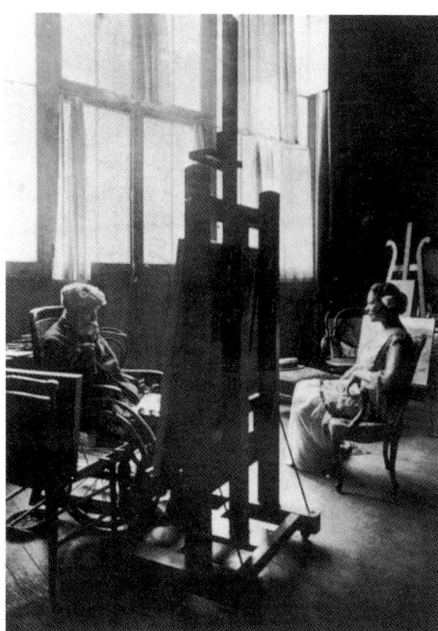

Renoir painting the portrait of Tilla Durieux (1880–1971) in the year 1914

Tilla Durieux (Ottilie Godeffroy), 1914
Oil on canvas, 92.1 x 73.7 cm (36⅜ x 29 in.)
New York, The Metropolitan Museum
of Art, Bequest of Stephen C. Clark

Claude Renoir tells the story behind the strange portrait of *Ambroise Vollard Dressed as a Toreador* (p. 270): "One day Vollard was out for a walk with us children. Suddenly he found his way barred by a herd of cows from the commune. He was terrified of animals so he offered a large reward to the cowherd in return for getting the cows out of his way. On my return home, I told my father this adventure. A few days later, Vollard lisped at my father: 'Tell me, Renoir, would you care to paint my portrait?' 'Yes', my father calmly replied, 'but only in a toreador's outfit'. Vollard was not disconcerted; he soon returned dressed as a toreador. The first sketch for this canvas shows Vollard with his sword in his hand and a dead bull at his feet. My father did not dare take the joke any further than that, however, and on the final canvas Vollard is shown sitting in an armchair with a rose at his feet. Vollard was no fool. He had gained a magnificent portrait that everyone knew about, and what is more, he took away with him a whole stack of canvases."

Renoir's *Portrait of Aline Charigot (later Madame Renoir*; p. 246) illustrates his development both in terms of technique and choice of subjects. The artist and his model were, as their son Jean recorded, a true love match. This was then a portrait of the woman that Renoir loved. She looks like a "fresh-faced farmer's wife": a radiant, good-natured countrywoman. Aline was a mischievous and spontaneous companion who kept him away from all the "ambitious seamstresses, failed florists, and ironing-women with broken irons – shameless hussies who only wanted to give up the trade they had learned and go in search of affairs". These women were held up to ridicule

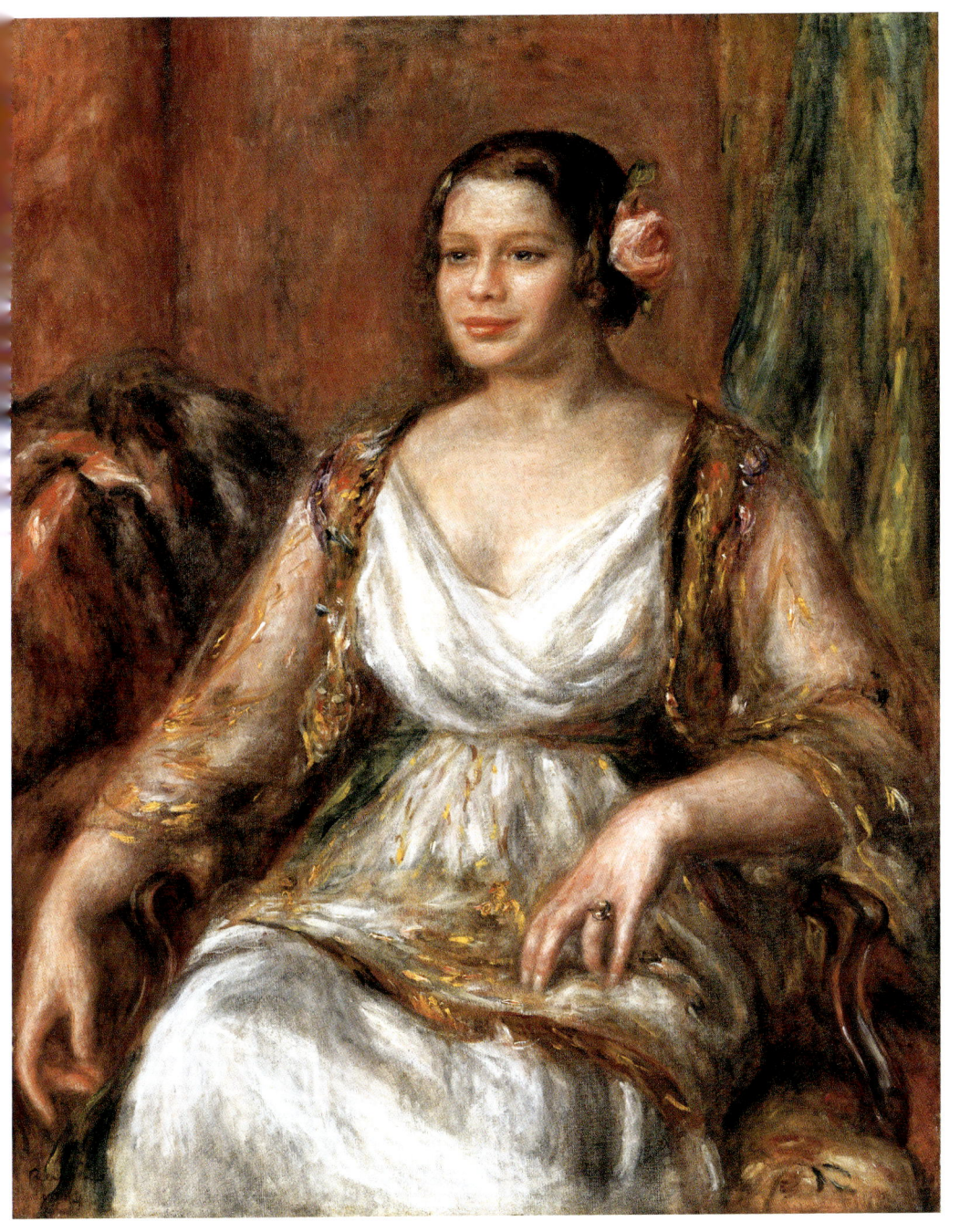

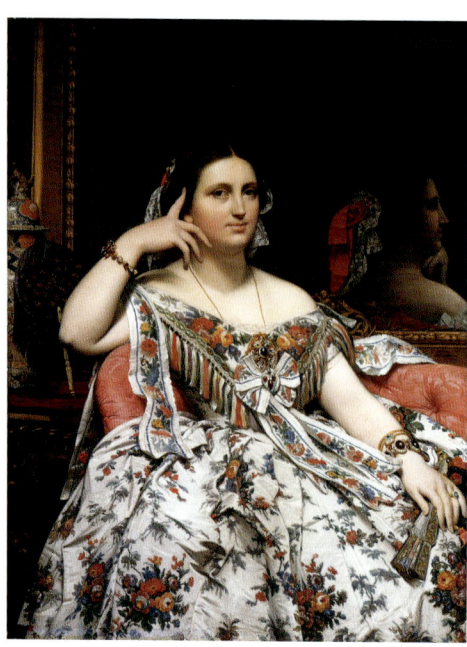

Jean-Auguste-Dominique Ingres (1780–1867)
Madame Moitessier, 1856
Oil on canvas, 120 x 92.1 cm (47¼ x 36⅜ in.)
London, The National Gallery

**Portrait of Misia Sert
(Jeunne femme au griffon)**, 1907
Oil on canvas,
92.5 x 73.5 cm (36½ x 29 in.)
Philadelphia, The Barnes Foundation

by the popular imagination. Aline, on the other hand, was a rustic Madonna. She was the subject of the *Maternity* series (pp. 386 and 387). Richard Guino created a sculpture based on these paintings in 1915, a year after Aline's death. It is like the final act of their love.

During the last part of his life Renoir, living at Les Collettes and confined to his wheelchair, spent his time painting numerous portraits of his children, his wife (*Madame Renoir*, p. 256), and Gabrielle the maid, who all enabled him to express his serenity and continual joy in life and painting. He had little time for commissioned work. The few exceptions to this rule include *Misia Sert* (p. 255), *Madame Colonna Romano* (p. 262), *Tilla Durieux* (p. 265) and *Portrait of Misia Sert* (p. 267). In all of these Renoir transforms his models into quintessential "Renoirs", in other words, tributes to Woman Triumphant. Each of them has been faithfully portrayed but they look as though they all belong to the same family. They are, as it were, Gabrielle's sisters. Renoir has placed the same rose in their hair, as if he wanted to make it his hallmark. Whether the subject is an actress, a countrywoman, or a bourgeoise, the same features reappear: a full face, rather pulpy like fruit, a pearly complexion and, above all, bright, slightly slanting eyes and fleshy lips. When Renoir painted nudes or bathers belonging to the same family, he gave them all the same idealised form.

Raymond Cogniat's account of Renoir's portraits makes the same observation. "Women are obviously Renoir's major, even unique, subject. He thinks of nothing else when he paints. Not only does the woman occupy the centre of the canvas, but any relief has disappeared and the background objects are more carefully depicted. She is not

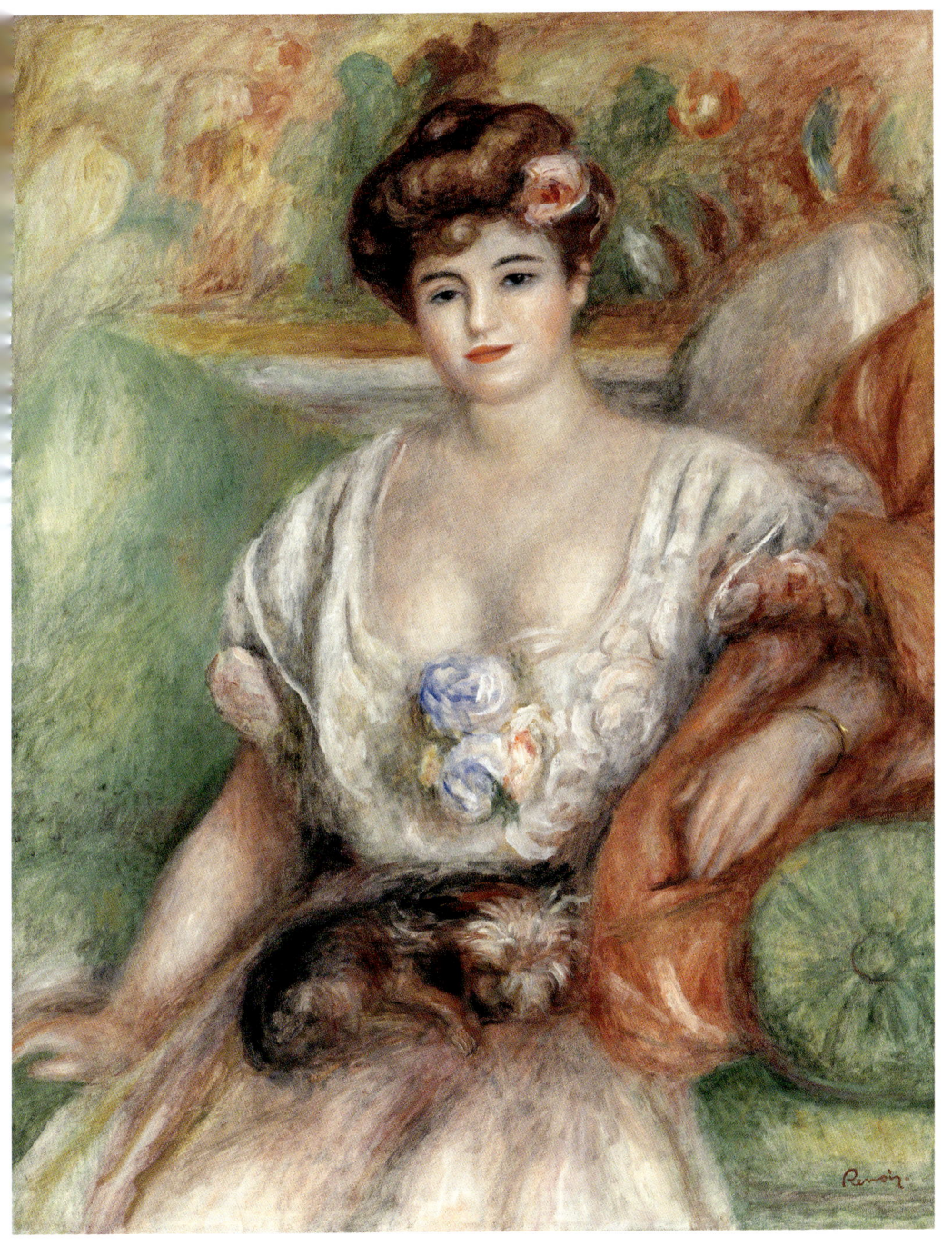

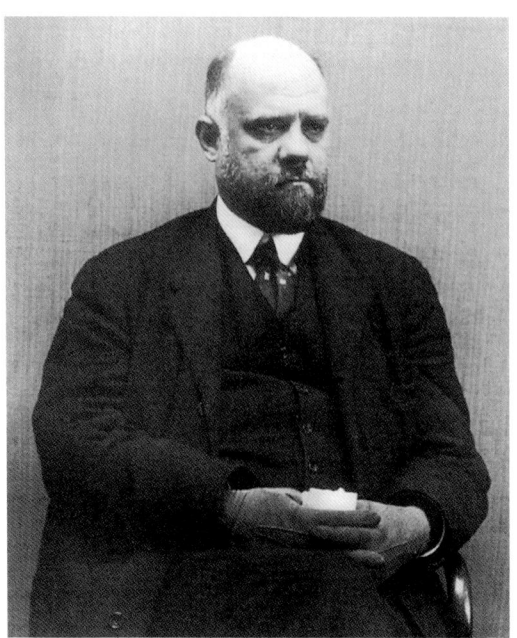

Ambroise Vollard
(1868–1939), c. 1915

Portrait of Ambroise Vollard, 1908
Oil on canvas,
81.6 x 65.2 cm (32¼ x 25¾ in.)
London, The Courtauld Gallery,
The Samuel Courtauld Trust

receiving light so much as radiating it." These are the family of giantesses or, in Matisse's word, "plane-tree women" whose necks, Aragon observed, thicken at the base. They are descended from the frescoes of Herculaneum and the paintings of Ingres. After Renoir they appear in the work of Matisse. It is obvious but amusing to note that these artists all paint the same picture of the same type of model in the same dreamy pose. They share the same Oriental vision of the ideal woman who is large and curvaceous and has a correspondingly peace-loving, unruffled temperament. Such women are nothing like Leonardo da Vinci's passionate creatures with narrow, bitter faces and eyes burning with excited arousal. Nor do they have the ecstatic look and ardour of Botticelli's virgins, who are maddened by divine temptations and whose bodies ripple in an ethereal dance. They are submissive women who think as infrequently as possible and are only too happy to lie about on sofas. They have more in common with (say) Titian's *Isabella of Portugal* in the Prado Museum, or Raphael's *Jeanne of Aragon* in the Louvre. They have large round cheeks and a languorous air. This comes from the "swollen", cylindrical neck with a thick base that they all have. Doctors have concluded that swelling in the neck is the first sign of hypertrophy in the thyroid gland and it is well known that women who suffer from this condition experience increased sexual pleasure. All of Ingres's women are goiterous, from *Thétis, Angélique* and *La Fornarina*, to the bathers in the *Turkish Bath*. Several of the models so beloved of Matisse, according to his grandson Claude Duthuit, died of the condition. Feminine curves are the link between Renoir's *Madame Colonna Romano* (p. 262) and Matisse's painting *Woman in Blue* (in tribute

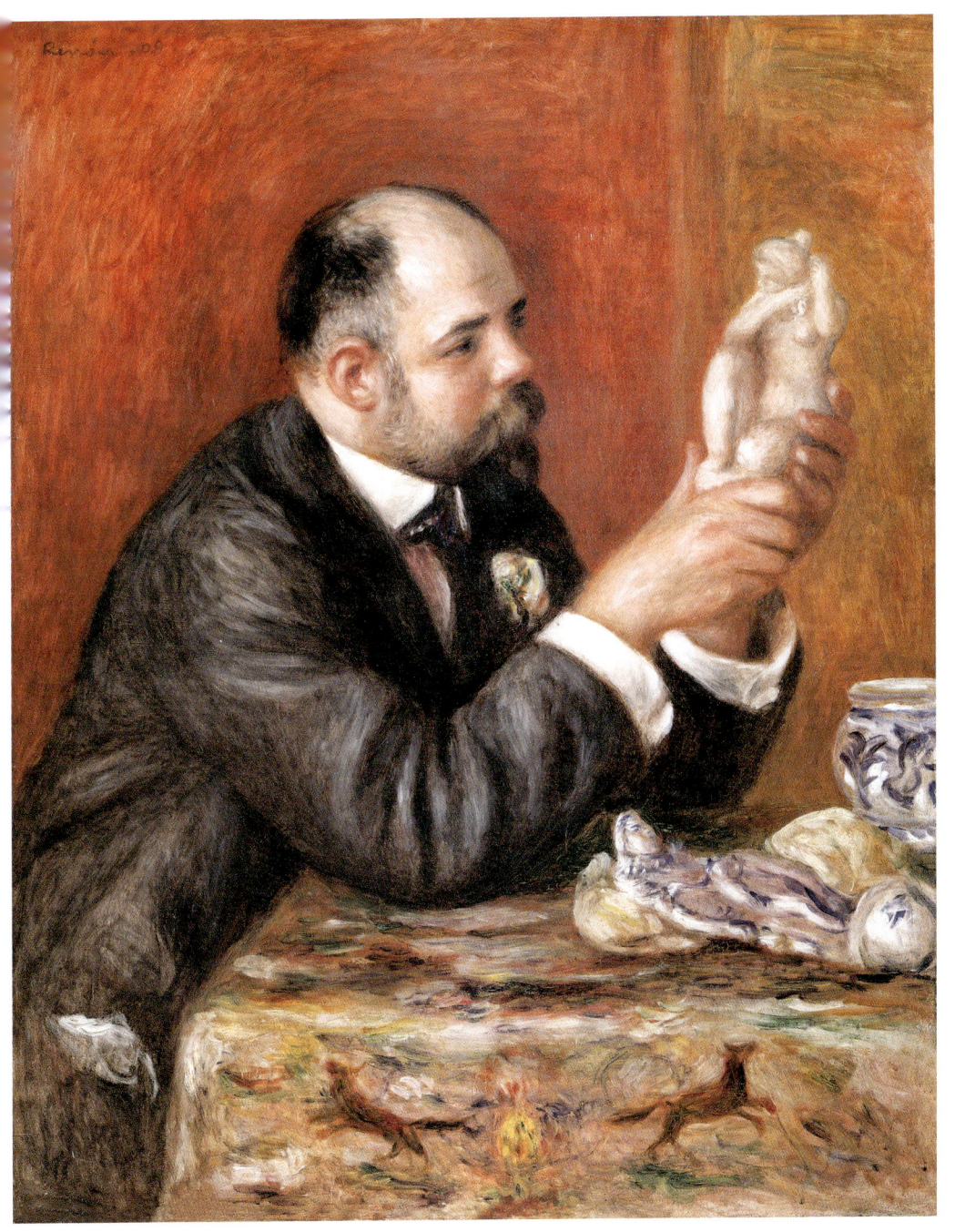

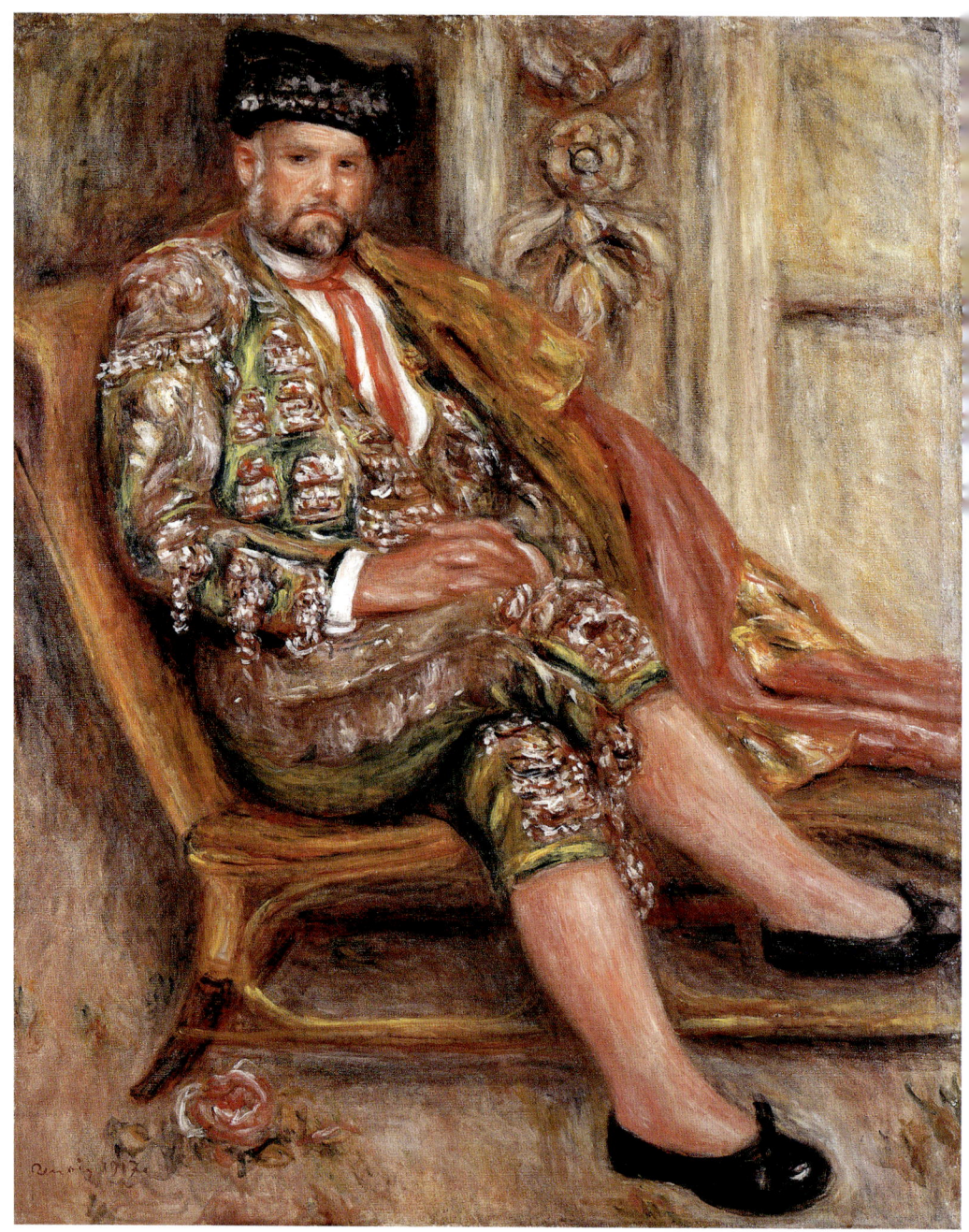

Ambroise Vollard Dressed as a Toreador, 1917
Oil on canvas, 103 x 83 cm (40⅝ x 32¾ in.)
Tokyo, Nippon Television Network Corporation

perhaps to Renoir, p. 263). Their common ancestor is *Madame Moitessier* (p. 266) whom Ingres no doubt discovered in Rome when as a young man he travelled there to study and copy the works of antiquity.

The last major commission that Renoir accepted was the portrait of *Tilla Durieux* (p. 265). Durieux, the great German actress, posed in an evening dress designed by Paul Poiret for the character of Eliza Doolittle in *Pygmalion*. Renoir's return to the celebrity portrait, which had enabled him to earn his living as a young man, appears to have taken him full circle. Durieux stares radiantly into space, as impassive as a figure on an Egyptian tomb or in a Roman fresco, an eternal monument to feminine beauty. In her memoirs, she tells how Renoir worked on the portrait four hours a day for two weeks, seated in his wheelchair (p. 264), and how his young assistant had to place his palette and paintbrushes in his hands. "I no longer want to paint portraits but I am happy to have done yours", he confided in her once the portrait was finished. "I have improved, wouldn't you say?"

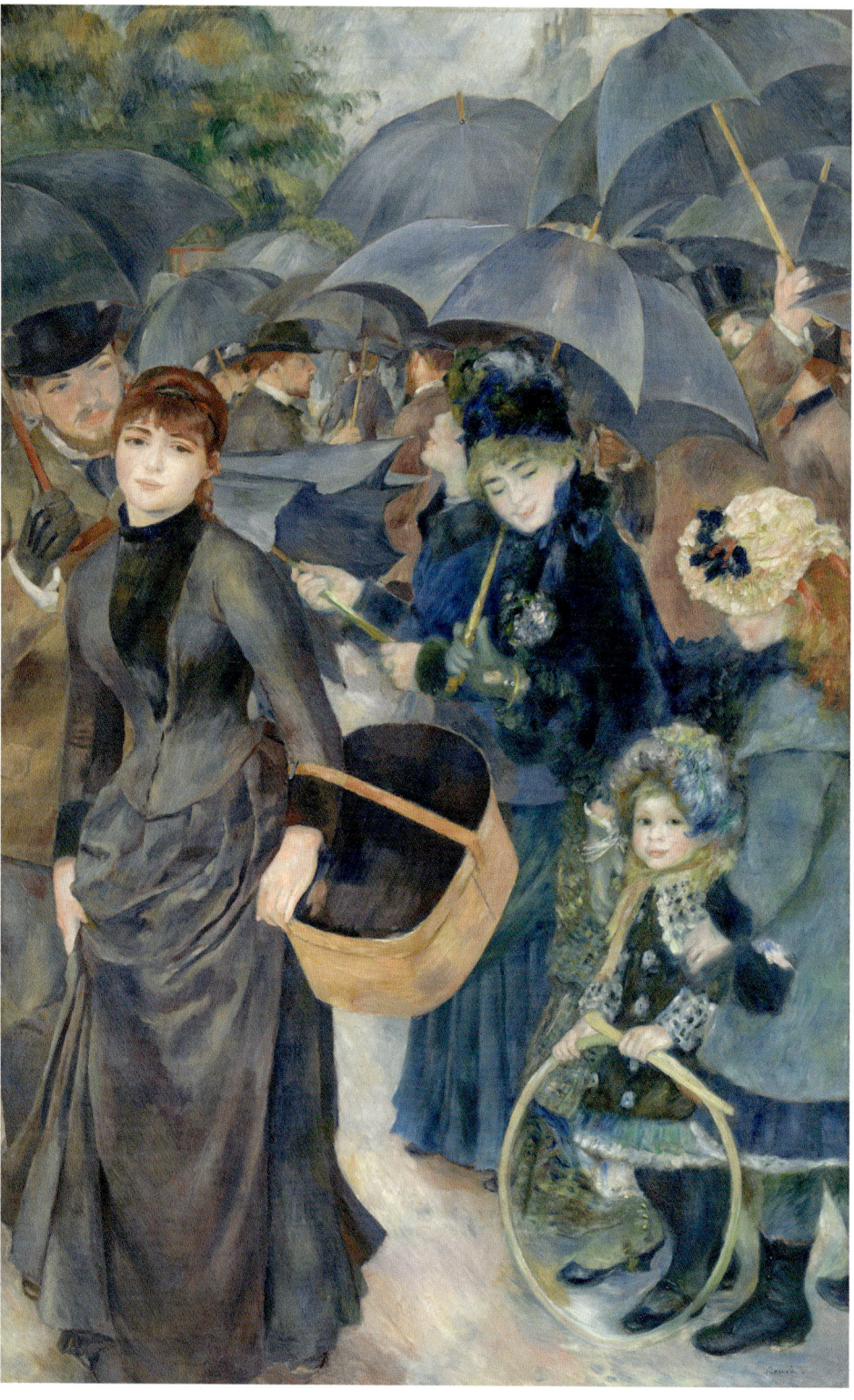

The Umbrellas, c. 1881–1886
Oil on canvas, 180.3 x 114.9 cm (71 x 45¼ in.)
London, The National Gallery,
Sir Hugh Lane Bequest

The Umbrellas represent a change in Renoir's
style and have the peculiarity of having been
painted in two separate periods. The right side
was produced in c. 1881, and still owes much to
Impressionism, but the left side was added in
c. 1886, and shows a carefully drawn representation in the style of Ingres.

The Harsh and the Pearly
1883–1897

Amateur collectors, who are always chasing a bargain, were in the market for Renoir's
paintings. So too, fortunately, were the much rarer breed of "purists", collectors and mer-
chants like Chocquet, Durand-Ruel and Bérard, whose purchases reflected their enthusi-
asms. There was also a third type of collector whom Vollard, after his conversations with
Renoir, described as "totally indifferent to, and even contemptuous of, the arts. He collects
paintings in the same way as others own racehorses. One member of this class of "major
collectors" was a certain Chauchard. He was so keen for everyone to know just how rich he
was that he ordered in his will that his most expensive paintings should be paraded in front
of his hearse." This type exists to this day. A major Japanese collector recently expressed
his desire to be cremated along with the Van Gogh he had bought in Paris. Gone were the
days when a marquess would bemoan the fact that his son, who had inherited a million
francs from his mother, had frittered it away: "If only he had bought some Impressionism," the marquess told Vollard, "in a few years he would have tripled his million." This
type of collector was beginning to wonder whether a collection that featured paintings by
Bouguereau, Carolus-Duran and others of their ilk was complete without a few by Impressionists such as Renoir. Vollard offered to sell a Renoir nude to one of his best clients,
Count Isaac de Camondo, who had become enamoured of French culture and had entirely
forgotten his Turkish-Jewish origins in the process. The Count was sceptical: "If this Renoir
of yours were younger, he might be able to cure himself of his excess of colour and learn to
draw. But what can you do with a painter, who is over sixty, and draws an arm and a thigh
like that?" he said, pointing to the various parts of the canvas with the tip of his cane.

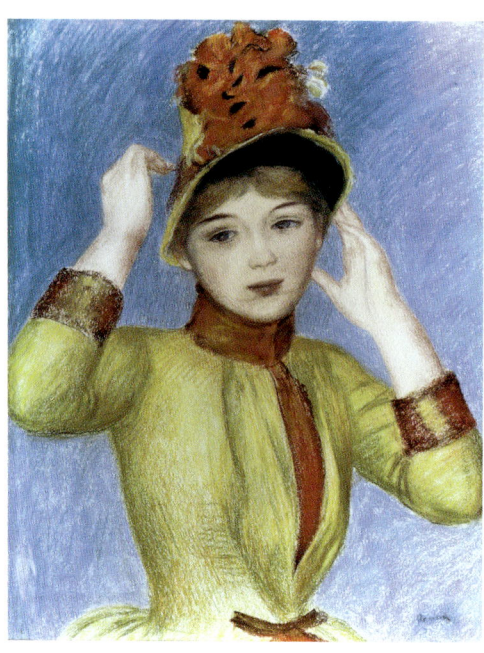

Bust of a Woman with Yellow Corsage, c. 1883
Oil on canvas, 42 x 32 cm (16⅝ x 12⅝ in.)
Private collection

PAGES 276/277
**Children in the Afternoon at Wargemont
(Marguerite, Lucie and Marthe Bérard)**, 1884
Oil on canvas, 127 x 173 cm (50 x 68⅛ in.)
Staatliche Museen zu Berlin, Nationalgalerie

"Just look at the colour of those cheeks! Do you know what Renoir lacks? A sense of *tradition*, that's what! You can tell that this man has no great love of the Louvre." The Count knew to sacrifice his personal taste if he realised that certain names were necessary for a great collection. "I shall eventually buy one or two examples of the craziest things Renoir has done", he told Vollard. "But nothing from the 1900s, mind you, nor even from 1896. And certainly nothing from '89, which is right in the middle of his *harsh period*. I once heard a famous critic say of Renoir's paintings from that period that they were 'fruits that will never ripen'. Find me some good things from the 1870s, even 1865, and Renoir 'women' of course. But watch out for the hands: I don't want any of those cook's hands that he so loves to paint. The secret is to find Renoirs that are not too obviously Renoirs. Always remember that they will eventually be donated to the Louvre. I would not even mind you going as far back as 1860. What I really want is some proper drawing", he explained. "But never tell anyone about my purchases. Every time I buy a painting, it makes the painter's value increase and interferes with my later purchases", he added and then, forgetting his own origins, commented: "Today's dealers are so Jewish!"

Drawing was indeed Renoir's preoccupation of the moment. After his trips to Italy, the painter spent more time in the Louvre, a source on which he drew abundantly. "In around 1883, there was a sort of rupture in my work", Renoir told Vollard. "I had gone as far as I could in my Impressionist phase, and had reached the conclusion that I could neither paint nor draw. I was in an impasse." The only way to extract himself from it was through tradition. "Today, we are all are geniuses, that goes without saying," he explained

Lucie Bérard (Child in White), 1883
Oil on canvas, 61.3 x 49.8 cm (24¼ x 19⅝ in.)
The Art Institute of Chicago,
Mr. and Mrs. Martin A. Ryerson Collection

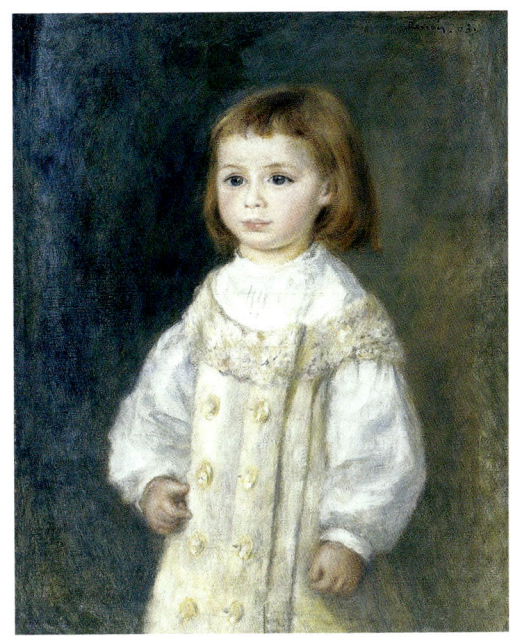

to Vollard, "but we can no longer draw so much as a hand. We know nothing about our craft. Yet it is was their craftsmanship that taught the Old Masters to produce the wonderful material and limpid colours that we try in vain to reproduce. The new theories will be of no help, I fear". He made a similar remark to Albert André. "There has been a move to replace apprenticeships with art schools", he told him. "Art school only teaches you to set your sights on winning awards, the Rome Prize, medals, and so on. It manufactures *official* painters. The state wants to become involved in protecting artists. But instead it has created a crowd of delinquents as well as distorting the public's judgement since the most heavily rewarded painter must, according to their logic, be the best. These painters imagine that they are truly extraordinary and that, by using blue instead of black, they will change the face of the earth. I have never allowed myself to become a revolutionary. I have always believed, and still do, that I am merely continuing what others have done, and done much better, before me".

Renoir's first attempt to escape from his impasse was the *Blonde Bather* (p. 338), which he painted in a rowing-boat in the Bay of Naples in 1881. His model was Aline Charigot, whom he went on to marry in 1890. She later told Julie Manet that this trip to Italy was like a honeymoon. There may well be some sentimental significance in the fact that the model is wearing a gold ring. Renoir executed this nude by studying the Old Masters. He took as his new models the Farnese Raphael and Ingres's painting *The Source*. Renoir turned his back on everything he had previously admired, such as the rendering of the atmosphere, and made style and accuracy in drawing of paramount importance. The

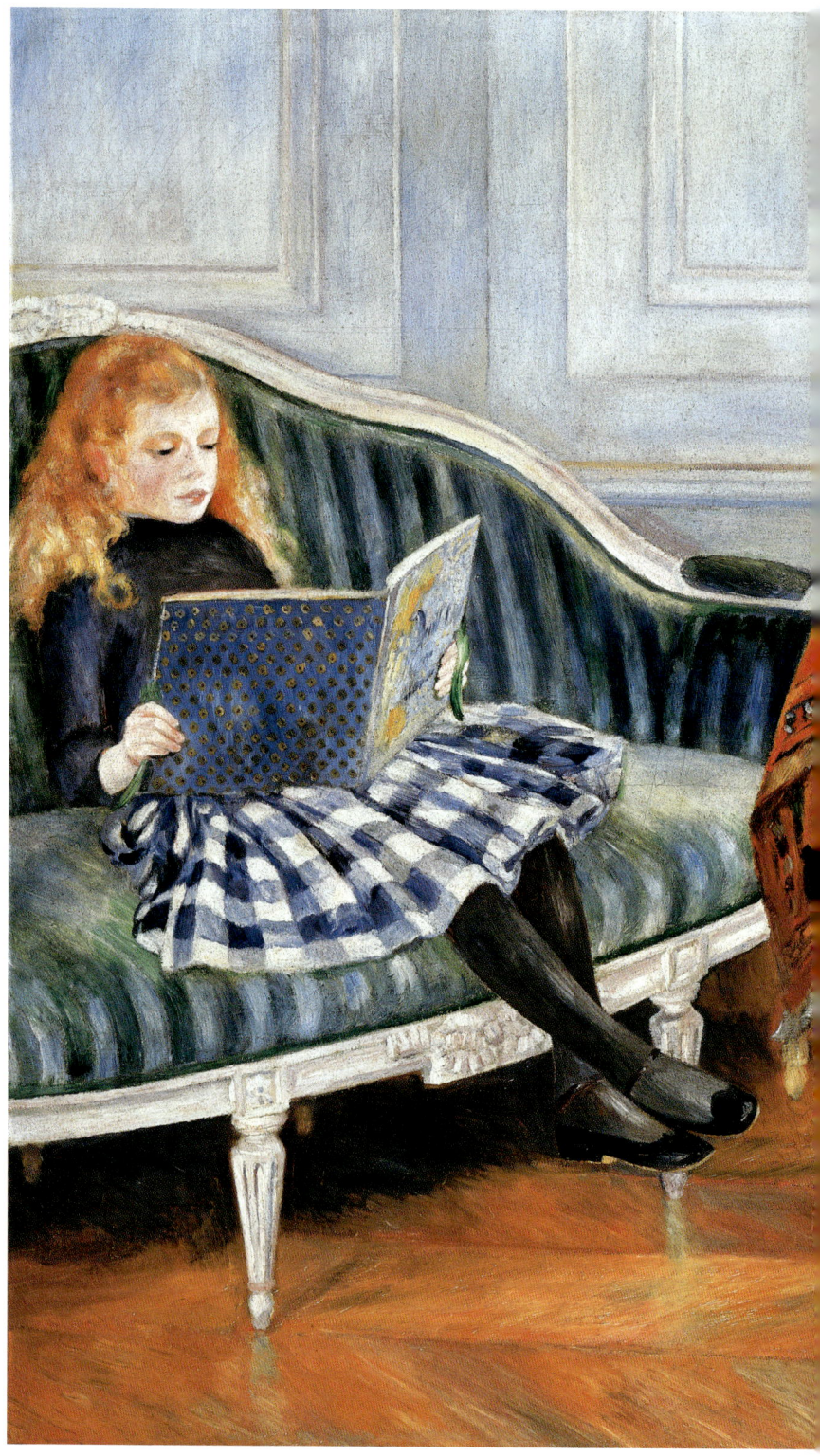

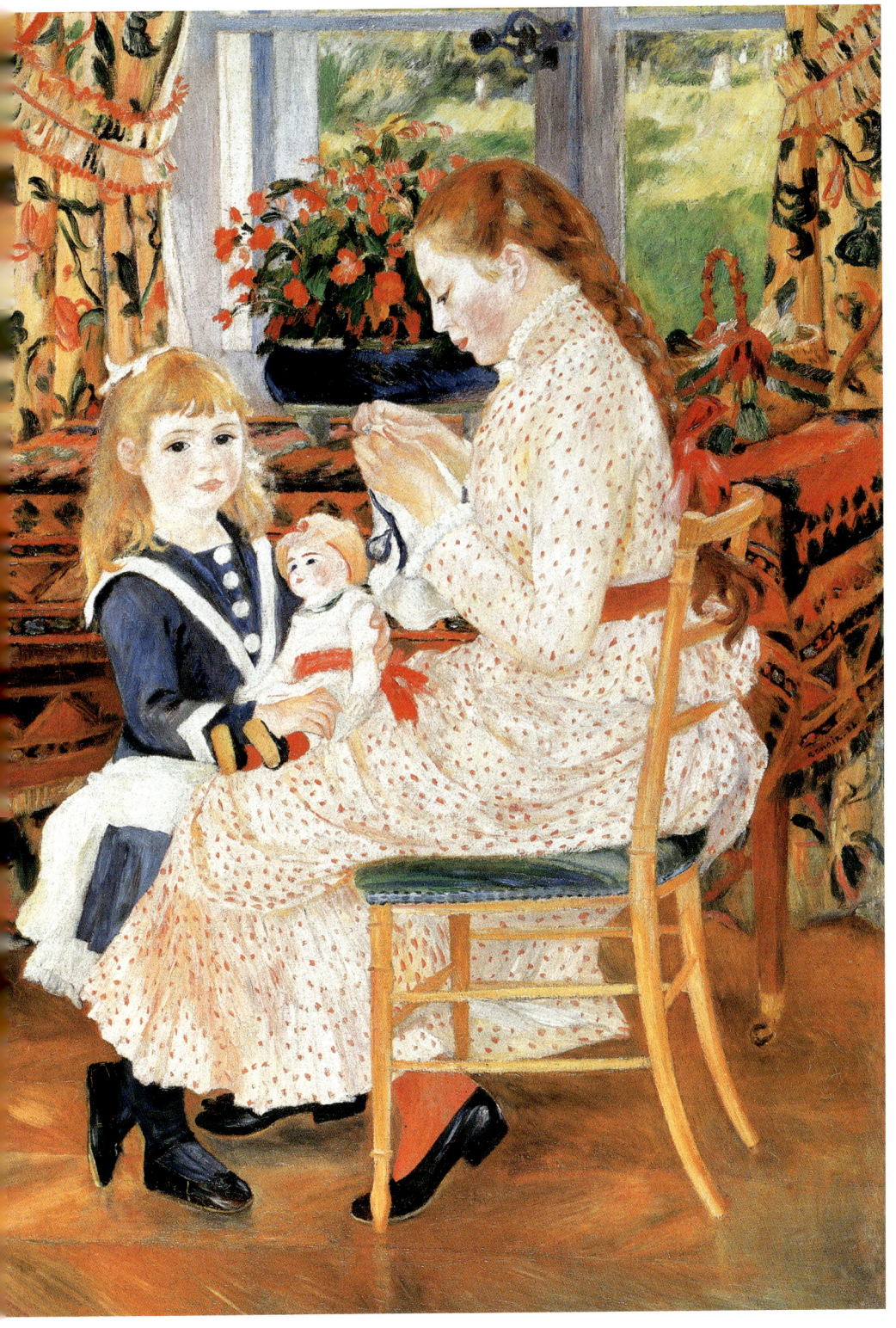

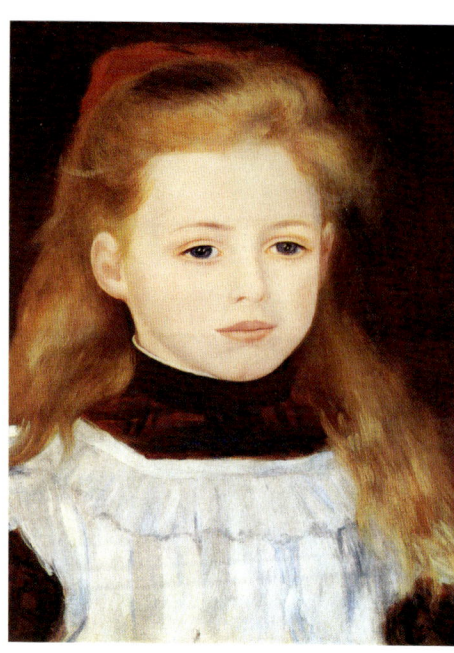

**Little Girl in a White Apron
(Lucie Bérard)**, 1884
Oil on canvas,
35 x 27 cm (13⅞ x 10¾ in.)
Private collection

By the Seashore, 1883
Oil on canvas, 92.1 x 72.4 cm (36¼ x 28½ in.)
New York, The Metropolitan Museum of Art,
H. O. Havemeyer Collection,
Bequest of Mrs. H. O. Havemeyer

nude is no longer a blurred subject under filtered light that breaks up the shapes but a monumental presence, invading the whole canvas with its pure, carefully drawn contours. The bay is a mere detail designed to highlight the central theme. The *Blonde Bather* herself is stunning in the brilliance of her pink-and-white flesh and the gold of her luxuriant tresses. The painting is the precursor of *The Great Bathers* (pp. 348/349). From this point on a single shadow is often enough for Renoir to make the viewer feel the weight of a breast, the slight bend of a hip, the curve of an arm or the twist of the body as it stands up. Renoir wanted to combine purity and voluptuousness, and his favourite subject was the female body, especially when naked. He had hitherto rather neglected the nude. He kept in mind the conclusion that, after much contemplation, Raphael had reached: "Do not try to achieve the impossible".

The Umbrellas (p. 272) represents this transitional phase perfectly. In this painting, Renoir's old and new trends are combined. It is unusual in that it was painted at two different periods. The right side was painted in around 1881 and still owes much to Impressionism. The left side, which was not completed before about 1886, shows clear signs of a greater attention to drawing, the new influence of Ingres, and the clear-cut style that this implies. Renoir clearly intended to apply his new principles to an open-air subject in which, unlike his colleagues, he did little to render atmospheric effects. The umbrellas are open but the rain is not even represented. Renoir seems keen to take on a challenge and demonstrate his intentions. What interests him is the way in which the figures are huddled together, the diversity of their gestures and attitudes. No doubt as a result of Cézanne's geometric

278

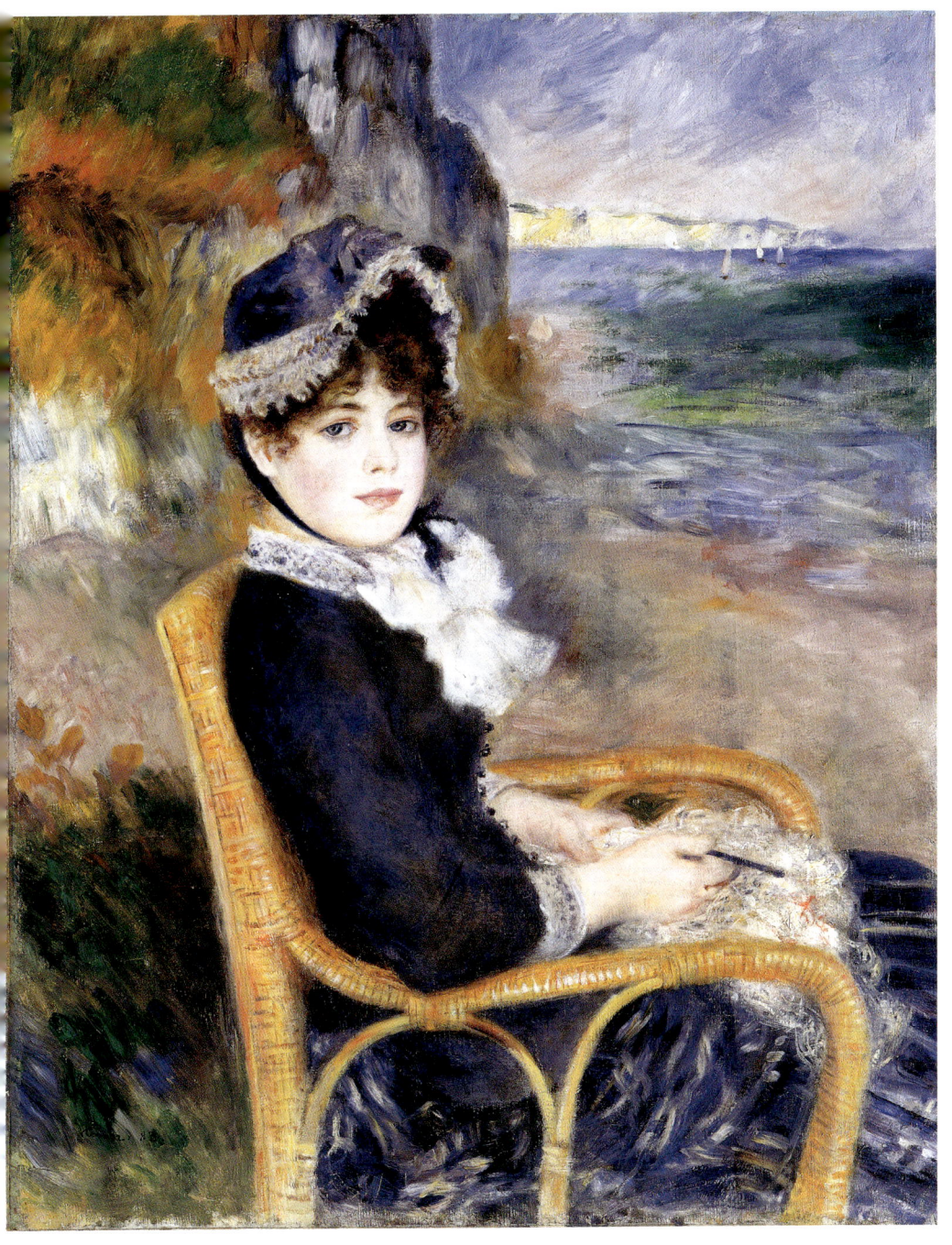

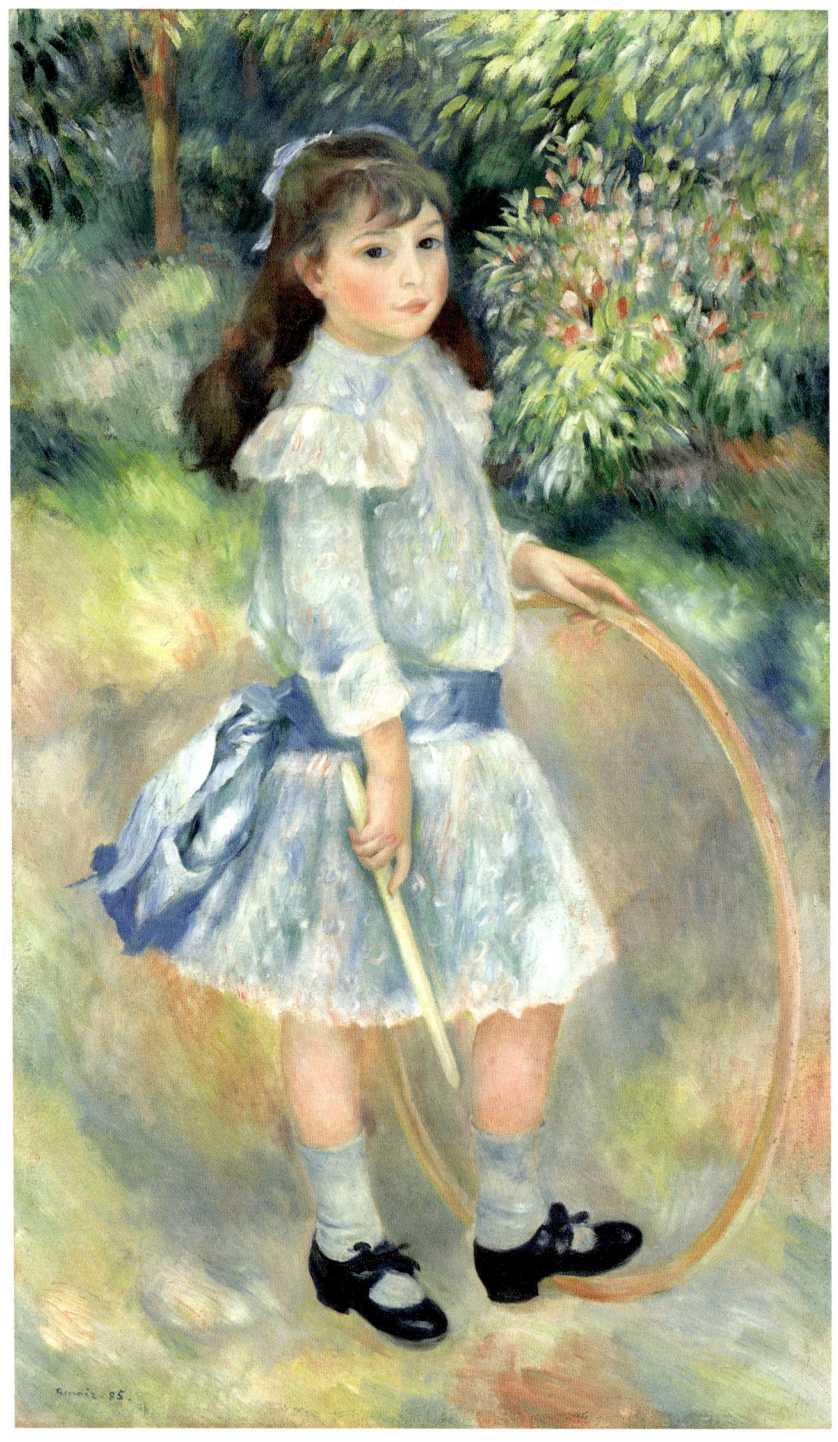

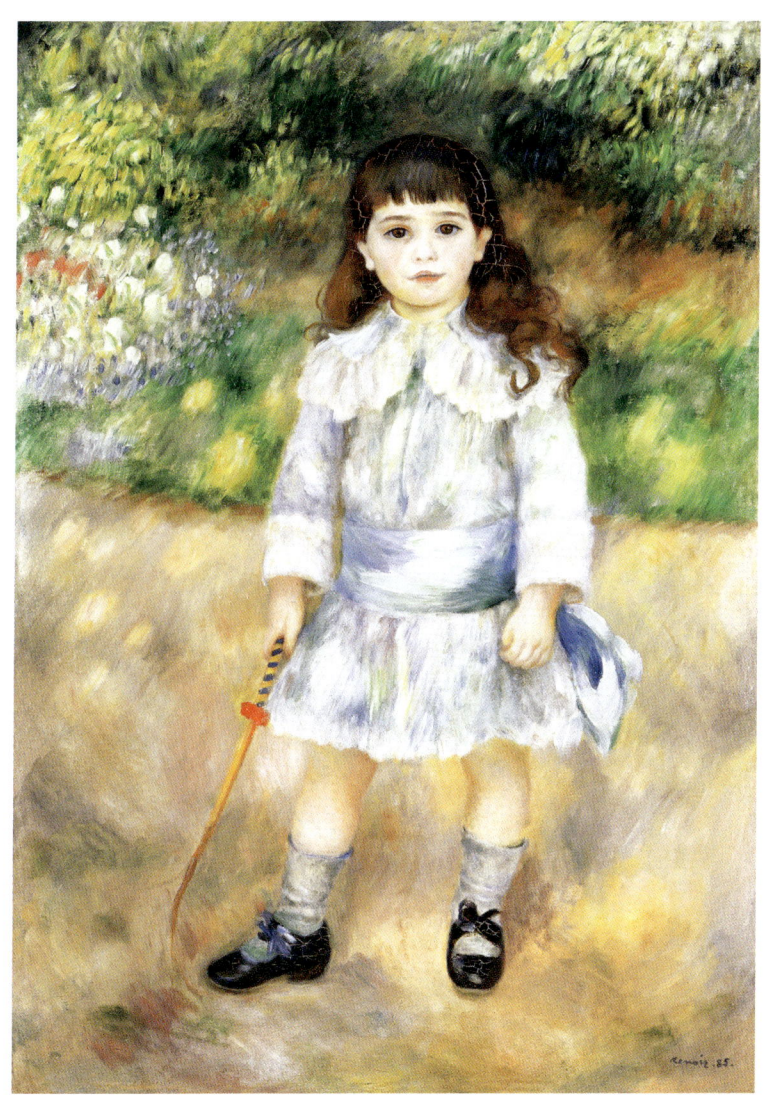

Girl with a Hoop (Marie Goujon), 1885
Oil on canvas, 125.7 x 75.6 cm (49½ x 29¾ in.)
Washington, D.C., National Gallery of Art,
Chester Dale Collection

Child with a Whip, 1885
Oil on canvas, 105 x 75 cm (41⅜ x 29⅝ in.)
Saint Petersburg, Hermitage Museum

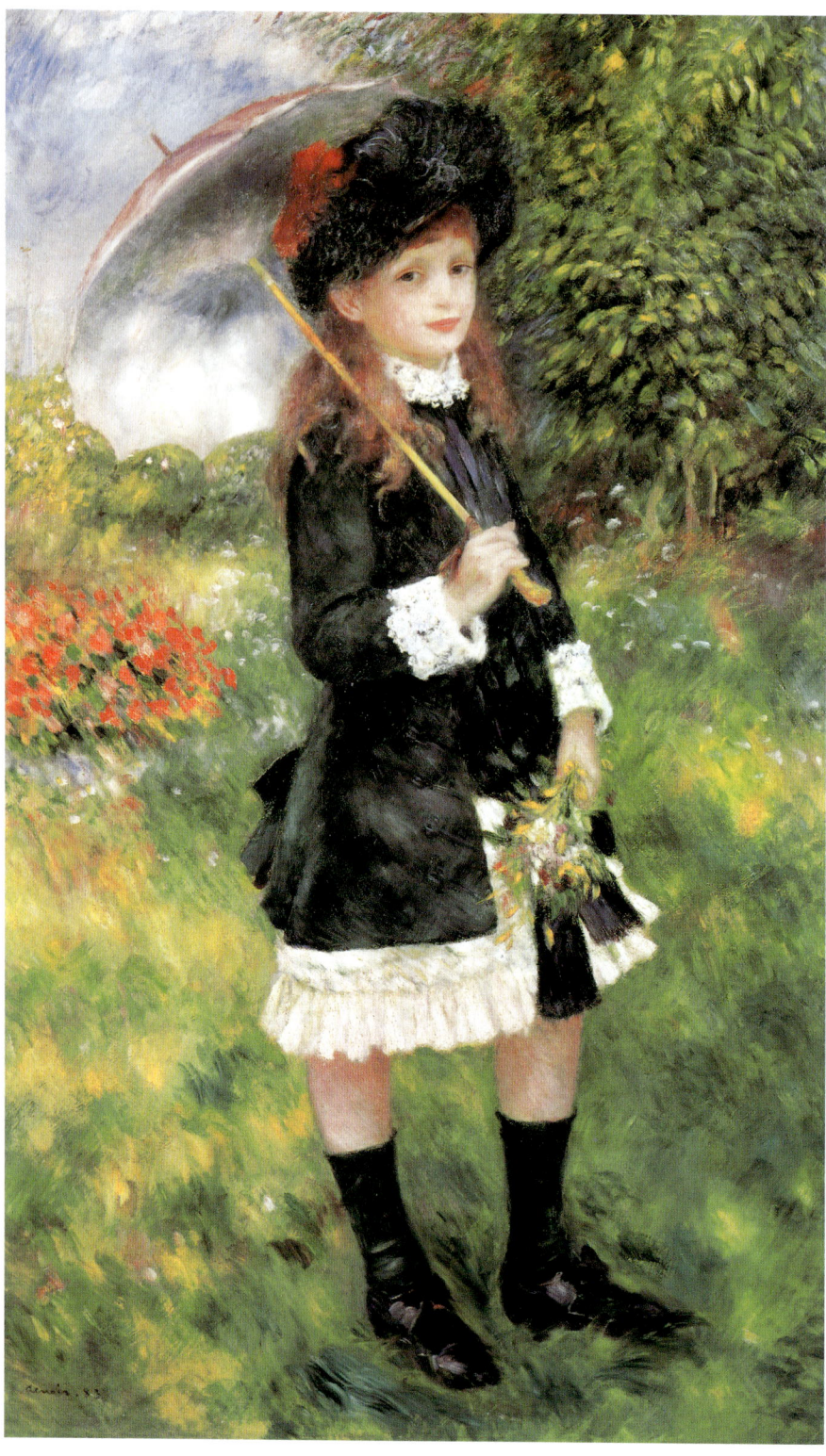

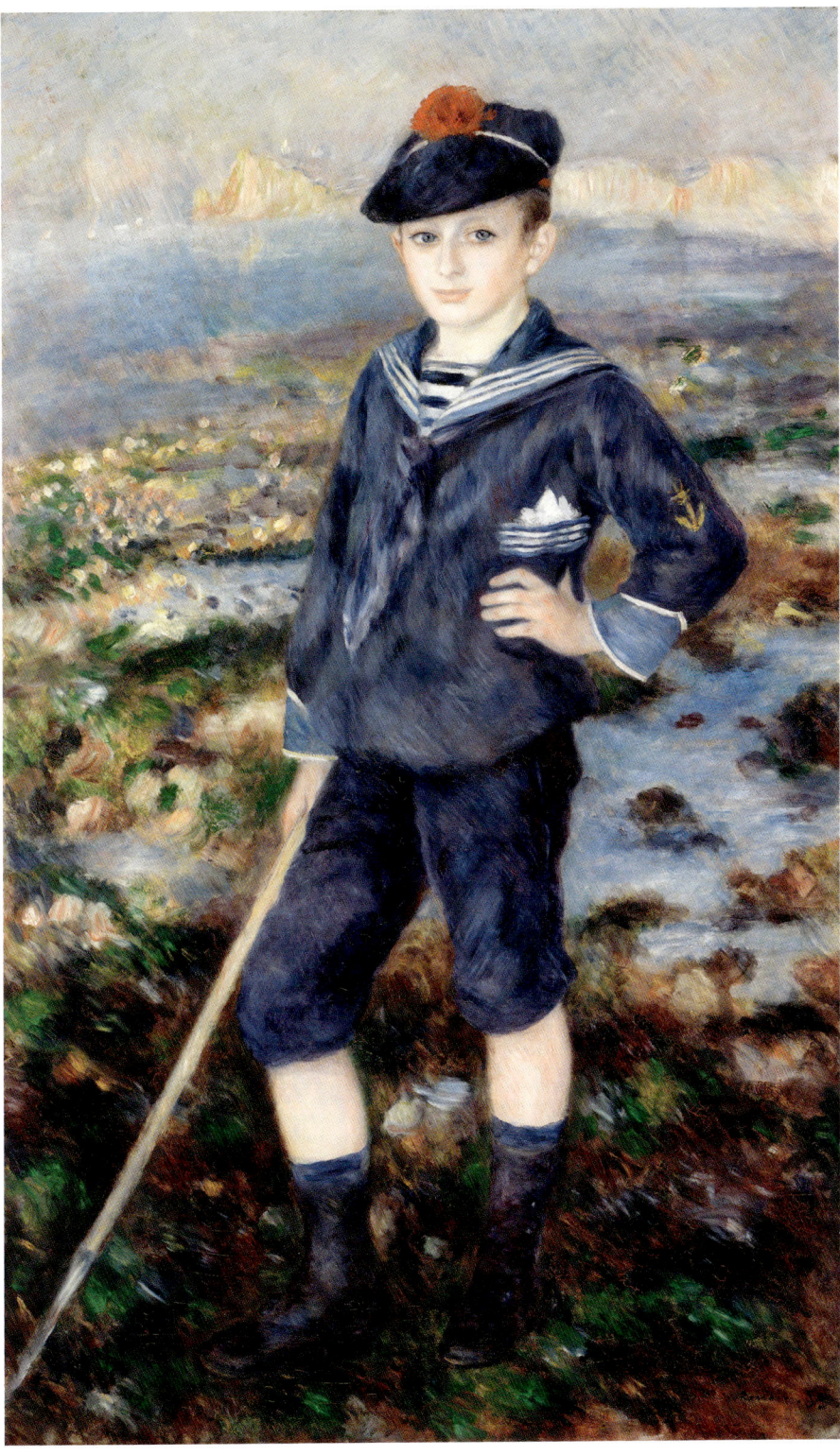

influence, he attempts to solve problems of space by means of the eternal circle. This is represented by the basket that the "harshly" painted young woman on the left is carrying, the hoop of the typically Impressionist child on the right, the shape of the umbrellas, and the circular grouping of the passers-by. The colour scheme is deliberately cooler on the left side and above, among the umbrellas, but a warmer and brighter scheme is used for the group containing the child and the woman on the right. During Renoir's Impressionist period, he made efforts to merge figures into the landscape. Here, his figures are made to stand out against the background. This gives the artificially grouped figures the un-pleasantly stiff pose of waxwork dolls, which is also manifest in the angle of the heads and the complexity of the drapery.

Even when Renoir takes on subjects more to his taste, such as *The Shepherdess, the Cow and the Ewe* (p. 305) or the portrait of *Young Girl with a Swan* (p. 303), he refuses to deviate from the demanding path he has chosen. These works are characteristic of Renoir's "harsh" period. They adopt a contrived, decorative style and exclude everything that looks natural. This is the very opposite of his true style and one which he was eventually to abandon. But it did enable him to take a great step forward in the 1890s. From his "harsh" period he retained (albeit in a less radical form) the technique of linear contour, which he combined with the palette and attractive subject-matter of his Impressionist years. The result has been called his "pearly" period, since it is typified by a pearly, iridescent technique that is also fluid and supple. His desire to transform his figures into sculptures bears the influ-ence of the Hellenistic carvings that he so admired in Naples. *Children in the Afternoon*

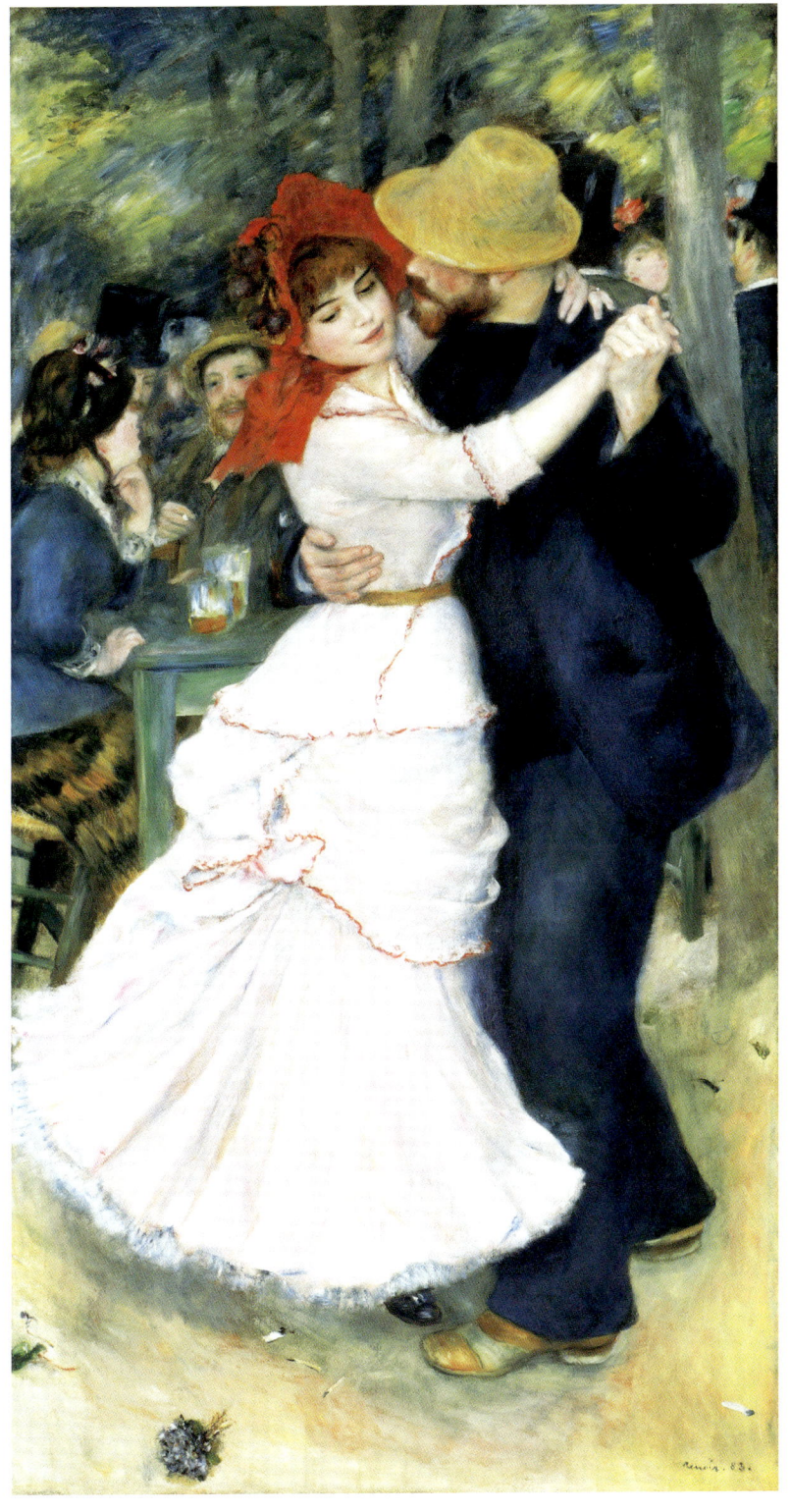

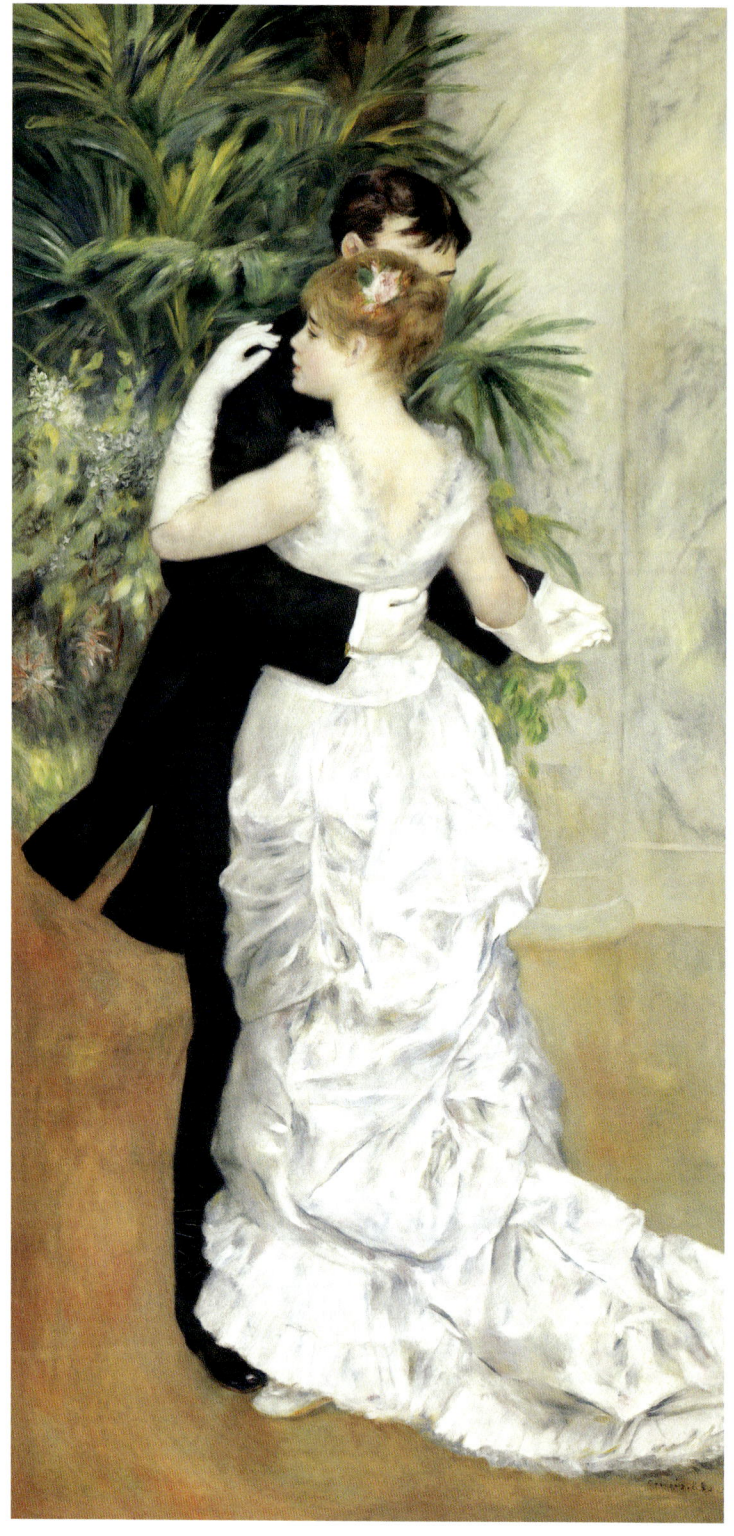

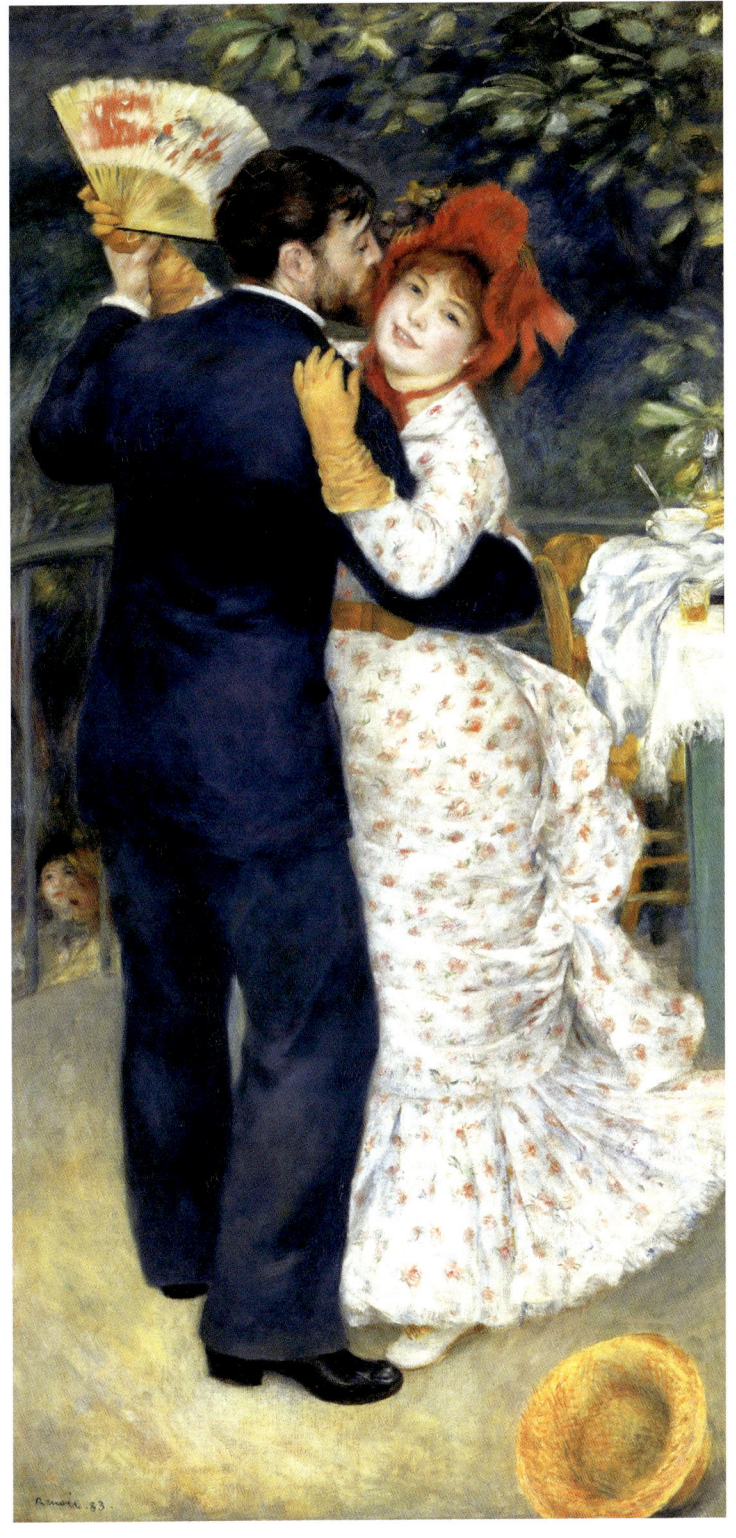

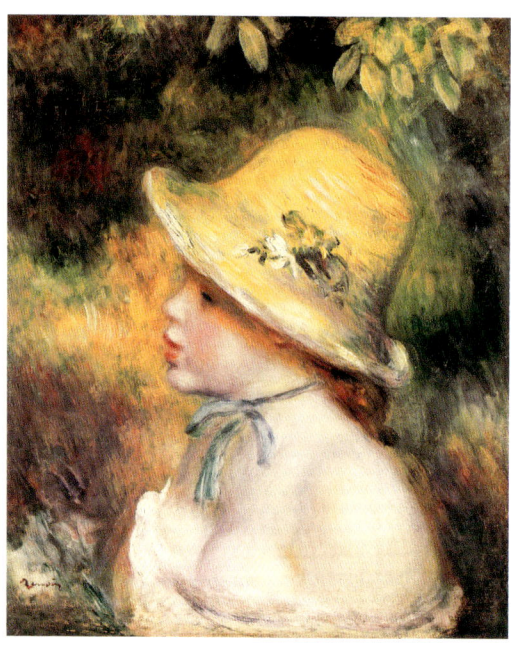

Young Girl with a Straw Hat, 1890
Oil on canvas, 46 x 38 cm (18⅛ x 15 in.)
Private collection

The juxtaposition of these two paintings of
Young Girl with a Straw Hat, one painted
around 1884, the other in 1890, is a perfect
example of Renoir's transition from his
"harsh" to his "pearly" period.

Young Girl with a Straw Hat, c. 1884
Oil on canvas, 54 x 43 cm (21⅜ x 17 in.)
Tokyo, Mitsubishi Ichigokan Museum

at Wargemont (pp. 276/277) reflects this influence. Roger-Milès suggested the influence
of Primatice and his school after 1905. Comparisons have also been made with Domenico
Ghirlandaio, whose frescoes Renoir may well have seen in Italy in 1881–1882, and with
Botticelli, since the Louvre purchased two Botticelli frescoes from Charles Ephrussi
in 1882. Renoir's attempts at sculpture invariably produced "petrified mannequins" or
"expressionless dolls" as they were dubbed. Those who were nostalgic for his "romantic
Impressionism" had cause for complaint.

Opinions, however, were divided. Some understood what Renoir was trying to do
and supported him. Paul Bérard, whose taste was ahead of its time, was one of the most
remarkable collectors of Renoir's paintings and followed him faithfully through all his
periods. Bérard, a banker and company director, did not merely commission him to paint
the portraits of all his children; he also befriended Renoir, introducing him to potential
collectors among his business acquaintances. The Bérards, who were a wealthy Protestant
family, met Renoir in 1879. They immediately became friendly. From then on until the
death of Paul Bérard, Renoir spent much time in his mansion at 20 Rue Pigalle, in Paris.
Here he depicted Bérard in a family setting, with a cigarette in his hand (p. 235). He also
painted Madame Bérard, whose sweet, gentle face radiates with kindness (p. 234). One
has only to compare these two portraits to contemporary photographs to see how artfully
the painter has portrayed his two sitters. Renoir also spent many happy summers at the
Bérard estate at Wargemont, near Dieppe. Wargemont held the same attraction for him
as Argenteuil and Chatou. He painted the Norman manor house on several occasions:

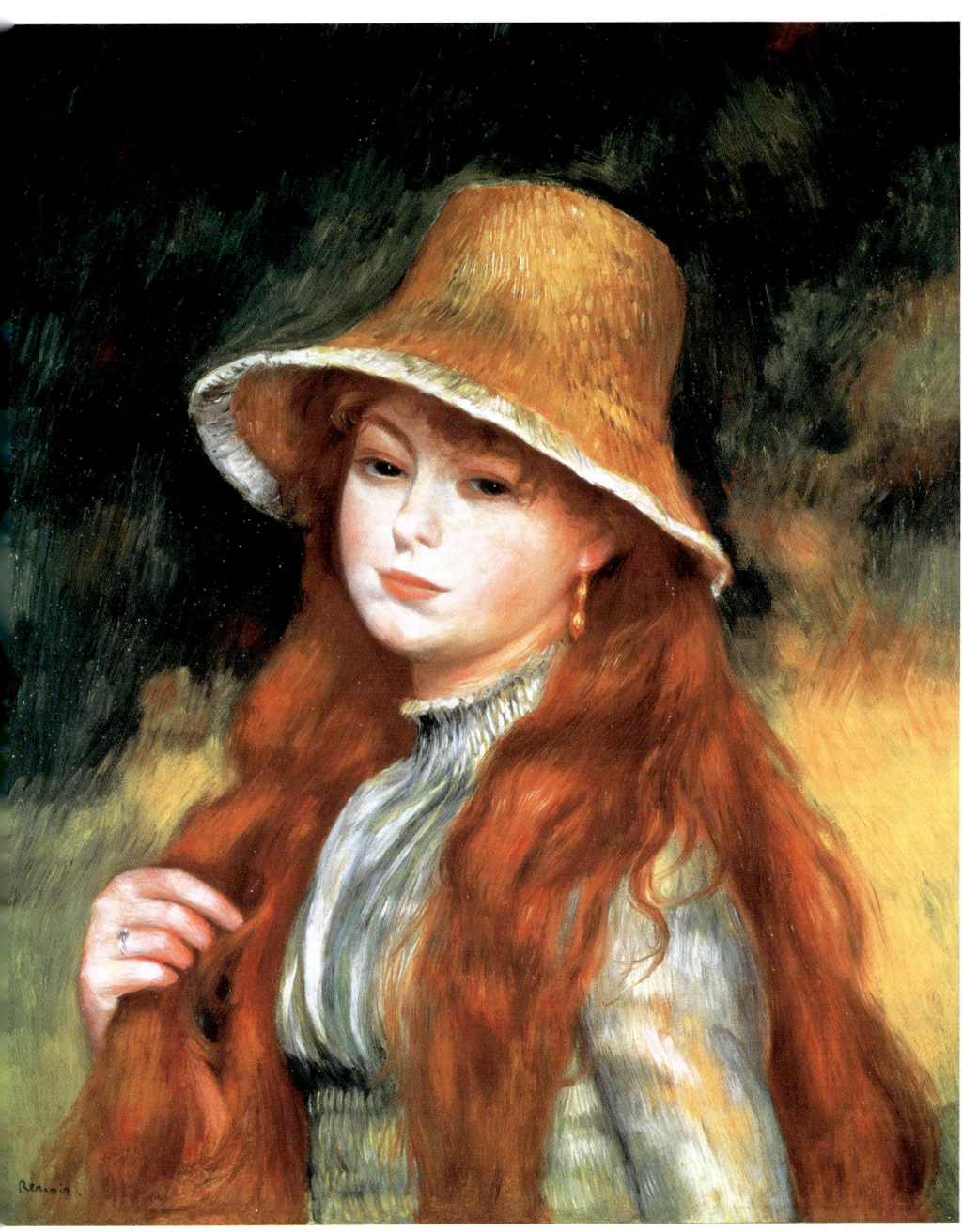

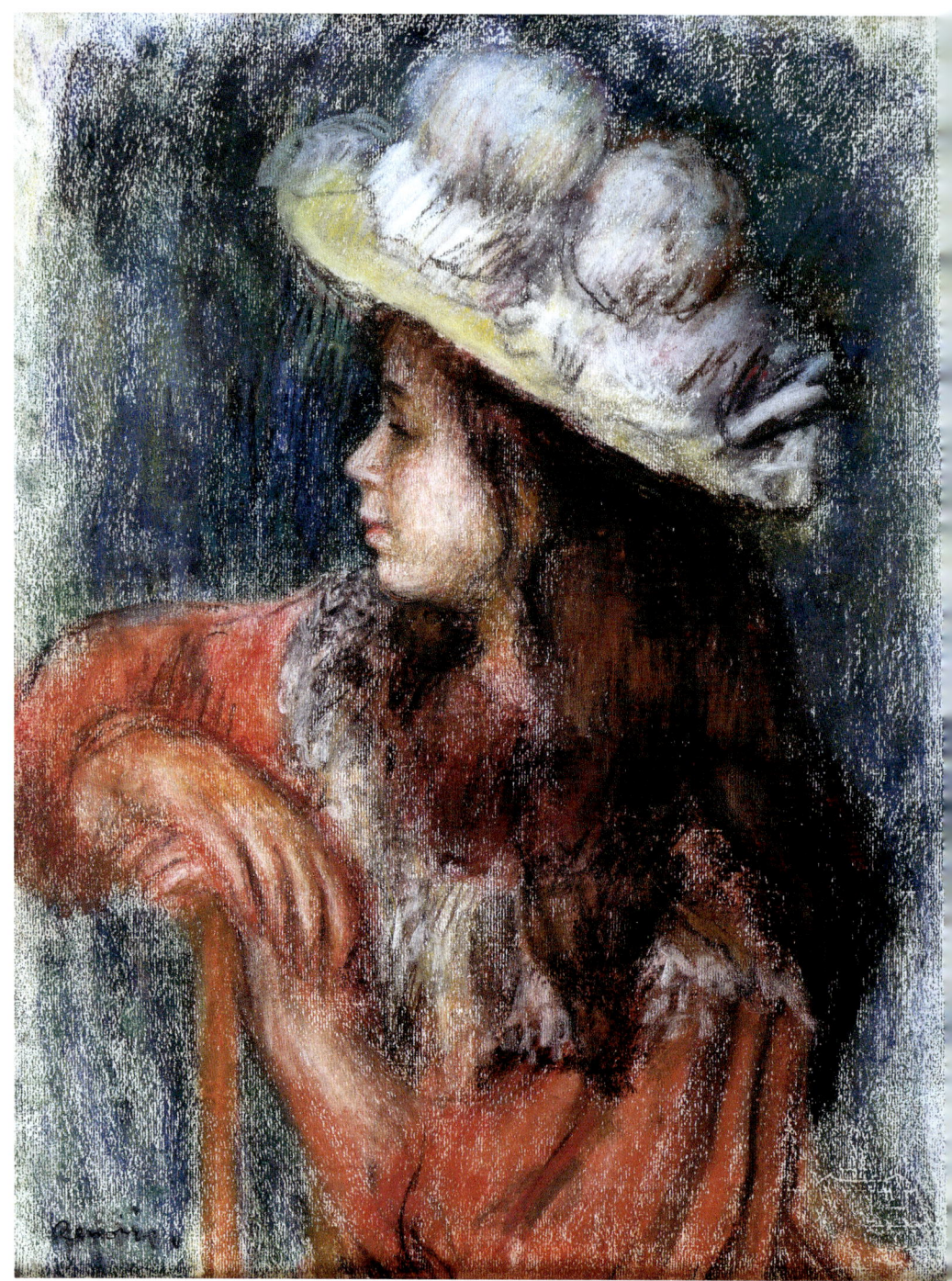

Nude in a Straw Hat, 1892
Oil on canvas,
41 x 32 cm (16¼ x 12⅝ in.)
Private collection

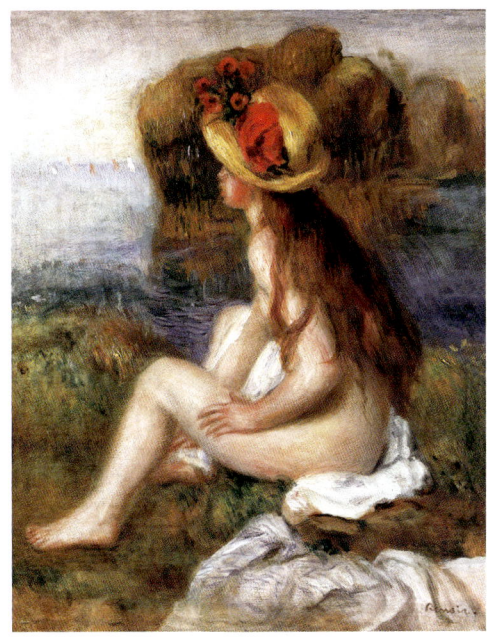

Young Girl Seated in a White Hat, 1884
Chalk, 57 x 47 cm (22½ x 18⅝ in.)
Paris, Musée Marmottan Monet

its brick façade, mellowed with the patina of age, stands out from the surrounding rose garden, which is sprinkled with flowers in full bloom (p. 140); in pure Impressionist style, the house cats play beside a copper bowl of geraniums (p. 170). Théodore Duret notes that, from 1879 onwards, Renoir painted each of the collector's children in turn (pp. 396, 399, 400/401, 403, 404). "While he was producing these portraits, Renoir was prudent enough not to scare his patrons off", Duret writes. "He refrained from using garish colours and stuck to a darker palette." The portraits pleased the parents, and their friends came especially to look at them.

The Château de Wargemont, on the road from Tréport, stood in spacious grounds near the coast. Renoir took advantage of the time he spent with the Bérards in the summer of 1879 to prepare a large composition on the beach at Berneval. He intended to submit it to the 1880 Salon. *Mussel-Fishers at Berneval* (p. 397) features four young girls; the one whose hair is tied back was also the model for *Gypsy Girl* (p. 144). Renoir was well known for his love of red hair. The collector Charles Ephrussi, a leading financier, was particularly susceptible to the charms of Renoir's young girls and owned several paintings of them. He bought the painting described by the Symbolist Jules Laforgue as "Renoir's dishevelled savage", which Renoir wanted to submit to the 1882 Salon. Ephrussi's habit of framing his paintings at the least expense possible frustrated his wishes. Renoir also painted a portrait of Marthe Bérard (*The Little Fisher Girl*; p. 396) catching shrimps. But by 1883, Renoir's style had changed. Bérard gave him the freedom to produce paintings in his new "harsh" manner. The first of these was the portrait of Lucie, their youngest daughter, who was three years old.

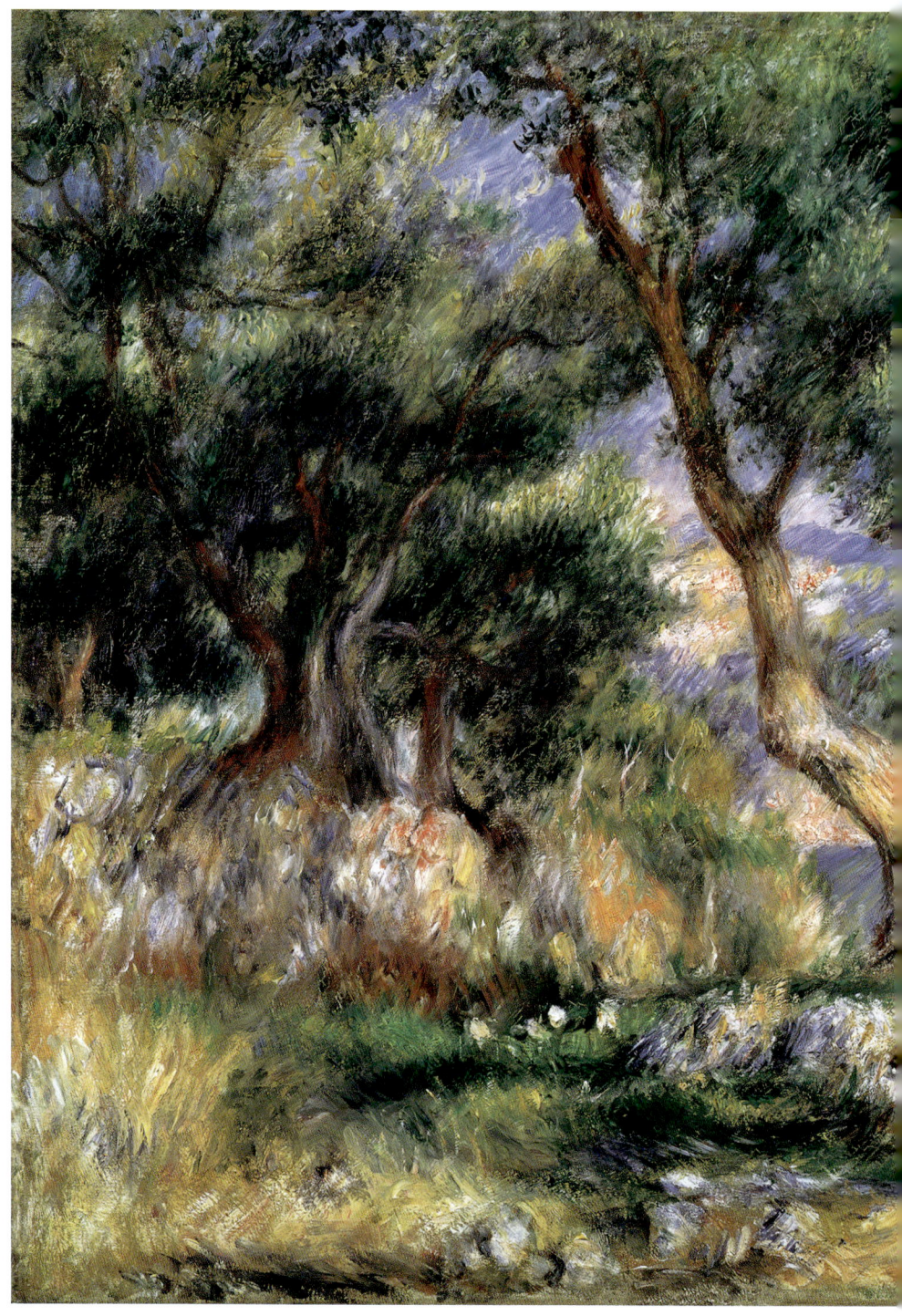

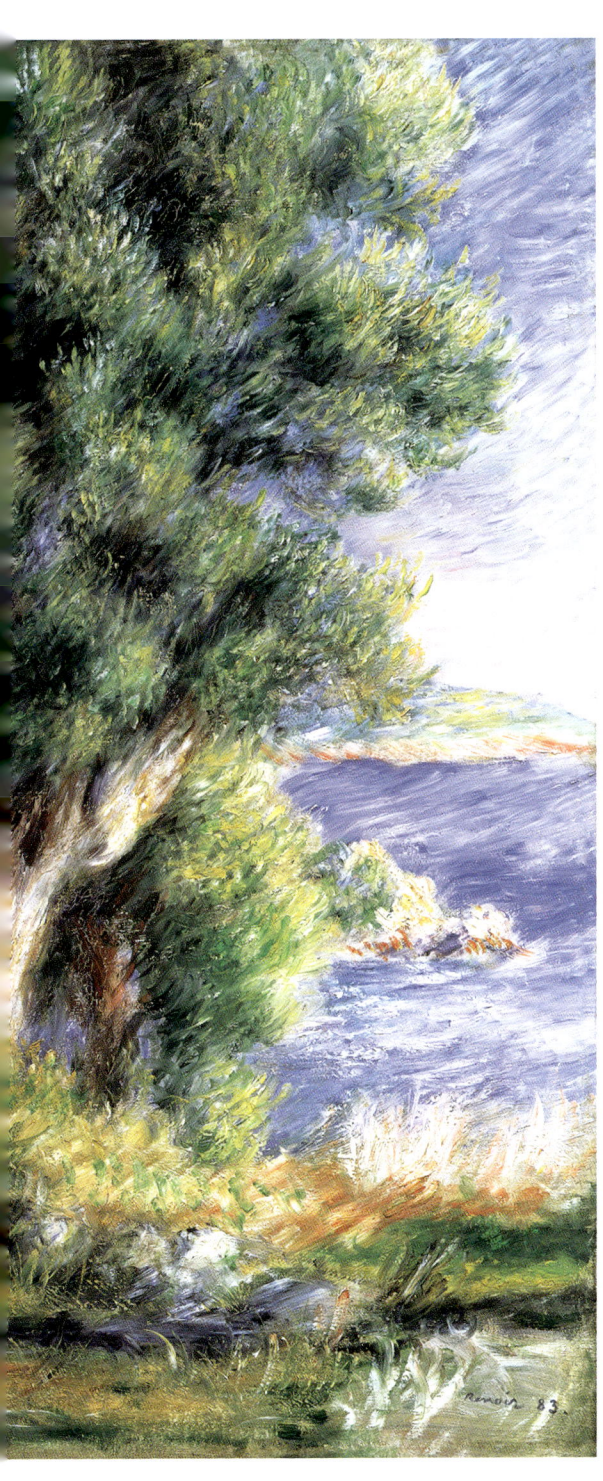

**Landscape on the Coast,
near Menton**, 1883
Oil on canvas,
65.7 x 81.3 cm (25⅞ x 32 in.)
Boston, Museum of Fine Arts,
Bequest of John T. Spaulding

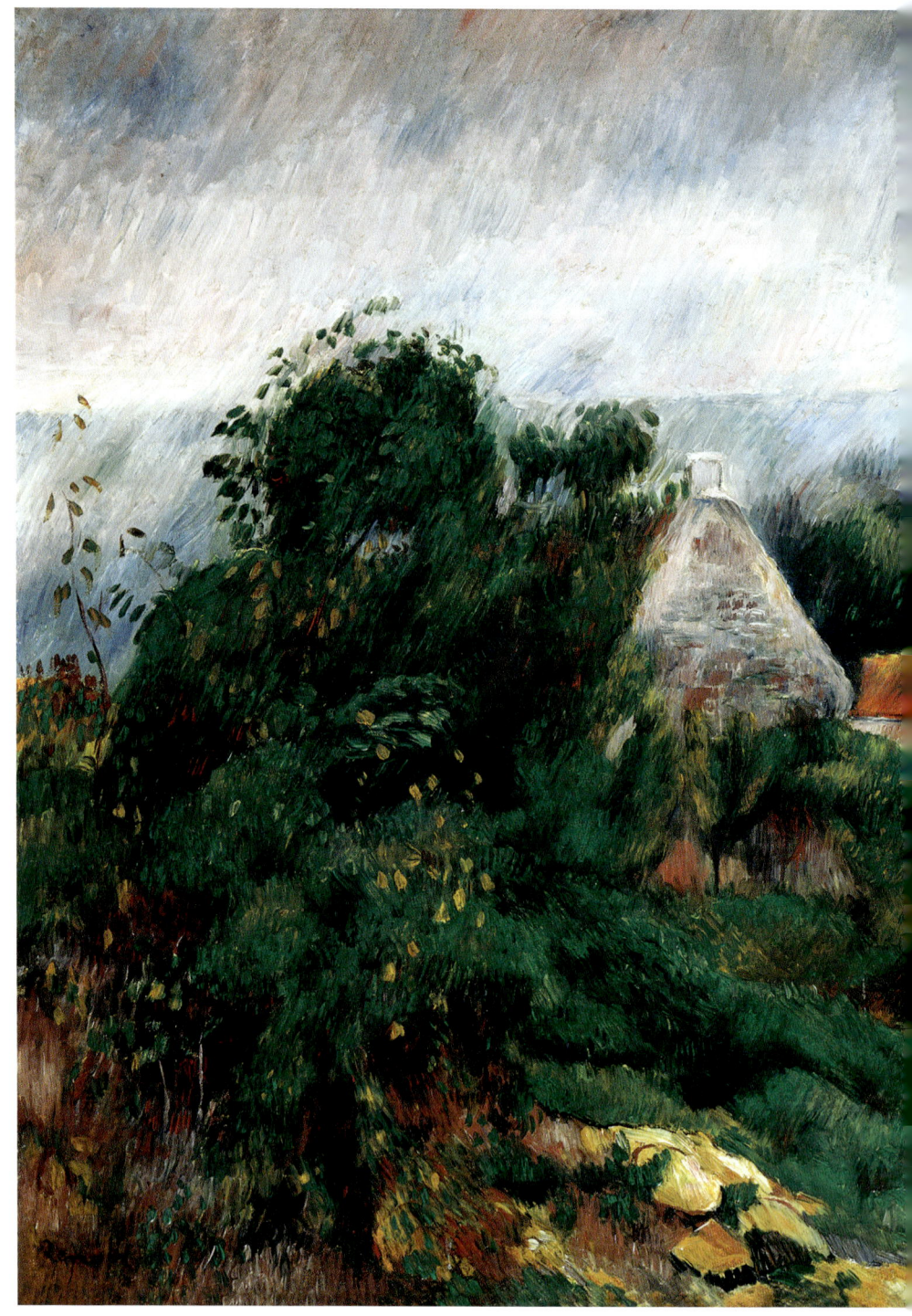

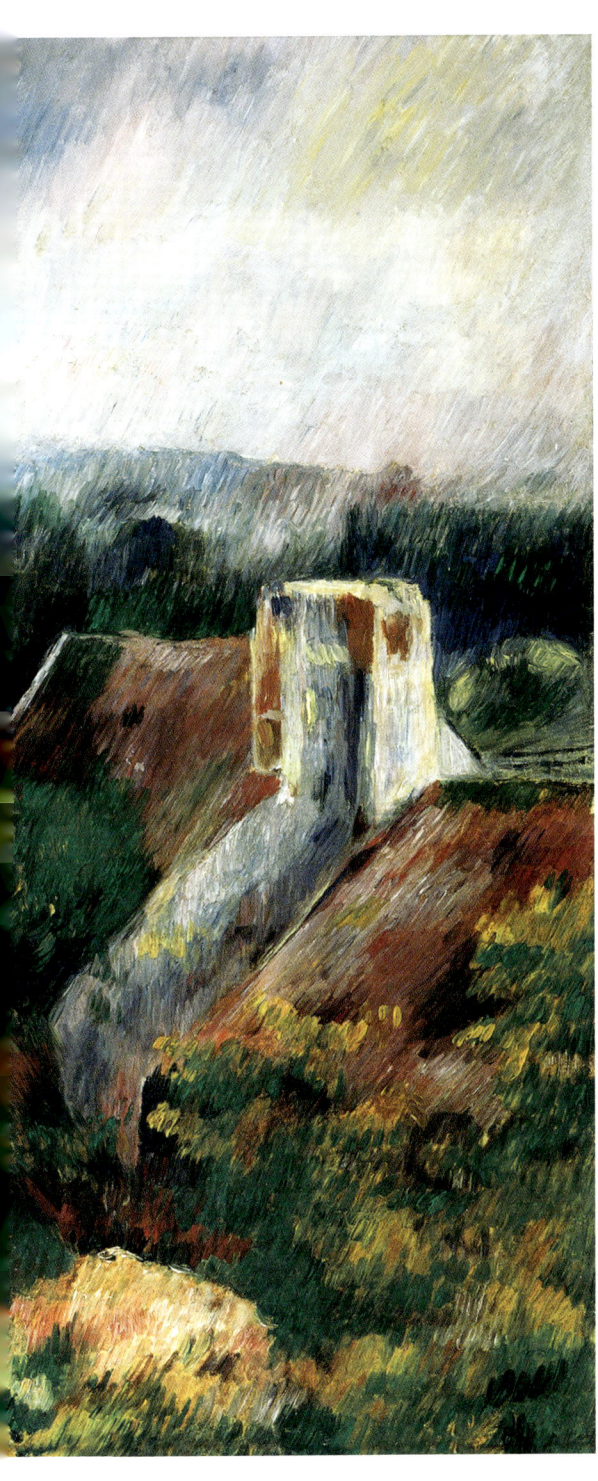

La Roche-Guyon, 1885/86
Oil on canvas,
46.5 x 56.1 cm (18⅜ x 22 in.)
Aberdeen Art Gallery & Museums

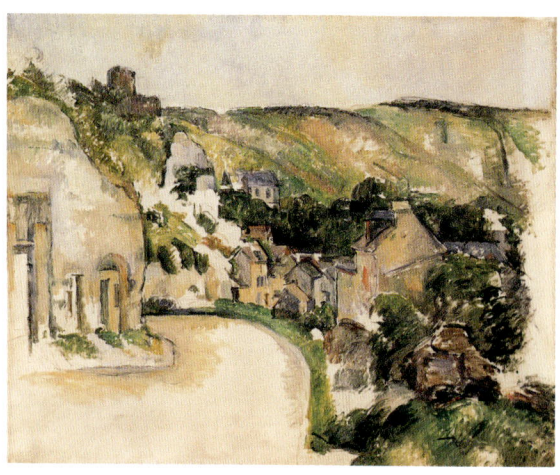

Paul Cézanne
A Turn in the Road at La Roche-Guyon, c. 1885
Oil on canvas, 64.1 x 80 cm (25¼ x 31½ in.)
Northampton, Massachusetts,
Smith College Museum of Art

Paul Cézanne
**Mont Sainte-Victoire,
Seen from Les Lauves**, 1902–1906
Oil on canvas, 63 x 83 cm (24⅞ x 32¾ in.)
Zurich, Kunsthaus Zürich

Lucie Bérard (*Child in White*; p. 275) shows this "living doll" transformed into a Spanish infanta. The portrait is very much in the style of Rembrandt. Its use of chiaroscuro and meticulous attention to detail are hallmarks of great academic painting and were beloved of Renoir's wealthy upper-class clientele. "I have spent a good deal of money on a lovely frame for Lucie's portrait", Bérard recorded. "I have hung it in a good spot in my study and Marguerite and I swoon with contentment when we look at it. But we cannot share our satisfaction with others. Many people say that the portrait shocks them."

Like *The Luncheon of the Boating Party* (pp. 156/157) and the portrait of *Madame Charpentier and Her Children* (pp. 388/389), the painting *Children in the Afternoon at Wargemont* (pp. 276/277) is done in a large format. It depicts the three Bérard daughters, Marthe (on the right, sewing), Lucie (the youngest, who stands holding her doll), and, Marguerite, who is busy reading a picture book on the left of the painting. It has been praised for its lack of shadow, the intensity of its tones, and the hieratic poses of the figures. These are said to give it the solemnity of a Renaissance work and, at the same time, the charm of a naïve painting. But the razor-sharp outlines reveal the harsh manner. Denis Rouart wrote of the painting that "one can only wonder what it would have been like if Renoir had reverted to type and freed himself from his self-imposed constraints. The atmosphere of the country house on a sunny summer afternoon deserved the full Renoir treatment every bit as much as *Moulin de la Galette* or *The Luncheon of the Boating Party*. You can imagine how he would have harmonised and integrated the various elements that here remain disparate". Renoir gives an admirably classical representation of

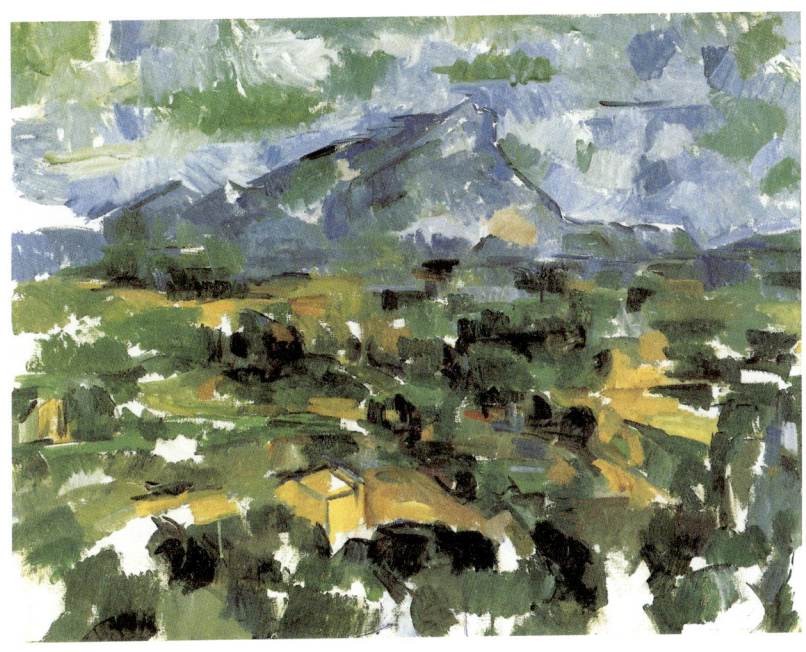

Lucie Bérard (p. 275). By placing her flowing locks, porcelain complexion, blue eyes and the folds of her blouse against a dark background, he gives her the same air of distinction and frigid grace that portraitists sought in the sixteenth century. The result is a painting in the primitive style.

In 1882 Durand-Ruel asked Renoir to start work on two large canvases on the theme of dance. He produced *Dance in the City* (p. 286) and *Dance in the Country* (p. 287). Durand-Ruel, as François Daulte argues, had no idea that he was helping the painter to move closer to his ideal style of painting. A third, slightly larger painting, *Dance at Bougival* (p. 285), should be added to these two masterpieces. In it the background figures are more clearly defined. These are the last great works that Renoir devoted to Paris and its environs. Critics vary in their responses to them. In the view of Julius Meier-Graefe, Renoir here replaces his Impressionist style with a "statue-like firmness" for the first time. John House notes how the close-up "life-size" figures invade the canvas. Renoir does not seem to try and insert them into the pictorial space, which is reduced to the area required. This probably shows his Italian influences. Instead of evoking an atmosphere, such as that of *Le Moulin de la Galette* (pp. 114/115), he concentrates on a single theme, that of a couple dancing close together. A drawing made for *Dance at Bougival* bears the following inscription in Renoir's hand: "She danced with delightful abandon in the arms of a blond man who looked like a boatman." *Dance at Bougival* captures the erotic ardour of the dancers in their tender and passionate pose. The boatman expresses his desire for the woman in an age-old gesture, by clasping her close to him. She abandons herself to him, conquered and consenting,

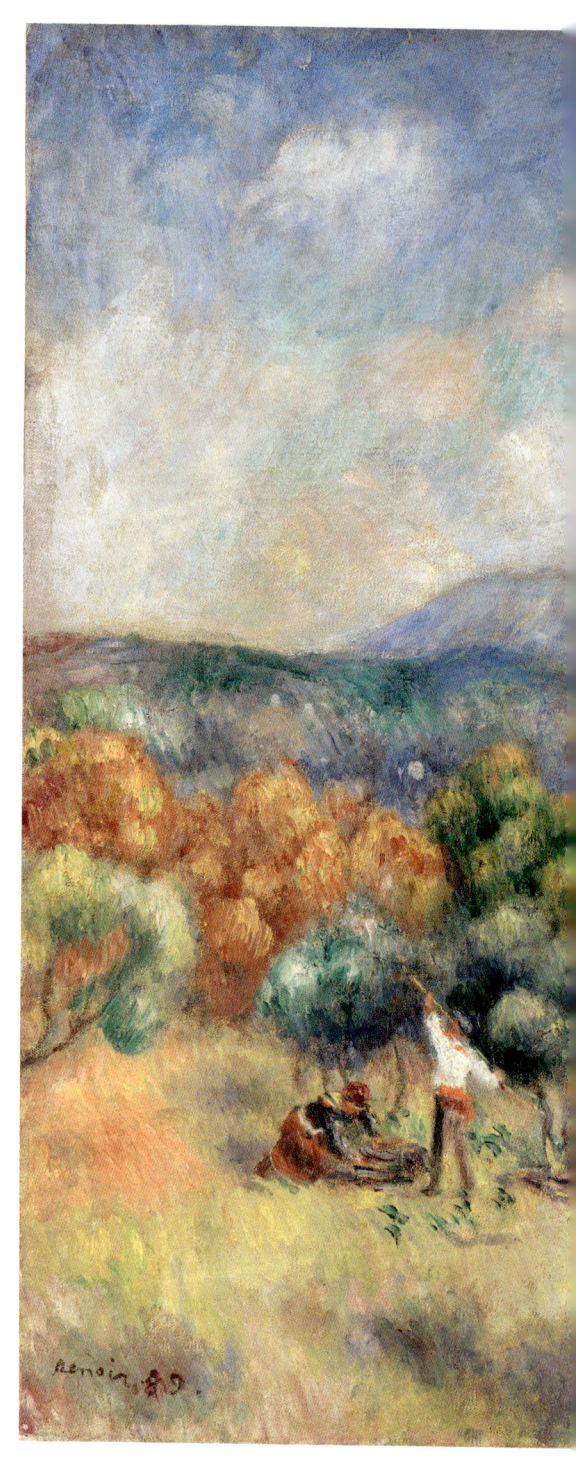

Montagne Sainte-Victoire, 1889
Oil on canvas,
54.4 x 65.5 cm (21½ x 25⅞ in.)
Philadelphia,
The Barnes Foundation

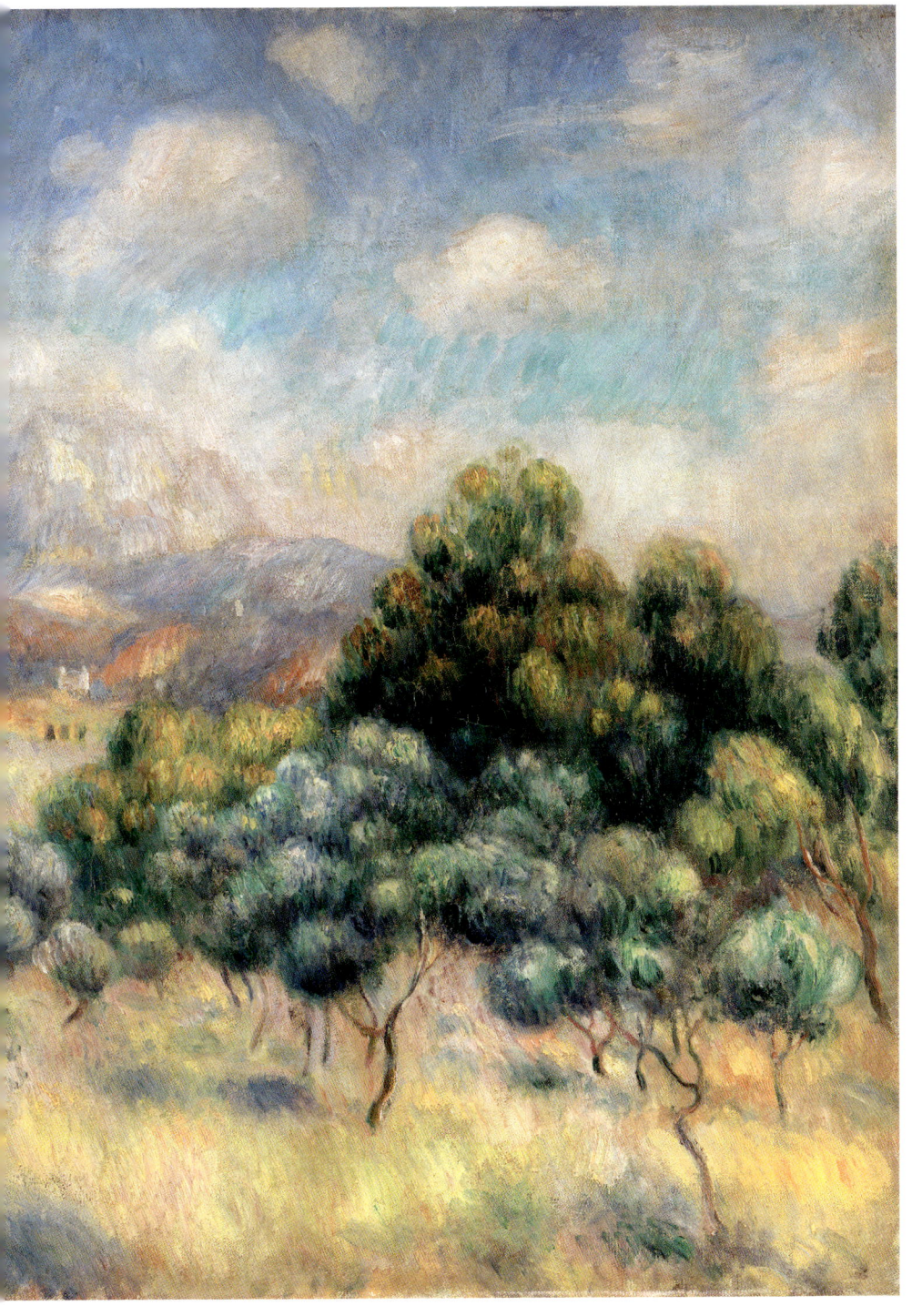

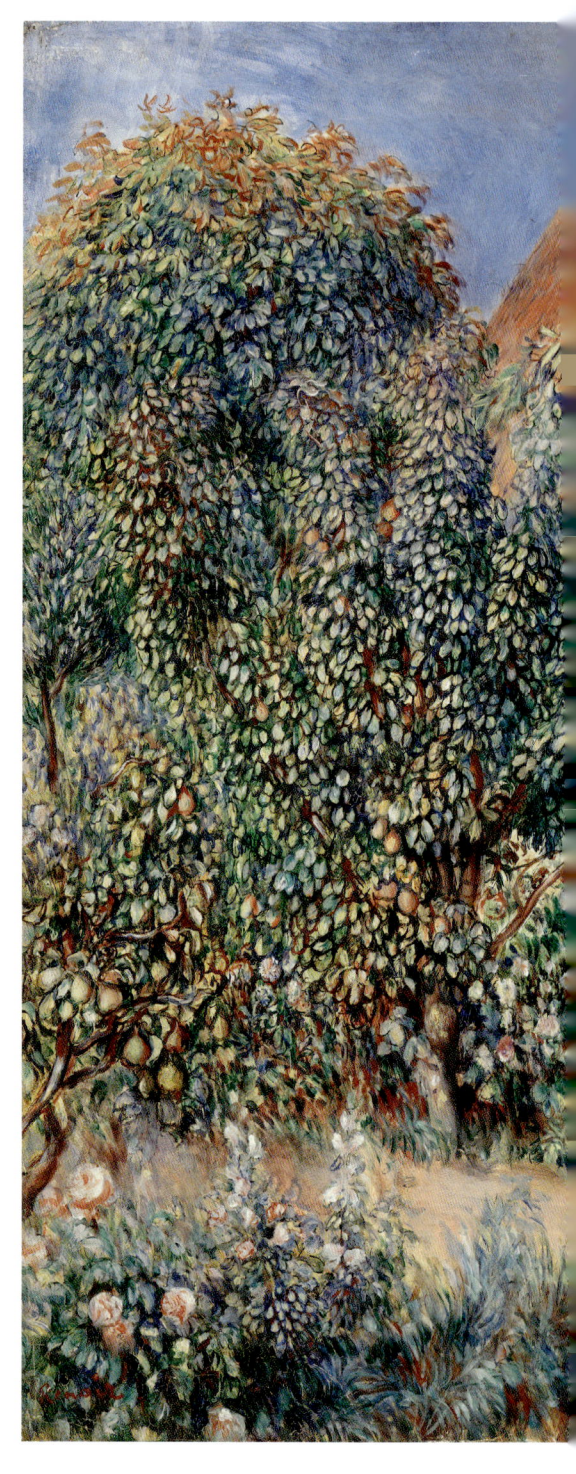

In Brittany, 1886
Oil on canvas,
54 x 65.4 cm (21⅜ x 25¾ in.)
Philadelphia,
The Barnes Foundation

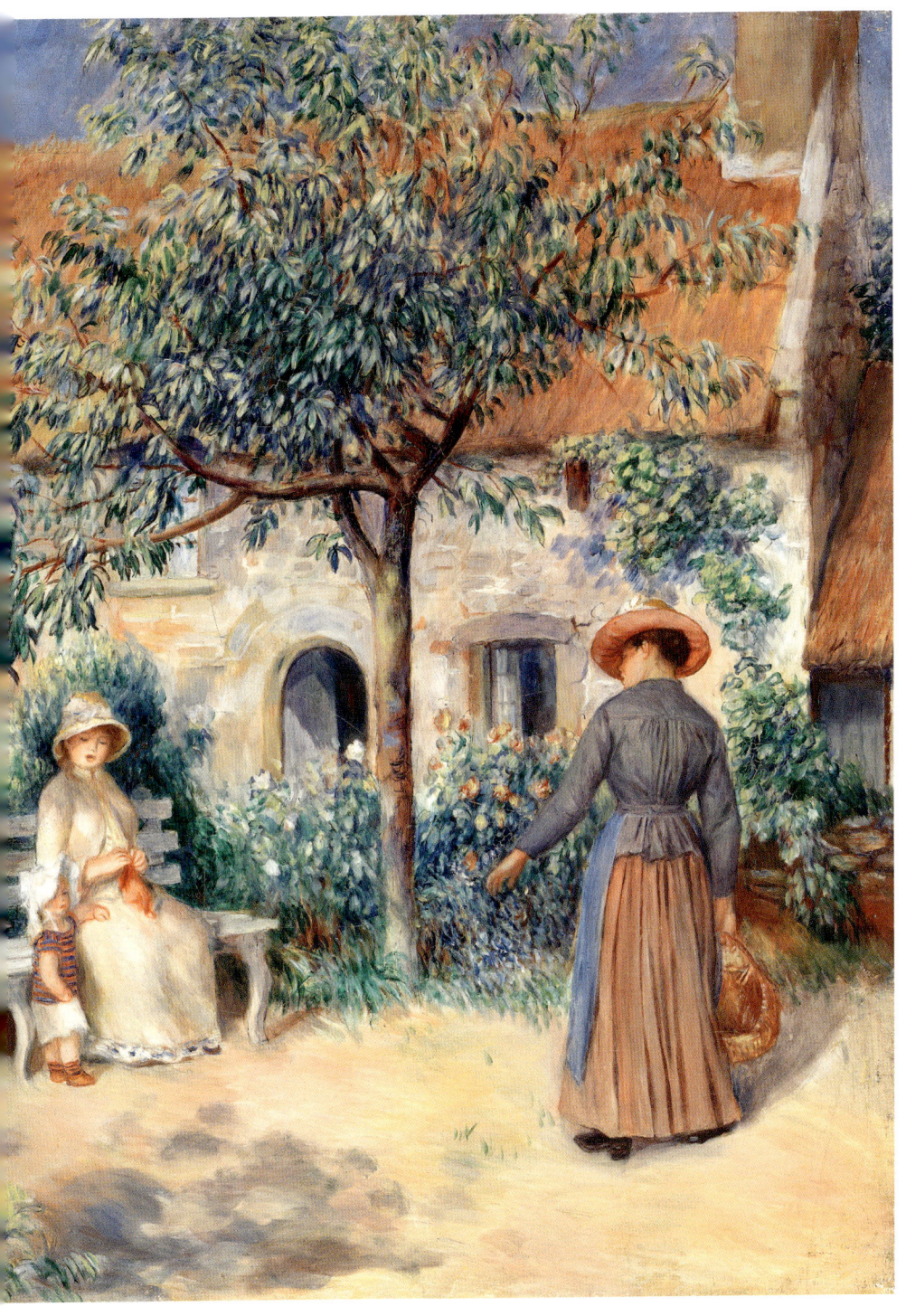

"her face hot with the blush of desire". The dashing boatman who posed for all three *Dances* was Paul Auguste Lhote, who had accompanied Renoir on his trips to Algeria and Italy and who was, according to Rivière, a close friend of his at the time. The dancer was a woman of outstanding beauty whose complexion, elegant features and magnificent figure had already attracted a number of painters. She began working as a trapeze artist at the age of fifteen, but a back injury ended her career in the circus. She became a model instead although, like Aline Charigot, she called herself a "dressmaker". She was simultaneously the mistress of Puvis de Chavanne and Toulouse-Lautrec – whom she hoped would marry her – as well of Renoir. Her name was Marie-Clémentine Valadon, and she would later become a famous painter in her own right under the name of Suzanne Valadon. She posed for *Dance at Bougival* and *Dance in the City* at seventeen years of age. At the time she was pregnant with a son, Maurice Utrillo; no one, including even perhaps Suzanne, ever knew which of the three painters was the boy's father. But in the circumstances it would have been difficult for him to avoid becoming a painter – and in time he did so.

Renoir chose Suzanne Valadon, with her youthfully slim figure, to incarnate urban chic. But he preferred to portray the more curvacious Aline Charigot in the robust setting of a country dance. Unlike the other models in Montmartre, Suzanne Valadon had a real gift for drawing. She was encouraged in this by none other than Degas, who was also perhaps attracted to her. She eventually became famous in her turn and able to live comfortably from her art. She wrote memoirs in which she described Renoir's passion for hats, the hours they spent together in milliners' shops, and the care with which he chose her

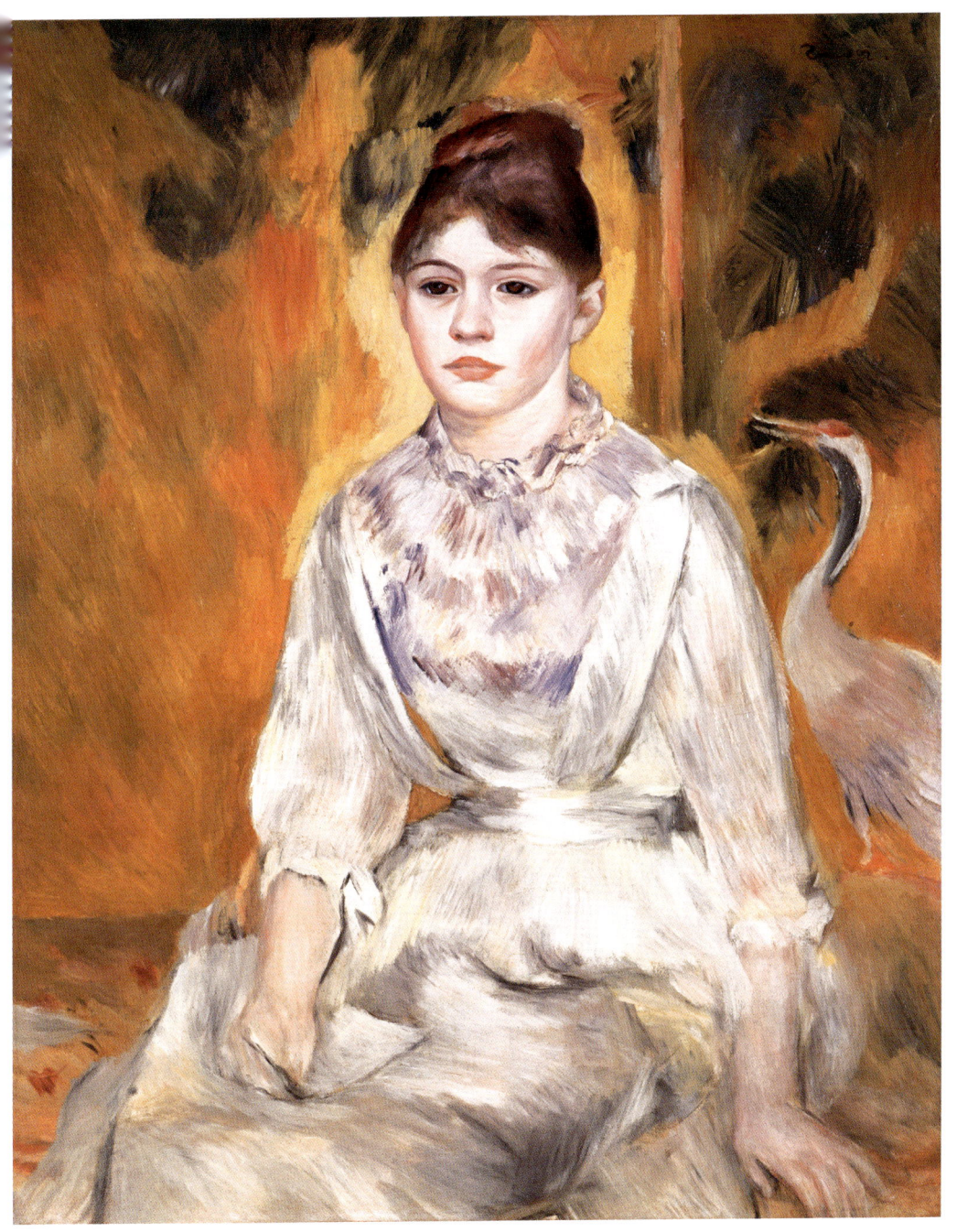

**The Shepherdess, the Cow
and the Ewe**, 1886/87
Oil on canvas,
53 x 64 cm (20⅞ x 25¼ in.)
Private collection

wardrobe for the two *Dance* paintings. Renoir depicts her with scrupulous fidelity in them, as he did in *Girl Braiding Her Hair* (p. 311) and *The Great Bathers* (pp. 348/349), for which she posed with Aline Charigot. Renoir, as has already been noted, was famous for giving his mistresses a valedictory portrait when he left them. He did this for Lise Tréhot *(Lise in a White Shawl)* and for Henriette Henriot, whose portrait is now in Washington (p. 91). Suzanne Valadon asked him to produce a smaller version of the large painting now in Boston. She insisted that he pay particular attention to her face, which is "hot with the blush of desire". This little-known masterpiece once again shows Renoir keen to please his favourite model of the time.

The drawing of the faces on the left side of *The Umbrellas* (p. 272), especially the young woman carrying a basket, is comparable to that of the children whom Renoir painted between 1883 and 1885. These include *Child with a Whip* (p. 281) and its counterpart, *Girl with a Hoop* (p. 280), portraits of Dr Goujon's children, as well as the brother-and-sister portraits of Robert and Aline Nunès, *Sailor Boy* (p. 283) and *Young Girl with a Parasol* (p. 282). In these paintings he succeeds in combining the rich colour of his open-air paintings with the careful drawing of his models. Renoir makes the most of the contrast between the background of the paintings, with their varying shades and brushstrokes, and the clothing of the models. The details of the hair and shoes give the compositions a focal point and precise tonal structure. The children stand like multicoloured garden statues and their faces look almost as if they have been carved in stone. The slight softening of their features suggests nevertheless that Renoir the sculptor remains, for all that, Renoir.

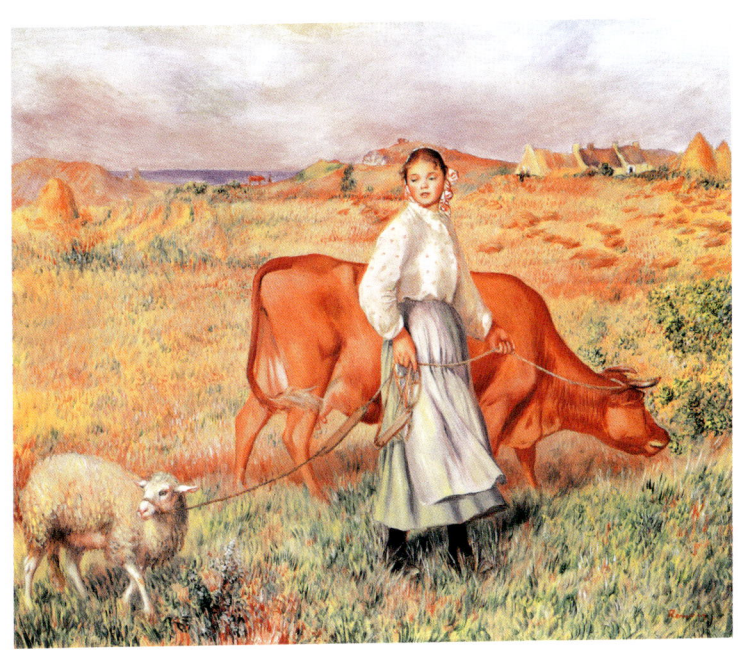

Renoir discussed these developments with Monet, who was painting nothing but land-scapes at that time. He stressed that he was seeking "the perfect model" because he was fun-damentally "a figure painter". In 1883 he wrote in similar fashion to Durand-Ruel: "I hope to return soon with a few canvases and documents so that I can continue painting pictures in Paris. I shall have in that way a source of real, graceful subjects on which to draw". He combined details from the sketches he had made on the beach to sculpt a number of "per-fect models", adding the familiarly simple gestures and expressions. Renoir's experience in Guernsey no doubt contributed to the atmosphere of the *Seated Bather* (p. 334). In a letter to Durand-Ruel, Renoir explained: "Here, people swim among rocks that also serve as changing-rooms, because there is nowhere else. There is nothing nicer than to see these men and women mingling among the rocks. The scene is more reminiscent of a Watteau landscape than of the real world. As in Athens, the women are not in the slightest con-cerned by the proximity of the men on neighbouring rocks. It is amusing to wander among the rocks and come upon young girls getting ready for a swim. Even though they are Eng-lish, they are not at all disconcerted".

Many years later, Renoir still reminisced to Vollard about the lack of false modesty shown by the English girls in Guernsey. The *Seated Bather* is drying herself on the rocks, with the sea lapping at their base, in an open-air setting recreated in a studio. The theme of the naked woman sitting beside water is both an eternal theme and one based on actual experience. This painting, as well as the magnificent *By the Seashore* (p. 279), can be com-pared with the *Dances* (pp. 285–287), since the technique remains supple and the contours

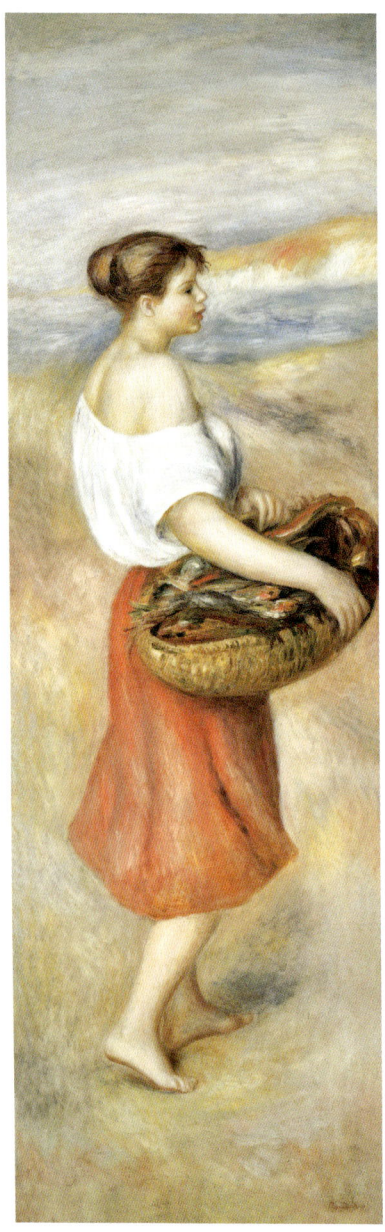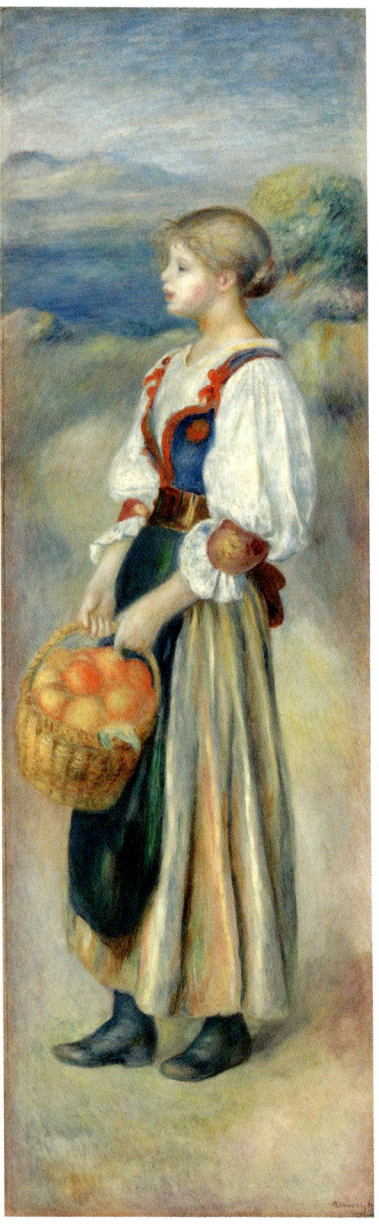

Girl with a Basket of Fish, c. 1889
Oil on canvas,
130.7 x 41.8 cm (51½ x 16½ in.)
Washington, D.C., National Gallery
of Art, Gift of William Robertson Coe

Girl with a Basket of Oranges, c. 1889
Oil on canvas,
128.8 x 41.8 cm (50¾ x 16½ in.)
Washington, D.C., National Gallery
of Art, Gift of William Robertson Coe

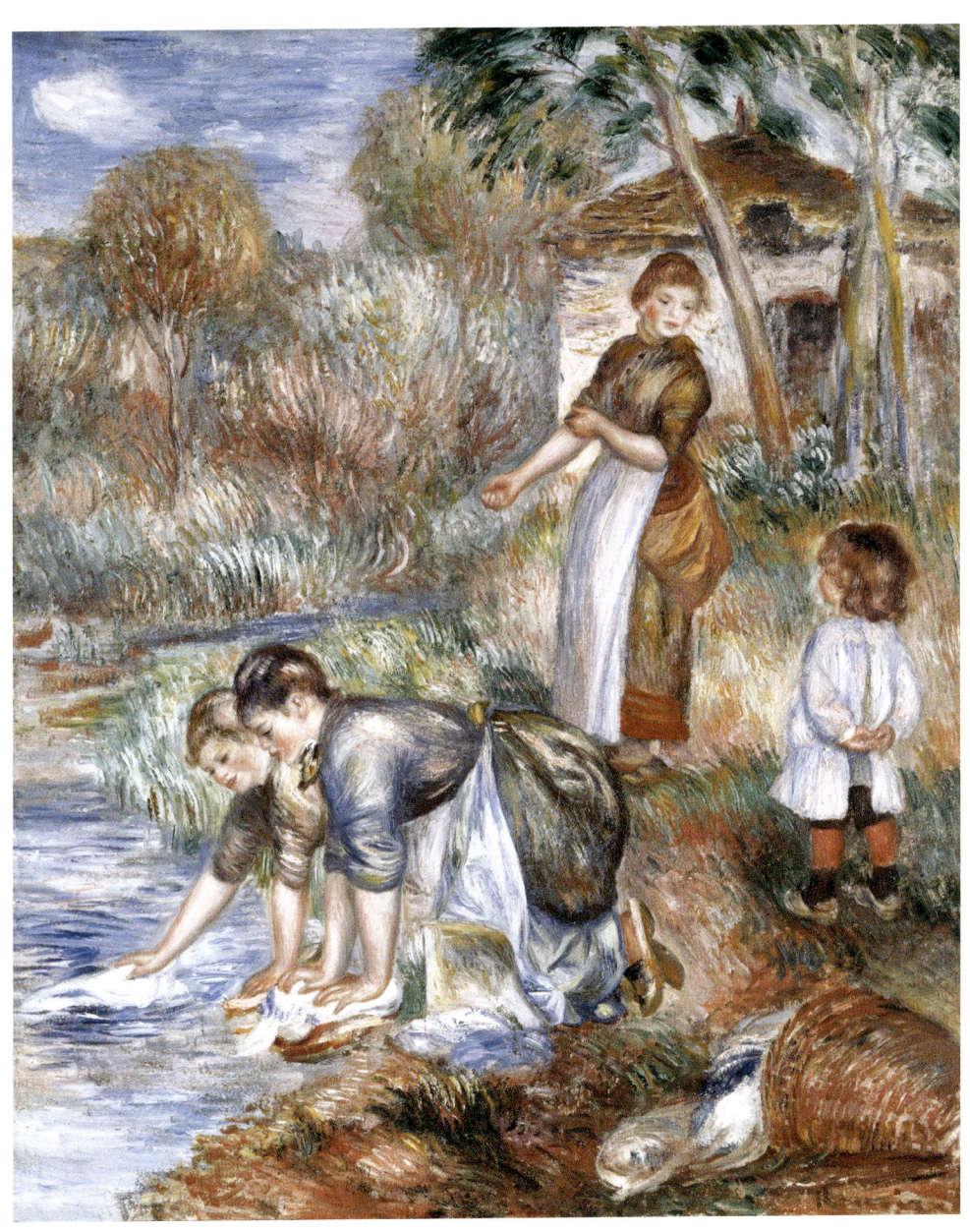

Washerwomen, c. 1888
Oil on canvas,
56.5 x 47.5 cm (22¼ x 18¾ in.)
The Baltimore Museum of Art,
The Cone Collection

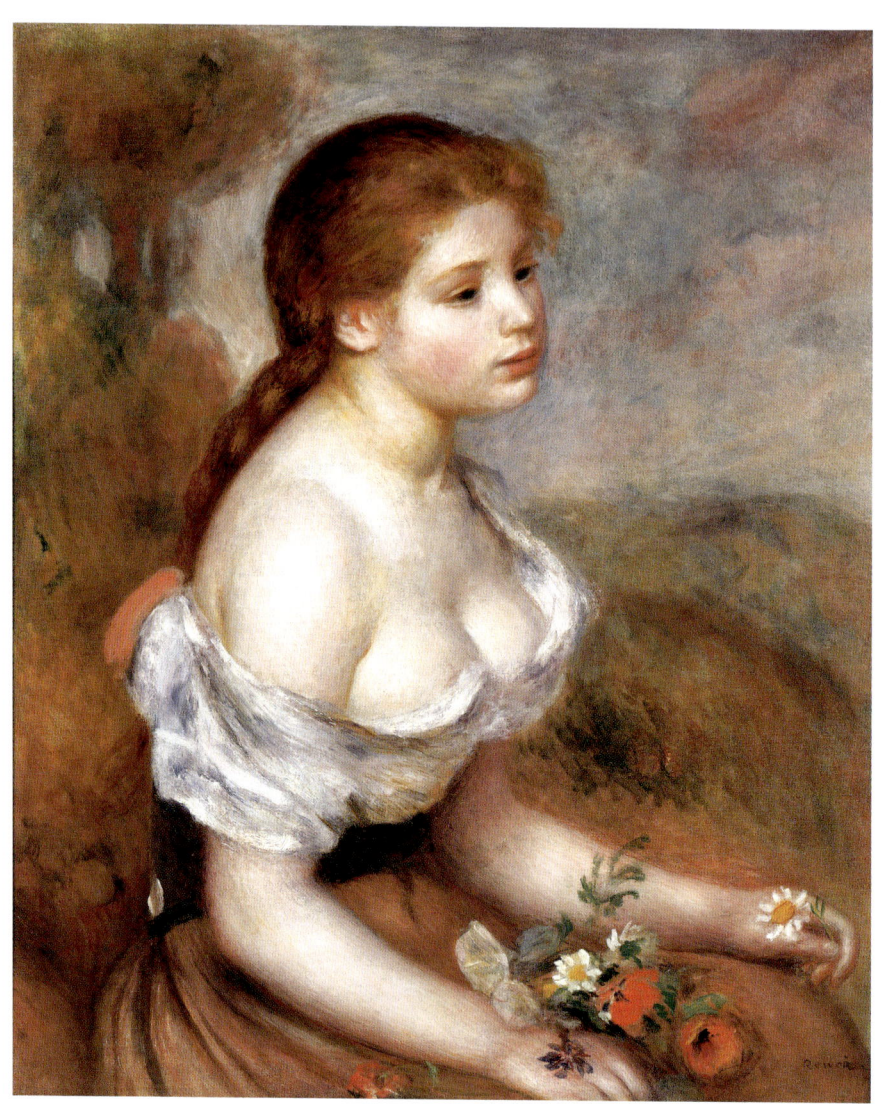

Young Girl with Daisies, 1889
Oil on canvas, 65.1 x 54 cm (25¾ x 21⅜ in.)
New York, The Metropolitan Museum of Art,
Mr. and Mrs. Henry Ittleson Jr. Purchase Fund

In the Meadow, c. 1888–1892
Oil on canvas, 81.3 x 65.4 cm (32 x 25¾ in.)
New York, The Metropolitan Museum of Art,
Bequest of Sam A. Lewisohn

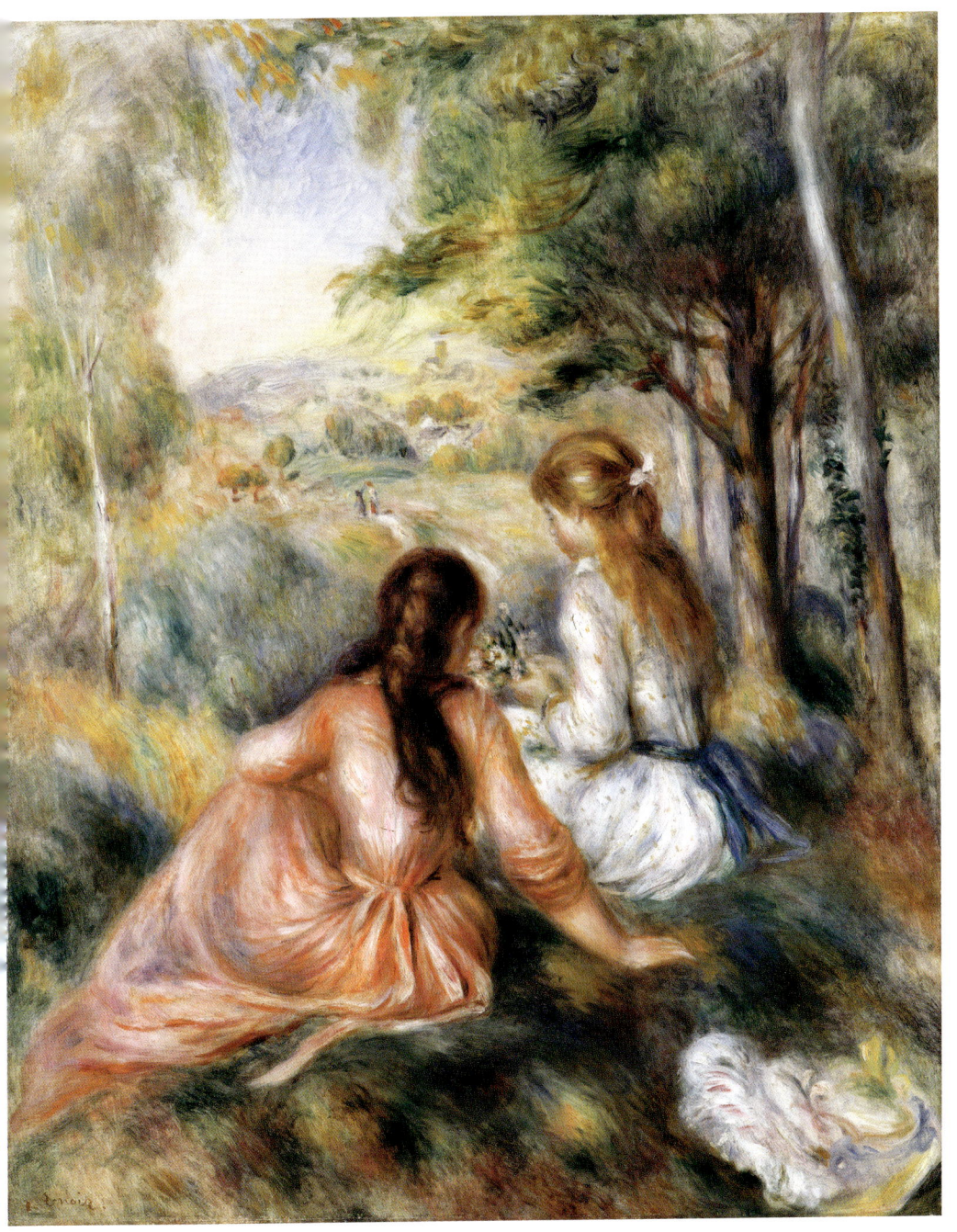

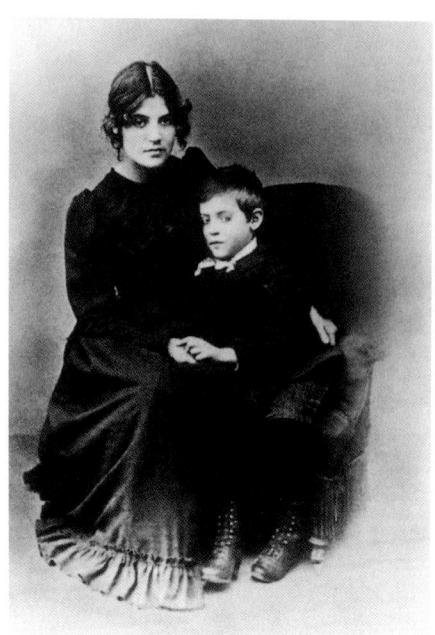

Suzanne Valadon (1865–1938) and
her son Maurice Utrillo, c. 1890

**Girl Braiding Her Hair
(Suzanne Valadon)**, c. 1886/87
Oil on canvas, 56 x 47 cm (22 x 18½ in.)
Baden, Switzerland, Museum Langmatt

are less harsh than they were to become in 1885. *Bather Arranging Her Hair* (p. 345), which
dates from 1885, is a case in point. Painted at the culmination of the period of technical
experimentation, the contours are more incisive and more sharply delineated. Suzanne
Valadon served as the model for this canvas. It owes much to *The Valpinçon Bather* by
Ingres in its composition and the majestic beauty of the figure. Titian's *Venus Rising from
the Sea* ("*Venus Anadyomene*"; p. 350) is also recalled in the opulence of the flesh and the
natural elegance of the arms which smooth down locks of hair. This gave a disturbing
charm to the women whom Renoir was soon to show bathing. Titian and Renoir shared
a fetish for female hair and this is apparent once again in *Girl Braiding Her Hair* (p. 311),
for which Suzanne Valadon also posed. This painting was among those most heavily
influenced by Ingres in this period, as is the drawing *Head of a Woman* (1883), which
may have been a preparatory study for a portrait.

In his quest for rigour, Renoir's work began to resemble that of Cézanne. To the background for paintings such as *Bather Arranging Her Hair* (p. 345), he applies colour in the
same way as Cézanne does to his still-life paintings. His thickly superimposed strokes
modulate the colour in contrast to the accurate and well-defined drawing. Ingres could
almost have painted the portrait in *Girl Braiding Her Hair* (p. 311) and Cézanne the background. Renoir sought to improve his technique for figure painting by studying Ingres
and Titian. But it was on Cézanne's rigorous version of Impressionism that he drew for
his background landscapes. This can be seen in the lovely unfinished watercolour, *Harvest*
(p. 315), in which he attempts to juxtapose these two opposing styles. Such attempts had

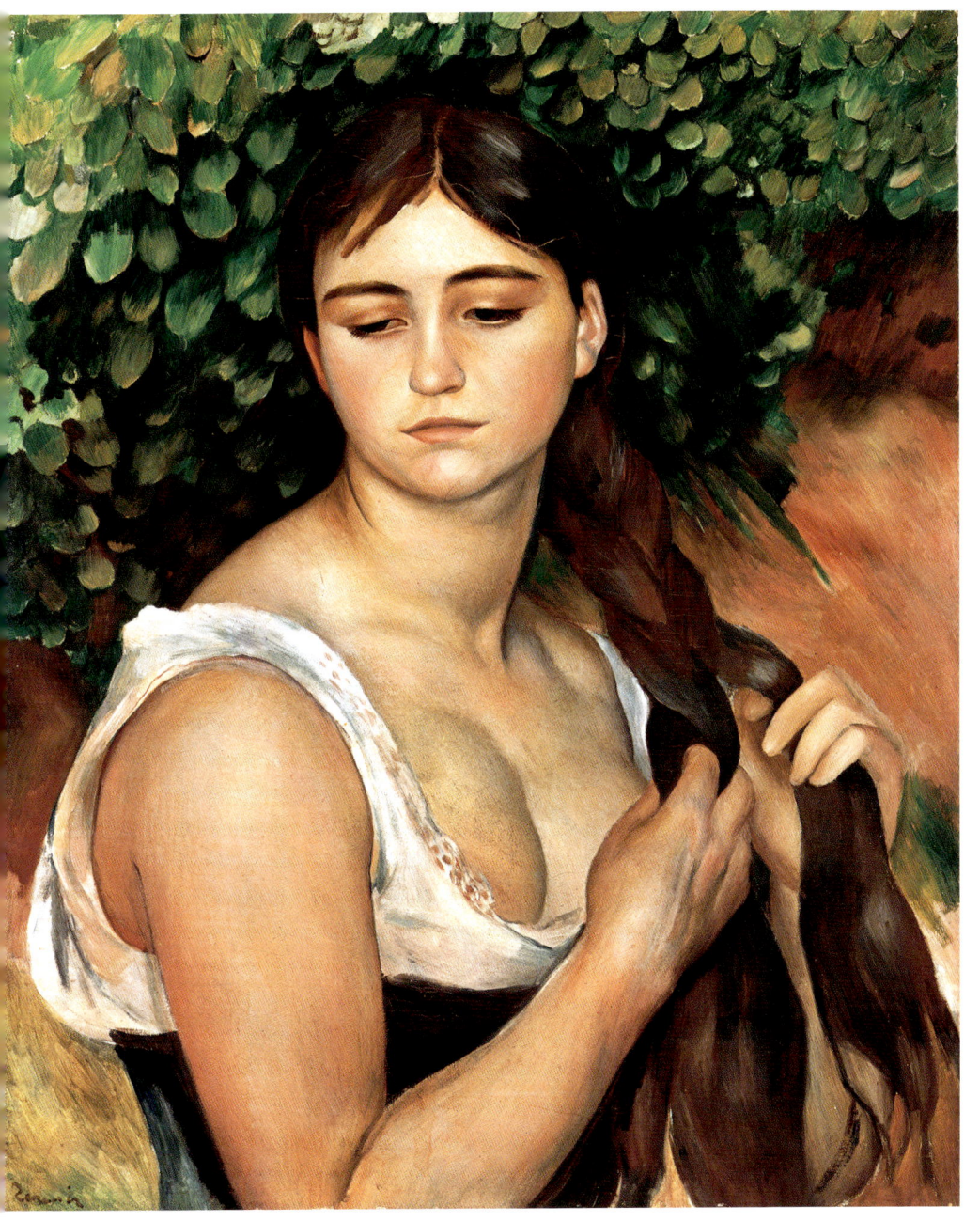

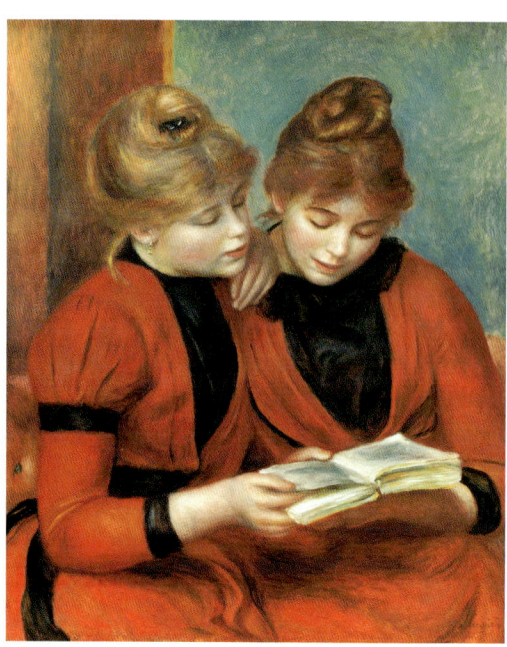

**Young Girls Reading
(The Two Sisters)**, c. 1889
Oil on canvas,
64 x 54 cm (25¼ x 21⅜ in.)
Private collection

Julie Manet, 1887
Oil on canvas,
65.5 x 53.5 cm (25⅞ x 21 in.)
Paris, Musée d'Orsay

begun as early as 1882, when he painted *Rocky Crags at L'Estaque* (pp. 178/179) at Cézanne's side. Renoir's oblique and parallel brushstrokes echo the much more rigorous "constructive stroke" that Cézanne used at the time to paint rocks. Renoir had just returned from Italy. He attempted to combine the lessons he had learned from Raphael with those of Cézanne, the order and simplicity of the former's wide structures with the skeletal formations which the latter detected in land masses. Even painting *Landscape on the Coast, near Menton* (pp. 292/293) in 1883 at Monet's side Renoir remained much closer to Cézanne than to his companion. Monet and Renoir were travelling along the Mediterranean between Marseilles and Genoa. They enthused about what they saw.

In a letter to Bérard, Renoir deplored the difficulty he was having in perfecting his own style of landscape-painting. "There are such lovely landscapes with distant horizons and the most beautiful colours", he wrote. "Unfortunately, our poor palettes cannot match them. However much trouble one takes, the wonderful bronzed tones of the sea become so heavy on the canvas." Renoir continued his quest but remained dissatisfied. Yet *Landscape on the Coast, near Menton* is magnificent. It owes its success as much to its orderly, classical composition – which Corot would have admired – as to the trees that provide a vigorous structural axis. These create a vista totally different from the dramatic contrasts and abrupt changes of plane that Monet adopted in the many paintings of cliffs that he made at this time. Renoir also achieves a subtle distribution of colour through the use of various techniques, depending on the natural texture of the features he painted. Sometimes he uses dabs of paint and at other times broad brushstrokes, which enliven the whole surface,

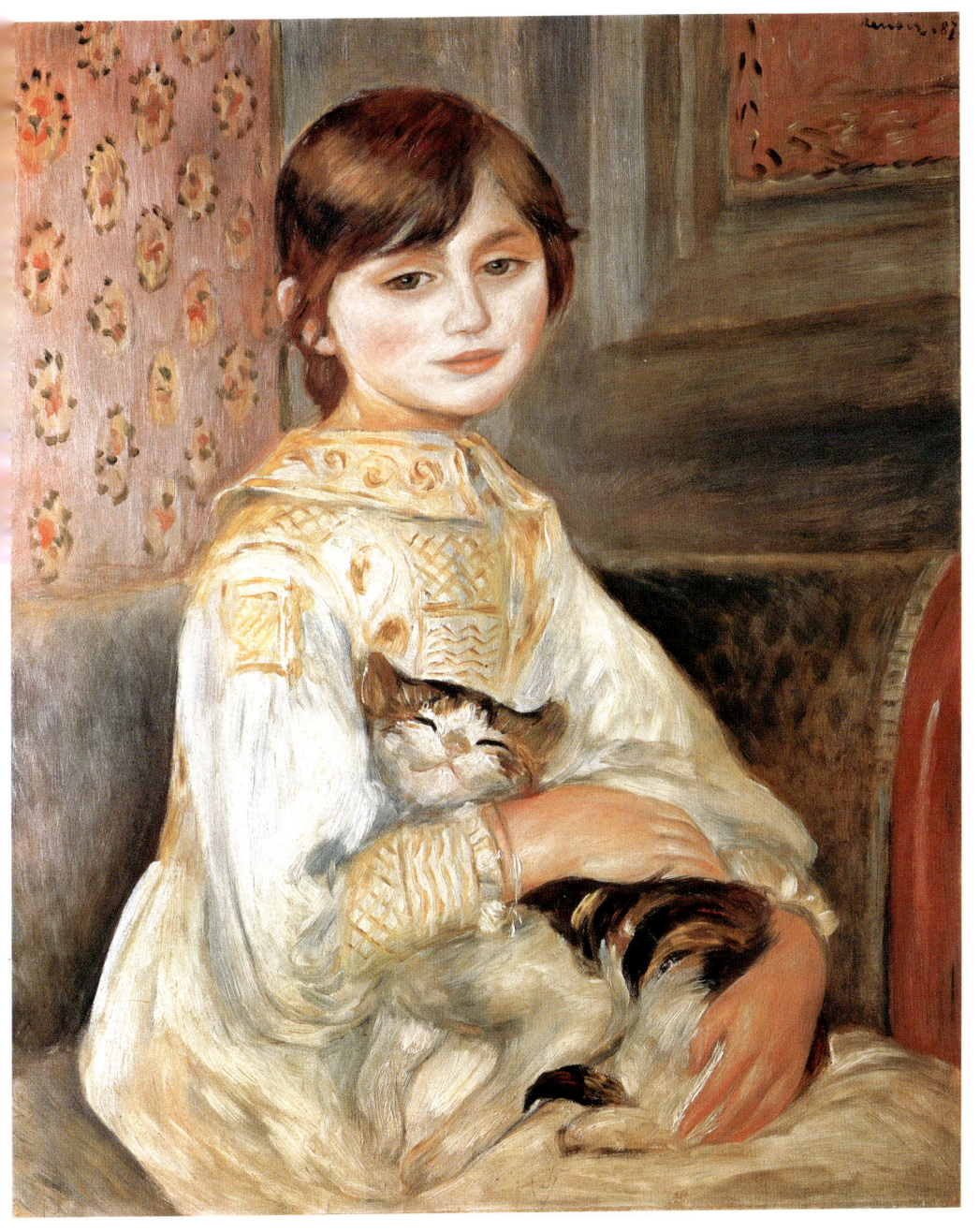

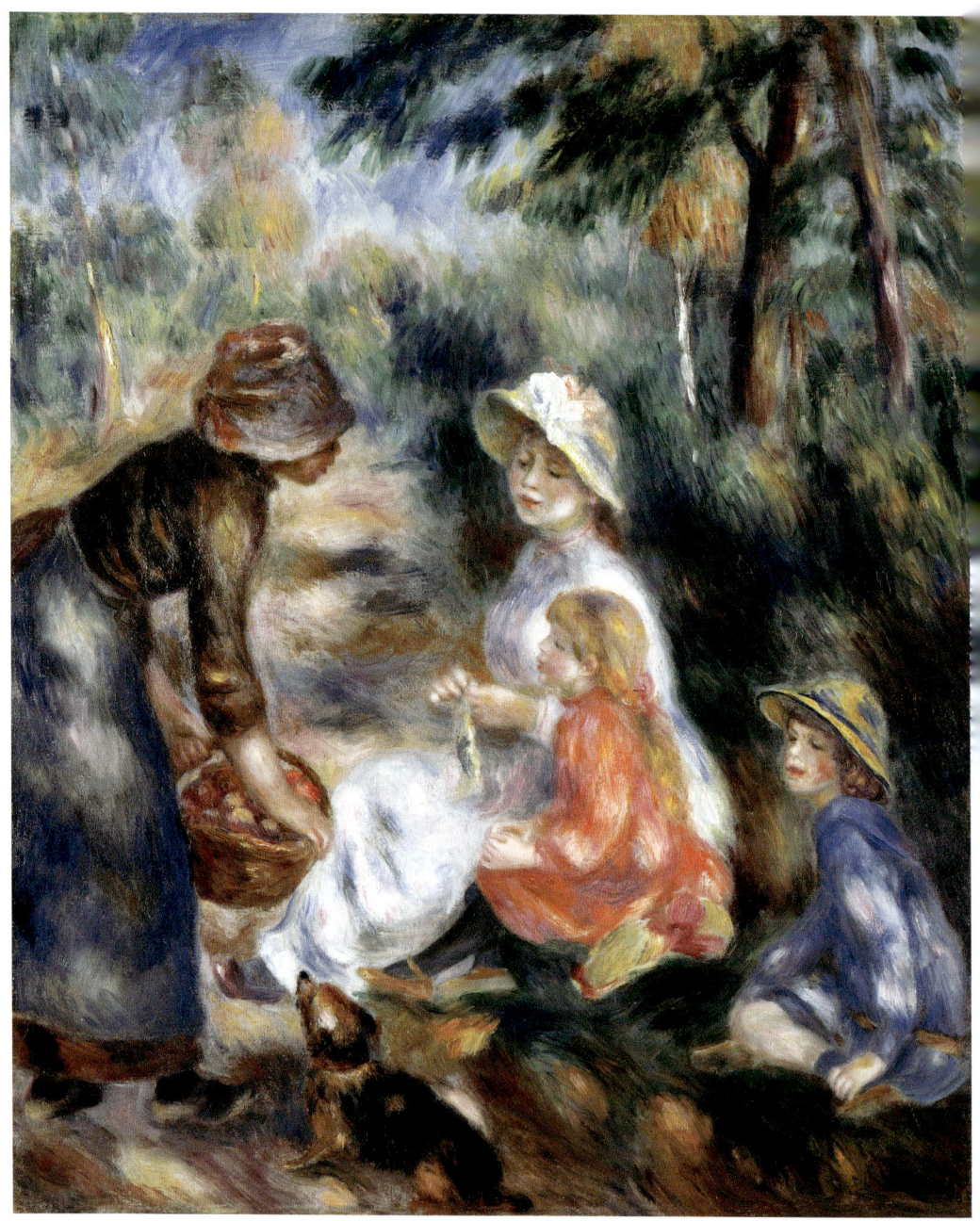

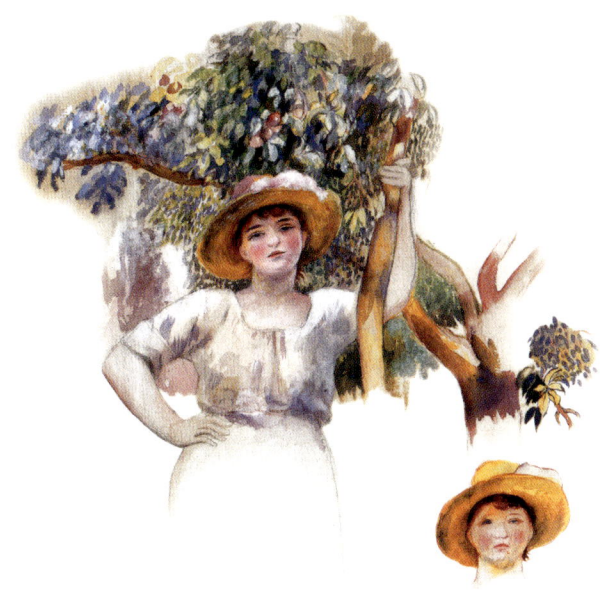

Harvest, c. 1885
Watercolour and chalk,
34 x 31 cm (13½ x 12¼ in.)
Paris, Musée du Louvre,
Département des
Arts graphiques

The Apple Seller, c. 1890
Oil on canvas,
65.8 x 54.5 cm (26 x 21½ in.)
The Cleveland Museum of Art,
Bequest of Leonard C. Hanna, Jr.

creating an undulating movement that runs through the grass, the tree trunks and the foliage. Distributed in this way, the colours add to the internal order of the painting and emphasise its structure.

Renoir and Cézanne were frequent painting companions. Together they painted the houses at *La Roche-Guyon* (pp. 294/295) in 1885/86 and then *Montagne Sainte-Victoire* (pp. 298/299) in 1888. On each such occasion Cézanne's influence waxed and Monet's waned. During the summers of 1885 and 1886, Renoir stayed at La Roche-Guyon, a town on the Seine between Paris and Rouen, a few miles from Giverny, to which Monet had recently moved. Cézanne came to join him for a short time in 1885. Cézanne's "constructive stroke" method involved structuring the surface of the canvas through a series of parallel strokes. It was much used by Renoir and *La Roche-Guyon* is one of his most extensive attempts in this direction. It uses diagonal strokes of even strength that unify the whole painting. Yet for all that Renoir remained Renoir. His Cézanne-style brushstrokes are less defined and tend to merge with each other in his usual way. Despite the evident tension between space and surface, the animation of the strokes and richness of colour lend the painting presence. But Renoir was still not satisfied. Two letters written at La Roche-Guyon in August 1885 betray his artistic uncertainty. In one of them, he asks Durand-Ruel not to come and see him while reassuring him that he has finally abandoned his "former clumsy efforts". In the other, he tells Bérard that he has prevented his dealer coming to visit him because "I want to find what I am looking for before I hand myself over".

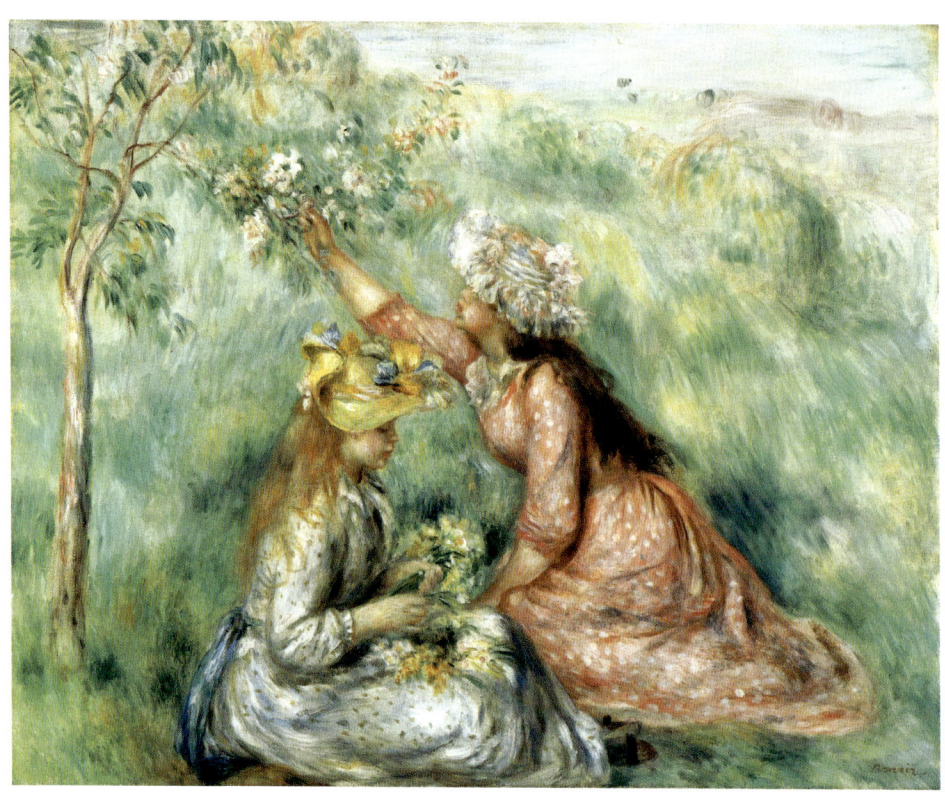

Girls Picking Flowers in a Meadow, c. 1890
Oil on canvas, 65.1 x 81 cm (25¾ x 32 in.)
Boston, Museum of Fine Arts,
Juliana Cheney Edwards Collection

Renoir moved effortlessly between the heavy toil
of the *Washerwomen* (p. 307) to the pursuits of
girls of good family, such as playing the piano in
town, walking in the country, picking flowers or
merely gossiping. These were subjects that not

only the artist liked very much, they also pleased
the public and purchasers. These creatures were
usually depicted in pairs, one of them blond and
dressed in blue and the other, dark-haired and
dressed in pink.

Young Girls at the Seaside, 1894
Oil on canvas, 55 x 46 cm (21¾ x 18⅛ in.)
Private collection

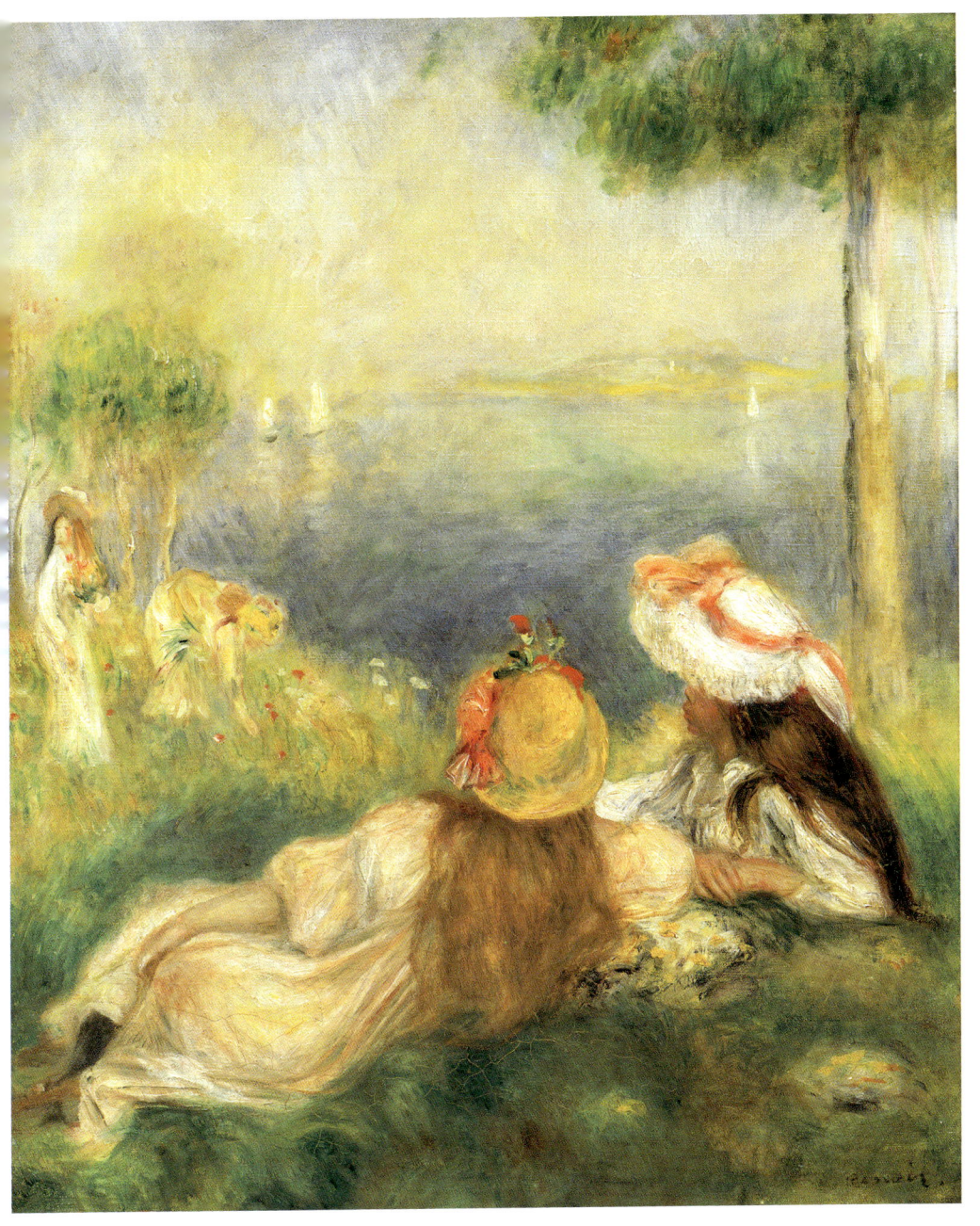

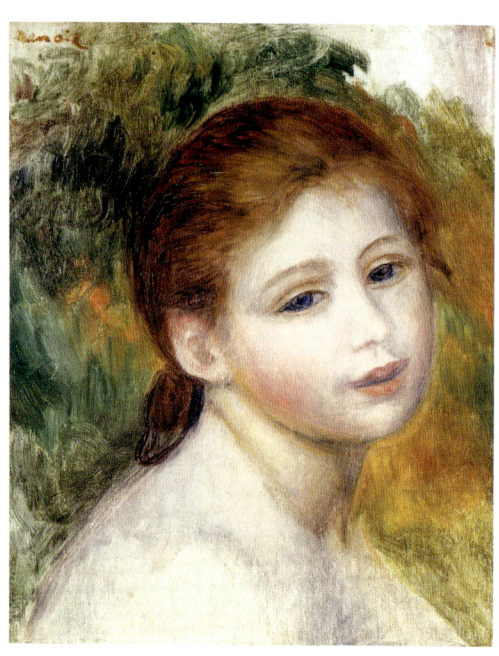

Head of a Woman, c. 1887
Oil on canvas, 42 x 32 cm (16⅝ x 12⅝ in.)
Private collection

A comparison between this *Head of a Woman*
with *Girl Sleeping*, painted ten years later,
clearly illustrates the difference between the
"sharp" period of the bust and the "mother-
of-pearl" period of the nude. In the meantime,
Renoir had moved on from the contour and
now produced a series of elongated, supple
brushstrokes juxtaposed, intermingling and
melting into each other to give the skin that
pearly look.

Girl Sleeping, c. 1897
Oil on canvas,
82 x 66 cm (32⅜ x 26 in.)
Winterthur, Oskar Reinhart
Collection "Am Römerholz"

In early 1888, Renoir rented a house called "Bellevue" near Aix-en-Provence from
Cézanne's brother-in-law. He wanted to learn how to paint like Cézanne and chose his
friend's favourite theme, Mont Sainte-Victoire (p. 297). He painted three views of the
mountain. At the same time Cézanne's methodical parallel brushstrokes became less dense
and regular, as if he too were seeking more flexible ways of translating his experience of
nature into a consistent pictorial form. Renoir, for his part, varied his parallel strokes both
in their strength and their direction. He allowed them to melt into the distance and the foreground, while in the foliage they appeared to go in all directions. Renoir's paintings of Mont
Sainte-Victoire are more welcoming and easily visited than those of Cézanne. He leads the
spectator by the hand towards the trees and then, step-by-step, right up to the mountain
in the distance. In Cézanne's work, the assonance of shape and colour and different spatial
planes represent nature as a monument to be admired but never entered. Renoir's painting
gradually returned to its original softness. For him, over-precision was synonymous with
sourness. He came to regret the precision so characteristic of this period, which he dubbed
"harsh". In *Girl Braiding Her Hair* (p. 311) this precision is applied not only to Suzanne
Valadon, whose face is as geometric as one of Cézanne's apples, but even to the background
foliage. Each of the leaves is painted with a separate outline as if it had been cut out of a
sheet of zinc. The same treatment of foliage occurs again *In Brittany* (pp. 300/301), painted
in the same year, which is now in the Barnes Foundation. In an unfinished preparatory
sketch of this painting, Renoir used the tip of his paintbrush to paint the leaves with such
precision that each of them looks like it has been drawn in pen and ink.

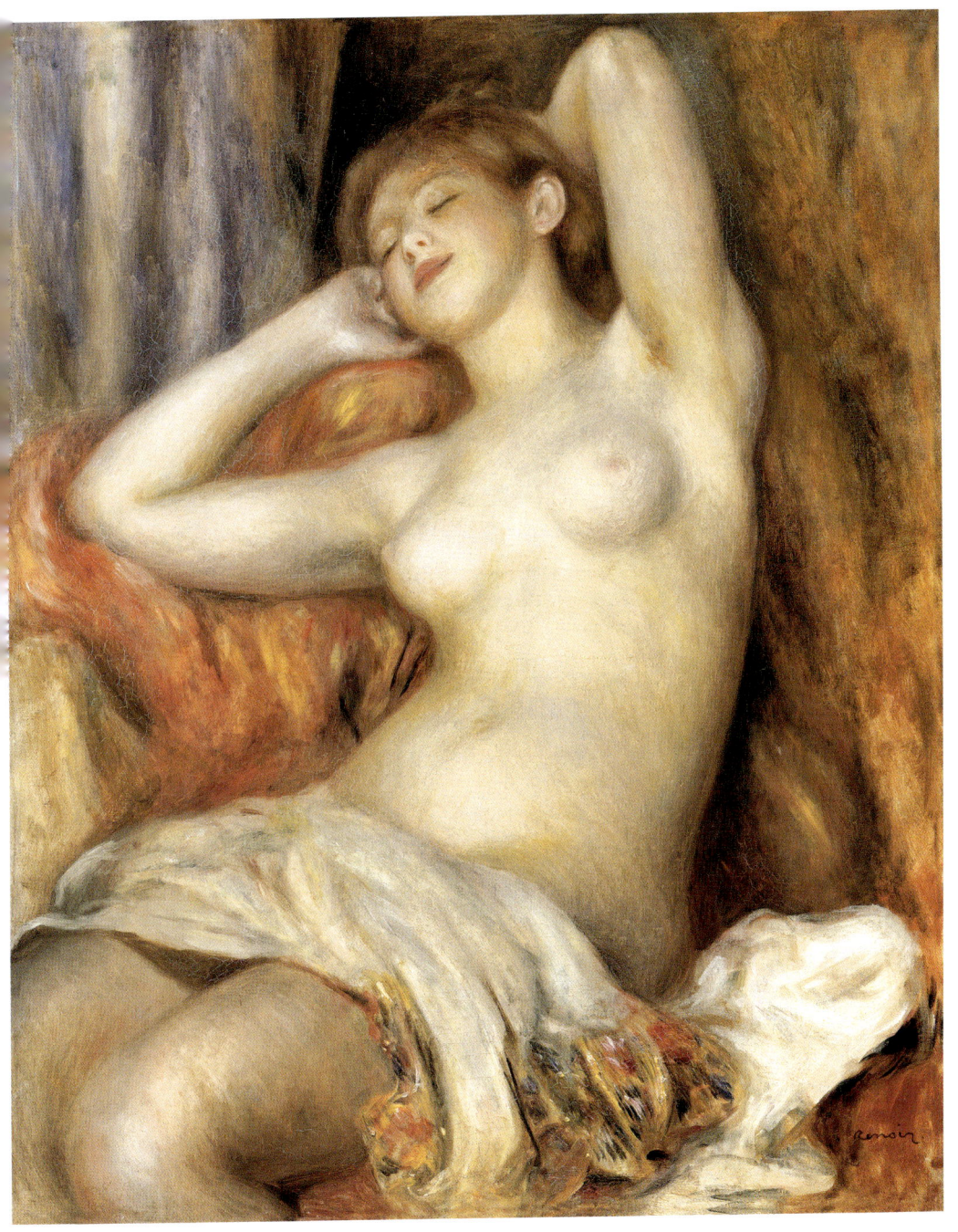

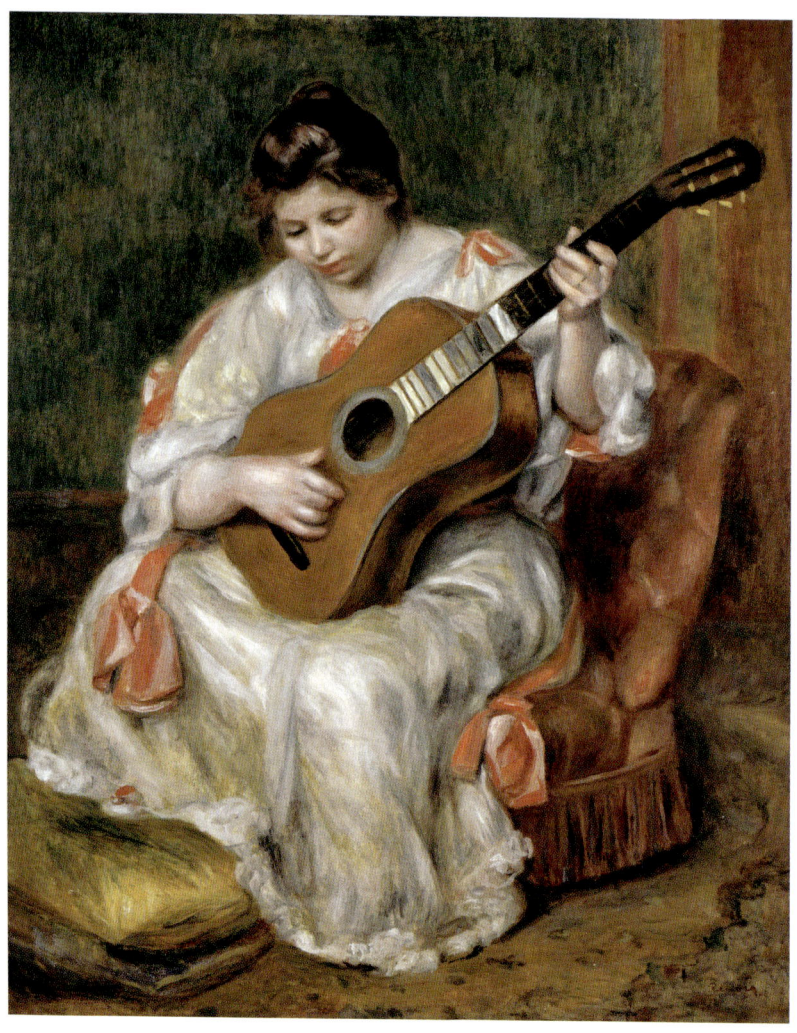

Woman Playing the Guitar, 1896/97
Oil on canvas, 81 x 61 cm (32 x 24 in.)
Lyon, Musée des Beaux Arts

The Daughters of Catulle Mendès, 1888
Oil on canvas, 163 x 130 cm (64¼ x 51¼ in.)
Private collection

The Daughters of Catulle Mendès was the
last painting to be sent to a Salon and it was
rejected. *Woman Playing the Guitar*, on the
other hand, was one of the first paintings
bought by a French museum, the Musée de
Beaux-Arts of Lyon. At the same time, *Girls
at the Piano* (p. 323), was acquired by the French
state, thanks to the intervention of Mallarmé, on
behalf of the Musée du Luxembourg in Paris.

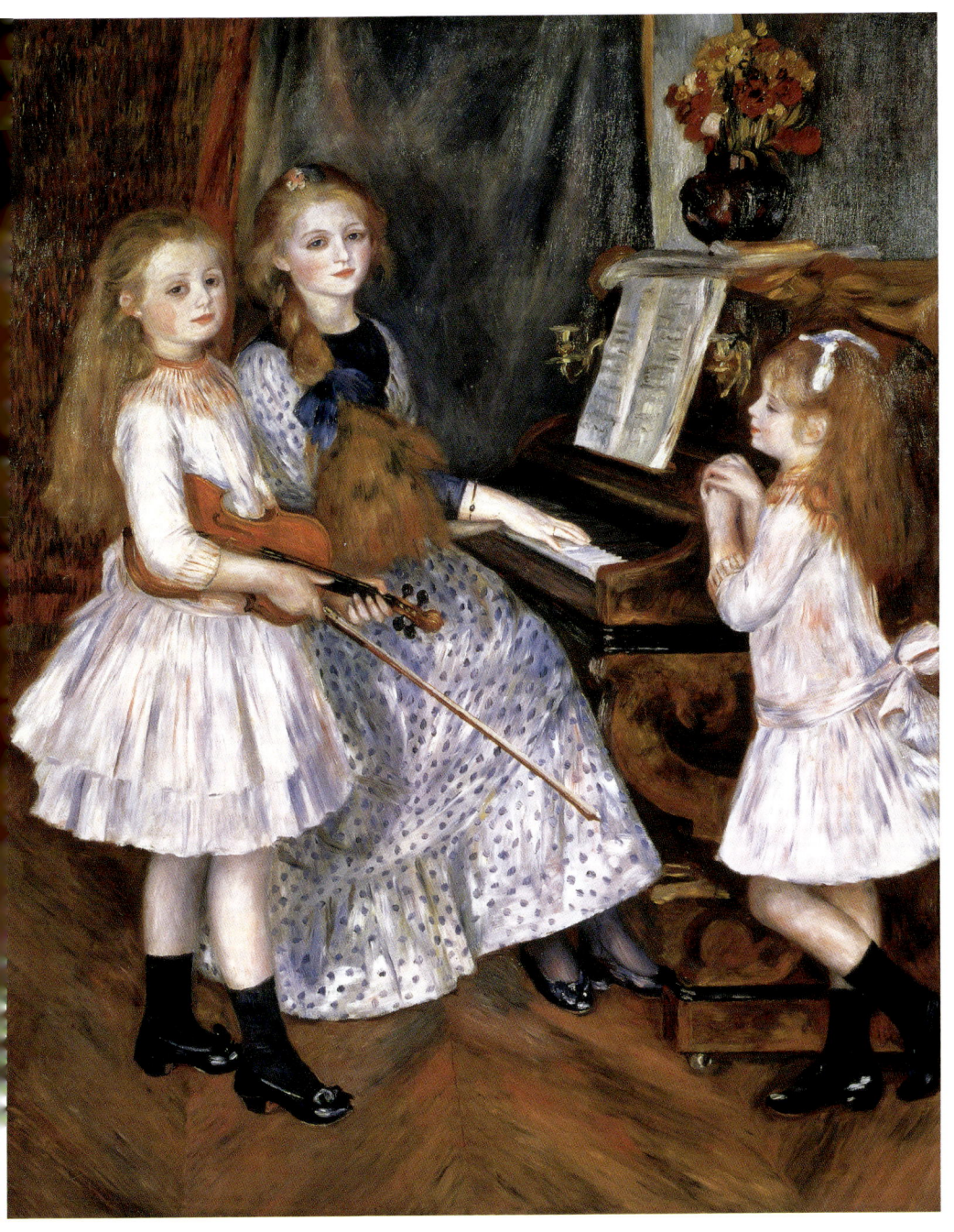

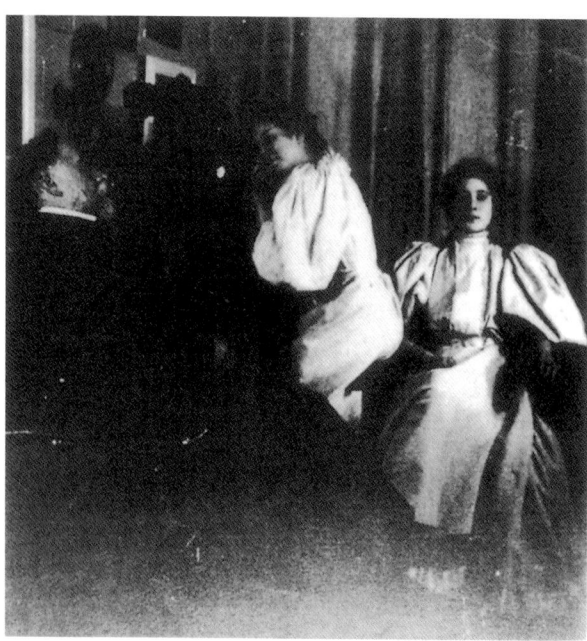

Yvonne and Christine
Lerolle, c. 1898

Girls at the Piano, 1892
Oil on canvas,
116 x 90 cm (45¾ x 35½ in.)
Paris, Musée d'Orsay

During this relatively short period, Renoir went too far in his attempt to master the art
of drawing. In the painting in the Barnes Foundation, he extends to the green setting the
same dryness and clarity of outline that he normally reserved for his figure-painting.
This is done in such an exaggerated fashion that the painter achieves exactly the opposite
of what he seeks. His diaphanous figures are placed against foliage that looks like nothing
so much as painted metal. These excesses were necessary if Renoir was at last to rediscover
his own true style. Having taken his Impressionism to excess, he now went to the extreme
of Ingres-like dryness, with *In Brittany* or *The Shepherdess, the Cow and the Ewe* (p. 305).
In *Young Girl with a Swan* (p. 303), however, the figures are painted in the opposite manner.
The clarity and precision with which the foreground figures are painted sets them apart
from their vague, misty background. The mistake is so obvious that it seems to have
provoked Renoir into a salutary reaction. The portrait of Julie Manet (p. 313) shows him
abandoning the discipline of Ingres in the course of 1887. The style of the face is still purist
in its geometrical roundness and in the almost perfect almond shape of the eyes, features
typical of Renoir. But the supple and sinuous technique shows not the slightest stiffness.
The practice of drawing the outline of shapes, thereby isolating them from their surroundings, has been abandoned. The crisis was over. Subsequent works reveal a new Renoir with
a surer and more balanced touch. He remained, of course, "the most changeable of men",
and his various periods overlapped. A fundamental division can nevertheless be made.
Any painting before 1890 falls more or less into Renoir's "harsh" period and anything after
that into his "pearly" one.

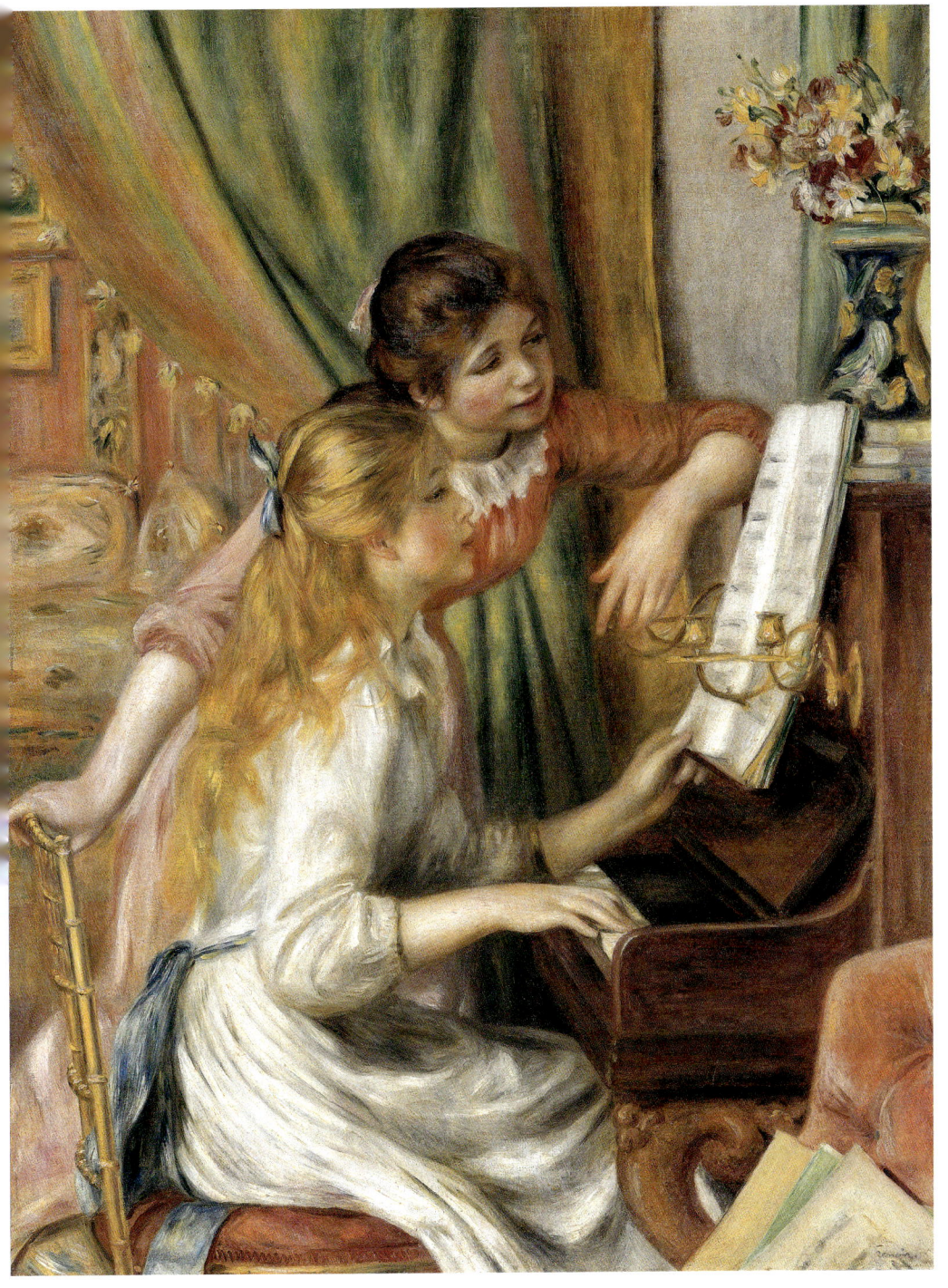

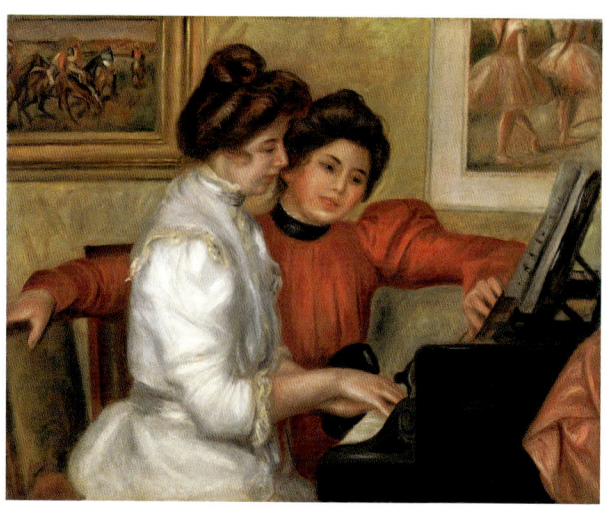

**Yvonne and Christine Lerolle
Playing the Piano**, 1897
Oil on canvas, 73 x 92 cm (28¾ x 36¼ in.)
Paris, Musée de l'Orangerie

Moss Roses, c. 1890
Oil on canvas,
35.5 x 27 cm (14 x 10¾ in.)
Paris, Musée d'Orsay

Painting nudes enabled Renoir to perfect his technique of rendering people, like statues, in high relief. From 1882 onwards, he had dreamed of painting a large-format composition which showed the interplay between several female bathers, some sitting on a riverbank, and others standing in the water. On his return from Italy, he began work on his *The Great Bathers* (pp. 348/349). He did not finish it until the spring of 1887; it was exhibited at the Salon that year. Renoir worked for a long time on the canvas and numerous studies reveal all the stages of its creation. His desire to recreate a link with traditional painting was so strong that he drew his inspiration directly from a bas-relief in lead by Girardon. Entitled *Nymphs Bathing* (1668–1670), Girardon's piece decorates the fountain in the Allée des Marmousets at Versailles. Ingres's *Odalisque* (1814) and Boucher's *Diana* (1742) also provided inspiration. The subject of Renoir's ambitious painting is enamel-like, the drawing of the female bodies carefully executed, and the outlining shadows well defined. Traces of the Old Masters are present and are no longer accompanied by artificial effects. There are no signs of stiffness in the work. Its exaggerated sensuality more than makes up for the few remaining manneristic emphases. Renoir finally found a way to paint womanhood in its natural state: the nude, which is the highest graphic expression of desire. *The Great Bathers* illustrates an ideal beauty, dissociated from any historical or geographical context, and finally marks Renoir's detachment from the prevailing naturalism. "One must paint according to the age in which one lives", he said at this time. "But it is in museums that one acquires a taste for painting that nature alone cannot give you".

In the autumn of 1885, Renoir finally agreed to visit Essoyes, Aline Charigot's home village. He stayed there several times and eventually even bought a house there. He painted

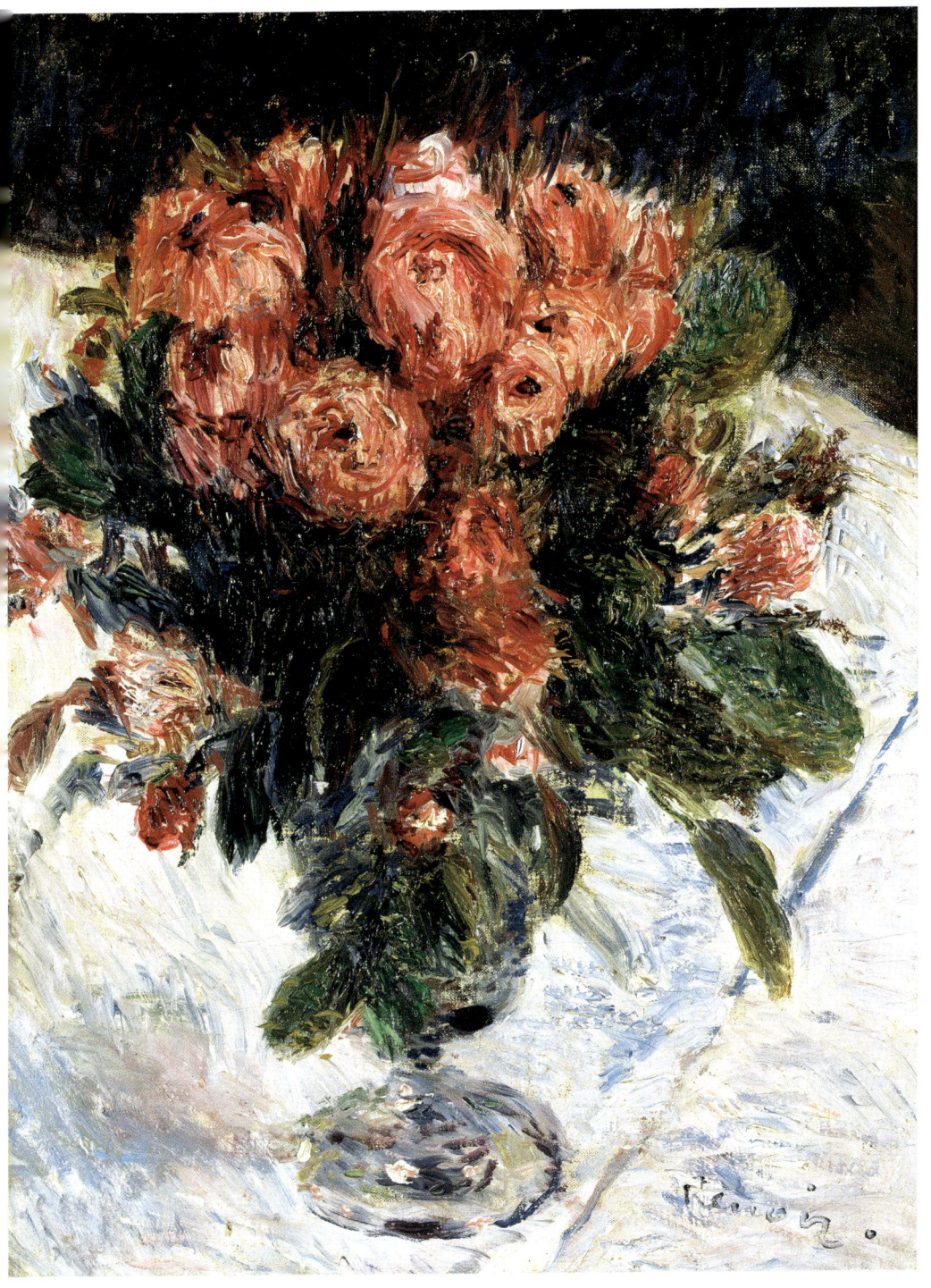

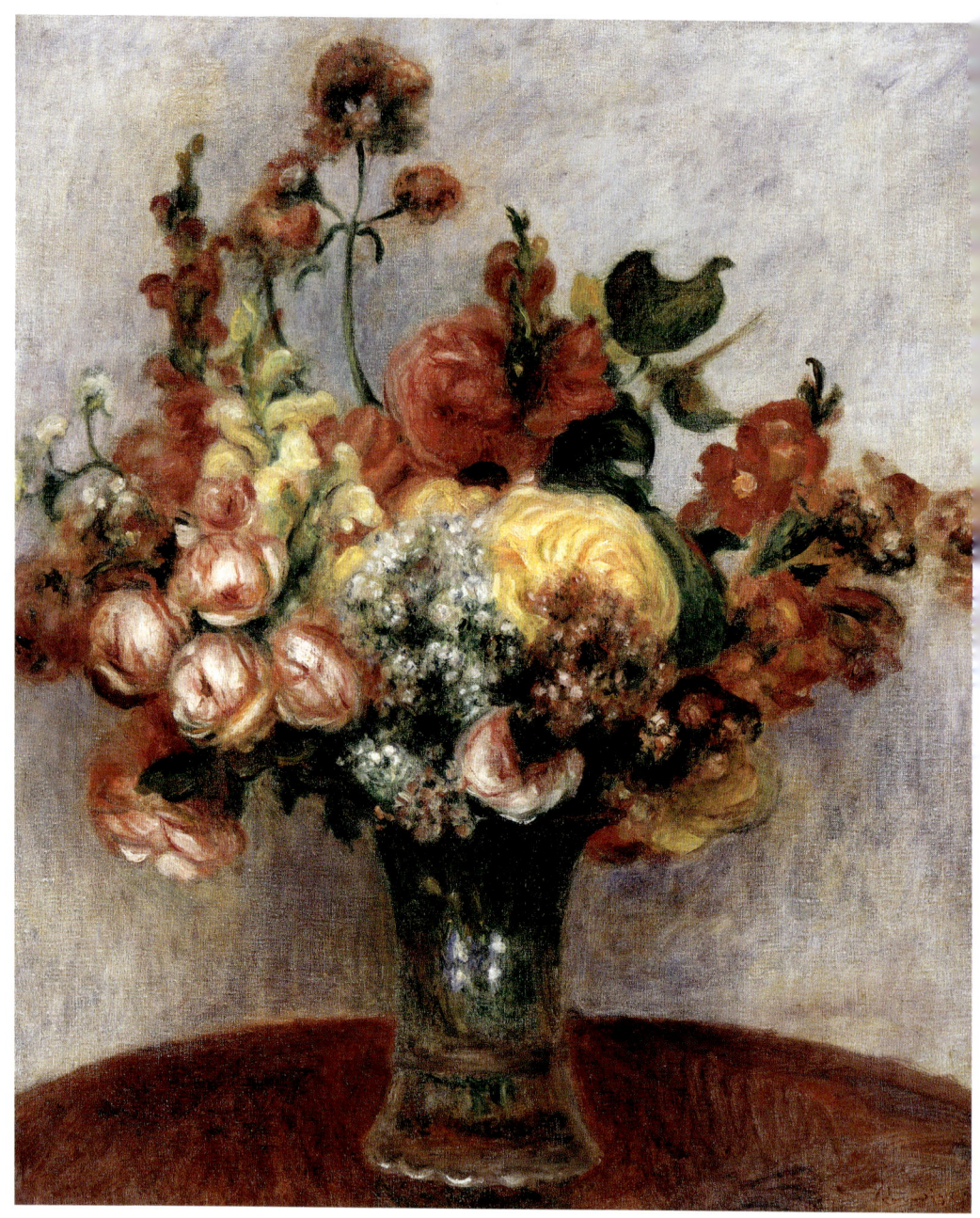

Young Woman Seated, 1890
Oil on canvas,
91 x 72 cm (35⅞ x 28⅜ in.)
Private collection

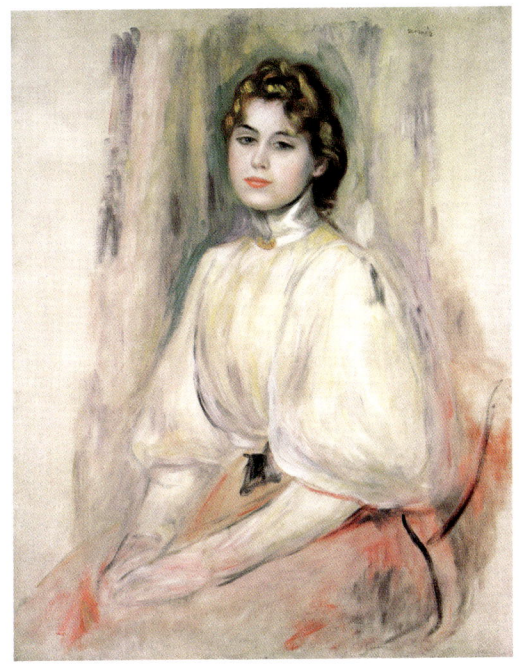

Flowers in a Vase, c. 1896–1889
Oil on canvas,
55 x 46 cm (21¾ x 18⅛ in.)
Paris, Musée de l'Orangerie

Washerwomen (p. 307) in Essoyes and wrote to Berthe Morisot: "I am staying with the peasantry in Champagne to escape from costly models. I am becoming more and more of a countryman". Fed up with the "stuffed shirts" of Paris, he was happy to paint peasant life and toil. Under his paintbrush, the vision soon becomes idyllic: a woman pushes back her sleeve and turns around to welcome the child watching the scene. The child is probably Renoir's first son, Pierre, who was born in March 1885. Renoir used Cézanne's parallel brushstrokes, but this time with no sign of dryness. Their undulating and varying rhythms are less rigid here than in a landscape such as *Montagne Sainte-Victoire* (pp. 298/299). *Washerwomen* merits all the painter's gentleness. The luminous colouring evokes pastel shades, with accentuated contrasts between warm and cool tones, and the heat is shown with a few touches of red and orange. Renoir later explained to his son Jean that such subjects were 'natural'. "It is good for women", he told him, "to crouch down to clean the floor, light a fire or do the washing. Their stomachs need to make such movements".

Renoir did not confine himself to rustic subjects such as *The Washerwomen*. Between 1888 and 1892, he painted a large number of canvases of young girls from good families playing the piano, reading, gossiping, taking country walks and picking flowers. The girls are depicted in pairs wearing brightly coloured dresses of flimsy fabric. These were subjects that the artist very much enjoyed painting. They also pleased his clients and the general public. The blondes are generally dressed in blue and the brunettes in pink. The setting, of sunny countrysides, delicate young girls, and flowers, offers the spectator a vision of harmony. Renoir is now at ease in Watteau's world, as well as that of Corot. He loves Watteau's

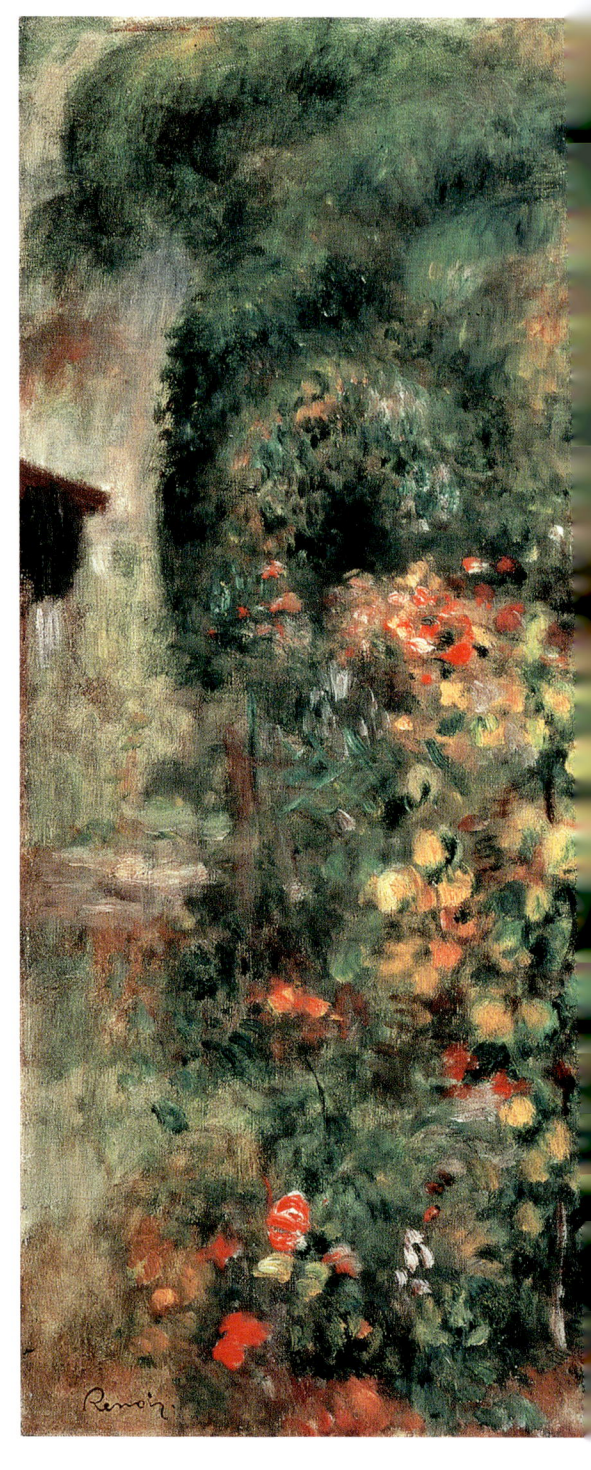

**Young Girls in a Garden
in Montmartre**, 1893–1895
Oil on canvas,
37 x 50 cm (14⅝ x 19¾ in.)
Private collection

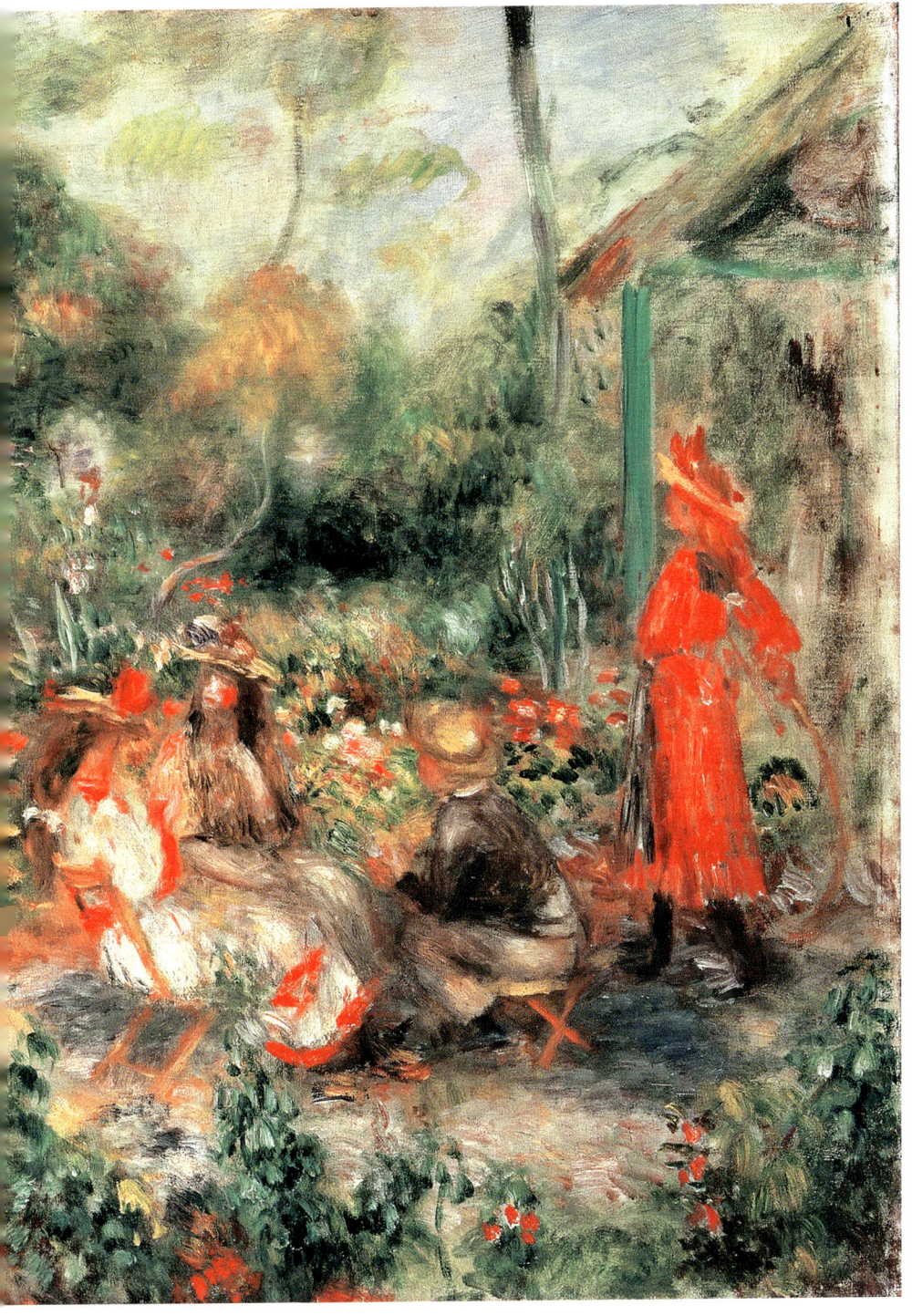

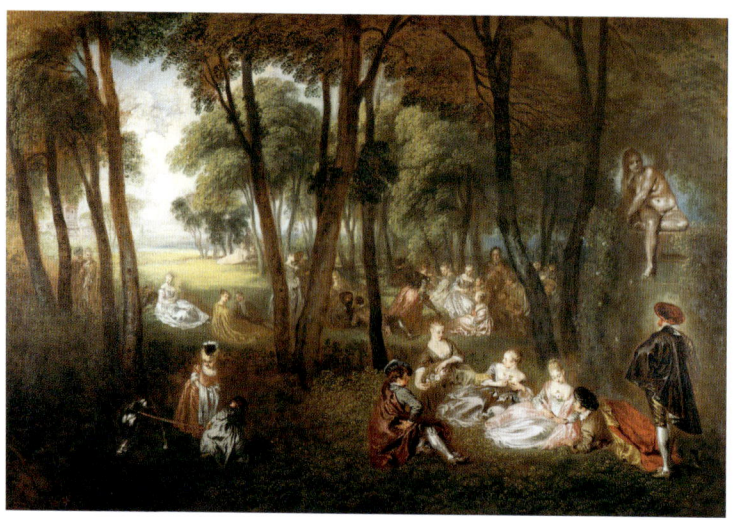

Jean-Antoine Watteau (1684–1721)
Fête galante in a Wooded Landscape, c. 1719–1721
Oil on canvas, 127.2 x 191.7 cm (50 x 75½ in.)
London, The Wallace Collection

Landscape at Beaulieu, c. 1893
Oil on canvas, 65.1 x 81 cm (25¾ x 32 in.)
Fine Arts Museum of San Francisco,
Mildred Anna Williams Collection

way of modelling shapes and suggesting space with the paintbrush rather than artificially separating painting from drawing and colour from line. He claimed that it was Watteau and Fragonard who helped him to escape from hard contours and rigid drawing in his *The Great Bathers*. Watteau's *Fête galante in a Wooden Landscape* (p. 330) bears a certain affinity to *The Beach at Guernsey* (c. 1895): the latter, painted a century or so later, differs from the former only in being more brightly coloured. Corot helped Renoir finally to solve the problems that landscape painting had long caused him. His Impressionist period had left him reluctant to use the studio when painting in the open air. But this was important in order to palliate the variations in the weather and the physical difficulties of working outdoors. From now on he quoted Corot to defend his practice of reworking studies made in the open air back in the controlled atmosphere of the studio. This allowed him to soften and unify the energetic and varied brushstrokes achieved outdoors, and to attain the delicacy he so admired in Corot's work. Corot also taught Renoir to reduce his palette and reinstate black, which he had banished regretfully in around 1875 from his landscapes, as his essential colour.

Renoir had always admired Corot – who, according to Picasso, "discovered the morning, as Renoir discovered young girls" – and this admiration attained its zenith during the 1890s. Renoir's delicately depicted landscapes became more brightly coloured versions of Corot's style in paintings such as *Girls Picking Flowers in a Meadow* (p. 316), *Young Girls at the Seaside* (p. 317), *The Apple Seller* (p. 314) or *The Washerwoman* (pp. 332/333). Corot's *Souvenir of Italy* (c. 1865) can be compared with Renoir's interpretation of it, or with a simi-

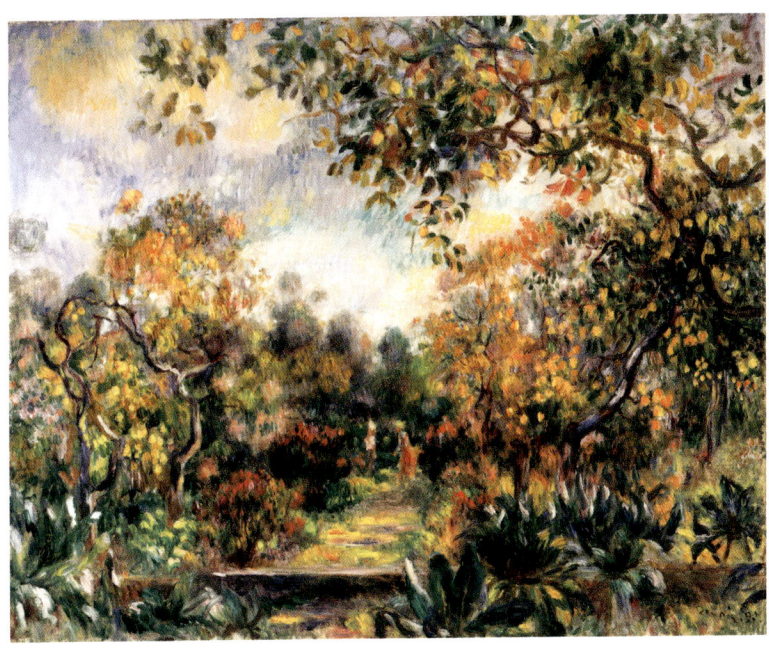

lar late landscape such as *Landscape with Figures at Cagnes* (c. 1916). The similarities are striking even though Renoir characteristically introduces figures to animate the landscape.

Renoir painted a whole series of girls at the piano (pp. 323, 324) in the 1890s, using his new "pearly" style. Nothing could be further from the style of *The Daughters of Catulle Mendès* (p. 321), which he painted at the height of his "harsh" period. This was the last painting that he submitted to the Salon, and it met with rejection. His aim in painting all these middle-class girls practising their scales was to try and get the French state to buy at least one version. This time, Renoir achieved his aim. After the intervention of Mallarmé, the state agreed to purchase *Girls at the Piano* (p. 323) for the Luxembourg Museum. Mallarmé, who had great influence as a poet and intellectual, had succeeded in convincing the Director of Fine Art, Henri Roujon. He was delighted. "I cannot congratulate you enough", he wrote to Roujon, "speaking both for myself and for all those around me, that a museum should have chosen to buy this important painting. It is a relaxed and liberated work by the mature Renoir". Nothing summarises better the "official" art of the new Renoir of the 1890s. Mallarmé, delighted at his friend's success, gave him the good news in a letter whose envelope he decorated, as usual, with a verse:

> "At the Villa des Arts, near Clichy Avenue,
> You'll find Renoir. He's working on a nude.
> The sight of one bare shoulder is all it takes
> To lighten both his palette and his mood."

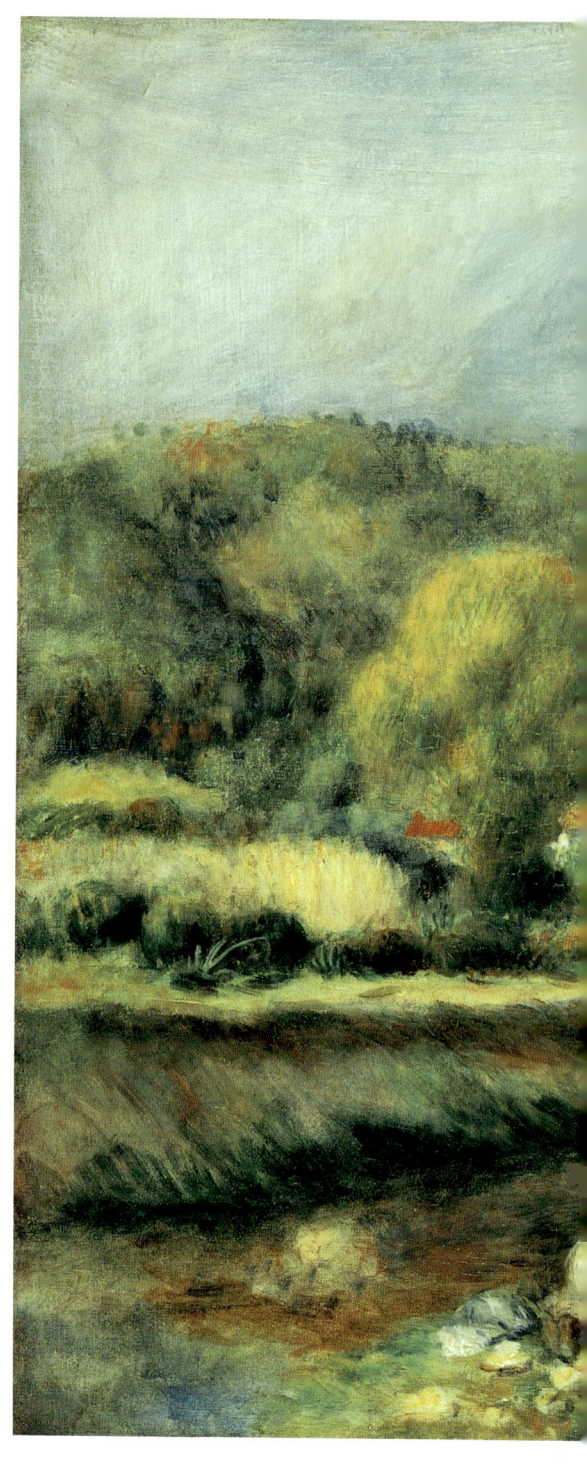

The Washerwoman, c. 1891
Oil on canvas, 46 x 56 cm (18⅛ x 22 in.)
Private collection

From the 1890s onwards, Renoir completely
abandoned his Impressionist theories and,
like Corot "painted the outdoors in his
studio". His landscapes were now full of
delicate brushstrokes, "highly-coloured
Corots" as it were, inhabited by figures in
the style of Watteau, inspired by his *Fête
galante in a Wooded Landscape* (p. 330).
He had finally combined the influences
of these two masters whom he so admired
and to whom he felt closer than ever
in temperament.

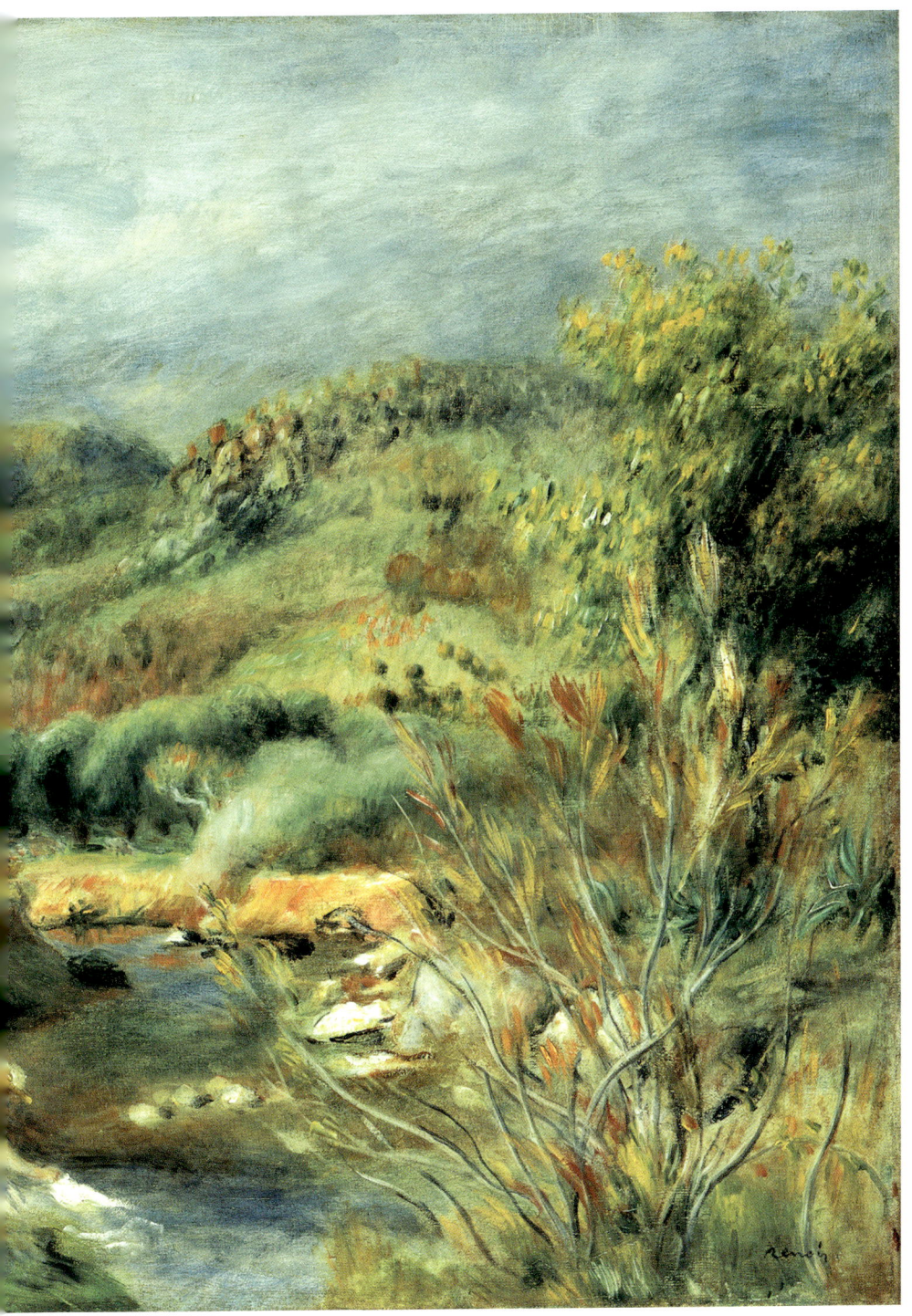

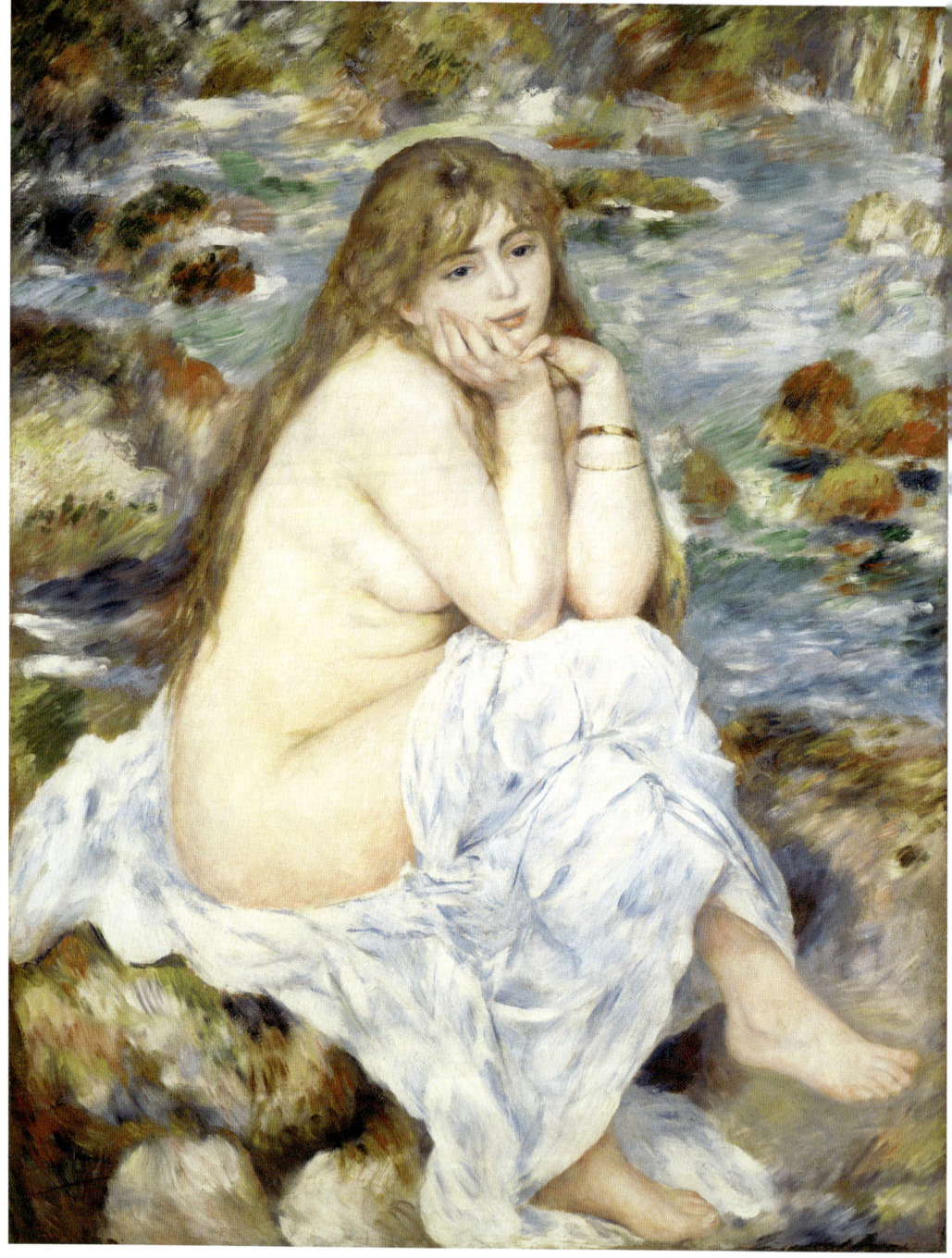

Seated Bather, c. 1883/84
Oil on canvas,
119.7 x 93 cm (47¼ x 36⅝ in.)
Cambridge, Massachusetts, Harvard Art
Museums/Fogg Museum, Bequest from
the Collection of Maurice Wertheim

Venus or Nini
1881–1919

In *The Symposium*, Plato explains that there are two types of Venus, one celestial and the other common. Renoir put the same idea more directly: "Nothing better will ever be invented than a naked woman (whether she is emerging from the sea or her bed, and whether her name is Venus or Nini". Academic but perfectly erotic nudes entitled *The Birth of Venus*, or *Susannah in the Bath*, could be exhibited at the Salon. English offers a distinction in the words "nude" and "naked". "Nude" refers to artistic nudity; "naked" means something altogether earthier like being "starkers" or "in your birthday suit". There was nothing nymph-like about Gustave Courbet's nudes. They look as if they have just got naked and an untidy pile of shawls, grimy petticoats, and muddy boots lies in a corner of the studio. "If you want me to do goddesses for you", Courbet grumbled, "then show me one!" Courbet, dubbed "the painter of low-life", disappointed Émile Zola when he abandoned social painting and was dubbed by him a "fleshmaker". But even the academician Henner was forced to concede, after he had seen *The Painter's Studio* (1855), that "no one had ever painted a nude woman so well". The model for *The Source* (p. 339) with her black hair, heavy thighs and thick ankles, is – as André Fermigier has noted – a Second Empire type of woman. Her popular figure was much closer in style to Édouard Manet's *Olympia* (p. 166) than to one of the goddesses exhibited at the Salon.

The new painters were criticized for debasing the nude and preferring a strong, healthy body and soft, velvety flesh saturated with erotic intentions. They were even charged with obscenity. The jury of the Salon accepted Manet's *Olympia* without so much as a second

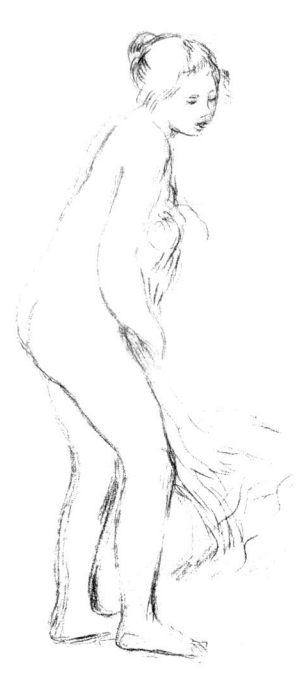

Bather, Drying Herself, 1896
Chalk. Private collection

Bather with a Rock, c. 1880
Oil on canvas, 92 x 73 cm (36¼ x 28¾ in.)
Paris, Musée Marmottan Monet

thought. This proved to be a mistake. Two guards had to be assigned to the picture permanently to prevent angry visitors from tapping it indignantly with their canes. The public and
the critics variously described Manet's creation as a "female gorilla" and an "over-adorned
courtesan". Manet had forgotten the cardinal rule of the Salon, namely, that a nude could
and indeed should be titillating, but only on condition that it was overloaded with historical and mythological allusions. Even Courbet had exploited this ambiguity. Yet Manet was
prepared to show, not a female nude stepping out of a well, but rather a young woman taking her clothes off for the first time. She was no classical nymph but a common prostitute,
waiting for her client, and "much too obviously naked and ready to exercise her profession
at a moment's notice".

Renoir had Courbet and Manet to thank for having already soaked up a good deal of the
criticism. His entrance into the domain of the nude had been well prepared. His intentions
though were pure. He did not want to paint prostitutes or "carthorses", as the Empress
Eugénie – who considered herself the reincarnation of Marie-Antoinette – described the
women in Courbet's *The Source* (p. 339) when it was exhibited at the Salon. Renoir's ambition was simply to paint the loveliest models in the most classical way without shocking
anyone. His "nymphs", as he called his "bathers", now became his primary concern; he also
found time for another of his passions, paintings of children. Moving from portraiture
to nudes was not a bad idea for someone as restless as he. Medals and decorations were
showered upon those painters who knew how to position their draperies in such a way as
to create suitably modest poses for subjects such as *The Source* or the *Vestal Virgins*. They

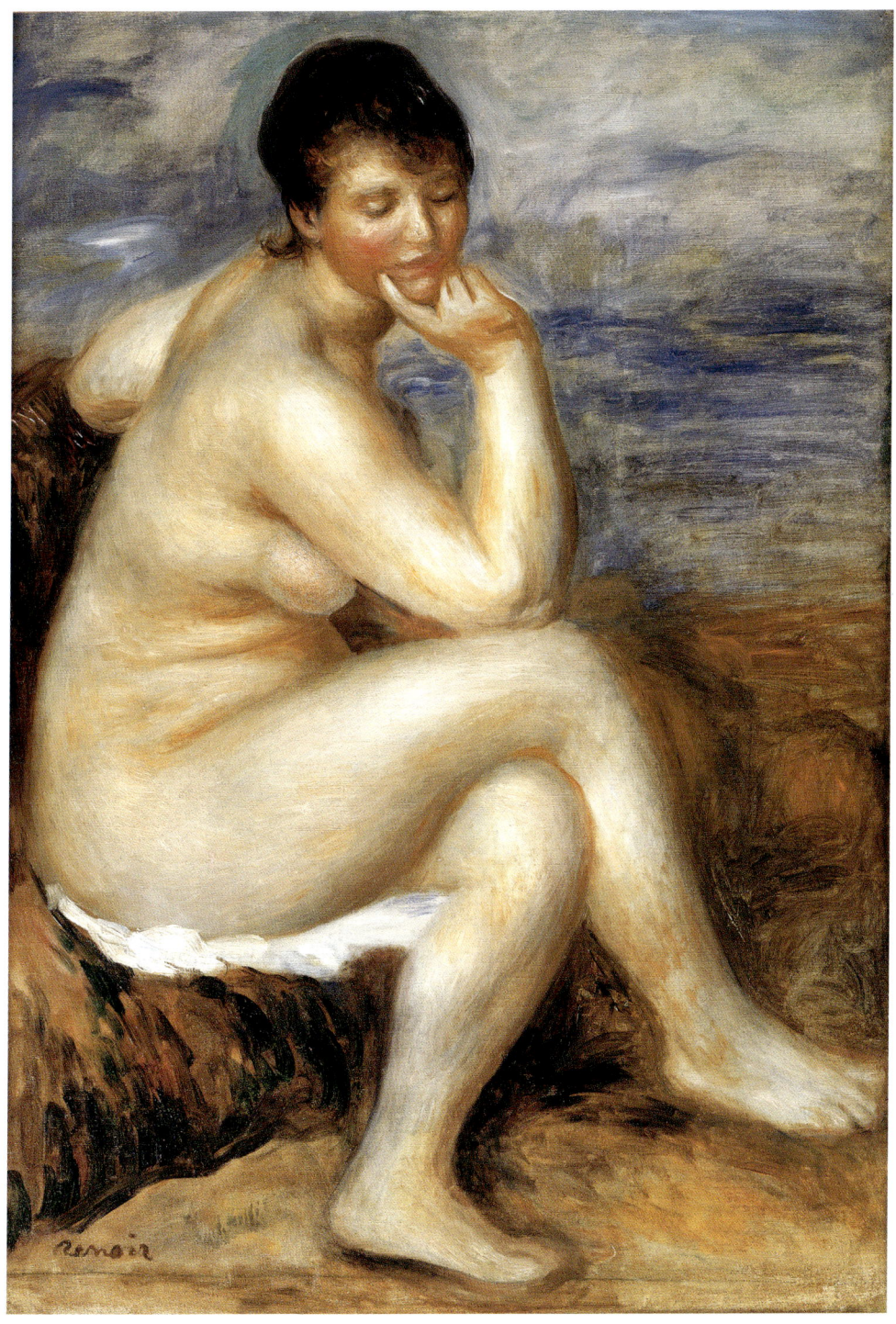

337

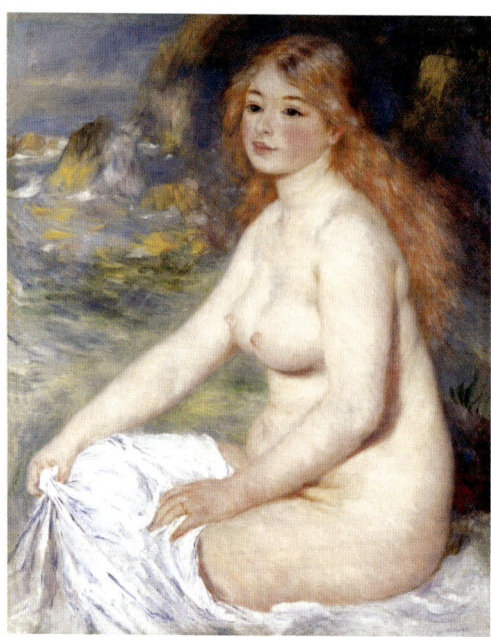

Blonde Bather, 1881
Oil on canvas, 81.6 x 65.4 cm (32¼ x 25¾ in.)
Williamstown, Massachusetts, The Clark

needed to reveal sufficient amounts of flesh on their Christian martyrs to awaken the appetite of the lions and the libido of the Salon clientele. The system worked. One wag created
a verse, supposedly sung by an artist's model: "Since I've been going from house to house /
I've shown it to old Bouguereau, / Bonnat did it in oil for me, / And Gervex used his water-
colours. / I've posed for all the greatest painters, / And starred in more than one life-class; /
Each day I feel I've missed my chance, / If I have not displayed my – nose!"

At this time the war of words between the academic "Pompiers" and the Impressionists
was at its height. Degas invented the verb "to bouguereau up" a painting, which meant,
"to paint with one's feet". Bouguereau was equally unimpressed by the Impressionists.
"These people", he sniggered, "have simply no talent. Look – they even place their models
in full sunlight. What do you do in full sunlight? Well, you screw up your face, and so do I."
He once asked a journalist: "Have you ever actually seen blue shadows? What do you think
is so clever about painting women who sweat rainbows?"

In the midst of all this sound and fury, one lone figure emerged. Ingres refused to be
pigeonholed. Throughout his life he placed his work in the classical tradition but, rather
like Manet, his own temperament constantly betrayed him. At this stage in his career
Renoir most admired, after Titian, Ingres and Corot. He took part in numerous discussions
in the Café Guerbois. "They reproached Corot for reworking his landscapes in the studio",
he recalled, "and they ranted against Ingres. I just let them talk. I believed Corot was right,
and I secretly took pleasure in the lovely belly in *The Source* and Madame Rivière's neck and
arm." His contemporaries carefully counted the number of vertebrae on Ingres's *The Large*

Gustave Courbet (1819–1877)
The Source, 1868
Oil on canvas,
128 x 97.5 cm (50½ x 38½ in.)
Paris, Musée d'Orsay

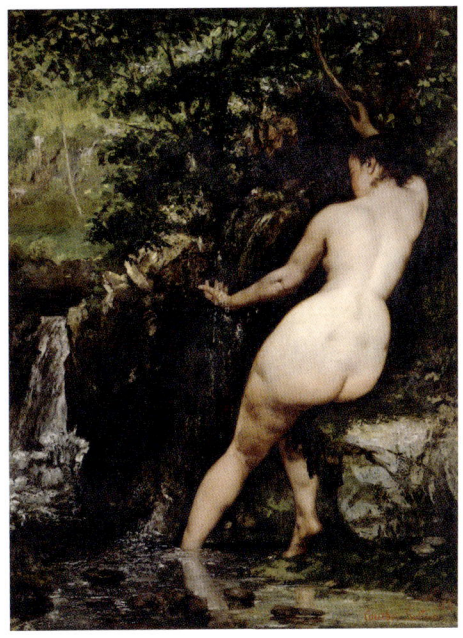

Odalisque (1814). She appeared to have three too many. "A woman's neck can never be too long", Ingres used to say. He loved to exaggerate a woman's figure, which he called "correcting nature by her own means". This Renoir appreciated and found liberating. Baudelaire had criticised such "corrections". But modern painters from Matisse to Picasso continued to make them and indeed went even further in this direction. "Here," Baudelaire jeered, "we find a navel that has wandered off to one side, and there, a breast pointing too far towards the armpit". Ingres's heroines, from *Thetis* to *Angélique*, were considered "goiterous". But their deformities are considered of no importance today in comparison with the plasticity and delirious eroticism of the painting.

Renoir was criticized for merging several perspectives in his final *Bathers*; for exaggerating the model's hips by combining views both of her profile and her back in *Female Nude in a Landscape* (p. 341); and for similarly combining profile and front views in *Blonde Bather* (p. 338). This may be partly due to the fact that Renoir encouraged his models to pose very freely. "Models are only there to fire me up", he used to say, "and make me dare to paint things that I could never have invented without them". Renoir appears to circle around his *Bather*, just as Picasso does when he simultaneously shows full frontal views of his models and their profiles. Renoir's experimentation clearly reflects his desire both to convey the physical presence of his nudes and to create an idealised vision of womanhood. In 1920, Élie Faure described how Renoir used these various angles of perception. At this time, Renoir's last works were attracting a great deal of attention from the Parisian avant-garde, and above all from its leading young painters, Matisse and Picasso. Their large

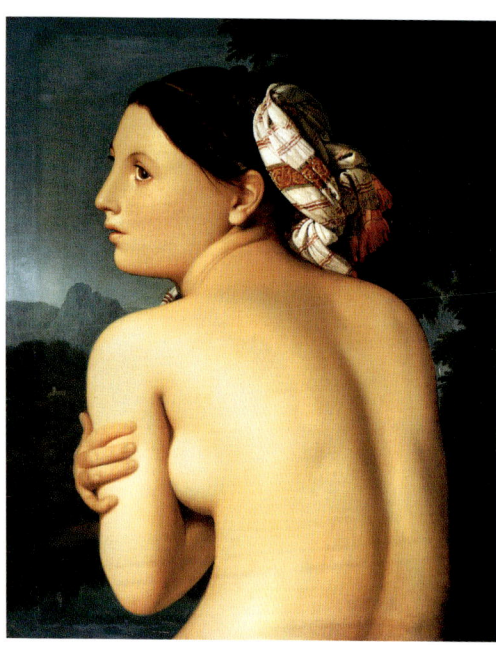

Jean-Auguste-Dominique Ingres
Back View of a Bather, 1807
Oil on canvas, 51 x 42 cm (20 x 16⅝ in.)
Bayonne, Musée Bonnat

**Female Nude in
a Landscape**, 1883
Oil on canvas,
65 x 54 cm (25⅝ x 21⅜ in.)
Paris, Musée de l'Orangerie

nudes, painted in the early 1920s, are an extraordinary fusion of Ingres and Renoir with the possibilities offered by the Fauvists' palette and the post-Cubist conception of space. Picasso's *Spring* (p. 358) is a case in point.

Another lesson that Renoir learned from Ingres was that to paint nudes "in the full light of desire", as Gaétan Picon so admirably put it. The beautiful bodies painted by Ingres are unaware of the desire they arouse. The same is true of Renoir's series of *Bathers*, who (if, of course, the paintings are accurately dated) appear innocent in early versions. Nothing could be more delightfully perverse. Degas, who had copied Ingres's *Saint Symphorien* in his youth, later admired him for abandoning large ceremonial compositions in favour of the everyday poses of women surprised by nudity. Degas embarked on paintings of women whose only preoccupation was washing, wiping, and drying themselves or combing their hair. "I want to show the species at its toilet, like a cat licking itself", he explained. Matisse, whose first teacher Bouguereau stated that he would never learn to draw, admitted that he had always been more drawn to Ingres's *Odalisque* than to Manet's *Olympia*. No doubt Ingres would have been surprised to see just how far Matisse and Picasso would go in their acts of distortion. For them, the additional vertebrae of the *Odalisque* and *Angélique*'s goitre are only the beginning. Some painters were lost in admiration for Ingres. Seurat's painting *Posers*, for example, shows a model from three different angles. He wanted to prove that his love of Ingres's pure lines could be reconciled with the modernity of his tone division and pointillist brushstrokes. Renoir, as Signac observed, loathed Seurat's painting: "He found it stupid, ridiculous, and devoid of all merit".

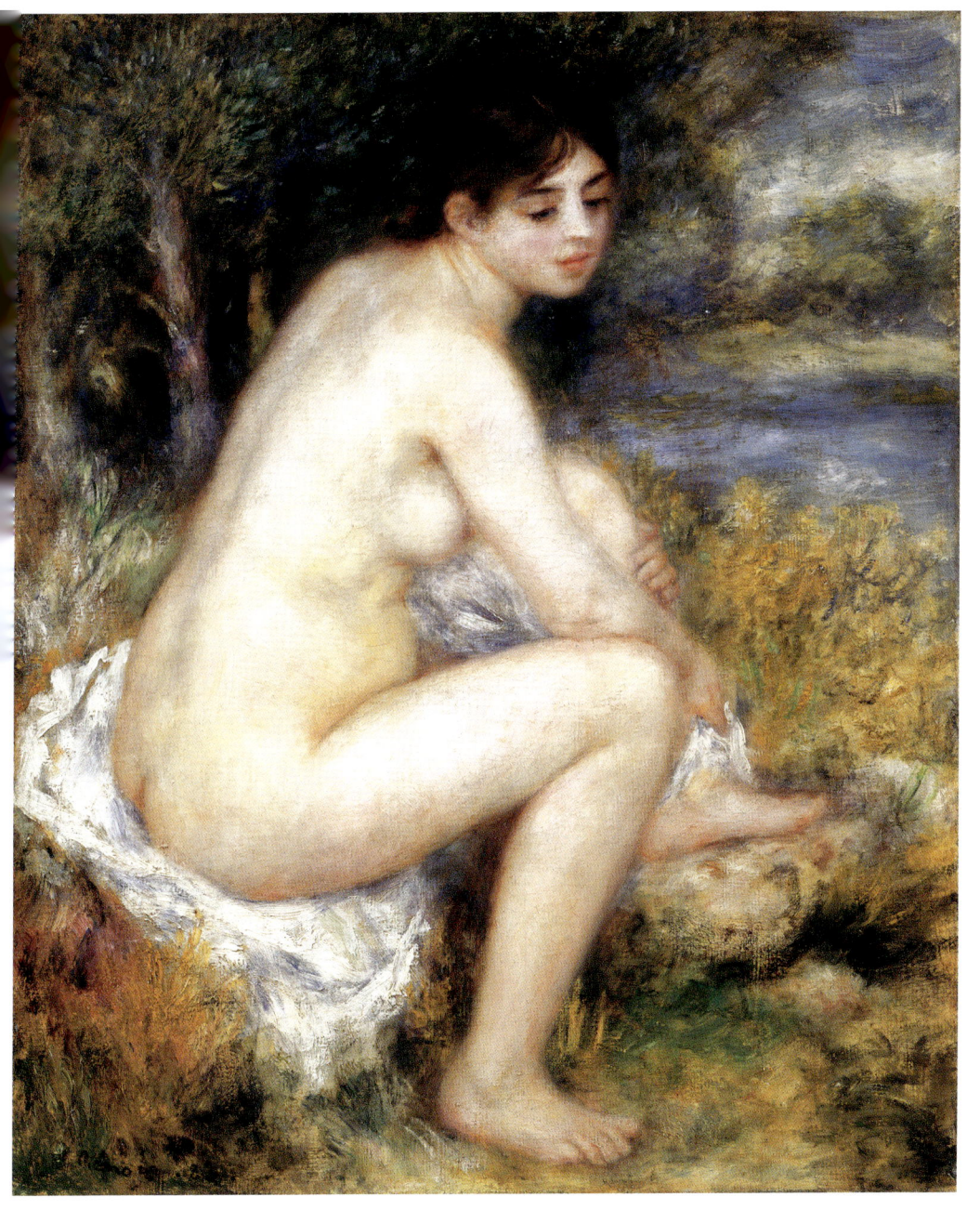

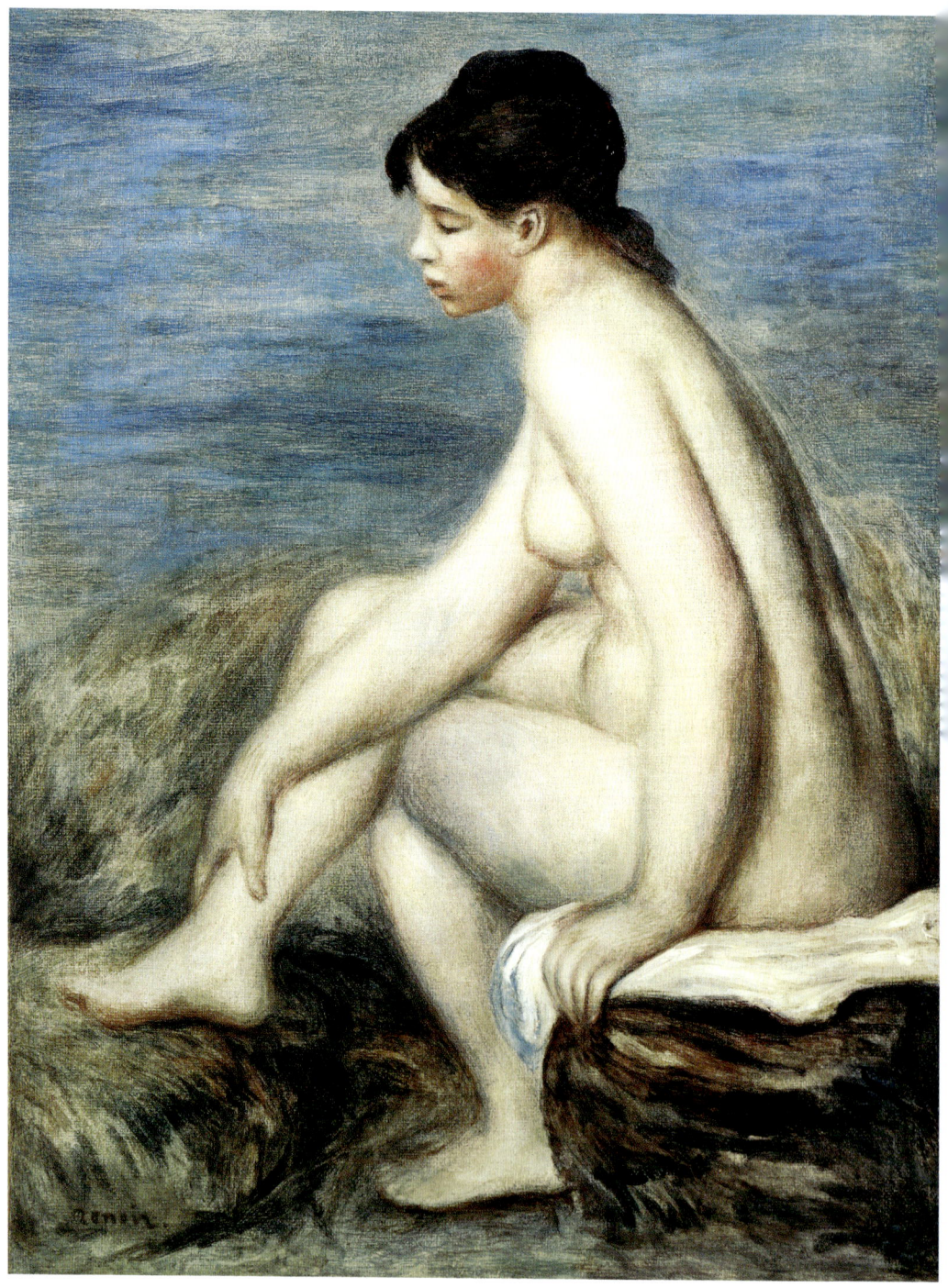

William Adolphe Bouguereau (1825–1905)
Nymphs and Satyr, 1873
Oil on canvas, 260.4 x 182.9 cm (102⅝ x 72 in.)
Williamstown, Massachusetts, The Clark

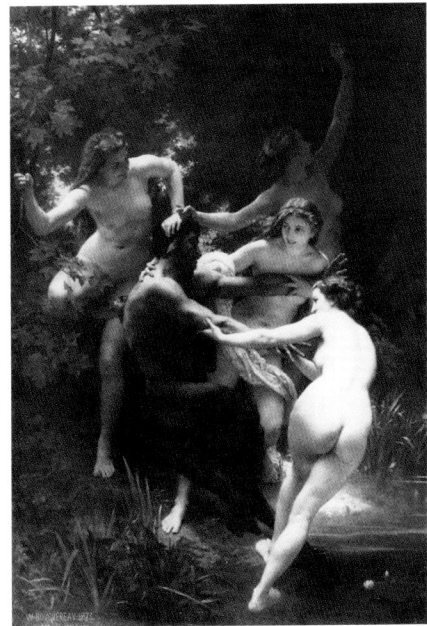

Seated Bather, 1882
Oil on canvas,
54 x 39 cm (21⅜ x 15⅜ in.)
Private collection

When Renoir painted a woman he wanted to give her fleshy curves asking to be touched rather than skin covered with pointillist dots looking like pimples. As the years passed and the influence of Ingres waned, he came closer to the precise tracing and softness of flesh of that other "painter of happiness", François Boucher. The latter was famous for teaching his students that, as he put it, "one should almost doubt whether a woman's body contains bones. They should be plump and delicate, with slender – though never thin – waists. Of the hundreds whom I have had undress in front of me, only one has possessed this high degree of beauty". Cézanne had difficulties talking to women. He seemed clumsy and unsophisticated to them and, when he came to paint his *Bathers*, was forced to seek inspiration from soldiers bathing on manœuvres and erotic postcards. Renoir never experienced such problems. "At one time (1868)," he recalled, "I often used to go and stay at the Fournaise inn. There I found all the beautiful girls to paint that I could wish for. One was not reduced then, as one is today, to following some little model around for an hour only to be called a dirty old man".

The Impressionists broke down the barriers of prejudice by bringing their own models with them. They disdained the elegant "court Venuses" of Winterhalter for the young "Ninis" of Montmartre with their pert *retroussé* noses, cornflower-blue eyes, and poppy-coloured lips. They took them for walks and sketched them from Chatou to Pontoise. You can almost smell the fried fish and wild strawberries in their paintings. Suzanne Valadon remembered how Renoir's visits to her grandparents' house put the servant-girls in a tizzy. One of them apologised for having left half the buttons on her blouse

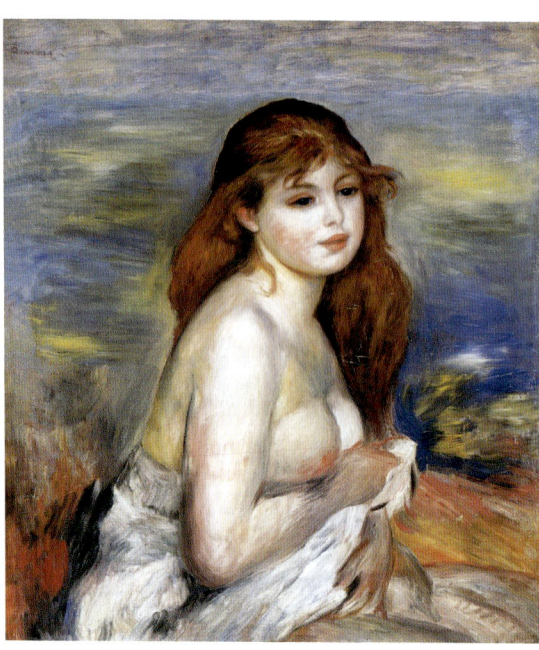

After the Bath (Little Bather), 1883
Oil on canvas,
60 x 54 cm (23⅝ x 21⅜ in.)
Oslo, Nasjonalmuseet,
The Fine Art Collections

Bather Arranging Her Hair, 1885
Oil on canvas,
91.9 x 73 cm (36¼ x 28¾ in.)
Williamstown, Massachusetts,
The Clark

PAGES 348/349
The Great Bathers, 1884–1887
Oil on canvas,
117.8 x 170.8 cm (46½ x 67¼ in.)
Philadelphia Museum of Art,
Mr. and Mrs. Carroll S. Tyson,
Jr., Collection

immodestly undone. "I've had enough, Madame, I just don't know what to do with it any more!" she exclaimed. Renoir could not restrain himself. "You've had enough of it?" he asked her. "Give them to me then!"

Why, one may well ask, did Renoir (with all these models at his disposal and his love of the female body) wait until he was forty years old before he started painting nudes? *Bather with Griffon Terrier* (p. 45) had of course won him his first, fleeting success, followed by *Nude in the Sunlight* (p. 121). There patches of light and shade surround the figure and the overlapping of shapes and the broken tones of the background reduce the contours to a minimum. Yet the modelling remains firm. There seems to be no reason why Renoir should not have gone on to paint a series of masterpieces in this style. The problem was that he loved women's bodies too much to want to destroy their figures by dappling them in light and shade as all good Impressionists were expected to do. He knew that contours were the best vehicle for painting nudes. Yet the Impressionists were doing their utmost to show that contours did not exist!

Renoir's development as a painter of nudes was stifled during his decade of adherence to the theories of Impressionism. Throughout this time he remained convinced that the nude ought to be simple and sculptural, like a column or an egg. He bided his time. His discovery of Raphael's Farnese frescoes and the ancient decorations at Pompei and Herculaneum were what provoked him to rebellion. His reaction was to produce his first nude, *Blonde Bather* (p. 338). Out of pure instinct and pleasure – he was after all in love with his model and future wife – he unconsciously solved all his problems. In this masterpiece, comparable

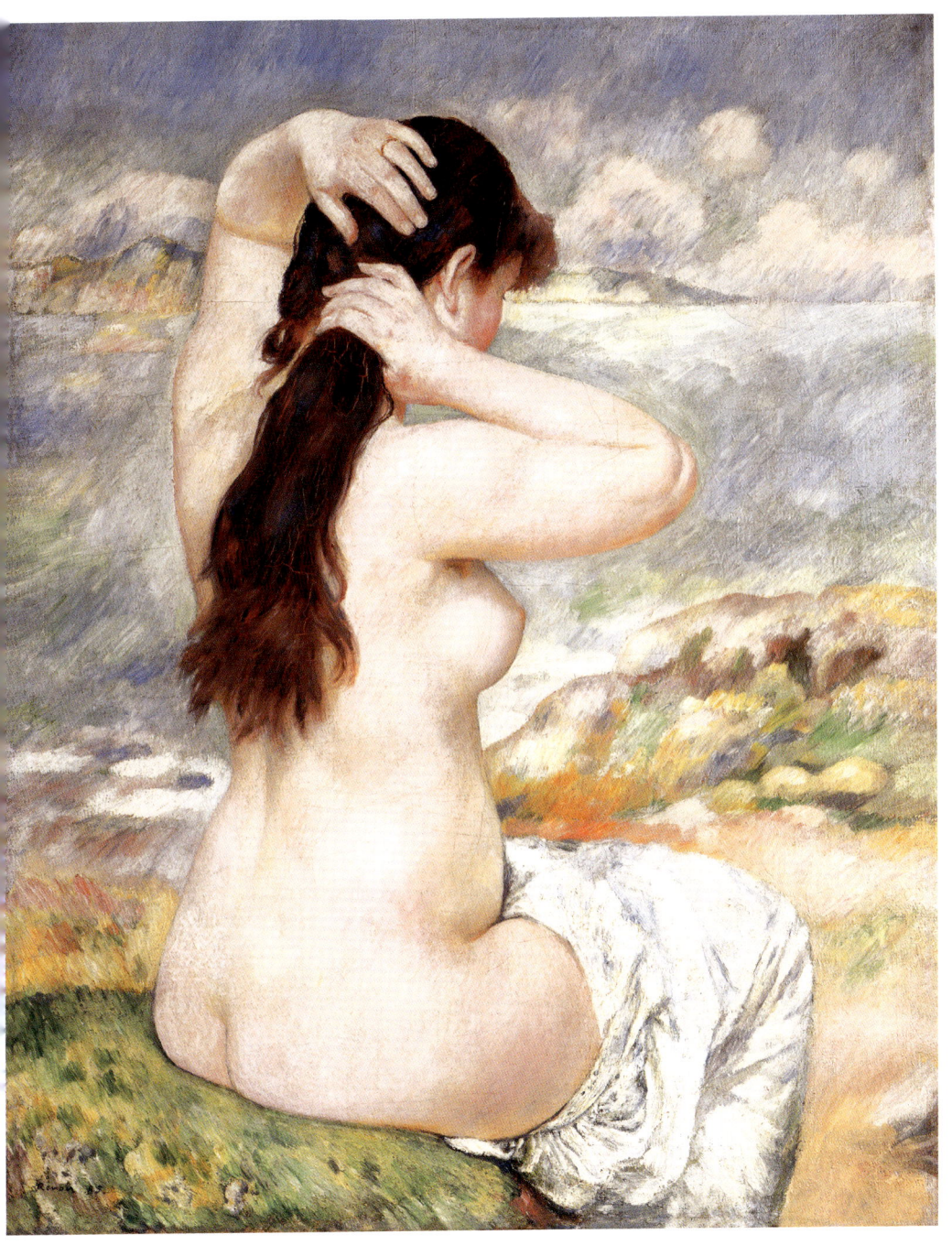

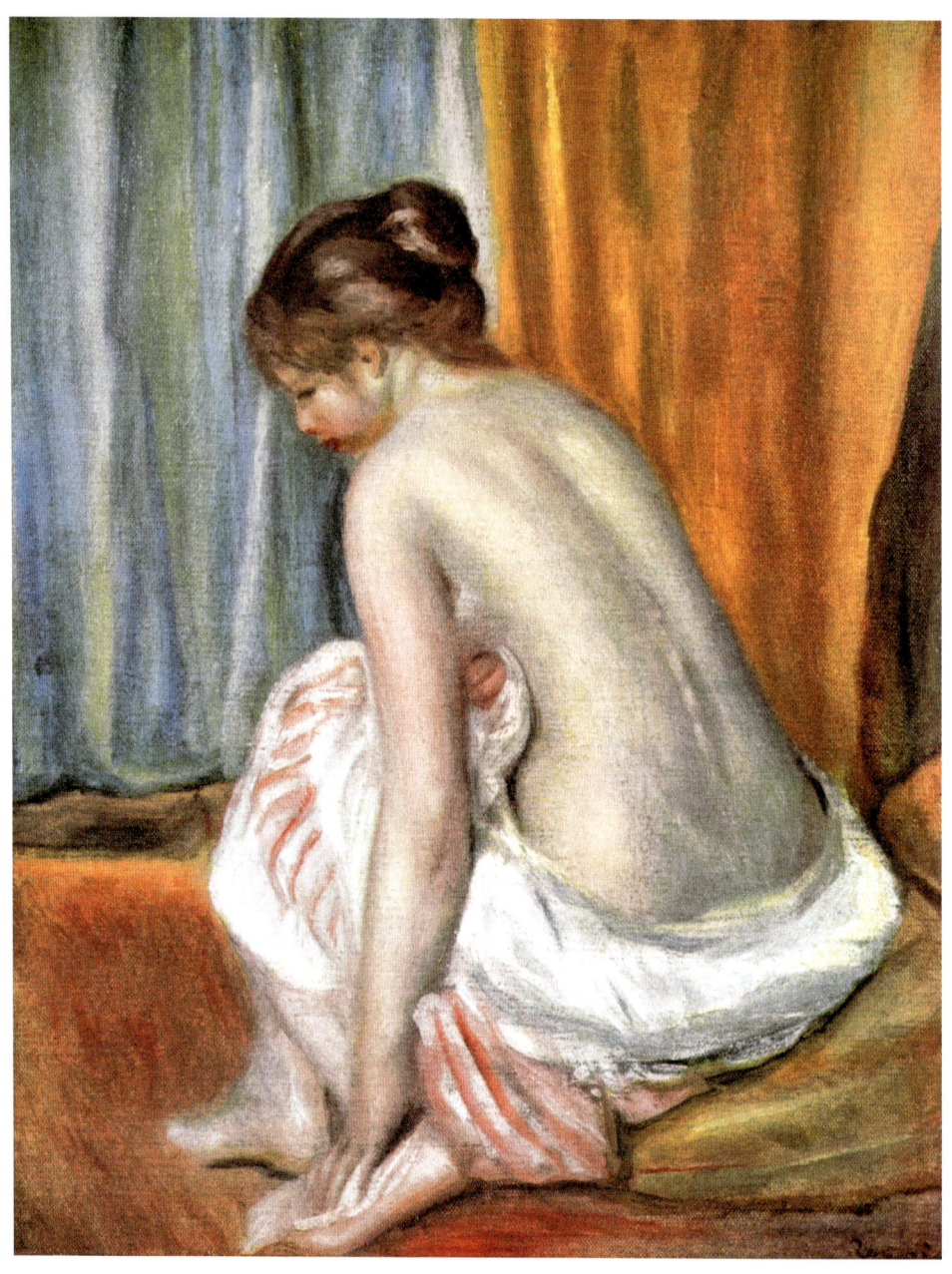

Back View of a Bather, 1893
Oil on canvas,
40 x 32 cm (15¾ x 12⅝ in.)
Private collection

Three Bathers by the Water, 1884/85
Sanguine, chalk,
108 x 162 cm (42⅝ x 63⅞ in.)
Paris, Musée d'Orsay

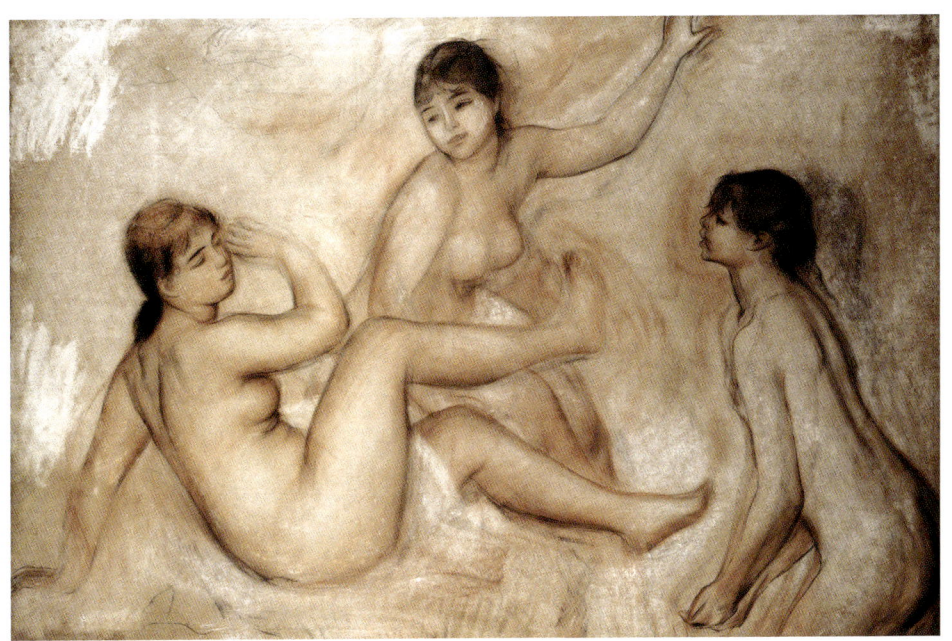

to Raphael's *Galatea* and Titian's *Venus Anadyomene* (p. 350), he produced a vision of feminine beauty that reflected his desire to exceed his direct experience of the model. Unfortunately, his subsequent researches caused him to forget this nude, whose skin was painted in a pearly glow, and who stands out from the background of her apricot-coloured hair and the blue of the Mediterranean. The opulent shapes that he was to multiply later in life are already present in this painting. No doubt they reflected those of the curvaceous Aline. But they also prefigure his subsequent tendency to exaggerate the female form in order to create an ideal of physical bulk worthy of the pyramids. Full of doubt and seeking the means to express his conception of the nude, he forgot the fortuitous inspiration that had led him to paint the *Blonde Bather* in this new style. For years afterwards he thought rationally about the problems that he had in fact instinctively solved that day.

Seated Bather (p. 334) is more lively and similar in feel to the *Dances* of the same period. It is a particularly successful attempt at what Renoir was trying to achieve, namely, to detach a sculptural nude against an Impressionist background. The flowing brushstrokes of the background make the water and rocks melt into an animated and brightly coloured background. This sets off the figure, which is treated in a very smooth manner and contains a reminiscence of the studies made in Guernsey of the young English girls who had no false modesty. Painted entirely in the studio, the painting is a superb representation of a naked woman sitting beside the sea, lost in a dream world and indifferent to everything happening around her. This age-old subject is one on which Renoir often worked subsequently.

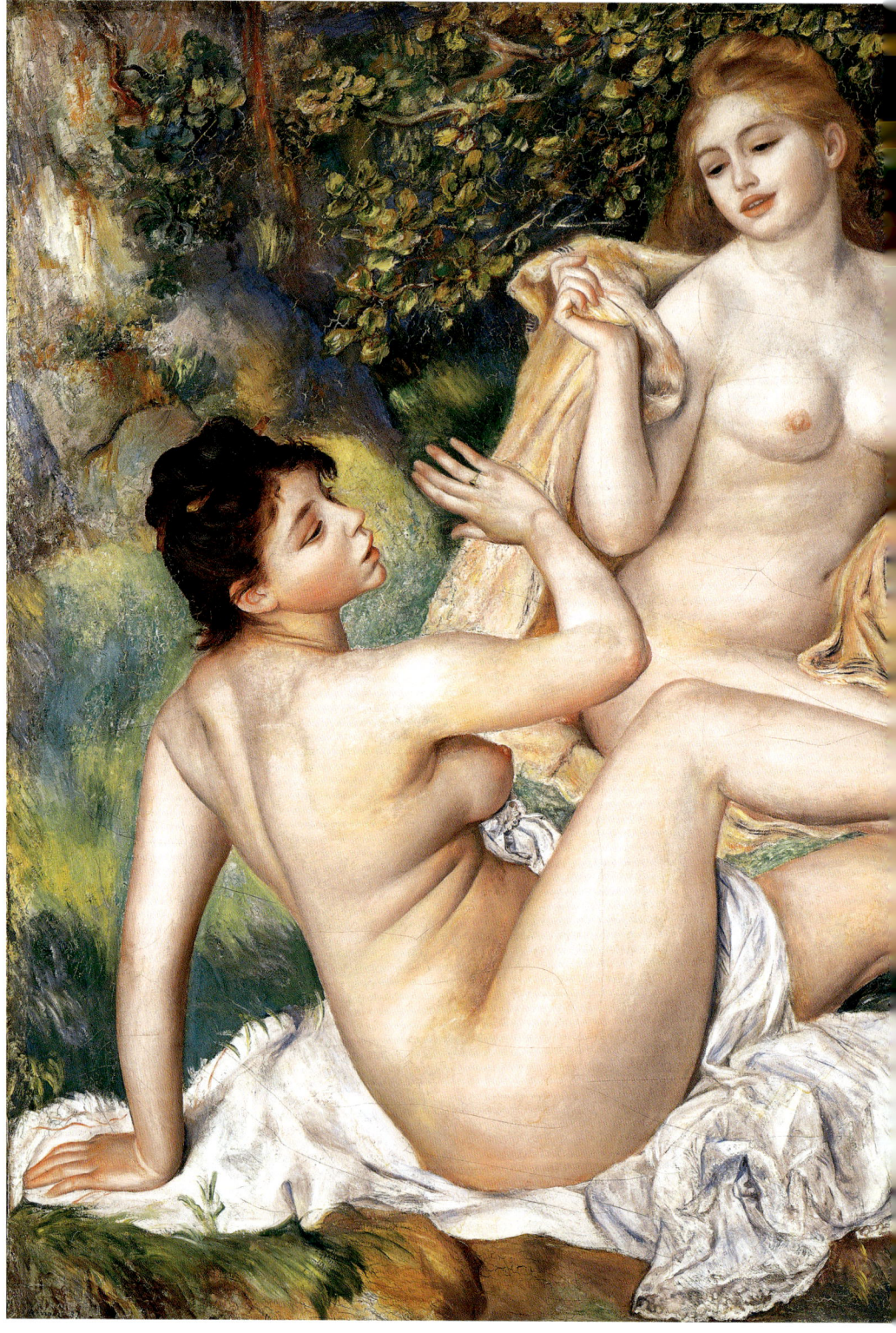

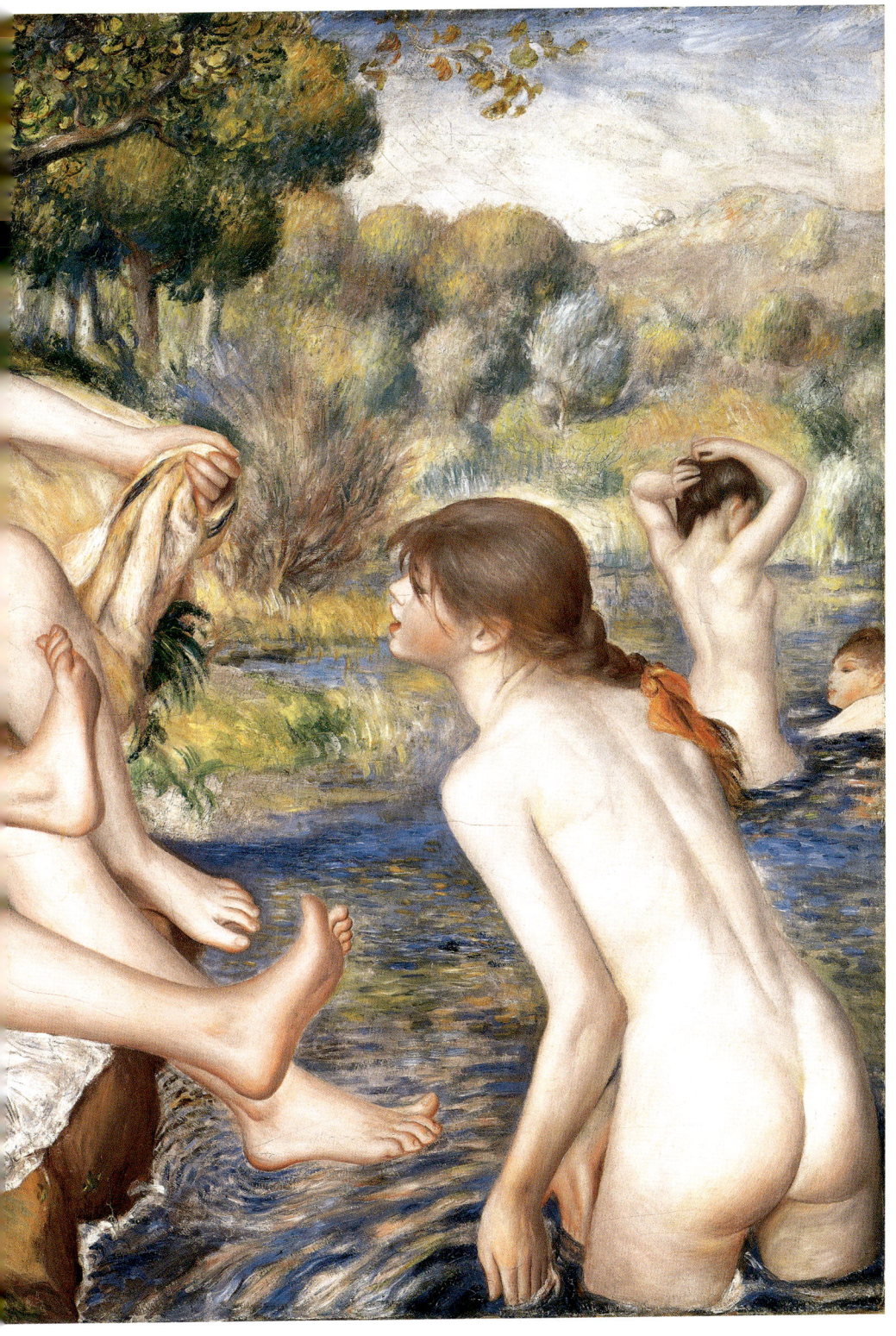

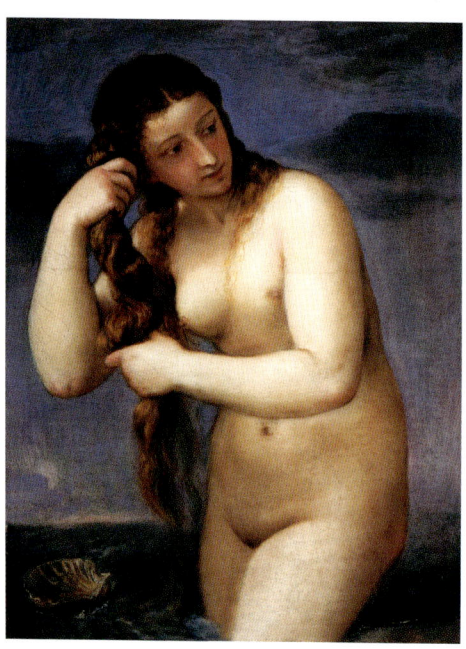

Titian
**Venus Rising from the Sea
("Venus Anadyomene")**, c. 1520
Oil on canvas, 74 x 56.2 cm (29¼ x 22¼ in.)
Edinburgh, National Gallery of Scotland

Renoir used to joke "Old Titian, not only is he
like me, but he is always pinching my tricks".
Three centuries after the heyday of the Italian
master, Renoir created an echo of Titian's *Venus*
in his *Bathers*. There was the same fullness of
the body, the same sensuality produced by giving the flesh a pearly glow, the same obsession
with flowing locks.

Study for **The Great Bathers**,
c. 1903–1905
Oil on canvas,
115 x 168 cm (45⅜ x 66¼ in.)
Cagnes-sur-Mer,
Musée Renoir – Les Collettes

Everything in the painting is composite, from the natural setting (containing no sky) to the
"elusive model", a pure invention of Renoir's imagination. In 1884, he complained about
this to Monet. "I am stuck in Paris where I am becoming extremely bored running after
the elusive model", he wrote. "I am a figure painter, which can be quite pleasant sometimes. But it is anything but when I cannot find the figures that I like". All of the features
of Renoir's new style, the monumental form of the imaginary model and the familiar
simplicity of gesture and expression, were now in place. Renoir succeeded in creating a
classical subject based on something he had experienced in real life.

Renoir painted a number of different *Bathers* during the period dedicated to technical
experimentation. Of these *Bather Arranging Her Hair* (p. 345), painted in 1885, is the most
Ingres-like in its incisive drawing and deeply shadowed contours. The divorce from the
Impressionist technique of merging figures with their surroundings was now complete.
Renoir's painting is highly experimental. Against the colourful background of an almost
abstract Cézanne-style landscape, the nude's silhouette is defined by a linear drawing
reminiscent of Ingres. It is coloured like a fresco with a surface borrowed from porcelain
or enamel painting. Despite Renoir's intense level of experimentation, the painting is a
masterpiece because he follows the technique of the founder of modern portraiture.
Titian brought out the temperament of his sitters by using melting tones and the technique
of "colourism", his transformation of Giorgione's "luminism". He used barely perceptible,
shadowless nuances that richly render the carnations. Meier-Graefe saw in *Bather Arranging Her Hair* a modern Venus: "*Venus Anadyomene* has not borrowed her charms from

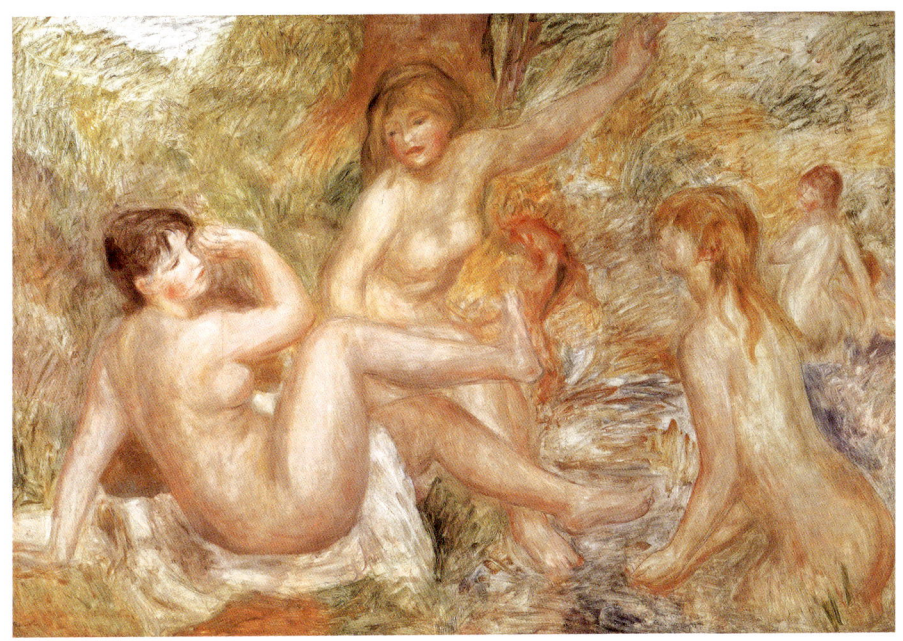

any antique sculpture", he said. "Her origins are much more plausible to our modern minds than that. She is a woman born of the sea-foam. Renoir uses his bright enamel-ling technique to produce her delightfully coloured setting and avoids the isolation of sculptural painting." Titian's influence on Renoir's nude painting reveals deeper affinities between the two artists. Both have a fetish for hair, which from Antiquity onwards has inspired poets. Homer considered Aphrodite to be the golden goddess and in Greek art the hair of Apollo, Dionysus, Artemis and the heroes was conventionally painted gold. "Come and indulge me, let your flowing locks caress our amorous embraces", Apuleus begs in Ovid's *Metamorphoses*. Titian and Renoir belong to the cohort of admirers of fem-inine tresses. Titian's numerous versions of *Madonna with Rabbit*, which Renoir admired in Italy, all endowed their subjects with magnificent manes of hair. So too did his *Venus Anadyomene* (p. 350). Renoir echoes Titian with his long-haired *Bathers*. With his *Venus of Urbino*, Titian had introduced a completely secular version of the female nude. Initially confined to Venice, this was later taken up by Rubens and then the eighteenth-century *Fêtes galantes*. It endures in Manet's *Olympia* and Renoir's *Bathers*. Here, just as in Titian's *Penitent Magdalene* (p. 176), the hair does more to reveal the breasts than to hide them. In Titian's *Venus* the model's hand, curved over the stomach and pubis, draws attention to her languorous charms instead of hiding them. The gesture itself is revelatory. In his *Bather* series, Renoir gradually passed from the modest nude to the complicit one and then to the nude who exhibits herself without caring about anyone else. Renoir saw Titian as his precursor. Titian painted women who, while decked out in the trappings of allegory,

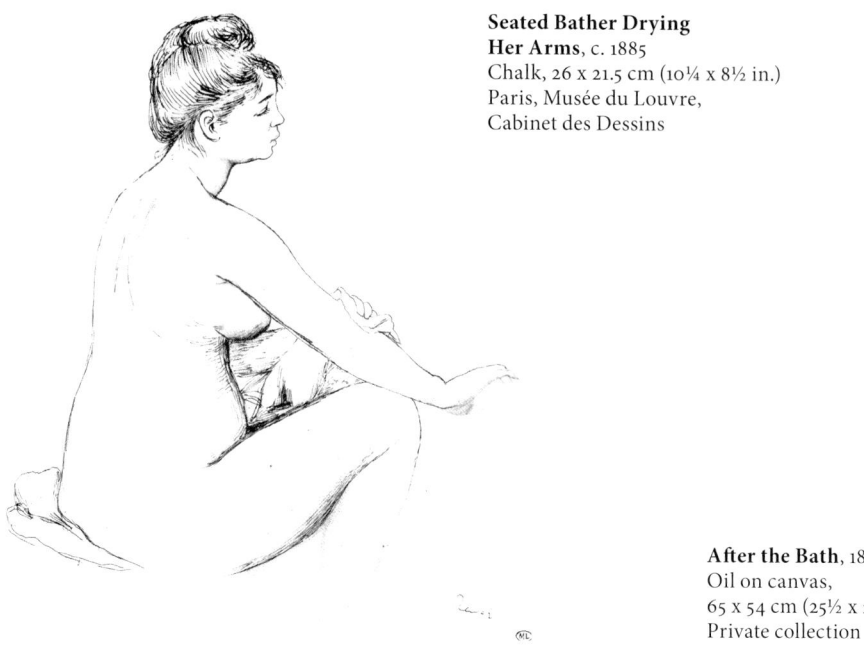

**Seated Bather Drying
Her Arms**, c. 1885
Chalk, 26 x 21.5 cm (10¼ x 8½ in.)
Paris, Musée du Louvre,
Cabinet des Dessins

After the Bath, 1888
Oil on canvas,
65 x 54 cm (25½ x 21¼ in.)
Private collection

revealed a naturally opulent, young beauty. After Titian, painting and the female nude would never be the same again. The wealth of his discoveries, and above all the poetic and sensual power that emanated from his work, had changed the very idea of painting. This is exactly what Renoir hoped to achieve in his own way. "What a pity I did not discover it earlier", he wrote from Italy to Durand-Ruel.

The Great Bathers (pp. 348/349) preoccupied Renoir from 1885 to 1887. Renoir could only emerge from his previous style by producing a large-format work that would summarise all the triumphs of French classical art from Girardon to Ingres. Kenneth Clark wrote of the painting: "Whether we consider this canvas as a work of art or a prodigious exercise of will, at any event, it released him from his uncertainties. In the next twenty years, a shrewd observer would still be able to find traces in his nudes of toil and calculation but they are cleverly concealed. These charming creatures sit on riverbanks drying themselves or splash each other with a perfect naturalness and spontaneity. They are fatter than classical models but have an appearance of Arcadian health. Unlike Rubens's nudes, their skin does not have the folds or wrinkles of a normal body but clings to their shape, like the fur of an animal. Through the natural way in which they accept their nudity, Renoir's nudes are no doubt more like the Greek models than all the nudes painted since the Renaissance and are not far from attaining the equilibrium sought in Antiquity between truth and the ideal". "When after three years of starts and restarts I completed the *Bathers*, which I consider my masterpiece," Renoir explained, "I sent the painting to an exhibition at Georges Petit's gallery. You would not imagine the abuse I received!

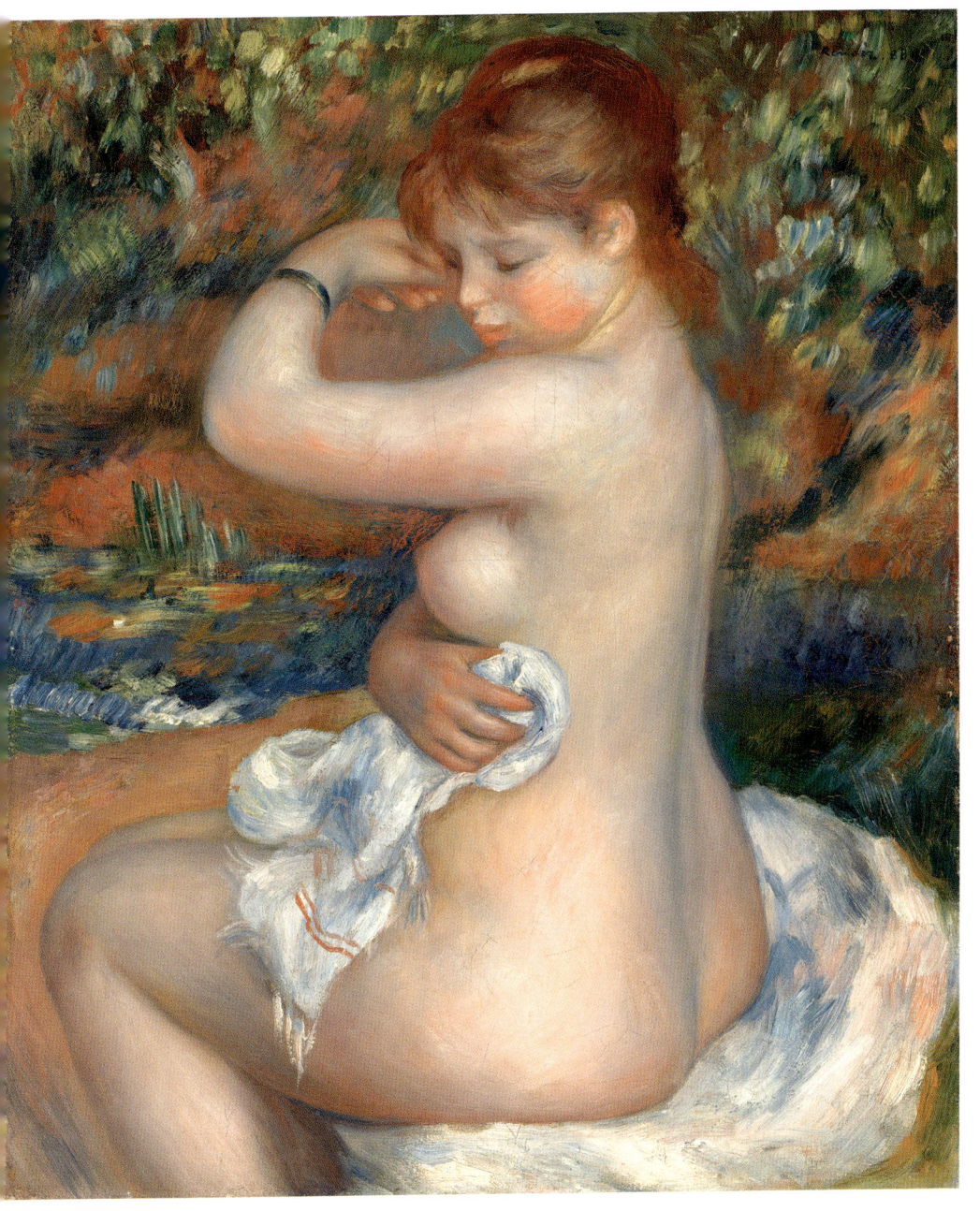

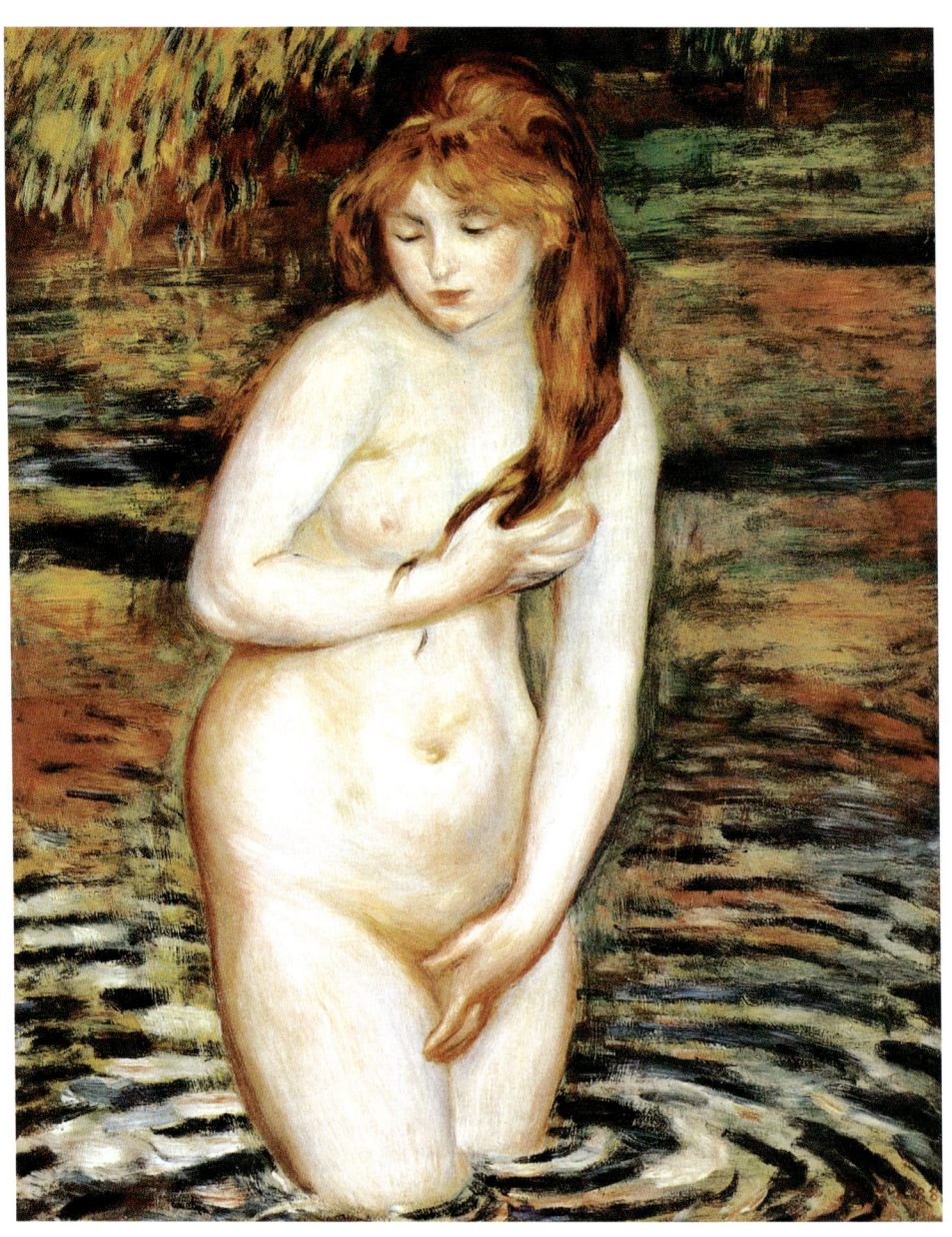

The Bather (After the Bath), 1888
Oil on canvas, 81 x 66 cm (32 x 26 in.)
Private collection

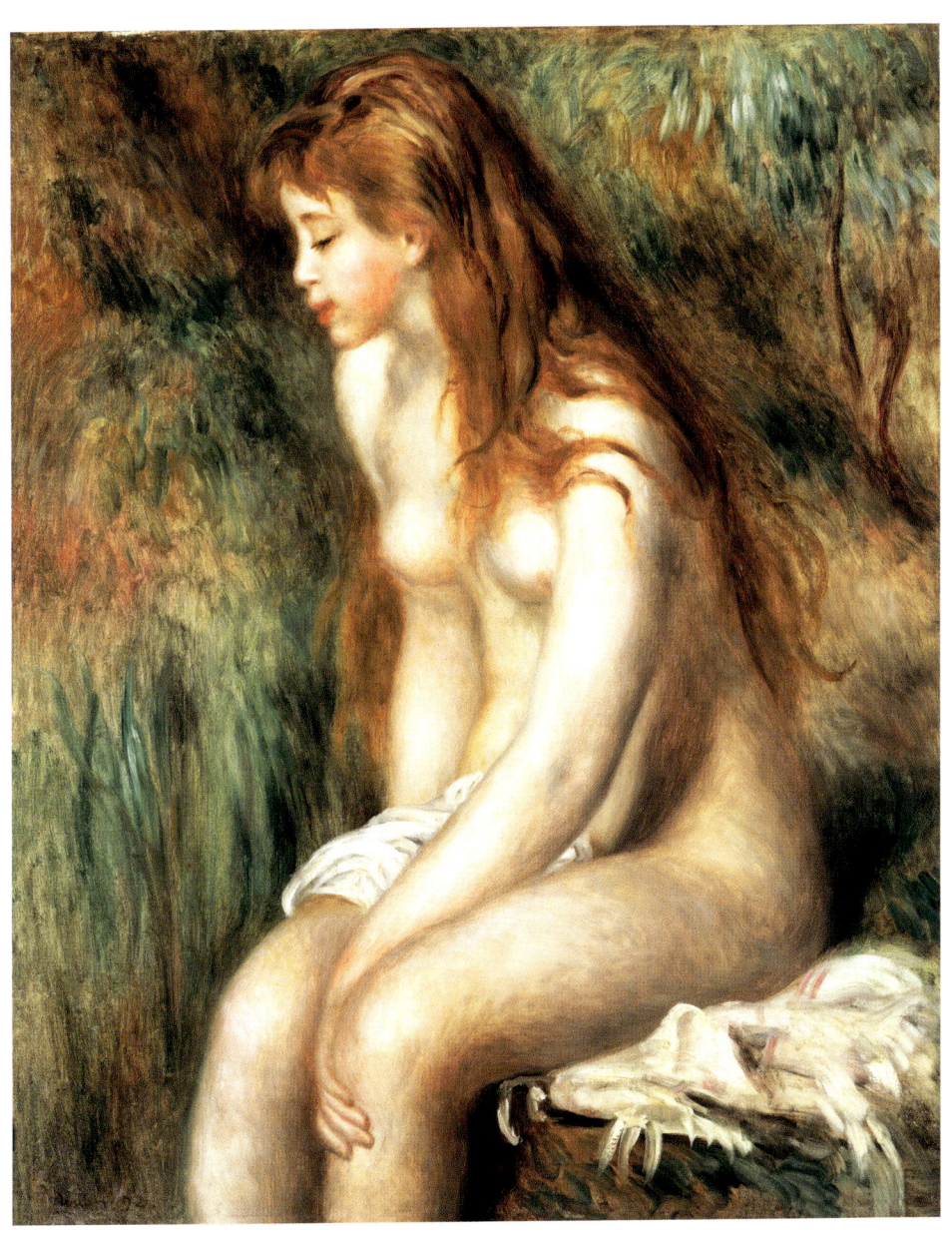

Young Girl Bathing, 1892
Oil on canvas, 81.3 x 64.8 cm (32 x 25½ in.)
New York, The Metropolitan Museum of Art,
Robert Lehman Collection

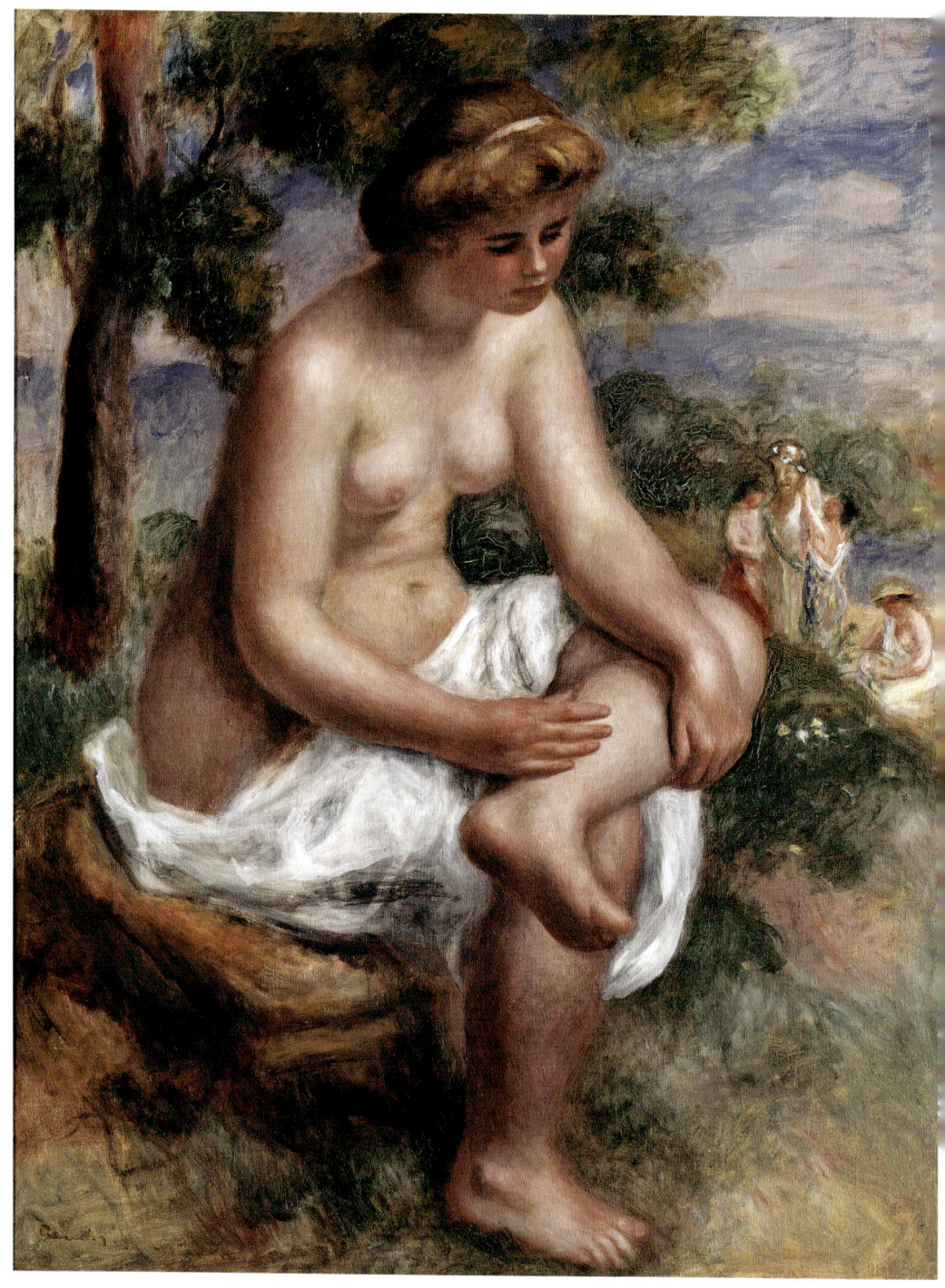

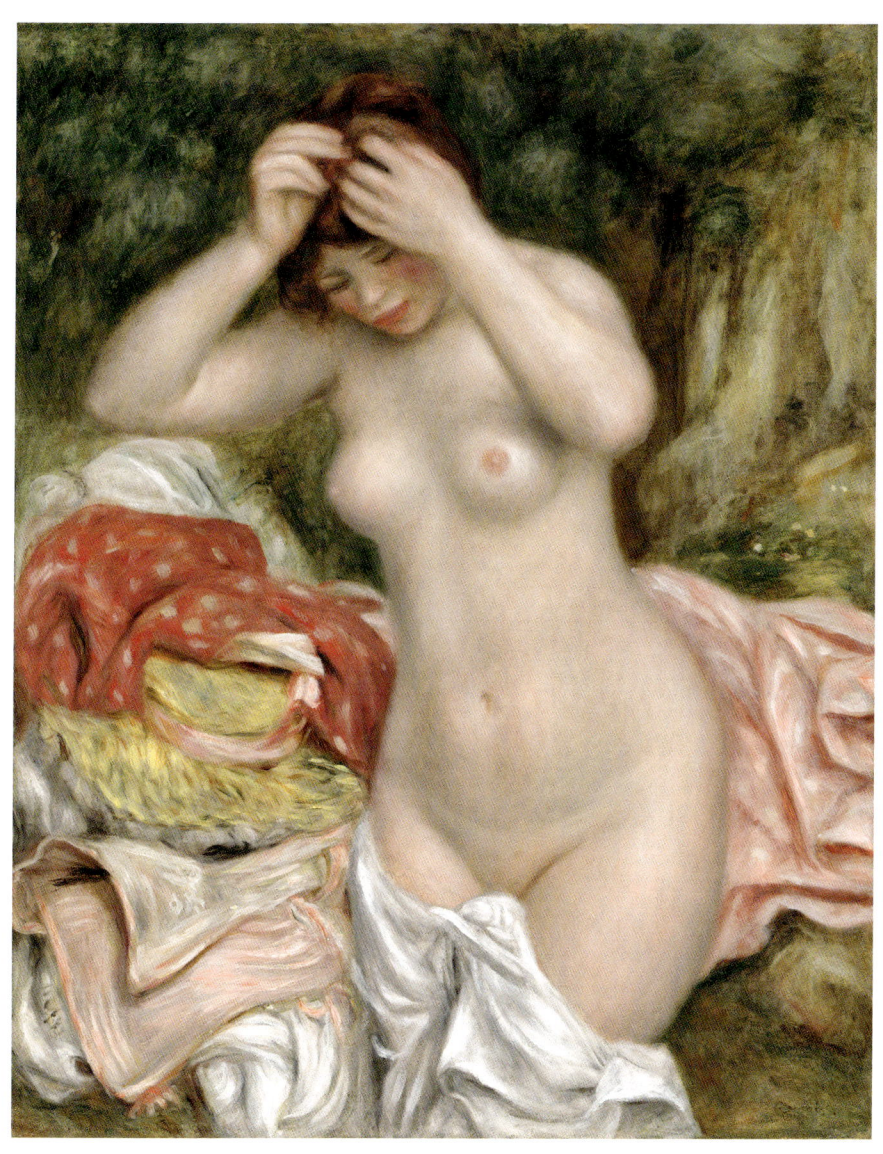

**Seated Bather in a Landscape
(Eurydice)**, 1895–1900
Oil on canvas, 115.9 x 88.7 cm (45¾ x 35 in.)
Paris, Musée Picasso

Bather Arranging Her Hair, 1893
Oil on canvas, 92.4 x 74 cm (36½ x 29¼ in.)
Washington, D.C., National Gallery of Art,
Chester Dale Collection

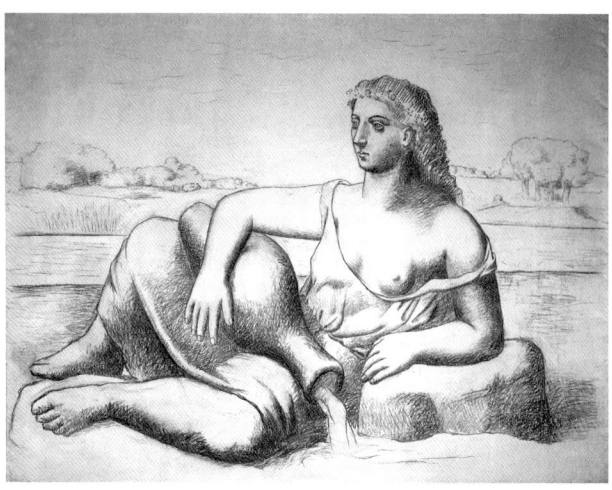

Pablo Picasso (1881–1973)
Spring, 1921
Pencil, 153.5 x 201 cm (60½ x 79¼ in.)
Paris, Musée Picasso

Bather Drying Her Leg, 1895
Oil on canvas, 51 x 41 cm (20 x 16¼ in.)
Paris, Musée de l'Orangerie

This time everyone, starting with Huysmans, agreed that I was all at sea; a few people even called me lazy. God knows how I had slaved away!" Laziness was not one of Renoir's vices. The composition is known to have been inspired by Girardon's lead bas-relief *Nymphs Bathing*. But before sketching the final version, Renoir made a host of drawings of the whole composition and studies of the details. These are of unexpected profusion and linear precision, and indicate his method of working. He also produced a series of pencil and sanguine drawings in the spirit of the subject, some of which depict an isolated figure (p. 352) and others an overall view (p. 347). He also produced oil sketches such as the one in the Musée Renoir in Cagnes-sur-Mer (p. 351). Far from being lazy or haphazard – as has often been thought of the Impressionists – Renoir considered these sketches as essential warming-up exercises. In the course of his researches, he noticed that a particular shape might be well suited to the dimensions of a small sheet of paper but not to the larger ones of a canvas. So he preferred not to use the procedure that consists of enlarging sketches from nature by means of graphs or squares. Instead he started by producing large drawings before tracing them on to the canvas.

Berthe Morisot admired Renoir's painstaking preparations after visiting his studio in the Rue Laval. "It would be interesting to show all these preparatory studies to the public, which generally imagines that the Impressionists worked at great speed", she noted in her 'carnet'. "I do not think that one can go any further in trying to paint a shape than by drawing it first. I find his nude women entering the sea as delightful as those of Ingres. He told me that he believes the nude to be one of the indispensable forms of art." The whole of French

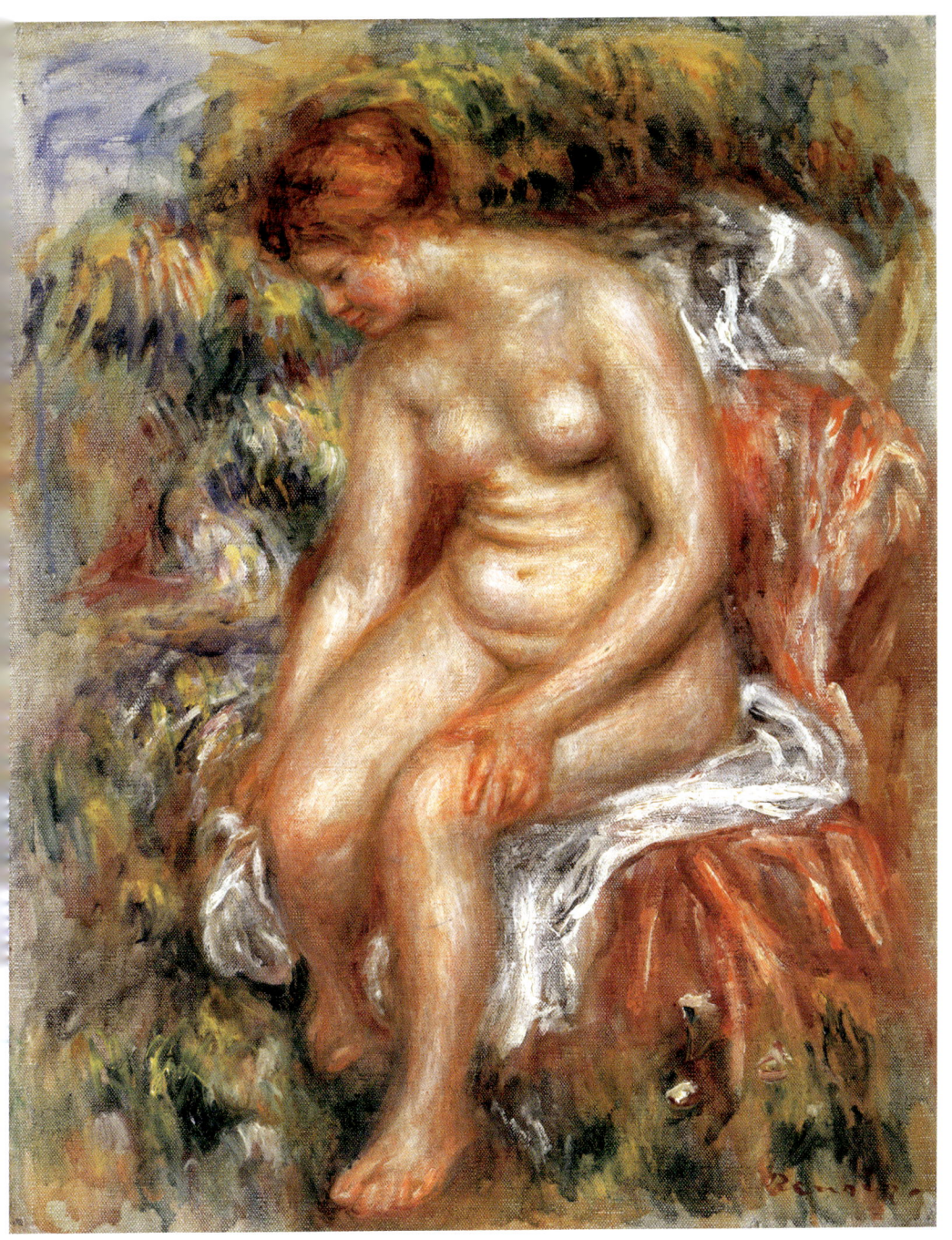

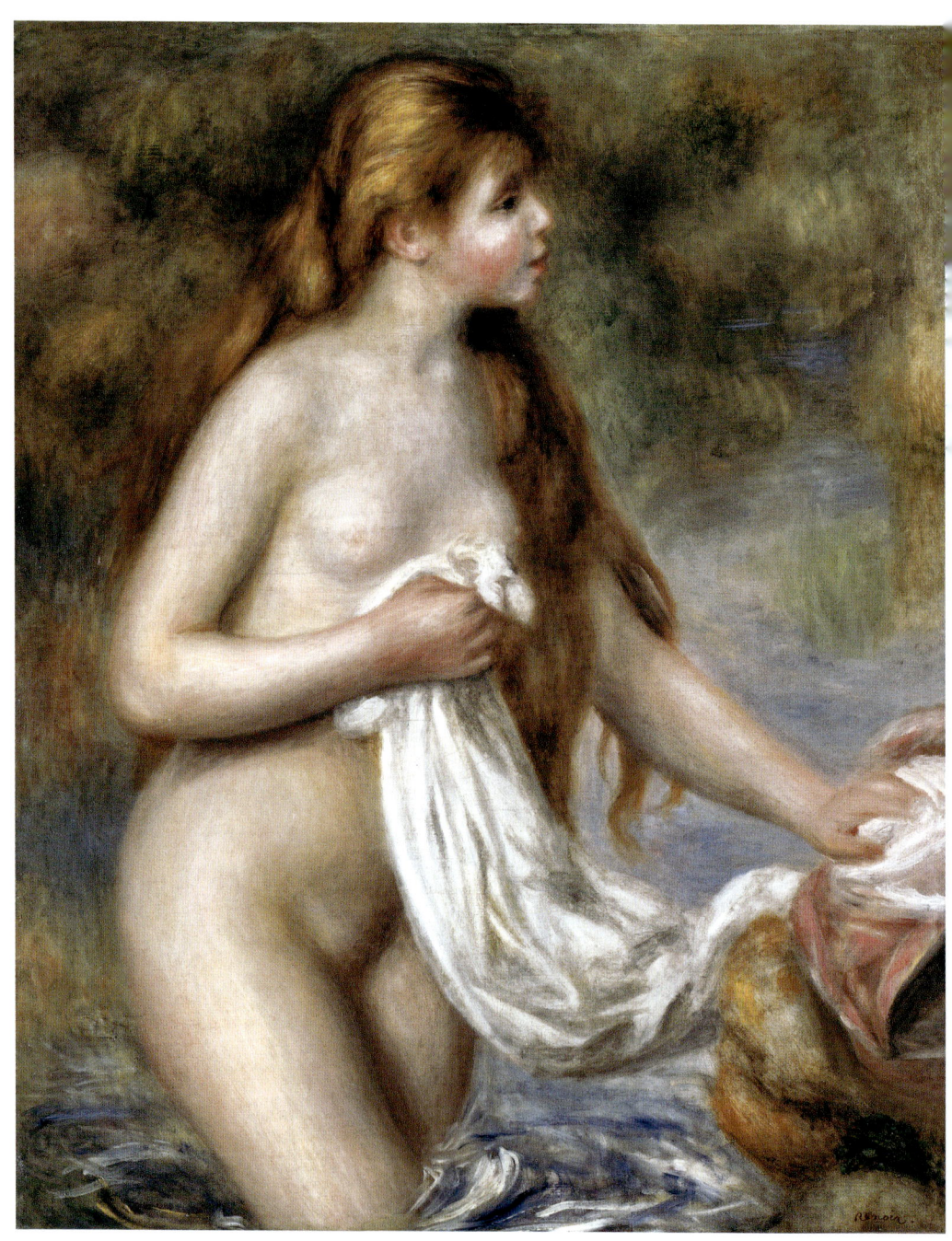

Long-haired Bather, c. 1895/96
Oil on canvas, 82 x 65 cm (32⅜ x 25⅝ in.)
Paris, Musée de l'Orangerie

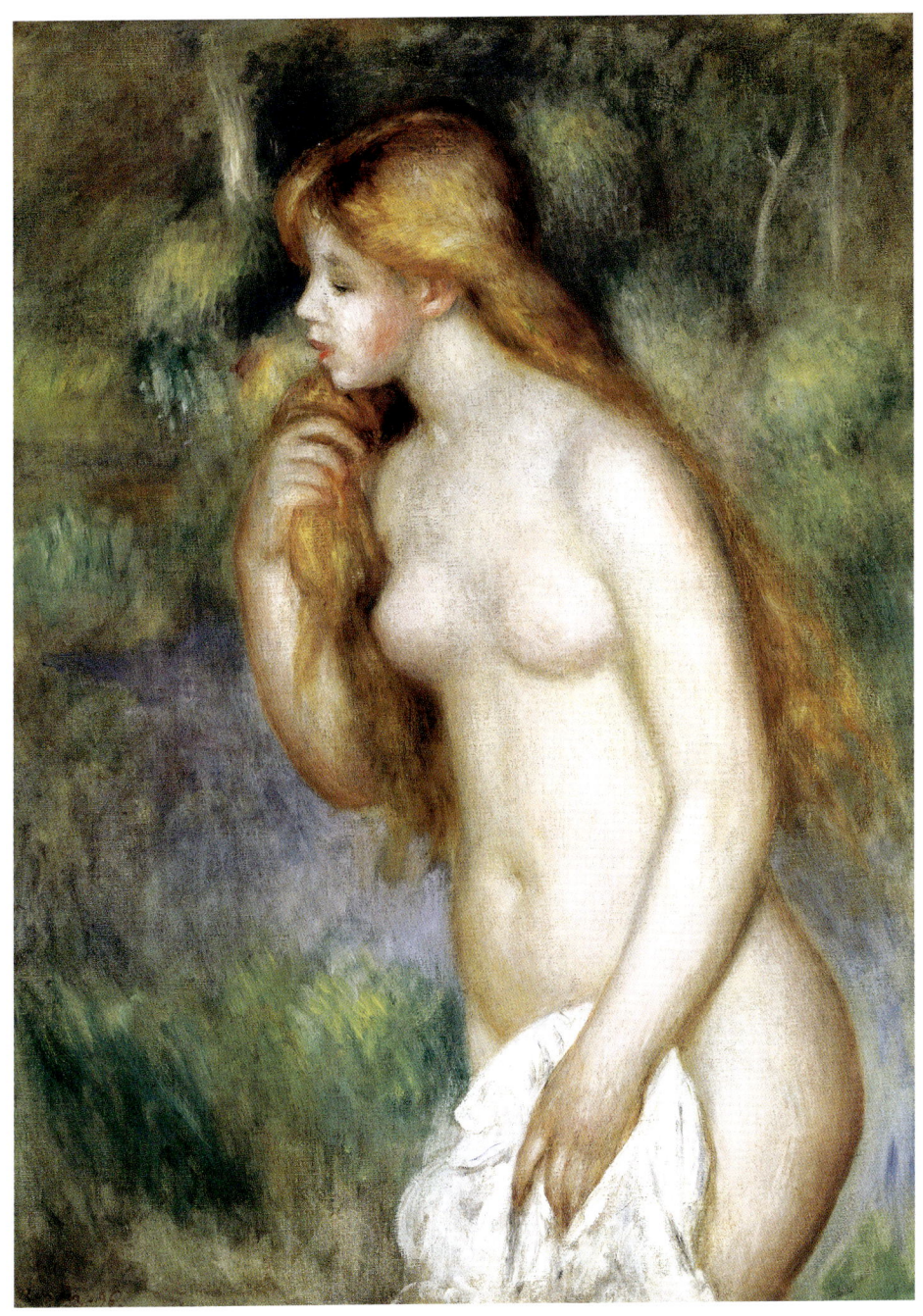

Bather Standing, 1896
Oil on canvas, 81 x 60 cm (32 x 23⅝ in.)
Private collection

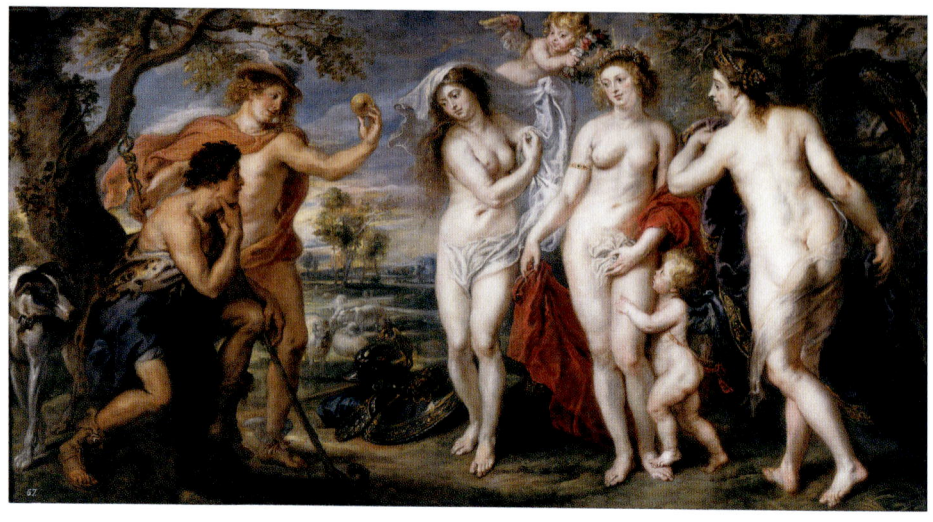

Peter Paul Rubens (1577–1640)
The Judgement of Paris, c. 1638
Oil on canvas, 199 x 379 cm (78⅜ x 149¼ in.)
Madrid, Museo Nacional del Prado

classical painting was brought together in Renoir. There was Girardon for the design, Ingres for the three-dimensional feeling and flowing lines, and Boucher's *Diana at the Bath* for the execution and tonality. Julius Meier-Graefe did not share the view that *The Bathers* were the summit of Renoir's work. But the painting did make an important contribution. "*The Bathers* are a rallying point. They provide art critics with the most valuable information. The work – Renoir's many friends who have rejected it should at least grant this – is quite unique. No other in nineteenth-century French art offers so many insights of this kind. Ingres would have been beside himself if anyone had thought him capable of showing four legs trampling on the same canvas. Among the twenty or thirty women in *Turkish Bath,* barely four feet are visible. Renoir breaks with traditional concerns about the need to preserve the solemnity of the pose. Something of the femininity of *Turkish Bath* has no doubt transferred itself to the *Bathers*; but there is so much to the Renoir that is lacking in *Turkish Bath*. Ingres's nude slaves are restricted to a narrow space and exist rather like women in a harem. They look like rare greenhouse plants. Renoir's young girls are free spirits out in the open air. Nature is their harem. Despite the severity of the line, no restraints appear to have been placed upon them." The idea that Renoir is a liberator of women might not please feminists. But it could be argued that anyone who loves women wants to set them free – as the mistresses of their own bodies.

The jibes and sneers with which any new trend in art is received always look inexplicable in hindsight. Renoir had often been attacked in the past. But the mockery that greeted this masterpiece is hard to understand and there are those indeed who criticise it to this day.

Study for **Bathers in the Forest**, c. 1897
Pencil, 26.7 x 23.5 cm (10⅝ x 9⅜ in.)
Private collection

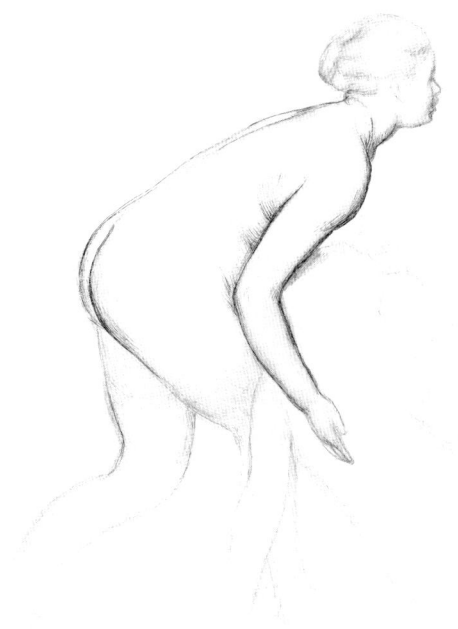

PAGES 364/365
Bathers in the Forest, c. 1897
Oil on canvas,
74 x 100 cm (29¼ x 39⅜ in.)
Philadelphia, The Barnes Foundation

The painting may well fall within the "harsh" period, but it also reveals Renoir's consider-able resources at this time. It combines the colour and luminous qualities of Impression-ism, the drawing skills learned from Ingres and Raphael, the fruits of his research into the clarity and simplicity of the fresco, the grace of his favourite eighteenth-century French painters, and above all the faces, bodies, and mischievous gestures that Renoir made his own and that retain a bewitching power to this day. Renoir for one understood why the ancient gods lusted after mere mortals.

In 1888, Renoir emerged from his most hermetic period of technical experimentation. He still wanted to reconcile the direct study of nature with participation in an artistic tradition and to combine clean-cut forms with the free play of strokes of colour. He decided to ignore the linearity of the Renaissance and Ingres. Instead he drew heavily upon Titian, Velázquez, Rubens, Rembrandt and Vermeer. Eighteenth-century French art and Corot were also crucial influences. Fragonard's *The Bathers* (p. 381) and Watteau's *Fête galante in a Wooden Landscape* (p. 330) helped him to soften the harshness of the contours in his *Bathers* and to diversify his technique. Making deliberate use of these diverse influences, he worked away at his canvas. The theme of idylls and nymphs that he adapted was an echo of eighteenth-century art. He then embarked on a long series of nudes in outdoor settings. These were mainly the young girls to whom he refers as "nymphs" in his letters. At first they were isolated and monumental figures, occupying the whole of the canvas. Then gradually, in around 1897, he started to create groups that move and play around in the landscape. It is as if Fragonard's *The Bathers* were suddenly

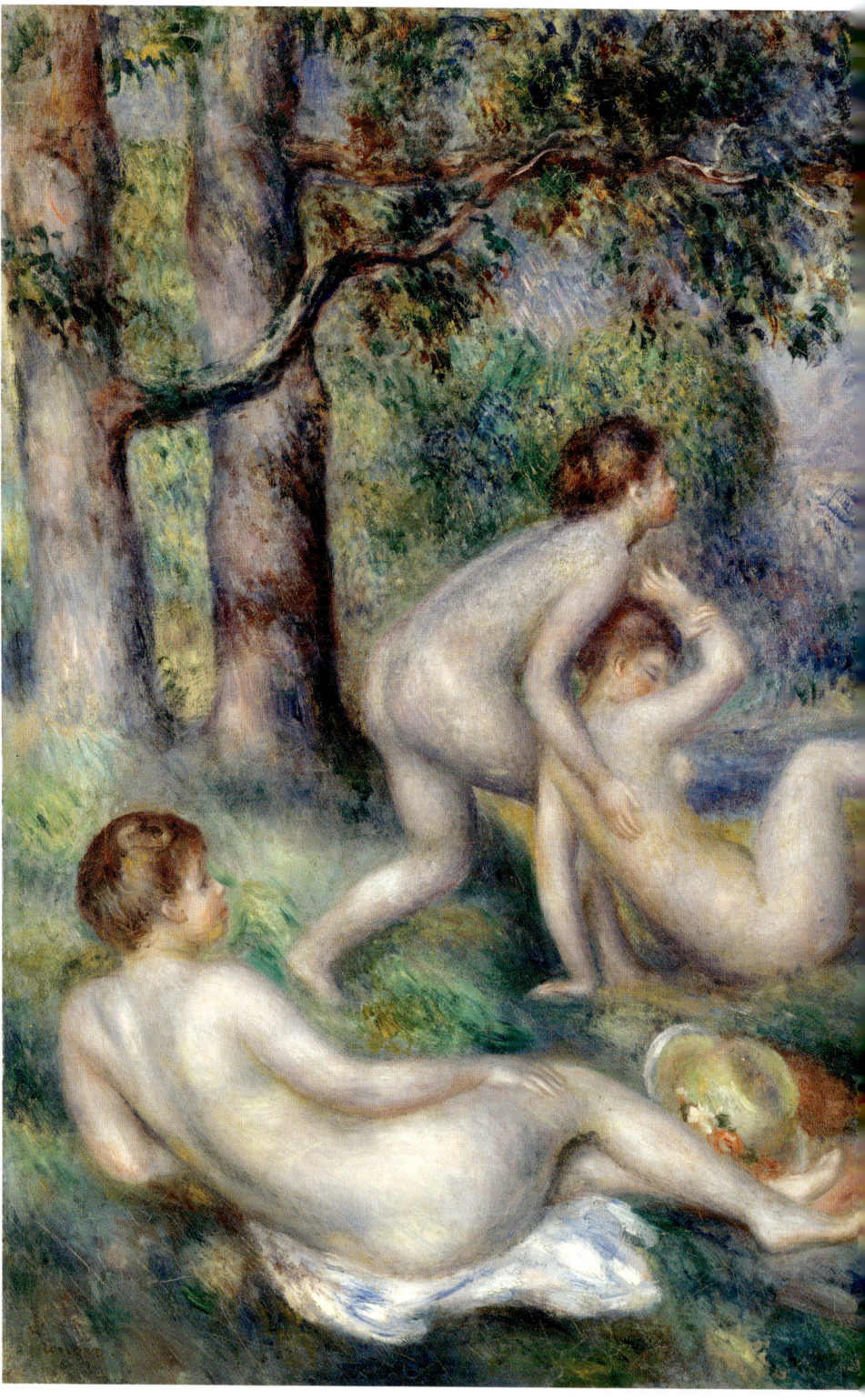

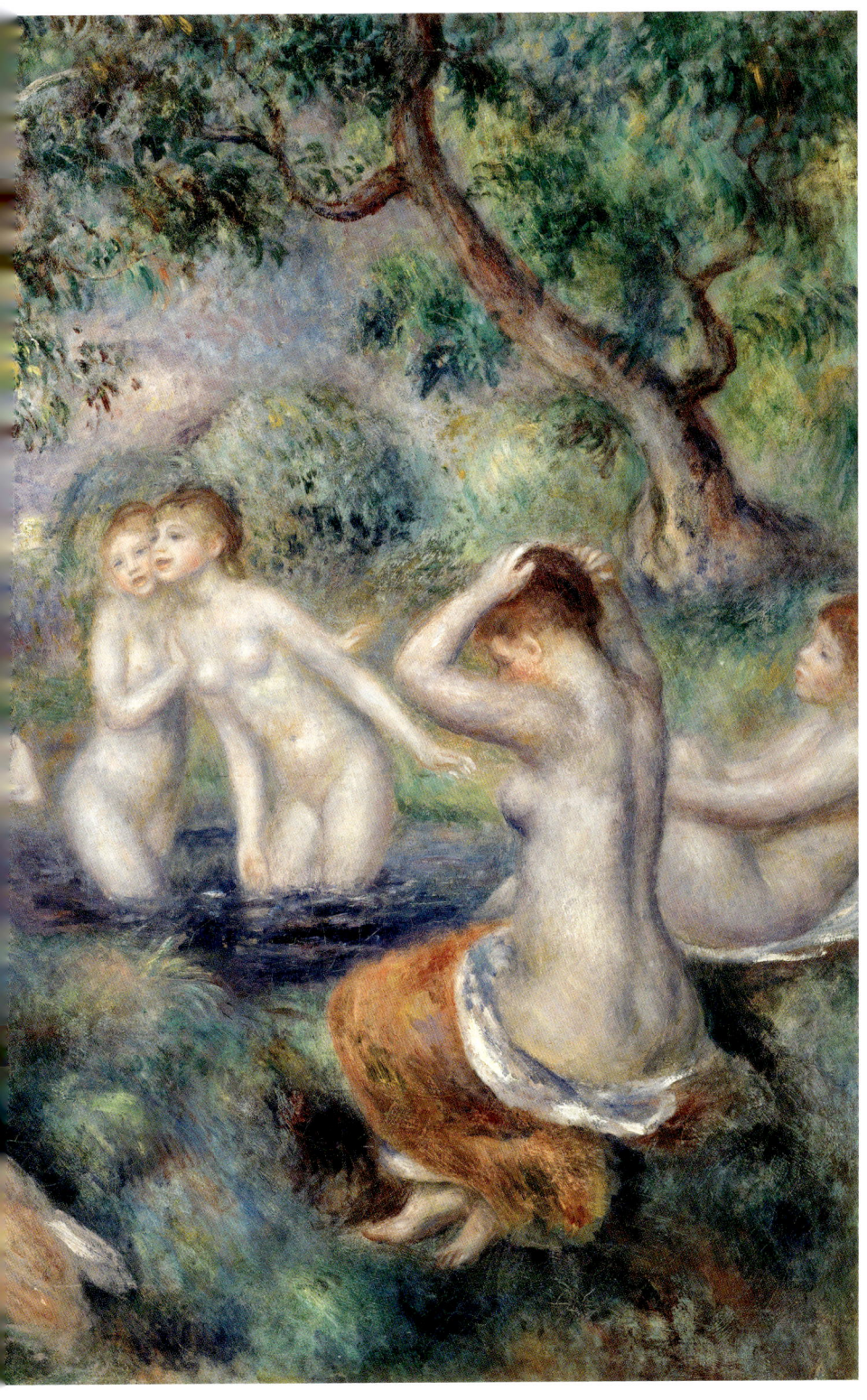

free to frolic in a Corot-style landscape. Renoir's *Bathers*, after undressing, wiping, drying themselves and arranging their hair, sit on a rock and daydream. Later they play about in a group, in *Bathers in the Forest* (pp. 364/365), or with a crab in *Bathers Playing with a Crab* (pp. 372/373).

Renoir announced to Berthe Morisot in 1892 that, like his friend Corot, he would "paint outdoor scenes in his studio". The result was *Young Girl Bathing* (p. 355) and *Bather Seated on a Rock* (1892). "I have just written to a model", he told Berthe Morisot. "I am resuming work in the studio while waiting for something better. I have spent a month looking at the sky and doing nothing else. I am going to paint outdoor scenes in my studio". He finishes on a note of justification: "Titian would certainly have worked in this way". The advantage of the studio was that it allowed Renoir to give free rein to his love of warm nuances, created from supple brushstrokes that subtly followed the shape of the nude. These delicate shades of pink and yellow rendered the flesh palpable in the play of light. Reduced to its most simple, almost abstract, expression, the background landscape harmonises in colour with the figure, whose outline is clearly detached from it without being outlined. Monet, who owned this *Bather Seated on a Rock*, criticised its conventional background as "looking like a piece of photographer's scenery". Monet tended to merge the figure with the background by treating it as an element of the landscape. In the *Bathers* series, Renoir deliberately rejects this approach. He re-establishes the figure as the focus of the painting. At the same time he establishes a link between his own form of art and the figurative tradition of the Old Masters.

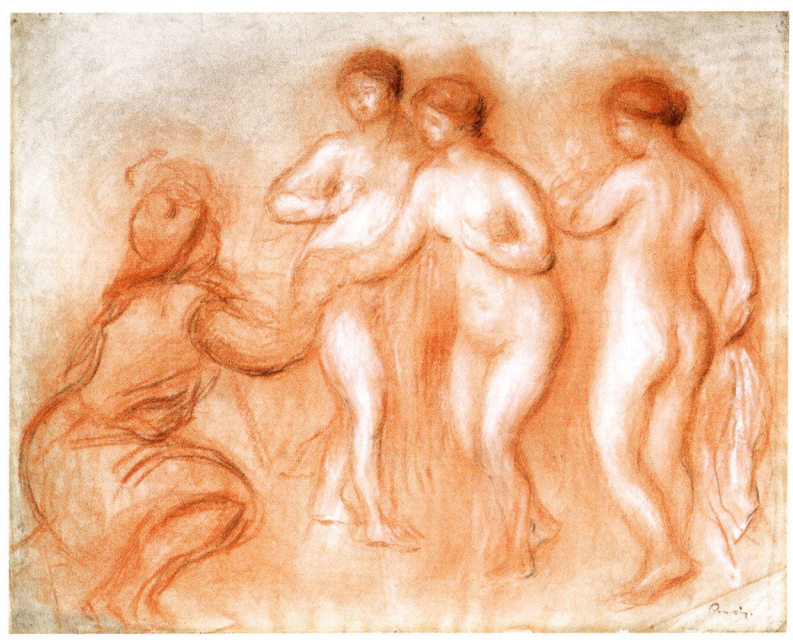

At the start of his series of *Bathers*, Renoir had chosen to paint innocent young girls who more or less concealed their naked bodies from the spectators while remaining apparently unaware of their presence. He sought to show a half-woman, half-child vision of beauty. From the turn of the century onwards, he painted freely what pleased him most, curvaceous models who are perfectly aware that they are being watched and who even appear to invite the viewer-as-voyeur into their show. Renoir displays a wicked streak when he represents a very young girl, such as *Long-haired Bather* (p. 360), who looks away innocently and does not even know that she is being watched. But the gesture that she makes with her towel unwittingly reveals her entirely naked body to the spectator. Geffroy describes these *Bathers* as "instinctive little creatures who are both children and women. Renoir paints them with both genuine affection and a malicious eye", he observes. "These sensual girls have no vices and do not even know what cruelty and responsibility are. But they are pleasantly awake to the realities of life. They exist as children, as playful young animals, and as flowers that absorb the air and the dew." Renoir's *Bathers* gradually increase in size and self-assurance. Those of the 1890s are shy young girls who try to protect themselves from the gaze of strangers. The *Bather with Loose Blonde Hair* (p. 371), painted around 1903, has removed her clothing; it lies like a coloured bouquet on the rock. Her curves are starting to become more generous. She holds up her heavy tresses and sneaks a furtive look around as if to check that her state of undress has had the desired effect on the viewer. She exhibits herself naturally and without shame and her gesture is a sort of sacrificial offering of her body. The *Bather Drying Her Right Leg* (p. 370), painted around 1910, is not remotely interested

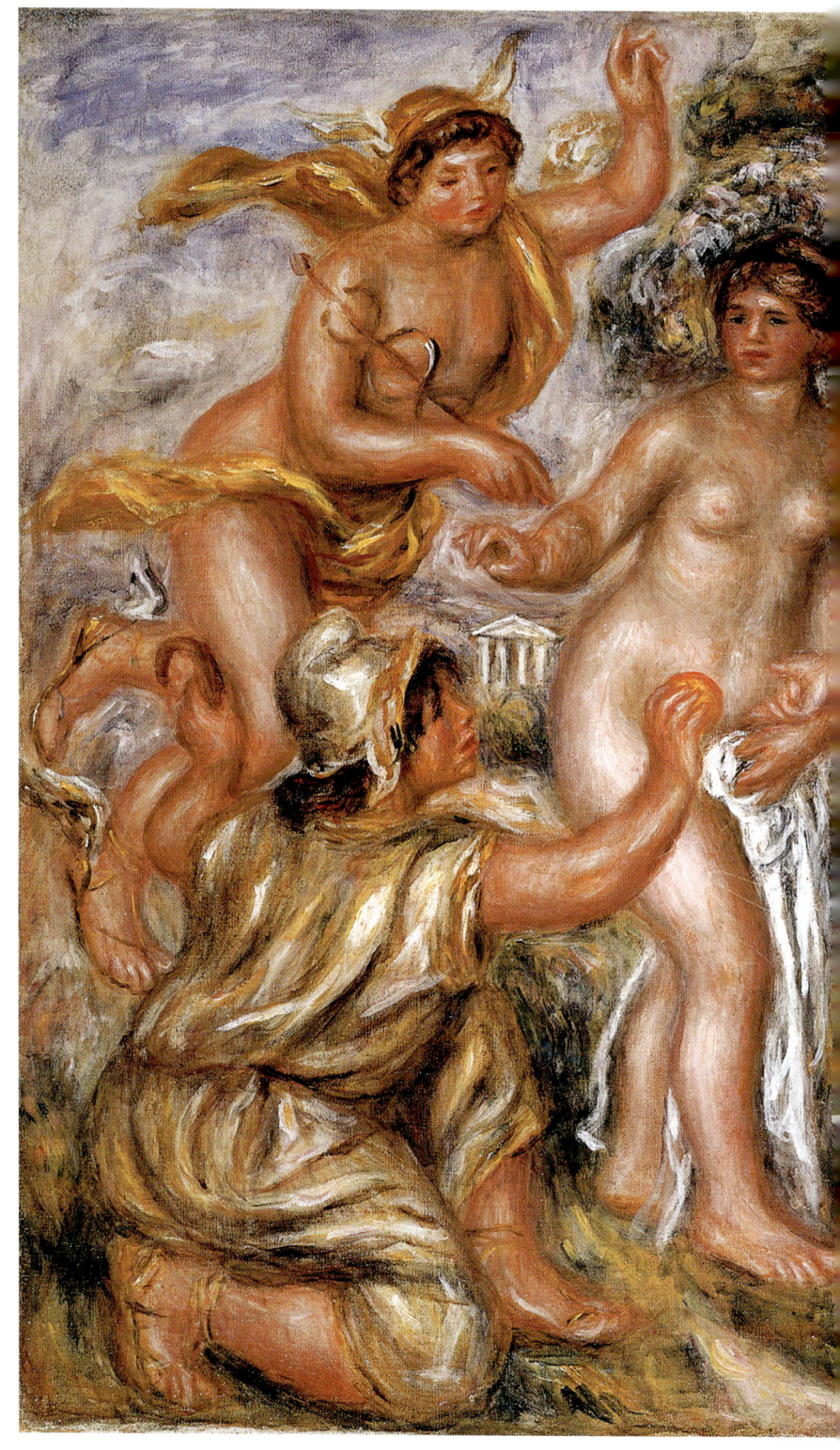

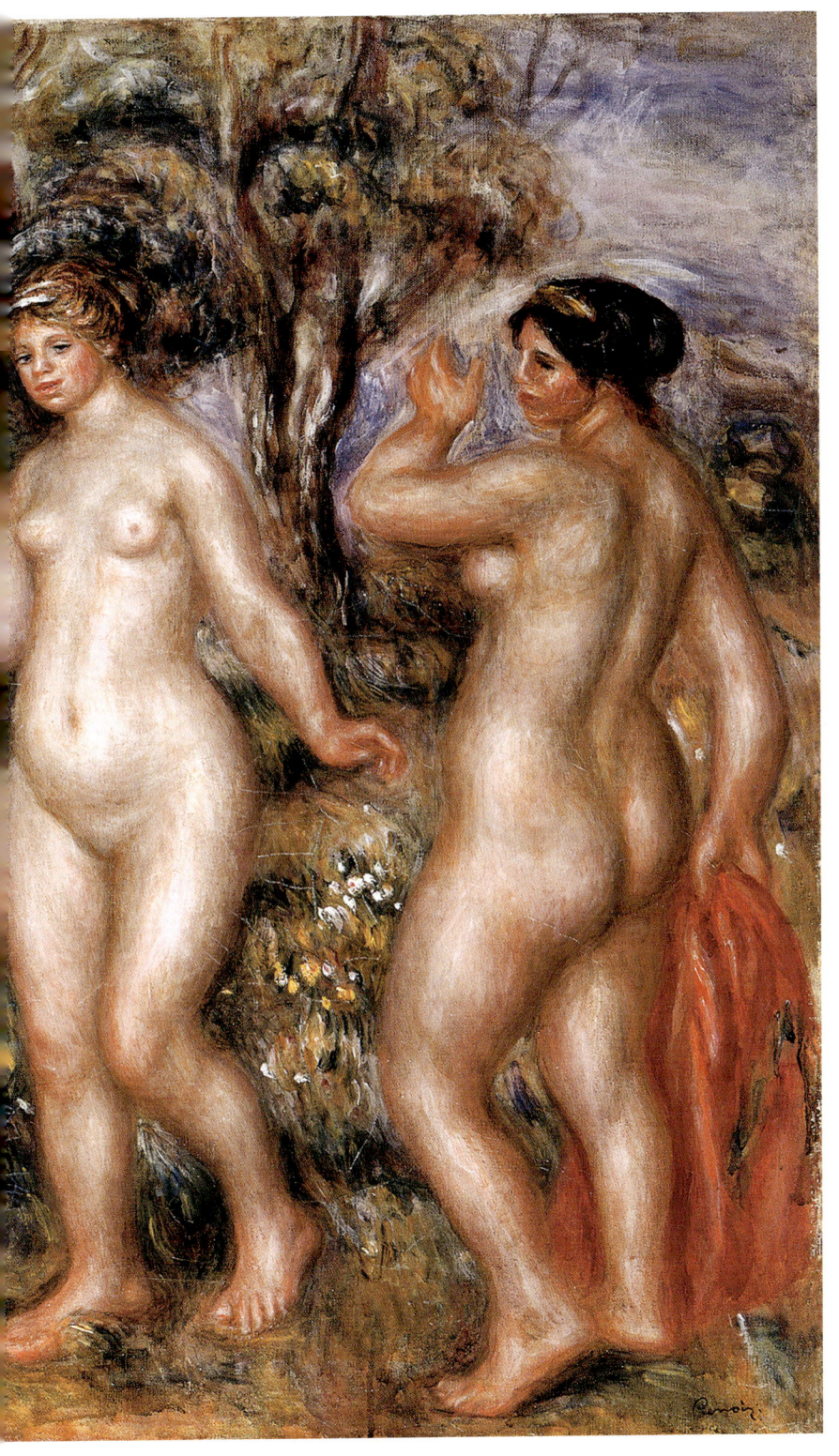

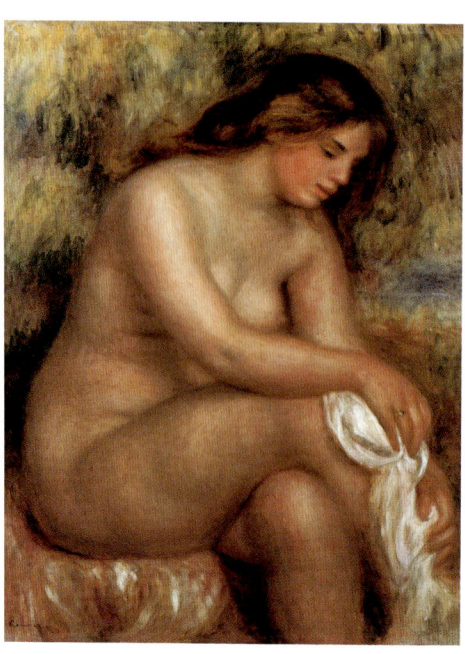

in knowing whether or not she is being watched. She is a serene woman, more mature and even more well-built than ever, busy drying herself. Camille Mauclair described the post-1900 nudes in the following terms: "Renoir hardly observes the outline of the figure, so attracted is he by the brilliance of the skin. For him, the female nude is a burst of lilac and mother-of-pearl that no model, no auburn-haired beauty with diaphanous skin, could possibly offer. She is 'his ideal clay' shown in her naked entirety. Like her academic sister, she seems to have neither age nor date nor origin. She comes, not from the groves of Academe, but from a proud and primitive land of dreams. One would have to travel to the colonies to see its like. Such ingenuous and sumptuous flesh he cannot have seen but only dreamed. Abundant tresses frame her small head. No thought has ever crossed her mind and she has the gentle eyes of an antelope. Her strong mouth is 'bleedingly naked'. Her lips are parallel and of equal size and shape. She possesses no intellectual faculties and does not invite the onlooker to avert his eyes from her enticing breasts or stomach in order to seek intelligence in her expression. She has the curves and mouth of a luscious fruit, and the unseeing eyes of a gentle beast. She blooms in a tropical setting in which false modesty is as unknown as vice and in which satisfaction is absolute." We are a long way here from Impressionism and its attention to atmospheric conditions. Renoir has entered the Golden Age and taken the spectator with him. Meier-Graefe claimed in 1912 that "a transfigured Rubens" was responsible for the "magnificent" bathers. Nine years earlier, when Renoir was busy painting the series of nymphs, he spoke to Wyzewa in lyrical terms about "the genius of Rubens, and the delightful trembling that one experiences when gazing at his paintings."

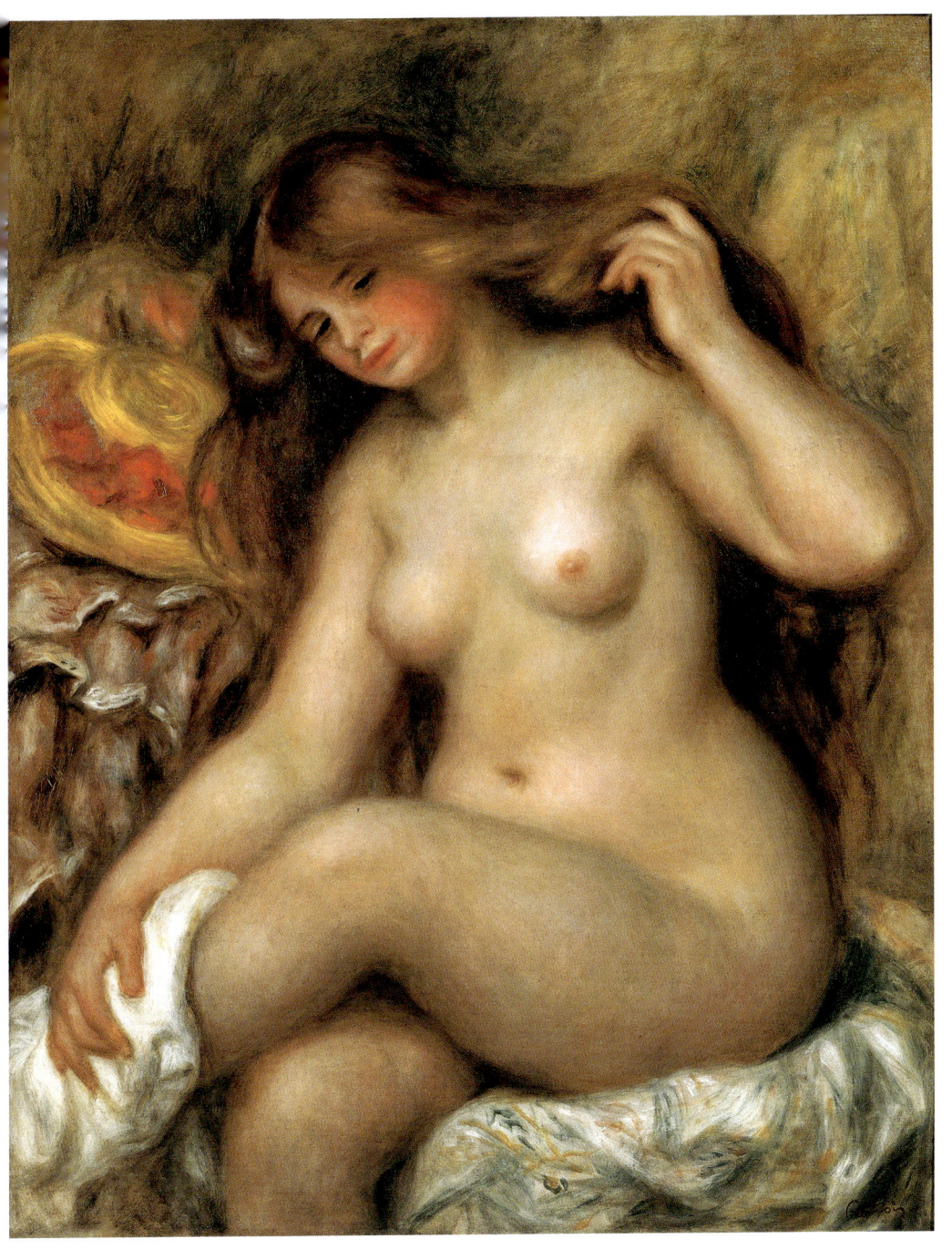

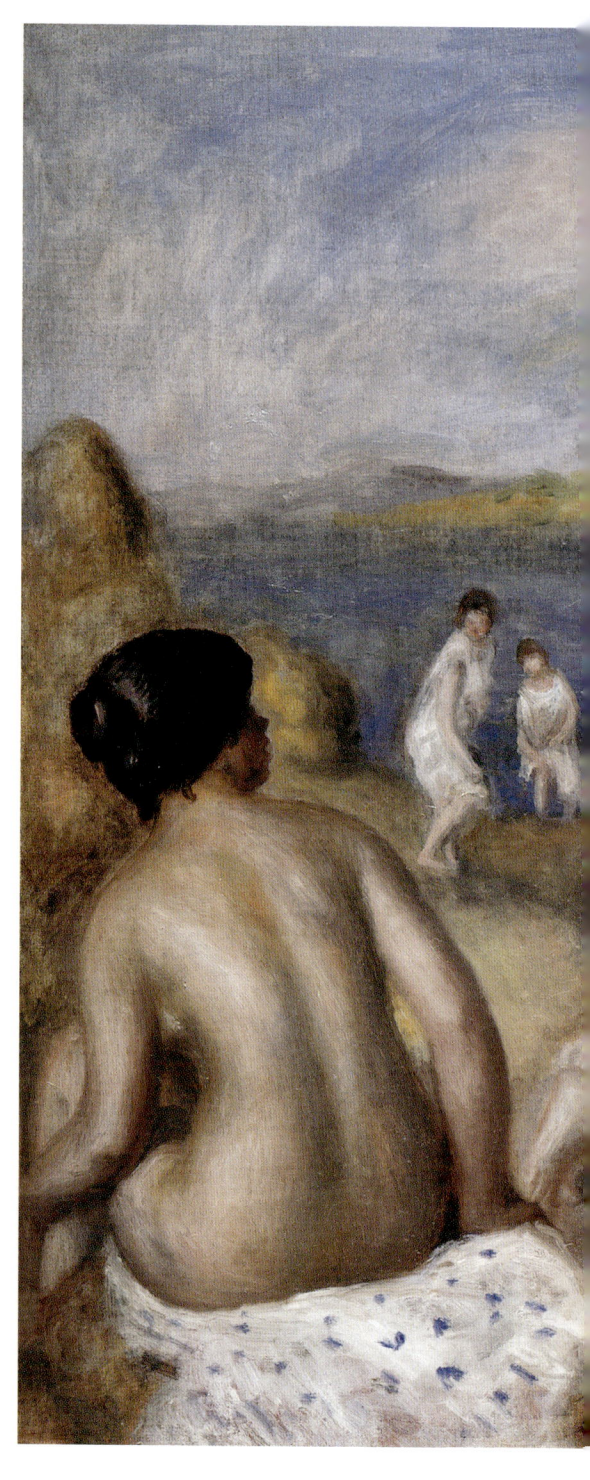

Bathers Playing with a Crab, c. 1897
Oil on canvas,
54.6 x 65.7 cm (21½ x 25⅞ in.)
The Cleveland Museum of Art,
Purchase from the J. H. Wade Fund

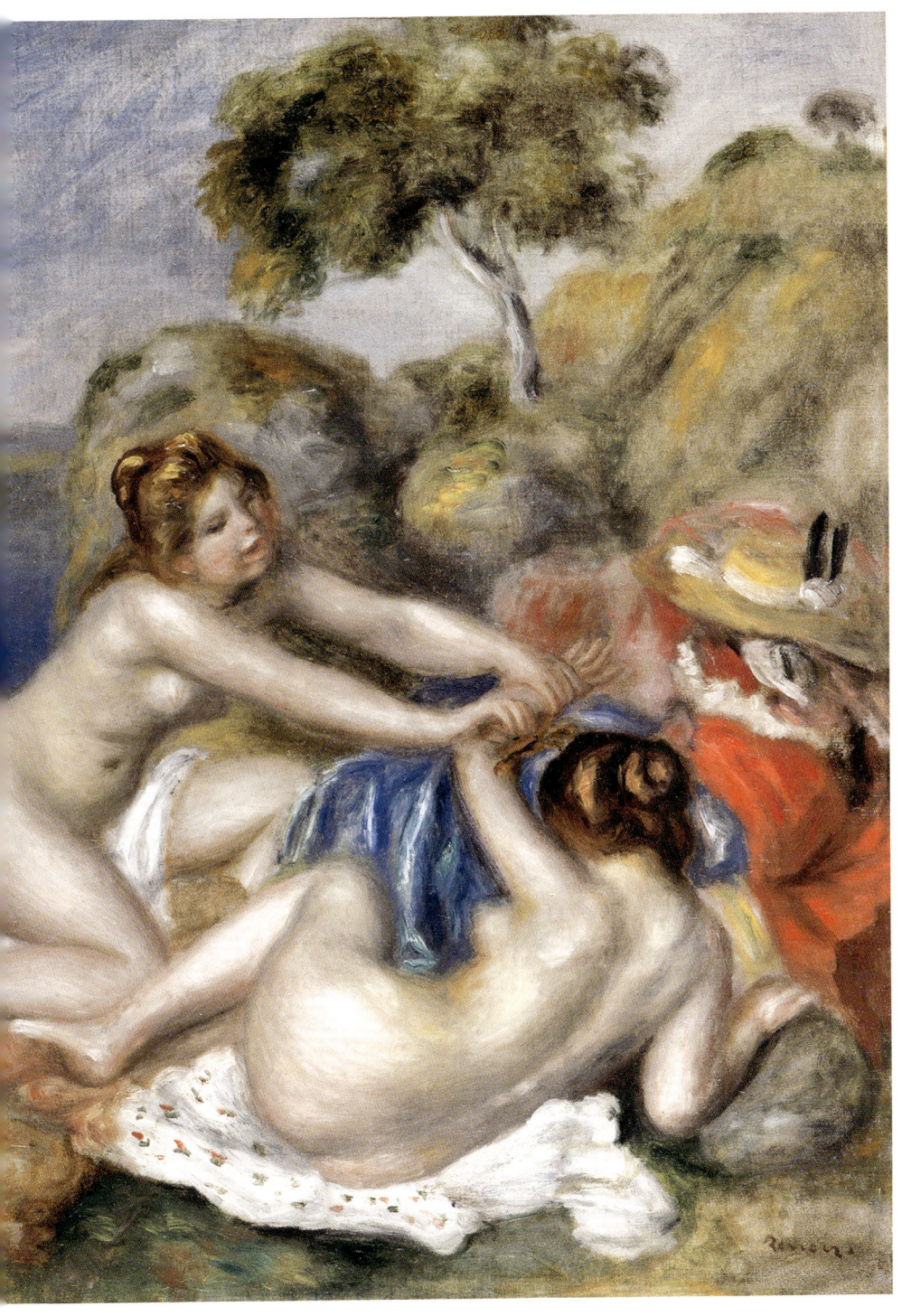

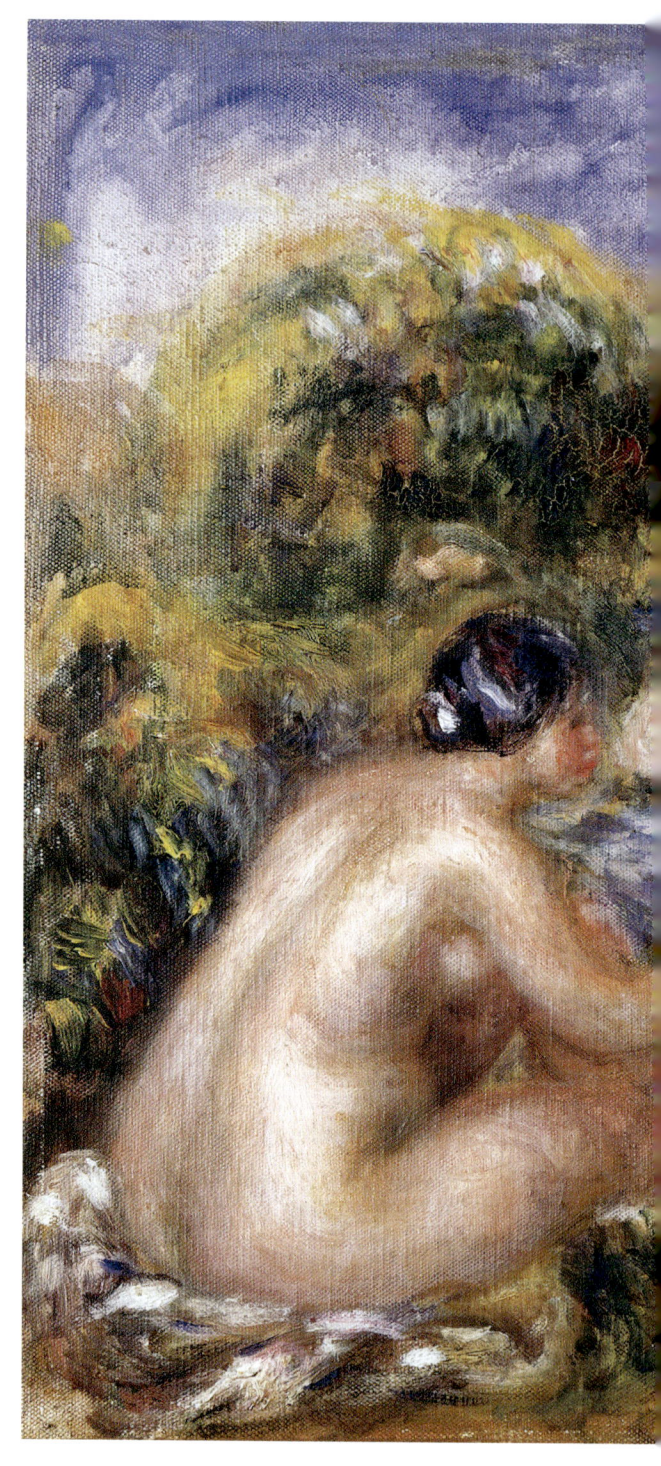

Bathing Women, c. 1915
Oil on canvas,
40.5 x 51 cm (16 x 20 in.)
Stockholm, Nationalmuseum

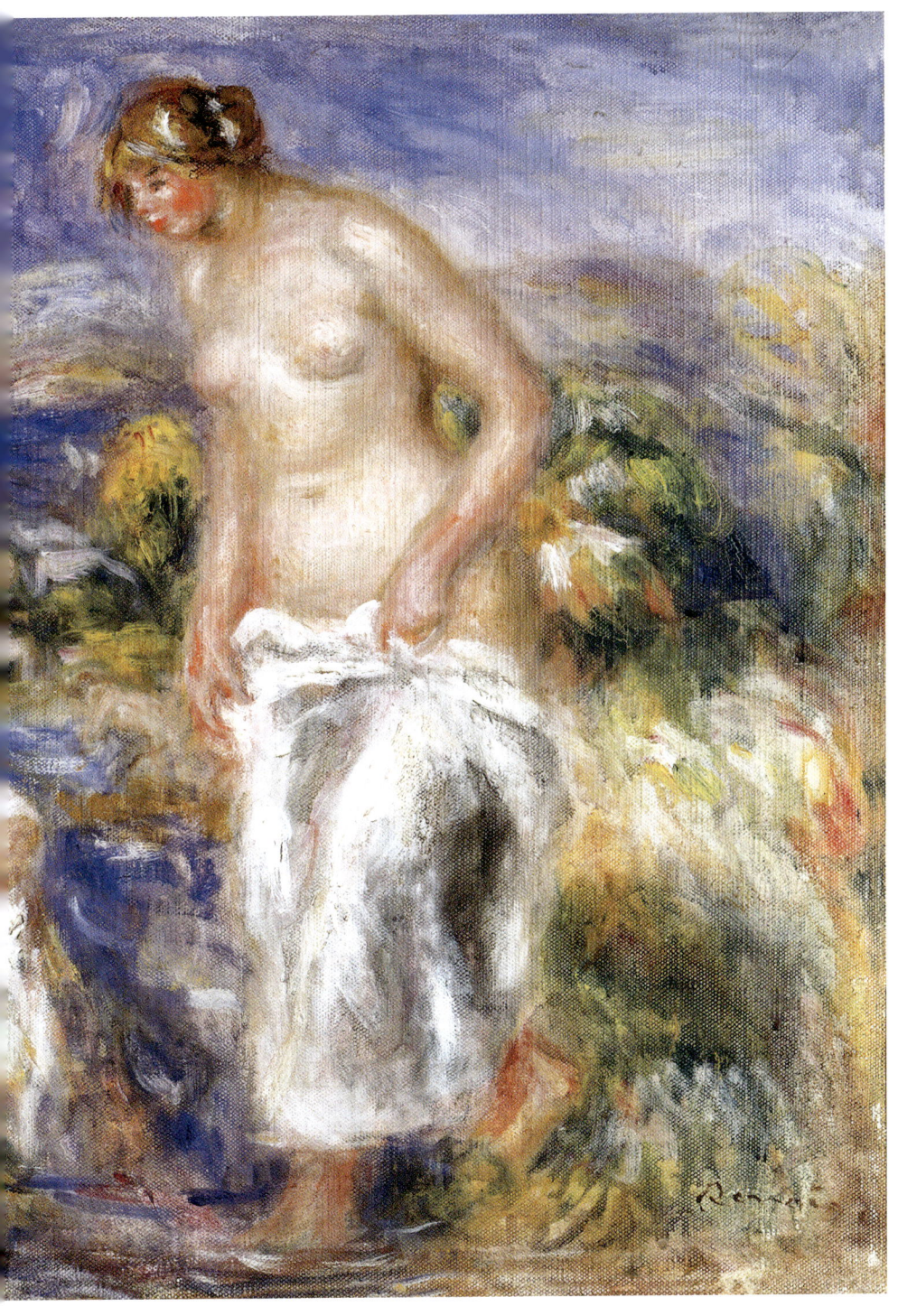

After the Bath, 1912
Oil on canvas,
67 x 52.5 cm (26½ x 20¾ in.)
Winterthur, Kunstmuseum

PAGES 378/379
Rest after a Bath, 1918/19
Oil on canvas,
110 x 160 cm (43¼ x 63 in.)
Paris, Musée d'Orsay

Renoir, now liberated, was able to forget Baudelaire's aesthetics of modern life, which had dominated his work between 1870 and 1880. He now took on subjects drawn from classical mythology and transformed his wife and maidservant into Olympian goddesses. In tribute to Ruben's *The Judgement of Paris* (p. 362) he painted his own version (pp. 368/369). It has the lushness of the earthly paradise that he perceived in his new home at Les Collettes, in Cagnes. The house was surrounded by olive groves and a country setting that he thought eternal. His maid Gabrielle posed as one of the three Graces (on the right). The other two were his favourite models of the period, Georgette Pigeot, and the model nicknamed "the Baker's Wife". An actor was supposed to represent Paris. But Renoir preferred to use Gabrielle, with whom he felt more at ease. He dressed her up in a Phrygian cap. "See how like a boy she looks!" he told Vollard. "I have always wanted to paint a Paris and had never before found the right model. What luck!" Renoir had painted an initial version of his *Judgement of Paris* in 1908, in which Venus holds out her hand to receive the golden apple (p. 472). In the final version, painted in 1913 and now in Hiroshima (pp. 368/369), Venus opens her arms wide and displays her beauty *au naturel* to Paris, the judge, as well as to anyone lucky enough to see the painting. The *Venus Victorious* pose served as the basis for *Venus Victrix* (p. 475), the sculpture that Guino later produced under Renoir's direction. Guino also sculpted a bas-relief of *The Judgement of Paris* (p. 473), showing the significance that Renoir attached to the painting. It would finally demonstrate to all and sundry that he had become a totally committed "classicist".

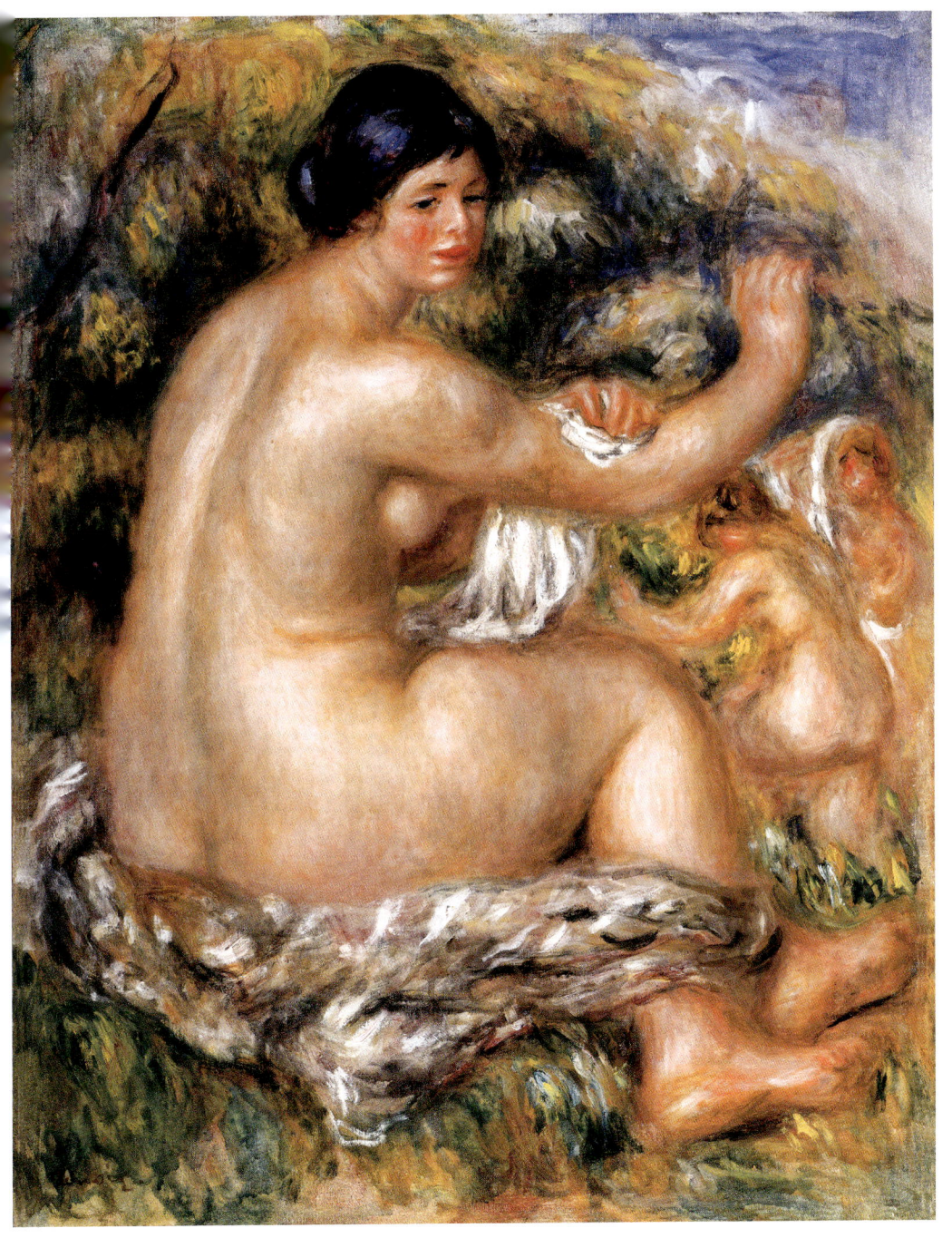

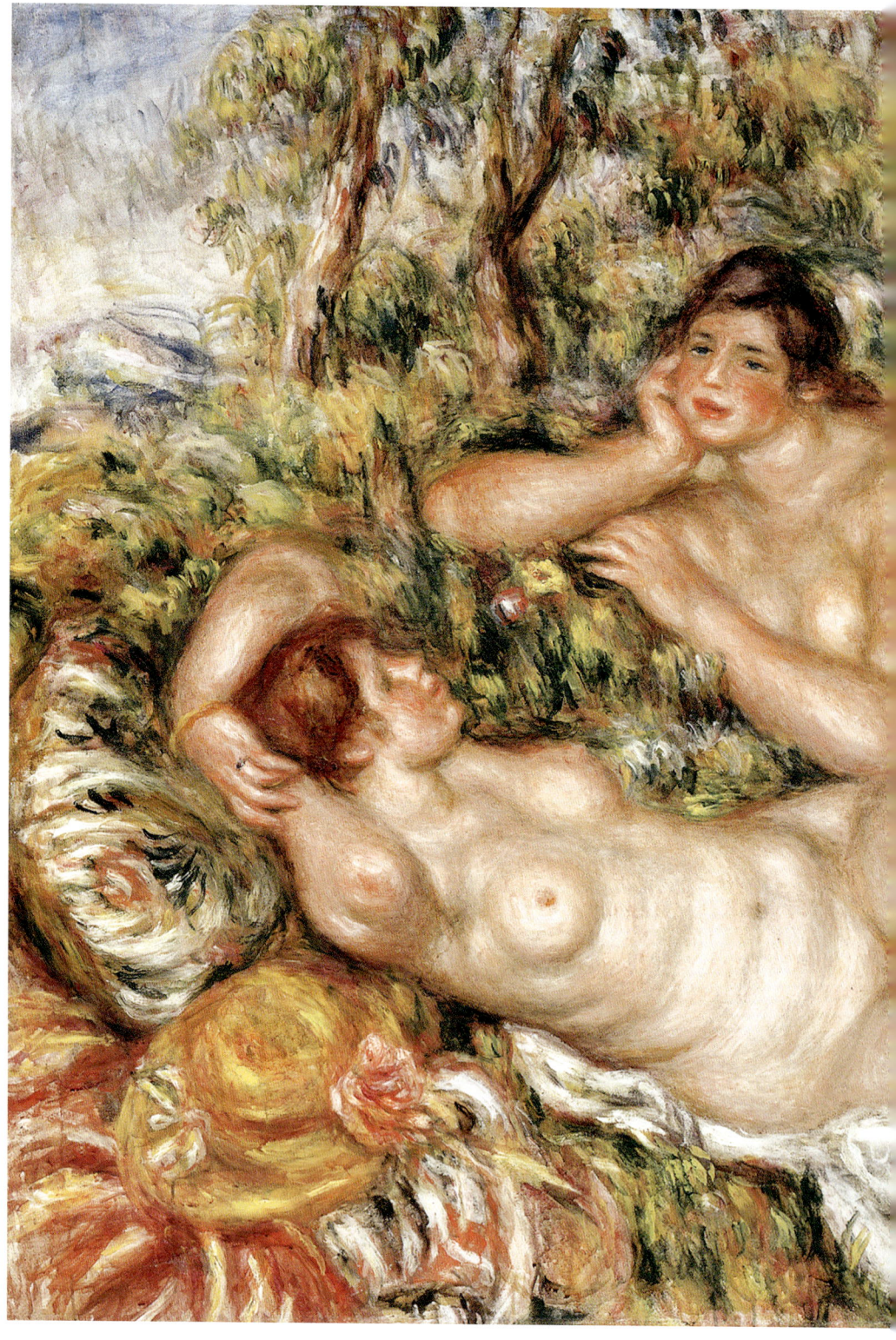

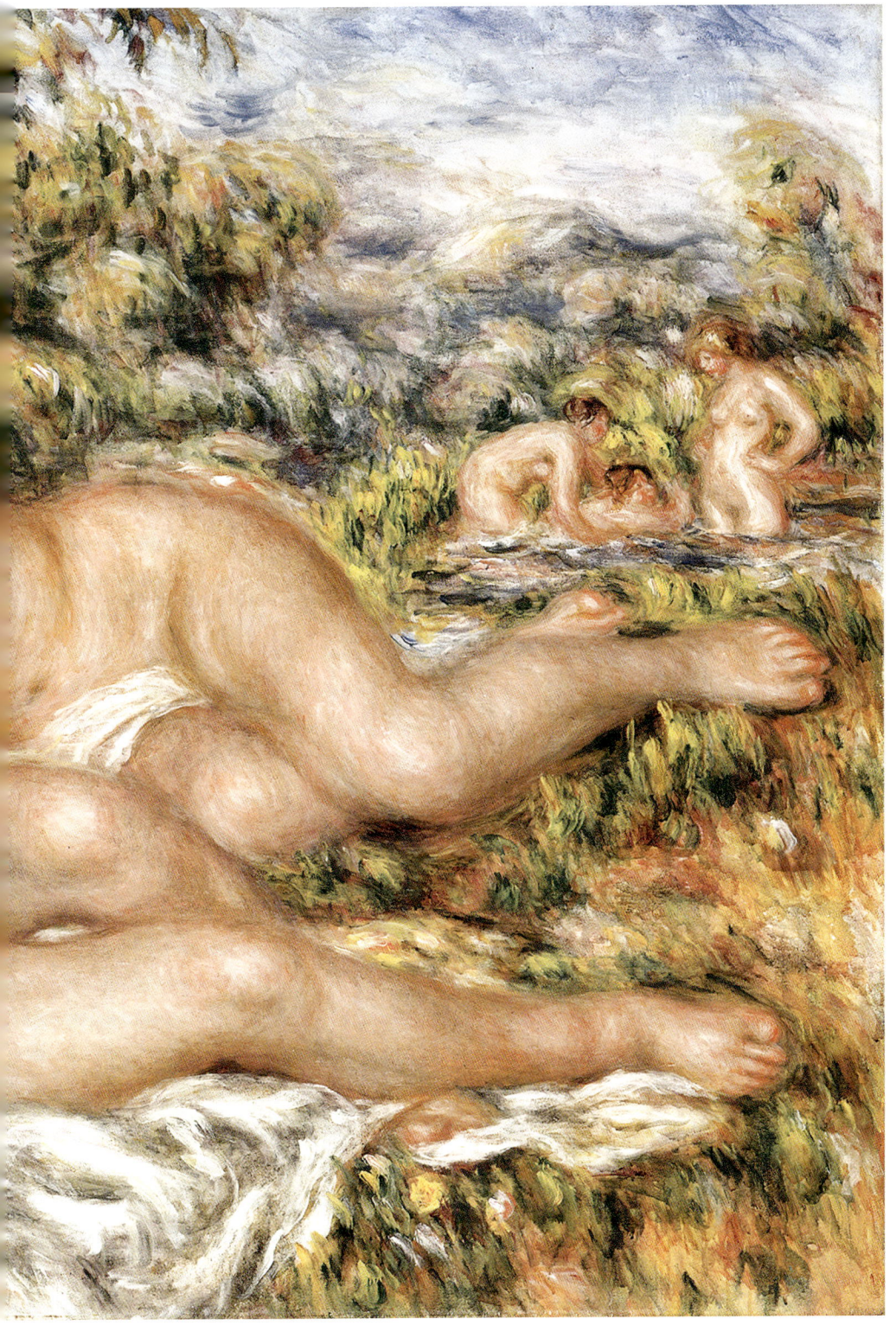

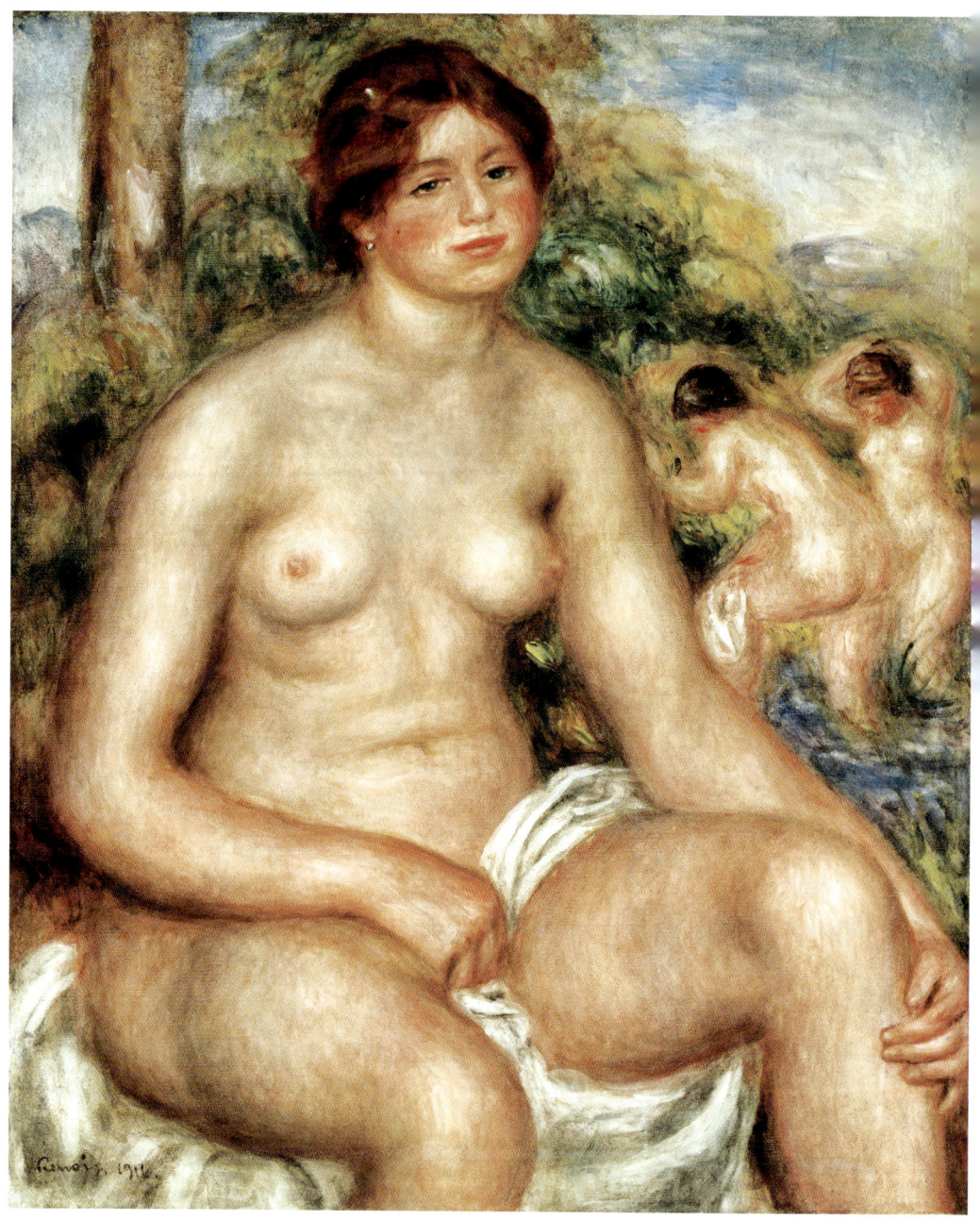

Jean-Honoré Fragonard
The Bathers, before 1756
Oil on canvas,
64 x 80 cm (25¼ x 31½ in.)
Paris, Musée du Louvre

Seated Bather, 1914
Oil on canvas,
81.1 x 67.2 cm (32 x 26½ in.)
The Art Institute of Chicago,
Mr. and Mrs. Lewis Larned
Coburn Endowment

PAGES 382/383
Bathing Group, 1916
Oil on canvas,
73.5 x 92.5 cm (29 x 36½ in.)
Philadelphia,
The Barnes Foundation

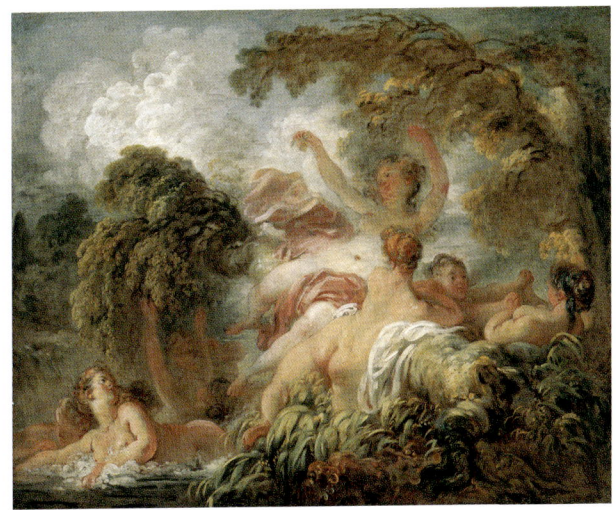

Renoir's pictorial confession of faith is huge. *Rest after a Bath*, which he completed in the year of his death (pp. 378/379). The *Seated Bather*, painted in 1914 (p. 380), represents his final preparatory step. It combines a monumental figure covering the whole canvas with a small group of bathers on the right. *The Bathers* is the ultimate expression of his most important theme, the female nude in a landscape, which he had first confronted thirty years previously in his Ingres-inspired *The Bathers* of 1887. Jean Renoir said of the *Bathers* that his father "considered them to be the climax. He thought that they summarised the research he had been conducting throughout his life and that they would also be a good springboard for his future research."

Albert André recorded the delight expressed by the aged Renoir when he spoke of his last *Bathers* painted in the Midi. "Look at the light on those olive trees, shining like diamonds, pink, then blue … and the sky playing across it", Renoir exclaimed. "It's enough to drive you mad. And those mountains over there that go past with the clouds. The whole thing looks like a Watteau background. Oh, and just look at that breast! Could it be sweeter or heavier? And the lovely golden fold just below it. You could go down on one's knees and worship it. If there were no such thing as breasts, I don't think I would ever have bothered painting figures at all".

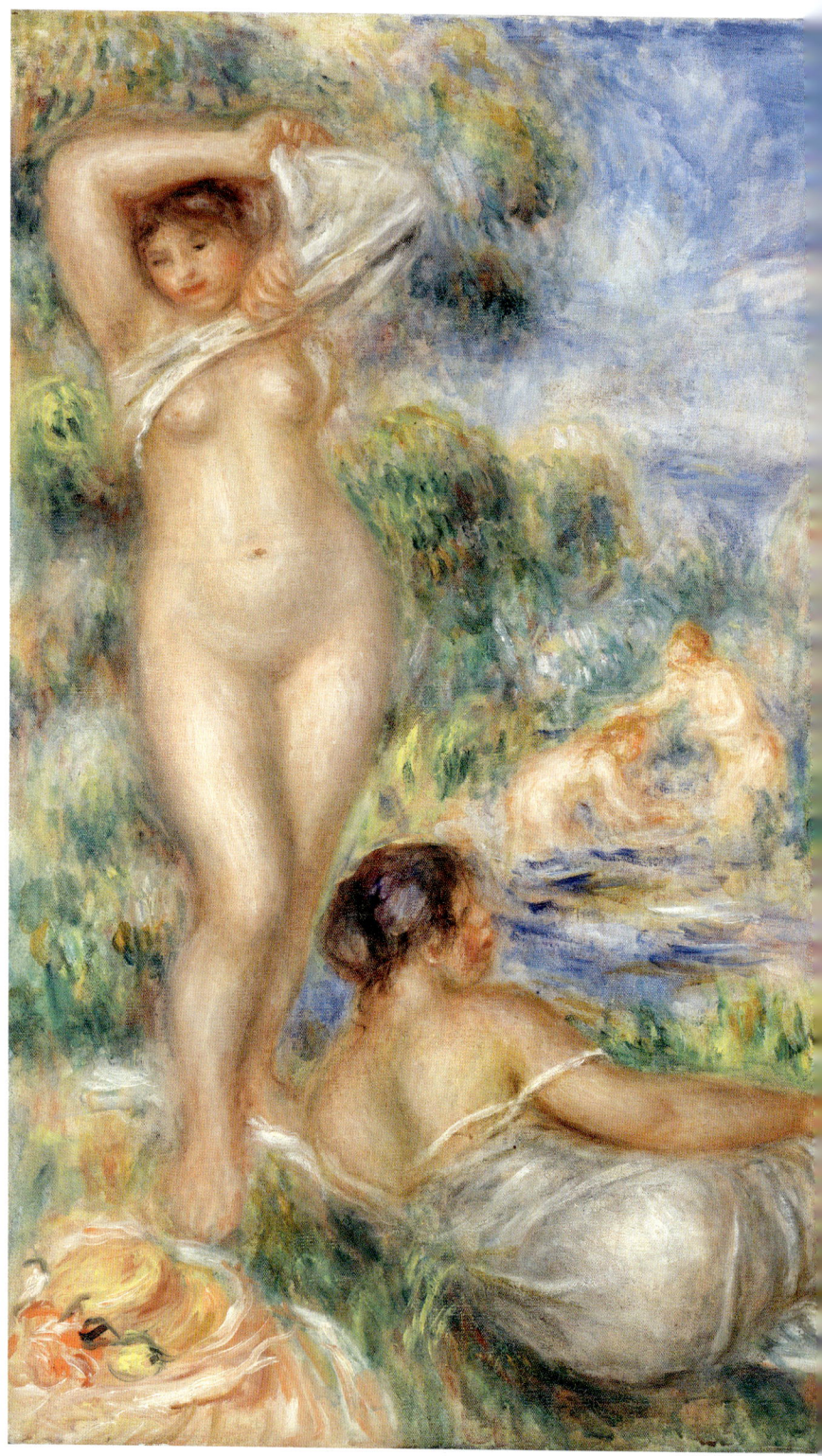

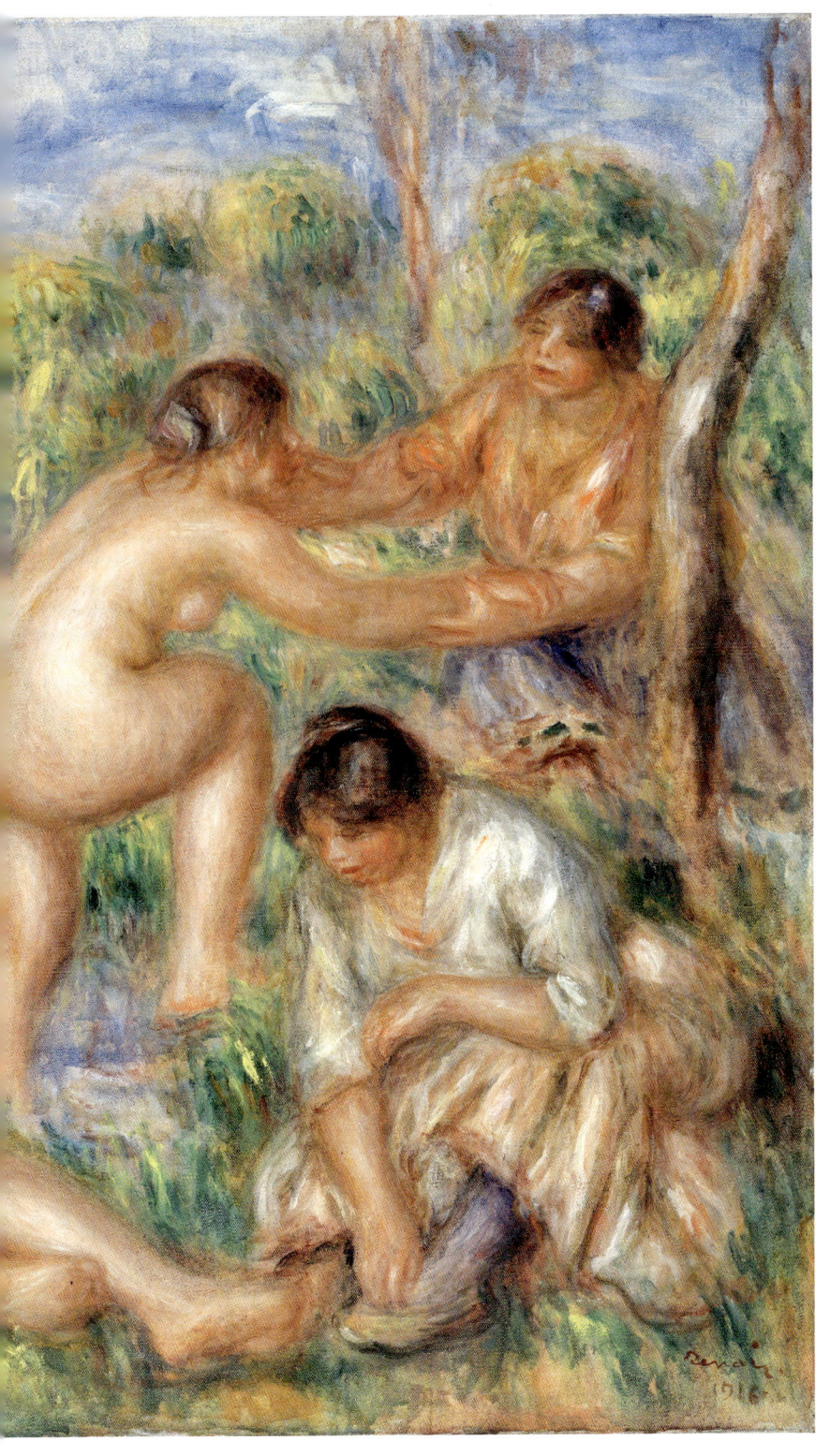

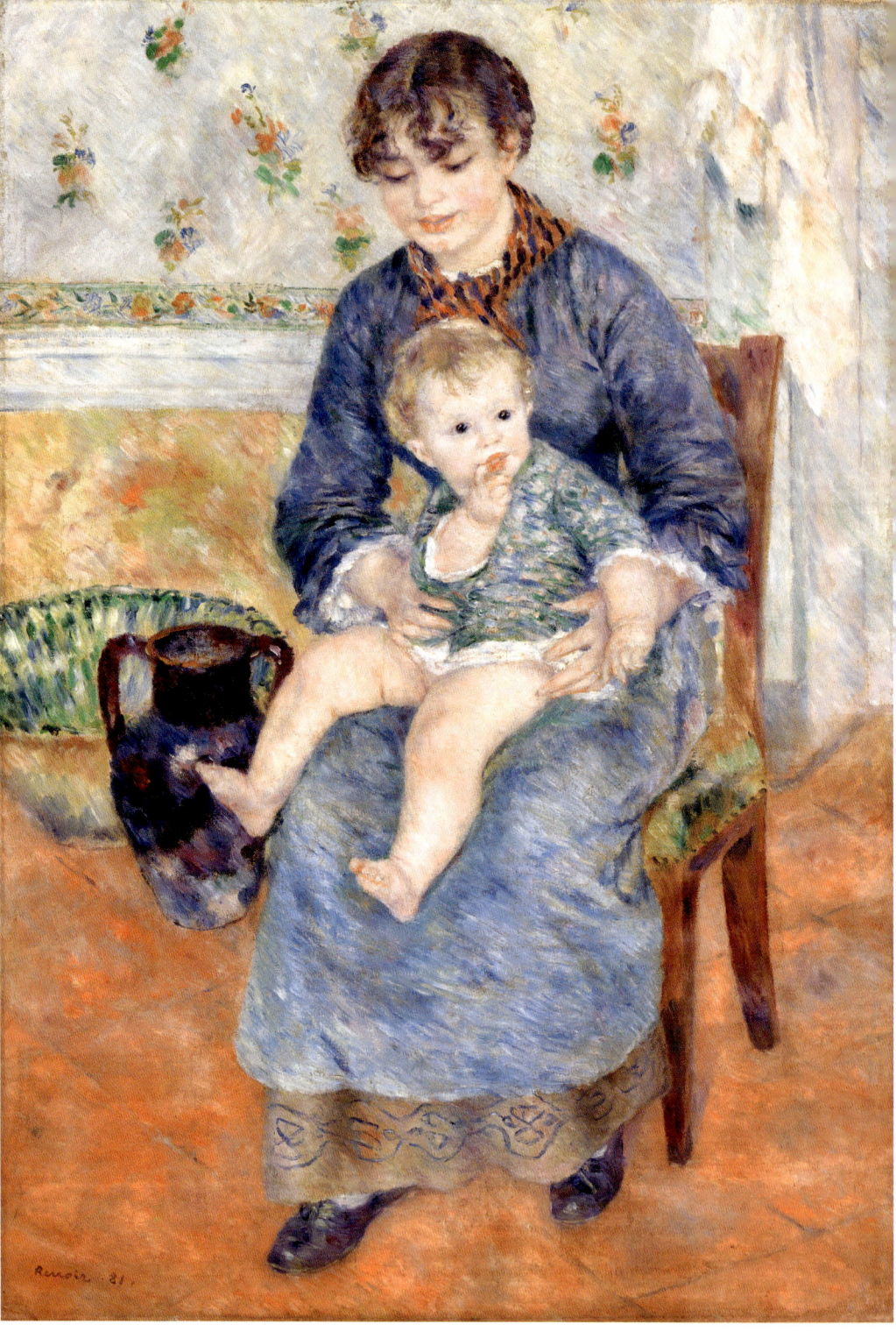

Baby Jesus and His Nanny
1876–1910

"My father's transition from bachelorhood to the status of a married man was more important, in my opinion, than any of the theories. He had always been restless and incapable
of staying put. One moment he was leaping into a train in the vague hope of enjoying the
filtered light on Guernsey, and the next he was losing himself in the pink reflections of
Blida. He had forgotten what it was like to have a home ever since he had left his parents'
house in the Rue des Gravilliers. All of a sudden, he found himself sharing an apartment
with a woman. There were meals at regular times, a nicely made bed, and his socks were
darned. To add to all of these advantages the arrival of a child, my brother Pierre, must
have caused a huge revolution in my father's life. The theories he heard expounded at the
Nouvelle Athènes café paled into insignificance beside the sight of a crease in the baby's
thigh. He started frantically drawing his son and, faithful to his own preoccupations,
attempted to render the look and feel of velvety, barely-formed skin. Renoir had rebaptised
his external world." Jean Renoir describes the birth of his elder brother, the future actor
Pierre, as an event that marked a turning point in his father's work. Vollard puts it in similar terms. "Another important aspect of Renoir's work is his studies of his children. These
'subjects' had fat, rosy cheeks from suckling at their mother's breast. If they had been fed by
a wet-nurse or from a bottle, like the rich children he painted on commission at the time,
they would have hardly moved him to take up his paintbrush."

Renoir's passion for the female form was only equalled by the tenderness he felt
towards the grace and freshness of children. He must have been overcome with

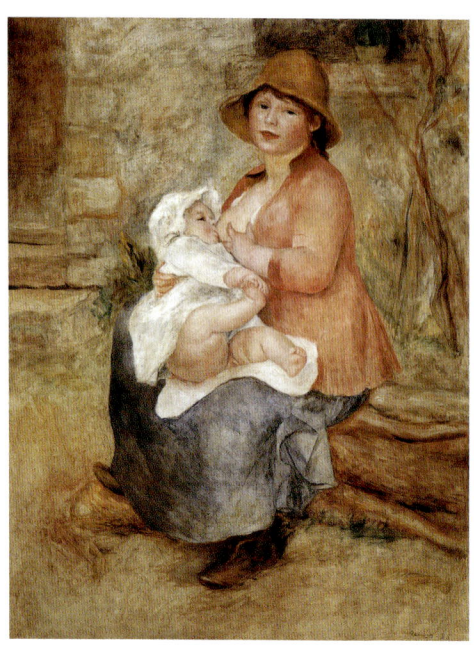

**Maternity – Baby at the Breast
(Aline and Her Son Pierre)**, first version, 1885
Oil on canvas, 92 x 72 cm (36¼ x 28⅜ in.)
Paris, Musée d'Orsay

**Mother Nursing Her Child
(Aline Charigot and Pierre)**, 1886
Oil on canvas, 74 x 54 cm (29¼ x 21¼ in.)
Private collection

emotion when he was able, for the first time, to paint both the woman he loved and their son. *Baby at the Breast*, also known as *Maternity* and *Mother Nursing Her Child* (pp. 386 and 387), which exists in numerous versions, is one of the tenderest renditions of the theme of mother and child. "Every woman who breastfeeds a child is a Raphael Virgin", the painter exclaimed, delighted at the way in which the line of Aline's breast and nipple was recalled in Pierre's hip and thigh. It was the perfect subject matter: Renoir could now combine family intimacy and eternity in his compositions. He remembered the pleasure he had derived from Raphael's *Virgin with a Chair* (at the Pitti Palace in Florence), which he described as "the most liberated, balanced, simple and living painting that you can imagine, arms and legs with real flesh, and what a touching expression of material tenderness!" Renoir, filled with the joys of fatherhood, excelled in capturing the child's most familiar gestures: he proudly shows his first son catching hold of his foot, as all babies do.

Maternity or *Mother Nursing Her Child* is a transposition of the *Blonde Bather* (p. 338). The model and pose are the same and so is the pyramidal shape of the monumental composition. Renoir painted a series of masterpieces that showed the woman of his life, first as the archetype of youthful beauty unveiled, then as a young mother inviting us to share her joy, and then again abandoning herself to the rustic pleasures of a *Dance in the Country* (p. 287). Like Rembrandt before him, Renoir displayed his wife's charms to all. After Aline's death in 1915, he produced a bronze sculpture

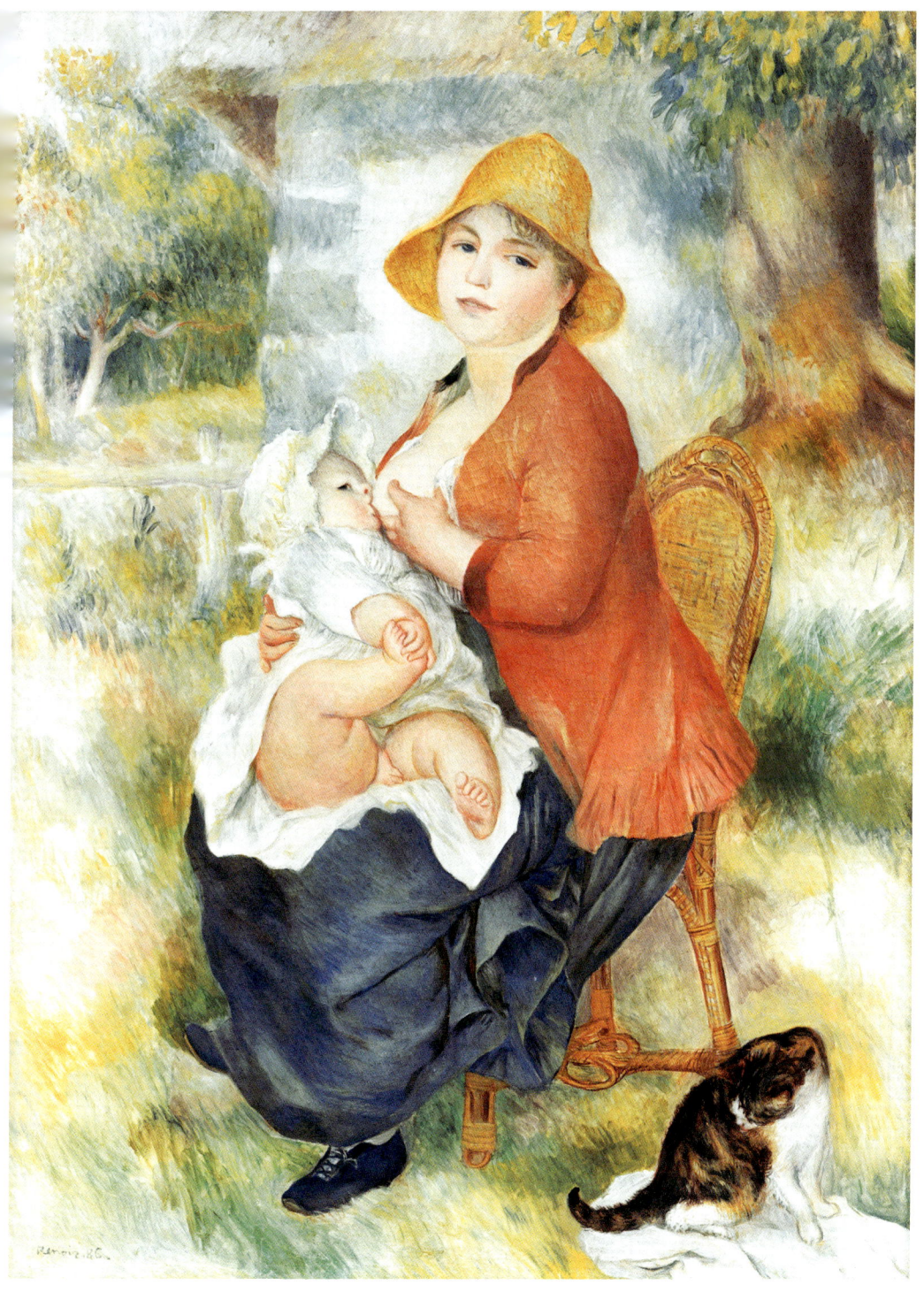

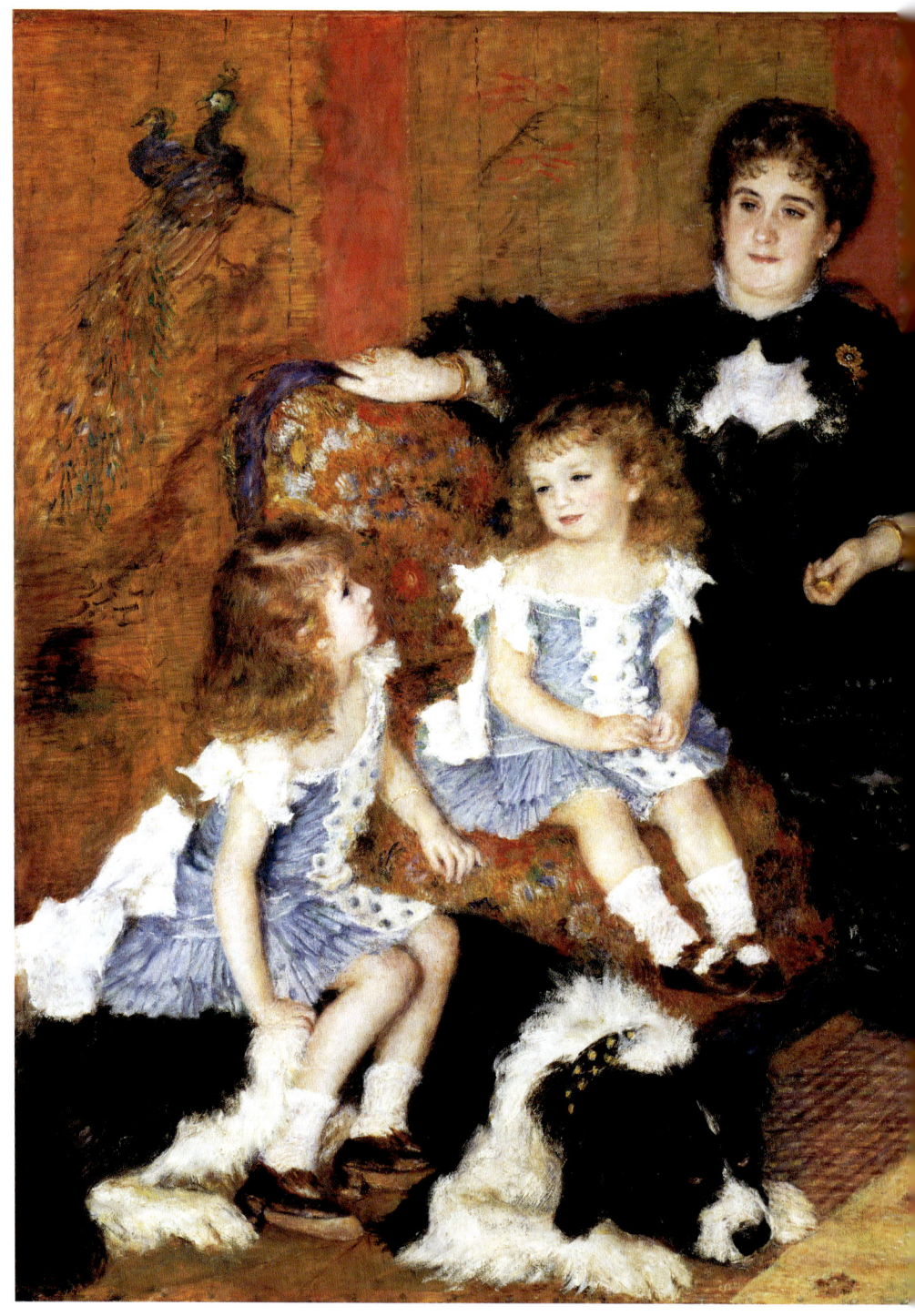

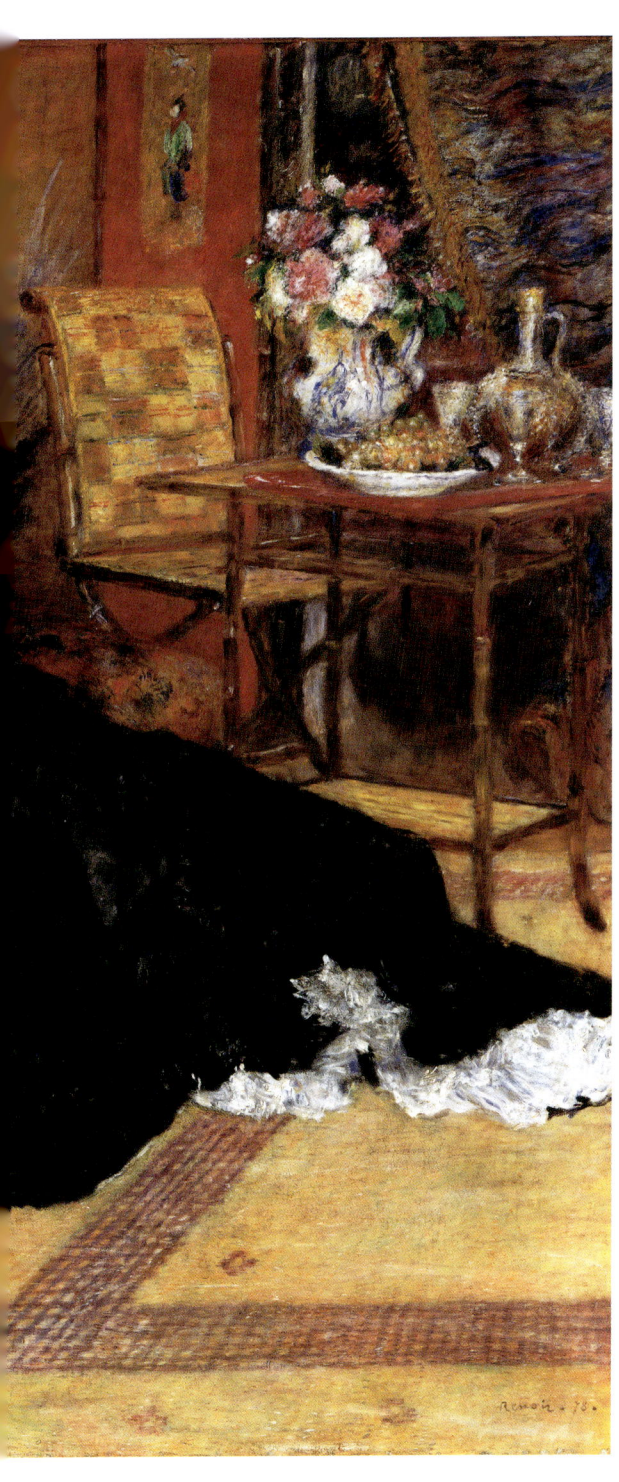

**Madame Charpentier and
Her Children**, 1878
Oil on canvas,
153.7 x 190.2 cm (60½ x 75 in.)
New York, The Metropolitan Museum
of Art, Catharine Lorillard Wolfe
Collection, Wolfe Fund

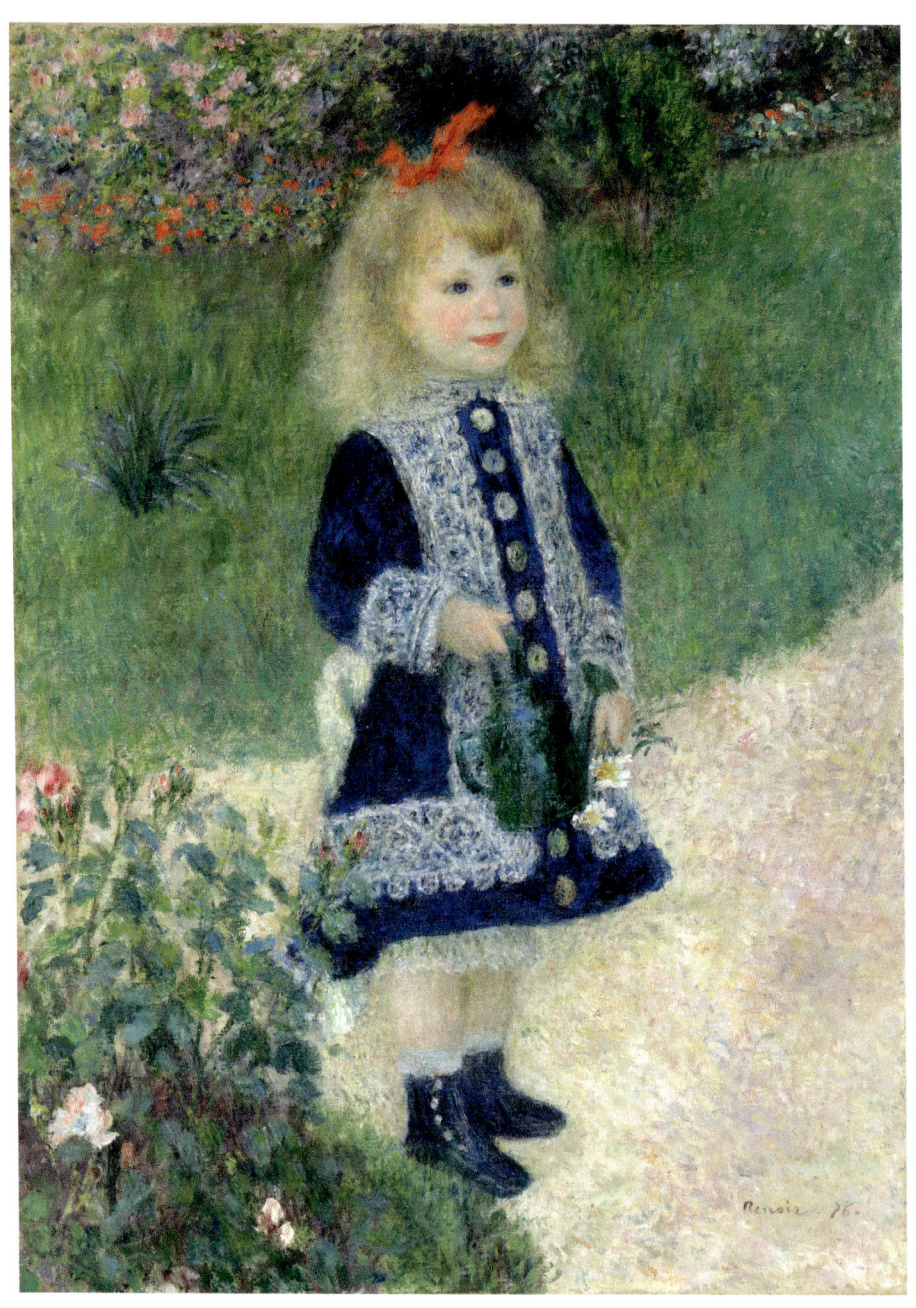

A Girl with a Watering Can, 1876
Oil on canvas, 100 x 73 cm (39¼ x 28¾ in.)
Washington, D.C., National Gallery of Art,
Chester Dale Collection

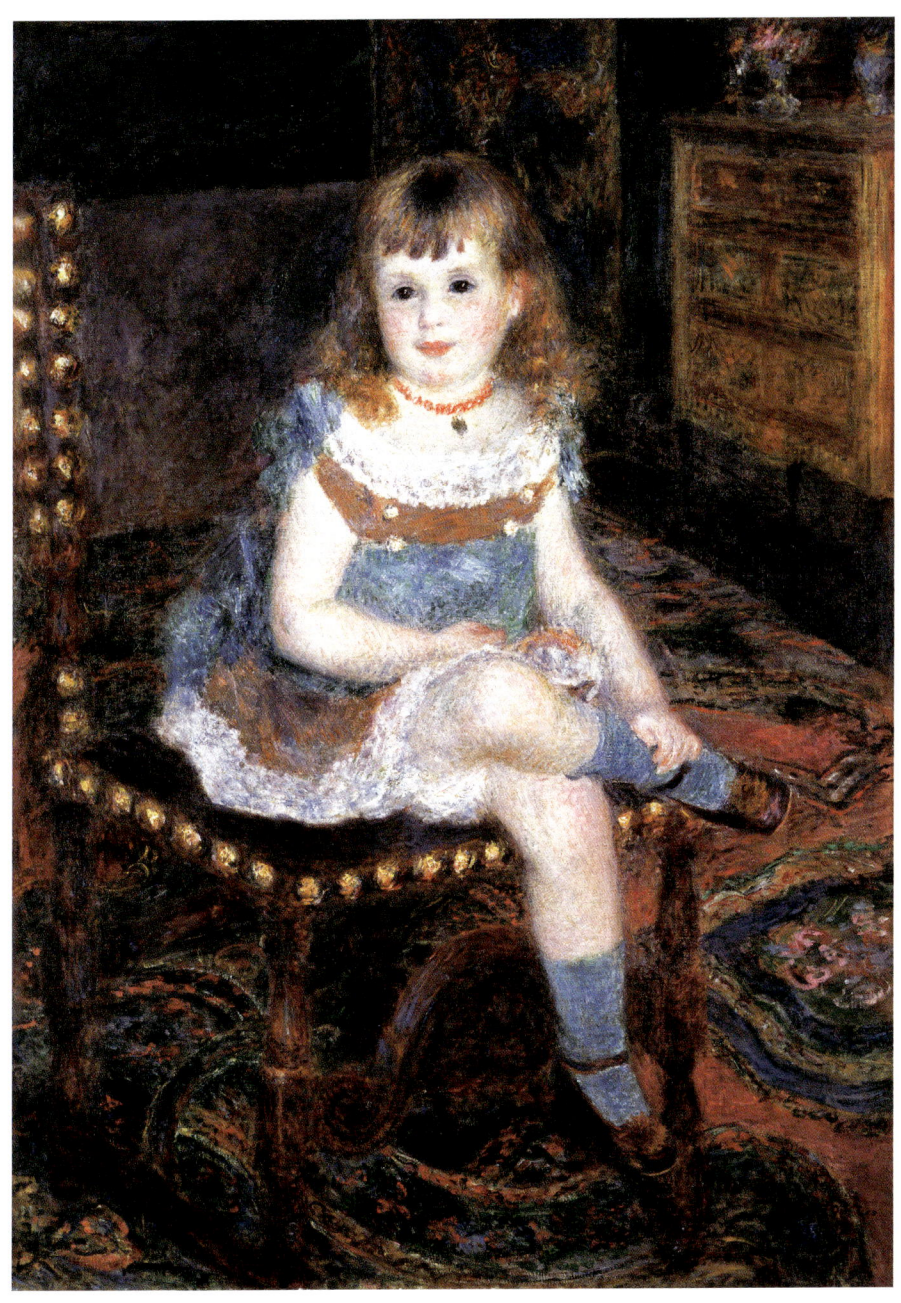

Mademoiselle Georgette Charpentier Seated, 1876
Oil on canvas, 97.8 x 70.8 cm (38⅝ x 27⅞ in.)
Tokyo, Artizon Museum,
Ishibashi Foundation

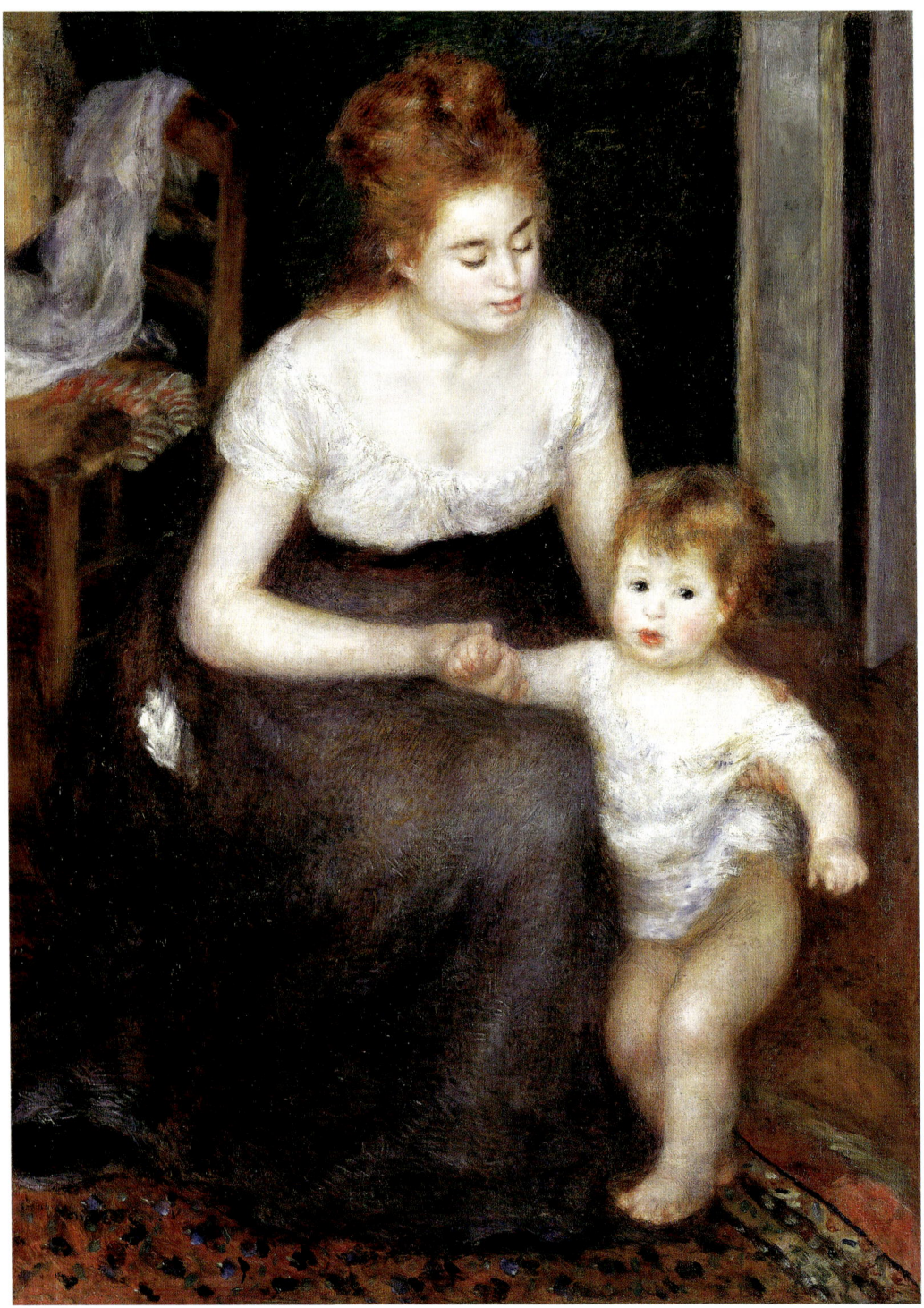

Peter Paul Rubens
**Helena Fourment with
Her Eldest Son, Frans**, c. 1632
Oil on wood, 145 x 102 cm (57 x 40¼ in.)
Munich, Bayerische Staatsgemälde-
sammlungen, Alte Pinakothek

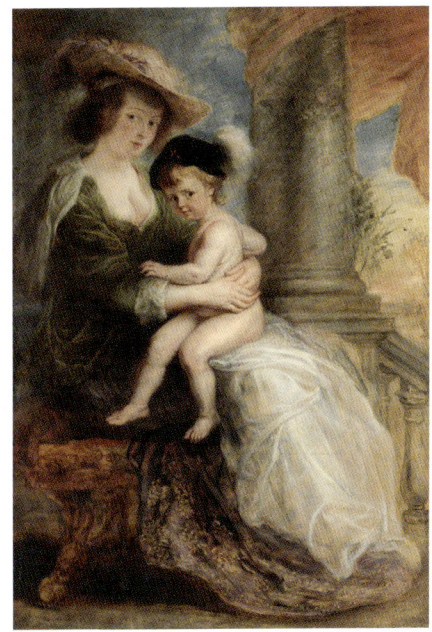

The First Step, 1876
Oil on canvas,
111 x 80.5 cm (43¾ x 31¾ in.)
Private collection

of this moment of happiness with the help of Richard Guino. He intended to decorate his grave with it.

Rubens similarly painted his young wife, *Helena Fourment with Her Eldest Son, Frans* (p. 393), representing her pink and fresh in a large hat that matched the roundness of her face. This intimate work reveals the true Rubens, who uses brushwork and palette to render fresh, tender gentleness. Renoir had already copied Rubens's portraits (*Helena Fourment with Her Children*), and he considered Hélène of Antwerp, "who was far more beautiful than Helen of Troy", to be Aline's alter ego across the centuries. Both painters see in their wives an exalted myth of feminine beauty at its most provocative. Renoir depicted child-women, luscious odalisques, and affectionate mothers in turn. Just as two parallel lines intersect in infinity, so Rubens and Renoir both come in their late periods to produce unrestrained and highly imaginative paintings. It is no coincidence that, like Rubens, Renoir painted *The Judgement of Paris* (pp. 362 and 368/369). Their Three Graces are huge amphoral offerings to fertile motherhood. Neither painter is disturbed by the eroticism of these naked bodies but indulges a keen appetite for shape, colour, and light. They present heavenly delights and gardens of love to the Graces, who show their nudity like an offering on the altar of nature.

In his delightful book about Renoir's portraits of children Michel Robida, Madame Charpentier's great-nephew, elegantly defined this aspect of the artist's work. "Renoir

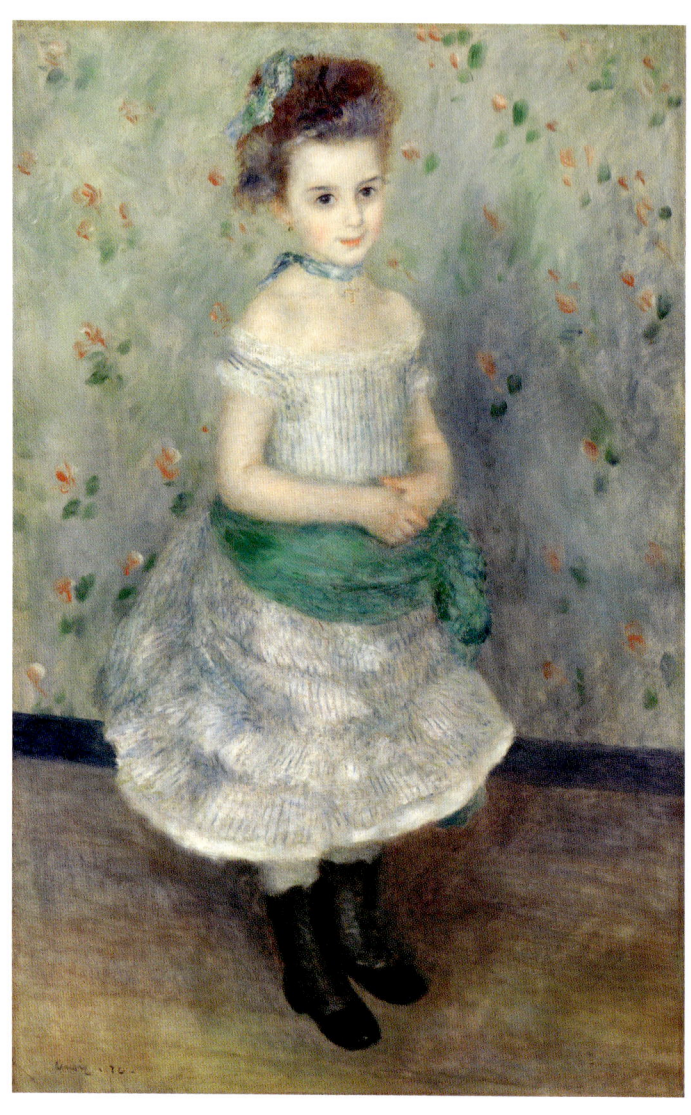

Portrait of Jeanne Durand-Ruel, 1876
Oil on canvas, 114 x 74 cm (45 x 29¼ in.)
Philadelphia, The Barnes Foundation

La Promenade, c. 1875/76
Oil on canvas, 170.2 x 108.3 cm (67 x 42¾ in.)
New York, The Frick Collection

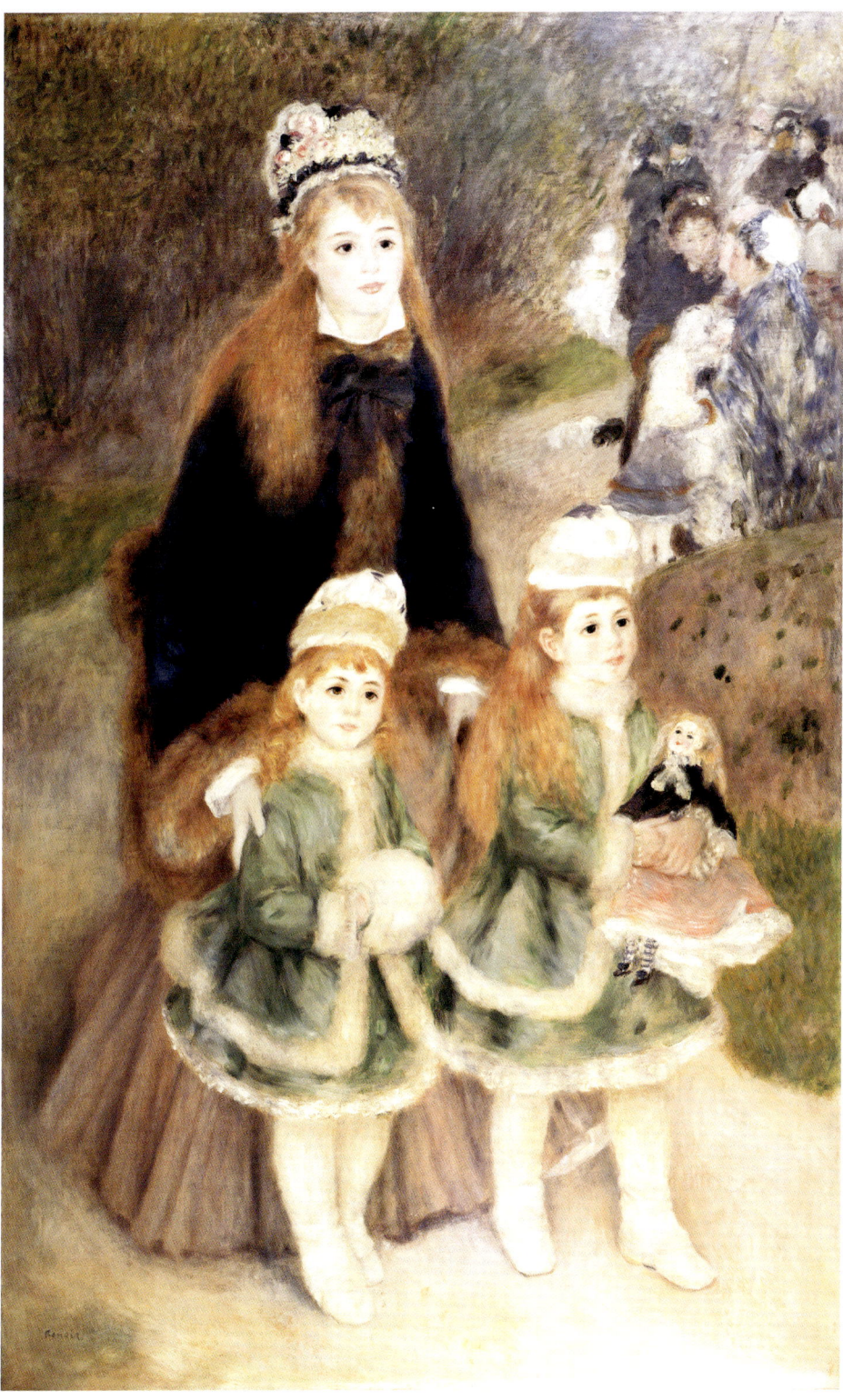

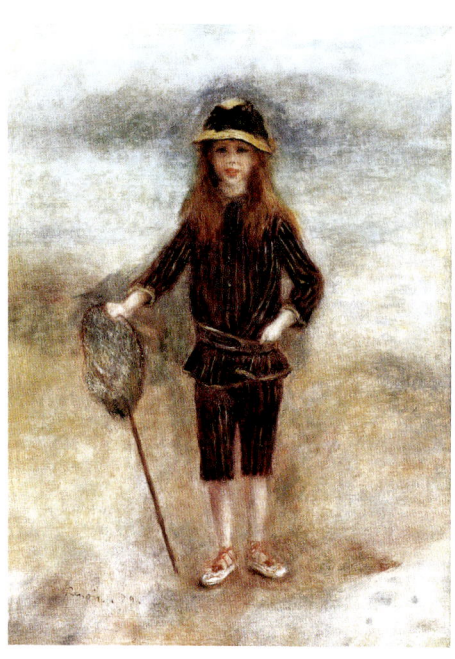

loved painting beautiful human beings", he observed. "That is why his portraits of children are so moving. He had the art of gathering children around him. The difficulty of making them remain still did not deter him. He was so agile with his brushes that he immediately captured their pose. Things did not always go smoothly between painter and model. Sometimes the child arrived in a sullen mood, bored, and determined to try the artist's patience. Renoir used flattery, stories, and exciting promises to win them over. He was always proud of his victory. From some of the portraits of children, such as those of the Cahen d'Anvers children, *Alice and Elisabeth Cahen d'Anvers* (p. 406), one can guess that Renoir was forced to accept his models just as their middle-class mothers had brought them to him: dressed in their best clothes, carefully washed and combed. In other studies of children, especially his own, Renoir had his models look untidy and dressed in their everyday clothes. He reproduced everything that he had in common with the child; this meant above naturalness and spontaneity. Renoir had a horror of everything that was prim and proper, stiff and unnatural. He disliked gardens that were too carefully maintained, preferring them to look slightly abandoned. At Les Collettes, his sons were allowed to trample on the lawns and climb the trees at will. Children for him were not just shapes and colours; he was interested in their natures. 'Women and children behave in the same way', he would say. 'Both are impulsive and obey their instinct alone. What makes them so dangerous is their power of seduction.'"

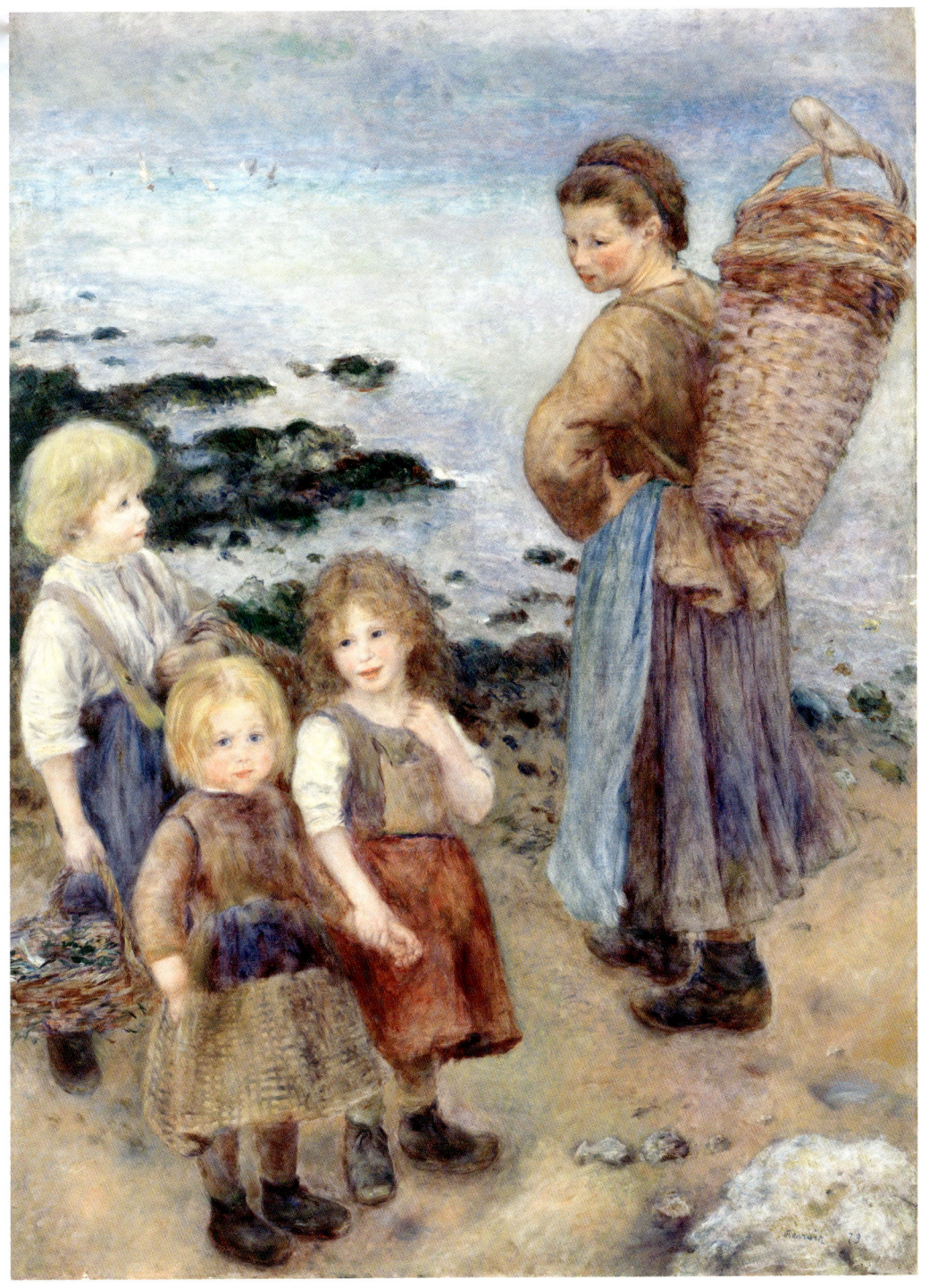

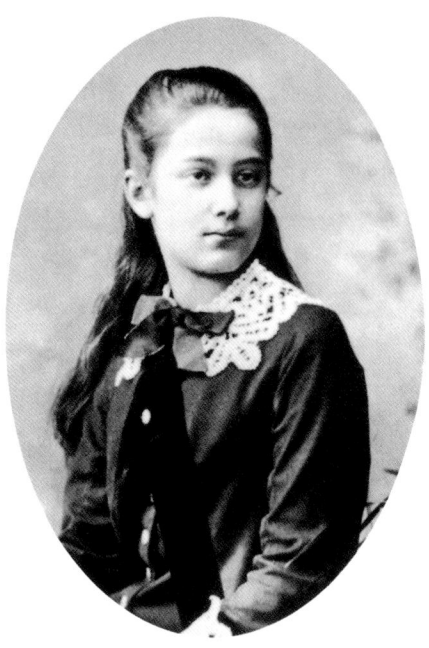

Thérèse Bérard, 1879

Thérèse Bérard, 1879
Oil on canvas, 55.9 x 46.8 cm (22 x 18½ in.)
Williamstown, Massachusetts, The Clark

PAGES 400/401
Sketches of Heads (The Bérard Children), 1881
Oil on canvas, 62.6 x 81.9 cm (24¾ x 32¼ in.)
Williamstown, Massachusetts, The Clark

Marcel Proust describes the famous portrait of *Madame Charpentier and Her Children* (pp. 388/389) in *Time Regained*, the final part of *In Search of Lost Time.* The success of the painting at the 1878 Salon launched Renoir's career. Proust considered it to be the most perfect evocation of its time. "Will not posterity, when it looks at our time," he asked, "find the poetry of an elegant home and beautifully dressed women in the drawing-room of the publisher Charpentier as painted by Renoir, rather than in the portraits of the Princesse de Sagan or the Comtesse de la Rochefoucauld by Cot or Chaplin?" The portrait of *Madame Charpentier and Her Children* was a milestone in more senses than one. It was a quintessentially Impressionist Renoir masterpiece, an artistic and financial success, and – last but not least – it was the Trojan horse in which Renoir entered the world of the wealthy middle classes. The lower class inner-city boy, who put on no airs and graces and befriended seamstresses and laundresses at the Moulin de la Galette, now mixed with Protestant and Jewish financiers and played by the arcane rules of old boy networks. Renoir felt at ease in this refined milieu, which promised him the new models and clients he sought. He was able to show a side of himself hitherto unexpressed. Marcel Proust knew Madame Charpentier and considered her to be a "ridiculous little bourgeoise". But he marvelled at the painting, which he considered "comparable to the most beautiful Titians". He explained what had happened to Renoir: "The artist may paint anything in the world that he chooses, but when beauty is awakened within him, the model for that elegance in which he will

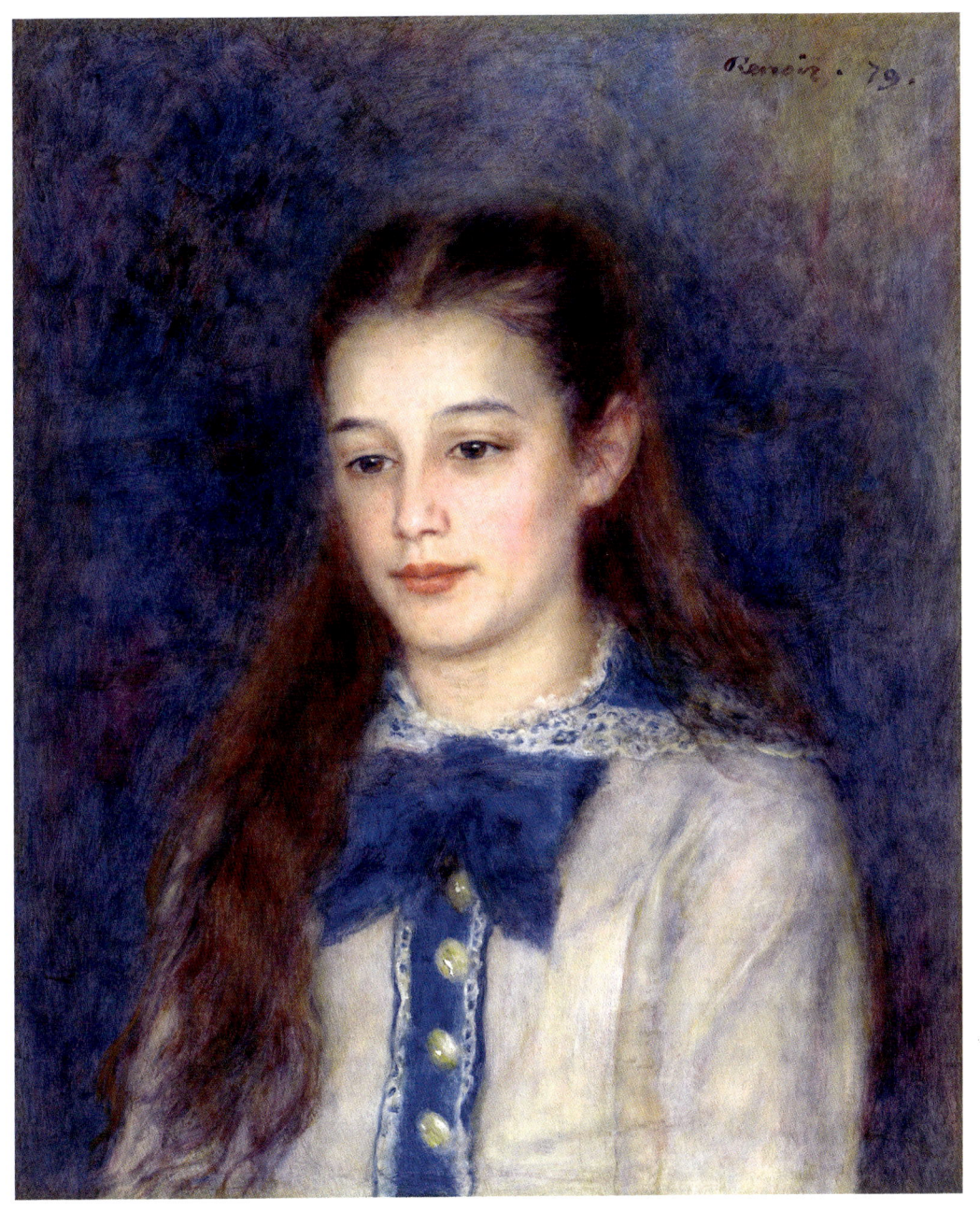

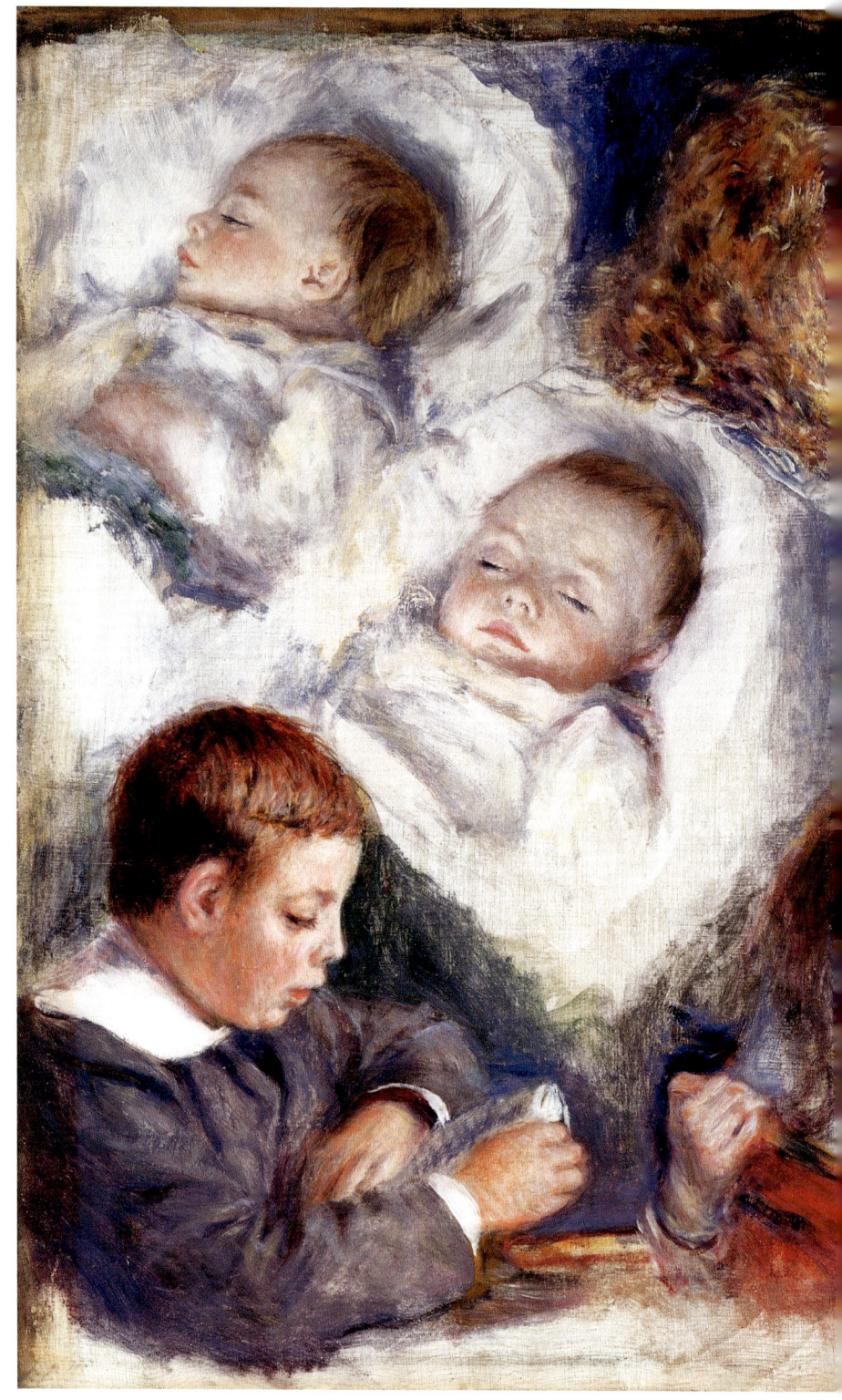

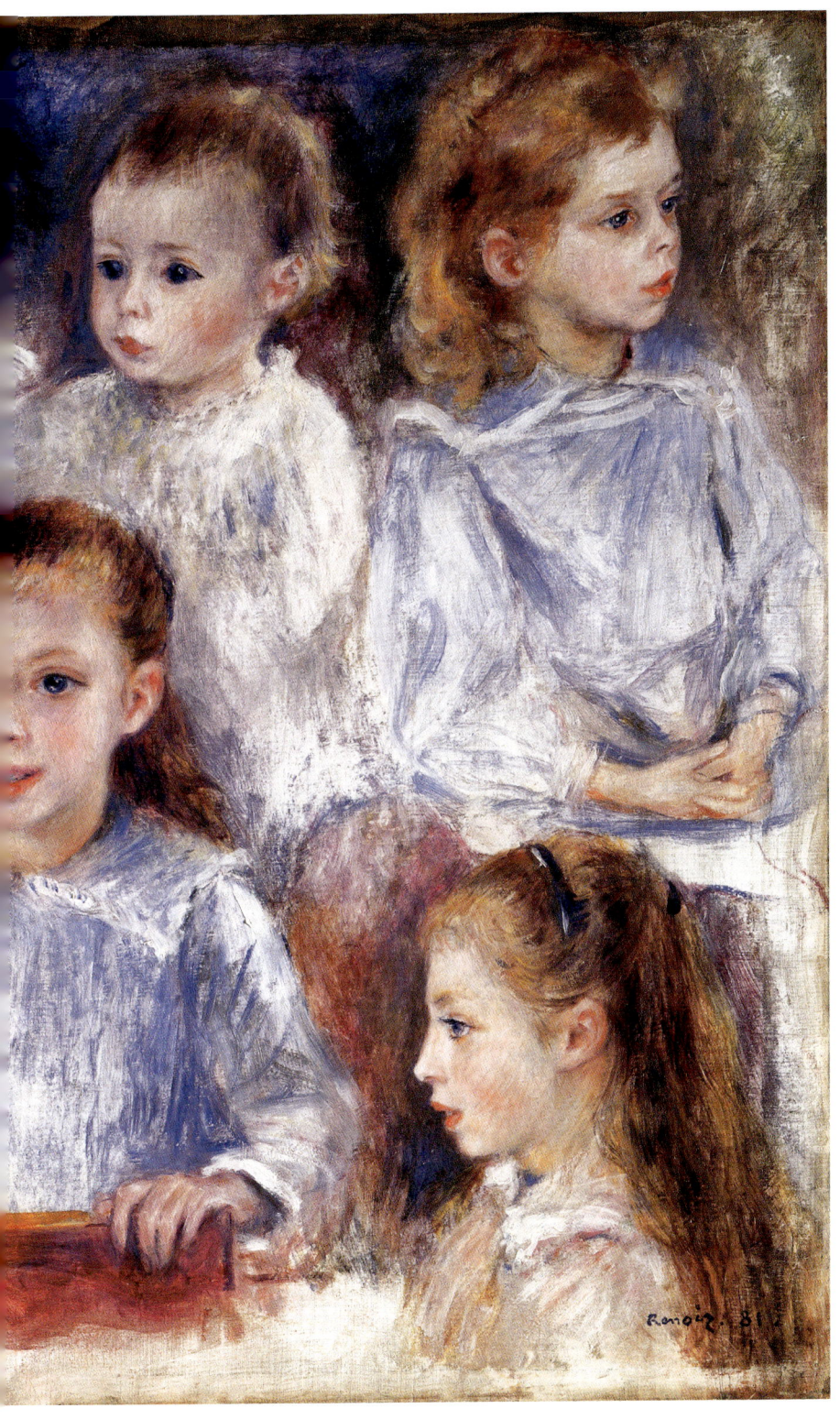

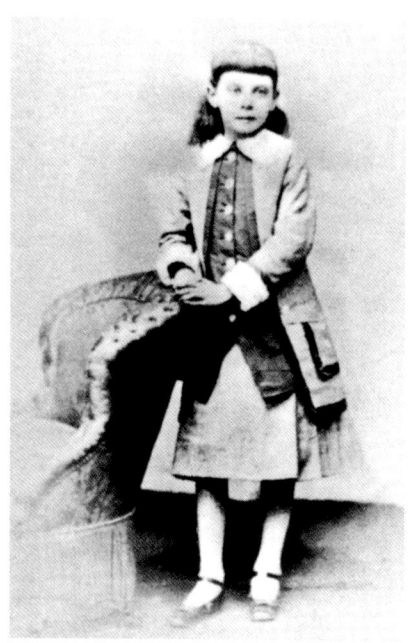

Marthe Bérard in 1879

Portrait of Marthe Bérard, 1879
Oil on canvas,
131 x 77 cm (51⅝ x 30⅜ in.)
Museu de Arte de São Paulo,
Assis Chateaubriand

find themes of beauty will be provided for him by people a little slightly richer than
he is himself, in whose house he will find what is not normally to be seen in the studio
of an unrecognised man of genius selling his canvases for fifty francs: a drawing-room,
with chairs and sofas covered in old brocades, an abundance of lamps, beautiful flowers, beautiful fruit, beautiful dresses." A detail in Renoir's painting shows his interest in
the décor, which he reproduces "without moving a single item of furniture", and also
his skill at being able to paint (like Velázquez) several paintings in one. There are two
lovely children with their dog, a portrait of a society woman in a magnificent dress,
and a rich still life. Despite his snobbery about the petty bourgeoisie, of whom the
Charpentiers were members, Proust nevertheless recognised the enormous importance of the role such people played in the discovery of little-known geniuses whom
they encouraged and supported.

Little children, whether rich or poor, delighted Renoir as they do the viewer of his
paintings. They are a key to the charm of his work. In the company of children he
became a child himself. He forgot all his theories and instinctively placed his technique at their service. "He took exquisite care and attention", wrote Arsène Alexandre
in 1892, "to depict the limpid, merry eyes of a child, the red mouths of women, and
the bright harmony of flowers. All of these go very well together. He always thought
he could draw with more suppleness, find still softer colours, and produce enamels
that looked even more alive. When he modelled these fragile things, he tried to

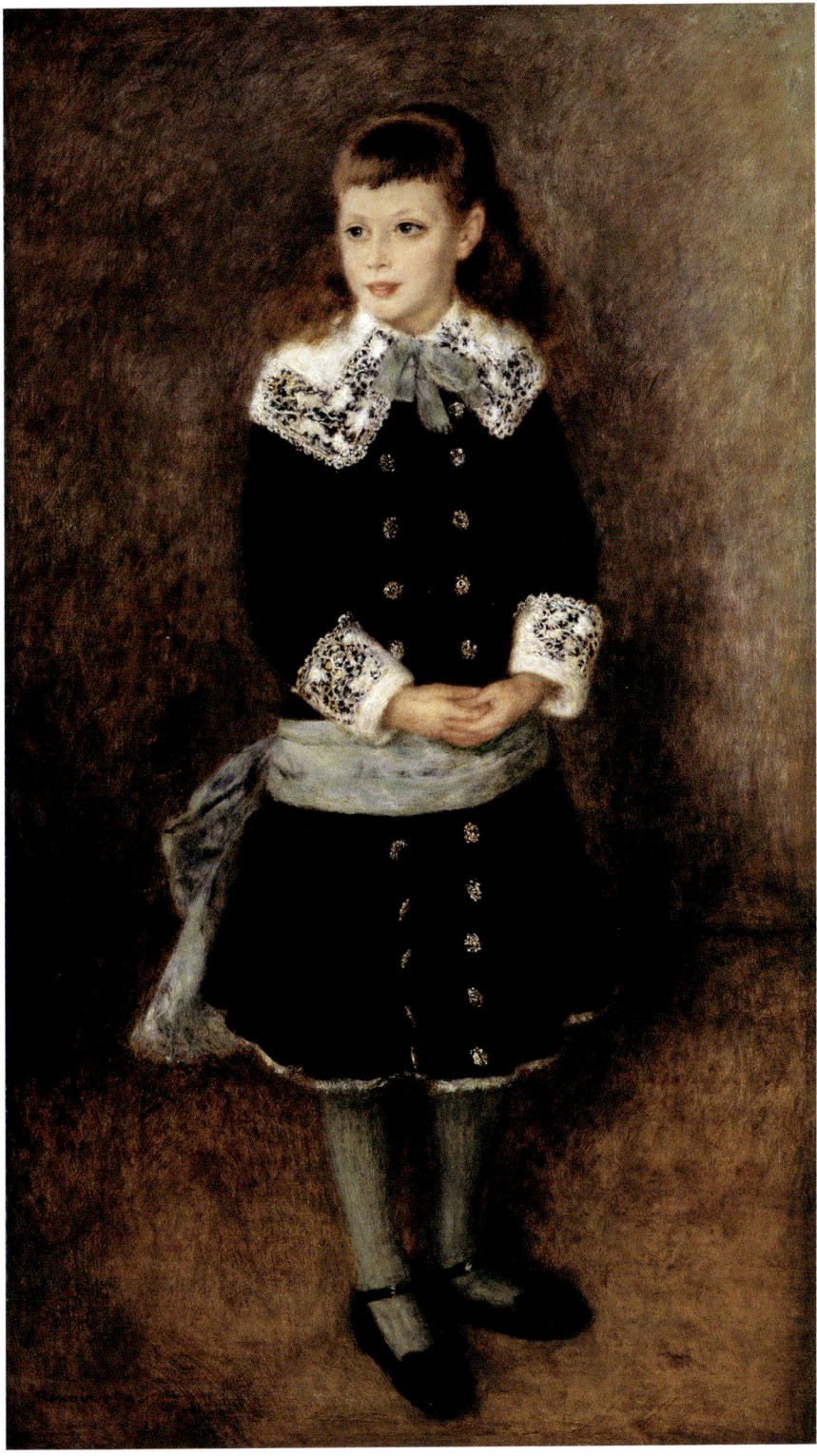

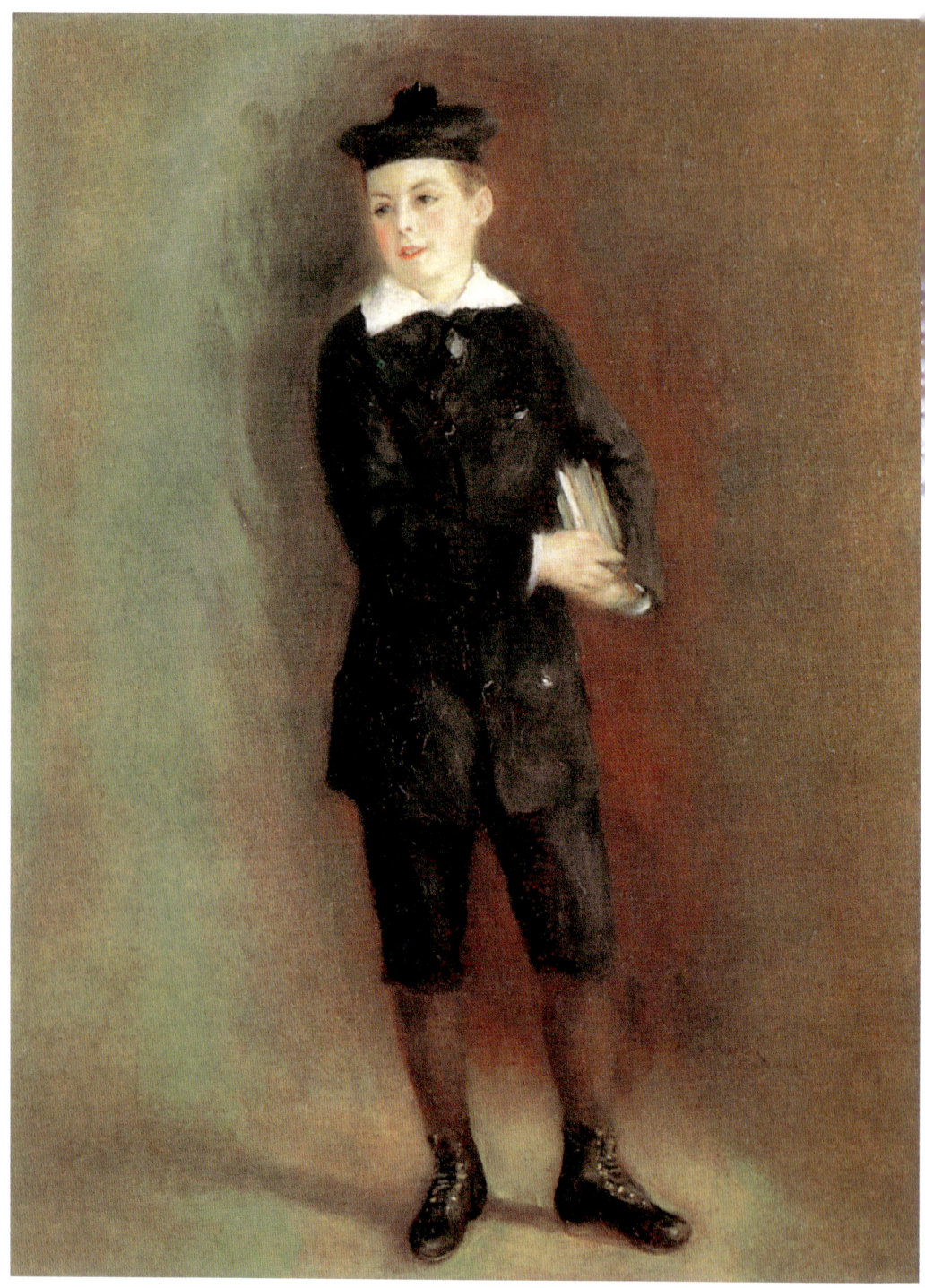

André Bérard, c. 1880

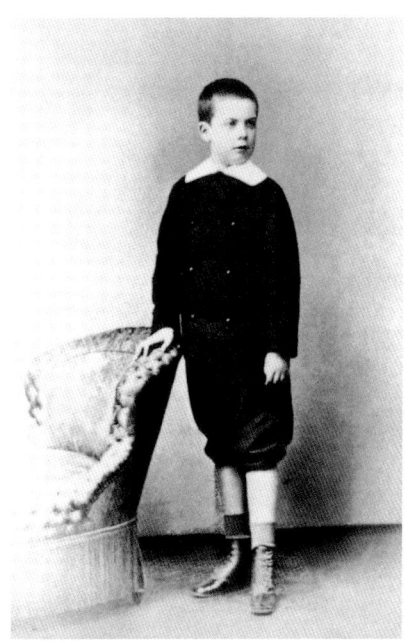

The Schoolboy (André Bérard), 1879
Oil on canvas, 61 x 46 cm (24 x 18⅛ in.)
Private collection

make them rare and alluring, like the loveliest plumage. He placed them in magical settings: among soft greenery in which the rays of the sun dance and break up into reflections; in intimate elegance among rare ornaments which he embellished with his colour palette; and in even richer and apparently intoxicated settings sprinkled with gold, emeralds, and rubies. His drawing, which even Renoir's most vehement adversaries never dared to attack to his face even at the height of their triumph, has a child-like grace. It is the work of a master painter who has kept, throughout life's disappointments and the anguishes of his art, the same candour and vivaciousness that he enjoyed at twenty years of age".

The children painted at the period are covered in lace, fur, satin, and ribbons. This is true of infantas such as *Mademoiselle Georgette Charpentier Seated* (p. 391) and *A Girl with a Watering Can* (p. 390), as well as *Portrait of Jeanne Durand-Ruel* (p. 394), *La Promenade* (p. 395), *Portrait of Marthe Bérard* (p. 403) and *Alice and Elisabeth Cahen d'Anvers* (p. 406). These children are dressed in the style of the period. Renoir used the frills and furbelows in their silky fabrics and light muslins to make the light play on their pearly, well-nourished flesh. But such pretty effects are not fundamental to Renoir's success in portraying people, and children in particular, "like ripe fruit".

When Renoir gave up commissioned portraits of "rich kids", he devoted himself with even greater pleasure, and equal simplicity, to portraits of other happy children – his own. Clients like the Charpentiers, the Bérards, the Cahen d'Anvers, the Durand-

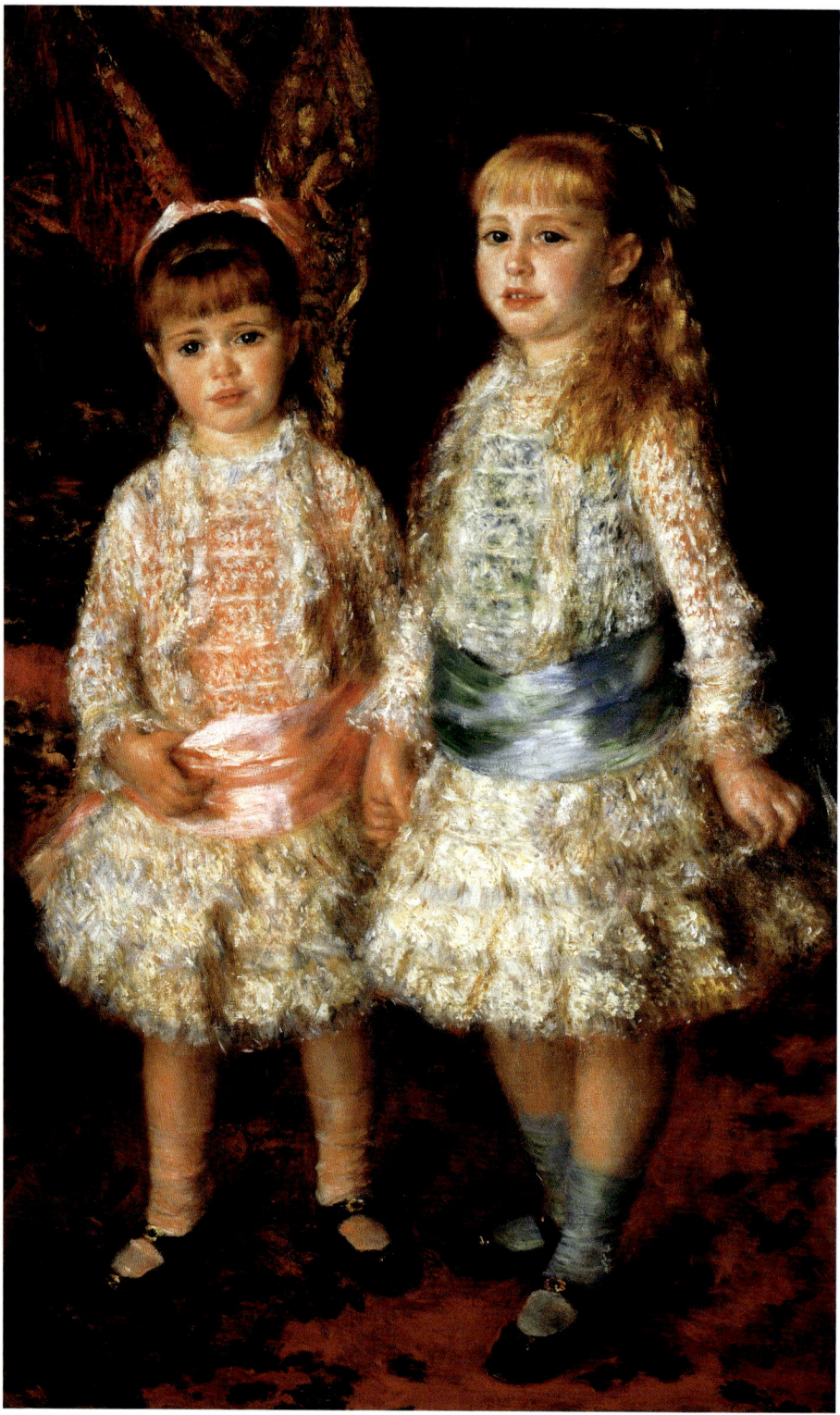

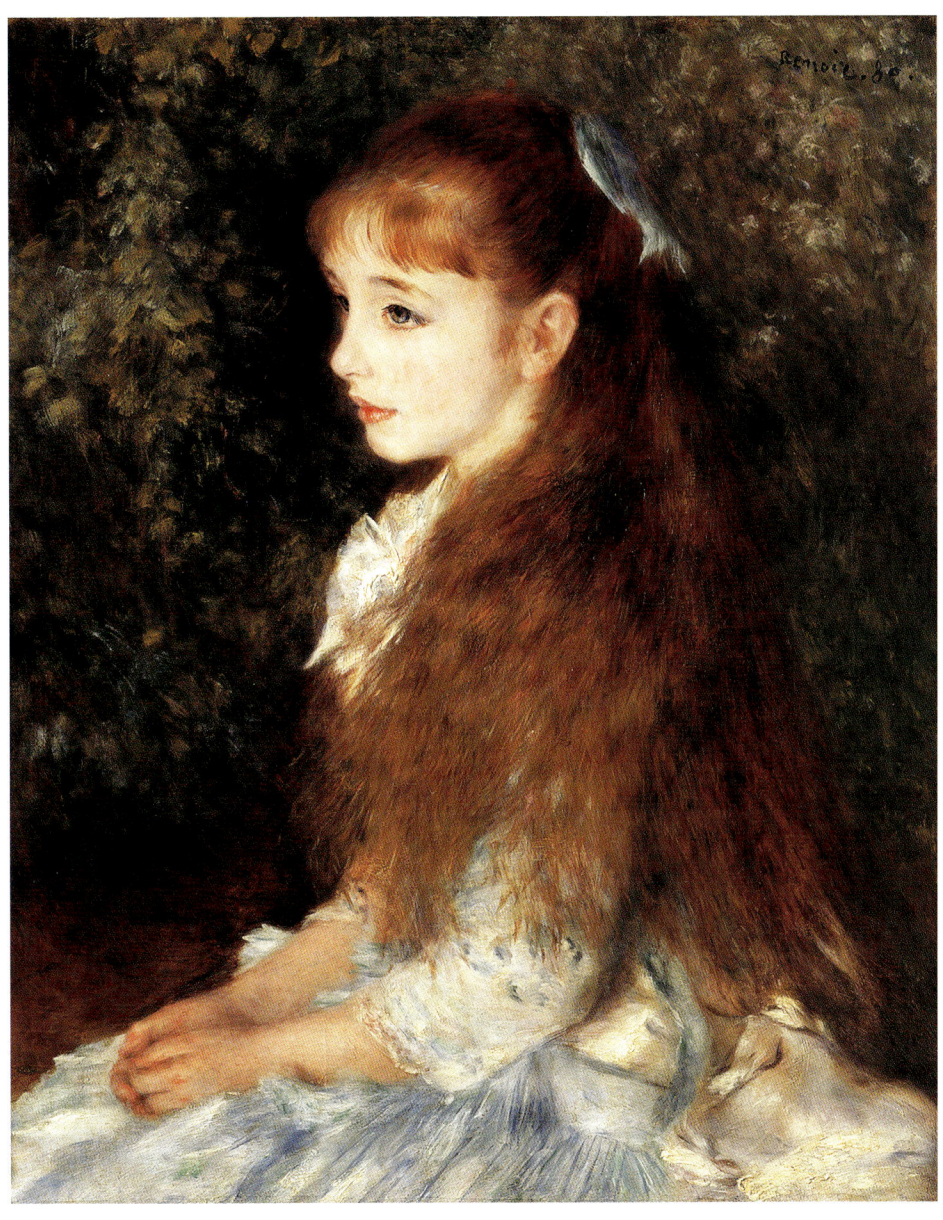

Alice and Elisabeth Cahen d'Anvers, 1881
Oil on canvas, 119 x 74 cm (46⅞ x 29¼ in.)
Museu de Arte de São Paulo,
Assis Chateaubriand

Mlle. Irène Cahen d'Anvers, 1880
Oil on canvas, 65 x 54 cm (25½ x 21¼ in.)
Zurich, Foundation E. G. Bührle Collection

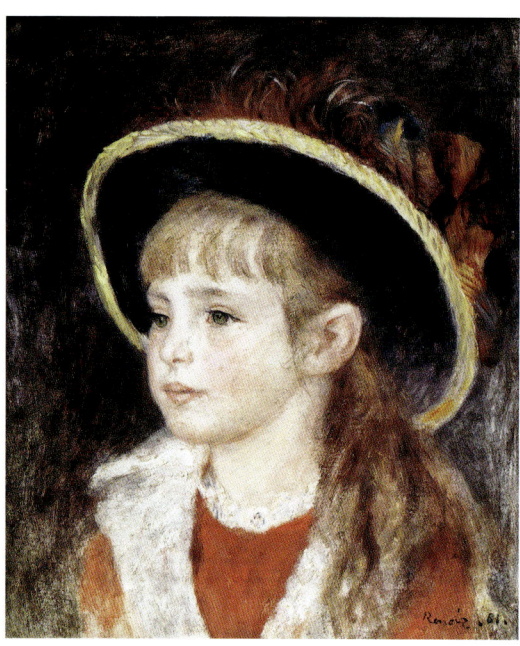

Jeanne Henriot (Girl in a Blue Hat), 1881
Oil on canvas, 40 x 35 cm (15¾ x 13⅞ in.)
Private collection

Le Jardin du Luxembourg, c. 1883
Oil on canvas, 64 x 53 cm (25¼ x 21 in.)
Private collection

Ruels and others knew that they were getting more for their money than a simple painted likeness of their offspring. Renoir's affection towards children always shined through. His friend Georges Rivière studied this phenomenon. "The candour of their movements and the spontaneity of their reactions make these children so attractive to painters who try to reveal the inner life of their models from their unconscious gestures. Children are always present in Renoir's work. He loved women, children and cats for the same qualities that he saw in them: the tenacity of their desire and their ability to satisfy it, regardless of the cruelty that this might inflict on others. The unconscious behaviour of women and children interested Renoir. It made him no more indignant than the patient manœuvres of a cat tracking a bird. It was this feeling that he most frequently expressed."

Renoir was primarily drawn, as he was in his portraits of women and his bathers, to the child's complexion and chubby flesh. But he also enjoyed depicting the play of light and reflections on secondary objects. In the Charpentier family portrait he gives almost as much prominence to the various items that are featured in the large canvas (the Japanese ornaments, flowers, fruit, crystal decanters and even the dog) as he does to the children. Matters were quite different when someone other than a banker, diplomat, or publisher had commissioned the portrait. Then the children were free to climb trees and tear their clothes instead of posing stiffly in their Sunday best. Renoir admitted to Duret that he could not tell whether or not his portrait of

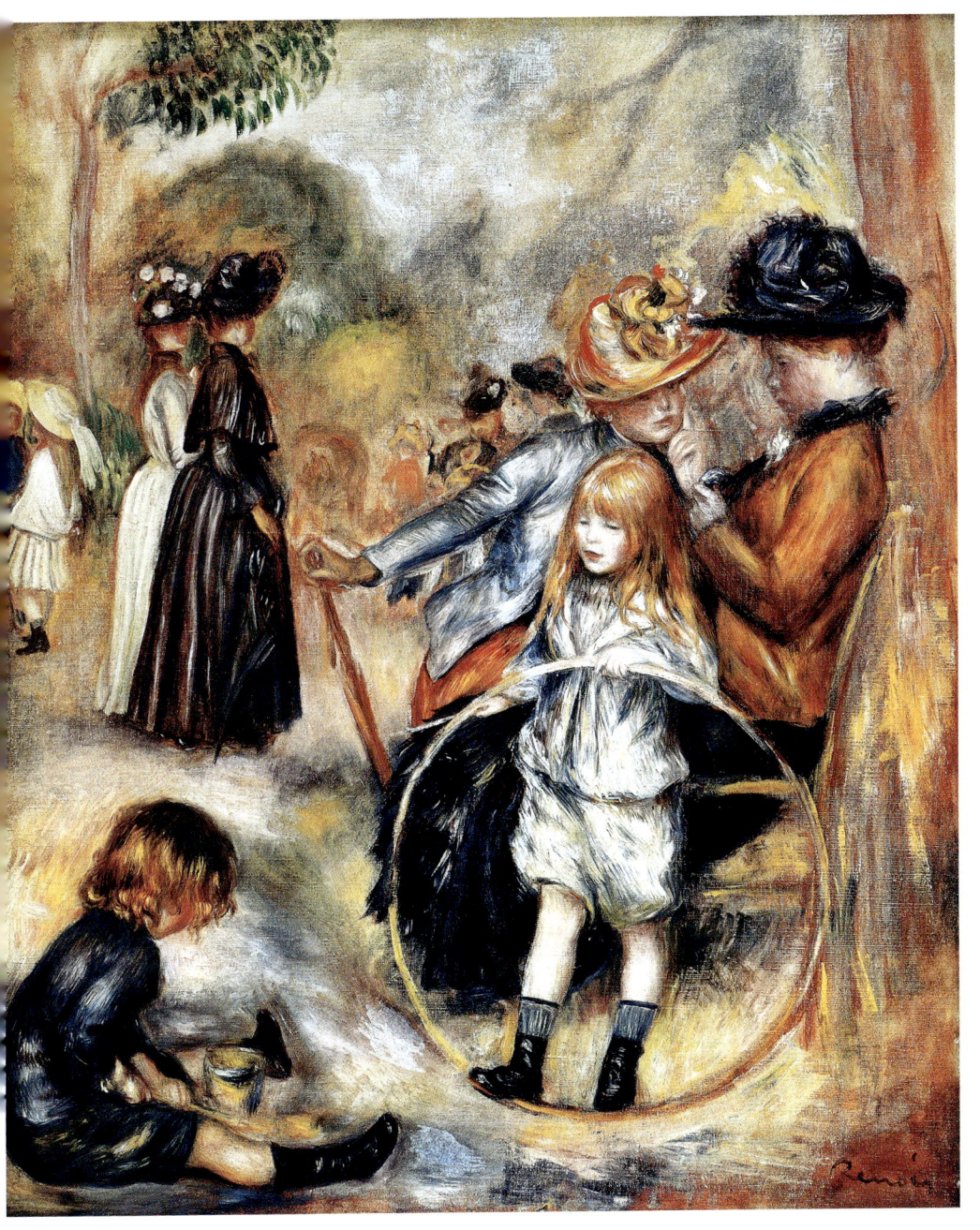

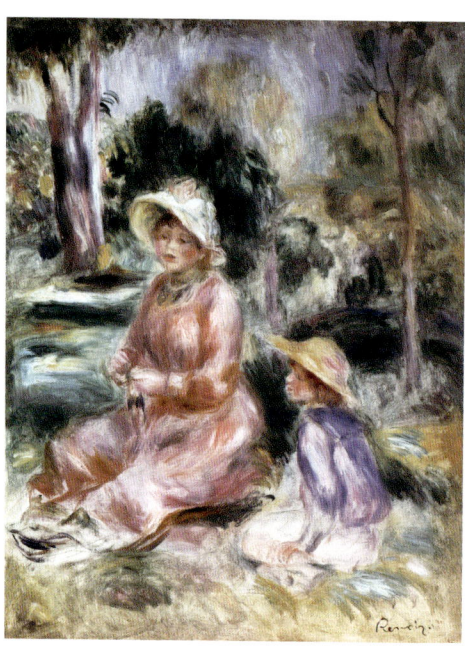

Madame Renoir and Her Son Pierre, 1890
Oil on canvas, 40 x 31 cm (15¾ x 12¼ in.)
Private collection

Children on the Seashore, Guernsey, c. 1883
Oil on canvas,
91.4 x 66.4 cm (36 x 26¼ in.)
Boston, Museum of Fine Arts,
Bequest of John T. Spaulding

Alice and Elisabeth Cahen d'Anvers (p. 406) was good. But he did know exactly what he thought of being paid late for the job. "As for the fifteen hundred francs from the Cahens," he told Duret, "permit me to say that I find the amount hard to swallow. It would be hard to be stingier. I'm having nothing more whatsoever to do with Jews". He preferred the Protestant diplomat and banker Paul Bérard, who paid up without being asked and even liked the paintings. Renoir treated him as a friend and, before starting the series of portraits of his children, sketched all their heads onto a single canvas. He kept *Sketches of Heads* (*The Bérard Children*; pp. 400/401) as an unfinished work and exhibited it in 1883. These heads enabled him to take notes for future portraits, observing the children from different angles and without their having to pose: according to Blanche, the little Bérard children were "savages who refused to learn to read and write, their hair was untidy and they were always running off to herd the cows in the fields". Renoir used the *Sketches of Heads* to compose *Children in the Afternoon at Wargemont* (pp. 276/277). This ambitious composition is characteristic of his Ingres period and came in time to rival *Madame Charpentier and Her Children* in popularity.

"The first time I ever saw Renoir painting", said Blanche, "was at Berneval-sur-Mer, near the castle in Normandy where Paul Bérard invited him to be his guest every summer. He made the fishermen's children pose in the open air. With their blond hair and pink, suntanned skin they looked like little Norwegians". Whenever

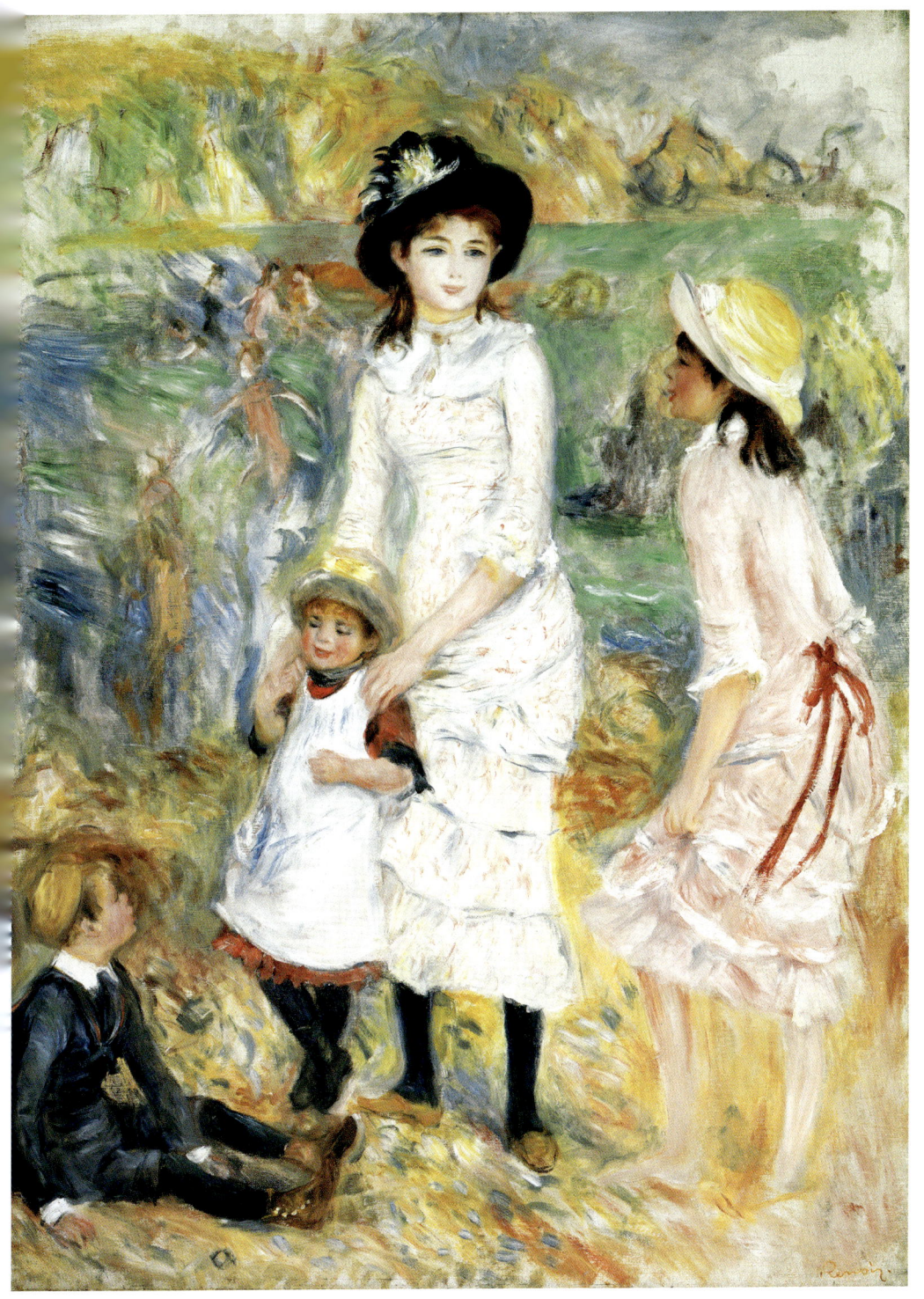

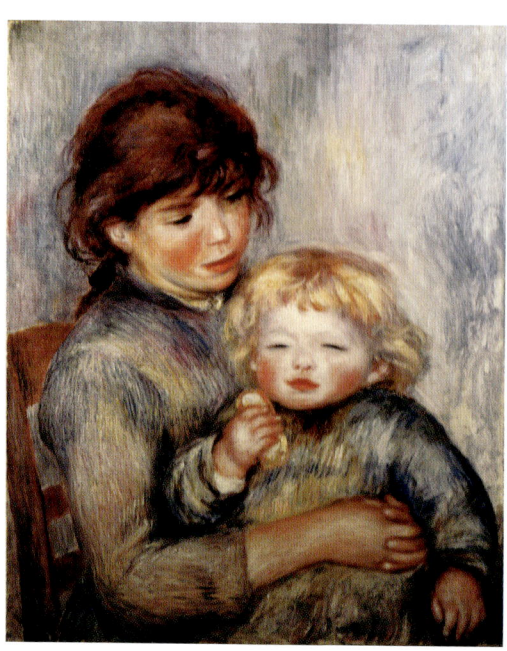

Maternity (Child with a Biscuit), 1887
Oil on canvas,
56 x 46.5 cm (22 x 18⅜ in.)
Private collection

**Mother and Child
(Aline and Pierre)**, c. 1886
Pastell, 79.1 x 63.5 cm (31¼ x 25 in.)
The Cleveland Museum of Art,
Bequest of Alexander Ginn 1977

he could, Renoir stopped painting commissioned portraits and sketched poor little imps, preferably female ones with abundant red hair, such as the *Gypsy Girl* (p. 144). Then he was free to paint as he wished and could try out a new technique by laying on translucent washes of colour. While apparently just amusing himself, he subjected his virtuoso achievements to a demanding plasticity. He used every stroke of colour to define volume and shape without needing to refer back to Ingres or Raphael. He was instinctively delighted with the fisherman's daughter. Her auburn locks, the brilliance of her skin, and the little curl falling over her left eye become a leitmotif particularly in the portraits of Gabrielle. He allowed no pathos – which was then considered *de rigueur* by academicians when they painted such children – to appear in the slovenly appearance of the girl with untidy hair and a torn blouse that reveals her naked shoulders. The portrait looks like a skilful snapshot of a young animal surprised for a moment and about to take flight once more. The red-headed girl so pleased Renoir that he featured her in *Mussel-Fishers at Berneval* (p. 397). This painting is less spontaneous, however, and was destined for submission to the 1880 Salon. For Renoir, the beauty of very young girls and flowers constituted a single theme that constantly inspired him to break out of the bounds of technical constraint. The very varied techniques used in *Little Girl Gleaning* (p. 415) marked the return to Impressionism echoed in *Gypsy Girl*. Renoir at last decided to revert to "the old style of painting, after long discussions with Durand, to the geranium

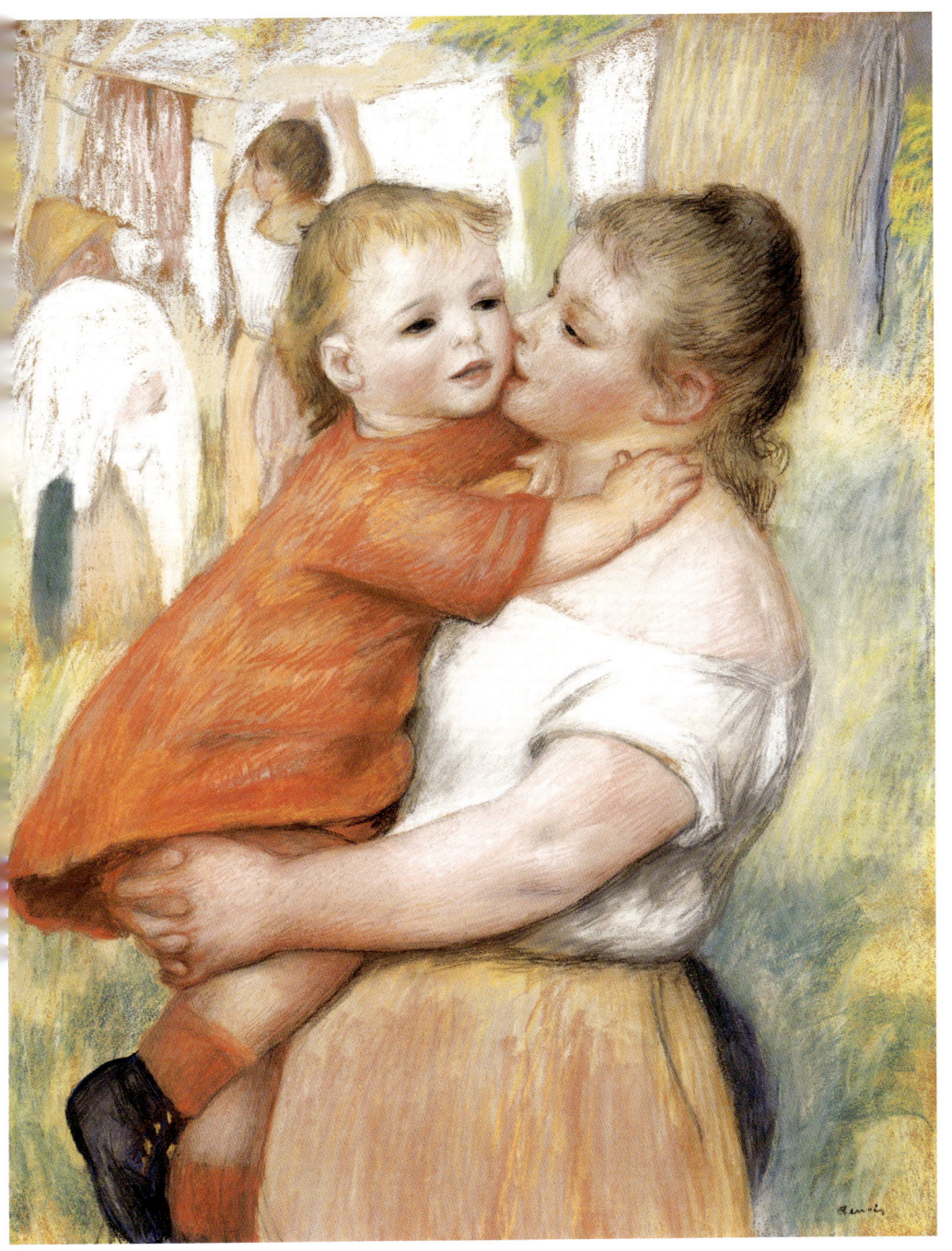

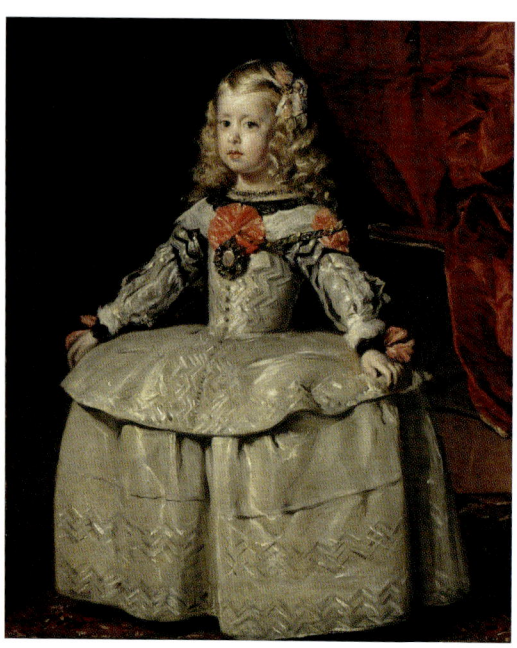

Diego Velázquez (1599–1660)
Infanta Margarita Teresa in a White Dress, c. 1656
Oil on canvas, 105 x 88 cm (41⅜ x 34¾ in.)
Vienna, Kunsthistorisches Museum

Little Girl Gleaning, 1888
Oil on canvas,
61.8 x 54 cm (24¼ x 21¼ in.)
Museu de Arte de São Paulo
Assis Chateaubriand

painting" (an allusion to the still life painted for Bérard in 1880, p. 170). But he had come a long way since then, as he insisted in his letters to his dealer. The Ingres-inspired harsh manner had disappeared and yet the figure is clearly detached from a richly diverse background. Renoir had digested the lessons taught by Corot and Cézanne. He was happy to combine a richly coloured setting and a vigorous and fragmented brushstroke with clearly structured shapes and compositions.

Renoir felt able to mix with his fellow artists without feeling bad about it, now that he had soaked himself in his artistic heritage and no longer needed to visit museums. Along with his soft spot for eighteenth-century French art, he had favourites among the Old Masters such as Titian and Rubens. He could produce "brightly coloured Corot" landscapes using Cézanne's style of brushwork. When Veláquez was preparing his portrait of the Spanish Infanta (*Infanta Margarita Teresa in a White Dress*, p. 414), he suddenly placed pink ribbons and flowers in their hair, exclaiming: "Now my composition will hold. All the tones will work together in relation to this rose: I have solved the colour problem!"

Renoir had seen Diego Velázquez's *Las Meninas* while travelling in Madrid with Paul Gallimard in June 1892. It inspired an ambitious new painting, *The Artist's Family* (p. 417). Renoir hoped it would be his definitive treatment of the theme of children and planned to donate the painting to the Louvre. Renoir's family poses against the woodland background of the cottage at 13 Rue Girardon, facing the

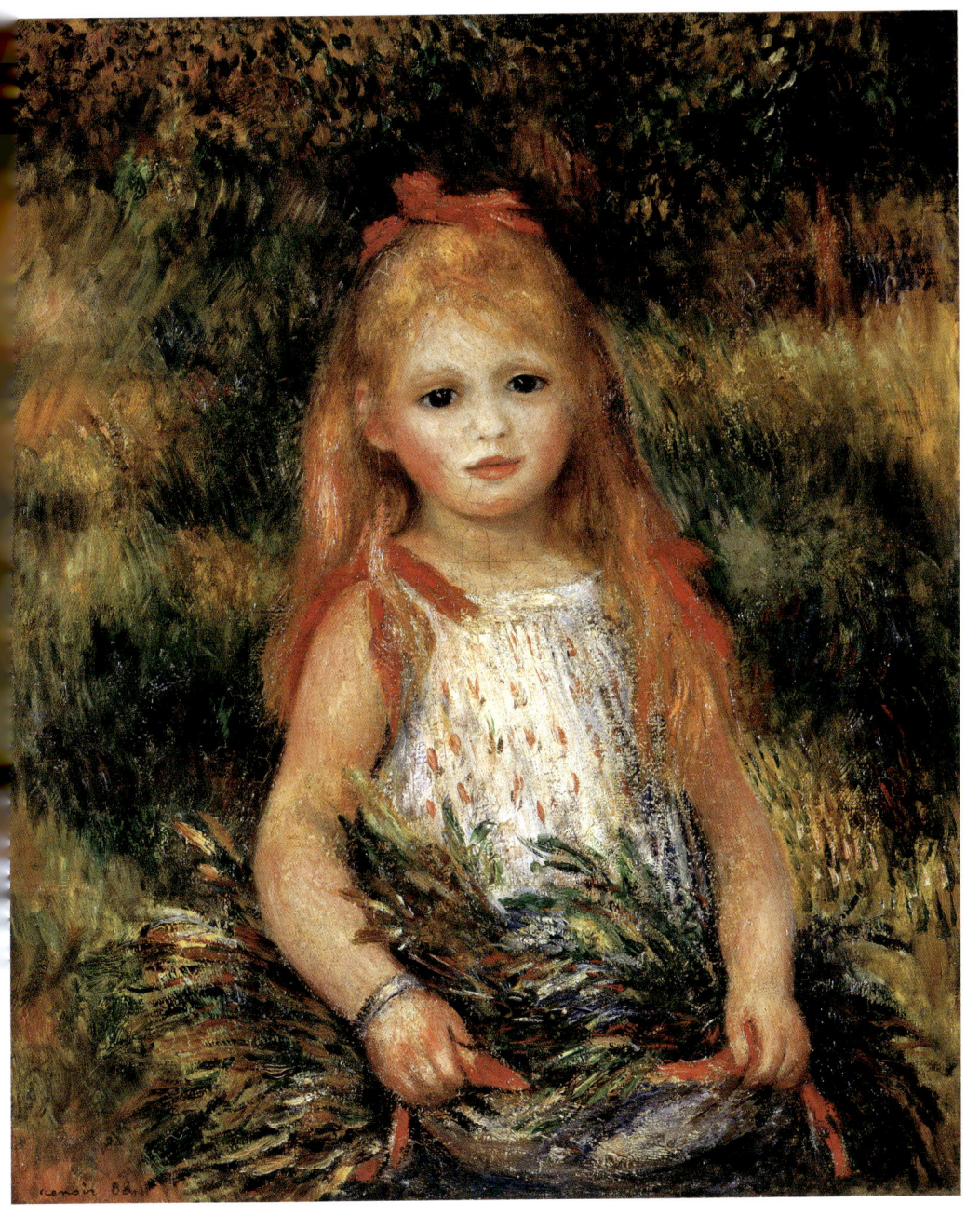

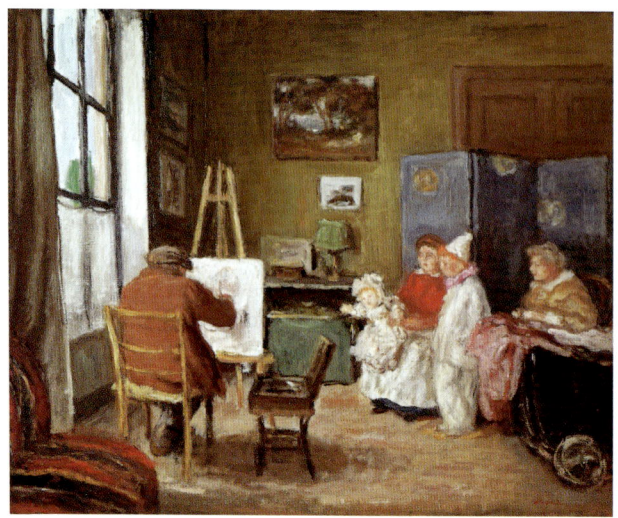

Albert André (1869–1954)
**Renoir Painting His Family
in His Studio at 73 Rue de
Caulaincourt, Paris**, 1901
Oil on canvas,
81 x 100 cm (32 x 39⅜ in.)
Cagnes-sur-Mer,
Musée Renoir – Les Collettes

The Artist's Family, 1896
Oil on canvas,
173 x 137.2 cm (68⅛ x 54 in.)
Philadelphia,
The Barnes Foundation

Château des Brouillards on the hill of Montmartre, to which they had moved in October 1890. Aline Charigot, now Madame Renoir, is wearing an imposingly large hat. The young boy in a sailor suit leaning against her affectionately is her eldest son, Pierre, who was eleven years old at the time. The younger son and future filmmaker, Jean, is not yet two; he is held by the maid, Gabrielle Renard, whom Renoir would immortalise in numerous portraits. The only missing element was the little girl that Renoir never fathered (Coco / Claude, his third son, had not yet been born). So the daughter of one of their neighbours was invited and, typically, Renoir asked her to play with her abundant tresses. She does so while glancing seductively at Pierre. One can already see her as the perfect bather. "The freshness", wrote Stéphane Mallarmé, "often consists – especially during this difficult period – of coordinating disparate elements." This Renoir achieved in a real *tour de force*. All of the themes that were dear to his heart are here. Against a country landscape there is a magnificent and imposing portrait of a woman. She may appear to be from the middle classes. But in fact, as Jean Renoir later said of his mother, "She always insisted on remaining what she was: the daughter of vineyard-owners who knew how to bleed a chicken, wipe a child's bottom, and prune grapevines". The theme of young people dressed up and flirting with each other is also present. So too is the theme described by Degas's ironic phrase as "baby Jesus in his nanny's arms". The bather, admittedly, is missing. But it takes little effort of the imagination to remove

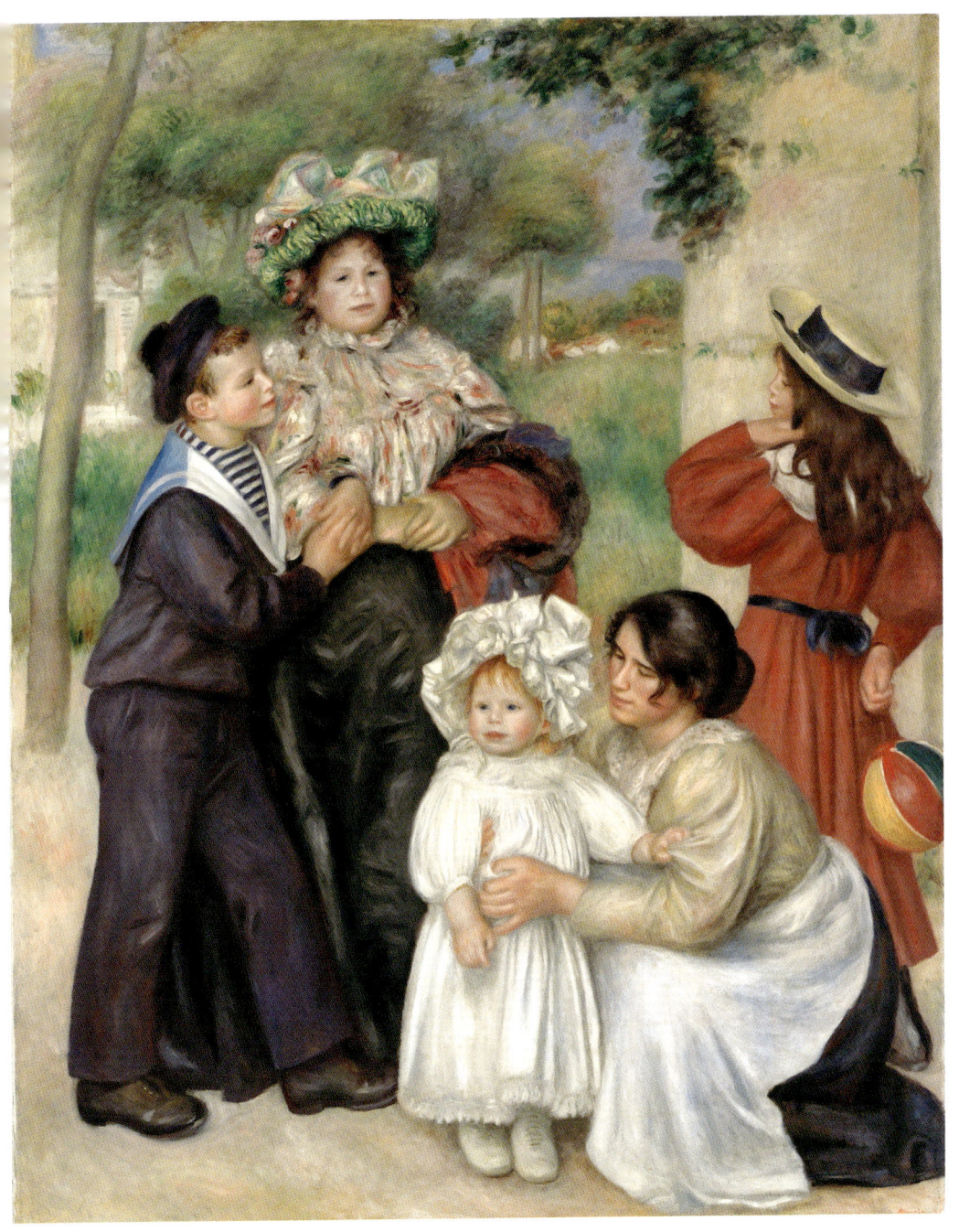

Claude Renoir Playing, c. 1905
Oil on canvas, 46 x 55 cm (18⅛ x 21¾ in.)
Paris, Musée de l'Orangerie

PAGES 420/421
**Portrait of Children
(The Children of Martial Caillebotte)**, 1895
Oil on canvas, 65 x 82 cm (25⅝ x 32⅜ in.)
Private collection

In this painting of children who are not his own,
Renoir chose to express his opinion that in the
battle of the sexes, the woman is an early victor.
Thus the little girl in pink is not looking at the
book on her knees but she is holding it such a way
as to make sure that her brother can only read it
with difficulty. She has also taken care to ensure
that the other books are out of his reach.

the clothing from the provocative little neighbour and picture her shaking herself
as she emerges from the water.

Colin B. Bailey reports: "In June 1896, Gustave Geffroy noted that as soon as it was
exhibited, everyone called this picture *Départ pour la promenade*: Renoir's family
out for a Sunday walk. In this epiphany of bourgeois married life – with Pierre in
the sailor suit customarily worn by the sons of the well-to-do – Renoir is coming
to terms with issues on which he had been ambivalent for some time: his wife, his
marriage, his family. Pierre, his first son, had been born out of wedlock in March
1885. Renoir married Aline only in April 1890, and not until August of the following
year did he introduce his wife and child to Berthe Morisot and her husband, good
friends of his for half a decade. 'I'll never be able to describe my astonishment at
meeting this heavy woman,' Morisot confided to Mallarmé in October 1891, 'whom I
had imagined, for reasons I cannot explain, more as a figure in one of his paintings.'
Six years later, the nomadic Renoir seems finally to have come to terms with par-
enthood, property, and conjugality. On 1 July 1895, he had consented to have Jean,
born the previous September, christened at the Eglise Saint-Pierre de Montmartre,
although he insisted to the child's godfather: 'We're doing the baptism without any
fuss.' In February 1896, just before starting *The Artist's Family*, he had experienced
real anxiety when Pierre fell with measles and Jean was at risk. Burning sulphur
in the boy's bedroom, he informed Julie Manet: 'Jean is superb at the moment, but

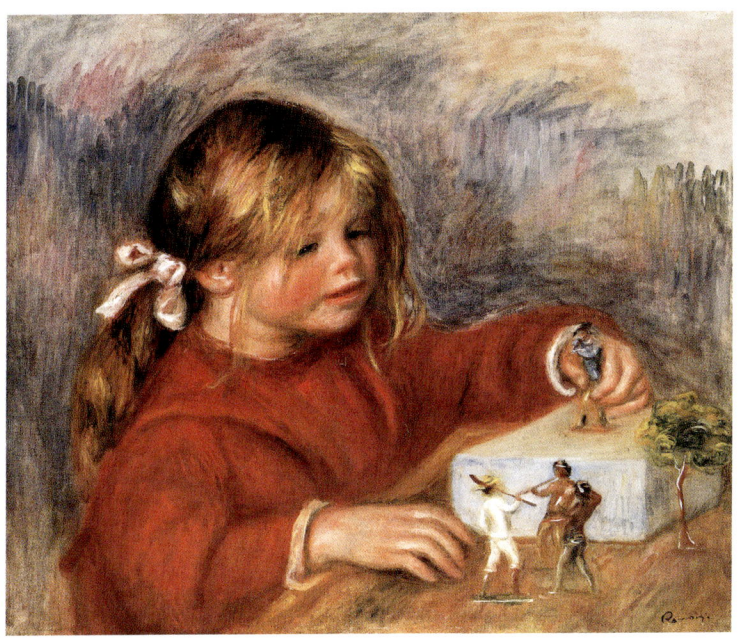

I'm still worried. At his age measles are unbearable.' Indeed, with his immaculately attired and fully recovered brood about to set forth in what Geffroy considered 'one of the finest groupings of human figures ever represented in painting,' Renoir does more than come to terms with bourgeois values – he positively embraces them, with a sureness of touch, a peerless technique, and a depth of affection and good humour that resonate and give pleasure one hundred years later and will doubtless continue to do so into the centuries to come."

Renoir loved painting pictures of "baby Jesus in his nanny's arms", the intense affection between a woman and her child. He renewed this traditional theme, for even though his paintings have no immediate religious significance, they are his most touching in human terms. The series began in 1876 with *The First Step* (p. 392). He took up the subject again in *Young Mother* in 1881 (p. 384). These were personal paintings that had not been commissioned; he treated them in the style and technique of the moment. The year 1887 saw *Maternity* (*Child with a Biscuit*; p. 412) and *Mother and Child* (*Aline and Pierre*; p. 413). The mother and child theme came into its own with the arrival of Gabrielle. The sixteen-year-old maid came from Essoyes in Champagne, like Madame Renoir, and entered service with the family one month before the birth of Jean. Gabrielle was a rosy-cheeked young peasant girl as tempting as ripe fruit. She was hired as a nanny on Renoir's standard prior condition that her skin "took the light". Not only did she go on to pose (in the nude and clothed) for more

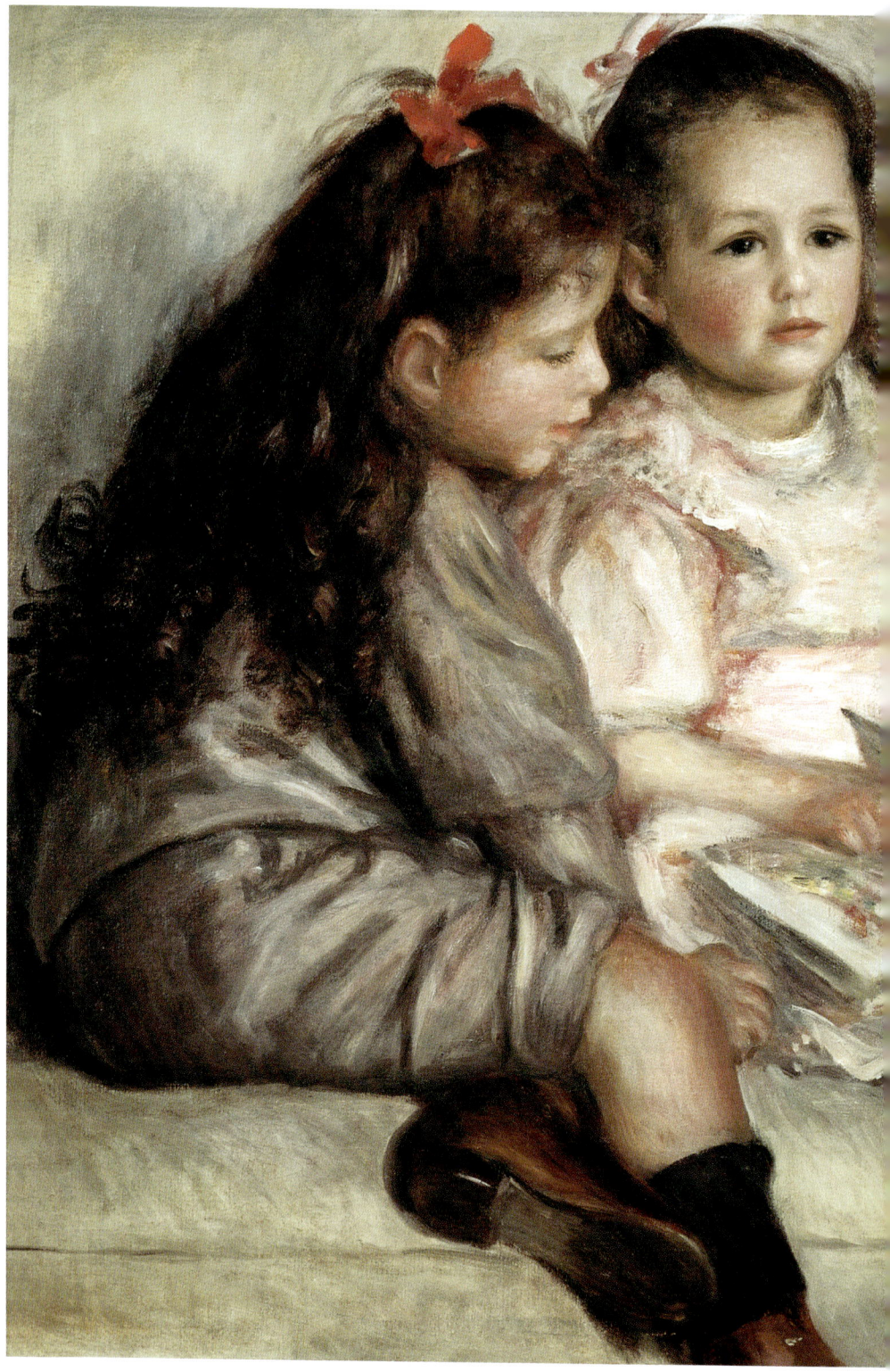

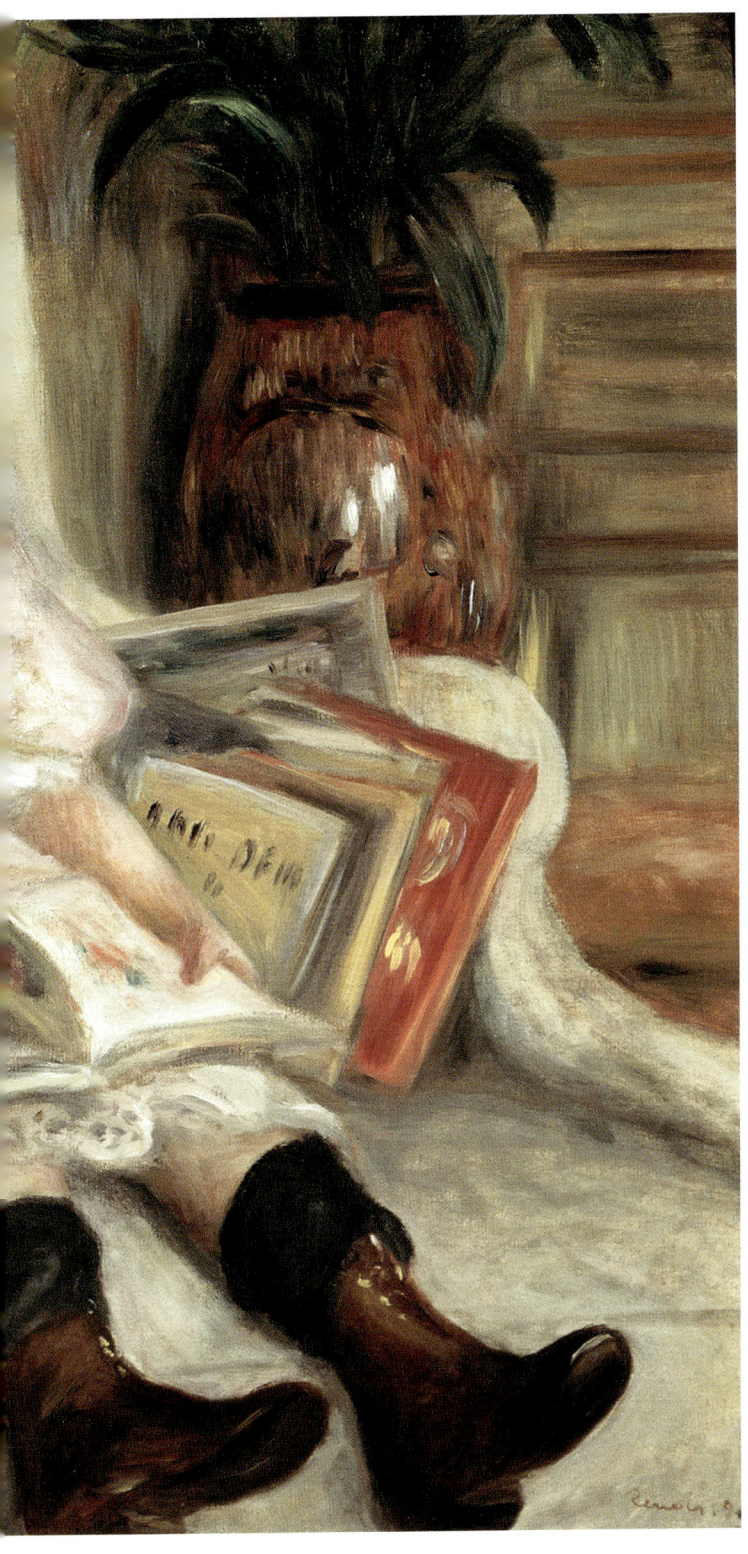

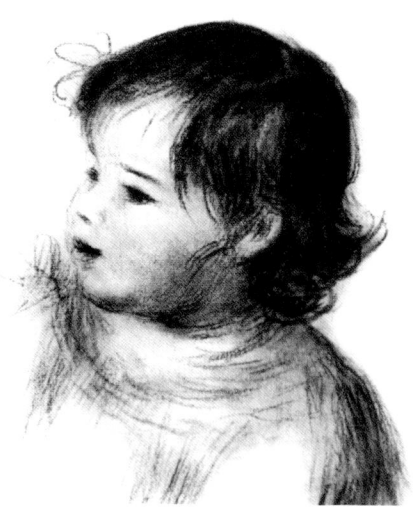

than two hundred paintings; she was also instinctively a second mother to the children. By the age of two, Jean had posed for his father in a whole series of paintings,
pastels, and drawings. *The Artist's Family* takes as its focus Jean, the baby Jesus in the
protective arms of the maid, Gabrielle. Beforehand Renoir had produced at least five
paintings such as *Child with Toys* or *Gabrielle and the Artist's Son, Jean* (p. 423) and
The Child with Its Nurse (p. 438). He would always find some excuse such as the child
sitting on his nanny's knee and playing with little animals or an apple. He studied
both his models intensely and explained his new passion to his fellow painter Congé.
"You need to be wrapped up in yourself to be able to use your head properly and
make things happen" he wrote. "At the moment I am constantly making faces at Jean
and I can assure you that, when I do so, I am working for myself and only for myself".

The portraits of Gabrielle with his sons are inseparable from Renoir's other
portraits of his children. Mary Cassatt, who admired her devotion, called her
"the marvellous Gabrielle, the only one with heart, his nurse and former model".
Renoir's three sons adored her. When she died in 1959, Claude mourned her passing.
"The whole world knows *Gabrielle with a Rose*, *Gabrielle in a Hat*, and *Gabrielle in
a Necklace*", he explained. "But only the two of us, my brother Jean and I, carried in
our hearts the portraits of a whole host of other Gabrielles. When we have gone,
nothing will be left". Gabrielle was not only the painter's favourite model. She was his
assistant, preparing his brushes and cleaning his palette, and such a strict nurse at

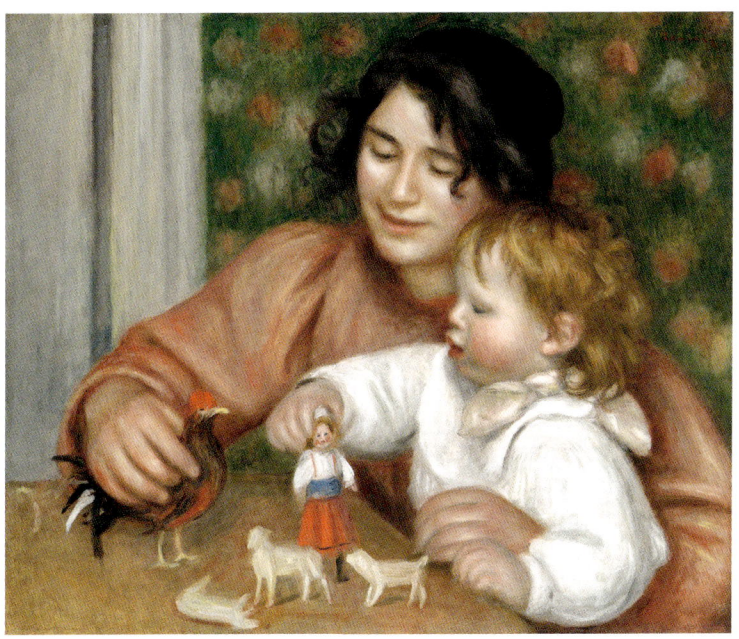

his sickbed that he would tell her jokingly to have the injection in his place. Numerous photos exist of Gabrielle at this time dancing (p. 462), playing the clown, or posing primly for a portrait (p. 465). Renoir, as was his wont, visibly softened her face in the portraits with the children and showed with great restraint the awakening of her maternal instinct.

Jean Renoir says of his father: "He would have found it improper to express his feelings to anyone else, perhaps even to himself, but they caught up with him as he stood before his easel". Then he showed her full of devotion and instinctive protection towards the children with whom she was playing. So too "his sharp but tender brush, caressing his children's napes and the little folds of their wrists," Jean continues, "announced his paternal love to the whole world". For him Gabrielle's finest quality was that she was already a "Renoir", which made it particularly easy for him to transform her into an eternal icon. He went as far as giving his other models her face and body, so perfectly did they match his conception of feminine beauty. A few days after Gabrielle's death a leading French weekly devoted a few pages to her memory. Renoir made the mistake of choosing some portraits for which, according to Claude Renoir, she had never posed. She was in them all the same.

A similar confusion exists in his portraits of children. Renoir's own sons were also "Renoirs": they resembled his perception of young children. Michel Robida visited Claude Renoir as an adult, at his art pottery studio in Menton, and was astonished

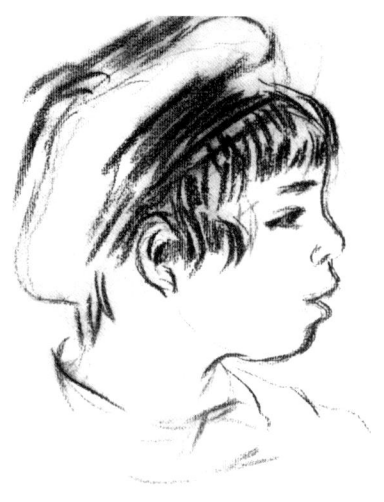

to see how closely he resembled the portraits painted of him as a child. "I once again had a revelation of the scrupulous probity that Renoir displayed towards his model," Robida recounts. "The first words I said to him, as he smiled back at me with the same almond-shaped eyes that still narrowed towards the temple, were: 'you look so much like your portraits!'"

In the various portraits, and especially their innumerable preparatory sketches (pp. 422, 424), it is hard to tell which of Pierre, Jean and Claude is which. The three bothers summoned the same images from their father and they looked so alike at the same age. This resemblance, caused by the love he had for his sons, disappears in the case of other children. The portrait of *The Children of Martial Caillebotte* (pp. 420/421) is a good example. Renoir has chosen a different theme from the one that motivated him to paint his sons. Renoir shows, as if on a stage-set of a children's theatre, that in the war between the sexes the woman wins very early on. The little girl dressed in pink is not reading the book on her lap but holding it in such a way that her brother can only read it with difficulty. She has also taken care to place the other books out of his reach. Rivière tells a story that illustrates the pleasure that Renoir felt in the inevitable female victory over the male.

"One afternoon, in the garden of his house in Essoyes, his attention was diverted to two children having a quarrel", Georges Rivière recalls. "The little girl, aged five or six, was defending herself against the anger of the little boy. 'Look at those kids',

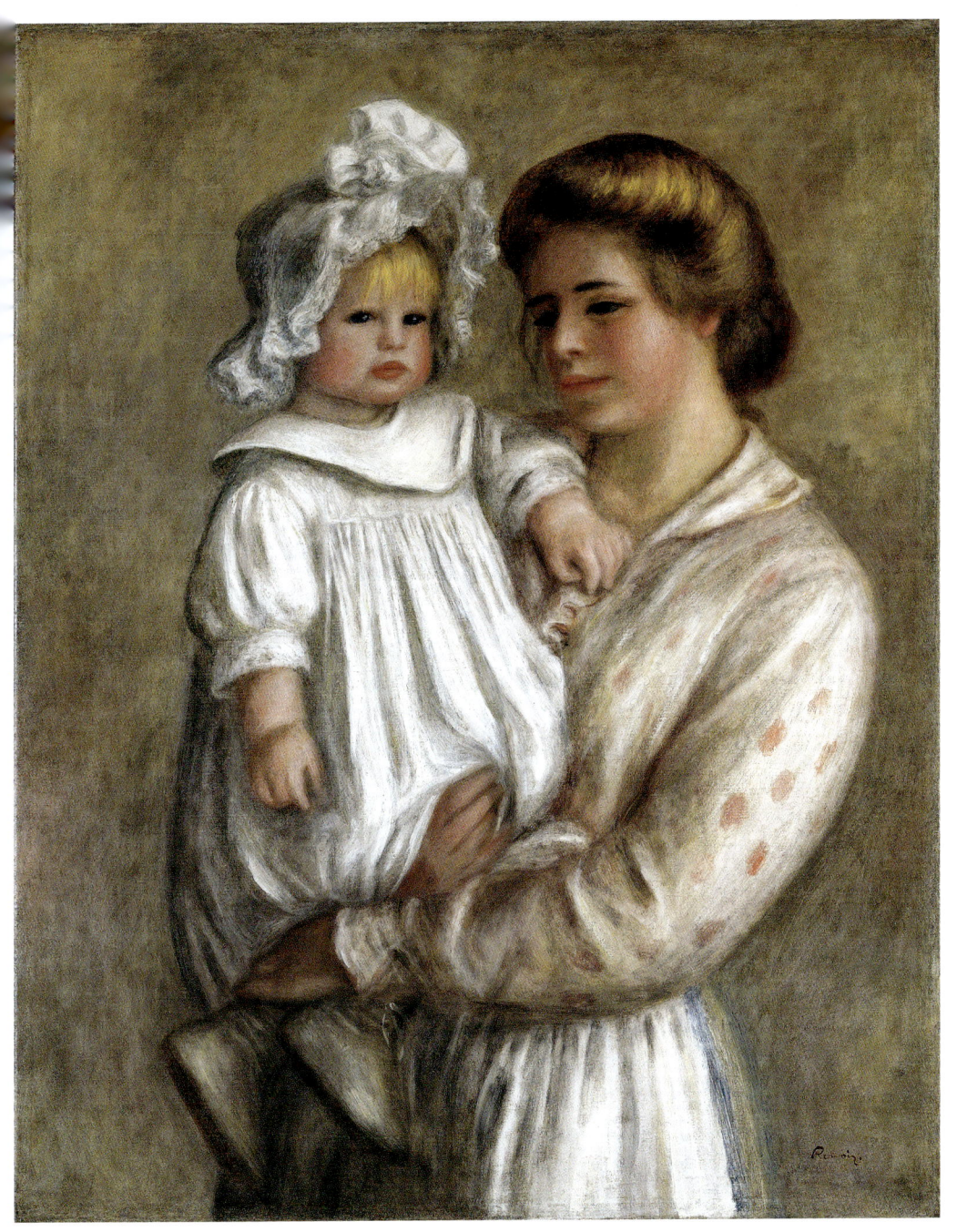

**The Artist's Son,
Jean, Drawing**, 1901
Oil on canvas,
45.1 x 54.6 cm (17⅞ x 21½ in.)
Richmond, Virginia Museum
of Fine Arts, Mr. and Mrs. Paul
Mellon Collection

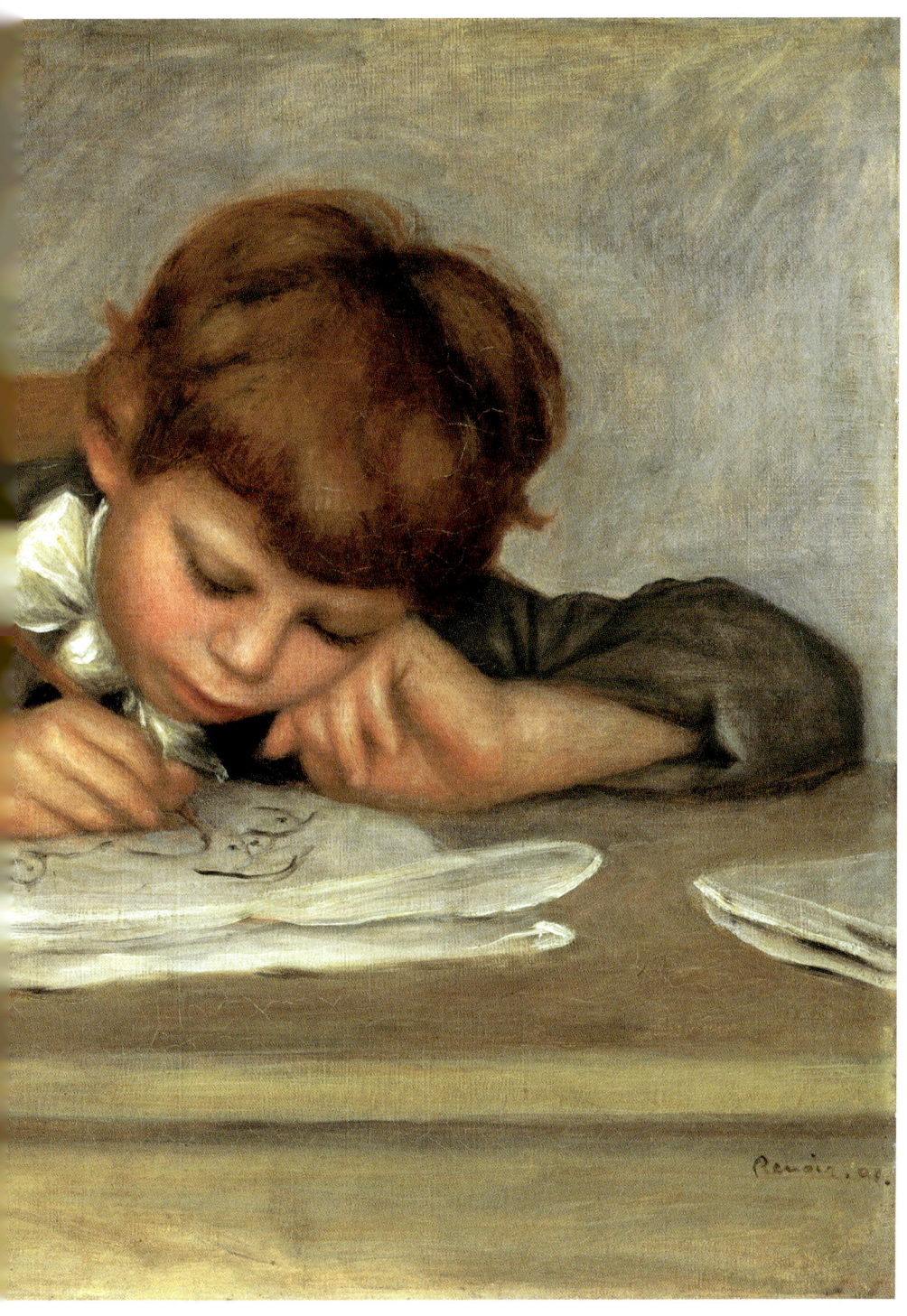

Coco Painting, 1907
Oil on canvas,
55 x 46 cm (21¾ x 18⅛ in.)
Private collection

remarked Renoir. 'They are already showing us the spectacle of the antagonism between the sexes. The little man gets angry and shouts away but the little girl will get the better of him.'" Renoir's portraits are not only hymns to the rounded flesh and lovely complexions of these little children but also a range of basic and simple colours organised in clear opposition between light and dark tones. The pinks, reds and browns delicately detach the figures from neutral backgrounds. The portraits are a chronicle of intimacy surprised.

Just as he released the captive slaves of Ingres' *Turkish Bath* and allowed them the complete freedom to frolic in the watery setting of *The Bathers,* Renoir could only think of children in a natural environment. He hated orderly gardens and primly beribboned children awaiting their portrait. At home Pierre, Jean, and Claude were allowed to run about, tear their trousers and trample on the grass. Not only did he not stop them running wild but he even actively encouraged and defended them when necessary. Claude Renoir told Michel Robida about the freedom that his father allowed him. "As a model, I did not have to stand in a fixed pose. I could run around all over the place. Sometimes I only had to stand still for three minutes. I served as a model only during bad weather. My father usually had a model for his studio or was beginning a landscape session. I was used for the little sketches unless it was for a definite painting such as the *Clown*" (p. 435). Work on this canvas was interrupted by a dispute about a pair of white woollen stockings, which Renoir insisted on adding

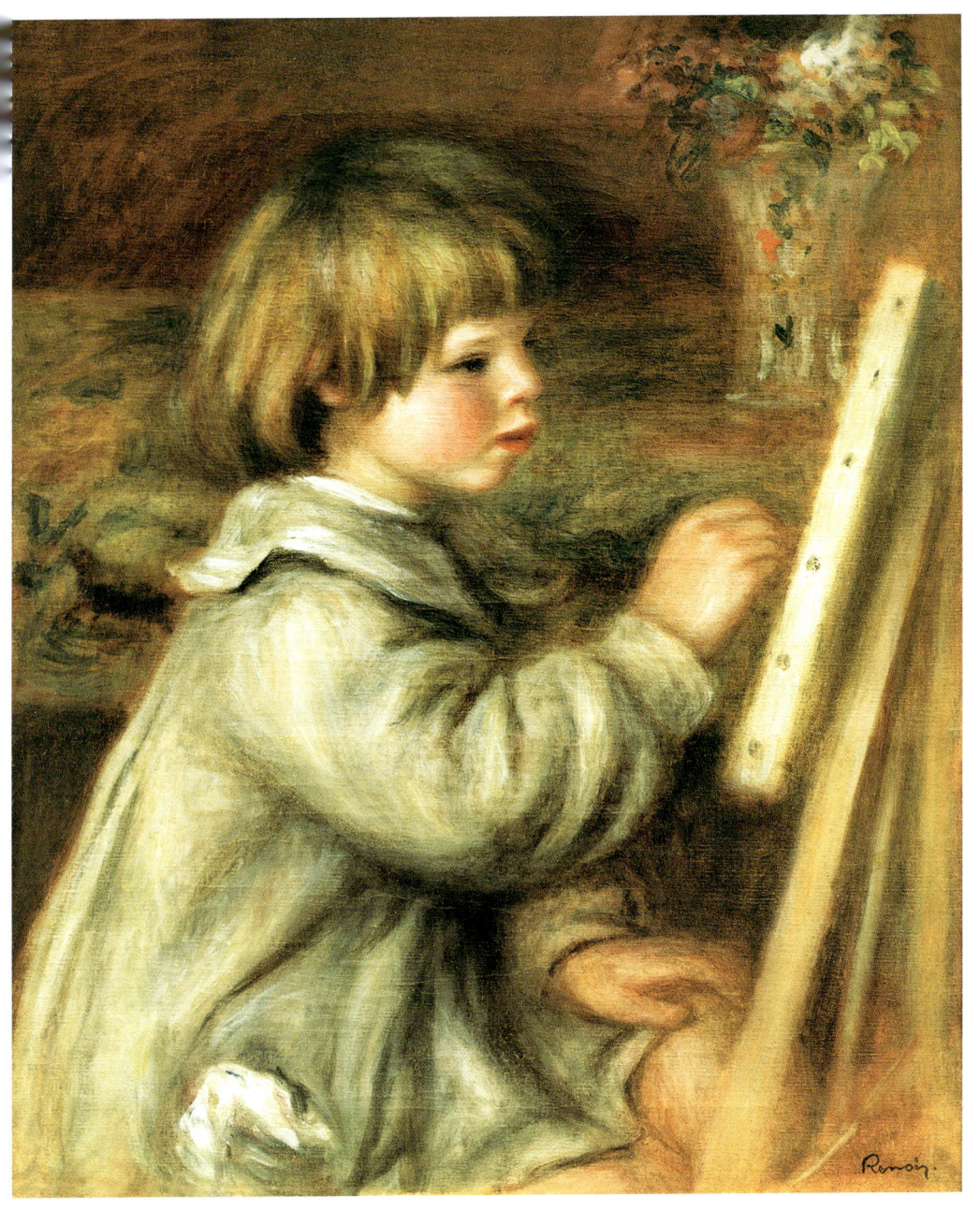

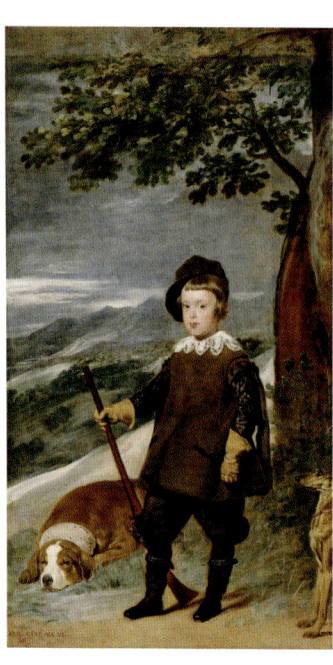

Diego Velázquez
Prince Baltasar Carlos as a Hunter, 1635/36
Oil on canvas, 191 x 103 cm (75¼ x 40⅝ in.)
Madrid, Museo Nacional del Prado

Jean as a Huntsman, 1910
Oil on canvas, 172.7 x 88.9 cm (68 x 35 in.)
Los Angeles County Museum of Art,
Gift through the Generosity of the Late
Mr. Jean Renoir and Madame Dido Renoir

Renoir liked to obliquely acknowledge the
influence of the Old Masters, especially
Velázquez whose portrait of *Prince Baltasar
Carlos as a Hunter* he parodied in *Jean as
a Huntsman*, going as far as making Bob,
Madame Renoir's dog, look very much like
that of the Spanish artist.

to the red suit, but which Coco hated. He remembered the incident well. "The
costume was completed with white stockings which I obstinately refused to wear.
To complete the painting, my father insisted on the stockings. But he was powerless.
They scratched me. So my mother brought some silk stockings, and they tickled me.
There were threats at first, followed by negotiations. I was promised, in turn, a good
hiding, an electric train set, boarding-school, and a box of oil paints. I finally agreed
to wear cotton stockings for a few moments. My father cooled his temper, which
was at boiling point, and finished the painting despite my writhing in contortions in
order to scratch myself. The train set and the box of oil paints were my reward."

Renoir kept *Claude Renoir in Clown Costume* until he died, although it could easily
have found its way into a museum. Claude maintained that the charm that his father
exercised on children during his work – he would make Gabrielle read Hans Christian
Andersen's fairy stories to them – extended to women. Many of them would never have
agreed to pose in the nude for anyone else. But they trusted his honesty and his quest
for a beautiful model.

It is no longer appropriate at this stage to talk of Renoir's "influences". But he
continued paying homage to, and parodying, Velázquez, Rubens and Watteau. The
"Coco Velázquez" paintings are so-called because, just as Velázquez had focused on
their pink bows in his paintings of the Spanish Infanta (p. 414), he now highlighted
the blond hair of his little models with a pink bow. The bow can be seen in portrait

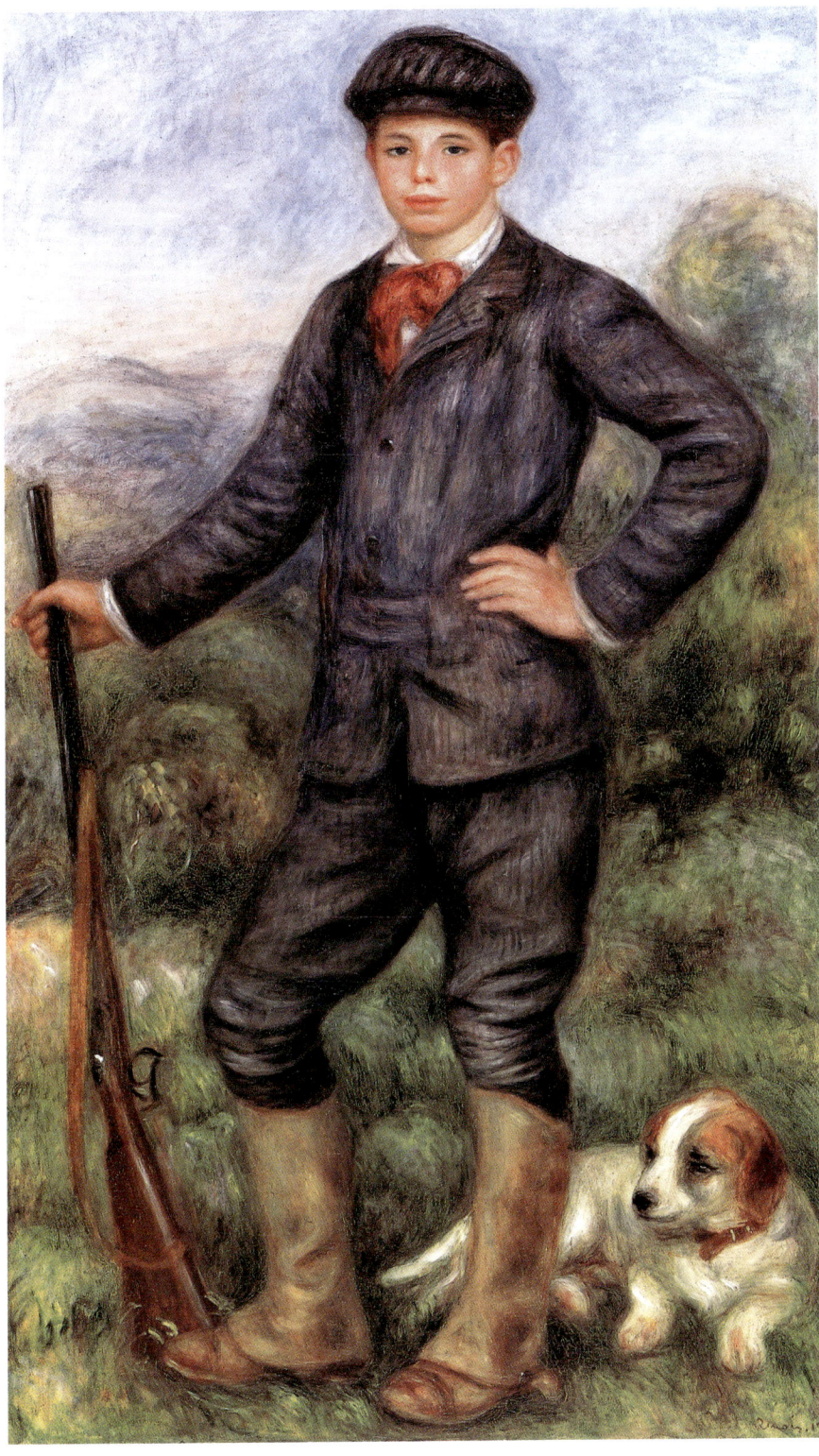

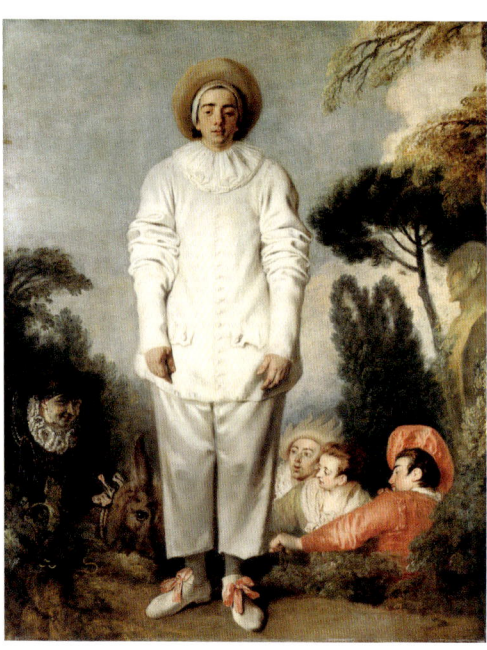

Jean-Antoine Watteau
Pierrot (formerly entitled **Gilles**), c. 1718/19
Oil on canvas, 185 x 150 cm (72⅞ x 59 in.)
Paris, Musée du Louvre

White Pierrot (Jean Renoir), 1901/02
Oil on canvas,
79.1 x 61.9 cm (31¼ x 24⅜ in.)
Detroit Institute of Art

after portrait, from *Claude Renoir Playing* (p. 419)*, Reading* (1905), and *Coco Paint-ing* (1905) to *Geneviève Bernheim de Villiers* (1910). According to Ambroise Vollard, Renoir rendered his homage to Velázquez in the form of a pastiche. "What I like so much about him", Renoir observed, "is the aristocratic touch that can always be detected in the smallest detail and the merest bow. The little pink ribbon worn by the Infanta Margarita incorporates all of the painter's art. What pretty things the eyes and the skin around them are! There is not a shadow of mawkishness. I am fully aware that the art critics dismiss Velázquez as a facile painter. What better proof could one have that he knew everything about his art! Only those who are completely skilled give the impression of spontaneity. A vast amount of research has gone into a painting that appears on the surface to be executed with such ease. What is more, he really knew how to use black. The execution of his paintings is divine. With mere dabs of black and white he was able to convey thick, heavy embroidery. And what about *The Spinners*! I know of nothing more beautiful. The background is all gold and diamonds. Wasn't it Charles Blanc who said that Velázquez was too down to earth? I can't understand why people always look for thinking in art! When I look at a mas-terpiece, I get a kick out of it. Another thing that I love about Velázquez is that he is full of the pleasure of painting".

The portrait of Coco dressed as a clown was a nod in the direction of Watteau's *Pierrot* (formerly entitled *Gilles*; p. 432). Renoir knew the painting particularly well since the

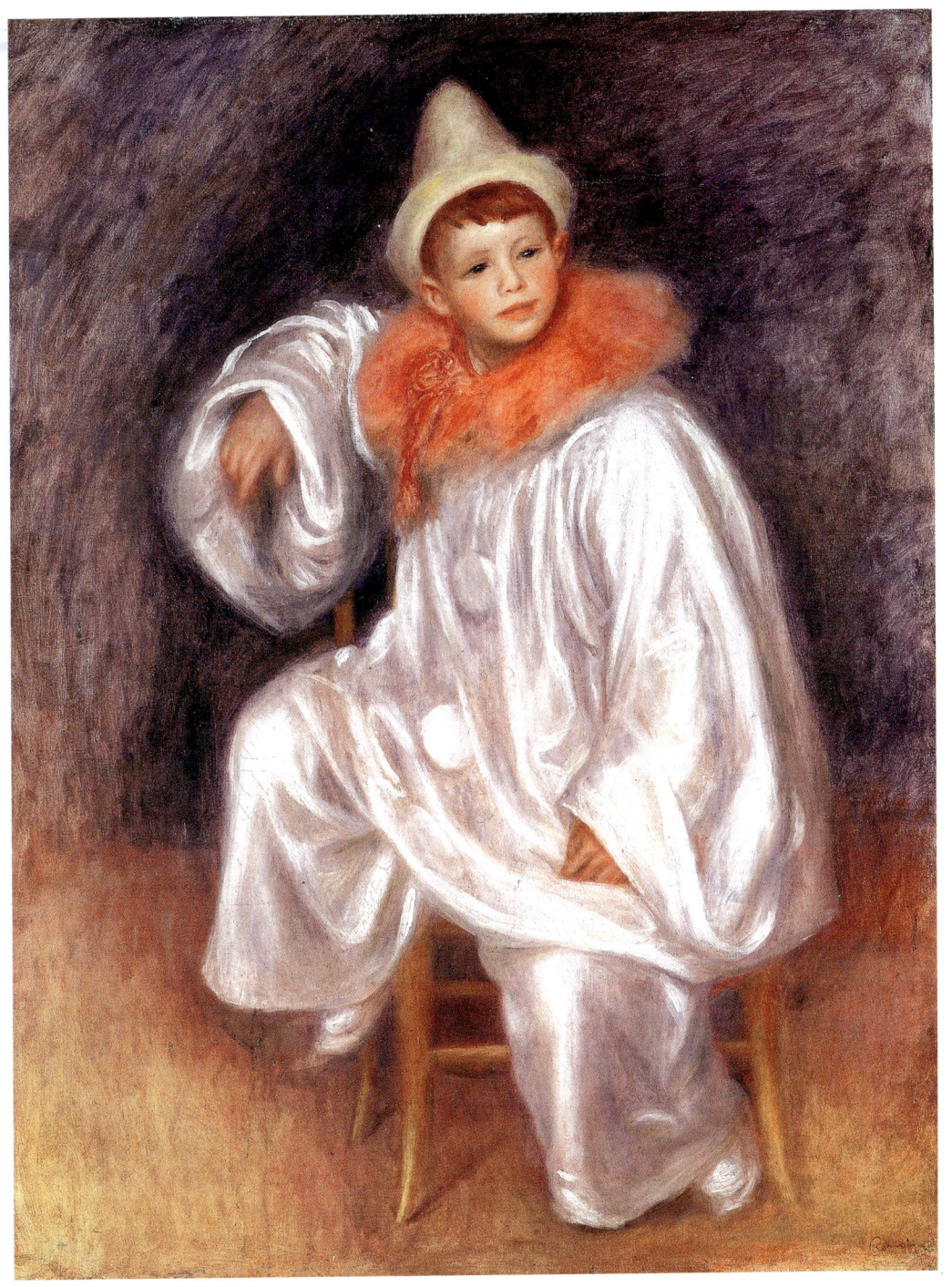

Claude (1913–1993) and Jean Renoir (1894–1979), c. 1910

Claude Renoir in Clown Costume, 1909
Oil on canvas,
120 x 77 cm (47¼ x 30¼ in.)
Paris, Musée de l'Orangerie

La Caze legacy had donated it to the Louvre in 1869. "Comparison with the haunting but enigmatic *Gilles* is instructive for several reasons", Colin B. Bailey writes in his *Renoir's Portraits*. "While Watteau may not have intended his street performer to appear sombre or melancholy, his painting was interpreted as such by successive generations. Watteau's sad clown, symbol of the misunderstood artist, was furthermore the spiritual godfather to Picasso's 'Saltimbanques' and 'Harlequins,' painted just prior to Renoir's *Clown*. Yet sentiment of this sort is thoroughly expunged from Renoir's portrait, as is the 'Anglo-Saxon melancholy' attributed to the circus performers themselves. While the reasons for dressing Claude as a clown may have been prompted by the family's nickname for him – originally Clo Clo, only later Coco – it was the opulent red costume that intrigued Renoir above all. ... Presented with admirable naivety, closer to the Douanier Rousseau's portraits of children than to Picasso's displaced bohemians and performers, *The Clown* brings to an end a long and respectable figurative tradition, while looking resolutely to the future in its insistence upon the means and materials of the painter's art. As such, it is Renoir's first twentieth-century masterpiece."

Jean Renoir in *White Pierrot* (p. 433) also avoided this fascination with the melancholic by appearing neither sad nor depressed. Jean-Baptiste Debureau, at the Théâtre des Funambules, had started the fashion and the Pierrot became the "pessimistic and macabre" symbol of an anaemic and decadent *fin de siècle*. On the contrary, Renoir's portrait shows Jean metamorphosed into a resplendent Pierrot,

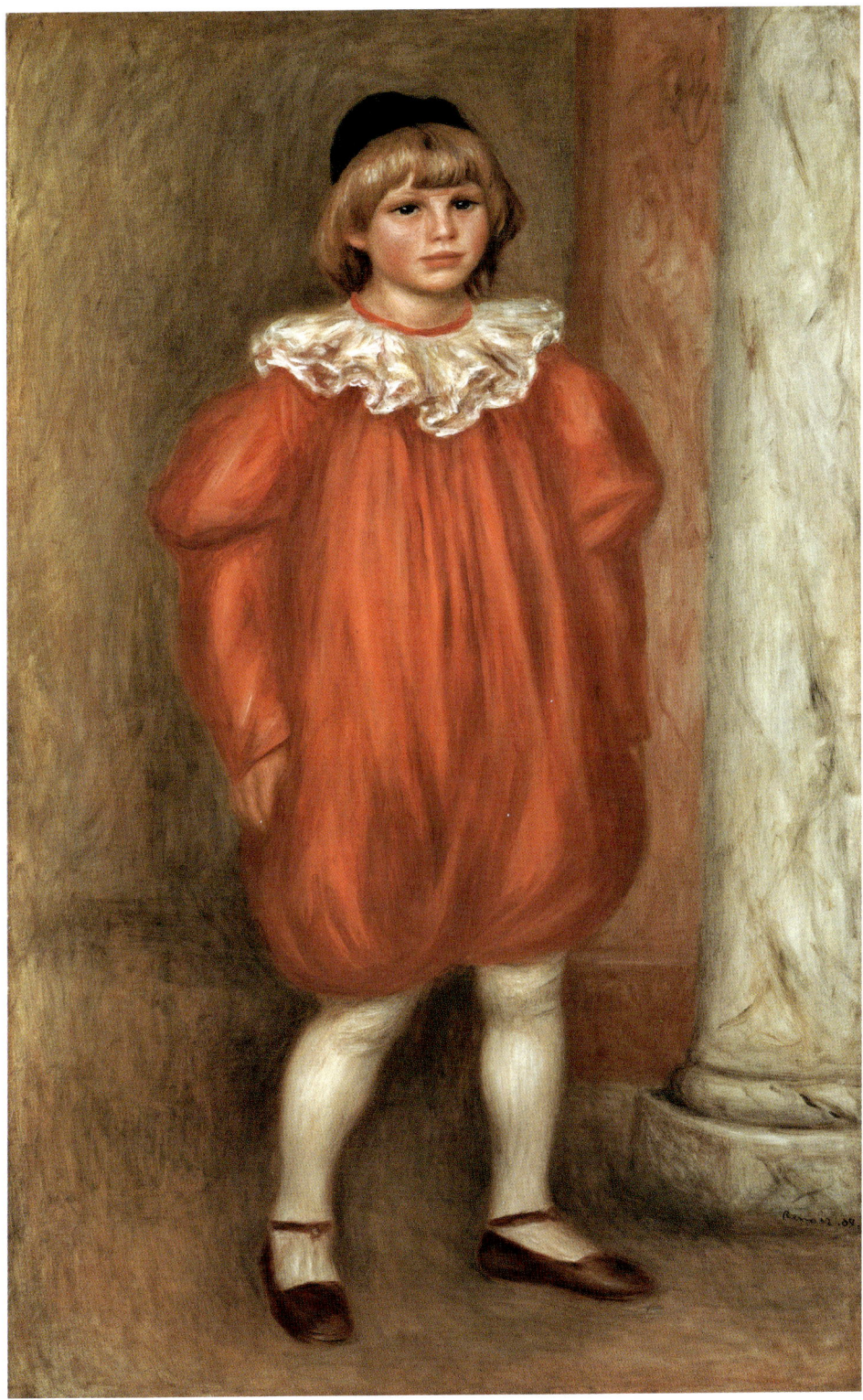

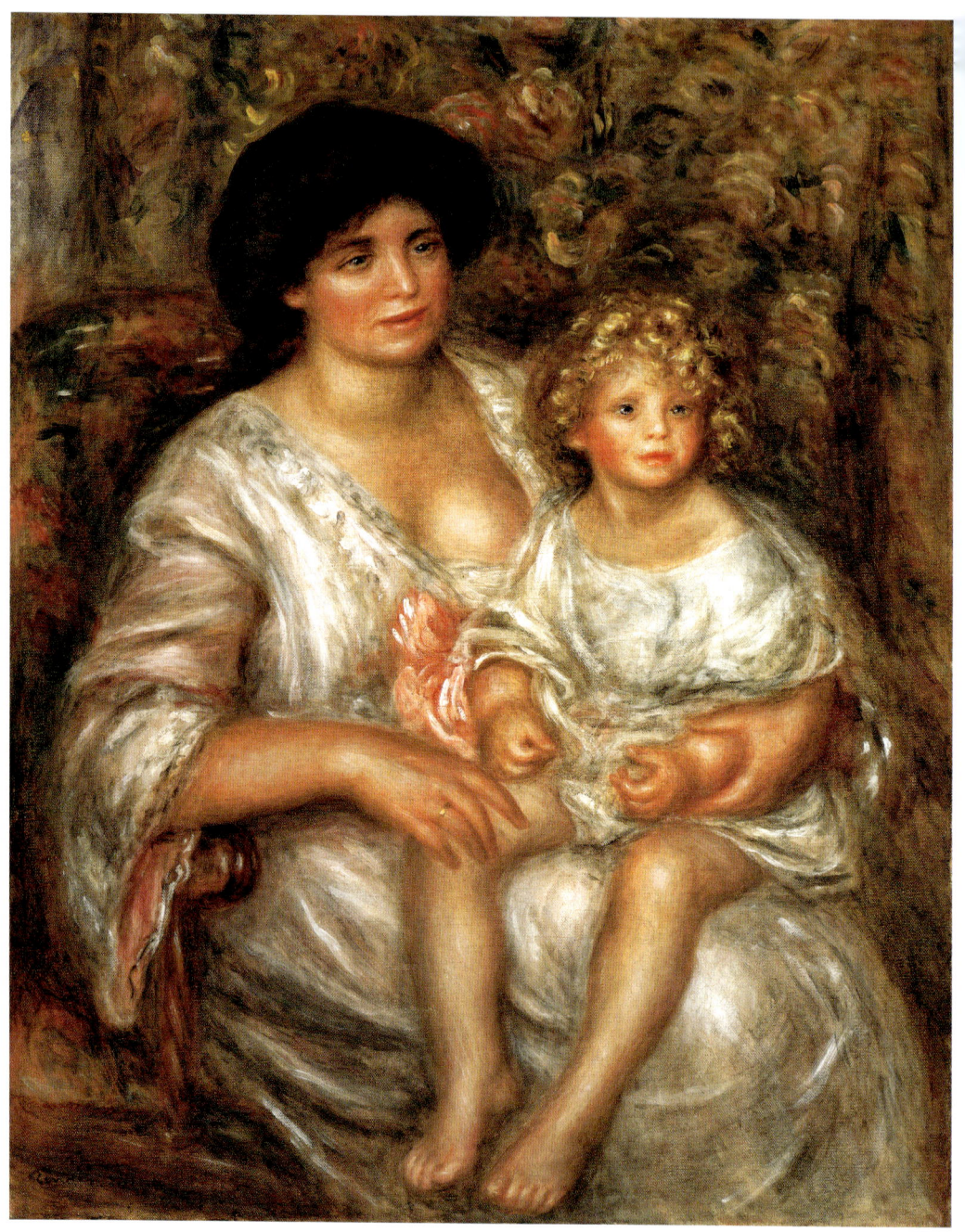

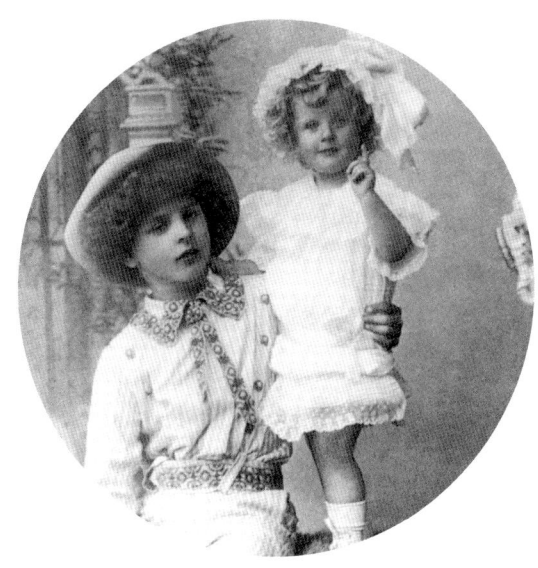

Mother and Child, 1910
Oil on canvas, 100 x 80.3 cm (39⅜ x 31⅝ in.)
Buffalo, Collection Albright-Knox Art Gallery

painted with a light and merry paintbrush. If Clo Clo the *Clown* was an allusion to
Watteau's *Pierrot*, *Jean as a Huntsman* (p. 431) is another homage to Velázquez and a
parody of his *Prince Baltasar Carlos as a Hunter* (p. 430), which Renoir had admired
in Madrid some eighteen years previously. The pose is exactly the same: even Madame
Renoir's dog has been made to look like the dog in the Velázquez painting. According to Jean Renoir, his father went so far in his homage as to buy an ornate frame
from an antique dealer in Nice and, believing it to be a seventeenth-century Italian
frame, had it regilded.

Renoir expressed to Durand-Ruel his admiration for Monet's huge *Waterlilies*.
Monet, he said, had more energy than he could muster, stuck as he was in a wheelchair and crippled by arthritis. Monet's example inspired him to continue painting
a few "large pieces". He had to invent a whole mechanical system, which enabled
him to hoist his wheelchair up to the desired height and raise or lower the canvas
with the help of a counterweight. "Paralysis prevented him from making a movement of more than twenty centimetres in length", Claude remembered. "So he had
to move the canvas continually under his brush". These huge vertical portraits were
the crippled old warrior's answer to the gossips who claimed that he could no longer
stand upright in front of his easel and could only paint figures lying down on land-
scape-format canvases. "Thanks be for painting that, late in life, still gives you
illusions and sometimes even joy," Renoir exclaimed to Jean.

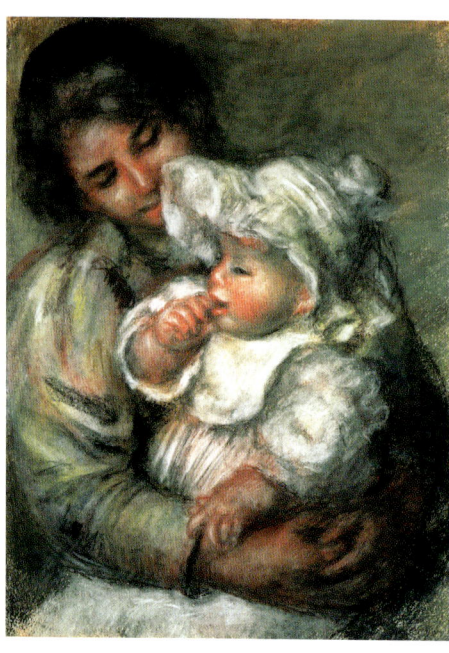

The Child with Its Nurse, 1895
Oil on canvas, 79 x 63.5 cm (31⅛ x 25 in.)
Private collection

The Promenade, c. 1906
Oil on canvas,
164.5 x 129.4 cm (64⅞ x 51 in.)
Philadelphia, The Barnes Foundation

The year 1910 was a great one for large-scale portraits. He painted his last version of what Degas called "baby Jesus in his nanny's arms". It was the portrait of *Mother and Child* (p. 436), which Dr Fritz Thurneyssen, a wealthy Munich intellectual and a recent convert to modern art, had commissioned from Renoir. He invited Renoir and his whole entourage, including the maids Gabrielle and Renée, to Wessling am See. The painting was a final tribute to Rubens and more specifically to his portrait *Helena Fourment with Her Eldest Son, Frans* (p. 393). Renoir confided to Walter Pach that although the Rubens in Munich abounded with magnificent colours, "the layer of paint was too thin". When dining at the famous Paris restaurant the Tour d'argent Vollard told the story behind the painting to Maurice Denis, Aristide Maillol, and Théo Van Rysselberghe. "The story is that this German fellow wanted Renoir to paint an intimate portrait of his wife. Renoir asked her to pull up the top of her dress, and the husband disappointedly exclaimed: 'Vot, does zat mean no nipples?'" The painting itself seems to confirm the anecdote. Betty Thurneyssen is seen revealing a rounded breast as if to suckle her child. But her three-year-old daughter Josephine Albertina, who is sitting on her lap, is much too old to be breastfed. Fritz Thurneyssen's wishes were fulfilled. Thanks to him, Renoir painted one of his most sensual portraits and an ecstatic version of motherhood. "It could be seen as a new type of Madonna", Meier-Graefe confirmed, "one who is not concerned with the divinity of her child."

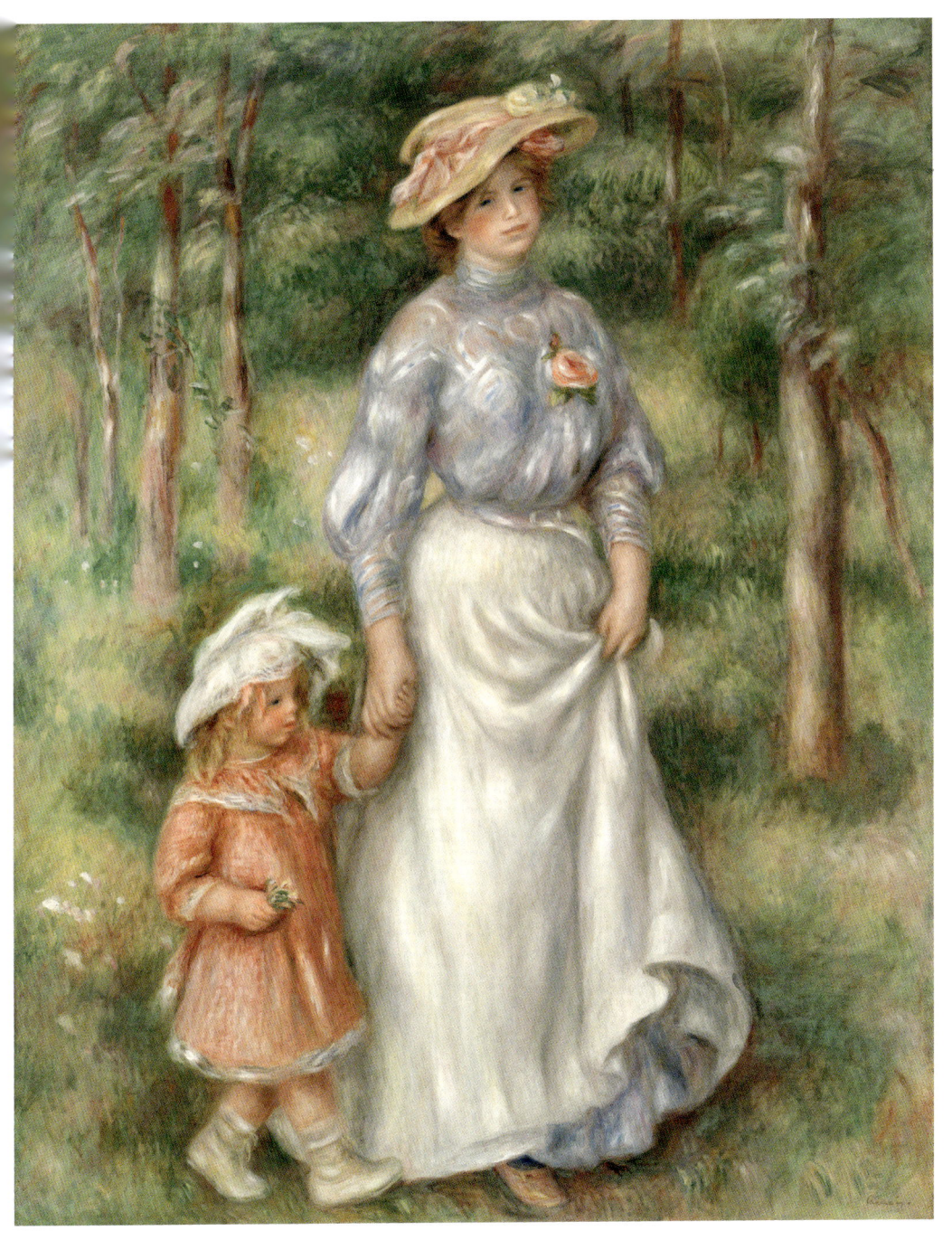

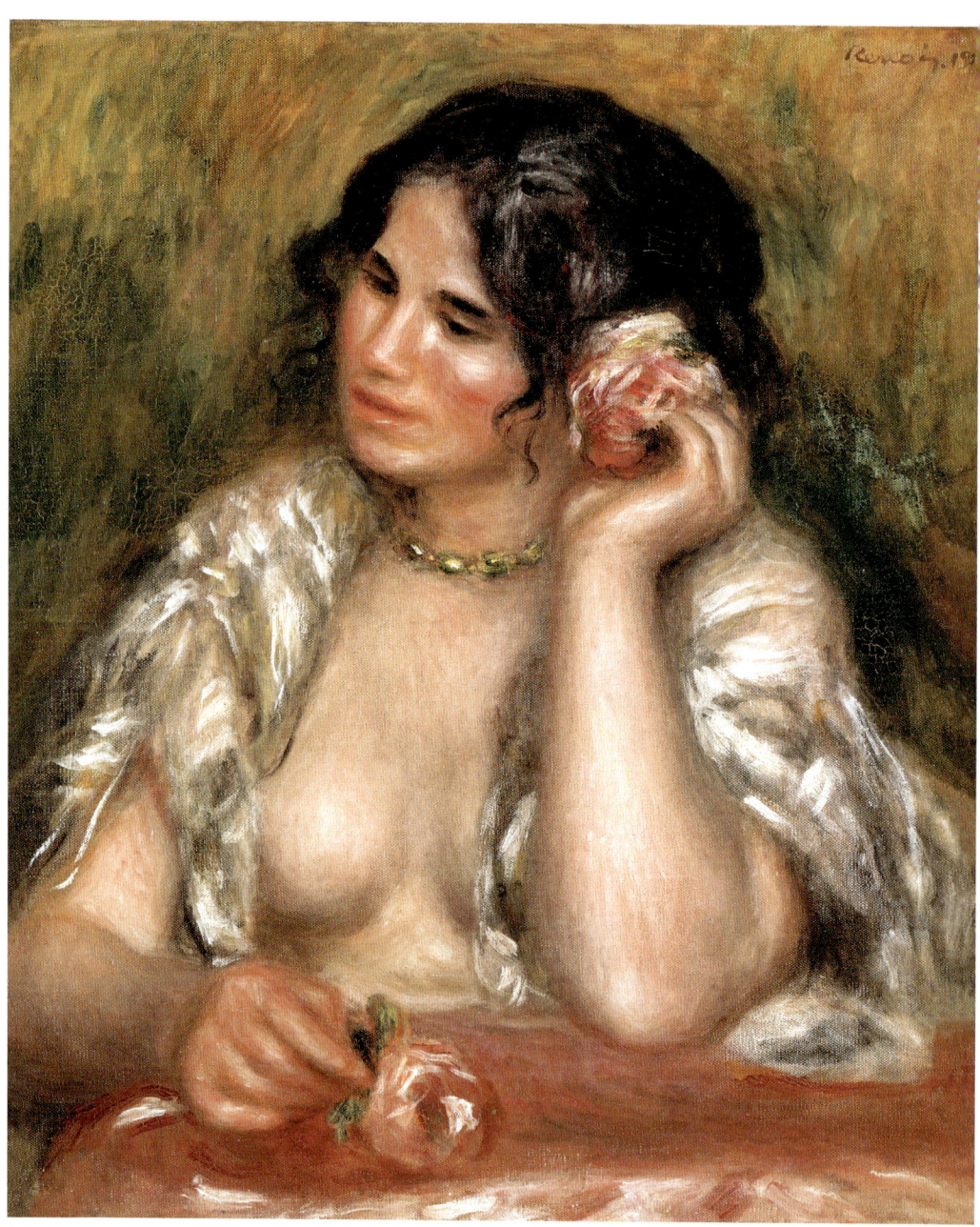

Gabrielle with a Rose, 1911
Oil on canvas,
55.5 x 47 cm (21⅞ x 18⅝ in.)
Paris, Musée d'Orsay

Venus Victorious

1900–1919

Renoir spent his last years in Provence. He felt that by living there, under the same Mediterranean sky as the ancient Greeks, he was reliving their myth of the Golden Age. "The Greeks were truly admirable people", he exclaimed. "Their lives were so happy that they believed that the gods themselves could find love with mortals alone. Earth was paradise to the Greek gods. That is what I want to paint." Renoir's time at Les Collettes can be summed up in these words. He attempted to re-create the idylls of Anacreon and the bucolic pleasures of Theocrites by attributing to the lavender-sellers of Cagnes and his beloved maid, Gabrielle, the grace and nobility of the Olympian gods. He painted fruitlike women to symbolize his love of life in his old age, which was one long tribute to womanhood. Wracked with terrible rheumatism, he sought relief at Les Collettes in the south of France. There he found models whose skin reflected the intense light of the region. With their harmonies of red and blue, these works represent the culmination of Renoir's research into the human figure. Nothing to him seemed too rich or magnificent when he depicted the supple and ample shapes of these Venuses. They were just that, delicious 'shapes', free of all psychological depth. Renoir continued to admire the woman in Ingres's *The Source* for having "nothing between her ears".

Rheumatism plagued Renoir relentlessly. With his paralysed fingers curled around his paintbrush he continued his work with as much application as ever. Durand-Ruel visited him in Cagnes in 1912. He found Renoir, as he put it, "in the same sad state, but still full of surprising strength and character. He could not walk, or even get up from his wheelchair. Two of us had to carry him everywhere. What bad luck he has had!

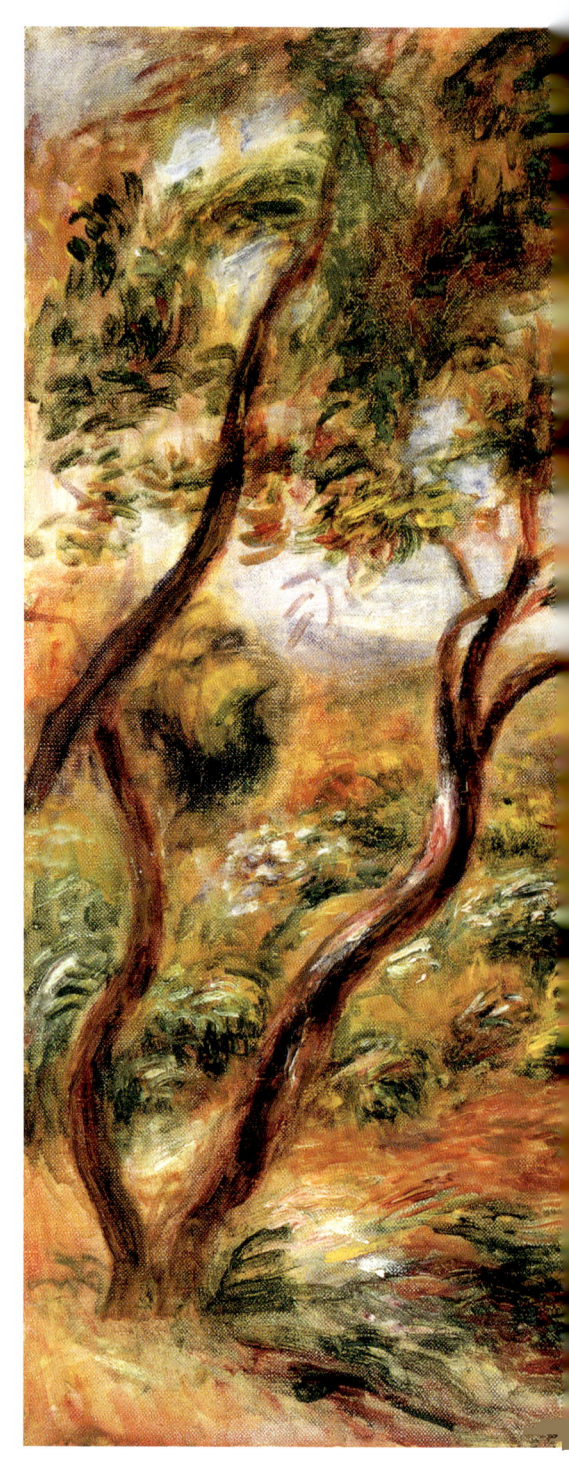

The Vineyards at Cagnes, 1908
Oil on canvas, 46.4 x 55.2 cm (18¼ x 21¾ in.)
Brooklyn Museum of Art,
Gift of Colonel and Mrs. E. W. Garbisch

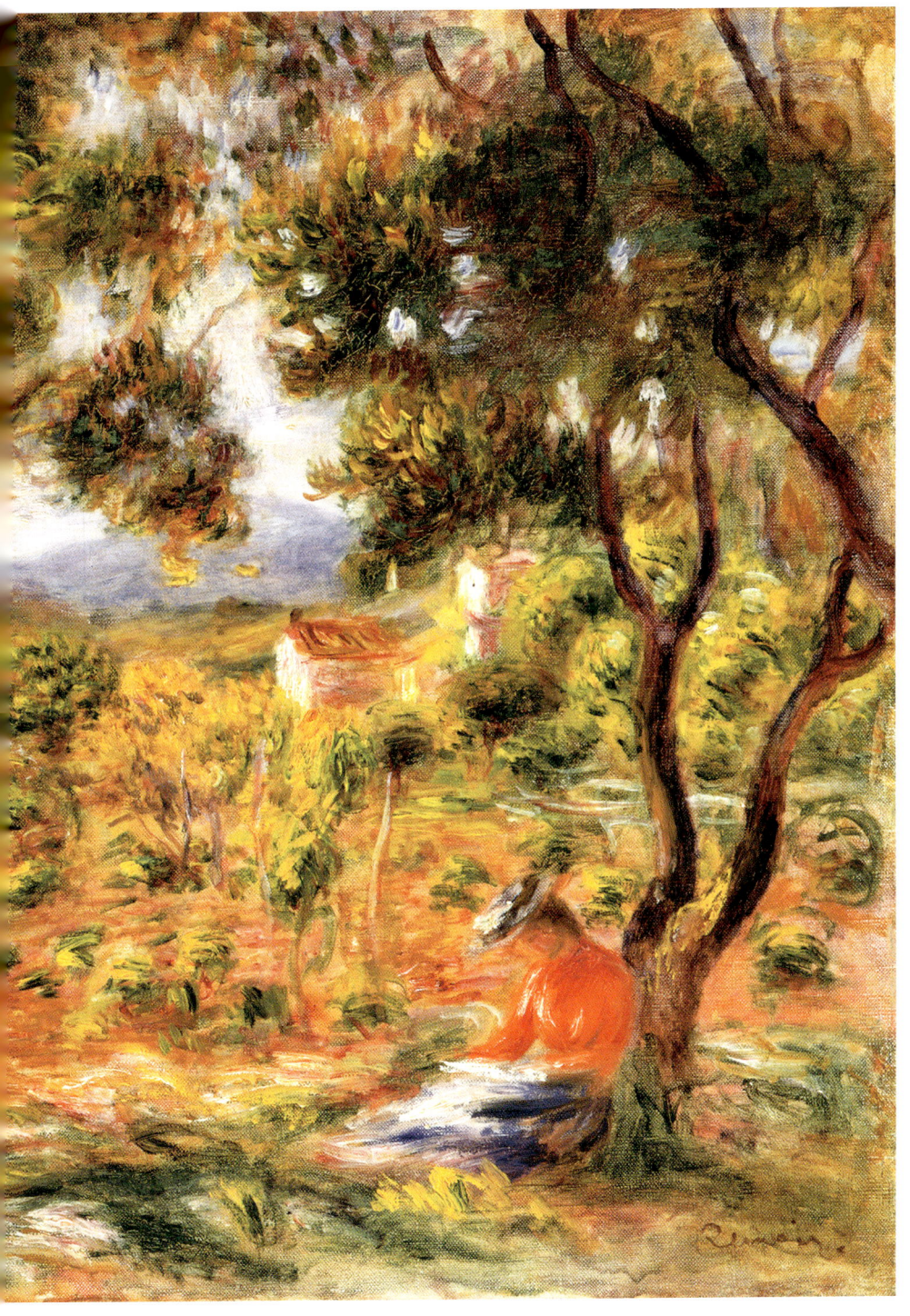

443

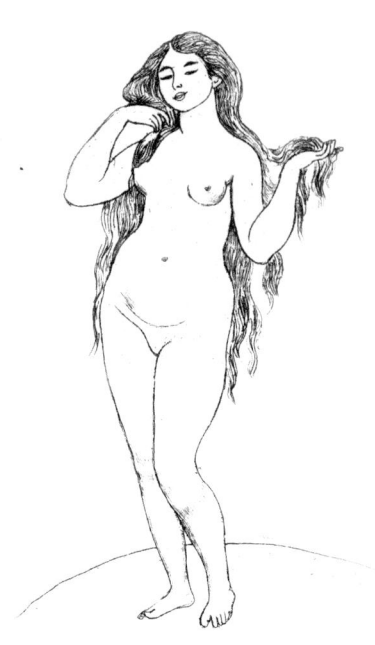

Venus – The Phenomenon of the Future, 1888
Frontispiece for the book *Pages*, published in 1891,
by his friend Stéphane Mallarmé
Etching, 17.1 x 11.4 cm (6¾ x 4½ in.)
Paris, Bibliothèque nationale de France

The Rhône and the Saône
Tapestry design for the
Gobelins factory, 1906
Oil on canvas,
92 x 74 cm (36¼ x 29¼ in.)
Private collection

Despite everything, he remained good-humoured. He was as happy as ever to be painting". Renoir first began to suffer from rheumatism in 1900 when his career was at its
zenith. With sure and painful progress it paralysed him. But it never stopped him from
painting and drawing. To look after his health he decided to go to Magagnosc and Le
Cannet. He finally decided to move to Cagnes in 1903. For six years he rented a spacious
apartment in a house in the Rue de la Poste for him and his family. Today, the house is
the town hall. The view from his windows stretched far into the distance, overlooking
the whole city and its surroundings. He used this to good advantage, often depicting the
houses and alleys of the old town, hemmed in only by the gently rolling hills. In most of
these landscapes, such as *The Vineyards at Cagnes* (pp. 442/443) and *Terrace at Cagnes*
(pp. 456/457) and especially the views of Cros-de-Cagnes, Renoir was able faithfully to
render the light of the Midi, the wonderful brilliance of the landscape with its warm,
crystalline hues indicating the close proximity of the sea. A photograph shows him
painting in front of the Villa de la Poste at Cagnes in 1903 (p. 482).

Soon afterwards Les Collettes was purchased. According to Claude Renoir, his mother
Aline used a threat hanging over the estate to persuade Renoir to agree to the purchase.
"This magnificent estate covering several hectares belonged to an old local family",
Claude recalls. "Ferdinand Deconchy, a friend of my parents, came over one day in 1907
to warn them that he had learned from the notary that a timber merchant was about
to acquire the rights to cut down all the olive trees. He was trying to beat down the price.
My mother got him on her side." This acquisition was one of the last important events

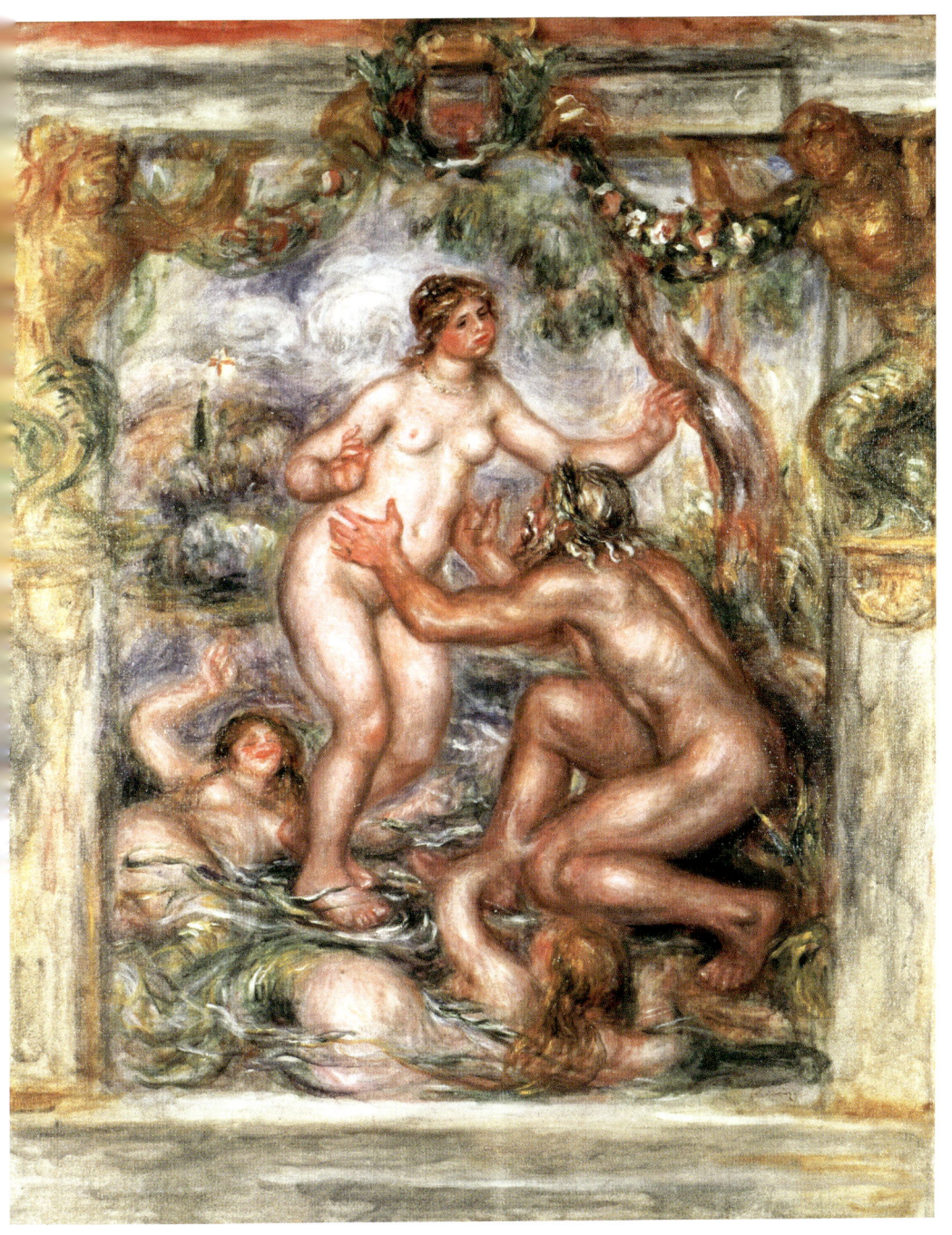

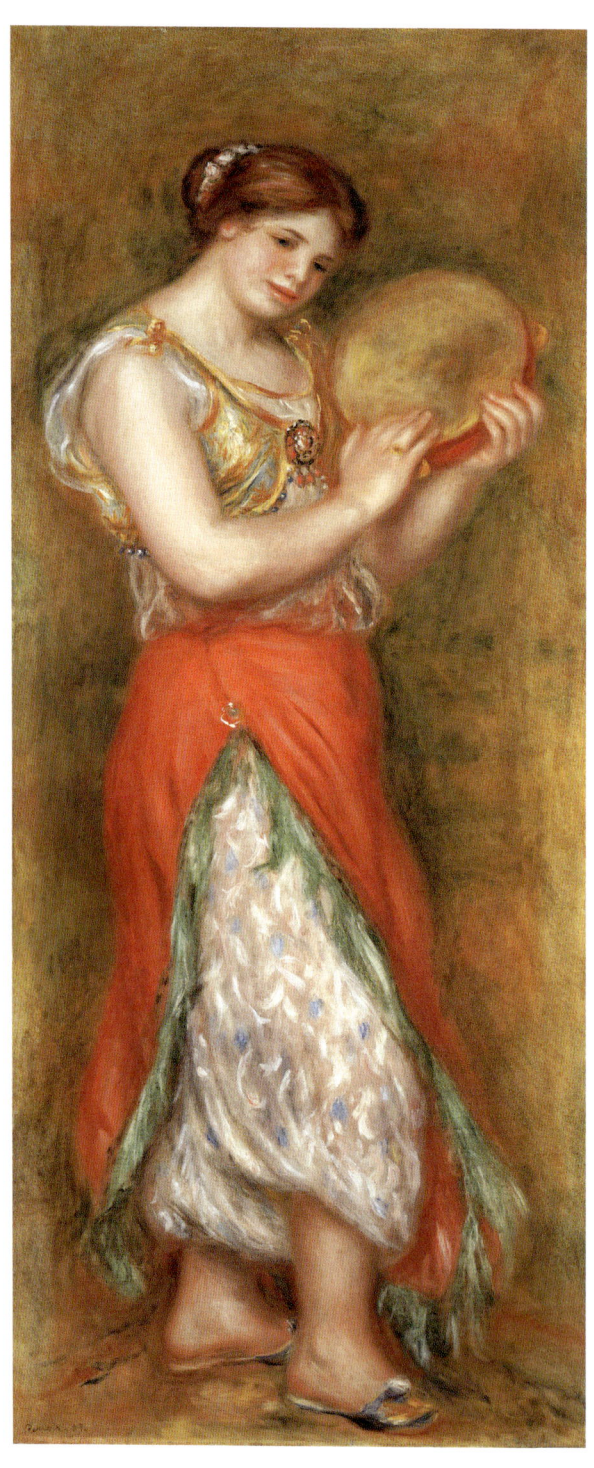

**Dancing Girl
with Tambourine**, 1909
Oil on canvas,
155 x 64.8 cm (61 x 25½ in.)
London, The National Gallery

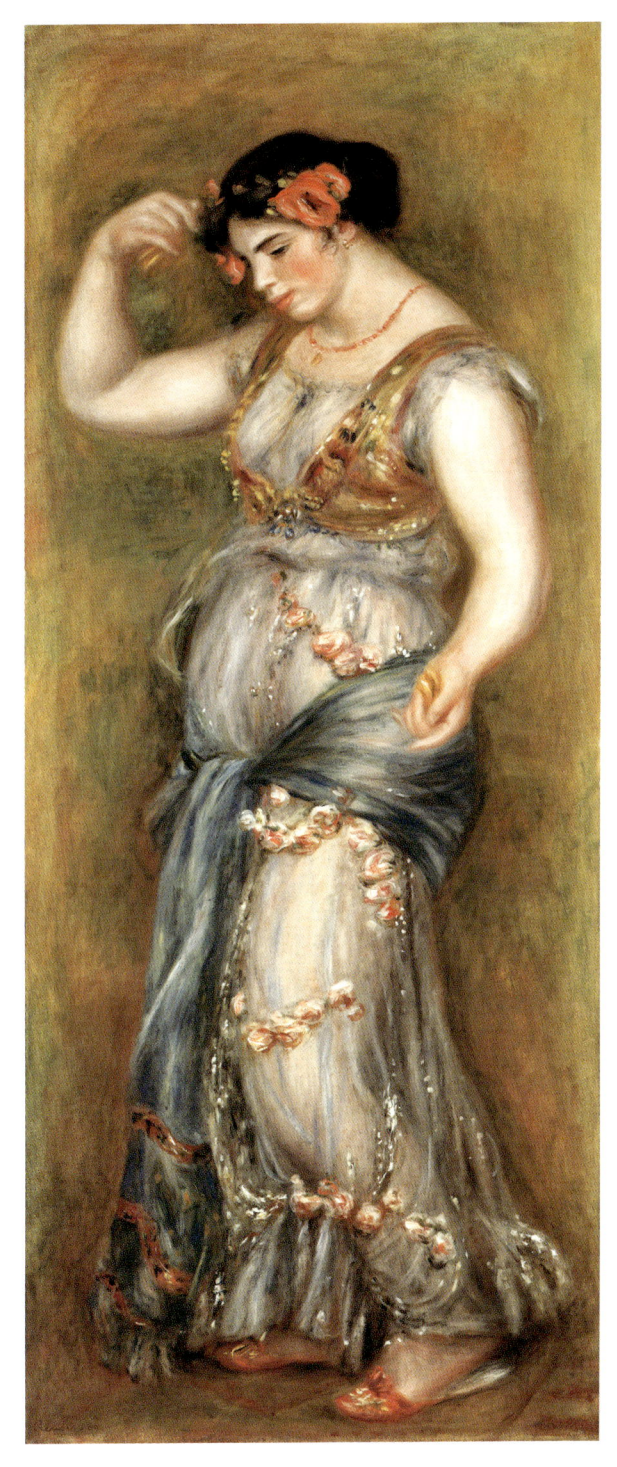

**Dancing Girl
with Castanets**, 1909
Oil on canvas,
155 x 64.8 cm (61 x 25½ in.)
London, The National Gallery

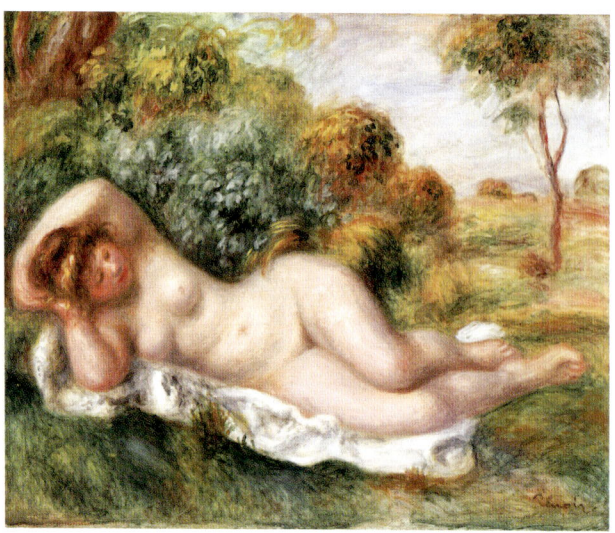

Reclining Nude (The Baker), 1902
Oil on canvas, 54 x 64.7 cm (21⅜ x 25½ in.)
Private collection

Ode to Flowers, 1903–1909
Oil on canvas, 46 x 36 cm (18⅛ x 14¼ in.)
Paris, Musée d'Orsay

in Renoir's life. He built a new stone house with living- and dining-rooms on the ground floor, and above it, bedrooms and a spacious studio. The surrounding olive grove, an ordered and luxuriant natural setting, was always a source of inspiration. Renoir never painted the house that he had built but the old farmhouse on the estate, which was for him, the centre of life there. It can be seen in *Woman Picking Flowers in the Garden of Les Collettes* (p. 459). Claude Renoir recalls how keen his father was to preserve the rural character of the estate. He even prevented the gardeners from uprooting the grass that grew on the paths. The natural setting corresponded to his pictorial vision. The old farm and its surrounding olive trees called for a human presence, female of course, to make it the "earthly paradise" that he sought to recreate at the end of his life. As Grappe said in 1933, "the farm at Les Collettes is the ideal setting for his flamboyant fantasies".

From Nice to Menton there were goddesses aplenty. They had skin that took the light well and came to pose regularly at his studio or outdoors. They populate landscapes in such paintings as *Landscape with River* (p. 450), *The Washerwomen* (p. 454), and *The Bathers* (p. 451). They reinforced the platoon of Venuses represented by Gabrielle, Madeleine Brune, Hélène Bellon, Joséphine Gastaud and Andrée Heuschling ("Dédé") who became Jean Renoir's first wife in 1920 (p. 483). All these women can be found in the numerous paintings of *Bathers* and *Washerwomen*, which represent the culmination of Renoir's research into figures in a landscape. Renoir's painting and his life were more closely merged than ever. "Ours was a house of women", explains Jean Renoir.

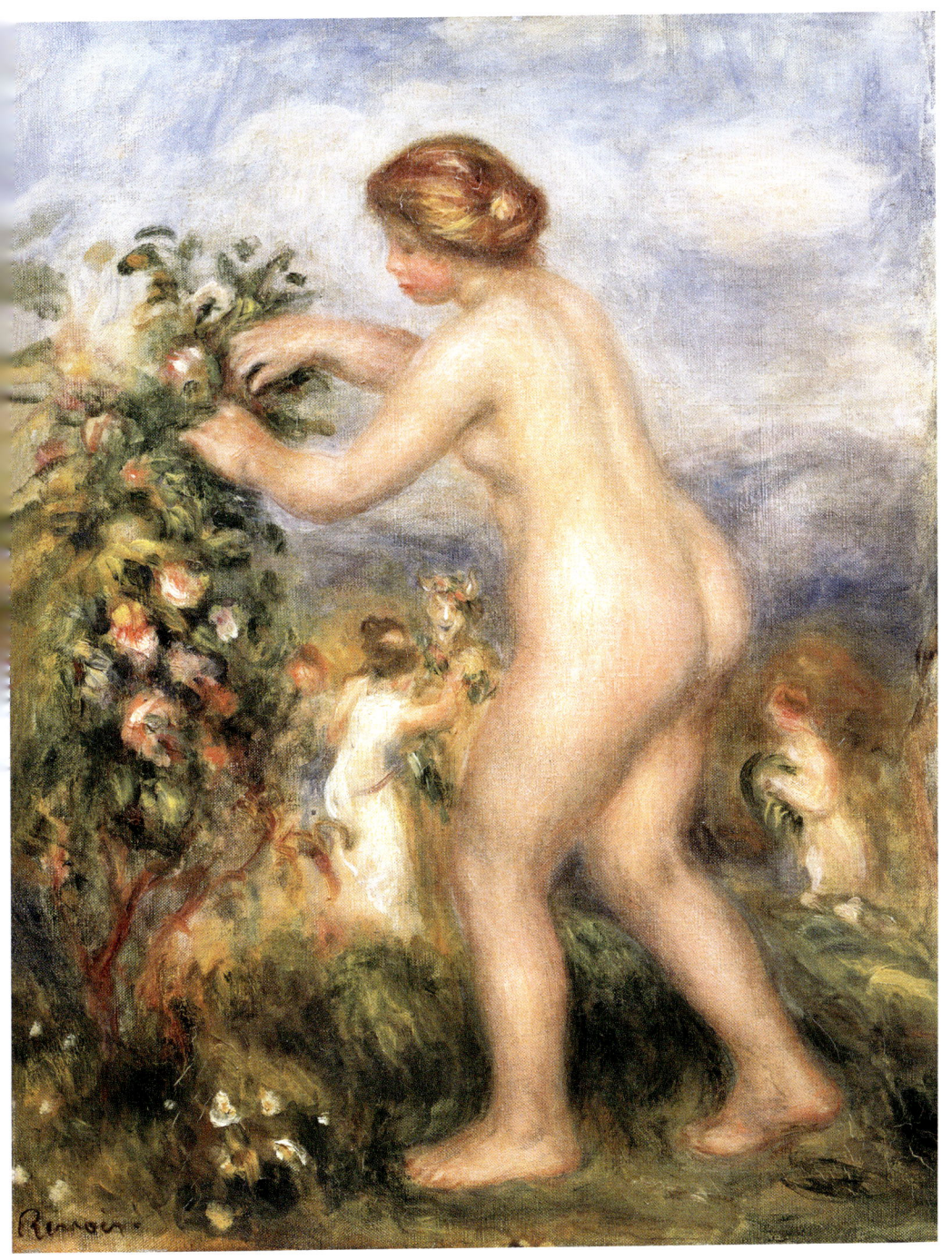

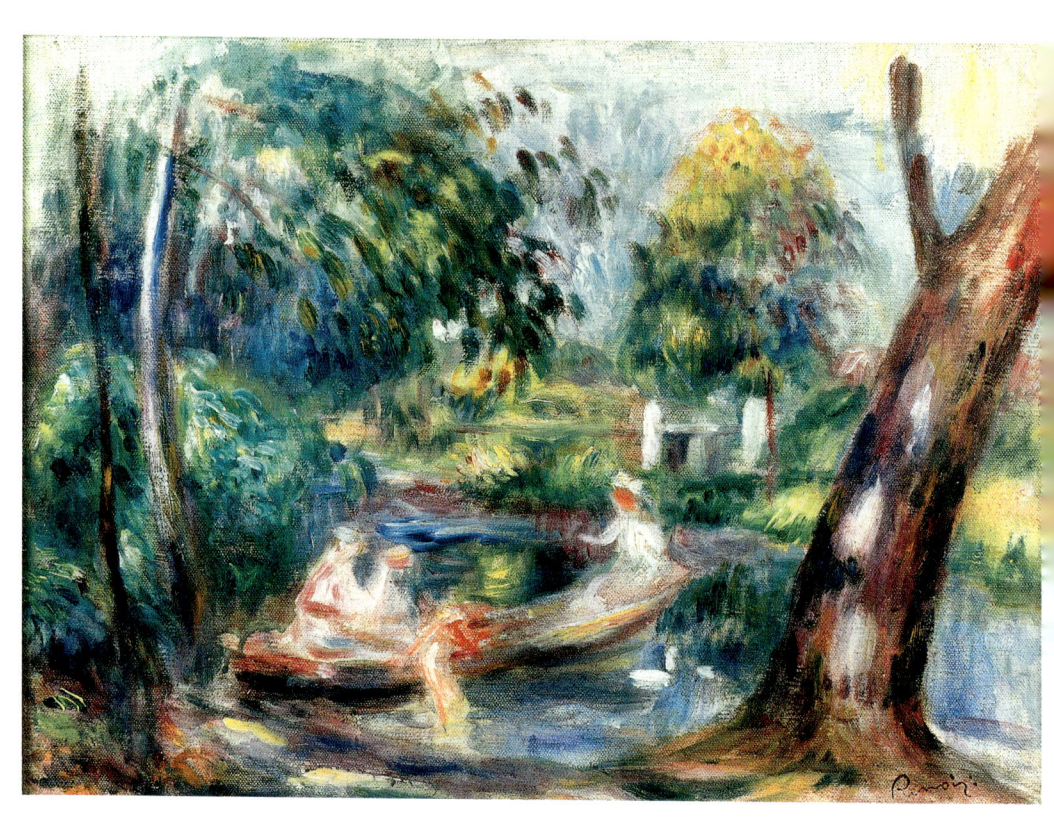

Landscape with River, 1910
Oil on canvas, 33.2 x 47.4 cm (13 x 18¾ in.)
Private collection

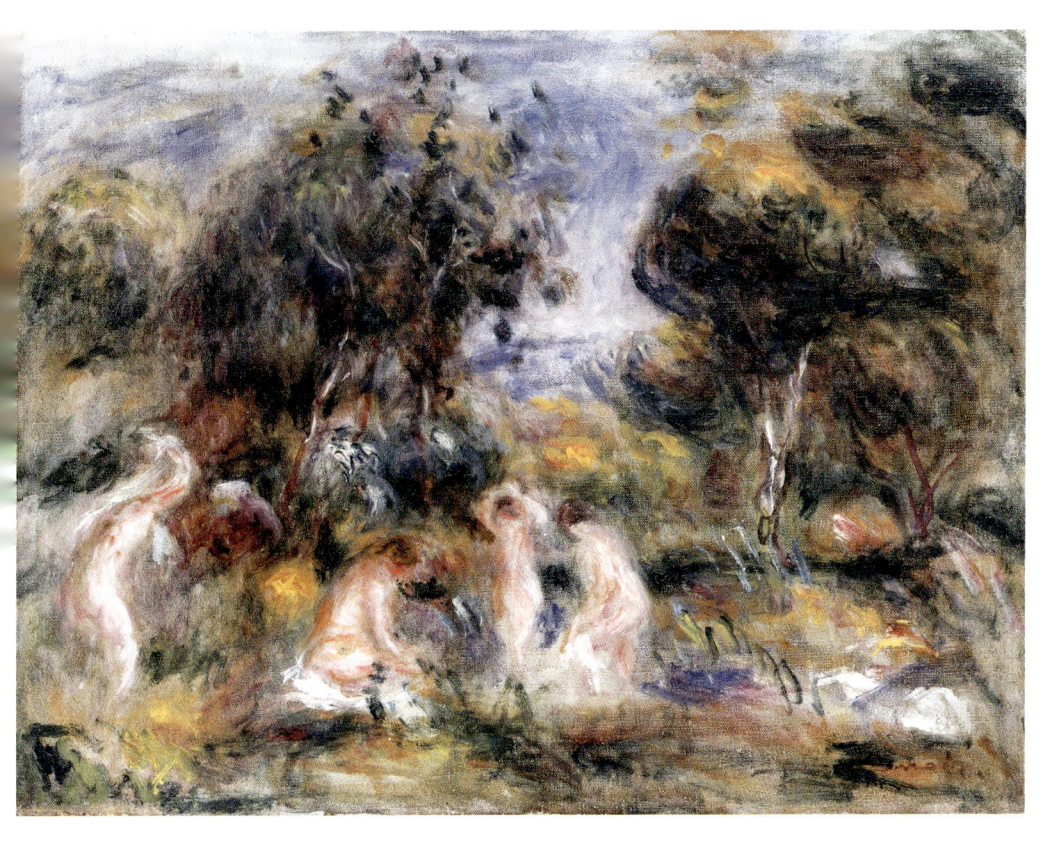

The Bathers, 1905–1910
Oil on canvas, 36 x 48 cm (14¼ x 19 in.)
Private collection

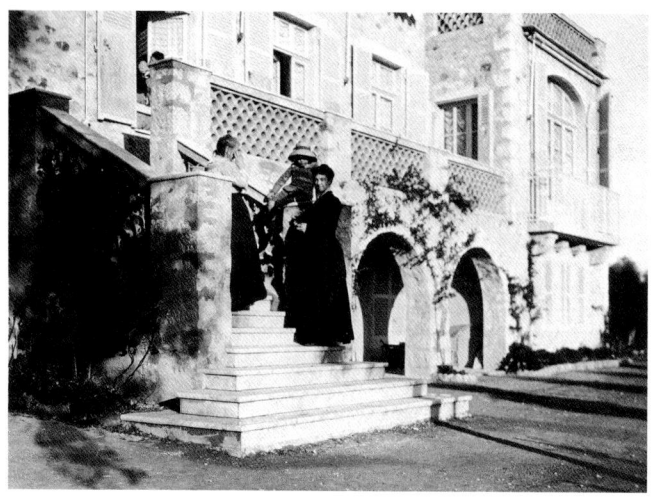

Madame Renoir, Coco and Madame Durand-
Ruel in front of the house at Les Collettes,
Cagnes-sur-Mer, 1910–1912

Meeting in the Garden, 1911–1915
Oil on canvas, 38 x 46 cm (15 x 18⅛ in.)
Paris, Musée d'Orsay

"My mother, Gabrielle, the girls, maids and models who filled it gave the house a dis-
tinctly anti-masculine feel. Sewing equipment was left out on the tables. Someone mentioned a woman lawyer to my father. He shook his head. 'I can't ever see myself sharing
a bed with a lawyer', he retorted." The man who boasted about loving illiterate women
wrote angrily to Philippe Burty in 1888: "I consider literary women, advocates and pol-
iticians, George Sand, Madame Adam, and all the others a terrible drag. They are mon-
sters, nothing but five-legged calves. Women artists are ridiculous, but female singers
and dancers are absolutely fine. In ancient and primitive times, women used to sing and
dance and were still women. Grace is woman's domain and her duty. I know full well that
such a view is considered disreputable these days, but what can I say? In ancient times
women sang and danced not to make money but simply for the pleasure of being graceful. There is too much money involved today. It takes away the charm." Renoir was worried about the Venuses of the future. "Gaining one thing always means losing another",
he confided to Jean. "You can't have everything. What women gain from learning, they
will lose in other parts of life. What really worries me is that future generations will make
love terribly badly." His deliberately ribald anxiety was genuine. He claimed that lack of
exercise would produce blue-stockinged girls incapable of enjoying sexual intercourse
to the full. "There will be fewer and fewer of those pretty tarts who lose their heads and
abandon themselves completely. Love, even of the normal kind, will become a form of
masturbation. When women were slaves they were really in charge. Now that they are
beginning to have rights, they will lose their power. When they are the equals of men,

452

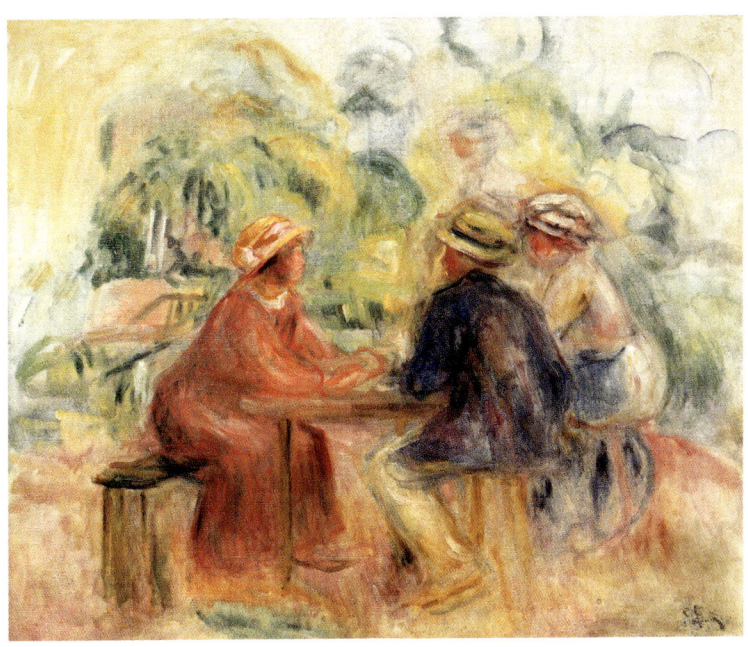

then they will know true slavery". He was surrounded by women and sons who looked like his paintings. "Sometimes he would put down his palette", Rivière recalls, "and gaze at them instead of painting. 'Why tire yourself out?' he would say to himself. What he wanted to create existed already."

Renoir said what he did out of love for women. He wanted them to keep what he saw as their true power by remaining feminine. He wanted Venus to be *The Phenomenon of the Future* (p. 444). This was his vision of an earthly paradise. To celebrate women better he tried to reproduce all of the five senses on a single canvas. To the magnificence of the female body he added the richness of the materials that touch it, fruitlike bodies that one wants to taste, the fragrance of flowers, and running water or musical instruments to delight the ear. At the end of his life, Renoir freely compared anemones to a woman's sexual organs and roses to the beauties of the female body.

The pink ribbon in the hair of Velasquez's infantas was transformed into the innumerable roses that he sprinkled in the hair and on the laps of his models as well as on the ground. In the famous *Gabrielle with a Rose* (p. 440) the model places a rose in her hair while holding another. After the wild flowers that adorned his paintings in his Impressionist period, roses now took on an almost obsessional character. The aim was not only to create a focal point of the same kind as the Velasquez hair-ribbon. It was also, as he explained to an astonished Vollard, "part of the researches into tone that I am making for my nudes". *Vase of Roses* (p. 471) finds its human correlative in the rosy-cheeked *Gabrielle in a Red Blouse* (1913). Like Picasso, who saw painting and eroticism

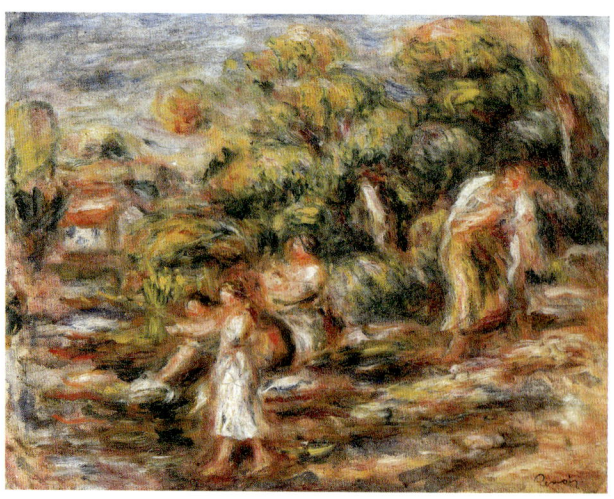

The Washerwomen, 1919
Oil on canvas, 28.5 x 38.5 cm (11¼ x 15¼ in.)
Private collection

Avenue through the Undergrowth, c. 1910
Oil on canvas, 55 x 46 cm (21¾ x 18⅛ in.)
Cagnes-sur-Mer, Musée Renoir – Les Collettes

as one and the same thing, Renoir associated the full-blown rose with a riper vision of feminine beauty.

Gustave Geffroy noted as early as 1894 that his final paintings of women reveal "Renoir's voluptuous art". *The Great Bathers* (pp. 348/349) contain "raw research and admirable application", he noted. "Renoir has worked hard to produce an intellectual and pictorial synthesis. The luminous purity of the Primitives, combined deliberately with the balanced drawing of Ingres, gave birth to a work of lingering charm." Renoir's final female portraits came from the very depth of his being. "Natural instinct was admitted into his conception", Geffroy continued. "Note the accurate constructions, their graceful young faces and shoulders, heavy breasts, the folds in their hips, their supple hair, the flesh tones harmonizing with their dark stomachs, the marbled veins showing on their bosoms, and their faces modelled in bright light. All of this is nature's bounty. Compare them to the beautiful women he had painted before, one with raised arms, another surrounded by clothing, both with healthy torsos and pink cheeks. The new women have feminine bodies but girlish faces. They have dainty, plump bodies that hardly appear to contain bones. Their round heads are shown almost in profile and their blushing expressions show them to be at the moment in life when youthful tranquillity gives way to the embarrassment of puberty. A girl, with her senses newly awakened, turns into a woman capable of love in front of our eyes. Renoir's favourite features in all of these women are a small forehead, which betrays gentleness and obstinacy, and a rather heavy jaw promising sensuality. Even in those portraits that least correspond

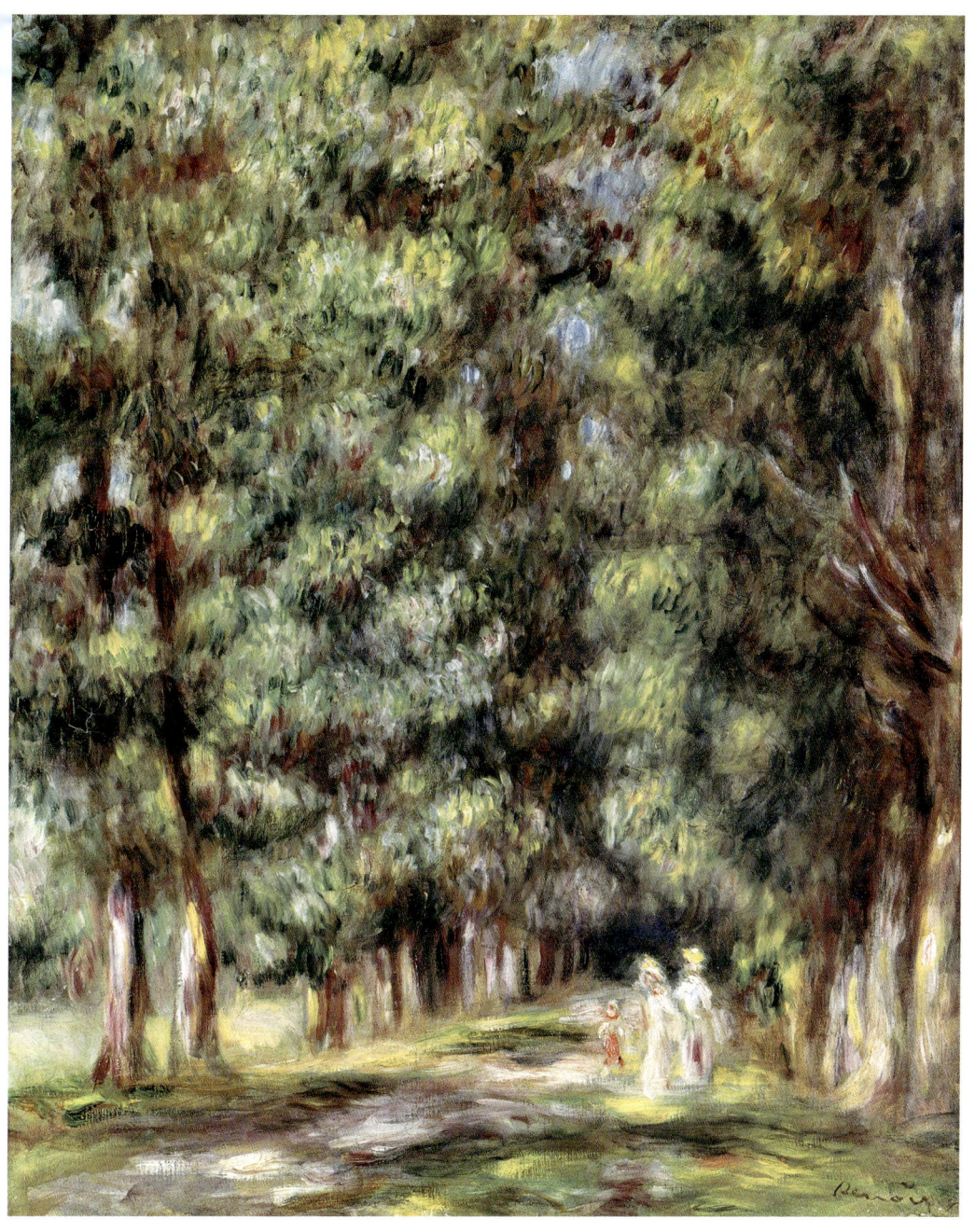

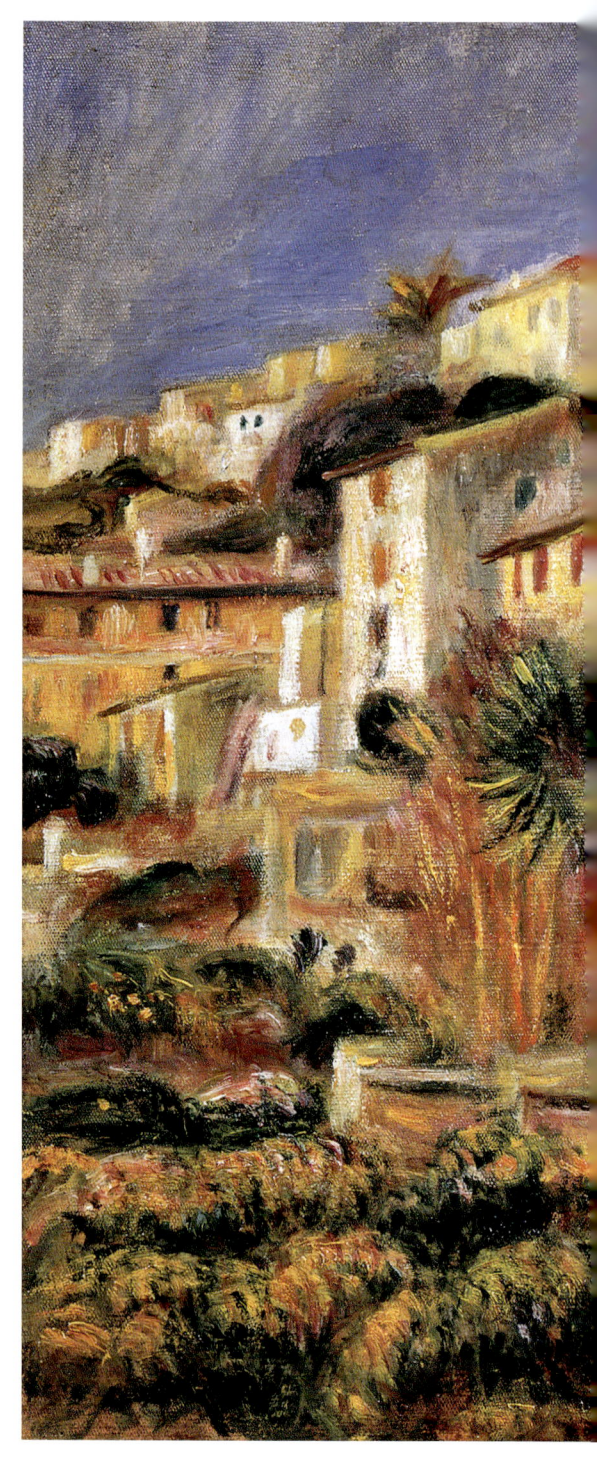

Terrace at Cagnes, 1905
Oil on canvas,
45.3 x 54.5 cm (17⅞ x 21½ in.)
Tokyo, Bridgestone Museum of Art

456

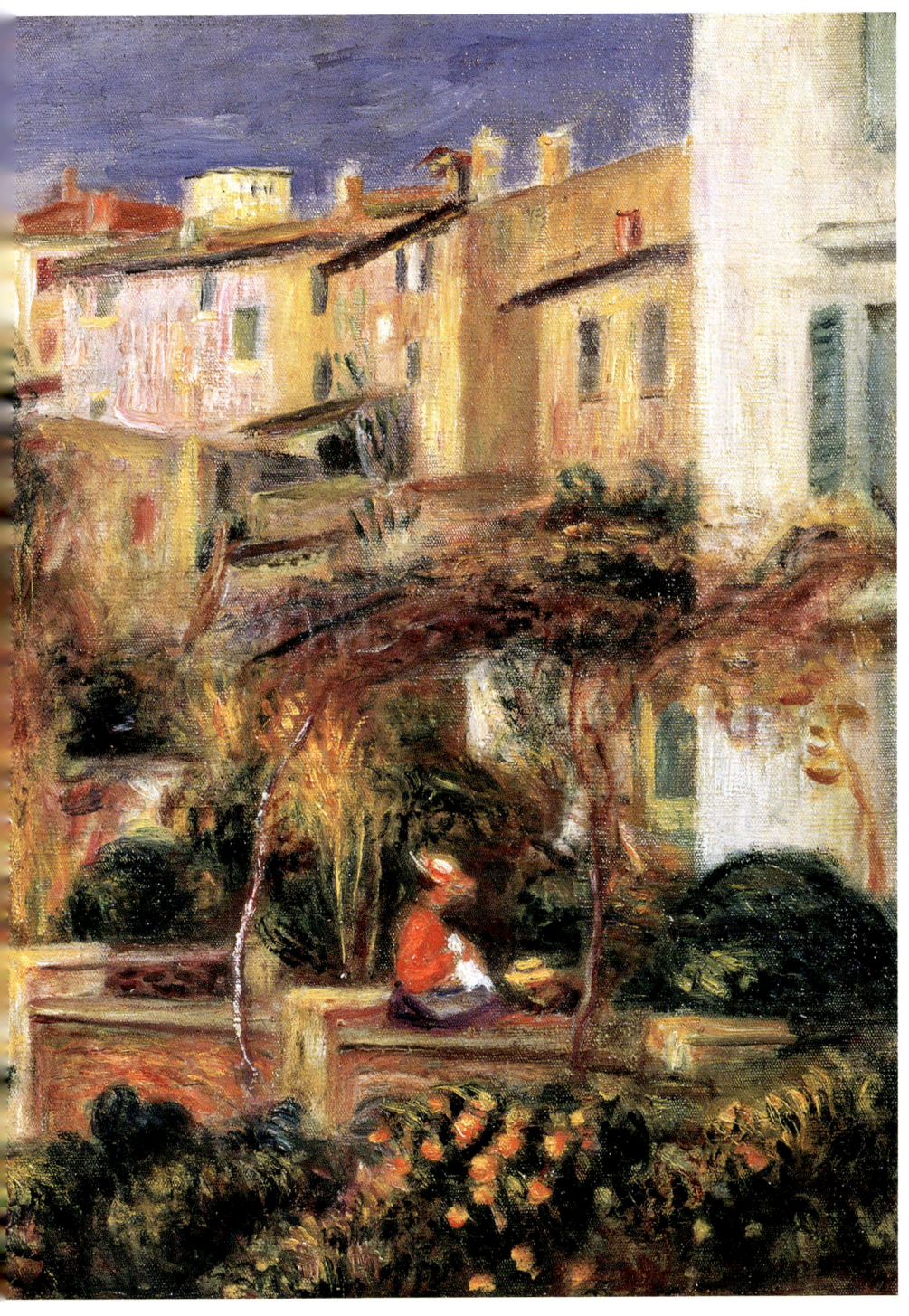

to his own desires, he adds from his rich imagination the features that he looks for in
a woman. In all the greatest painters of women you find this same instinctive choice.
They all create a beauty that is haughty, passionate, melancholy and charming. By these
means they transmit their desire and reveal the inner workings of their minds".

Gabrielle remained Renoir's archetype of womanhood. Jean Renoir has left an affectionate portrait of her, which makes it easier to understand what Renoir saw in her.
"When my mother was pregnant with me, she had the idea of bringing a cousin of hers
from Essoyes to help her. Gabrielle Renard was fifteen years old and had never been
outside her native village before. The nuns had given her a good education. She could
sew and iron and by the age of ten she knew how to tell the vintage of a wine, tickle trout
without being caught by the gamekeeper, herd cows, bleed a pig, find grass for the rab-
bits and collect dung from horses coming back from the fields. Dung was precious stuff.
People waited, with shovels and buckets in hand, for steaming lumps of it to fall on the
white road. Every kid in Essoyes was proud of the family dung-heap: it had pride of
place in the centre of the courtyard, and they were always looking for fresh supplies.
Epic struggles ensued between them. Gabrielle generally emerged victorious but with
her clothes in tatters. Gabrielle only put shoes on in the mornings to go to lessons with
the nuns. In the evening, as soon as she left, she took them off. When the nuns met her in
the street, they told her that a barefoot little girl would never become like Mademoiselle
Lemercier, the pride of the village, who wore a veil, had passed her school certificate,
and was engaged to a colonial civil servant. Gabrielle replied that she did not want to be

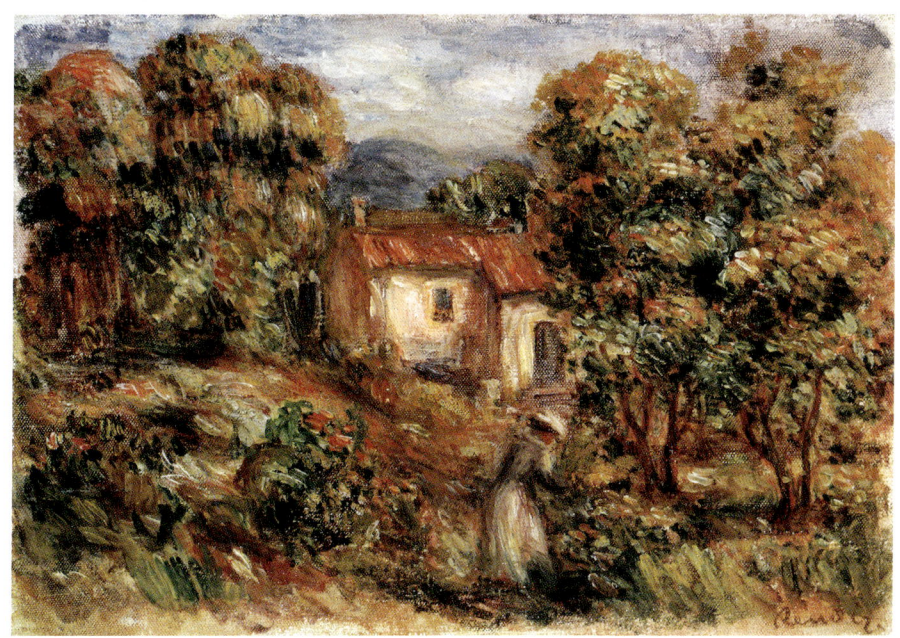

like Mademoiselle Lemercier. The nuns generally managed to give their pupils a veneer of good breeding. With Gabrielle, however, they failed completely. When she arrived at the Château des Brouillards, she expressed volubly her surprise at finding no dung-heap in the garden. The following day, my mother knocked on her door. There was no reply. Gabrielle was in the street, playing with the local kids. My mother thought this was a good sign. All that she asked of her young cousin was to play with me when I was born".

Gabrielle did not merely help with the household chores and look after Jean. She soon became the model to whom Renoir most frequently turned. At first she posed as the Nanny in the "baby Jesus" paintings. From 1900 onwards Renoir was without a model; she agreed to pose in the nude on a regular basis and did so with perfect ease. She had what Renoir considered to be the two essential qualities in a model: a skin colour that caught the light, and the kind of body and features that corresponded to his vision of womanhood. Between 1903 and 1907, the painter produced a series of recumbent odalisques of Gabrielle. These were reminiscent of Ingres in their subject matter but very different in style. A soft brushstroke and deliberately restrained palette replaced the harsh, drawn contours. Maurice Denis wrote about them in his review of the 1905 Autumn Salon, in which one of these *Recumbent Nude* paintings was exhibited. "Renoir, who in any case is no longer an Impressionist in any way, triumphs with his latest style of robust and abundant nudes", he concluded. "He reminds one of the Raphael of *The Fire* and the *Farnesine*. Note that his skilful execution of the flesh has in no way compromised his freshness and ingenuity."

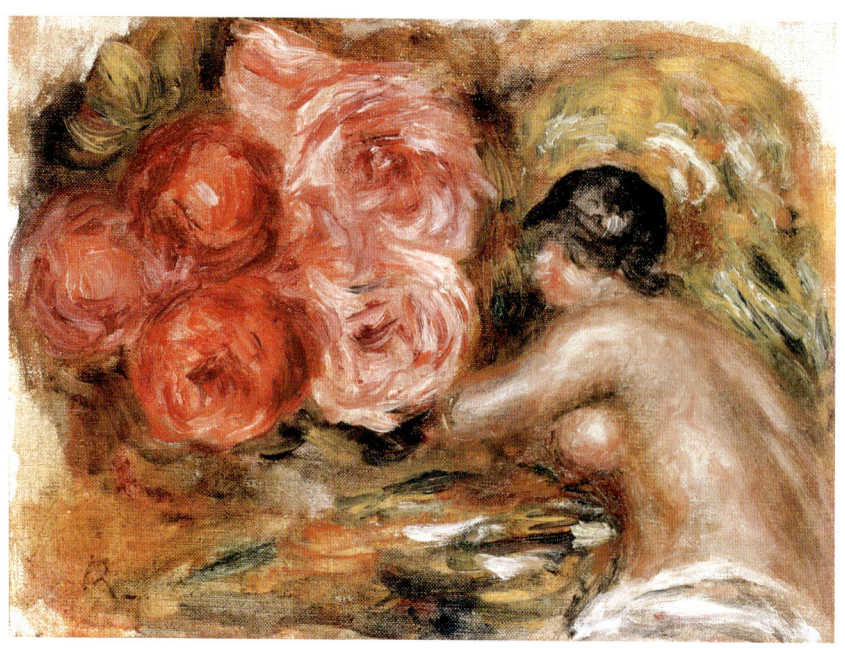

The model for *Nude on Cushions* (pp. 466/467), which belongs to the same series, was probably not Gabrielle but a similar model to whom Renoir gave the same features and pose. Renoir cited Titian's *Venus with an Organist*, which he had seen in Madrid in 1892, as the inspiration for his nude's pose. "The limpidity of that rump makes you want to stroke it", he told Vollard. "When you look at this painting you can see what a pleasure it was for Titian to paint. When a painter shows me that he gets a kick out of painting something, he gives me the same kick." Renoir now had his nudes pose unambiguously as objects of admiration. Gabrielle did not only pose naked. Between around 1907 and 1910, Renoir frequently depicted her in floating, semi-transparent veils that open at the front to reveal her breasts. These timeless masterpieces include *Gabrielle with a Rose* (p. 440), *Female Semi-Nude* (p. 463), and *Gabrielle with Jewels* (p. 464). Roses become a metaphor for breasts in these paintings. The spectator can feel that all the frills and furbelows are about to drop away and reveal the naked body in all its transparent glory. This is a seductive woman ready to offer herself up to the painter's gaze and then to all those who look at her portrait.

Renoir described to Walter Pach his methods at this time. "I arrange my subject according to my taste and then I just go on and paint her, like a child would", he explained. "I want to find a red loud enough to ring like a bell, and if I don't manage it at first, I add reds and other colours until I do. There is nothing more intelligent to it than that." In 1909 he explained to Schnerb that he had found the colour for one of his paintings, of Gabrielle no doubt, by using "a single tone". He constantly tried to obtain

Roses and Study of Gabrielle, c. 1907
Oil on canvas, 36 x 48 cm (14¼ x 19 in.)
Private collection

The pink ribbons filched from Velázquez's
infantas and transposed into Coco's hair, were
transformed into roses to adorn Gabrielle's tresses.
Renoir never hid the fact that, for him, the rose
symbolised the female sexual organ, an intimate
reflection of woman's carnal beauty. When he had
completed a nude painting he sometimes used the
colours remaining on his palette to sketch a few
roses. When Vollard expressed astonishment at
such profusion, Renoir replied, "this is research
into skin tones that I am doing for the nudes".

richer effects with simple means. He reduced his palette to retain maximum control
over his materials and results.

"Some paintings from the last period", wrote Meier-Graefe in 1912, "are like young
wines: they need to age. Renoir paid attention at that time neither to the material quality
of the paints he used nor to his technical use of them. He believes that this is the reason
for the inadequacy of his earlier work. Today, he thinks about the effect that time will
have on his colours and colour contrasts and so deepens all the tones. These, especially
the lacquers, soften slightly after a time. Hence the exaggerated redness of certain flesh
tones. The colours need time to 'settle' for a few years before they blend perfectly into a
smooth enamel. Many people find his palette mawkish. Such 'delicate' judgements lack
the delicacy required to appreciate true worth. People who buy paintings by the dozen
transform the Renoir at which they are looking into a crude image of itself. The result is
reminiscent of those dreadful impressions in three colours where all the delicate shades
of colour have been reduced to barley sugar pink, violet blue and blinding white, the
hallmark of bad taste in painting. These people cannot see the rich and original shades
located between these worn-out extremes of colour. They have the same mentality as
those so-called literati who think that the rhyme 'eyes' and 'sighs' necessarily belongs
to bad verse written by schoolgirls. Perhaps the vision of someone who started out as a
painter of porcelain is a true reflection of the symbolism of colours of his time and these
are fairly banal. But, in my eyes, it is a rare advantage that one can still discover this
popular theme in Renoir's richest variations."

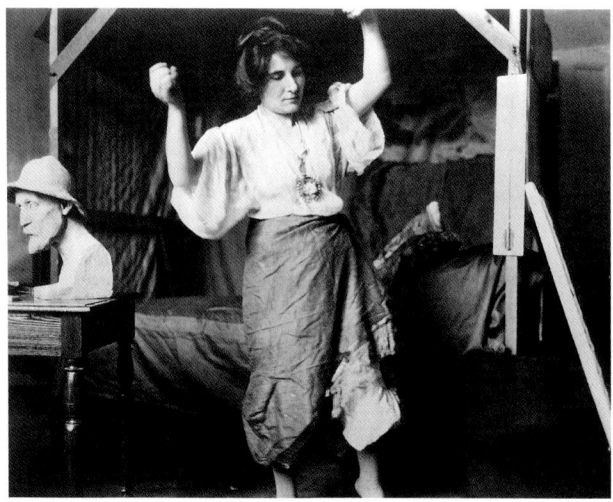

Bust of Renoir by Aristide Maillol
(1861–1944) and Gabrielle dancing in
the studio at Cagnes-sur-Mer in 1910

Female Semi-Nude, c. 1908
Oil on canvas, 65.5 x 53.5 cm (25⅞ x 21 in.)
Private collection

Many of Renoir's admirers flinched when they saw *Reclining Nude – The Baker* (the nickname of one of his models, p. 448) and the *Ode to Flowers* (p. 449). One critic gave the Barnes Foundation's *Bathing Group* (pp. 382/383) and *Young Women in the Country* (1916), now in Besançon, the unflattering nomenclature "pneumatic goddesses". Another critic expressed his fear that "these windbags would burst if pricked with a pin" and called Renoir's women "creatures haunted by apoplexy". A third critic reinforced these views by calling them "rubber lobsters afflicted with elephantiasis". The thickness of their legs and arms, their rolls of fat and the red colour of their skin were disliked by the critics. Renoir's reply was simple: "I am struggling to make my figures become one with their background landscape ... I am a poet, and poets must dream." Max-Pol Fouchet comments: "Renoir seeks to achieve union with those earth forces from which womanhood cannot be dissociated. Women, in these paintings, are gigantic life bearers, fecund like the prehistoric fertility goddesses. The redness of their flesh is the red of blood and fire". He is referring to the *Venus Victorious* paintings. "What I like about painting", Renoir commented at this time, "is that it has an air of eternity about it". Even today, exhibitions neglect late Renoir.

The reputation of his later works would no doubt improve if they were allowed greater exposure. Great painters, from Toulouse-Lautrec to Picasso and from Renoir to Matisse, have gone on evolving right to the end. They all suffer from a tendency of critics to judge their last period as one of senility. It is in fact the peak of their art and the moment at which they open up new paths for their successors.

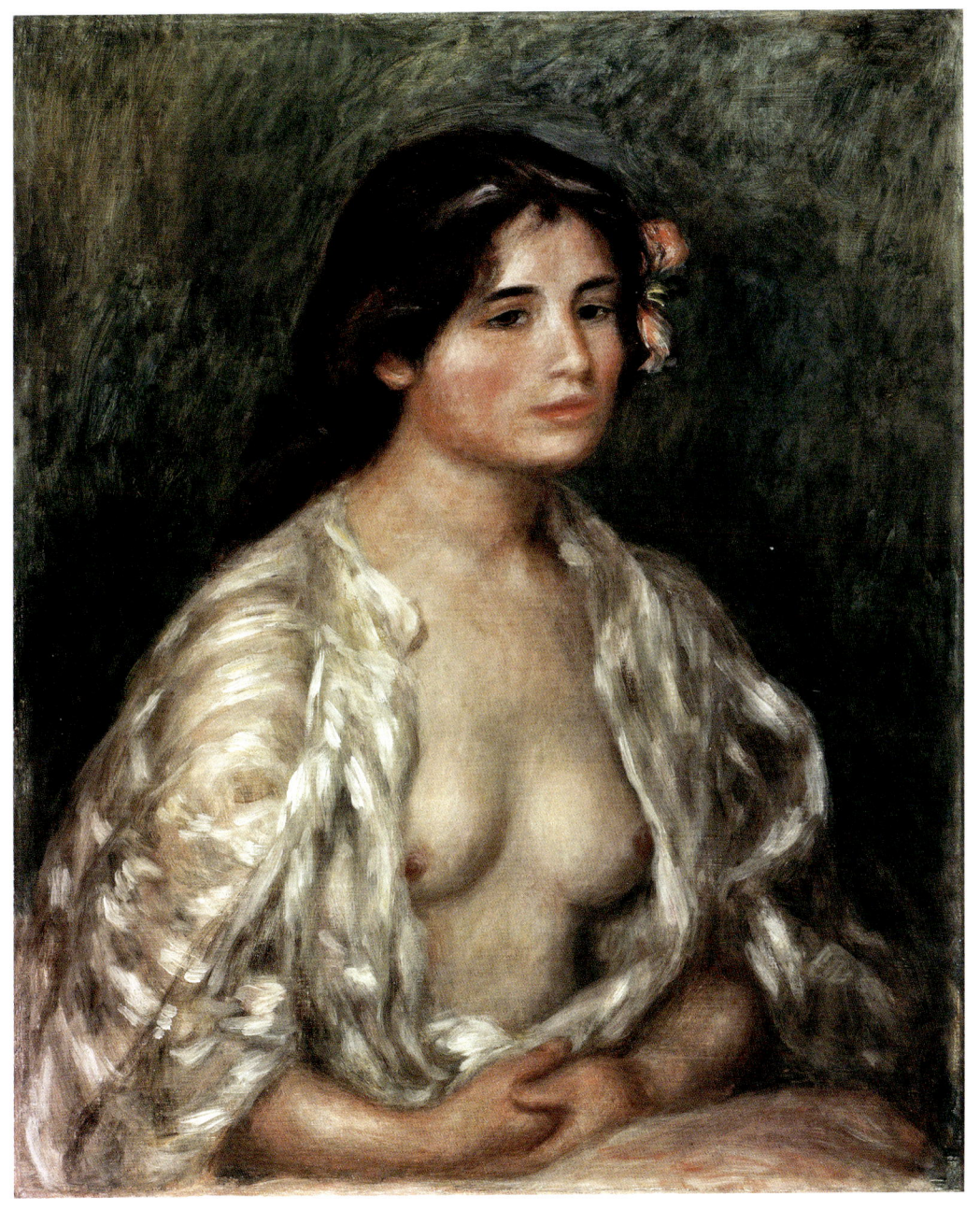

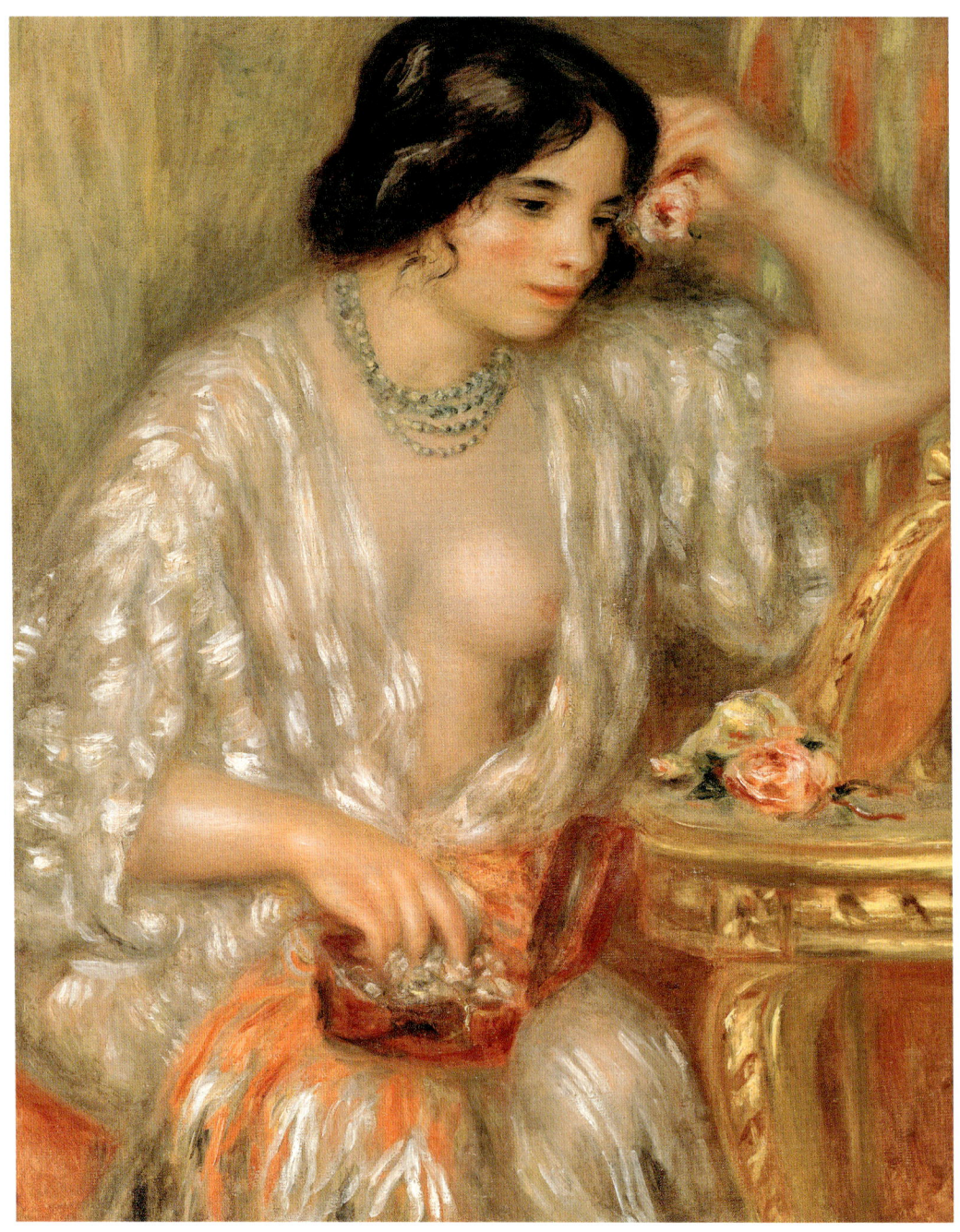

Gabrielle, 1910–1912

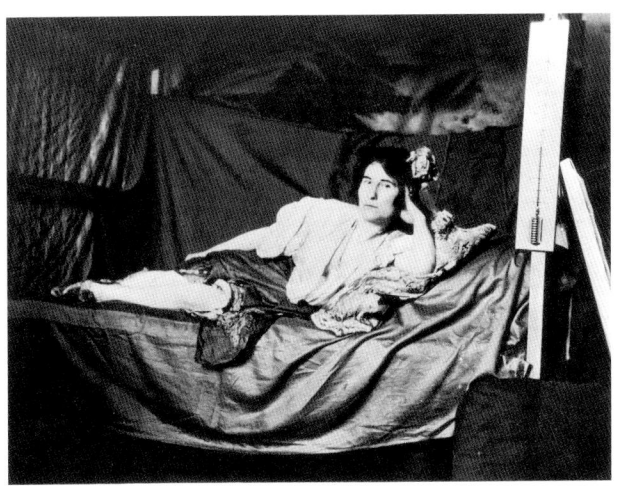

Gabrielle with Jewels, c. 1910
Oil on canvas, 82 x 65.5 cm (32¼ x 25¾ in.)
Private collection

In 1961 the English sculptor Henry Moore, whose monumental female sculptures owe something to Renoir's late nudes, finally persuaded the National Gallery in London to acquire two large late Renoir paintings, *Dancing Girl with Tambourine* and *Dancing Girl with Castanets* (pp. 446 and 447). These are said to have been inspired by the performances of La Belle Otéro; for a long time they decorated Maurice Gagnat's living room. Moore used the occasion to publish a statement in which he expressed his admiration for Renoir's late representations of women and argued that he had proved himself to be superior to Maillol and the equal of Rembrandt.

The opinion of such an outstanding modern artist is worth more than that of all the critics put together. "Whoever doesn't like those girls doesn't understand what Renoir was trying to do", Moore wrote. "The two pictures must represent at least three or four months of continuous work at the best period of Renoir's life. A tremendous amount of application went into the painting of them, a great deal of real ambition; they represent a big effort to produce something worthy of the museums. If you copy nature as it is, as Renoir was mainly doing during his earlier Impressionist period, you can't really show the form that underlies appearances. Nature is too complicated, and to make a work of art out of it you have to simplify, to invent a system of vision. In painting, where you have to reduce everything to a flat surface with only colour and texture, you have above all to simplify the lighting. Renoir hit on this method of lighting the model, as it were, simply from his own eyes; so that all his surfaces are subject to a logical system of lighting which explains the form. In these pictures he has learned to fit his forms into space.

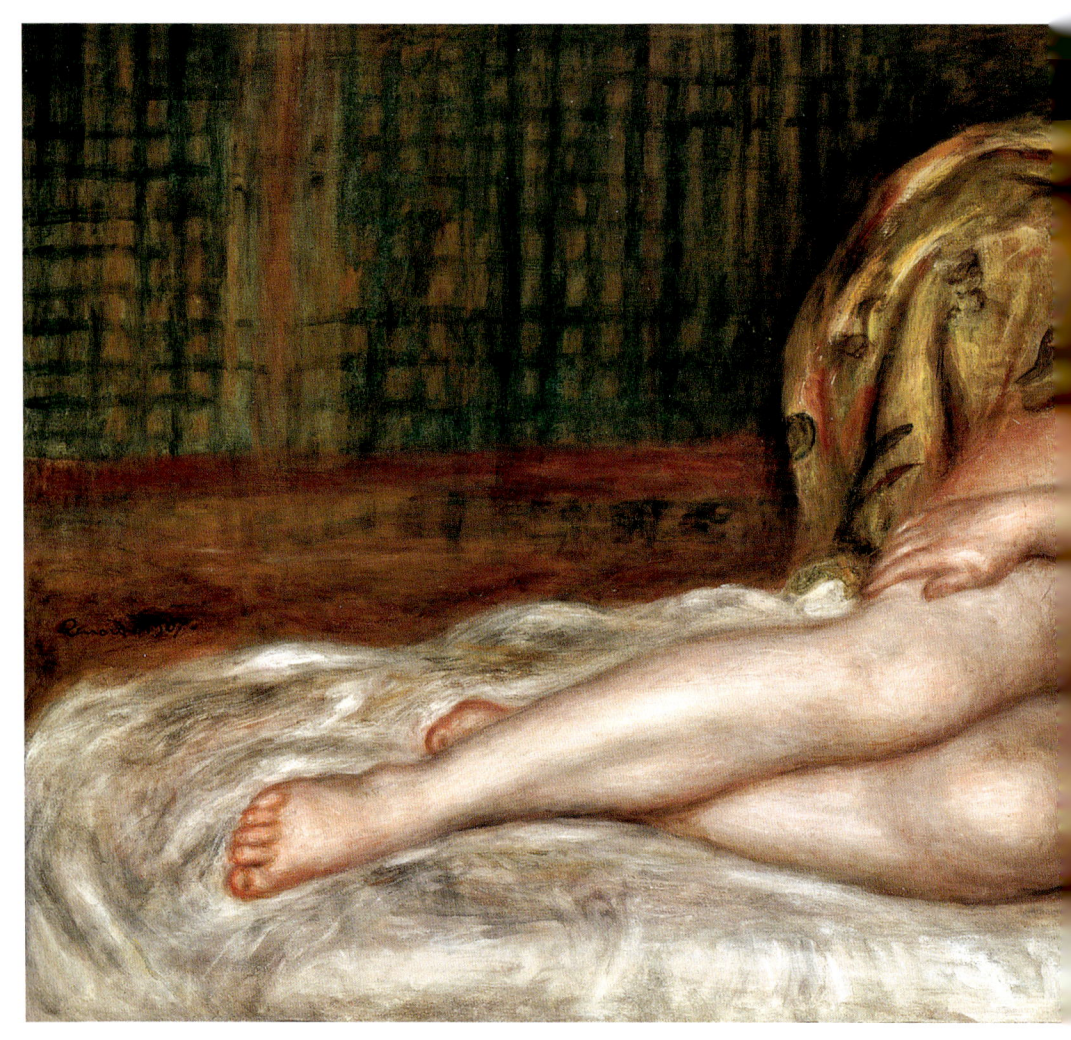

Nude on Cushions, 1907
Oil on canvas, 71 x 156 cm (28 x 61½ in.)
Paris, Musée d'Orsay

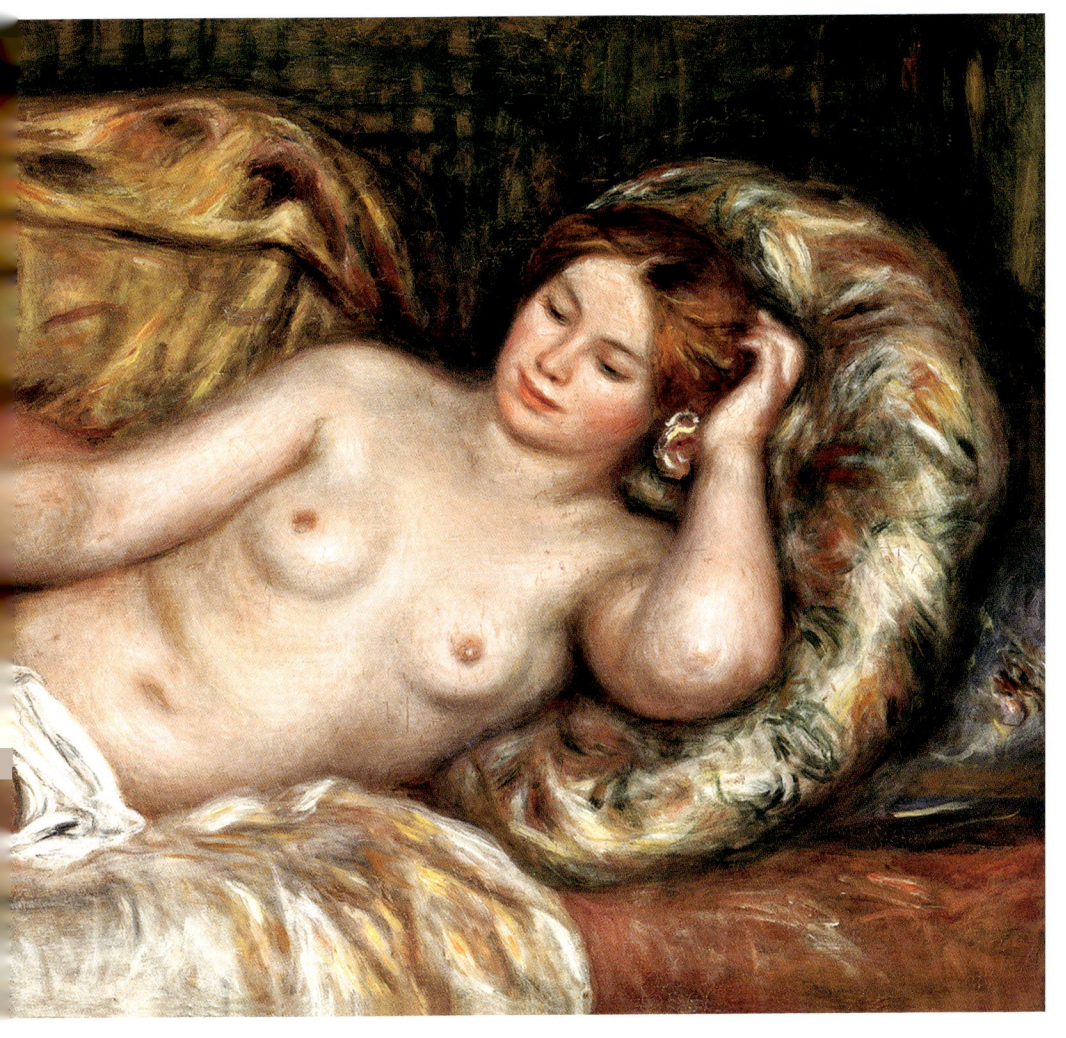

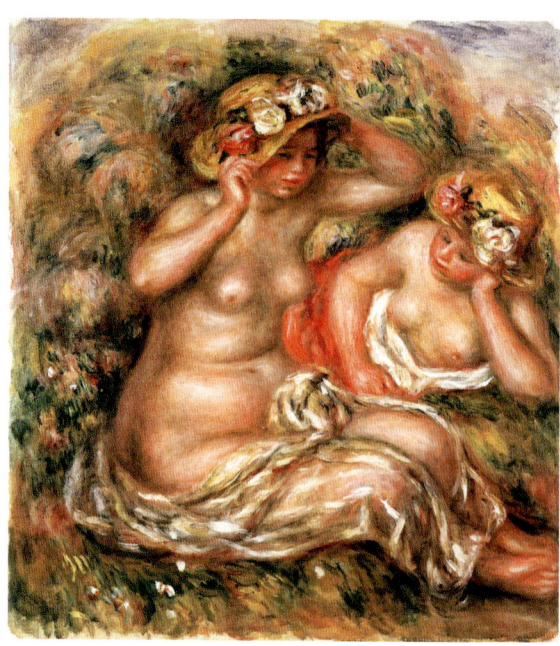

Two Nudes Wearing Hats, 1919
Oil on canvas,
32 x 34 cm (12⅝ x 13½ in.)
Private collection

The Bather at the Fountain, 1914
Oil on canvas,
55 x 47 cm (21¾ x 18⅝ in.)
Private collection

The shapes of these two girls are melted into the background; so that what you see and feel about them comes from inside the forms, not just from the outlines, as it did earlier, in his hard-edge paintings. And yet these rounded forms have a marvellous supple rhythm, such as people are apt to associate only with outlines. What one likes about them is that, though they are so monumental, yet, if you compare them, for instance, with Maillol's sculptures, they have none of the stiffness which these are apt to have. They make me realise that Renoir was really a much greater sculptor than Maillol. And, in addition, what lovely passages there are of delicious painting and wonderful colour! There are so many subtleties in the painting of them which one goes on discovering that I never know which I like the better of the two. One day it's one, another day it's the other. One could say most of these things if these were 'abstract' pictures. But they are anything but that; Renoir tried to put into them all that he felt about women. The way he dressed them up is a key to this. For me their costumes only emphasise the sculptural grandeur of them, as Rembrandt wanted to do when he dressed up Saskia. Renoir didn't just paint these girls as he saw them about the house, as he did in so many of his smaller, more everyday pictures. When they came into his studio in the morning to pose, they didn't just take their clothes off either. The whole ceremony of getting dressed up would help to make the occasion important. The pictures represent, I'm sure, a significant episode in Renoir's career, a special effort; that's why I think they are not just ordinary pictures for private collectors, why I believe they are the kind of pictures we should have in the National Gallery."

468

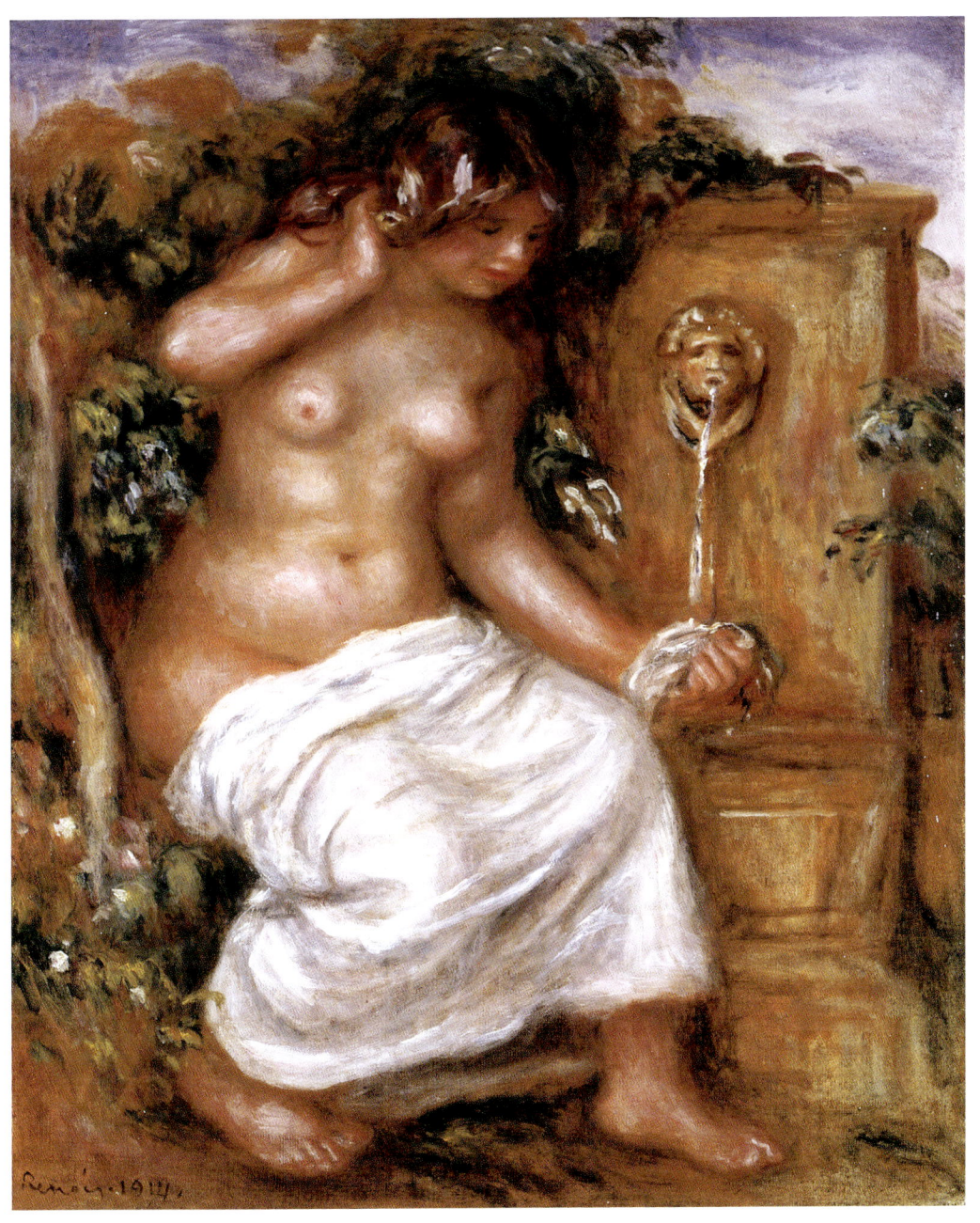

Vase of Roses, 1919
Oil on canvas,
37 x 31.5 cm (14⅝ x 12½ in.)
Private collection

Kenneth Clark, former director of the National Gallery, shared Henry Moore's opinion. He posed the more general question of how it was that Renoir managed to convey the qualities of plenitude and harmony, which the Greeks had discovered, while also lending his representations of the female body a warm reality. "Talking of Renoir's nudes as if they were ripe peaches that he could pluck merely by holding out his hand", he wrote, "is to forget his long struggle with the classical style, a struggle that continued after the victory of 1887. It is in sculpture that Renoir's Venus reaches perfection, and, through a curious paradox, this master of oil painting exercised less of an influence on painting than he did on modern sculpture, in which it was decisive. The series of Nudes that Renoir produces between 1885 and 1919, the year of his death, is one of the most captivating tributes to Venus ever rendered by a great artist, and brings all the threads together in this long chapter. Praxiteles and Giorgione, Rubens and Ingres, different as they are from each other, would all have recognised him as their successor. Like him, they would no doubt have talked about their work as a simple but skilled representation of outstandingly beautiful individuals. Artists ought always to express themselves with such simplicity. But in fact, they were all seeking an image that was the result of the meeting of their memories, their requirements and their artistic convictions: souvenirs of the most ancient works of art, the requirements of their personal sensitivity and the conviction that the female body expressed the order and harmony of the world."

Despite being confined to his wheelchair, and having to grasp his paintbrush between his arthritis-ridden fingers, Renoir continued to put his lifelong dreams on to canvas

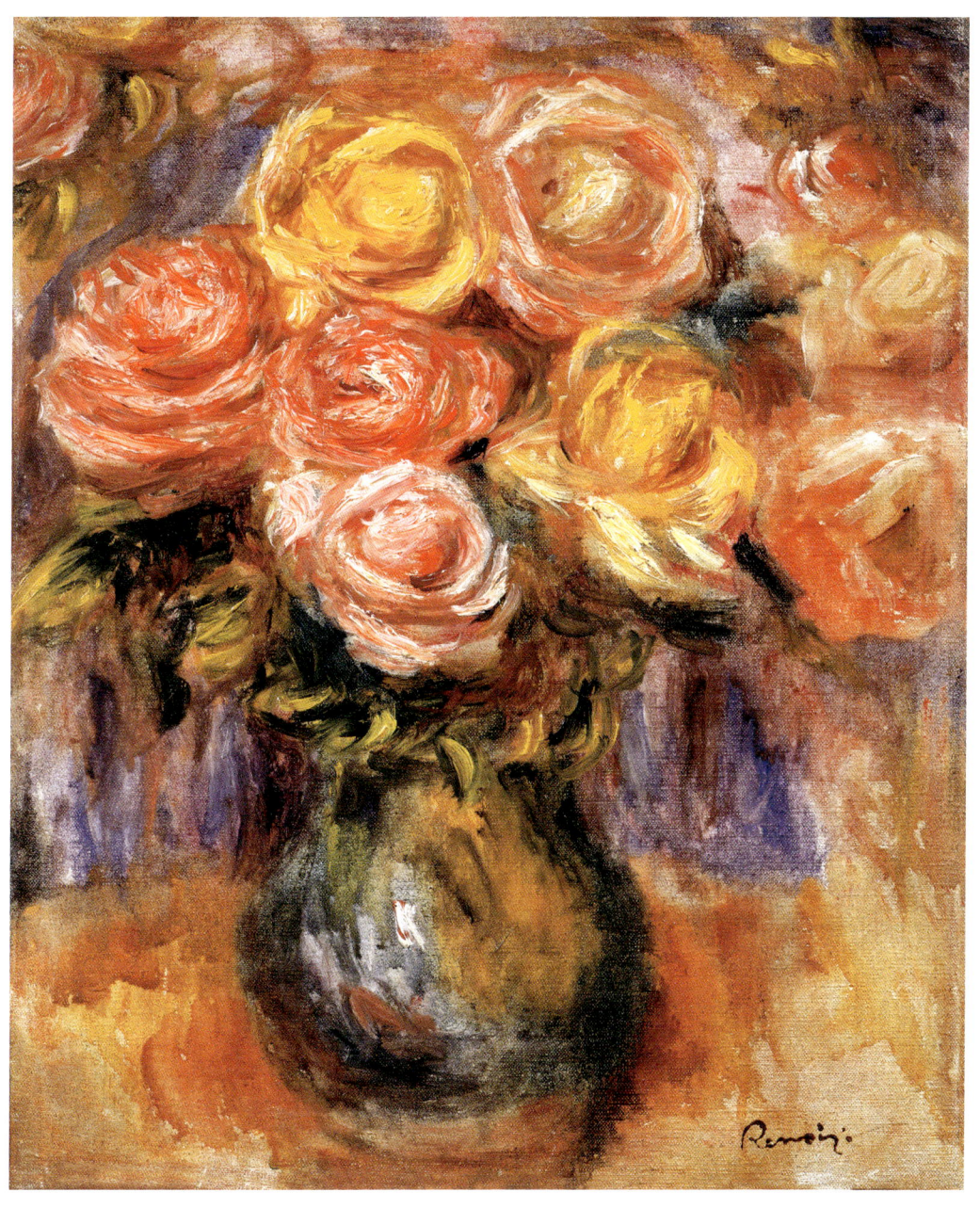

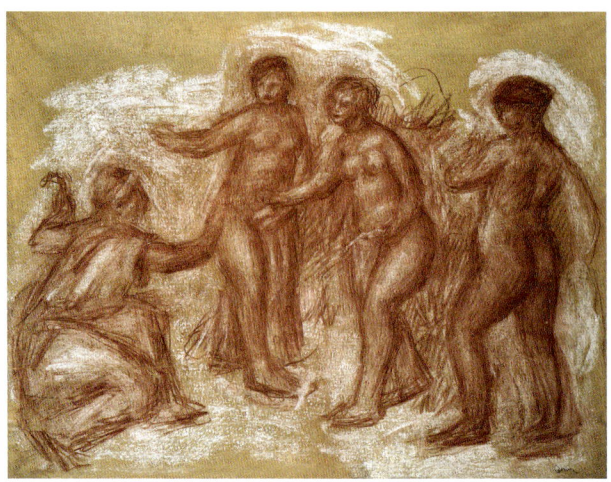

Study for **The Judgement of Paris**, 1908
Sanguine and white chalk on tracing paper,
transferred to canvas, 75 x 103 cm (29⅝ x 40⅝ in.)
Paris, Musée du Louvre, Cabinet des dessins
(Fonds des dessins et miniatures, Musée d'Orsay)

Pierre-Auguste Renoir – Richard Guino
Study for **The Judgement of Paris**, 1914
High relief, painted plaster,
76.2 x 94.5 x 10 cm (30 x 37¼ x 4 in.)
Paris, Musée d'Orsay

with equal fervour. He took everything as an excuse to magnify the body of women, the splendour of their complexions, and the curvaceous shapes of the *Bathers* that give them the status of goddesses. The flower-like girls, whom he had exalted during his youth, unconsciously evolved into women ripe as fruits. He increasingly preferred to place his nudes in natural settings in paintings such as *The Baker* (p. 448), *Ode to Flowers* (p. 449), *The Bather at the Fountain* (p. 469), and *The Rhône and the Saône* (p. 445). Renoir's women, lying beside springs or in the midst of a sunlit grove, recall their artistic ancestry. In renewing links with the great tradition, Renoir became something he had long aspired to be – a great classical painter. His feminine ideal took him back to mythology. The landscapes in which he places his nymphs belong to an Arcadian world in which nudity signifies the organic accord between woman and nature. His maidservants, whether as bathers or washerwomen, have faces with slightly almond-shaped eyes, snub noses, and the sensual mouth that he always loved. They have imposing and fecund forms with massive thighs like heavy columns. Theirs is a sculptural monumentality. To sculpt them was, then, an inevitable step.

"We must find Renoir hands!" Vollard exclaimed. Maillol was approached but made his excuses: he had his own sculpture to do. He suggested instead his best student, a Catalan like himself, named Richard Guino. The result was a miraculous osmosis between the two temperaments. What started as way of satisfying Vollard's financial greed became Renoir's final and triumphant means of expression. *Venus Victrix* (p. 475), *The Large Washerwoman* (1917), and *Maternity* (1916) took three-dimensional shape. Few pieces were sculpted –

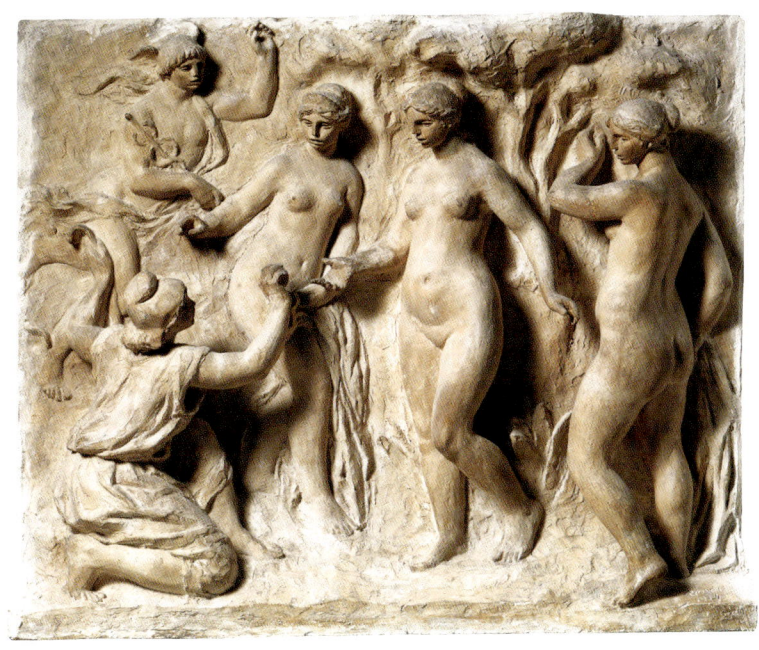

only ten – but they are among the masterpieces of French sculpture. "This is important", Jean-Louis Ferrier stresses, "because the tiny world of art critics tends to dismiss Renoir's blushing late nudes as 'blackcurrant jam'. Nothing could be further from the truth. Their transposition into statues confirms this. Renoir, his body weakened by rheumatism, fills these women's bodies with strength, volume, and a monumental presence".

Sculpture in the twentieth century has been dominated by painters. These include Degas with his horses and dancers, Matisse and his nudes, Picasso, Braque, Léger and many more. They seem to approach sculpture as a test and a challenge for their painting – and its ultimate flowering. Renoir is one of their number. He is by nature the last of the ancient Hellenic artists. "Renoir alone rediscovered the anthropomorphic vein of ancient civilisations", wrote Pierre Francastel. "He was the only one to have found spontaneously in the human body the means to express the whole of the perceptible universe". There could be no more fitting end to Renoir's work than *The Judgement of Paris* (p. 473) and the radiant effigy of *Venus Victrix* (p. 475). For in them he celebrates one more his most enduring inspiration: the glory of women.

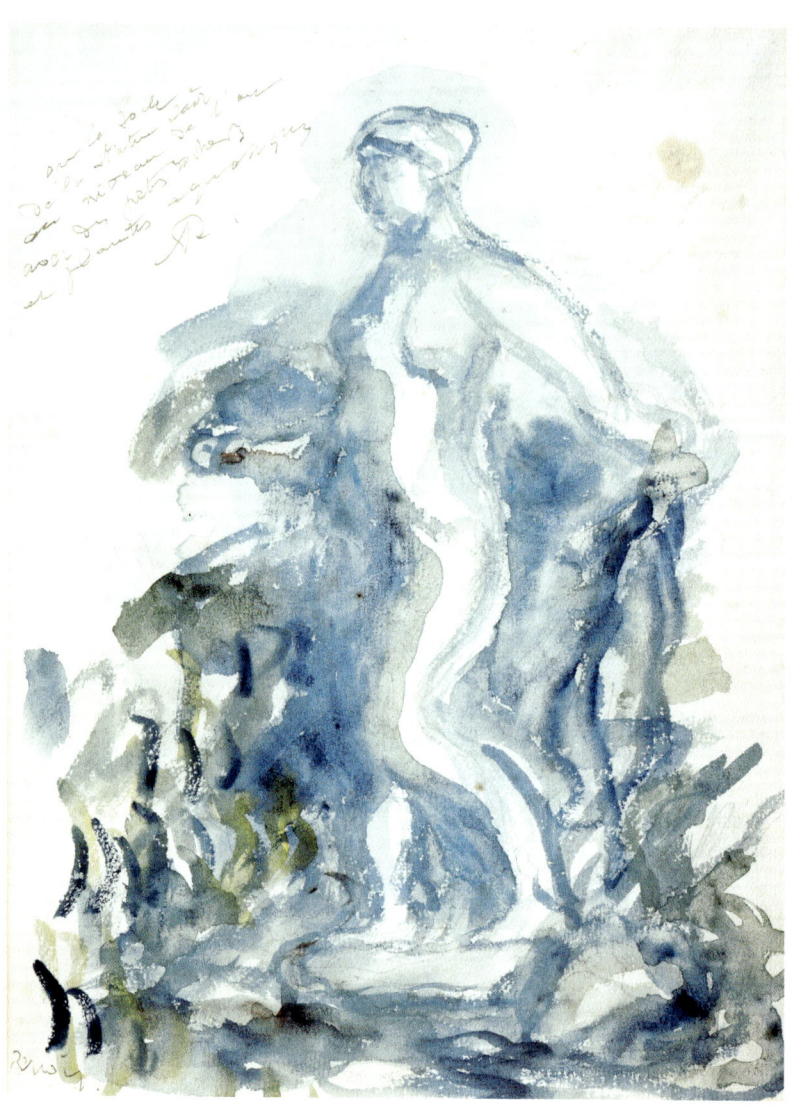

Study for **Venus Victrix**, 1914
Watercolour, 31 x 23 cm (12¼ x 9 in.)
Musée des Beaux-Arts de la
Ville de Paris, Petit Palais

Venus Victrix, 1916
Bronze, 181 x 111 x 78 cm (71⅜ x 43¾ x 30¾ in.)
Musée des Beaux-Arts de la
Ville de Paris, Petit Palais

474

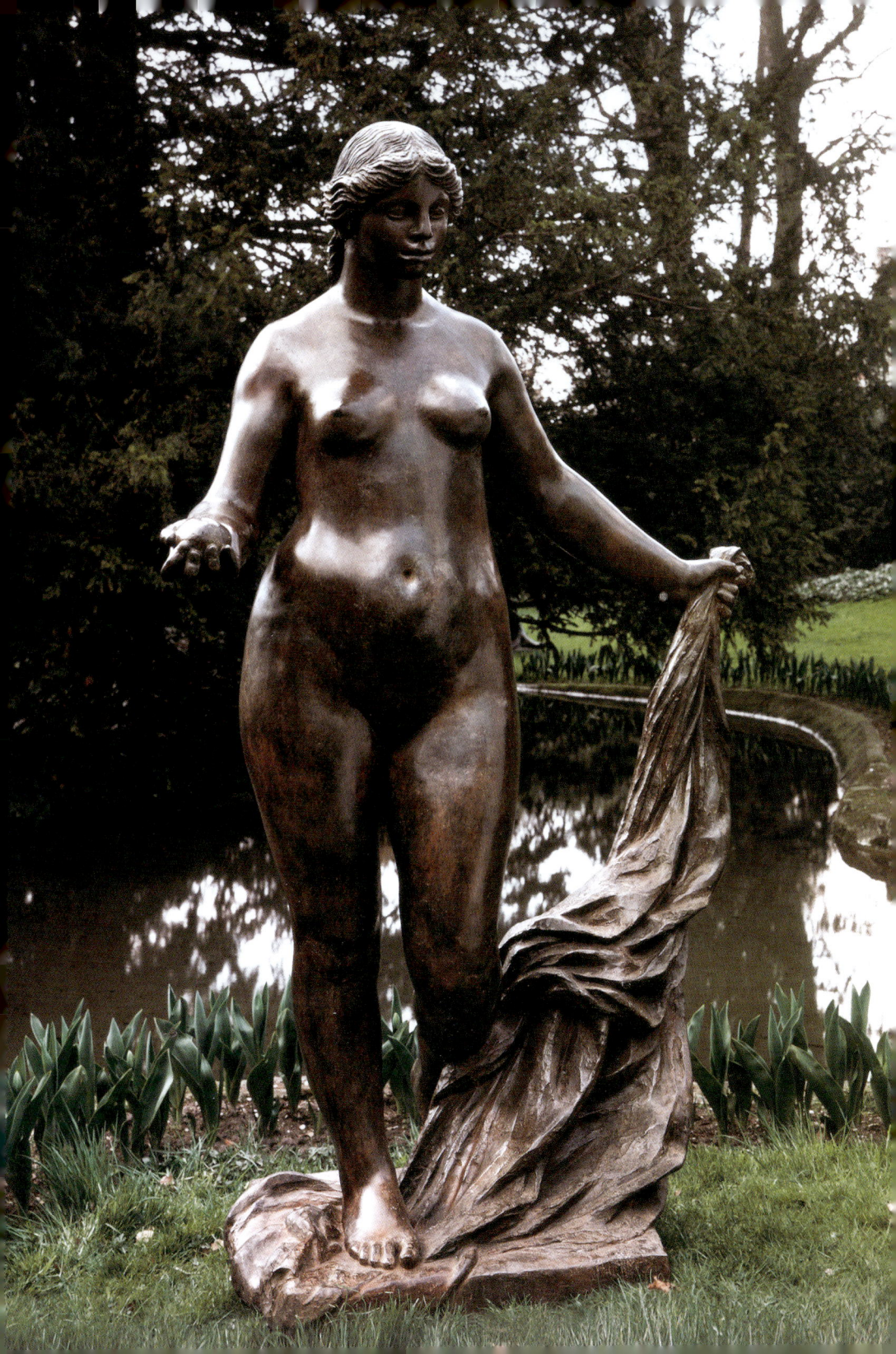

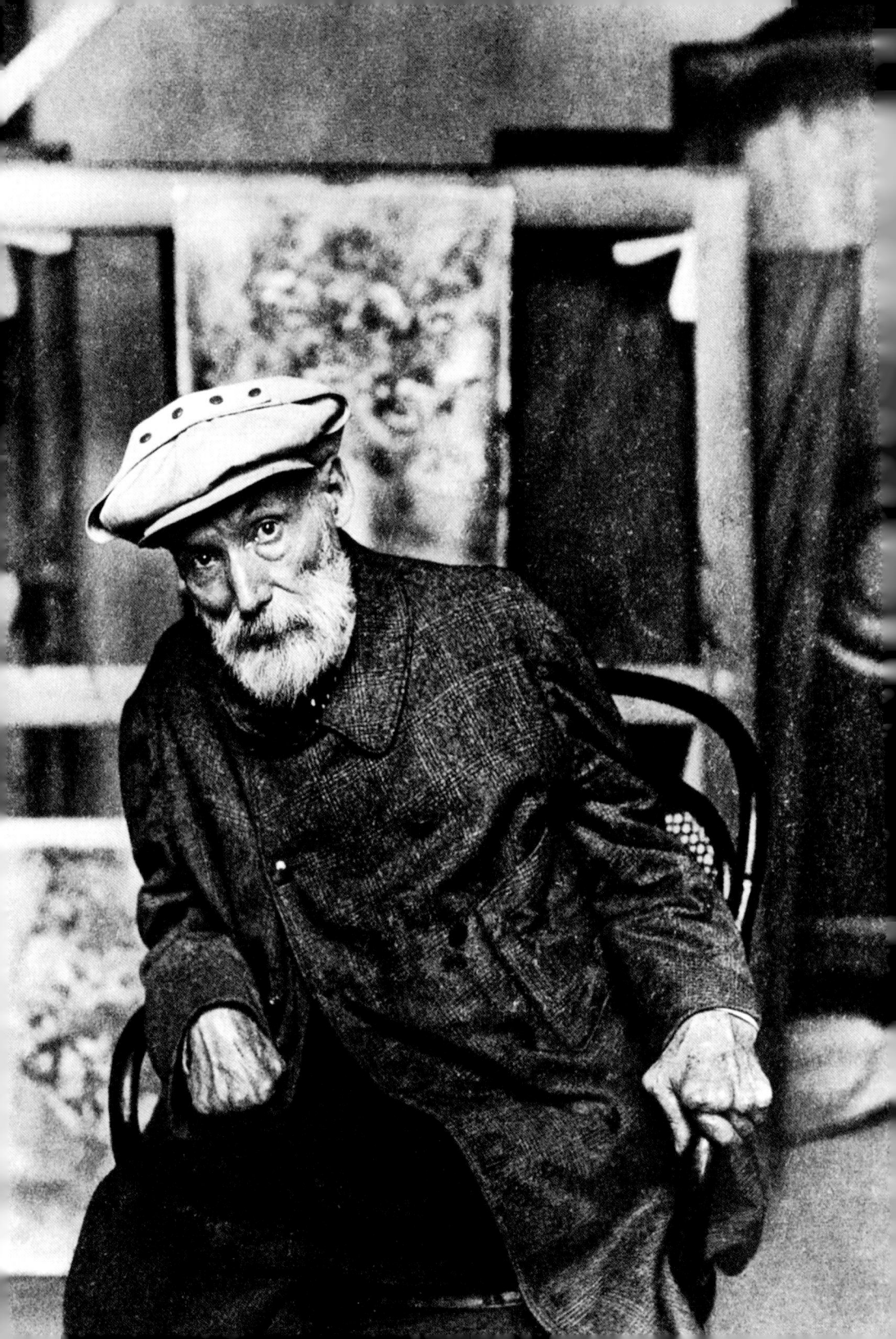

Chronology

1841 Birth of Pierre-Auguste Renoir in Limoges to Léonard Renoir, a tailor, and Marguerite Renoir (née Merlet), a seamstress. He is the sixth of their seven children.

1844 The Renoir family moves to Paris.

1848 Attends a school run by the Christian Brothers. The young composer Gounod teaches him singing and opera.

1854 Is apprenticed to a porcelain-painter by the name of M. Levy. Paints plates and vases before graduating to fans. Also attends a school for the decorative arts run by the sculptor Louis-Denis Callouette.

1855 His father opens his own tailor's shop under the name of Raynouard.

1859 Becomes a professional artist in the workshop of Monsieur Gilbert, a "specialist in blinds on religious themes and imitations of stained glass windows".

1860 Obtains permission to copy paintings in the Louvre and engravings in the Bibliothèque impériale.

1861 Enters the studio of Charles Gleyre at the École des Beaux-Arts. Monet, Sisley and Bazille join him the following year. Copies the works of antiquity and his favourite Old Masters as well as sketching live models. Is awarded average marks for his work.

1862 Visits the Louvre with Fantin-Latour. Meets Pissarro, Cézanne, Díaz, Courbet, Corot and Daubigny. Paints landscapes in the Forest of Fontainebleau. Becomes a close friend of the painter Jules Le Cœur.

Renoir in his studio, 1912

1863 Rejected by the Salon. Destroys his painting *Nymph with a Faun* in anger.

1864 Paul Renouard, a pupil of Gleyre, is awarded tenth place out of 106 in the competitive examination for drawing and sculpture. Renoir's entry for the Salon, *La Esmeralda*, is accepted but he later destroys it in disgust at its dark palette.

1865 His parents move to Ville-d'Avray. Stays with Sisley in Paris and with Jules Le Cœur in Marlotte. There meets Lise Tréhot, who becomes his model and mistress. Exhibits his portrait of Sisley's father (p. 31) at the Salon.

1866 Period of close friendship with Sisley and Le Cœur. The three friends go for walks together in the Forest of Fontainebleau and lodge with one another. Renoir shares a studio with the more affluent Bazille; Monet, who is penniless, frequently stays with them.

1867 Moves to Chantilly. His painting *Diana* (p. 44) is rejected by the Salon. Signs a petition, drawn up by Bazille, appealing for those rejected by the Salon ('Les Refusés') to be awarded their own exhibition.

1868 Shares a studio near the Café Guerbois with Bazille, whom he thanks for his hospitality by painting his portrait (p. 19). Meets Manet and his friends Degas, Duret, Zola, Burty and Silvestre. Jules Le Cœur's architect brother Charles commissions Renoir to decorate the ceilings of Prince Georges Bibesco's mansion. *Lise* (p. 33) is accepted by the Salon and acclaimed by the critics.

1869 Works with Monet, who now lives in Bougival. They paint *La Grenouillère* side-by-side (pp. 52–59). Exhibits two paintings at the Galerie Charpentier in Paris.

1870 Henri Fantin-Latour paints *A Studio at Batignolles* (p. 9 bottom), which features Manet, Otto Scholderer, Renoir, Astruc, Zola, Edmond Maître, Bazille and Monet. *Bather with Griffon Terrier* (p. 45) and *Odalisque* (pp. 50/51) are

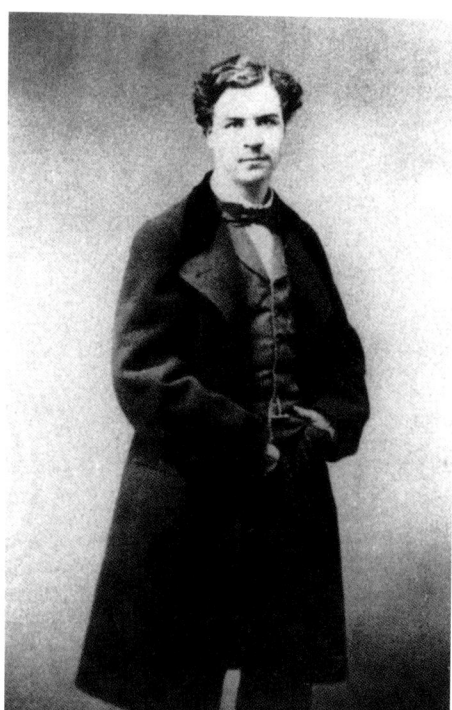

Pierre-Auguste Renoir, c. 1860

Degas. Sets up house in the Rue Saint-Georges. Becomes friendly with Georges Rivière but quarrels with the Le Cœur family after making advances to their eldest daughter.

1874 The first Impressionist Exhibition, held in the studio of the photographer Nadar in the Boulevard des Capucines in Paris. Renoir exhibits six paintings, including *The Theatre Box* (p. 87) and *The Parisian Woman* (p. 89). The venture ends in scandal and huge commercial failure. Father Martin buys *The Theatre Box* from Renoir for next to nothing. Death of Renoir's father.

1875 Organises an auction of his paintings and those of his friends in order to pay off their debts. Renoir's twenty paintings fetch the paltry sum of 2,251 francs. Uses the money to rent a studio in the Rue Cortot in Montmartre. Meets two future patrons, the collector Victor Chocquet and the publisher Georges Charpentier.

1876 Works in the garden of his studio in the Rue Cortot (p. 118). Paints a *Nude in the Sunlight* (p. 121) of his new mistress and model, Margot Legrand. Begins *Le Moulin de la Galette* (pp. 114/115). Stays with the Charpentier family and the writer Alphonse Daudet, producing portraits and decorative paintings for his hosts.

1877 In the face of hostile criticism, Renoir urges Rivière to publish the periodical *L'Impressionniste* in which he takes an active part. Exhibits twenty-one canvases at the Third Impressionist Exhibition. Earns 2,005 francs from the sale of fifteen canvases and a pastel sketch at another auction. Meets the statesman Gambetta and solicits an appointment as curator of a provincial museum. Paints the portrait of the pastry chef Eugène Murer (p. 231).

1878 Illustrates Émile Zola's *The Grog Shop*. Sells three paintings for a mere 157 francs.

1879 Decides no longer to exhibit with the Impressionists. *Madame Charpentier and Her Children* (pp. 388/389) is hung in the place of honour at the Salon, thanks to the social standing of its subject, to critical acclaim. The portrait of *Jeanne Samary* (p. 130), his new mistress, is hung and received less well. Stays on the Normandy coast with his new patrons, the Bérard family, whom he met at the Charpentiers'.

1880 Breaks his right arm after a bicycle accident; enjoys "working left-handed". *Mussel-Fishers at Berneval* (p. 397) is accepted by the Salon but

accepted by the Salon. Enlists in the Tenth Chasseurs on the outbreak of war between France and Prussia. Falls ill. Bazille is killed at Beaune-la-Rolande.

1871 Renoir is demobilised and returns to Paris at the height of the Commune. Obtains permission from his friend Raoul Rigaud, the Prefect of Police, to travel between Paris and his parents' home in Louveciennes. Rents a studio in the Rue Notre-Dame-des-Champs and renews his friendship with Monet.

1872 Monet introduces Renoir to Durand-Ruel who buys *The Pont des Arts, Paris* (pp. 28/29), which is exhibited in London. The Salon rejects *Interior of a Harem in Montmartre* (*Parisian Women Dressed as Algerians*; p. 47) on the grounds that it is excessively erotic. Signs another petition for a Salon des Refusés.

1873 Exhibits *Ride in the Bois de Boulogne* (p. 209) at the Salon des Refusés and sells *Lise* to Théodore Duret, whom he met through

badly hung. Zola suggests reorganising the Salon. Stays on the Isle of Chatou, at the home of Alphonse Fournaise, where he starts work on *The Luncheon of the Boating Party* (pp. 156/157). Meets his future wife Aline Charigot, a young seamstress from Essoyes, who poses for him with her dog.

1881 Period of doubt about the value of his own work and about the virtues of Impressionism. Takes a trip to Algeria, in the footsteps of Eugène Delacroix, and then travels to Italy. Raphael's frescoes in Rome make a particularly strong impression. Studies the paintings of Pompei. On a rowing-boat in the bay, he paints Aline as the *Blonde Bather* (p. 338) in a new style that will revolutionise his art.

1882 Paints the portrait of Richard Wagner (p. 252) in only thirty-five minutes while staying in Palermo. On his return to France, paints alongside Paul Cézanne at L'Estaque. Catches pneumonia and returns to Algeria to convalesce.

1883 First Renoir retrospective (of seventy works), held at 9 Boulevard de la Madeleine. Duret writes in his preface to the catalogue: "Among the Impressionists I would choose Claude Monet for landscapes and Renoir for portraits". The Salon accepts his portrait of *Madame Clapisson* (p. 237). Goes to the Côte d'Azur with Monet to paint, visiting Cézanne on the way back to Paris.

1884 Auction of Manet's works at the Hôtel Drouot. Renoir is sad that he cannot afford "a souvenir of his deceased friend". The Union Générale crisis leaves Durand-Ruel facing bankruptcy. Renoir and Monet encourage him to sell their paintings cheaply.

1885 Aline gives birth to Renoir's first son, Pierre, the future film actor. Caillebotte agrees to be the child's godfather. The Renoir and Cézanne families stay at La Roche-Guyon. Berthe Morisot holds dinners with Renoir, Mallarmé and Degas.

1886 Berthe Morisot visits Renoir's studio, admiring his maternity paintings (pp. 386, 387) and *The Great Bathers* (pp. 348/349). Renoir's international standing grows. Eight canvases are displayed in Brussels, at the 'Cercle des XX', and thirty-eight in New York by Durand-Ruel. Spends time in Essoyes, Aline's hometown.

1887 *The Great Bathers* is exhibited by Georges Petit to mixed reviews. Renoir is criticized for

changing his style. Stays with his friends the Murers in Antwerp where he is reunited with Camille Pissarro. "I chatted to Renoir. He told me that former fans of his, Durand – everyone in fact – are angry with him for trying to leave his romantic period behind", Pissarro writes to his son Lucien.

1888 Stays with Cézanne at the Jas de Bouffan, Aix-en-Provence. An infection leaves part of his face paralysed. Undergoes electrotherapy. Illustrates *Pages* by his friend Stéphane Mallarmé with a frontispiece entitled *Venus – The Phenomenon of the Future* (p. 444), which belongs with the *Bathers* series.

1889 Refuses to exhibit his later works at the Exposition Universelle, because he is dissatisfied with them. A further stay in Provence.

1890 Finally marries Aline Charigot, at the town hall of the ninth arrondissement in Paris. Refuses a state honour. "My congratulations to him", wrote Monet to Caillebotte. "The honour might have come in handy, it is true, but to succeed without it is so much better". Exhibits a painting, *The Daughters of Catulle Mendès* (p. 321), at the Salon for the last time.

1891 More time spent in Provence. Death of Victor Chocquet. Introduces Aline to Berthe Morisot.

1892 The French government buys *Girls at the Piano* (p. 323) at Mallarmé's suggestion.

Renoir and his son Coco, 1901–1902

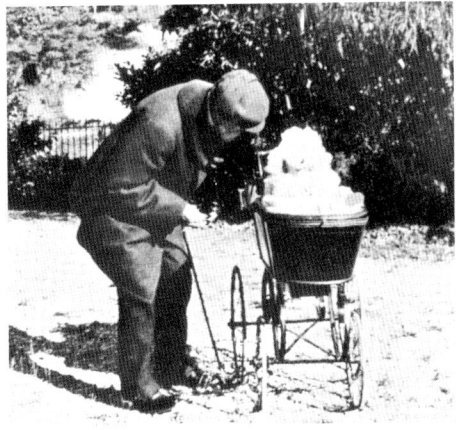

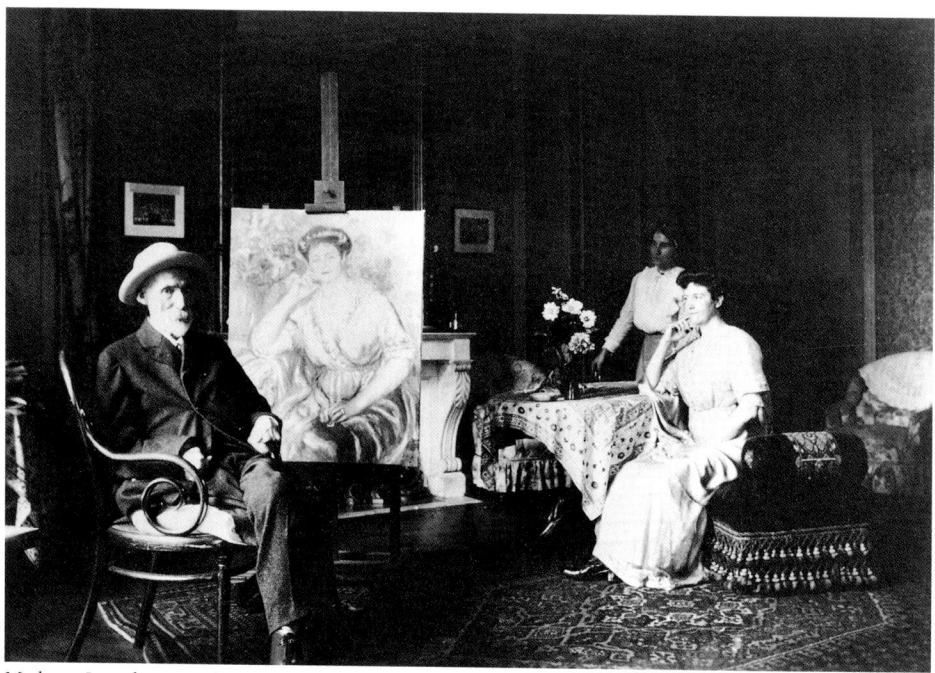

Madame Joseph Durand-Ruel, posing for Renoir, Gabrielle standing, Saint-Cloud in 1911

A retrospective featuring 110 paintings is held at the Durand-Ruel gallery. Meets Émile Bernard. Travels to Madrid with Gallimard; admires the Infanta paintings and *Las Meniñas* by Velázquez in the Prado.

1893 Sees Paul Gauguin's work, whose exoticism he dislikes, at Durand-Ruel's. Meets Jeanne Baudot, who becomes his pupil.

1894 Death of Gustave Caillebotte. Renoir, as the executor of his will, attempts to persuade Roujon, the Director of Fine Art, to accept the Caillebotte bequest to the Luxembourg Museum and the Louvre. Gabrielle Renard, Aline's cousin, comes to Paris to look after the children. She is to become Renoir's favourite model. Birth of a second son, Jean, the future filmmaker. Renoir's rheumatism worsens. Meets Ambroise Vollard and Albert André, his future biographers and (in Vollard's case) art dealer.

1895 Death of Berthe Morisot. Renoir becomes the guardian of her daughter, Julie Manet. They all move to Brittany. Renoir buys a house at Essoyes and quarrels with Cézanne.

1896 Renoir, Monet and Degas organise a Berthe Morisot retrospective at the Durand-Ruel gallery. Death of Renoir's mother, aged eighty-nine.

1897 The Caillebotte bequest (including six paintings by Renoir) is finally placed in the Musée du Luxembourg.

1898 Discovers Cagnes and returns to Paris full of enthusiasm. Attends the funeral of Stéphane Mallarmé at Valvins and visits a Rembrandt exhibition in Amsterdam. Falls out with Degas after he sells Durand-Ruel a Edgar Degas pastel, *The Dancing Lesson*, which he had inherited from Caillebotte.

1899 Death of Sisley. Moves to Cagnes in order to nurse his worsening rheumatism.

1900 Exhibitions of his work by Bernheim-Jeune in Paris, Durand-Ruel in New York and at the Universal Exposition increase his renown. Finally accepts the Legion of Honour. "I have allowed myself to be decorated", he writes to Monet. "Whether or not I have made a mistake, I still value your friendship."

1901 Birth of Claude, nicknamed Coco, the painter's third son. The Lyons Museum purchases *Woman Playing the Guitar* (p. 320).

1902 Moves to Le Cannet where Aline joins him with Jean and Claude. Albert André works alongside him. Experiences further deteriorations to his health (the atrophy of a nerve in his left eye and attacks of rheumatism).

1903 Death of Pissarro. From now on spends every winter in Cagnes.

1904 Makes a formal complaint against imitators of his work. Thirty-five paintings are shown in a "Renoir Room" at the Salon d'Automne in Paris.

1905 Fifty-nine works are exhibited in a major Impressionist exhibition arranged by Durand-Ruel at the Grafton Gallery in London. A further nine paintings are displayed in the Salon d'Automne of which he is made honorary president.

1906 Death of Cézanne. Maurice Denis visits him in Cagnes.

1907 Sale of Georges Charpentier's collection after his death in 1905. *Madame Charpentier and Her Children* (pp. 388/389) is bought by the Metropolitan Museum of Art. Buys the Les Collettes estate in Cagnes.

1908 A series of exhibitions held in Paris, New York and London. Makes Les Collettes his permanent home.

1909 Receives a number of guests in the new house he has built for himself; these include Albert André, Jacques-Émile Blanche and Paul Durand-Ruel. Opposes a plan to erect a monument to Cézanne, writing to Monet, "a painter should be represented by his painting alone".

1910 Retrospective held in Venice. Travels to Munich and stays with the daughter of Édouard Bérard, Mrs Thurneyssen, whom he paints with her daughter (p. 436). On his return finds himself so crippled by rheumatism that he can no longer walk.

1911 Publication of the first biography of Renoir, in French and German, by Julius Meier-Graefe.

1912 Now able to paint only if his paintbrushes are placed in the palm of his hand and if his fragile skin is protected against the brushes by a piece of fabric.

1913 Five of his works are exhibited at the Armory Show in New York. Jean Renoir enlists in the French army. Vollard suggests to Renoir that, with the help of Aristide Maillol's protégé Richard Guino, he produce some sculptures. "When Vollard first mentioned sculpture, I told him to go to the devil, but on reflection I let myself be talked into it".

1914 Works on a tapestry design for the Gobelins factory of Neptune kissing Venus. Gabrielle leaves to marry an American painter. Receives a visit from Rodin, whose portrait he draws. Germany declares war on France. Both his sons are wounded. Aline visits Pierre in Carcassone and Jean in Luçon.

1915 Jean is wounded a second time, this time in the leg. Aline visits him and dies upon her return. Renoir returns to Paris to receive Jean on his discharge from hospital. They begin conversations that will eventually serve as the basis for Jean's biography of his father.

1916 Invites the sculptor Guino to visit him at Essoyes and to cast a bust made from a study of his late wife. The bronze of *Venus Victrix* (p. 475) is exhibited at the Paris Triennale.

Renoir, his wife Aline and son Claude, called "Coco", 1912

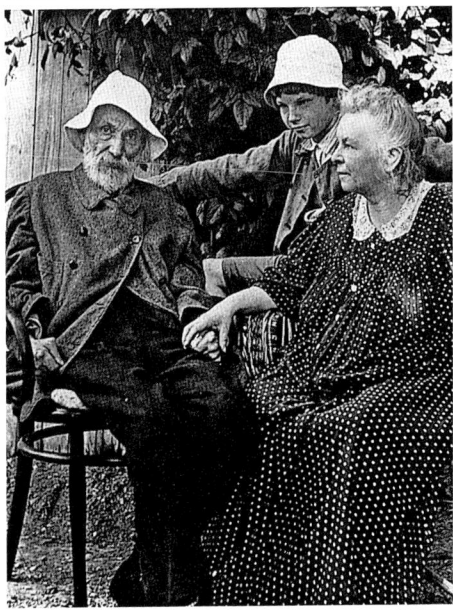

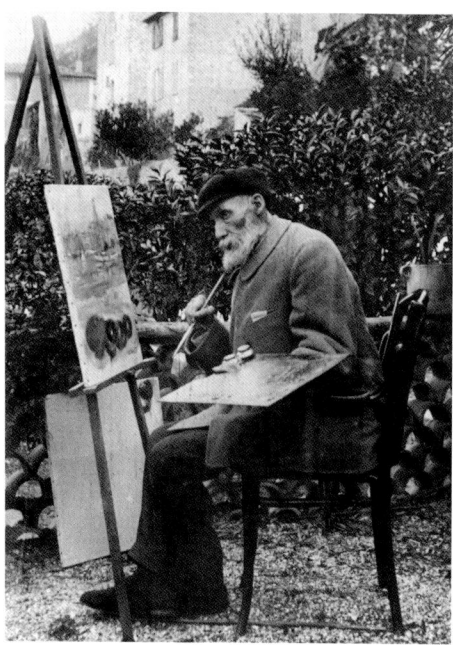

Renoir painting in front of the Villa de la Poste
at Cagnes in 1903

1917 Purchase of *The Umbrellas* (p. 272) by
the National Gallery in London. A group of
British artists and collectors pays tribute to
Renoir on this occasion. Death of Degas.
Matisse visits Renoir in Cagnes. Renoir
teaches ceramics to his son Claude.

1918 End of World War I. Renoir's health
deteriorates further; gangrene is diagnosed
in his foot.

1919 Made a Commander of the Legion of
Honour. In triumph, Renoir, "the pope of painting",
is carried aloft in his wheelchair right inside the
Louvre Museum so that he can view his portrait
of *Madame Georges Charpentier* (p. 229), which is
now on display in the La Caze room. He asks to
be allowed to pause on the way so that he can
admire *The Wedding at Cana* by Veronese for the
last time. Returns to Cagnes and dies of pulmon-
ary congestion at Les Collettes on 2 December.
Only a few hours before his death, according to
Jean Renoir, he asks for a palette and brush to be
brought to him so that he can paint some flowers.
He hands them back to his nurse, murmuring,
"I do believe that I am finally starting to get
the hang of it".

Renoir in a wheelchair with Andrée Heuschling
(1900–1979), called "Dédé", 1915

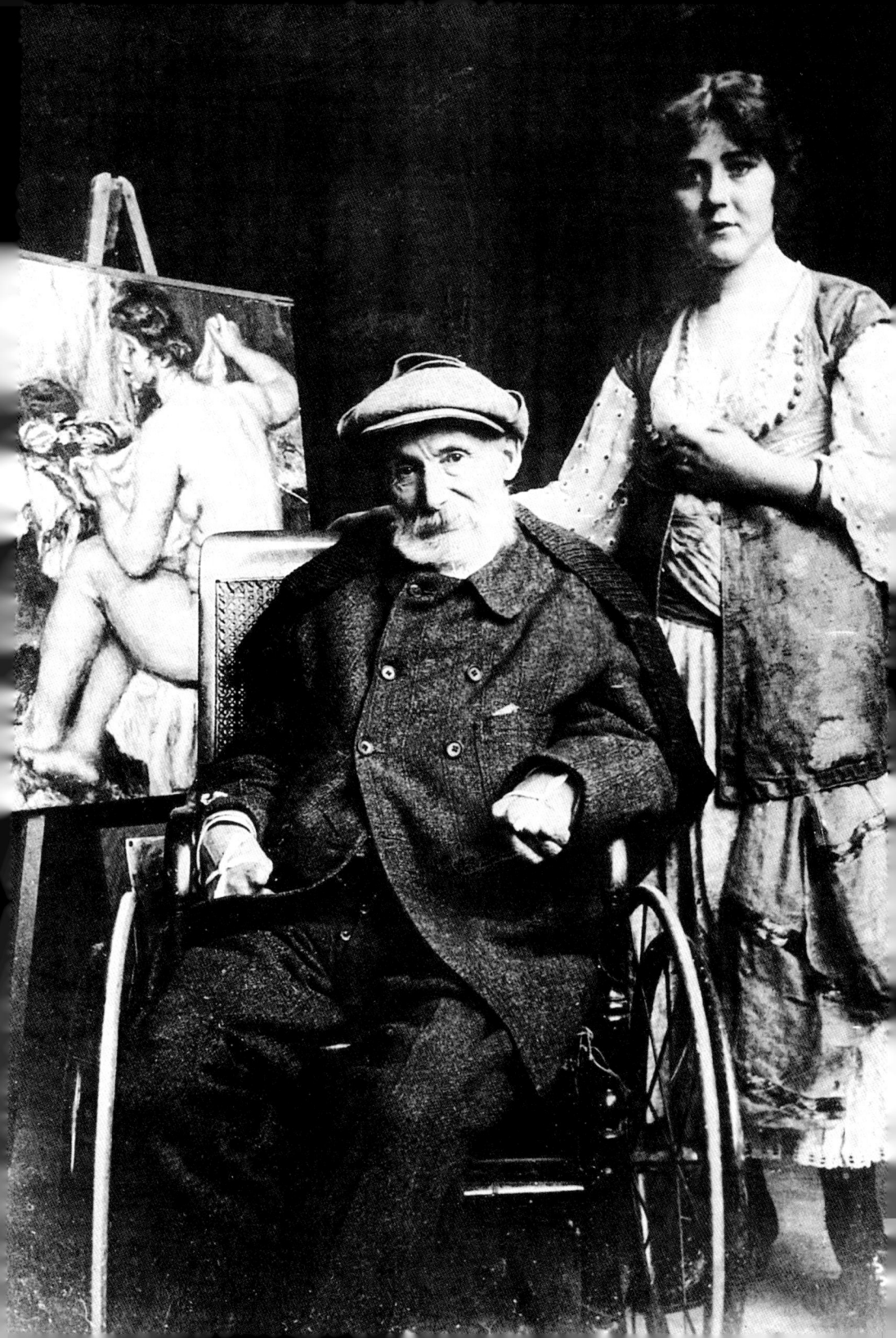

Selected Bibliography

J. MEIER-GRAEFE, *Renoir,* Munich, 1911; French edition, Paris, 1912; republished, Leipzig, 1929

A. VOLLARD, *Renoir,* Paris, 1919 and 1920

A. ANDRE, *Renoir,* Paris, 1919 and 1928

TH. DURET, *Renoir,* Paris, 1924

G. COQUIOT, *Renoir,* Paris, 1925

A. BARNES and V. de MAZA, *The Art of Renoir,* New York, 1935

J. REWALD, *Renoir Drawings,* New York, 1946

W. PACH, *Renoir,* New York, 1951

J. BAUDOT, *Renoir, ses amis, ses modèles,* Paris, 1951

M. BERR de TURIQUE, *Renoir,* London, 1952

D. ROUART, *Renoir,* Geneva, 1954

M. DRUCKER, *Renoir,* Paris, 1955

M. ROBIDA, *Renoir et les Enfants,* Lausanne, 1959

J. RENOIR, *Renoir, mon père,* Paris, 1962; English edition *Renoir, my father,* Boston, 1962

H. PERRUCHOT, *La Vie de Renoir,* Paris, 1964

S. TOMINAGA, *Renoir,* Tokyo, 1969

E. FEZZI, *Renoir,* Paris, 1969

F. DAULTE, *Renoir,* Milan, 1971

D. WILDENSTEIN, *Renoir,* A l'École des Grands Peintres, Vergeures, Paris, 1980

B. EHRLICH WHITE, *Renoir, His Life, Art and Letters,* New York, 1984

G. NÉRET, *Renoir – 60 chefs-d'œuvre,* Fribourg (Switzerland), 1985

G. NÉRET, *Les Impressionnistes, de la révolte à la consécration,* Fribourg (Switzerland), 1985

M. HOOG, N. WADLEY, *Renoir, un peintre, une vie, une œuvre,* New York, 1987; Paris, 1989

P. H. FEIST, *Pierre-Auguste Renoir,* Cologne, 1993; republished 2016

A. DISTEL, *Renoir "Il faut embellir",* Paris, 1993

C. B. BAILEY (ed.), *Renoir Portraits: Impressions of an Age / Les Portraits de Renoir – Impressions d'une époque,* exh. cat., The National Gallery of Canada, Ottawa / The Art Institute of Chicago / Kimbell Art Museum, Fort Worth, 1997/98, Paris, 1997

C. B. BAILEY (ed.), *Renoir Landscapes 1865–1883,* exh. cat., The National Gallery, London / Philadelphia Museum of Art / The National Gallery of Canada, Ottawa, 2007/2008, London, 2007

G.-D. DAUBERVILLE, *Renoir: Catalogue raisonné des tableaux, pastels, dessins et aquarelles,* 5 vols, Paris, 2007–2014

A. O'CONNOR (ed.), *Renoir in the 20th Century / Renoir au XXe Siècle,* exh. cat., Musée d'Orsay, Paris / Los Angeles County Museum of Art / Philadelphia Museum of Art, 2010, Ostfildern, 2009

K. SAGNER (ed.), *Pierre-Auguste Renoir – wie Seide gemalt, l'effet de la soie,* exh. cat., Kunstsammlungen Chemnitz 2011, Munich, 2011

N. ZIMMER (ed.), *Renoir. Zwischen Bohème und Bourgeoisie: Die frühen Jahre / Renoir. Between Bohemia and Bourgeoisie: The Early Years,* exh. cat., Kunstmuseum Basel, 2012, Ostfildern, 2012

C. B. BAILEY (ed.), *Renoir, Impressionism, and Full-Length Painting,* exh. cat., The Frick Collection, New York, 2012

C. POMMEREAU (ed.), *Renoir père et fils – Peinture et cinéma,* exh. cat., Musée d'Orsay, Paris, 2018

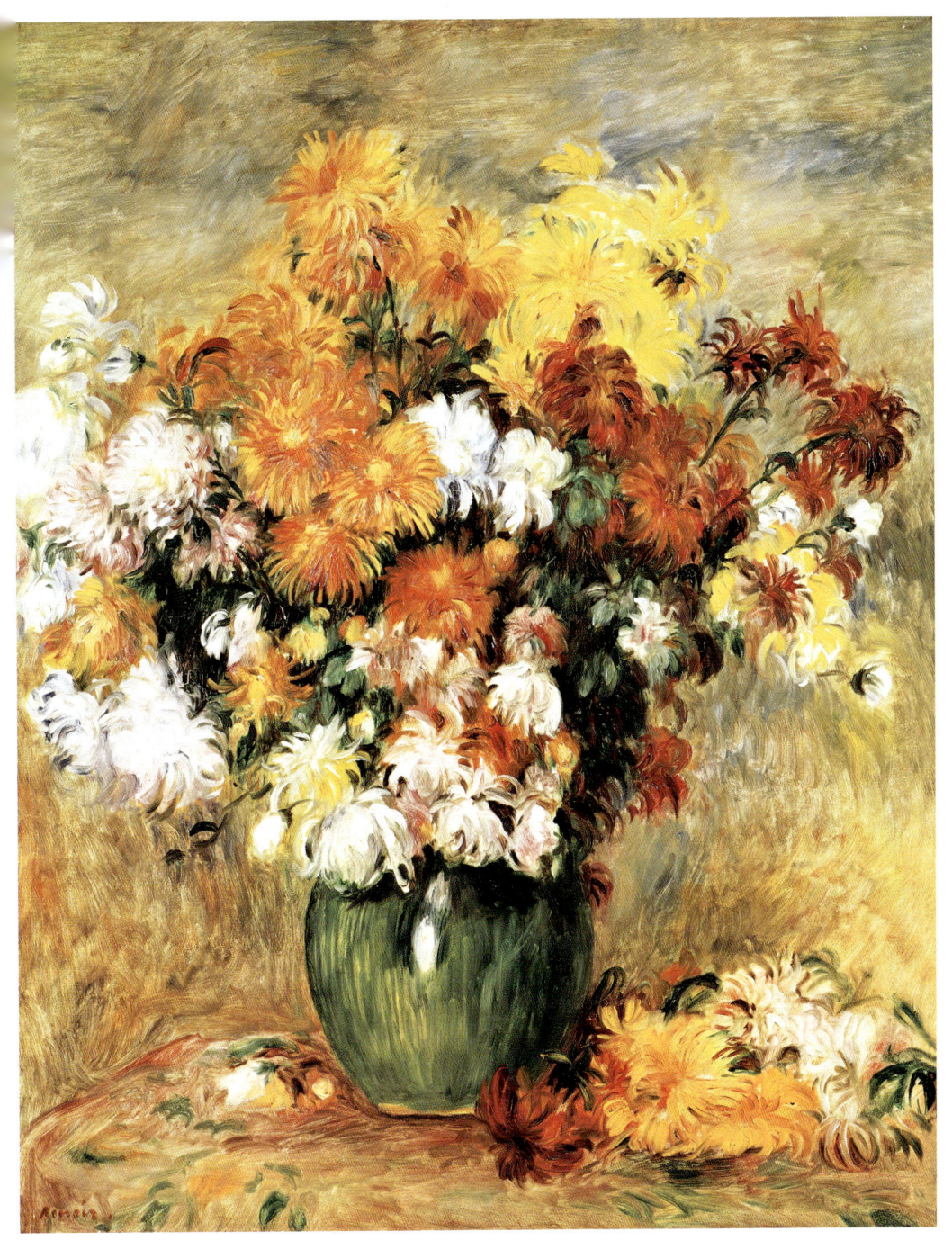

Acknowledgements

The author and publisher would like to express their grateful thanks to Caroline Durand-Ruel Godfroy, as well as to Daniel Wildenstein and Marie-Christine Maufus, for their invaluable assistance and contribution to the knowledge of Renoir's work, in their willingness to make available the Durand-Ruel et Cie archives and those of the Wildenstein Institute, respectively.

The editor and publisher have made every effort to obtain permissions and pay royalties for use of the copyright to the photographs on which the illustrations are based, as required by law. Anyone who believes they have rights to any of these images and who has not been contacted is requested to get in touch with the publisher. The owners of the works are listed in the captions unless they wished to remain anonymous or if the editor was not aware of their identity. The publisher would appreciate being informed of any incomplete or inaccurate information as well as any changes which may have occurred since the time of writing.

The publishers wish to thank the museums, private collections, archives and photographers who granted permission to reproduce these works and offered their support in the creation of this book. Unless otherwise stated, the copyright in the illustrated works is owned by the collections and institutions listed in the picture captions or the author's archive.

PAGE 485
Bouquet of Chrysanthemums, c. 1884
Oil on canvas, 82 x 66 cm (32¼ x 26 in.)
Rouen, Musée des Beaux-Arts

Photo Credits

Imprint

**EACH AND EVERY TASCHEN BOOK
PLANTS A SEED!**
Each year, we offset our annual carbon emissions
with carbon credits at the Instituto Terra, a
reforestation program in Minas Gerais, Brazil,
founded by Lélia and Sebastião Salgado. To find
out more about this ecological partnership, please
check: www.taschen.com/institutoterra.
Inspiration: unlimited.
Carbon footprint: (almost) zero.

Want to see more? Visit taschen.com to view our
current publications, browse our latest magazine,
and subscribe to our newsletter.

© 2026 TASCHEN GmbH
Hohenzollernring 53, D–50672 Köln
www.taschen.com

Original edition: © 2001 TASCHEN GmbH

Printed in Bosnia–Herzegovina
ISBN 978–3–8365–9209–3

PAGE 2
Girl with a Fan, c. 1879
Oil on canvas, 65.4 x 54 cm (25¾ x 21⅜ in.)
Williamstown, Massachusetts, The Clark

PAGE 4
On the Terrace, 1881
Oil on canvas, 100.4 x 80.9 cm (39½ x 32 in.)
The Art Institute of Chicago, Mr. and Mrs.
Lewis Larned Coburn Memorial Collection

© for the work of Richard Guino:
VG Bild-Kunst, Bonn 2026
© for the work of Pablo Picasso: Succession
Picasso/VG Bild-Kunst, Bonn 2026

Conception and text: Gilles Néret, Paris
Translation: Josephine Bacon, London